Joseph Story and the American Constitution

Marble statue of Joseph Story,
by William Wetmore Story. (*Courtesy of Fogg
Art Museum, Harvard University*)

JOSEPH STORY
and the AMERICAN
CONSTITUTION

A Study in Political and Legal Thought

WITH SELECTED WRITINGS

by James McClellan

Foreword by Stephen B. Presser

UNIVERSITY OF OKLAHOMA PRESS : NORMAN AND LONDON

BY JAMES MCCLELLAN

(with Russell Kirk) *The Political Principles of Robert A. Taft* (New York, 1967)

Joseph Story and the American Constitution (Norman, 1971)

(with Kenneth Redden) *Federal Regulation of Consumer-Creditor Relations* (Charlottesville, 1982)

Liberty, Order and Justice: An Introduction to the Constitutional Principles of American Government (Cumberland, 1989)

(editor, with M. E. Bradford) *Debates in the Federal Convention of 1787 as Reported by James Madison* (Richmond, 1989)

(editor, with George Carey) *The Federalist.* Student Edition (Dubuque, 1990)

Library of Congress Cataloging-in-Publication Data

McClellan, James, 1937–
    Joseph story and the American Constitution : a study in political and legal thought with selected writings / by James McClellan.
        p.   cm.
    Reprint. Originally published: Norman : University of Oklahoma Press, 1971.
    ISBN 0–8061–0971–8 (cloth)
    1. Story, Joseph, 1779–1845.   2. United States—Constitutional law.
KF8745.S83M34   1990
342.73'0092—dc20
[347.30092]   90–33798
ISBN: 0–8061–2290–0 (pbk.)

In Memory of My Parents,
James Charles and Florence Stewart McClellan

Foreword
By Stephen B. Presser

Joseph Story is the thinking man's John Marshall. Story supplied the citations, tried to reconcile the constitutional doctrines, labored to build a soaring edifice of nationalist commercial jurisprudence through erudite opinions, lectures at Harvard Law School, and dense books, while Marshall garnered virtually all the glory with a little law encased in some deft and ringing phrases.[1]

I wrote those words in a review of another splendid biography of Joseph Story,[2] but they were inspired by my reading of the first edition of James McClellan's feisty and delightful book. McClellan argues convincingly that virtually all of the accomplishments in constitutional law for which we ritually praise John Marshall are more properly attributable to his more bookish colleague, Story. Marshall's creative construction of the Constitution, and, perhaps, Marshall's unwillingness to anchor his broad and sweeping words with much in the way of citation have been enormously useful to liberal interpreters of the Constitution since the days of the New Deal. Marshall's contemporary lionization is in rather stark contrast to the near total popular ignorance of Joseph Story. While Story and Marshall shared a nationalist vision of the Constitution, Story made the mistake of articulating clearly his elitist and conservative version of that nationalism, and found himself out of popular favor from the time of Taney on.

Moreover, as McClellan demonstrates, Story's version of American jurisprudence was infused not only with a proper regard for the ancient and modern philosophers, such as Aristotle, Cicero, and Burke, but with heavy reliance on an expressly Christian natural law. In our modern secular era this is regarded as unacceptable at best, and wildly bigoted at worst. Perhaps this helps explain how the book you hold in your hands, a book originally written with what must have been the rather modest aim of setting the record straight with regard to the relative contributions of Story and Marshall, could have ended up as one of the principal causes of a virtual revolution in the writing of American legal history.

[1] Stephen B. Presser, "Resurrecting the Conservative Tradition in American Legal History," *Reviews in American History* 13:526–533 (1985).

[2] R. Kent Newmyer, *Supreme Court Justice Joseph Story: Statesman of the Old Republic* (Chapel Hill, 1985).

It was the first edition of this book, along with still another fine biography of Joseph Story,[3] that prompted Morton Horwitz to write his now famous scathing attack on what he called "lawyers' legal history."[4] Horwitz excoriated McClellan, Gerald Dunne (the other Story biographer), and Roscoe Pound, for good measure, for engaging in too uncritical and too simplistic an interpretation of American law. Horwitz thought that the Story biographies were too self-servingly panegyrical, and missed what he took to be the extraordinary legal contradictions and transparent instrumentalism in Story's work.

Horwitz proceeded to write his own attempt to set the record straight, his Bancroft Prize winning *Transformation of American Law* (1977),[5] in which nineteenth-century American law in general and Joseph Story in particular, were presented not as the products of philosophical or religious thought, but of raw economic determinism. To a very great extent Horwitz's passionate and brilliant work dominated the writing of legal history for the next decade, and the leftward slant of his book was also reflected in the work of many Critical Legal Studies scholars who turned to legal history.

The irony of Horwitz's attack on McClellan, however, was that following his 1977 book, Horwitz and his Critical Legal Studies colleagues eventually seemed to become more and more interested in examining the cultural, philosophical, intellectual, and religious aspects of the thought of nineteenth-century lawyers and judges that McClellan had found central to Story's work. McClellan may have simply been about ten or fifteen years ahead of his time.

The reissue of McClellan's book thus arrives at a propitious moment. Most American legal historians are now more concerned with the complex of ideas now called "Republicanism," the notion of Aristotelian "civic virtue," which has been recently discovered to have been as important as Lockean liberalism in the formation of the Constitution and early American law. Moreover, American historians are beginning to understand that Christian religious thought may have been as vital as "Republicanism" to early American politicians and lawyers. McClellan did not use the trendy word "Republicanism" to describe or analyze what he found, but there is much here from which legal and general American historians can still learn.

Probably the most attractive feature of McClellan's work in this regard is what he offers us in the way of recapturing the conservative tradition that Horwitz was perhaps a bit too quick to dismiss. This is not the conservatism of a Meese or even a Rehnquist, with their borrowing of some

[3] Gerald Dunne, *Justice Joseph Story and the Rise of the Supreme Court* (New York, 1971).
[4] Morton Horwitz, "The Conservative Tradition in the Writing of American Legal History," *American Journal of Legal History* 17:275–294 (1973).
[5] Morton Horwitz, *The Transformation of American Law 1780–1860* (Cambridge, 1977).

states' rights ideas from Thomas Jefferson. This is the real thing, the conservatism of the Federalists of the 1790s, a conservatism profoundly influenced by the aristocratic English example and displayed on the bench by men like Samuel Chase, James Wilson, William Paterson, and Oliver Ellsworth.

If it is true that the Supreme court will be embarking in a more conservative direction as the century comes to a close, and if it is true, as even the scholars of the left now seem to be sensing, that there is more to law than mathematical rationality or economics, perhaps those on the bench and off can profit from another look at McClellan's splendid foray into the religious and philosophical aspects of our most intellectually gifted Supreme Court Justice.

Preface

MY primary objective in this book is simply to supply a basic philosophical and theoretical understanding of Justice Story's constitutionalism, and in this respect my findings may be regarded as a prolegomenon to the study of Story's jurisprudence in the future. This book is not a biography, therefore, although a great deal of biographical material has been included to introduce the reader to Joseph Story as a person, to illustrate the formative influences on his thought, and to clarify his position on a particular political or legal issue. Nor is this a systematic study of the nature and extent of Story's influence upon constitutional development—though I hasten to add that I have not been indifferent to the question of Story's permanent effect upon the Constitution and have endeavored to show that many of his more important opinions have become an integral part of our fundamental law. Nor will the reader discover a definitive treatment of the history of the Marshall and Taney Courts or of Story's contributions to private law.

During his long and resourceful career as Dane Professor of Law at Harvard and as associate justice of the Supreme Court, Story became a worldwide authority on the subjects of equity and conflict of law. He is often regarded as the father of admiralty law; and he has exercised an enormous influence on American patent law, trust law, the law of negotiable instruments, and many other fields of commercial law. But these are topics beyond the purview of Story and the Constitution.

On this subject I intend not only to provide an understanding of Story's constitutional doctrines, but also to elevate a relatively obscure figure to his rightful place in American history. If I seem to have overstated my case, or to have been too harsh in my criticisms, it is only because certain factors have aligned themselves against a proper reception of the man and his ideas. Not the least of these is the stature of Chief Justice Marshall in American history, which over the course of time has assumed such immense proportions as to overshadow that of Mr. Justice Story. John Marshall was a lovable man, who possessed great intellectual and rhetorical prowess. Owing to the brilliance of Marshall, however, and to the limited nature of our past inquiries, we have failed to perceive the steady, permeating rays of Story's influence. I am persuaded that Marshall's contributions have been somewhat overestimated when compared to those of Story. For this reason the book is partly a "revisionist" interpretation of the roles both have played in the development of the American Constitution, especially in the early nineteenth century.

Story's relative obscurity may also be attributed to the general neglect of legal history; and, more specifically, to the neglect of ideas in American legal history, ideas which may or may not be revealed in the documentary remains of the past or spelled out in a lawyer's brief, but which were "in the air" all the same, coloring the environment and conditioning the climate of opinion.

Legal scholars, political scientists, and historians have surely missed a rich vein in neglecting to study law in relation to political philosophy and political theory. As a result, the common law foundations of our political thought are rarely explored in any depth, and the role of the Supreme Court in shaping our attitudes as well as our political, economic, and social institutions has been greatly minimized. I have found the combination of law and theory to be most fruitful in a study of Joseph Story, who was a lawyer in a variety of ways: as a writer and teacher immersed in its history, principles, and philosophy, and as a jurist who plunged into the thicket of political and constitutional theory. By failing to view legal history as the history of ideas, we invite misunderstanding of our institutions and their origin and, as in the case of Joseph Story, relegate many deserving individuals to the intellectual backwaters of time and thus to obscurity. For to study Story on the Constitution is to study to no small extent the place of natural law in constitutional law and history.

One of the great problems he faced as a member of the Supreme Court was the confusion and controversy surrounding the natural law philosophy. Rejecting the newer interpretations of natural law as represented in Locke and Rousseau, Story adopted what was essentially a Burkean, or traditional, natural law philosophy, which he wielded as a powerful instrument of jurisprudence. This interpretation is the general theme of my study and provides the book with whatever unity it may have.

Since the time of Story, the concepts of natural law and natural justice have fallen into an eclipse that has lasted more than a century. Such notions are no longer formally acknowledged as worthy of study or as guiding principles of jurisprudence. Most social scientists and legal scholars have adopted the Benthamite attitude that natural law is a legal fiction, the idle play of the imagination. Ignoring the fact that improvement in the law and in the art of government was often the result of the application of the moral principles of the natural law to the practical affairs of man, many have in effect dismissed as irrelevant and uninstructive more than a thousand years of legal development.

"History is the only true way to attain a knowledge of our own condition," Savigny, an admirer of Judge Story, wrote in 1815. While this may be an overstatement of the case for legal history, on the other hand it is true that today there is a near total disregard for this important subject. That a comprehensive history of American law has never been written is indeed a sad commentary on our times. Today's law students often graduate from the universities knowing little or nothing of legal history or legal philosophy. Seeming to despise the past, the legal world has turned to positivism and its vagaries in search of an elusive, "pure" science of law, much in the same way political scientists are now turning in increasing numbers to "behavioralism" in search of a "pure" science of politics. The only genuine knowledge, contend the positivists, is "scientific" knowledge. Any metaphysical question that does not lend itself to the methods of science or empirical proof should not be asked; it is "unscientific," and consequently "unintellectual," to make value judgments or to raise questions pertaining to the intellectual and ethical attributes of a particular political system, set of laws, or judicial decision.

To the positivist, concepts such as religion, culture, justice, virtue, and liberty are relative, and therefore meaningless. To the legal positivist—and he is a dominant figure in almost any law school today—the question that he invariably poses to his students asks what the law *is*, not what it *should be*. This narrow focus on the law as declared by the judges and legislatures is what Judge Story inveighed against, and what threatens to reduce the lawyer to the intellectual compass of a technician who simply recites cases, makes the proper citations, and dares not question the wisdom of the laws. The crucial consideration, holds the positivist, is not what is *good* law, but what *is* law or *how* it came into being. Hence it is impossible for the positivist to tell right from wrong, a just law from an unjust law, a good government from an evil one.

An ally of utilitarianism, legal positivism first took root in Germany. Hans Kelsen, who with Rudolph Stammler founded the neo-Kantian school of jurisprudence, represented every tenet of the traditional conception of rule of law as a metaphysical superstition. A state, he insisted, could not act "illegally" because "Every expression of the life of a State, every act of State, is a legal act."[1] The founder of the neo-Hegelian school, Josef Kohler, reached similar conclusions, asserting that there were no universal truths or eternal standards of right conduct.

The legal positivists were influential outside Germany, and their doctrines spread to the United States, where they were embraced by the rising school of jurisprudence known as "legal realism." Its most illustrious spokesman was Justice Holmes, who scoffed at natural law and thought it best if "every word

---

[1] Hans Kelsen, "The Pure Theory of Law" (trans. by C. H. Wilson), *Law Quarterly Review*, Vol. LI (1935), 534. "The Pure Theory of Law," he concluded, "denies that it can ever be the task of legal science to justify anything. Justification implies judgment of value, and judgment of value is an affair of ethics and of politics, not, however, of pure knowledge. To the service of that knowledge, legal science is dedicated." *Ibid.*, 535.

of moral significance could be banished from the law altogether." Justice Holmes, in fact, proclaimed that he did "not know what is true."[2]

But Holmes *did* know what was true; and like the natural law jurists he acted upon certain values, consciously or unconsciously. His opinions, as we all know, revealed a libertarian bias, a strong commitment to the need for vigorous protection of free speech and press, but less enthusiasm for economic due process or "liberty of contract." And it seems abundantly clear that today's doctrines of jurisprudence and the rejection of natural law have not "neutralized" the Constitution or rendered judicial opinions any less immune from value judgments.

In the modern Court the attack on natural law in the name of impartiality continues unabated, Justice Black being its most vociferous foe. He strongly criticized Justice Frankfurter in *Adamson* v. *California* for having suggested that "In the history of thought, 'natural law' has a much longer and much better founded meaning and justification"[3] than the doctrine that the first eight amendments to the Constitution can be incorporated wholesale into the Fourteenth. Professing self-restraint, complete objectivity, and a value-free, mechanistic jurisprudence, Black informed his colleagues that natural law was an "incongruous excrescence on our Constitution" which only served to "degrade the constitutional safeguards of the Bill of Rights and simultaneously appropriate for this Court a broad power which we are not authorized by the Constitution to exercise."[4] These are the words of a jurist who has gone as far as any member of the Supreme Court to stretch the meaning of the Constitution and expand federal judicial power! Fearful that the subtle workings of natural law might be influencing Justice Harlan, Black dissented in a recent decision involving the "right of privacy," insisting that this "mysterious" philosophy of natural law had been "repudiated" by the Supreme Court.[5] Like Holmes, Black seems unaware of his own partisanship in defense of absolutist libertarianism. The point is not simply that the spirit of natural law, as Otto Gierke observed, can never be extinguished, but that a completely value-free jurisprudence is both undesirable and impossible.[6]

Purporting to be "objective," the positivists and those under their influence delude themselves; they disavow values while at the same time they impose them. Leo Strauss has quite properly remarked that there is "a mysterious pre-established harmony between the new political science and a particular

[2] Oliver Wendell Holmes, "The Path of the Law," *The Mind and Faith of Justice Holmes* (ed. by Max Lerner), 78–79; "The Soldier's Faith," *ibid.*, 20.

[3] 332 U.S. 65 (1947).

[4] *Ibid.*, 70, 75.

[5] *Griswold* v. *Connecticut*, 381 U.S. 516 (1965).

[6] See Arthur S. Miller and Ronald F. Howell, "The Myth of Neutrality in Constitutional Adjudication," *University of Chicago Law Review*, Vol. XXVII, No. 4 (Summer, 1960), 661–95.

version of liberal democracy. That version of liberal democracy is not discussed openly and impartially. . . . The new political science looks for laws of human behavior to be discovered by means of data supplied through certain techniques of research which are believed to guarantee the maximum of objectivity; it therefore puts a premium on the study of things which occur frequently now in democratic societies: neither those in their graves nor those behind the curtains can respond to questionnaires or to interviews. Democracy is, then, the tacit presumption of the data."[7]

And to this, Russell Kirk adds cogently: "Although, generally, the behaviorists treat with indifference or contempt the questions of transcendent knowledge and of moral beliefs, their own predilection for molding society into a thoroughly democratic, egalitarian, strifeless unity necessarily brings them face to face—however disconcerting this may be—with religious and moral influences upon politics. . . . By disavowing all 'value judgments,' the behaviorists are cast back upon personal prejudices, popular slogans, and self-interest as models for society. Democracy, equality of condition, and social unity—not to say monolithic society—are the goals which appear, explicit or implied, in their writings."[8]

The claims of positivism, it would appear, do not always conform to the results. But more important, legal positivism, to confound the matter further, is often driven by the force of its inner "logic" to a position of neutrality between the free society and its totalitarian enemies. It is a short walk from the positivistic doctrine that law should be viewed as a form of regulated force, that the only true law is the command of the sovereign, to the idealization of the state and "scientific" socialism. If, as the positivists say, man is incapable of knowing justice, freedom, religion, and virtue, is not any system acceptable? Perhaps it is no mere coincidence that "In Hitler Germany and in Fascist Italy, as well as in Russia," legal positivism enjoyed some of its first and greatest successes among the intellectuals, establishing the belief "that under the rule of law the state was 'unfree,' a 'prisoner of the law,' and . . . must be released from the fetters of abstract rules. A 'free' State was the one that could treat its subjects as it pleased."[9]

Despite repeated assertions of faith by many intellectuals that basically democratic societies such as ours are incapable of succumbing from within to totalitarianism, there is no denying that over the past years the government of the United States has moved steadily in the direction of unlimited political

[7] Leo Strauss, "Epilogue," *Essays on the Scientific Study of Politics* (ed. by Herbert J. Storing), 326.

[8] Russell Kirk, "Segments of Political Science Not Amenable to Behavioristic Treatment," *The Limits of Behavioralism in Political Science* (ed. by James C. Charlesworth), 53, 54.

[9] Friedrich A. Hayek, *The Constitution of Liberty*, 239.

power and increased control of the individual in his daily affairs. "As an augury of things to come," Professor John Hallowell warns us, "realistic jurisprudence certainly suggests that tyranny is an inevitability. For the only way out of the intellectual and moral anarchy underlying the realist's conception of the law is tyranny. If force alone, as Justice Holmes believed, is the only possible arbiter of our 'deep-seated preferences,' if moral judgments are nothing more than expressions of individual taste and preference, and if law, as Jerome Frank declares, is simply what men arbitrarily declare it to be, then we have no choice but to submit our differences to the arena of force."[10]

A vindication of natural law, however, is not within the scope of this study. It is only my hope that, in the voice of an influential jurist such as Joseph Story, this most splendidly conceived utterance in America will be recognized at least as the life force that it once was, thereby deepening the understanding of American institutions in our own day.

In the past, the influence of natural law ideas upon the development of case law in particular has been questioned by some legal scholars, who have suspected that judicial references to natural law or natural rights were nothing but "rhetorical flourishes" adhering to no fixed standards. A popular text of jurisprudence, for example, asks whether "judicial references to 'natural law,' 'natural rights,' 'natural justice' signify the influence or acceptance of natural-law or natural rights philosophy in any of its definitive versions." The author concludes that "without more evidence (as to the particular case) the answer must be negative."[11] The reader may judge whether I have offered sufficient evidence to substantiate my claim that the answer must be Yes.

Joseph Story was one of the few men of his time who sensed, however faintly, the impending crisis in Western legal thinking and sought to establish an ethical and moral basis for authority through the incorporation of traditional natural law principles into America's institutional framework. His natural law, therefore, forms an essential part of our constitutional heritage, linking our jurisprudence to past, present, and future. It also plays a vital role in the dramatic struggle for the preservation and extension of individual liberty. Tracing the strains of that philosophy is the task to which the reader is invited to turn.

JAMES McCLELLAN

Hampden-Sydney, Virginia
March 21, 1971

[10] John H. Hallowell, *Main Currents in Modern Political Thought*, 367. See also his *Moral Foundation of Democracy*, *passim*.

[11] Edwin W. Patterson, *Jurisprudence: Men and Ideas of the Law*, 372.

Acknowledgments

IT is a pleasure to acknowledge the various institutions which have assisted me in the preparation of this book. The libraries of Emory University and the University of Virginia went far beyond their customary generosity in providing me with research materials, courteous assistance, and a quiet place to work. The Library of Congress, the National Archives, Henry E. Huntington Library, Pierpont Morgan Library, the William L. Clements Library at the University of Michigan, the Essex Institute, the Cincinnati Historical Society, the Historical Society of Pennsylvania, the Maine Historical Society, the Massachusetts Historical Society, the New Hampshire Historical Society, the New-York Historical Society, and the libraries of Harvard College, Christ's College (Oxford University), and North Carolina, Texas, and Yale universities not only have been equally helpful, but also have kindly permitted me to print passages, or whole letters, from their manuscript collections. I wish to extend my thanks to the Fogg Art Museum of Harvard University, the Boston Athenaeum, and again to the Essex Institute and Massachusetts Historical Society, for having allowed me to print photographs of paintings, statues, and busts of Joseph Story in their possession. The Essex Institute also permitted me to reproduce the photograph of Story's home in Salem, Massachusetts.

Not the least deserving of my gratitude are Emory University and the Earhart Foundation. Grants from these institutions made it possible for me to prepare and publish this book.

In the course of completing this publication, I have accumulated many obligations to individuals, not all of whom can be adequately acknowledged here. I am especially indebted to Professors Robert J. Harris and George W. Spicer of the University of Virginia, George Carey of Georgetown University, and the late Willmoore Kendall of the University of Dallas, all of whom read portions of this book. Their acute observations were invaluable, as were those of my former colleague Francis W. O'Brien of Rockford College. I am also grateful to the descendants of Joseph Story, especially Peter de Brant and Julian Story, who responded promptly and cheerfully to my letters of inquiry. Mr. de Brant kindly permitted me, with the assistance of professors George

Cuttino and Regis Courtemanche, to reproduce from his personal collection several photographs of members of the Story family.

A special note of appreciation is also due Professors R. Kent Newmyer and Gerald T. Dunne. They obligingly read the entire manuscript. Their counsel and learning, as well as their writings on Justice Story, were a constant source of reference and reflection. Mary Jane Guy also helped at every stage of the study as typist, editor, and critic.

But one of my deepest obligations, by far, is to Russell Kirk. His encouragement in this venture has been unflagging from the start. I shall forever be in debt to him for taking an interest in the work and for offering to read the manuscript in entirety. His searching eye uncovered errors of fact and judgment, and his shrewd comments on style were particularly helpful. Dr. Kirk's face-saving criticisms, as well as those of the scholars named above, enhanced a work which otherwise would have fallen even shorter of their high standards of scholarship.

Contents

Illustrations

Joseph Story and the American Constitution

Implicit in every decision where the question is, so to speak, at large, is a philosophy which, however veiled, is in truth the final arbiter. It accepts one set of arguments, modifies another, rejects a third, standing ever in reserve as a court of ultimate appeal. Often the philosophy is ill-coordinated and fragmentary. Its empire is not always suspected even by its subjects. Neither lawyer nor judge, pressing forward along one line or retreating along another, is conscious at all times that it is a philosophy which is impelling him to the front or driving him to the rear. None the less, the goad is there. If we cannot escape the Furies, we shall do well to understand them.

JUSTICE CARDOZO, *The Growth of the Law*

CHAPTER I

The Man and His Times

College was never in a worse state than when I entered it,—Society was passing through a most critical stage. The French Revolution had diseased the imagination and unsettled the understanding of men everywhere. The old foundations of social order, loyalty, tradition, habit, reverence for antiquity, were everywhere shaken, if not subverted. The authority of the past was gone. The old forms were outgrown, and new ones had not taken their place .... The state of morals among the students was anything but good.

WILLIAM ELLERY CHANNING, *Memoir*

OF the many tributes to Joseph Story as author, teacher, and jurist, none seems more lasting than that in the Cathedral of Saint John the Divine in the city of New York. Encased in the magnificent stained glass of the Lawyer's Bay is a small medallion of Story. He is with old friends. Solon, Hammurabi, Bracton, Grotius, Marshall, and other immortals stand close to his side. Major medallions of the Justinian Code, the Magna Carta, the Mayflower Compact, and the American Constitution surround him. The law of nature, scarcely shrinking from a comparison with the larger scenes, is represented by a smaller medallion slightly below and to the right of Story. The theme of the setting is "the gradual revelation of Law and Order throughout the world, with the Ten Commandments as the fundamental basis."[1] To the man who sought to proclaim the ways of God to man through the natural law, the Constitution, and the common law, this tribute is truly fitting.

The artist's selection of his subject's vocation is no less appropriate. Story is pictured as Dane Professor of Law at Harvard University instructing his students. That modestly remunerated chair, to which he brought all the luster of his high judicial character, was dearer to him than the Supreme Court bench he adorned for some thirty-four years under John Marshall and Roger Brooke Taney; more important to him than all of his successes in doctrinal writing, including his famed *Commentaries on the Constitution, Equity Jurisprudence,* and *Conflict of Laws,* which stand even today austere and indisputably grand in libraries across the country. Above all else, Joseph Story wanted to be re-

[1] Edward Hagaman Hall, *A Guide to the Cathedral Church of Saint John the Divine in the City of New York,* 63.

membered as a teacher of jurisprudence. He was, in fact, proudest of his title "Professor," and he placed it on the title pages of all his books. Only at the insistence of his publisher, Charles Sumner tells us, did he finally consent to add, "Justice of the Supreme Court of the United States."[2]

Story's reputation, like that of the Harvard Law School which he helped to found, increased with his years. Tradition later took up his name and handed down stories and anecdotes of his prowess at the bar and in the classroom. "Such appears to me to be the law in the case," John Marshall is said to have remarked once at a Supreme Court conference, "though I have not, I confess, looked much into the books. . . . If I am correct, our brother Story here . . . can give us the cases from the twelve tables down to the latest term reports."[3] In tales told by his students one gets an inkling of Story the eccentric and beloved scholar. On one occasion a fire alarm sounded while Story was delivering a lecture. "As the engines went clanging by," an admiring pupil recalled, "we began to peer out the windows, and our interest was so plainly shown in the matter of the fire . . . the judge took a look out the window himself, just as a large volume of smoke burst up from a nearby building, and said, 'Run, boys, run! *Inter ignes, silent leges.*' We ran, and the Judge followed."[4] And run he did throughout life, it seems, at a gallop. Some master spirit within him drove him at a feverish pace to great accomplishments which few in his profession have equaled before or since. His energies and feats as author, teacher, and jurist were so amazing as to stagger the imagination of even his most active contemporaries.

Aside from his reputation as a man of law, Story plays a prominent role in the social and intellectual history of the country—a fact which only in our own time is coming to be recognized.[5] In his own way, and at his own leisure—whenever he could salvage a moment from his tremendous teaching and juridical responsibilities—Joseph Story was a prophet and a preacher of the old school, striving wholeheartedly to spare his countrymen from a sterile modernism, pointing their gaze to that symmetry and balance of character which has seemed to many a noble mind the true goal of human endeavor. In drawing rooms and at the podium, one might hear his Olympian voice, re-

---

[2] "Tribute of Friendship: The Late Joseph Story," Boston *Daily Advertiser*, Sept. 16, 1845, reprinted in *Life and Letters of Joseph Story* (ed. by William W. Story), II, 618. Hereafter this work will be cited as *Life and Letters*.

[3] As quoted in William Plumer, Jr., *Life of William Plumer*, 205–206.

[4] Account of Daniel Saunders of Lawrence, Mass., a student in 1844, as quoted in Charles Warren, *History of the Harvard Law School and Early Legal Conditions in America*, II, 55.

[5] See, for example, Vernon Parrington, *Main Currents in American Thought, 1800–1860: The Romantic Revolution in America*, 299–303; R. Kent Newmyer, "A Note on the Whig Politics of Justice Joseph Story," *Mississippi Valley Historical Review*, Vol. XLVIII, No. 3 (Dec., 1961), 480–91. See also chapter 7, *infra*.

sisting with every gesture the thrust of innovation, if it was to encroach upon established truths in morals, literature, and politics.

Strange, that within a few generations his name would be almost entirely forgotten, except among the more learned of the legal profession. If, perchance, one should visit his native Marblehead, a charming little village nestled on the rocky Massachusetts shore not far from Boston and Salem, he would sadly note how the town has already begun to erase from memory its most famous inhabitant. The house in which Story lived as a boy still stands, but it serves today as an apartment instead of a national monument, and its whereabouts is known only to a few. There is a Story School, but no recollection exists among the townspeople of anyone named Joseph Story ever having lived in Marblehead. In Abbot Hall—which overlooks Marblehead's quiet, narrow streets, small business establishments, and sturdily constructed homes of the Federalist era—a large oil portrait of Story hangs in public view; yet the employees who daily pass beneath it squint in bewilderment at the mention of his name.

Happily, some thirty miles away in Cambridge, his silent presence may still be felt by students of the Harvard Law School. They have probably crossed the threshold of Story Hall or ambled down Story Street, which juts off Brattle on the way toward the house in which the judge and his family lived from 1829 until the time of his death. Surely they have viewed his many portraits and busts scattered across campus.

The late Story Professor of Law, Roscoe Pound, saw the need some twenty years ago to invigorate the memory of the man whose chair he honored. Under his guidance the statue of Joseph Story, carved by Story's son, William, was moved from Mount Auburn Cemetery and placed within university walls. Seated and gowned, with uplifted, emphatic hand, the majestic figure of Joseph Story now looks down like a father upon the students who enter and leave Langdell Hall. "One might take him there either as delivering a judgment in court or explaining a principle from his Harvard chair," commented Henry James when he first looked upon that artistic masterpiece. It expressed for James, as it must have for others, the character that made him exclaim, "What a lovable great man!"[6]

THE POET OF MARBLEHEAD

The eldest of eighteen children, Joseph Story was born in the small fishing village of Marblehead on September 18, 1779, three years after Thomas Jefferson penned the Declaration of Independence. Cradled in the revolutionary struggle of Massachusetts and nurtured by the intoxicating spirit of nineteenth-century romanticism, he was sure to follow a line of intellectual development as irregular as the New England coastline.

[6] *William Wetmore Story and His Friends*, I, 23–24.

As a youth who roamed the lonely beaches, shallow inlets, and rude territory of his native town, Story witnessed firsthand the overwhelming and triumphant wave of English individualism that swept across the Old Bay State. Later, as a diligent young man at Harvard College immersed in the *Odes* of Horace and the poetry of Milton and Pope, he intently observed the ebb of that wave, and the onrushing of a new, more powerful one, born in the storming of the Bastille and the ferocity of the French Revolution. He could not wholly avoid the influence of the revolutionary tide that lapped about him. Yet, reared in a Calvinist household and coming to appreciate early in his youth the attributes of a disciplined, orderly life, Story developed, under the watchful eyes of admonishing parents, an imaginative capacity and a breadth of spirit and intellect which eventually ran at crosscurrents with his age.

Indeed, as time wore on, Story seemed to many of his contemporaries a mere refuge of tradition and reaction amidst the flux of his turbulent era. It is true that Story, like so many early nineteenth-century conservatives—Orestes Brownson, Coleridge, and Wordsworth come immediately to mind—embarked upon life with a firm belief in the perfectibility of man and a suspicion of institutional restraints on the individual. But unlike many men of his day, he was never severely embittered by the democratic experiment when its ideals had lost their attraction. A man of jolly dimensions, with an evident taste for good living, Story had weathered the storm of revolution and reaction, the whirlwinds of progress, without losing a jot of that healthy, broad benevolence with which nature had enveloped his heart.

Thus, the nature of his early inspiration and training, under parental tutelage, indicates the mold but not the direction his mind was to take. While traditional patterns of morality were etched upon his soul to last a lifetime, his orthodoxy and conservatism were only fully realized years later, after a regrettable flirtation with radicalism as a young man.

Even before he emerged onto the national scene, Story was a fit candidate for Jefferson's natural aristocracy. Sharing with Herman Melville the honor of having a father who participated as an "Indian" in the Boston Tea Party, he acquired early in age a strong sense of history, tradition, and patriotism. His father, Dr. Elisha Story, had also been associated with the "Sons of Liberty." He had fought at the side of Thomas Marshall and General Washington during the American Revolution, serving as surgeon during the Jersey campaign in 1777.

Although firmly attached to Washington and Adams, Elisha Story was a member of the Republican party, and young Joseph adopted the same paradoxical attachments. A simple and generous man devoted to his family, the elder Story was a successful Marblehead physician, amply providing his son with amenities, both material and moral. He instilled in young Joseph a stern New England morality, balanced by a strong sense of religious toleration.

His mother, Mehitable (Pedrick) Story, encouraged his interest in reading, urging him often to excel in his work: "Now Joe, I've sat up and tended you many a night when you were a child," she chided in his formative years, "and don't you dare not to be a great man."[7]

Story recollected, however, that he had learned little from books as a child. His sensibilities instead were awakened by phantasms of his Marblehead, where "ghosts, hobgoblins, will-o-wisps, apparitions, and premonitions were the common, I might almost say the universal subjects of belief; and number-less were the stories of haunted houses, and wandering spirits . . . that were told at the fireside, and filled my imagination with all sorts of preternatural fears."[8] Days devoted to careless idling and gazing upon the sleepless ocean had steadily pumped the lifeblood of the locale, all of its color and romance, into his veins. One need only glance at *The Power of Solitude*, a contemplative, poetic effusion written at about the age of twenty-one, to see the effect of this childhood experience. Faintly limned in somber couplets is the portrait of a wide-ranging spirit, a sensitive, almost brooding lover of nature—a solitary with a keen desire for truth.

To appreciate the high and subtle quality of Story's talents, one has only to pit him against his age and the rationalists pure and simple, like Jeremy Bentham, whom it bred. Life played upon Story in richer and more varied ways. It touched him into response through associations having a more human character, a warmer and deeper color of emotion, drawn as much from family and professional ties as from his early surroundings. As a result, Story brought to bear upon his court decisions and treatises a broader understanding of human problems than the average jurist would subscribe to, and a more compendious accumulation of imaginative experience. Much of this approach stems from the fact that he had the romantic ferment in his blood.

Story also traced his strong love of literature to those superstitious inhabi-tants of Marblehead who spun romantic tales and legends of the sea.[9] The pith of old books was the marrow of his bones, and literature, next to juris-prudence, was his greatest love. He admired the works of Coleridge and Tennyson, but preferred the pre-Romantic English writers, heirs of the Augustan school and the classics. Among his favorites were Cowper, Gold-smith, and Gray, men who sought the natural, the simple, the sublime, and the pathetic within traditional poetic bounds.[10] If his literary tastes, like Lamb's,

---

[7] *Life and Letters*, I, 2–3.

[8] Joseph Story, "Autobiography," *The Miscellaneous Writings of Joseph Story* (ed. by William W. Story), 10. Hereafter this work will be cited as *Miscellaneous Writings*. Many of the papers collected in this volume were originally published by Justice Story under the title *The Miscellaneous Writings, Literary, Critical, Juridical and Political of Joseph Story* (Boston, 1835).

[9] Story, "Autobiography," *Miscellaneous Writings*, 10.

[10] *Ibid.*, 38.

inclined toward poetry bathed in the beatitude of a grander age, his approach to the law was no less romantic. As medieval as Sir Walter Scott, Story, who had once fancied himself "the veriest knight-errant in romance,"[11] sought adventure in ancient writs and old court cases. In more ways than one he was, as Charles Sumner proclaimed, the "Sir Walter Scott of the common law."[12]

It was at Marblehead Academy that Story developed a proficiency in Latin and Greek and a genuine interest in the classics and English literature. His formal education came to a temporary halt in the fall of 1794, when he withdrew from school in protest against an undeserved and severe beating inflicted by the schoolmaster. A disdainful and proud Story continued his studies unaided, determined to enter Harvard College.

Early in the winter of 1795, at the age of sixteen, he was escorted by his uncle, Isaac Story, to Cambridge, only to discover he had first to pass an entrance examination and equal the current attainment of the freshman class before enrolling. "This circumstance," Story recalled, "at first discouraging, gave by its success a new imposture to my mind, and taught me the valuable lesson of a reliance on my exertions. I have always thought it gave a strong impression to all my subsequent course of life."[13] Given only six weeks to learn the material, Story returned home and without benefit of tutor, mastered grammar, rhetoric, logic, the works of Sallust, the *Odes* of Horace, two books of Livy and Homer, and three of Xenophon's *Anabasis*. Returning to Harvard, he was again offered for examination and obtained his matriculation.[14]

At Harvard, Story was a conscientious student and severe taskmaster, graduating second in his class behind William Ellery Channing in 1798. Already a recognized scholar and poet in the academic community, he was given the traditional honor of delivering a poem at commencement.[15] He later burned that work in one of his many fits of protest against the age in which he lived, embarrassed that he, the archfoe of metaphysics, should ever have been drawn to its captivations. The poem was entitled "Reason."[16]

The Cambridge days also stimulated Story's romantic temperament to a republican fever, driving the fullblooded patriot-poet headlong into a general defense of the Enlightenment. The basic contradictions between eighteenth-century English liberalism and French revolutionary radicalism were not apparent to Story the poet as they were to Story the jurist. The impingement of startling events and ideas from abroad on progressive Harvard students

---

[11] Story to Samuel Fay, Sept. 6, 1801, *Life and Letters*, I, 77.

[12] "Tribute of Friendship," *Life and Letters*, II, 615.

[13] To Mr. Agg, Aug. 17, 1827 ("Autobiographical Letter"), Joseph Story Papers, Massachusetts Historical Society (cited hereafter as Story Papers, MHS).

[14] Story, "Autobiography," *Miscellaneous Writings*, 13–14.

[15] *Ibid.*, 17.

[16] *Ibid.*, 37.

likewise demanded of Story a reassessment of moral and political values. It briefly induced a religious skepticism and a contempt for "the shackles of the world and its customs."[17] Accusations that his ideas were colored with the "tinge of romance"[18] only served to stoke the fires that burned within him. Even his Harvard classmates admonished him to temper his idealism, but with little success. "Laughing is an innocent thing. But, believe me, Story, you will have frequent reason to cry," warned one student. "Your ingeniousness will be your snare. . . . [don't] be displeased, Story, if I should recommend to you careful perusal of the Bible, ardent love of its doctrines, obedience to its precepts, early piety and religion. 'Tis the only way to happiness. Truth is truth."[19]

Too independent to accept the advice of his peers, Story naïvely envisioned a private and national destiny along the primrose paths of utopianism. The reproach of elders was "but the calculating meanness of individual experience, which content to walk in the common road, knows not that flowers as well as thorns could blossom in the paths of life."[20] At twenty-one Story recommended Rousseau. Truths discovered through reason and impulse were far more reliable than those derived from the mundane process of experience or religion.

Even in the pink of his modernity, however, Story was never constitutionally attracted to radicalism, nor did he for a moment assume the ineffable smartness of the new young radicals. During his "radical" period the theme of the romantic movement, that the individual had a just claim to emancipation from outward restraints by reason of an inherent natural goodness, ran counter to his true disposition. He later grew to abhor the new crop of romantic poetry, certain that the untrammeled outpouring of oneself in feeling degenerated into lawlessness and the effacement of ethical distinctions. He found the romantics relied "too much on extravagant events, characters and passions, far removed from common life, and farther removed from general sympathy."[21]

Drawn as he was, then, in these early years, to men of Southey's fiery temperament and radical thought, the quiet, redolent tones of olden literature still echoed in the antechambers of his mind. Southey's sentiments of justice and liberty excited him pleasurably, but Story was more attracted to his native integrity: "Our degeneracy alone prevents us from perceiving his merit. As a poet, he is *inter magnates*; as a politician, equitable and humane . . . He is now

---

[17] Story to Fay, Jan. 6, 1801, *Life and Letters*, I, 79.

[18] Story, letter written June 21, 1800, *ibid.*, 78.

[19] Leonard Woods to Story, Sept. 12, 1796, Joseph Story Papers, William L. Clements Library, University of Michigan (hereafter cited as Story Papers, Clements Library).

[20] Letter written June 21, 1800, *Life and Letters*, I, 78.

[21] Joseph Story, "Characteristics of the Age," A Discourse Pronounced at Cambridge, before the Phi Beta Kappa Society of Harvard University, Aug. 31, 1826, *Miscellaneous Writings*, 367.

my favorite."[22] With equal enthusiasm his fingers tripped lightly through the political tracts of Junius, that "philosophic citizen of the world,"[23] who appealed to Story as a prolocutor of universal truths. His infatuation with Rousseau, however, seems to have been more on the order of sensationalism and romance than intellectual commitment. Nearly in the throes of ecstasy, Story wrote to his lifelong friend, Samuel Fay, in 1798: "I perceive by a hint of your letter, that you have read Emilius. Pray write me your opinion of it. I know you admire it. Read his Eloisa and be crazy."[24]

Thus, when the distant tremors of the French Revolution were being felt in the Federalist homes of Boston and Salem, Story responded with jubilant poetic utterance, framed, ironically, in conventional Popian couplets:

> So chained by tyrant power in cursed Bastile,
> Whose weeping walls uncounted wrongs reveal,
> Fate's hopeless victim, prey of cankerous care,
> On torture feeds and surfeits on despair.
> But hark! the portal on its hinges jars,
> And freedom's arm unbolts the ponderous bars.
> Enwrapt in flames she melts his chain away
> And leads the astonished captive forth to day.[25]

The truths which had inspired Story to assume this apocalyptic pose he later came to believe were at best only a spurious, holiday view of existence. A broader experience might have rendered the young man from Marblehead less likely to indulge in a violent and theatrical rupture with the age after the fashion of Rousseau, or to risk the delicate and perilous task of a breach with the past.

Nevertheless, it is evident that even as a student, Story was able to taste that true felicity which is accompanied by stability, independence, and contentment —a felicity too seldom desired only because it is too little known, but which every man may cultivate within. Contrary to what the title of the poem ("The Power of Solitude") might suggest, its young author was no extravagant misanthrope, who would compel mankind to retire into forests, to inhabit dens and caves, and to live only with wild beasts. Few men seem more completely satisfied that man is born for society, or seem to have grasped all the social duties of life than Mr. Story. It is not in tumultuous joys, in the noisy

---

[22] Story, letter written in 1799, *Life and Letters*, I, 80–81. At this time Robert Southey was an ardent republican and convert to Coleridge's pantisocracy.

[23] *Ibid.*, 81. According to Story's son, "his opinions of the letters of Junius became entirely changed in after life." *Ibid.*

[24] Sept. 6, 1798, *ibid.*, 75–76.

[25] *The Power of Solitude*, a new and improved edition, containing "Fugitive Poems," 25. His opposition to the French Revolution increased with age. See, for example, *Miscellaneous Writings*, 663.

pleasure of public entertainments, in blindly following the chimeras of ambition or the illusions of self-love that men must expect to feel the charms of those reciprocal ties which unite them to society. Under the peaceful shades of solitude, the mind of man regenerates, and his faculties for human compassion acquire new force:

> By moral musings social feelings start,
> And mould to truth the sympathies of heart.

Although the work is imitative in subject, theme, and style of Thomson, Zimmermann, and Pope, slavish in its use of classical allusion, and not wholly free from bombast or learned discourse, it reveals a unique balance, social and personal, to be admired in one standing at the threshold of experience.

What emerged from those venerable shades of Harvard College was, then, a friend to humanity, a sensible and virtuous individual, and an honest citizen, who chose, through the medium of poetry, and later the law, to enlighten the minds of his fellow creatures upon a subject most interesting to them: the attainment of virtue and happiness. In whatever station of life thereafter Story chose to navigate the freighted and noble cargo of his thought, be he poet, public man of affairs, or jurist, one would surely discern the same reverence for society, the same stress on intellectual attainment and personal contentment.

The return home from Cambridge in 1798 left the young graduate in a state of despondency and uncertainty. College friends were going their separate ways, to be seen no more; a career would have to be taken up, and a means of livelihood attained. The stimulating world of books and intellectual companionship at Harvard had, he quickly discovered, alienated him from provincial Marblehead, that backward little hamlet of "general poverty" where there was "little room for the pride of scholarship, or the triumph of superior knowledge."[26] Stimulating letters from former classmates, such as the one which arrived from Berlin in the summer of 1799, however, kept him abreast of the times, offered sound advice, revived fond memories, and provided temporary escape from isolated Marblehead. "We shall, Joe, find that the hours we passed in those walls will be some of the pleasantest during life," sighed the correspondent, "however glad we were to get out of sight of them. The joys of Harvard are not justly appreciated by those who are in the immediate enjoyment; it is to us only, who have bid adieu to her venerable walls, that their true value is known; like the blessings of liberty, they are contemned by those who profess them, and valued by those out of whose reach they are placed."[27] The situation in Germany, he reported, was ominous; radicalism, like that apparently attractive to Story, had carried the day, with disastrous consequences: the "fondness of the Germans" for belles-lettres "has been much

[26] Story, "Autobiography," *Miscellaneous Writings*, 7.
[27] Thomas Welsh to Story, June 17, 1799, Story Papers, Clements Library.

weakened by the doctrines & writings of the philosophers of the Parisian school; the exertions of the latter have been incredible, & their success proportionate to their exertions—the populace of letters are almost to a man infected with the holy doctrine of liberty & the rights of man ('equality' is now laid aside)."[28]

Hundreds of miles to the south of Marblehead, but almost a decade earlier, another young man whose path Joseph Story was destined to cross read similarly unfavorable accounts of revolutionary developments in Europe. Gouverneur Morris, American minister to France, had been sending home reports of "the scarlet and revolting phases of the French Revolution that came to the Virginia lawyer,"[29] John Marshall. As for Marshall, little persuasion was necessary to turn him against the armed doctrines of the French radicals. In 1792 he was a conservative lawyer, a Federalist, and an honored patriot who had fought beside Washington at Valley Forge and in the Virginia ratification struggle of 1788 to secure the adoption of the American Constitution.

Not surprisingly, then, Morris' candid descriptions of the Jacobin atrocities had an immediate and lasting impact on Marshall. The youthful and ingenuous Story, now more removed from the ghastly activities of the Terrorists, required additional time to see the relationship between the ideas and the events; he would also need the sobering influence of his chosen career before coming around completely to Marshall's point of view. The legal profession provided just such an influence, and Story's decision to undertake the study of law, therefore, proved to be a major turning point in his thinking—though this was not realized at first either by Story or his acquaintances.[30]

Story embarked upon a legal career apparently "for the lack of anything better to do."[31] As was customary in these times—there being an acute shortage

[28] *Ibid.*

[29] Albert J. Beveridge, *The Life of John Marshall*, II, 8. Writing to Robert Morris, Gouverneur Morris related on one occasion that the owner of a quarry had demanded damages because so many corpses had been dumped into his quarry that they "choked it up so that he could not get men to work at it." These victims, he continued, were "the best people," killed "without form of trial, and their bodies thrown like dead dogs into the first hole that offered." Other accounts of the Revolution by Morris were equally shocking: "(September 2, 1792) the murder of the priests . . . murder of prisoners . . . . (September 3) The murdering continues all day . . . . (September 4th) And still the murders continue." As quoted *ibid.*, 7. According to Beveridge, Marshall had access to Gouverneur Morris' letters as Robert Morris' attorney and business associate.

[30] Edward Everett, Massachusetts statesman, orator, educator and friend of Story, later recalled as editor of the *North American Review* that "Mr. Justice Story was of the democratic party, and shared the general views of that party, on questions of constitutional politics; but with a mind of too legal a cast, to run into wild revolutionary extremes." "Story's Constitutional Law, *North American Review*, Vol. XXXVIII (Jan., 1834), 82–83.

[31] Gerald T. Dunne, "Joseph Story: The Germinal Years," *Harvard Law Review*, Vol. LXXV, No. 4 (Feb., 1962), 719.

of law schools—he turned to the legal profession for instruction and persuaded Marblehead's leading Federalist lawyer, Samuel Sewall, to take him on as a student-apprentice. Unlike Marshall, whose formal "training" in the law consisted of six casual weeks of lectures at the College of William and Mary,[32] Story encountered an exhaustive and protracted course of legal study. The Essex County Bar of Massachusetts into which he sought admission was one of the strictest in the country. Attorneys admitted to practice were required not only to offer proof of a college education and three years of study under a lawyer, but also to obtain the consent and recommendation of the bar.[33]

Compounding his difficulties was Sewall's political career, which separated teacher and pupil for months at a time. Being a member of the Congress, Sewall was often in Philadelphia, leaving Story to fend for himself in Marblehead. From Sewall's office Story sadly wrote to his friend, Samuel Fay:

Conceive, my dear fellow, what is my situation, doomed to spend at least ten years, the best of my life, in the study of the law,—a profession whose general principles enlighten and enlarge, but whose minutiae contract and distract the mind. Ambition is truly the food of my existence, and for that alone life is desirable. Yet, hard lot! Those favorite studies, those peculiar [literary] pursuits by which I have fondly (however vainly) hoped to attain celebrity, are ravished, and I must content to be a *plodder* in order to be what the world calls a *man*. Yet it is the part of cowardice to shrink, and of imbecility to hesitate. I have determined, and will execute.[34]

And execute he did. Sewall's frequent absences found the young apprentice once again thrown back on his own resources. He would have to master the law almost entirely on his own. Accustomed to exploring the haunts of poetry and gazing upon the lofty structures of the great masters of prose, Story was initially repelled by the "back-letter" philosophers. He thought law dry. Soon he was lost in the complex passages of the commentators. His spirits reached a nadir when he found—as Kent,[35] Blackstone,[36] and others had before him— that *Coke on Littleton* was almost incomprehensible. "I took it up," recalled Story, "and after trying it day after day with very little success, I sat myself

[32] Beveridge, *Life of Marshall*, I, 154. Chancellor Kent read law for three years in the Poughkeepsie law office of Attorney General Egbert Benson before being admitted to the bar in New York; Daniel Webster spent less than a year in the law office of Christopher Gore, Boston Federalist, but read widely and intensely. For an excellent discussion of legal education in the post-Revolutionary era, see Anton-Hermann Chroust, *The Rise of the Legal Profession in America*, II, Chapter 4.

[33] Chroust, *Rise of the Legal Profession*, II, 35.

[34] Sept. 6, 1798, *Life and Letters*, I, 71.

[35] John Theodore Horton, *James Kent: A Study in Conservatism*, 37. Webster "complained of 'murdered' Latin and the agonizing perplexities of *Coke on Littleton*." Maurice G. Baxter, *Daniel Webster and the Supreme Court*, 4.

[36] David A. Lockmiller, *Sir William Blackstone*, 17. Blackstone complained that *Coke on Littleton* was "too much for Hercules."

down and wept bitterly. My tears dropped upon the book, and stained its pages."[37] But Story persevered, until at last he could "see daylight."

Blackstone's *Commentaries on the Laws of England*, the first introductory book for the use of law students in Anglo-American law, posed fewer problems. In sharp contrast to Coke's crabbed commentary on Littleton's summary of medieval law, Blackstone's comprehensive treatment of eighteenth-century English law was free of technicalities and stylistic gaucheries. Even so, Story experienced some difficulty, as did American lawyers generally, in applying Blackstone to American law, and turned to Sewall for a practical solution to the question of the applicability of the common law to American common law. "The difficulty you suggest as occurring in the reading of Blackstone," wrote Sewall encouragingly from Philadelphia in the winter of 1799, "shews a proper attention to what must be the principal aim of your studies; the knowledge of the laws of *your* country is requisite to a Counsellor & Practitioner."[38] Therefore, he advised, it is necessary first

to examine the *theory* & general doctrines & the *origin* of the municipal law, & descending from generals to particulars, to discover the *partial* applications & *limits* of the [English] system. In this last course you are engaged, & it is apparent that this must be the most scientific, & you need not fear that when you have the law of England as a system of *political, moral* & *economic* rules, you will find any difficulty in ascertaining the variations which our situation & difference of manners and general policy have required.[39]

Having once acquired a knowledge of the English law, Sewall continued, Story should then commence a reading of Massachusetts laws,

and in them you will discover all the local and positive variations of the general system. . . . You are to view, then, Blackst[one] & other books which you will be put to read, as affording you tenets & doctrines of which some are directly & plainly applicable & of full obligation in this country as well as in England; rules & principles of indirect effect, & other parts, tho[ugh] inapplicable, abrogated or disused, have a logical utility, seeming to connect the system & thereby aiding the memory in retaining the parts of it which have been adopted, & serving also in many instances to explain & harmonize them.[40]

Thus was Story instructed in the law of the young Republic, at a time in American history of widespread aversion to everything English, especially the traditional common law.[41] As will become more clearly evident later, the

37 "Autobiography," *Miscellaneous Writings*, 19–20.

38 Feb. 12, 1799, Story Papers, Clements Library. Emphasis supplied.

39 *Ibid*. Emphasis supplied.

40 *Ibid*. Sewall's letter is an interesting document in American legal history. Additional and extensive portions are reproduced and discussed in chapter 4, *infra*.

41 See, for example, Chroust, *Rise of the Legal Profession*, II, 3–92; Roscoe Pound, *The Formative Era of American Law*, ch. 4; Howard Mumford Jones, *O Strange New World*, 273–350.

teachings of Blackstone and the advice of Sewall permanently influenced his thinking, and all his life he remained as devout a son of English legal institutions as a Holt, a Mansfield, or a Burke. The fervid radicalism of Jean Jacques would soon be displaced in Story's mind by the unruffled conservatism of Blackstone; and the reckless denunciations of the common law by Story's fellow democrats, countered by Sewall's encomiums, had no discernible effect on his thinking. He readily shared Sewall's belief that "that system of written & unwritten reason which our fathers brought with them to this country and very early adopted as the bond of the social order" was unquestionably "their noblest inheritance from their native country."[42]

With Coke and Blackstone behind him, Story was now prepared to undertake a reading of the cases. Busily engaged in matters of state, Sewall tardily responded in the spring of 1800. "I have not intentionally neglected your inquiries as to your studies," he apologized. "Plowden and Saunders are the two authors to be first read as reporters; these I presume you have gone thro[ugh]. Coke's reports, if you can borrow a modern edition of them, are well worth your attention." Likewise, the Massachusetts reports "are all to be read . . . . At my return I shall attempt to review with you some of the elementary treatises which you have read, and assist you in arranging your learning. But your memory is the best commonplace & deposit & I have myself found that principles of law are better remembered as well as more accurately understood when applied in reporter's cases, than drawn from [a] book of elementary maxims & reasons."[43]

Appointed to the Supreme Judicial Court of Massachusetts, Sewall, however, was unable to fulfill his promises, and toward the end of his apprenticeship, Story was compelled to move across the harbor to Salem to complete his legal study in the offices of Samuel Putnam. Having by this time digested a prodigious amount of law, Story now "breathed a purer air" and swore to his utmost satisfaction he "had acquired a new power."[44]

But the transformation from Story the poet to Story the lawyer was still incomplete. In 1804 he decided to publish "A New and Improved Edition" of his poem "The Power of Solitude." The earlier edition had appeared in 1802.

[42] Sewall to Story, Feb. 12, 1799, Story Papers, Clements Library.

[43] Sewall to Story, Apr. 3, 1800, Story Papers, Clements Library. Story apparently followed his teacher's advice. His son recalled years later, "His knowledge of the law had scarcely any boundaries. . . . [H]e had read nearly everything of any value in the range of jurisprudence. And he remembered with wonderful accuracy what he had read. It did not, however, lie in his mind like a dull, cumbrous load of facts, cases, rules, and precedents, but like a living organization held together and vivified by principles. But not only this; he remembered all the leading cases in every branch of the law, by name and volume, and many of them by page." William Wetmore Story, *Conversations in a Studio*, II, 448–49.

[44] Story, "Autobiography," *Miscellaneous Writings*, 19–20.

It "is such as I should not wish to meet in any library," Story remarked years later, "it is so rusty & youthful a collection. The latter is far more extensive."[45] His Massachusetts critics, however, were unable to discern any improvement in quality. Ridiculed and scoffed, the poem nevertheless piqued Story's Federalist tantalizers, who were closely scrutinizing his every thought and deed. "It has much puzzled my brain to find for what purpose you want the P. of Solitude," wrote Richard D. Harris to Leverett Saltonstall. "I have ransacked my imagination in vain for a cause . . . . It is said that the author after many revisions & corrections, after much labor & sweat has sent a copy of his production to London for publication. The fellow is not content to be thought a fool at home, but must even go abroad to be laughed at. See what comes of vanity. Should he prove worthy of notice, the receivers will no doubt give him a taste of their 'birch.' "[46] Story was unable to sustain with equanimity such repeated attacks, and his second poetic endeavor met the fate of the Harvard poem. Buying up as many copies of the work as he could find, he set them to the torch and despairingly watched a lifetime ambition smoulder in the ashes.

Had the critics been more kind, there is little doubt our subject would have commanded the necessary reassurance to pursue a literary career. But there were other problems frustrating his literary aspirations, more personal and social in nature. "Captain Nichols," recorded the Reverend William Bentley (December 3, 1800), an acute observer of the local scene and opponent of Story, "wishes to dissolve an intimacy formed between his daughter & Story the Poet of Marblehead."[47]

Story's literary dilettantism is of no small importance in assessing the quality of his mind or the fullness of his character. There was hardly a lawyer renowned in those times for extent of capacity or greatness of exploit, who had not left behind him some memorial of lonely wisdom and silent dignity. Possibly "another Ovid" was Alexander Pope's estimate of Mansfield's unexplored literary talent. Sir William Blackstone "lisped in numbers," as did most great American lawyers of the early nineteenth century. William Wirt, the Tuckers of Virginia, John Pendleton Kennedy, William Gilmore Simms, Philip Pendleton Cooke, Richard Dana, Hugh Swinton Legaré, and William Wetmore Story, to mention only a few, divided their talents into literary and legal pursuits. As Thomas Nelson Page has noted, "Their profession called forth the exercise of the highest intellectual powers, and necessarily they occasionally strayed into the adjoining domain of letters."[48] There is truly something to be said for this "seeming aptitude of second-rate poets to become first-rate jurists."[49]

45 To Agg, Aug. 17, 1827, Story Papers, MHS.

46 Apr. 27, 1803, Leverett Saltonstall Papers, Massachusetts Historical Society.

47 *The Diary of William Bentley, D.D.,* I, 358 (cited hereafter as Bentley, *Diary*).

48 "Authorship in the South before the War," in *The Old South: Essays Social and Political,* 67.

Story actually developed somewhat of a reputation as a man of letters in later years. A multivolume anthology entitled *A Library of American Literature*, published in 1888, offered a selection of his poetry and prose,[50] and William Story recounts that one day Rufus Griswold—journalist, literary critic, discoverer of poets and poetesses such as the renowned Mrs. Osgood, and the protector of Edgar Allan Poe—approached him on the streets of Boston in regard to a book he intended to publish, *Prose Writers of America*, which would contain extracts from all the leading writers of the country. He requested of William any particular passages Judge Story should like to have printed, and suggested that the judge also be persuaded to sit at his leisure for a portrait painter, either Inman or Page, so that he could "adorn a picture gallery of all the distinguished authors in England and America."[51]

Convinced it was better to delve than to soar, however, Joseph Story chose the law as the profession most amenable to his true talents and ambitions. Pegasus had carried him only so far as the wind in his quarter of experience would allow. Rather than risk the perils of falling short of poetic brilliance, Story chose to invest his inexhaustible fund of energy and genius in more promising stock. Bidding "A Lawyer's Farewell to the Muse," Story nevertheless continued to write under its spell, partly to satisfy his romantic inclinations and partly from an early belief that "truth is never more forcibly impressed than when it appears in the substantial forms of historic truth, or the sportive fablings of mythology."[52] But it was when he discoursed and wrote of law that the real power of his intellect was shown.

THE SALEM LAWYER

"It can not be unknown to you," wrote the Republican congressman from Salem, Jacob Crowninshield, to a member of the Jefferson administration in 1802, "that we have very few republican lawyers in Massachusetts. It is a fact that nine tenths of the bar are federal & uniting together with the judges, who are federal to a man, we have a formidable body against us which time only can remove. A young republican lawyer is almost a phenomenon. Still this County affords one, & we are indeed proud that we possess Mr. Joseph Story. He is at present in the Inferior Courts, & hints are already given out that he will not be received in the Supreme Court because Jacobins are not wanted there."[53]

[49] Dunne, "Joseph Story: The Germinal Years," *Harvard Law Review*, Vol. LXXV, No. 4 (Feb., 1962), 719.

[50] Edmund Clarence Stedman and Ellen Mackay Hutchinson, eds., *A Library of American Literature*, IV, 421–26.

[51] James, *William Wetmore Story*, I, 79.

[52] Story, "Proem," *The Power of Solitude*, 1–2.

[53] To Levi Lincoln [?], Nov. 26, 1802, Letters of Application and Recommendation during the Administration of Thomas Jefferson, 1801–1809 (Appointment Papers),

No sooner had the young Salem lawyer sprung from the law office of Samuel Putnam than a pack of Federalists was unkenneled at his heels to run him down. Attempts to prevent his practicing law, whether real or imagined, were unsuccessful, however, and in July of 1801 he gained admission to the Essex bar and opened a law office in Salem. Being a Republican in a society dominated by Federalists, however, made the legal profession initially onerous for Story, and clients did not immediately flock to him. "Mr. Story is marked out for destruction, he has aided the cause of the Gover't & the people,"[54] observed Crowninshield in 1802. The Federalists "had a 'Court Ball' last week and no republican was asked ... [they] voted to exclude certain persons among whom we find our names, Silsbee, Story ...."[55]

In addition to social and professional ostracism were public vituperations, which engendered a settled hostility between Story and the Federalists. "For several years after I came to the Bar I stood there the solitary & unaided supporter of Mr. Jefferson's administration," recalled Story, "[and] political excitements were not then, as now, assuaged by the milder courtesies of private life."[56] A group of horrors was pressed upon the public imagination regarding the character of this young man to prop the cause of good government and sound morals. "I was brought up in the heart of Essex County Federalism," recounted a student of Story's, "and it may illustrate the intenseness and stubbornness of political animosity of these times when I say that all through my boyhood I heard Joseph Story's name as synonymous with all that is evil and hateful, on the sole ground of his activity as a leader of the Democratic party."[57]

Story scoffed at charges he was "a deist, a defender of suicide, an eccentric phenomenon, a violent Jacobin,"[58] but the conduct of the accused sometimes contained little of the calm dignity of innocence. This is not to say that Story displayed all the uneasiness of guilt, but only that he was too excitable and proud to be coerced into silence if the situation called for a show of physical as well as mental strength in defense of principle. His vindications of political

---

National Archives. This letter, written from Salem and in the hand of Crowninshield, has been tampered with by an unknown party. The last page, containing the names of the sender and recipient, are missing, and the name of one person identified in the letter has been carefully cut out, apparently with scissors. See also Crowninshield's letter to Richard Crowninshield, on November 15, in Dunne, "Joseph Story: The Germinal Years," *Harvard Law Review*, Vol. LXXV, No. 4 (Feb., 1962), 714–15.

[54] To Richard Crowninshield, Nov. 24, 1802, in Dunne, "Joseph Story: The Germinal Years," *Harvard Law Review*, Vol. LXXV, No. 4 (Feb., 1962), 714–15.

[55] *Ibid.*

[56] To Agg, Aug. 17, 1827, Story Papers, MHS.

[57] Andrew Peabody, *Harvard Reminiscences*, 56.

[58] Story to Fay, Feb. 28, 1801, *Life and Letters*, I, 87.

belief frequently touched off a rowdy response, even to an exchange of blows or a street brawl.

"Election approaches," recorded Pastor Bentley (April 2, 1803), and "this day Mr. Story and Hearsay Derby had an open engagement at fisty-cuffs. The passions of party rise, & had any provocations ensued afterwards, the utmost resentment would have been discovered."[59] On another occasion an entry in Bentley's *Diary* (February 22, 1805), ran, "Mr. Martin & Story had a fight, & since that time affairs are more quiet."[60] Theodore Parker recalled an instance during which Story was "on account of his political opinions, knocked down in the street, beaten, and forced to take shelter in the house of a friend, whither he fled, bleeding, and covered with the mud of the streets."[61]

Story was fond of delivering patriotic orations. In 1800 he delivered his first eulogy (which he later condemned as "poor and in bad taste,"[62] probably for its strong Republican overtones), on the death of George Washington, thereby marking the formal beginning of a public career.[63] His decision to join the party of Mr. Jefferson was probably based more upon filial devotion than philosophical conviction. "My father was a Republican, as contradistinguished from a Federalist," said Story, "and I had naturally imbibed the same opinions."[64] But a close friend thought Story's "ardent temperament, his want of experience, his consequent overestimate of the virtue of man, and ignorance of the disturbing influences of passion and selfishness" explained his decision to join the Jeffersonian Republicans. "His democracy was the dream of a young and pure mind, glowing with visions of an ideal commonwealth, which were to be realized by the removal of all restraints, and by leaving men free to indulge their natural impulses."[65] No doubt, however, the emphasis upon national unity among New England Republicans, and secessionist sympathies among certain Federalists, reinforced the correctness of his choice. "A Virginia republican of that day was very different from a Massachusetts republican," explained Story, "and the anti-federal doctrines of the former state then had and still have very little support or influence in the latter state, notwithstanding a concurrence of political action upon general subjects."[66]

[59] *Diary*, II, 18.

[60] *Ibid.*, 142.

[61] *Additional Speeches, Addresses, and Occasional Sermons*, I, 178.

[62] *Life and Letters*, I, 84.

[63] Joseph Story, "An Eulogy on General George Washington," Written at the Request of the Inhabitants of Marblehead and Delivered before Them on the Second Day of January, 1800.

[64] "Autobiography," *Miscellaneous Writings*, 20.

[65] "Biographical Notice of Mr. Justice Story," *American Review, A Whig Journal*, Vol. III (Jan., 1846), 68–69. The anonymous writer identifies himself only as one who "was, for many years, honored by his friendship and his confidence," and now writes "with suffused eyes and a trembling hand." *Ibid.*, 82.

[66] "Autobiography," *Miscellaneous Writings*, 27. The Louisiana Purchase, the Electoral

An inordinate deference to the sovereignty of the federal state was a fixed principle dominating the mind of Joseph Story throughout his political and juridical career. "I was and always have been a lover, a devoted lover, of the Constitution of the United States, and a friend of the union of the states. I never wished to bring the government to a mere confederacy of states; but to preserve the power of the general government given by all the states in full exercise and sovereignty for the protection and preservation of all the states."[67]

A political enigma was this Jeffersonian Republican who warmly supported the Federalist theory of government. "I was at all times a firm believer in the doctrines of General Washington," Story confessed, "and an admirer of his conduct, measures and principles during his whole administration. . . . I read and examined his principles, and have made them in a great measure the rule and guide of my life."[68] In a letter dated March 24, 1801, Story expressed admiration for "Washington, Adams, Pinckney, Pickering and other illustrious men, who are supposed to be the touchstones of party." These leading Federalists, said Story, "have always received my unreserved public approbation. The late administration has always been the theme of my praise, though in some individual measures my judgment has differed from that of more enlightened statesmen."[69] Significantly, one of the "individual measures" from which Story dissented was the Sedition Act of 1798.[70]

Story's political views and affiliations encompassed a broad field of conflicting theories. He wore the badge of a Jeffersonian Republican, but it would seem a more stalwart Federalist never graced the American political scene. Although a member of the Republican party throughout his career in the Massachusetts legislature and the United States House of Representatives, he refused to truckle to Republican policies and consistently offered or opposed measures against the wishes of his party; yet he never joined Federalist ranks. Among Republicans his party loyalties were often deemed questionable. Federalists thought him a radical Jacobin. But basically he was an independent

---

Amendment Act, and other Republican measures convinced such Federalist senators as Tracy and Hillhouse of Connecticut and Pickering of Massachusetts that the continued allegiance of their states to the federal union would result in their destruction by democracy. See Henry Adams, *History of the United States of America*, I, 160, and William A. Robinson, *Jeffersonian Democracy in New England*, 36. Fisher Ames believed most southern politicians were "Jacobins." Ames, *Works*, 310, cited in Robinson, *ibid.*

[67] Story, "Autobiography," *Miscellaneous Writings*, 27.

[68] *Ibid.*

[69] To Captain Ichabod Nichols, Mar. 24, 1801. Joseph Story Papers, University of Texas (cited hereafter as Story Papers, Texas). During his senior year at Harvard, Story had drafted a nationalistic memorial endorsing President Adams' policy in the undeclared war against France.

[70] Story to Harrison Gray Otis, Dec. 27, 1818, Harrison Gray Otis Papers, Massachusetts Historical Society (cited hereafter as Otis Papers, MHS).

belonging to no party. A gentleman in Boston once asked Story during these times whether his political sentiments were Federal or Jacobinical. "Neither," retorted Story, "but that I was a person *sui generis.* 'He that is not with us is against us,' replied he, and I was accordingly dubbed a political heretic."[71]

Even during the height of his "radicalism," Story's feelings were strongly enlisted in more moderate ranks:

It has frequently been asserted that my political opinions are Jacobinical. This I absolutely deny. Though I am not on the *extreme* of what are denominated federal principles, I feel myself a *Federalist* in the noblest sense. I respect the constituted authorities of my country, as much as any man. I venerate the constitution of my country as the grand palladium of our rights and liberties. I detest the arts and designs of ambitious demagogues, and as far as my feeble influence has extended, have unhesitatingly opposed their injurious maxims. . . .

It has been my misfortune, but not my crime, to have once entertained doubts respecting Christianity. This has ever been viewed by me an unfortunate circumstance, to remove which, I have labored and read with assiduous attention all the arguments of its proof. . . . I have never been an infidel . . . . I verily believe Christianity necessary to the support of civil society, and shall ever attend to its precepts as the pure and natural sources of private and social happiness.[72]

Such were the sentiments of Salem's most unpopular, maligned lawyer, sentiments which Story's antagonists were unwilling to accept as palliatives for his conduct as a partisan of the Republican cause. Although he had steeled himself to endure the persecution and abuse of the Federalist clique, there were moments when he nearly broke under the strain. "I never look back upon this period without surprise," reminisced Judge Story from his armchair in 1827, "that I was not driven to change my residence. In fact, I had it in serious contemplation to remove several times; but the turn of public events & my growing practice, stimulated by professional pride, induced me to remain in Salem."[73]

By 1803, Story's legal practice was becoming more lucrative, in spite of these considerable political and social handicaps. In a year or two, he says, business flowed in upon him;[74] and the entries of his Case Record Book for the years

[71] Undated and Unaddressed Letter, *Life and Letters,* I, 81.

[72] Story to Captain Nichols, Mar. 24, 1801, Story Papers, Texas. Captain Nichols was the father of Lydia Nichols, who at this time was being courted by young Joseph. Story's beseeching letter was an attempt to persuade the captain that he was not the radical the inhabitants of Salem had made him out to be, despite the fact he was a Republican and had adopted the Unitarian faith while a student at Harvard. Story's Unitarianism caused many to look upon him as an atheist. In 1832 he became head of the Unitarian Association.

[73] To Agg, Aug. 17, 1827, Story Papers, MHS. See Story to Hon. G. Duval, Mar. 30, 1803, *Life and Letters,* I, 103; Story to G. W. Prescott, Dec. 19, 1804, Joseph Story Papers, Harvard University.

[74] "Autobiography," *Miscellaneous Writings,* 21.

1802–1804 substantiate this claim. Story's first client, one Benjamin Kimball, blacksmith, sought his assistance regarding a small debt owed him by Roger Balch, "yeoman." For his services Story collected four dollars. During this first year as a struggling young lawyer, Story represented some eighty clients, primarily as a collector of debts, including those owed his father, Dr. Elisha Story. Rarely did he receive a fee of more than five dollars, and his ledger indicates that not all his clients were inclined to pay. In his second year his practice doubled, as the number of clients rose to 158. Now small entrepreneurs—"Trader," "Mercht.," "Baker," "Mariner"—begin to appear in the book of entries. Fees doubled, sometimes tripled. By the third year Story had risen from a tyro to an established, respected lawyer. With December not recorded he could boast of 183 clients, many of whom were well-to-do members of the community.[75]

Much of his rapid success can surely be attributed to his skill as a lawyer. "Such ... was the force of his industry, his capacity, his attention to business, and his cordial and attractive manners—so general was the conviction of the sincere conscientiousness of his views, that the rigor of political prejudice began gradually to be relaxed in his favor. He gathered around him good clients, and, what was better, good friends."[76] Doubtless too, Story's reputation for honesty and fair play was a contributing asset. Samuel Putnam related

the faithful manner in which he [Story] practiced with us there. The habit of that [Essex] Bar was to disclose freely to the adverse counsel, the points which were to be controverted, or admitted, whereby much expense to clients was saved. What out of court was agreed to be admitted was always admitted on trial; and so much trouble and expenses of witnesses was [sic] prevented. No traps were set. But the debateable [sic] ground was maintained with as much earnestness, as was consistent with good breeding. And in all this your father well-played his part. Those agreements were uniformly verbal—but always performed.[77]

The year 1805 brought forth Story's first major book of law, *A Selection of Pleadings in Civil Actions*,[78] marking him as a serious and industrious young advocate whose knowledge of the law was more than *rudis indigestaque*

---

[75] Case Record Book, Jan., 1802–Dec., 1804, Joseph Story Papers, New-York Historical Society (cited hereafter as Story Papers, NYHS).

[76] "Biographical Notice of Mr. Justice Story," *American Review, A Whig Journal*, Vol. III (Jan., 1846), 69.

[77] To William Story, May 28, 1846, Samuel Putnam Papers, Essex Institute.

[78] *A Selection of Pleadings in Civil Actions*, Subsequent to the Declaration, with Occasional Annotations on the Law of Pleadings (Salem, 1805). "The design of the following selection," said Story, "is to facilitate to the American student the practice of special pleading. A variety of English books on this subject are at once elaborate and learned. Yet such is the difference of our customs, statutes, and common law, that they will be found, in many instances, inadequate to supply the necessities of our own juridical practice." *Ibid.*, iii.

moles. A greatly needed work, published at a time when American law books were practically nonexistent, it unraveled the procedural mysteries of the common law and provided inexperienced American lawyers with new insight into the complexities of formal pleading in American courts. Story's son recalled many years later that "This work was received very favorably by the profession, and for a long time was the sole book of forms used in this country. Professor Greenleaf [of the Harvard Law School] says 'its appearance, with its valuable body of notes, gave a new impulse to study in this department of professional learning, and after the lapse of forty years is still resorted to with all the confidence originally reposed in it.' "[79]

There is yet another evaluation of Story's *Selection of Pleadings* handed down to posterity by an unknown critic, which suggests that some members of the Federalist bar of Massachusetts may well have entertained less enthusiastic opinions about the book. Convinced of Story's ineptitude, an anonymous reviewer of Federalist persuasion assured the readers of the fashionable *Monthly Anthology and Boston Review* that the book was a vulgar exhibition of bad taste and impoverished scholarship. The author's annotations and commentaries "have increased the bulk and cost of the book, without increasing its value. So far as we have examined the notes, they contain only that common place learning, which every student, who has read Blackstone ... must be presumed to possess. Any man, tolerably well read in the law, might make from a dozen law books, with such notes and dissertations as Mr. Story's, nearly as many books as he could make from different combinations of sound from the same number of harp strings."[80]

Pausing with the indignant grace of an eighteenth-century savant, the reviewer complimented Story for his diligence and industry, which "in this world of ours, where the air we breathe seems to inspire sloth, and where indolence is more contagious and more fatal than the pestilence ... is no moderate praise."[81] But the temptation to debunk and destroy this Republican upstart was compelling; here was an opportunity to give the brazen young lawyer from Salem a stern lecture on legal ethics and professional responsibility. As spokesman for the profession, the reviewer performed his task admirably, informing poor Story that his fellow lawyers would regard the book as an insult to their intelligence and a threat to the integrity of the profession. Such a book, he implied, deserved to go down to a common and obscure grave with the author's earlier publication of like nature. "Whatever may have been the real motives, or the success of Mr. Story in the works he has published," surmised the reviewer with stinging sarcasm, "it seems no

[79] Story, *Life and Letters*, I, 112.

[80] "Review of Story's Pleadings," *The Monthly Anthology and Boston Review*, Vol. II (1805), 484.

[81] *Ibid.*, 488.

more than candid to presume he meant to be useful, and to relieve in some degree, the necessities of the profession. Of Mr. Story's 'Precedents of Declarations,' the profession have formed an opinion. The publication of that form book has saved many an indolent student or careless practitioner from the intolerable evil of thinking, and from the labour of consulting the English entries. The compilation, which now claims our notice, partakes of the same character."[82] Indeed, respectable lawyers would question

whether such books as Mr. Story makes are advantageous to the publick or to the profession. To gentlemen, whose industry and talents entitle them to confidence, these books are but *Primers*. To those, who are not entitled to confidence, they are mischievously useful. They afford to professional men but a very superficial knowledge, and tend to make them copyists instead of students. But the greatest injury these books do to society is the enabling some men to get a living in the character of lawyers, whose knowledge and whose moral delicacy are far removed from being subjects of commendation.[83]

If the reviewer's comments provoked many a laugh, Story's book surely roused an equal amount of anxiety. Behind the caustic remarks of the reviewer was a keen awareness of the revolutionary impact such a book might have on legal practice. By simplifying common law pleading, a book such as Story's might allow many an untutored lawyer to argue any case in a court of law. This possibility in turn could lead to a democratization and flooding of the profession, and work an economic hardship on established lawyers. So frightened were members of the Massachusetts bar of Story's book that they demanded licensing; and the supreme court quickly established new rules for practice, including formal examinations.[84]

To attribute the reviewer's hostility toward *A Selection of Pleadings* solely to political or economic motives, however, would be to ignore his genuine concern over the dignity of the law and the integrity of lawyers. The legal profession, especially in Massachusetts, which boasted one of the most outstanding and best-organized bars in America, prided itself upon the complexities of pleading. Such impediments foiled the amateur and put all lawyers to the test of scholarship. The learned and successful lawyer was a student not only of existing law but also of legal history and legal philosophy. In the course of his private search for correct precedents and principles, he had examined all the original sources—the *Corpus Juris Civilis*, the writings of the great legal thinkers, and the statutes and reports, both English and American.

---

[82] *Ibid.*, 483. According to a letter written by Richard Dana to William Story, Judge Story's first legal work, *American Precedents of Declarations* (Boston, 1802), was published anonymously. Dana to Story, May 3, 1851, *Life and Letters*, II, 321.

[83] "Review of Story's Pleadings," *The Monthly Anthology and Boston Review*, Vol. II (1805), 483.

[84] Oscar Handlin and Mary Handlin, *Commonwealth: Massachusetts, 1774–1861*, 79–80.

He was privy to the subtle workings of jurisprudence and to the ideas and practices which had contributed to its downfall and success. He knew where he was going because, in a sense, he knew where he had been. He believed, in short, that the only good lawyer was the self-taught lawyer, and he tended to view commentaries and other such short cuts with misgivings. Story himself came to adopt such views, and in his later years often criticized those who sought an oversimplification of pleadings and of the common law in general. But he was his own worst enemy. His legal treatises tended to undermine the rigorous scholarship which he forcefully advocated in others.

If the devastating review of Story's book was a true reflection of legal sentiment in Massachusetts, perhaps, then, Story's unpopularity in certain legal circles did not stem simply from his identification with the Republican party. In the mind of the reviewer, Story was more than an outcast and a dangerous influence in the profession. He was presumptuous, arrogant, and personally obnoxious:

For the honour of American taste and literature, we wish, that the author had exhibited more modesty, than in applying to his works the words, which Lord Coke applies to some of his Reports. "*Illud a docto lectore peto, vel ut corrigat sicubi erratum invenirit vel saltem ne partem aliquam reprehendat, donec totum studiose perlegerit, unde forte fiet, ut pauciora criminetur.*" The language of great men should be sacred to great occasions. But experience proves, that it is much more easy to adopt the language, than to rival the merit of that illustrious Judge, whose works will ever preserve to themselves that rank among lawyers, which the Illiad holds among the poets.[85]

To Story, certainly, the reviewer's thankless and humiliating commentary was neither discriminating nor altogether just. Whatever the merits of the book, it sold widely; and Story's practice continued to prosper.[86] "At the time of his elevation to the bench, his professional income was not less than five

---

[85] "Review of Story's Pleadings," *The Monthly Anthology and Boston Review*, Vol. II (1805), 488. "This I ask from the Judge, that he either correct an error wheresoever he will find it, or at least in some degree restrain himself while he carefully surveys the case, from which perhaps it will happen that he will condemn a fewer number."

[86] In 1805, Story was retained by William Orne, a wealthy Salem merchant, to prevent the construction of a bridge threatening Orne's wharf (Massachusetts Historical Society *Proceedings*, 2nd Series, Vol. LXVII [Oct., 1941–May, 1944], 174). In 1806 he appeared before the supreme court of Massachusetts in *Kilham* v. *Ward* (2 Tyng [Mass.] 236 [1806]) and the supreme court of New Hampshire ("Autobiography," *Miscellaneous Writings*, 23–25). In 1808, Story argued for the constitutionality of the embargo laws (*United States* v. *William*, 28 Federal Cases 614, No. 16,700 [1808]). In *Rust* v. *Low* (6 Tyng [Mass.] 90 [1809]), Story appeared with Nathan Dane as co-counsel and proved to the satisfaction of Chief Justice Theophilus Parsons—in a brilliant stroke of research— that the decision of Lord Hale controlling the case at hand was erroneously decided (see Story, *Life and Letters*, I, 116-18); he also argued before the United States Supreme Court in *Fletcher* v. *Peck* (6 Cranch 87 [1810]) on behalf of the Georgia claimants.

thousand dollars a year; a very large sum, considering the place and the period."[87]

Whatever the intended effects of the review, it failed to damage noticeably his growing reputation for competency among many members of the bar,[88] or to discourage him from undertaking similar works. Indeed, well before his appointment to the Supreme Court in 1811, he was a proven legal scholar. In 1809 he edited Chitty's *A Practical Treatise on Bills of Exchange* and in 1810 and 1811 brought out new editions of Abbott's *A Treatise of the Law Relative to Merchant Ships* and Lawe's *A Practical Treatise on Pleading in Assumpsit*. At this time he had also completed three manuscript digests, similar to Comyn's *Digest*, before abandoning the task.[89] Story's early ability to edit scholarly works of law while simultaneously carrying on an active law practice, dabbling in local and national politics, and writing poetry and editorials for the Republican Salem *Register*, was prophetic of his indefatigable industry and literary prolificness as a teacher and judge, which later astounded the legal profession throughout America and Europe.

Story was also moving well beyond the hornbook stage of politics during this period of professional ascendancy, although his first public office was more the result of accident than design. Administrative confusion, originating in an amusing exchange of misread letters, brought him a surprise appointment as commissioner in bankruptcy in 1802. The mix-up began in May of that year, when the Reverend Isaac Story of Marblehead, Joseph's uncle, wrote to Thomas Jefferson, informing the president that he wished to leave the pulpit and obtain a post as commissioner in bankruptcy. An ardent democrat, Isaac reassured Jefferson of his loyalty, which he had demonstrated only the year before in a Fourth of July oration sent to the president.[90] On August 5, Jeffer-

[87] "Biographical Notice of Mr. Justice Story," *American Review, A Whig Journal*, Vol. III (Jan., 1846), 71. Story actually suffered a reduction in salary in accepting a position on the Supreme Court—which paid only $3,500 a year. William Pinkney of Baltimore, king of the American bar, was appointed minister to Russia in 1816, and offered Story his legal business, with an annual income of about $20,000. Tempted, Story nevertheless declined the offer, preferring instead his judicial career. (See Story, *Life and Letters*, I, 278–79.) Story's income in 1811, probably the highest in Essex County, has also been estimated to have been $7,000. A general account of lawyer's incomes during this period is given in Chroust, *Rise of the Legal Profession*, II, 87–90.

[88] In 1806, Story, along with Samuel Putnam, Edward Livermore, William Prescott, and Nathan Dane, was appointed by a rule of court to be official examiner of persons seeking admission to the study and practice of law for the Essex bar. Chroust, *Rise of the Legal Profession*, II, 131.

[89] Copy in the Harvard University Law Library; see Story, *Life and Letters*, I, 119–20.

[90] Isaac Story to Jefferson, May 8, 1802, Letters of Application and Recommendation during the Administration of Thomas Jefferson, 1801–1809 (Appointment Papers), National Archives. Isaac also intimated that due respect for patronage in Marblehead would be politically profitable. "No town in All New England is so united in republican

son obligingly dispatched a reply to Isaac, notifying him of the appointment; however, "the name of your son, Joseph, is that which was . . . in the commission. He was represented to me as a lawyer of eminence & a man of virtue & respectability, & as we have confined these appointments entirely to lawyers & merchants, I have assumed you would be as much gratified by his appointment as your own, and under that presumption destined the place for him."[91] Two weeks later an exasperated office seeker was searching for a suitable answer to the president, as well as another position. "I have just received a line from you," Isaac replied, "informing me that the commission, which I received, was designed for Joseph Story of Salem. . . . He is not my son, but my Nephew." Perhaps the president might wish to consider appointing Isaac as collector at Newbury Port?[92] (Two days later Isaac changed his mind, asserting that he was confident of his abilities to act as a commissioner of bankruptcy after all.[93] Whether Story's hapless uncle received any appointment is not known.)

Intervening on Story's behalf, Representative Crowninshield turned to Washington in the fall of 1802, in the hope of obtaining for his friend a more lucrative post. "The President has lately honored him with the appointment of Commissioner in Bankruptcy, but there does not two failures happen a year in this County, so that no pecuniary advantage can be derived from it."[94] Envisioning Federalist conspiracies, the impassioned and irascible Crowninshield foresaw the death of the Republic and of republicanism, lest the Federalists be purged from office at once, and vacancies created for deserving partisans like Story.[95] "I am compelled by the urgent calls of friends of gov-

principles, & in favor of President Jefferson, as the town of Marblehead," he told the President. "This appears conspicuously in the votes of governor: Mr. Gerry had 254 votes, & Mr. Strong only 24 . . . . Governor Clinton, when at Boston, made the same remark. He said that Marblehead was the most republican town, he knew of." In a postscript, Isaac further noted: "You will find my Brother's name on the list of Representatives, that voted in favor of an address being presented to you by the legislature of Massachusetts."

[91] To Isaac Story, Aug. 5, 1802, *ibid*.

[92] To Jefferson, Aug. 18, 1802, *ibid*.

[93] Isaac Story to Jefferson, Aug. 20, 1802, *ibid*.

[94] Jacob Crowninshield to Levi Lincoln [?], Nov. 26, 1802, *ibid*.

[95] Crowninshield's account of the Salem newspaper war and his charges of interference with the freedom of the press by Federalists are interesting documents. The Salem *Gazette*, a Federalist paper, was guilty, he declared, of "pouring out the most foul mouthed abuse against the President, and scattering the vilest detraction & most scandalous invective against the Secretary of the Treasury and Atty General particularly." More recently it has "gone into the still lower & more contemptible acts of slandering private families. . . . As to ourselves (I mean the Crowninshield family generally) we are able to bear it . . . but I feel for my republican friends." On the other hand, the Salem *Register*, a Republican paper, innocent of wrongdoing, was subject to constant harassment by Federalist authorities. "Mr. Carlton, the Editor of the Register, has long been marked out by some leading federalists in this County; he was to have fallen at an early day, a

ernment & by my own sense of public duty," he declared, "to state to you the necessity there is for further removals in Essex .... Late events in this County demonstrate the absolute necessity of something more being done to check the career of federalism; if it falls hard on some individuals they can thank their party for it." Why not, then, appoint Joseph Story a naval officer at Salem?[96] "The friends of Mr. Story (and these are every republican of any consequence in the County) would be much pleased," reckoned the congressman, "if Government would give him some employment worthy of him, & the place now held by Mr. Pickman the naval officer has been mentioned as the only one here he could accept, as it would not confine him too much."[97] But Story thought otherwise. His profession was more important to him now, and

---

victim on the altar of persecution, but the scheme was not quite matured." Now he has been dragged into court: "a prosecution was determined upon, and the Supreme [Judicial] Court sitting here last week gave them an excellent opportunity. Complaint was accordingly made against the Register, & the majority of the Grand Jury being federal, a bill has been found for a libel against Mr. Pickering, and the printer has been obliged to give bonds. I am told this article is not libellous, but you will know when a court is federal a poor republican printer stands no chance for mercy,—and the grand object is to crush the Register & with it as they foolishly expect the republican principles in this quarter; but I already perceive the public indignation runs high against the promoters of this prosecution, & I rather expect before another year comes round, they will be sick of it. Still they will perhaps have obtained one of their favourite points, the draining the pocket of the printer of all the spare cash which he has accumulated." Perhaps "this victim will . . . escape from the fangs of his pursuers," along with Joseph Story, who likewise is fleeing "a host of enemies, determined to crush him." *Ibid.*

[96] *Ibid.* "Mr. Story," Crowninshield testified, "is a young man of great worth, few indeed possess powers equal to him, & I venture to predict . . . that he will shine as a bright star in Massachusetts." Furthermore, "his political writings have rendered the most essential service to the Government. His enemies are too acquainted with the fact, & therefore they persecute him." They are "determined to crush him in a profession where talents & abilities . . . can not always support the profession & command success, especially when a whole court of a hundred rivals are secretly plotting the destruction of every person possessing opposite political opinions to their own." But the administration must not delay, "and we should be certain of retaining him in the County. This is of considerable importance to the republican cause, for we run some risk of loosing [sic] him, Propositions having been made to him to go into one of the Southern States, where there is no question but he wd. meet with more encouragement." (*Ibid.*) Story seriously considered taking up residence in Portsmouth and in other cities to the south, especially Baltimore, but eventually abandoned the idea.

[97] *Ibid.* "With respect to the present naval officer," wrote Crowninshield, "I wish to say but little. He is decidedly opposed to the governmt., & all his near relations and friends (particularly those bearing the same name) are most violently hostile to Mr. Jefferson's Administration .... The late conduct of the federalists has convinced me that we are bound by a sacred duty to keep no measures with the party, & I believe wd. have been the better policy at first to have swept the whole board of officers at once, & not left a federalist standing." *Ibid.*

he declined the appointment "without hesitation, expressing my determination to devote my life to the law."[98]

Following up an earlier appointment to a committee to revise the city ordinances in 1802, Salem placed Story on its school committee in 1804 and also bestowed upon him the high honor of delivering the annual Fourth of July oration, a major event in those days of patriotic zeal. Thirsting for revenge, the Republican lawyer of Salem, now a man of power and prestige, mounted the speaker's platform and proceeded to thrash his critics. It was a political harangue the Federalists neither forgave nor forgot. Dr. Johnson's quip that "patriotism is the last refuge of scoundrels" must have been on the lips of every indignant Federalist in the audience. The oration was generally regarded as "a red flag to the Federal bull."[99]

Still under the spell of the Enlightenment, enthusiastic about the possibilities of democracy, Story stressed the virtues of republicanism: "It is the boast of a representative government, that the voice of the people is distinctly heard; that deliberation precedes action; that the interests of the whole are not abandoned to the mercenary projects of the few. . . . Away then with these shallow declamations against republican governments."[100]

Again addressing himself to the Federalist party, Story reminded his fellow patriots of the contempt monarchies had shown for civil liberties and the rights of property.[101] Waxing eloquent, he pointed out the true and terrible result of royalism: "Corruption and crime have not fled the imperial purple. Debauchery and murder have too often usurped the palace; and stifled the voice of complaint, before it reached the throne. The energy of a monarchy is the mere result of the absolute control of one will over many; of an individual opinion, unchecked but by the suggestions of ambition or revenge."[102] The theme of Story's elocution was a plea for national unity, patriotism, and the abolition of factious politics. "We are all federalists, all republicans," contended Jefferson's New England supporter. There were, therefore, no grounds for "the vehemence of party."[103]

---

[98] To Agg, Aug. 17, 1827, Story Papers, MHS. See Story's letter of refusal to Gabriel Duval, comptroller of the treasury and later a justice of the Supreme Court, in Story, *Life and Letters*, I, 102–104.

[99] Josiah Quincy, Jr., *Figures of the Past*, 189.

[100] "An Oration," Pronounced at Salem, on the Fourth Day of July, 1804, 26.

[101] *Ibid.*, 21–26.

[102] *Ibid.*, 25.

[103] Story always regretted "that there are factions in our country that are openly endeavoring to destroy the confidence of the people in the Constitution. It seems as if in New England the Federalists were forgetful of all the motives for union and were ready to destroy the fabric which has been raised by the wisdom of our fathers. Have they altogether lost the memory of Washington's farewell address?" (To Captain William Story, Jan. 3, 1809, as cited in Warren, *History of the Harvard Law School*, I, 273.) "I wish

This boundless chauvinism and love of Union, reflected in a contempt for party strife, engendered in him a fierce hatred of factional politics and secessionist movements throughout life. Again and again his correspondence and public papers harked back to the familiar eighteenth-century principle that found its classic exposition in the tenth *Federalist*. On the other hand, the oration was also a defense of Jeffersonian Democracy, and this he later rejected. At one point in the speech, he had gone so far as to question "Why the alarum bell [is] forever ringing . . . against innovation, reform, and philosophy."[104] Later in life, when asked by Daniel Webster about his Fourth of July oration, Story flatly repudiated it. "I thought the text very pretty, sir, but I looked in vain for the notes. *No authorities were stated in the margin.*"[105] Ever eager to dissociate himself from his Jeffersonian past, Story assuredly censured the speech without pausing to reflect that many of the principles he had always cherished were also included in the philosophy conveyed on that celebrated day of Independence in 1804.

Such was the nature of Story's political thought. One could always find his conservatism and liberalism overlapping, balancing, as it were, that eighteenth-century constitution he carried in the back of his mind or behind his breast pocket. It is little wonder that his contemporaries questioned his political convictions. Nor is it surprising that Story himself was unable to pinpoint his exact position on the political spectrum. On a later occasion he confessed bewilderment with the changing names and policies of the competing partisan organizations: "I seem to myself simply to have stood still in my political belief, while parties have revolved about me; so that, although of the same opinions now as ever, I find my name has changed from Democrat to Whig, but I know not how or why."[106] In the end, it was a coalescing of incongruous political sympathies and affiliations which led Story from a discreet Jeffersonian Federalism to the Whig party of Webster and Clay, to do battle with Jacksonian Democracy.

A cursory review of Story's activities in the Massachusetts legislature and United States House of Representatives bears out the truth of his repeated assertions that politics and party were distasteful to him. Held in check by deep-seated religious convictions and traditional values, Story followed an independent course throughout his life, acting and reacting to the formidable dictates of conscience, thus avoiding the conformism of the party process. In 1805 he was elected at the age of twenty-six to represent Salem in the Massa-

---

to God," wrote Story at an earlier occasion, "there were more among us who had talents to expose & firmness to resist the arts & machinations of party." To George W. Prescott, July 30, 1808, Alexander C. Washburn Papers, Massachusetts Historical Society.

104 "An Oration," 21.

105 Quincy, *Figures of the Past*, 189.

106 *Life and Letters*, I, 540.

chusetts legislature. His legal background specified that he should lead his party in matters concerning courts and law. A major problem of Massachusetts at this time was the question of an independent judiciary, and Story immediately responded in favor of an increased salary for judges on the Supreme Judicial Court of Massachusetts, much to the delight of the Federalist party.[107] The issue arose in 1806, when Theophilus Parsons, a leading Federalist and outstanding Massachusetts lawyer, refused to accept the chief justiceship vacated by the resignation of Francis Dana. Parsons had insisted that judicial salaries be increased and placed on a "Permanent and Honorable basis."

Isaac Parker, recently appointed to the court, prevailed upon Story, who was chairman of the legislative committee examining the issue, and persuaded the young legislator with facts and figures that existing salaries were neither equitable nor constitutionally suitable. "[I]t is obvious," wrote Parker, "that no lawyer in respectable practice can go upon the bench without a sacrifice hardly to be expected; that none who are now upon the bench can remain there without great interruption to their happiness on account of almost perpetual absences from their families, without great personal fatigue & anxiety of mind. And without continual dread of leaving their families in a state of poverty, which a steady pursuit of private professional business would have avoided."[108]

---

[107] See Story's "Report on the Salaries of the Judiciary," *Miscellaneous Writings*, 58–62. The *Columbian Centinel*, a Federalist newspaper, declared on April 12, 1806, that "In elective governments, the spirit of party may find its way into councils of State. . . . The Judiciary interposes its corrective influence. It brings the laws to the touchstone of the Constitution. It arrests the progress of Executive violence. Judges, holding office during good behavior, honorably paid, able, virtuous, few in number, personally responsible for abuse of power, are the very soul of republican government." For Republican reactions, see the *Pittsfield Sun*, August 16, 1806, and the Boston *Independent Chronicle*, January 19, 1807. "It is astonishing," said the *Independent Chronicle* on June 15, 1809, "that the people should be indifferent to the abuse continually committed by a body clothed with powers injurious to the rights and liberties of their fellow citizens; who claiming to be independent of the authority which created them, set the laws at defiance whenever they please—one day explain away a statute; and another, substitute a forced construction."

[108] Parker to Story, May 31, 1806, Story Papers, Clements Library. "Although it may be thought by some improper for any member of the court to interest himself personally in this affair," Parker flatly stated, "I confess I can see no reason why any reserve should be maintained, between one department of the government deriving its support from another, and the one to whom it is to look for aid." Totalling his travel and living expenses for the year, Parker amply demonstrated why some members of the court "according to the standard of the present times are poor." His salary of $2,000 was quickly reduced by $500, as a result of expenses incurred while riding 2,000 miles a year on circuit duty; annual rent on his modest home was $350; wood for fuel came to a cost of $75; $200 more for "The hired person" to assist the family during his absences; $60 for a horse and chaise; and $300 for the education of his children, one of whom was enrolled at Exeter Academy. "Upon adding these items to the sum which attending the circuit will cost," he concluded,

Story responded with a bill to increase the salaries of the chief justice and associate justices to $2,500 and $2,400 respectively. "Animated and vehement" debate, led by Story, resulted in the bill's passage, and according to Story, "the bill must have been lost, but for my efforts."[109] As chairman of a committee concerned with judicial reform, Story recommended on June 15, 1807, three judicial bills, one of which advocated the establishment of a separate court of equity.[110] The bill, however, failed to get a third reading.[111] Again, in 1809, he advocated a second bill to increase judicial salaries to $3,500 for the chief justice and to $3,000 for the associate justices, which, after lengthy and heated debate, finally passed.[112]

These varied efforts by Story to strengthen the independence of the Massachusetts judiciary were clearly indicative of a thoughtful and maturing conservatism; moreover, they show that almost from inception, Story's constitutional principles were at times in direct conflict with Jeffersonian Republicanism. Still in an infant stage of development, the American republic had not as yet demonstrated a firm attachment to the doctrine of separation of powers and checks and balances, and Republicans were prone to eye it with suspicion. Like the American Constitution itself, however, the institutional structure of Massachusetts government embodied the uniquely American concept of a balanced constitution and rejected the pure doctrine which had briefly dominated American politics in the 1770s. In fact, "It was in the Massachusetts Constitution of 1780 . . . that the new philosophy of a system of separated powers which *depends upon* checks and balances for its effective operation was first imple-

---

"it will be found that less than $500 are left for the maintenance of a family of Nine or Ten in food & clothing, for the common hospitalities of life, & for those various incidental expenses which cannot be foreseen or prevented." Parker estimated that his annual income before coming to the bench was $3,500.

Story replied, seeking more information and advice from Parker (see Parker to Story, June 8, 1805, *ibid.*). Samuel Sewall also offered Story suggestions to improve his bill on the judiciary. Sewall to Story, Jan. 29, 1806, and Sept. 27, 1806, *ibid.*

[109] To Edward Everett, Nov. 1, 1832, *Life and Letters*, I, 135.

[110] Story's committee report is reproduced in Gerald T. Dunne, "Joseph Story's First Writing on Equity," *American Journal of Legal History*, Vol. XIV, No. 1 (Jan., 1970), 76–81.

[111] R. Kent Newmyer, "Joseph Story: A Political and Constitutional Study" (unpublished Ph.D. dissertation, University of Nebraska, 1959), 33. For further discussion of Story's activities in the Massachusetts legislature see *Ibid.*, 26–39; Dunne, "Joseph Story: The Germinal Years," *Harvard Law Review*, Vol. LXXV, No. 4 (Feb., 1962), 725–27.

[112] Newmyer, "Joseph Story," 34. On other issues, too, Story abandoned party. He was, for example, the only member of his party who voted against a Republican scheme to push through an unethical, if not unconstitutional, rule of procedure (see *Columbian Centinel*, Jan. 24, 1807). Similarly, he refused to participate in the fraudulent redistricting of the Massachusetts senatorial districts in 1811, despite its guaranty of a Republican majority. Story to Fay, March 10, 1812, *Life and Letters*, I, 240–42.

mented. This Constitution embodied the results of the ideas of John Adams, and, more important, perhaps, of the Essex Result."[113] Reverting to the democratic idealism of the revolutionary period, the Jeffersonian Republicans became increasingly fond of a pure separation of powers and critical of the balanced constitution. The latter they viewed, together with Abbé Sieyès and the French revolutionaries, as a surreptitious device calculated to reintroduce the despicable ideas of monarchy and aristocracy. The only truly democratic constitution, they argued, was that which required all of the branches to be directly responsible to the people. Then, every branch "would at once be equally subordinate to the true sovereign power. There would therefore be no need for checks and balances. Pure republicanism, said Jefferson, can be measured in no other way than in the complete control of the people over their organs of government."[114]

Appalled by the activities of the Federalists in state courts, as well as their clandestine alliance with the federal judiciary in the partisan enforcement of the Sedition Act, Republicans declared war on the national judiciary in the first administration of Jefferson—as witnessed by the Judiciary Act of 1802, legislative attacks upon the courts, Republican hostility towards *Marbury* v. *Madison*, impeachment of federal judges, and the trial of Aaron Burr. At the state level, the Jeffersonian assault against the independence of the judges was equally virulent. In 1808–1809, for example, the Ohio legislature in a single sweeping action removed from office all the justices of the peace and more than one hundred judges, including three supreme court justices, and all the presiding and associate judges of the courts of common pleas.[115] Indeed, the

[113] M. J. C. Vile, *Constitutionalism and the Separation of Powers*, 148. In 1775, Massachusetts returned to a form of government based essentially upon the royal charter of 1691; but the scheme was unpopular, and in 1778 a new constitution was drafted and submitted to the people, but rejected. The forerunner of the constitution of 1780 (which Adams drafted), the reply from Story's Essex County to the proposed constitution of 1778 was the work of Theophilus Parsons. Parsons applied the doctrine of separation of powers, but also insisted upon additional safeguards, in keeping with the traditional English idea of a balanced constitution. "Thus was the whole emphasis of the mid-eighteenth-century theory of the balanced constitution transformed. The ideas and vocabulary that had formerly been applied to monarchy, aristocracy, and democracy were firmly transferred to the legislative, executive, and judicial branches of government. Whereas in contemporary England the separation of powers was a necessary, but subordinate, element of a system in which three *classes* check and balance each other, in America the checks and balances became a necessary, but subordinate, element of a system in which the *functionally divided branches* of government can maintain their mutual independence." *Ibid.*, 151. Emphasis supplied.

[114] *Ibid.*, 165.

[115] Chroust, *Rise of the Legal Profession*, II, 47. Early state legislatures, Chroust points out, "did not hesitate to interfere with the traditional functions of the courts. They enacted statutes reversing judgments of the courts in particular cases; they attempted to admit to probate wills previously rejected by the courts on good legal grounds; and they sought

Jeffersonian philosophy of the inherent virtue and sovereignty of the common man was antithetical to the Federalist idea that a propertied, conservative élite should interpret laws and impose them upon the majority. But Joseph Story, the Republican lawyer from Salem, did not agree. He cast his lot with the Federalists and stood stoutly behind the judges.

In his unsuccessful effort to establish a chancery jurisdiction, however, Story stood alone. Equity, not widely popular among Federalists, was inimical to Puritan morality, for it relieved persons of their obligations. And Republicans were hardly disposed to look upon it favorably, as it expanded the use of judicial discretion in interpreting and applying the law, thereby placing the legal process farther beyond the realm of legislative authority.[116]

Story's attempt to secure judicial reform resulted in frequent attacks by Republican newspapers.[117] "The Republicans have suffered much," recorded Bentley on March 12, 1808, "from the infidelity of Story. . . . [the] political character of this man is very doubtful among us."[118] Conservative papers complimented Story for his work in the legislature,[119] and certain Federalist leaders were apparently eager to convert him to their cause. When Story began

---

to dictate the details of administration of particular estates. By special laws they validated particular invalid marriages, and they attempted to exempt a particular wrongdoer from liability from a particular wrong for which his neighbors would be held liable by the general law as administered by the courts. They suspended the statute of limitations for a particular litigant in one case, and for particular and specified litigants they dispensed with the statutory requirements for bringing suit for divorce." Perhaps the decisive factor in undermining the independence of the judiciary, Chroust concludes, "was the almost universal tendency to pay little or no salaries to judges. When Jeremiah Smith, a truly prominent lawyer, was appointed Chief Justice of New Hampshire in 1802, the salary attached to this office was a mere $850.00 per annum. . . . When the Court of Appeals was organized in Kentucky, the annual salary of each judge was originally set at $666.66." Of the original thirteen states, seven (Virginia, Connecticut, Georgia, Rhode Island, North Carolina, South Carolina, and New Jersey) placed the selection of the judges in the hands of the legislature. Judges in New York were selected by a special Council of Appointment, and in Pennsylvania and Delaware by the executive and legislature together. Massachusetts, New Hampshire, and Maryland authorized the governor and council to make the appointment. *Ibid.*, 44–46.

116 See Pound, *Formative Era of American Law*, 155. Massachusetts courts did not have equity jurisdiction until the end of the nineteenth century. "Probably the decisive factor in our reception of English equity was Story's *Equity Jurisprudence*. With much art, whether conscious or unconscious, he made it seem that the precepts established by the decisions of the English Court of Chancery coincided in substance with those of the Roman law . . . and hence were but statements of universal principles of natural law universally accepted in civilian states." *Ibid.*, 156.

117 See the Pittsfield *Sun*, Aug. 16, 1806. Story recalled later he "was denounced by Republican papers" for his efforts to increase judicial salaries. To Everett, Nov. 1, 1832, *Life and Letters*, I, 135.

118 *Diary*, III, 348–49.

119 See *Columbian Centinel*, June 17, 1809.

his first trek south in 1807 as a lobbyist for the New England Mississippi Land Company, the eminent New England Federalist, Harrison Gray Otis, wrote to Robert Goodloe Harper:

I shall in a few days, give to a Mr. Story from this place a line of introduction to you, at his particular request, and will thank you to pay him such attentions as may be consistent with your convenience and leisure. He is a young man of talents, who commenced Democrat a few years since and was much fondled by his party. He discovered however too much sentiment and honour to go *all lengths* and acted on several occasions with a very salutary spirit of independence, and in fact did so much *good* that his party have denounced him, and a little attention from the right sort of people will be very useful to him and to us.[120]

A bipartisan interest group, the New England Mississippi Land Company since 1804 had lobbied the Congress unsuccessfully for a compensation law, in the hope of indemnifying its shareholders, who were innocent purchasers of the infamous Yazoo lands. The company's leading claimants included a Republican United States district attorney for Massachusetts, George Blake; Samuel Dexter, Federalist congressman and former secretary of war under Adams; Gideon Granger, Jefferson's postmaster general; James Sullivan and Peres Morton, prominent Massachusetts Republicans; and Federalist Samuel Sewall, Story's law teacher from Marblehead. Story also had connections with the Yazooists, through his second wife, Sarah Waldo Wetmore, whose father, Judge William Wetmore of the Boston Court of Common Pleas, was one of the original investors in the New England Mississippi Land Company.[121] Upon his election to the Congress, Story replaced Ezekiel Bacon, a Republican from western Massachusetts, as the company's chief spokesman in the House of Representatives, and shortly thereafter was retained, along with Sullivan and Harper, as counsel for John Peck, a director in the company, to argue that

---

[120] Apr. 19, 1807, Samuel Eliot Morison, *The Life and Letters of Harrison Gray Otis, Federalist, 1765–1848*, I, 283. On May 5, 1807, Story wrote to Otis that he was journeying south and would like a letter of introduction (Otis Papers, MHS). See also George Cabot to Timothy Pickering, January 28, 1808, Henry Cabot Lodge, *Life and Letters of George Cabot*, 377.

[121] C. Peter Magrath, *Yazoo: Law and Politics in the New Republic. The Case of Fletcher v. Peck*, 68. On December 9, 1804, Story married Mary Lynde Oliver, who died on June 22, 1805, less than seven months after their marriage. Two months later, his father, Dr. Elisha Story, passed away. Deeply wounded, Story confessed to his friend, Samuel Fay, that he had reached the depths of misery. "I have just crawled into my office," he wrote, "and am now endeavoring to drown all recollection in the hurry of business. . . . So exquisitely was she adapted to suit the character of my mind, that I doated on her with distracted fondness, and on her bosom found the never-failing solace of my cares. We were united by the tenderest ties. . . . You knew my father . . . . My attachment to him from my earliest years had been very great." (Oct. 8, 1805, *Life and Letters*, I, 114–15.) On August 27, 1808, Story and Sarah Wetmore were wed in Boston.

case in the United States Supreme Court.[122] In 1809 and 1810, Story and Harper appeared before the Court in the case of *Fletcher* v. *Peck*, asserting to the satisfaction of the judges that the Georgia act of 1796 repealing the original grant was a violation of the contract clause of the Constitution.

In the fall of 1808, Story was elected a member of the United States House of Representatives to fill the vacancy in Essex, South District, caused by the death of Jacob Crowninshield. He took his seat on December 20 and again flouted Republican party policies by advocating an increase in the size of the navy. Republicans, convinced that any newly constructed ships would be quickly destroyed by the British, tabled Story's proposal.[123] Story also proposed a bounty on fish and the hiring of unemployed seamen on coastal gunboats. Neither proposal was adopted. His attempt to repeal Jefferson's embargo (which he had formerly defended in Massachusetts as a "temporary expedient"), however, was more successful.

Stepping gingerly into the midst of a national crisis, the freshman congressman quickly rose to a position of influence. To his colleagues he was a cynosure of censure and praise; but Story saw himself as a detached and amused spectator. His ability to laugh, even at himself, carried him through many an ordeal, be they of a political or social nature. Politics he could never really take seriously. Nothing endears him to us more than his charming account of a New Year's Eve party at the White House in 1809, in which he finds himself done up like a dandy amidst the pomp and trumpery of American politics.

It was not a little amusing to see federalists & republicans here mingled together & striving to shew who could exhibit the most pleasant & good humour. I also, as you may imagine, was determined to figure among the group. So I threw off my boots & pantaloons, arrayed myself in black underclothes, seized my *double bowed shoes* & marched in great state to the scene of action. I could hardly avoid smiling at myself so suddenly metamorphosed into a beau, dressed off in black ribbons in abundance

---

[122] "I shall with much pleasure," wrote Bacon wearily, "resign into your hands next winter the sole management of *Yazooism* in the national councils." (To Story, June 1, 1808, as quoted in Dunne, "Joseph Story: The Germinal Years," *Harvard Law Review*, Vol. LXXV, No. 4 [Feb., 1962], 738.) Earlier that year Story had written to Morton, "Yesterday I presented a petition to the House of Representatives to be heard at their bar in defense of the Georgia Claim," and "After a debate in which the partisans of the South were as usual extremely bitter, it was rejected by a very great majority." Story endeavored to explain why the House rejected the petition, and expressed little hope of success. However, "The action of Fletcher v. Peck is entered; & as yet I am not instructed what counsel to engage in the argument. Probably it must be continued. By the course of the Court, an abstract brief of the whole case must be given to each of the seven judges. This has not been prepared & would require great clerical labor. Mr. Granger has not yet returned. I deem it of importance to consult him before definitely acting on the subject." To Bacon, Feb. 13, 1808, Fogg Papers, Maine Historical Society.

[123] For Story's speeches in favor of an increased naval establishment, see *Annals*, Debates of the House (1808–1809), 907, 976–77, 1031–32, 1078, 1079, 1095.

& with a deep, aye very deep, ruffle by way of armament. . . . Pray take a passing glance at me, if you please. I stepped into the drawing room, made my bow to the President, & with my *hat under my arm* marched around with majestic steps in diplomatic style offering congratulations to all my acquaintances.[124]

Story gave rein to a compromising attitude toward the embargo, but was soon convinced of its hopelessness.[125] The repeal brought dishonor upon the Republican party, and Story's opposition, which Jefferson alleged was the cause of the catastrophe, earned him a reputation of duplicity. "I ascribe all this," wrote Jefferson,

to one pseudo-republican, Story. He came on (in place of Crowninshield, I believe) and staid only a few days; long enough, however, to get complete hold of [Ezekiel] Bacon, who, giving in to his representations, became panic-struck, and communicated his panic to his colleagues, and they to a majority of the sound members of Congress. They believed in the alternative of repeal or civil war and produced the fatal measure of repeal.[126]

About January 20, after less than a month in Congress and before the vote for repeal of the embargo, Story left Washington, bored and disgusted with party politics, declaring he "would not continue in the public councils for a salary of $10,000 per annum."[127] Returning home, the Salem lawyer refused to run for re-election, preferring to "look out upon the political world without being engaged in it."[128] If many of the inhabitants of Salem were suspicious of Story's "pseudo-republicanism," at least Federalists were amused by his sudden departure from Washington. "By the way," queried the Salem *Gazette*, "what has become of the bounty on . . . fish? Has Mr. Story deserted his post, and left the fish to swim as chance directs?"[129]

How was it possible for a man of integrity and independent course to exhibit himself to his contemporaries in a posture of paradox and conflicting ideals? While his optimistic view of the nature of man darkened gradually to one of pessimism and dismay, in certain convictions Story never wavered. A

[124] To Mrs. Story, Jan. 3, 1809, Story Papers, NYHS.

[125] An excellent account of Story's role in the repeal of the embargo is given in Newmyer, "Joseph Story: A Political and Constitutional Study." See also Newmyer, "Joseph Story and the War of 1812: A Judicial Nationalist," *The Historian*, Vol. XXVI, No. 4 (Aug., 1964), 486–501; Dunne, "Joseph Story: The Germinal Years," *Harvard Law Review*, Vol. LXXV, No. 4 (Feb., 1962), 730–34, 737–45; Dunne, "Joseph Story: 1812 Overture," *ibid.*, Vol. LXXVII, No. 2 (Dec., 1963), 240–78.

[126] To Henry Dearborn, July 16, 1810, *Writings of Thomas Jefferson* (Library ed.), XII, 399.

[127] To Fay, Jan. 9, 1809, *Life and Letters*, I, 182.

[128] Story to Nathaniel Williams, Nov. 30, 1811, *ibid.*, 201. Story served again in the Massachusetts legislature (becoming its Speaker) from 1810 until his appointment by President Madison to the United States Supreme Court.

[129] Salem *Gazette*, Feb. 14, 1809.

belief that the welfare of the nation was most secure in a strong union which could resist, through the Supreme Court, the machinations of party and the disorder of sectionalism directed his thinking from early manhood. His early distrust of legislative bodies, and, after the accession of Andrew Jackson, of presidential power, led him to believe that only a powerful judiciary could save the country from political and social ruin.

The greatest cause of confusion over Story's politics stems from the fact that he was associated with a party whose philosophy, for the most part, he could not accept. Consequently, he was often identified with policies he actually opposed. This, when considered with his strong independency, rendered him a true political phenomenon. Moreover, it was precisely Story's ability to stand apart, to survey political strife from a distinct vantage point, that enabled him to maneuver in the field of politics as a legislator, and later in law as a jurist, without compromising principle.

Story's preliminary and distasteful experience in politics profoundly influenced his views toward popular government. He deplored Congress' inability to deal effectively with current problems in a statesmanlike manner. "On near approach, I find that my imagination had greatly swelled the magnitude of things. . . . Everything here seems in a dead calm. While the whole nation are anxiously looking upon Congress, a stupor, or an indifference pervades that body."[130] Equally discomforting was the mediocrity of the American legislator. With the single exception of John Randolph of Roanoke, wrote Story, "I have not marked as yet a single man of transcendent talents. . . . I am told that there are fifty members in the House who mingle in debate. I say mingle, because many of them must confuse and embarrass, without enlightening; and many must talk without matter or point."[131] Nor did Story later demonstrate a faith in the ability of the common man to correct this situation. What few qualified leaders there were "carry not all the weight, that they deserve. But men of lower views & humbler acquirements possess an influence, which is sometimes an overmatch for political wisdom & experience."[132]

Brief as it was, then, Story's legislative experience in Massachusetts and in Washington had a lasting effect. When coupled with his earlier distaste for party politics, it conjured up in his mind doubts about the wisdom of popular assemblies and unchecked popular sovereignty. Had not Jefferson's party irresponsibly attacked Blackstone's first maxim that the judiciary must be independent? The fathers of the Constitution, who, by abridging their wants, had found time to cultivate their minds, were in Story's eyes far superior to the

---

[130] To Fay, Feb. 16, 1808, *Life and Letters*, I, 162.

[131] To Fay, Feb. 13, 1808, *ibid.*, 157–58. At the same time, however, Story had nothing but praise for the Supreme Court. See Story to Fay, Feb. 16, 1808, *ibid.*, 162; Story to Fay, Feb. 25, 1808, *ibid.*, 166–68.

[132] Story to David Daggett, Dec. 31, 1818, Joseph Story Papers, Yale University.

plodding sons of gain now in control of government. In short, Story's political fling seems to have made him acutely aware of the inherent dangers of democratic extremism. This conservative attitude of Story's, it has been noted, "tempered a bent for innovation with a reverence for the old . . . majority despotism with a sense of transcendent right."[133] Even before Story's philosophy of law had matured, he had learned what some regard as the first rule of modern politics: that enlightened conservatism, upholding order and restraint, is the countervailing force which makes democracy work. "Without this admixture of lawyer-like sobriety with the democratic principle," observed Tocqueville, "I question whether democratic institutions could long be maintained."[134] On the eve of his appointment to the Supreme Court, Joseph Story was asking the very same question.

MR. JUSTICE STORY

Thomas Jefferson, still binding the wounds the Marshall Court had inflicted upon him, had retired to Monticello when news arrived in the fall of 1810 that Associate Justice William Cushing of the United States Supreme Court was dead. To no avail the weary Jefferson had waged a long and unremitting war against the federal judiciary, the common law, and lawyers generally.[135] The opportunity to pack the Court and bend its will to that of the majority had come at last. Cushing's death reduced the Court to three Federalists, three Republicans. "Old Cushing is dead," chortled Jefferson. "At length, then, we have a chance of getting a Republican majority in the Supreme Judiciary."[136] But we must be careful in picking a replacement, he warned his Republican friends, for "It will be difficult to find a character of firmness enough to preserve his independence on the same Bench with Marshall."[137]

President Madison was perfectly willing to comply, but who possessed the necessary qualifications? Any man highly trained in the principles of Blackstone and the common law was out of the question. Jefferson had always disliked lawyers, as Madison was well aware. "When . . . the honeyed Mansfieldism of Blackstone became the student's hornbook," wrote Jefferson, "from

[133] Gerald T. Dunne, "The American Blackstone," *Washington University Law Quarterly*, Vol. 1962, No. 3 (June, 1963), 327.

[134] *Democracy in America* (ed. by Phillips Bradley), I, 276.

[135] Criticism of the common law is a recurrent theme in Jefferson's writings. See, for example, Jefferson to Edmund Randolph, Aug. 18, 1799, *Writings of Thomas Jefferson* (Library ed.), X, 128–29; Jefferson to Judge John Tyler, June 17, 1812, *ibid.*, XIII, 165–68; "Observations on the Force and Obligations of the Common Law in the United States, on the Occasion of Hardin's Case in Kentucky," Nov. 11, 1812, *ibid.*, XVII, 410–15.

[136] To Albert Gallatin, Sept. 17, 1810, as quoted in Charles Warren, *The Supreme Court in United States History*, I, 402.

[137] Jefferson to Gallatin, Sept. 27, 1810, *Writings of Thomas Jefferson* (Library ed.), XII, 429.

that moment, that profession . . . began to slide into toryism, and nearly all the young brood of lawyers now are of that hue. They suppose themselves to be Whigs, because they no longer know what Whiggism or republicanism means."[138] Madison's range of selection was further narrowed by the requirement that the new appointee be a New Englander, inasmuch as he would be riding the First Circuit a good portion of the year. Remembering Story's role in the repeal of the embargo, and the influence he had exerted over Ezekiel Bacon, Jefferson advised Madison against the appointment of either. "Story and Bacon," he warned Madison, "are exactly the men who deserted us. . . . The former unquestionably a tory, and both are too young."[139] The only logical choice, concluded Jefferson, was Levi Lincoln, his former attorney general. The president assured Jefferson that Lincoln would get the appointment. Story and Bacon were not being considered for the position. "Lincoln is obviously first presented to our choice," wrote back Madison. "Granger is working hard for it. . . . Neither Morton, nor Bacon, nor Story have yet been brought forward."[140]

On January 3, 1811, the Senate confirmed the appointment of Lincoln; but Lincoln, who had insisted from the start that his failing eyesight made him unequal to the task, persisted in his refusal to serve, and Madison was forced to make another choice. Jefferson was fond of Gideon Granger, his former postmaster general, but Madison passed him over, perhaps because Granger was pressing his candidacy too hard. Instead, Madison picked the obscure federal revenue collector of Connecticut, Alexander Wolcott. The Senate wisely rejected the nomination by a vote of 24 to 9. Madison responded with a third nominee, John Quincy Adams, and the Senate endorsed the appointment unanimously. Adams, however, refused to budge from his diplomatic post in Saint Petersburg. Like Jefferson, Adams was no friend of Blackstone's science. "I entertain some very heretical opinions upon the merits of the *common law*, so idolized by all English lawyers and by all who parrot their words in America," explained Adams to his aged father in turning down the appointment.[141] Legal studies, he politely informed the exasperated Madison, "were never among those most congenial to my temper."[142]

Ezekiel Bacon now recommended to Madison the thirty-two-year-old Salem lawyer, Joseph Story. Madison, having nearly exhausted the list of candidates, apparently appointed him out of desperation.[143] On November 18,

---

138 To Madison, Feb. 17, 1826, *Writings of Thomas Jefferson* (Memorial ed.), XVI, 156.

139 Oct. 15, 1810, *Writings of Thomas Jefferson* (ed. by Paul L. Ford), XI, 150–52.

140 To Jefferson, Oct. 19, 1810, as quoted in Warren, *Supreme Court in United States History*, I, 407.

141 July 21, 1811, *Writings of John Quincy Adams* (ed. by Paul L. Ford), IV, 145.

142 June 3, 1811, *ibid.*, 95.

143 Resentful, and scarcely appreciative of Story's contributions to their cause, old-line Federalists could never bring themselves to forgive Story for his youthful republicanism.

1811, the Senate approved the nomination of Story, youngest man ever to sit on the Supreme Court.

James Madison, President of the United States of America.

To all who shall see these presents,—Greeting:

KNOW YE, That reposing special Trust and confidence in the Wisdom, Uprightness and Learning of Joseph Story, of Massachusetts, I have nominated, and by and with the advice and consent of the Senate, do appoint him one of the Associate Justices of the Supreme Court of the United States; and do authorize and empower him to execute and fulfill the duties of that office according to the Constitution and Laws of the United States; and to Have and to Hold the said office, with all the powers, privileges and Emoluments to the same of right appertaining unto him the said Joseph Story during his good behavior.[144]

In less than ten years, Joseph Story, embattled lawyer, political rebel, seeker of a free, just, and cultivated democracy, had reached the top of his profession. His rise from a nobody, against the pressures of social, political, and professional adversity, to the highest court in the land, within this span of time, can only be regarded as phenomenal. His appointment was the signal triumph of his life, and he blushingly took it without a moment's hesitation. "For this distinguished favour," he wrote James Monroe, secretary of state, "I beg leave thro[ugh] you to express to the President my most unfeigned and grateful acknowledgments. The high responsibility of the office, & an unaffected sense of the difficulty of sustaining it with the dignity due the U.S., impose on my mind unusual diffidence and embarrassment. I accept of the office with a sincere desire to promote the happiness & honour of my Country; and if I shall in any tolerable degree attain the end, the burthens and duties

As late as 1827, Timothy Pickering was reminding others that "Judge Story while at the bar was an insidious democrat, attending all the caucus meetings in this region, and naming all his partisans in opposition to the federalists. Possessing considerable talents, and uncommon industry, he finally became so . . . conspicuous in his profession as to be selected by Madison to fill a vacant seat on the Bench of the Supreme Court. Having this momentum, on the *shoulders* of democracy, to the place which gratified his existing ambition, he sought for better company; and never appeared more happy than when in the Society of respectable federalists." (To William Coleman, Apr. 30, 1827, Timothy Pickering Papers, Massachusetts Historical Society. Quoted in part in Shaw Livermore, *Twilight of Federalism*, 208). Isaac Parker, however, thought Story should be forgiven; see chapter 5, note 2, *infra*. For a fuller discussion of Story's appointment to the Court, see Morgan D. Dowd, "Justice Joseph Story and the Politics of Appointment," *The American Journal of Legal History*, Vol. IX (1965), 265–85.

[144] James Madison, Nov. 18, 1811, Dept. of State, Miscellaneous Permanent Commissions, Vol. C., National Archives.

will be borne with the greatest cheerfulness."[145] Indeed, it was to be no easy or trivial duty, but Story was as well prepared in the law as almost any man who has ever been appointed to the Court.

A blessing to some, a catastrophe to others, Story's appointment was also as ironic as it was fortuitous. A mere stroke of luck had placed upon the high bench one of the great jurists of all time. Singlehandedly Story wove a whole *corpus juris* into the American legal system, producing, in addition to his three edited works, nine major commentaries, drawn from his class lectures, within the short space of twelve years. Each, a major success, went through several editions, some even into the twentieth century. His circuit opinions, not to mention those delivered on the Supreme Court, comprise some thirteen volumes.[146] Articles, statutes, law reports, and speeches constitute a smaller part of his countless accomplishments in the building of a viable American common law.[147]

[145] Nov. 30, 1811, Dept. of State, Acceptances and Orders for Commissions, 1789–1829, National Archives. "I avail myself of the present opportunity," Story added, "to express my gratification at the manly & honorable course pursued by the Government in its foreign negotiations; and my perfect confidence in its impartiality, wisdom, and integrity."

[146] For an account of Story's activities at the circuit court level, see R. Kent Newmyer, "Joseph Story on Circuit and a Neglected Phase of American Legal History," *American Journal of Legal History*, Vol. XIV, No. 2 (Apr., 1970), 112–35. Story once confided to a fellow jurist: "I have sometimes said, to particular friends, if my name shall happen to go down to posterity, my character as a Judge will be more fully and accurately drawn in the opinions of the Circuit Court than in the Supreme Court. In the former I speak for myself upon full research & deliberate considerations & in the exercise of my own free Judgment. In the latter I speak for the Court, & my own opinions are modified, controlled, & sometimes fettered by the necessary obedience to the opinions of my Brethren. This may well account for the different manner in which I treat subjects at Boston & at Washington." (To Joseph Hopkinson, Feb. 16, 1840, Joseph Hopkinson Papers, Historical Society of Pennsylvania [hereafter cited as Hopkinson Papers, HSP]). The First Circuit, which Judge Story rode covered the states of Massachusetts, New Hampshire, Rhode Island, and Maine. In Massachusetts all the sessions were held in Boston; in New Hampshire, alternately at Portsmouth and Exeter; in Rhode Island, at Providence and Newport; and in Maine, at Portland and Wiscasset. In 1838, Judge Story estimated that "in the course of the discharge of my judicial duties, including my journey to Washington and back," he traveled 1,896 miles a year, in addition to some 200 other miles for frequent trips between Boston and Cambridge on circuit business. (To John Forsythe, secretary of state, July 28, 1838, Dept. of State, Miscellaneous Letters, General Records, Record Group 59, National Archives.) Other members of the Supreme Court responding to Secretary Forsythe's inquiry gave the following estimates for annual travel in the discharge of their court duties: Justice Barbour (1,498); Justice Wayne (2,370); Justice Thompson (2,590); Justice McLean (2,500); Justice Catron (3,464); Justice McKinley (10,000!); Chief Justice Taney (458) (*ibid.*). "Theoretically," notes Gerald T. Dunne, "the system kept the Supreme Court justices in touch with local law and current practice. It also often made couriers of aging men, guaranteed that dockets fell further behind, and provided a built in bias on appeals taken to Washington." (Dunne, "Joseph Story: The Salem Years," *Essex Institute Historical Collections*, Vol. CI, No. 4 (Oct., 1965), 317.

But here was the irony: Jefferson had strongly recommended that Cushing's successor be capable of resisting the doctrines of John Marshall. Madison unwittingly appointed a man who literally sat at the right elbow of the chief justice for nearly a quarter century, guiding his hand in the drafting of major opinions, giving him wholehearted support and advice on legal questions which seemingly covered not only the entire domain of the common law, but nearly every clause of the Constitution. Furthermore, this "judge of last resort" was appointed against the strict advice of Jefferson, dean of the states' rights school and father of the democratic philosophy. Story would become within Jefferson's lifetime a leading nationalist, a self-acclaimed conservative and follower of Edmund Burke, and the most outspoken opponent of Jefferson on the Supreme Court. Marshall himself could not have appointed a more congenial ally.

The famous Story-Marshall friendship was a cornerstone in the development of American constitutional law. Usually united on the great constitutional issues of the day, Story and Marshall shackled state power, expanded the scope of national authority, and in so doing, determined the future of the Republic for years to come. Marshall found Story to be a helpful and enthusiastic supporter in the *Dartmouth College* case,[148] *Cohens* v. *Virginia*,[149] *McCulloch* v. *Maryland*,[150] and *Gibbons* v. *Ogden*.[151] Likewise, Story could depend upon

---

[147] Under the terms of his acceptance as Dane Professor of Law at Harvard, he agreed to prepare his lectures for publication. Within a short space of twelve years, Story, already burdened with judicial and teaching duties, not to mention other responsibilities, produced in rapid succession nine major commentaries, the first of which, *Bailments*, appeared in 1832. His *Commentaries on the Constitution* (3 vols.) was published in 1833, followed by *Conflict of Laws* in 1834. For a discussion of the latter work, see: Ernest G. Lorenzen, "Story's Commentaries on the Conflict of Laws—One Hundred Years After," *Harvard Law Review*, Vol. XLVIII, No. 1 (Nov., 1934), 15–38; Kurt H. Nadelmann, "Joseph Story's Contributions to American Conflict Law: A Comment," *American Journal of Legal History*, Vol. IV (1961), 230–53, and "Marginal Remarks on the New Trends in American Conflicts Law," *Law & Contemporary Problems*, Vol. XXVIII, No. 4 (Autumn, 1963), 860–69. Story's *Equity Jurisprudence* (2 vols.) was published in 1836, followed by *Equity Pleadings* in 1838, *Agency* in 1839, *Partnership* in 1841, *Bills of Exchange* in 1843, and *Promissory Notes* in 1845. These commentaries, each a pioneering endeavor, enjoyed immediate success and went through many editions. Their significance in American law, however, has not been closely examined by the legal profession. No comprehensive evaluations of Story's contributions to equity and admiralty law, for example, have been undertaken. See, however, Gerald T. Dunne, "Mr. Justice Story and the American Law of Banking," *American Journal of Legal History*, Vol. V (1961), 205–29; Frank D. Prager, "Changing Views of Justice Story on the Construction of Patents," *ibid.*, Vol. IV (1960), 1–21.

[148] *Trustees of Dartmouth College* v. *Woodward*, 4 Wheaton 518 (1819).

[149] 6 Wheaton 262 (1821).

[150] 4 Wheaton 316 (1819).

[151] 9 Wheaton 1 (1824).

Marshall's concurrence in such important decisions as *Martin* v. *Hunter's Lessee.*[152] Of the many factors pointing to why "Marshall and Story may be considered one and the same person," few seem more fundamental than their mutual distrust of democratic government, and loss of faith in the people's steadiness, moderation, and self-restraint. Marshall's biographer asserts that "no man in America was less democratic in his ideas of government"[153] than the chief justice; but surely Story outdid his friend on this score.

That Story harbored deep reservations about the democratic trend in America became more noticeable as the years passed. The virulence of the struggle between the Supreme Court and the state of Virginia; the increasing sectional strife between North and South: these barometers of decline and decay forecasting the War between the States led Story to the unhappy conclusion that the Union he and Marshall strove to preserve was doomed. "The old notions of republican simplicity," he told Bacon in 1818,

are fast wearing away, and the public taste becomes more and more gratified with public amusements and parade. . . . I have long been satisfied that the nation was in danger of being ruined by intestine divisions; and fortunately, among men of real talent, and real virtue, and real patriotism, there are now few, if any, differences of opinion. But a new race of men is springing up to govern the nation; they are the hunters after popularity, men ambitious, not of honor, so much as the profits of office,—the demagogues . . . who follow not so much what is right as what leads to a temporary vulgar applause. There is great, very great danger that these men will usurp so much popular favor that they will rule the nation; and if so, we may live to see many of our best institutions crumble in the dust.[154]

Engrained in his mental constitution was a growing conviction that enthusiasm for party or cause, especially the liberal democratic cause, was inconsistent with intellectual balance and high moral standards. Jacksonian Democracy, ushering in the spirit of leveling and riotous partisanship, confirmed his fears that American democratic institutions were a failure. In the hands of roughnecks and radicals, the Constitution was a travesty. A nation could not long survive government by brute force and impetuous majorities. By the 1840s, Judge Story had given up all hope that men of understanding and good will could any longer "make a stout & strong resistance to the inroads of a low & mischievous Democracy. For my own part I think, that we have fully tried the Experiment of a Representative Republic; & that it is a failure on our part. The vital principles of the Constitution are uprooted & disregarded in the blind fury of party spirit. I look now to the dissolution of the Union as inevitable, & at no very distant period."[155]

[152] 1 Wheaton 304 (1816).
[153] Beveridge, *Life of Marshall*, IV, 61. See also ch. 6, note 128, *infra*.
[154] Mar. 12, 1818, *Life and Letters*, I, 311.
[155] Story to Richard Peters, Nov. 27, 1842, Richard Peters Papers, Historical Society

The votaries of radicalism not infrequently become its bitterest adversaries. The visions, the hopes, the theories of youth, revealed in their true light by the lamp of experience, prudence, and practical wisdom, are impugned by the seasoned veteran, who warns his children not to repeat the mistakes of the father and tenders apologies to old enemies, that he might be forgiven. "I like as much to see a young man democratic, as an old man conservative," Story told his son in later life, for "when we are old, we are cautious and slow of change, if we have benefited by experience."[156] No doubt the famous judge had his own stormy career in mind. In matters of politics, Story came to agree with Burke that experience is the best teacher. "The truth is & it ought not to be disguised," he ultimately confessed to the Federalists, "that many opinions are taken up & supported at the moment, which at a distance of time, when the passions of the day have subsided, no longer meet our approbation. He who lives a long life & never changes his opinions may value himself upon his consistency; but rarely can be complimented for his wisdom. Experience cures us of many of our theories; & the results of measures often convince us against our will that we have seen them erroneously in the beginning."[157]

CULTURE AND ANARCHY

'The century into which Joseph Story had ventured as a young man of twenty-one was growing steadily democratic, socially, politically, and intellectually. Although not yet reshaped into an industrial class structure, the society of the seaboard colonies, fabricated by mercantile and landed aristocracies, and a hardy yeomanry, was slowly beginning to unravel. Financiers,

of Pennsylvania (hereafter cited as Peters Papers, HSP). At a dinner at Judge Story's, attended by Jeremiah Mason, Josiah Quincy, George Ticknor, and a British visitor, Lord Morpeth, "The judge our host," recorded Morpeth in his diary, "talked with incessant but pleasant and kindly flow; the conversation approached very near to treason against their own constitution; they pronounce it an utter failure, especially with respect to the election of fit men." (Diary of Lord Morpeth, Dec. 11, 1841, as quoted in Arthur M. Schlesinger, Jr., *The Age of Jackson*, 323.) "Down till the election of Andrew Jackson in 1828," James Bryce wrote many years later, "all the Presidents had been statesmen in the European sense of the word, men of education, of administrative experience, of a certain largeness of view and dignity of character. All except the first two had served in the great office of secretary of state; all were known to the nation from the part they had played. In the second period, from Jackson till the outbreak of the Civil War in 1861, the Presidents were either mere politicians, such as Van Buren, Polk or Buchanan, or else successful soldiers, such as Harrison or Taylor, whom their party found useful as figureheads. They were intellectual pigmies beside the real leaders of that generation— Clay, Calhoun, and Webster . . . . Europeans often ask, and Americans do not always explain, how it happens that this great office . . . is not more frequently filled by great and striking men." *The American Commonwealth*, I, 83, 77.

[156] Story, *Life and Letters*, I, 98–99.

[157] Story to Otis, Dec. 27, 1818, Morison, *Life and Letters of Harrison Gray Otis*, I, 122–23.

capitalists, and land speculators were replacing rural proprietors. "But whatever the experiences of any group," Oscar and Mary Handlin have written in their economic history of Massachusetts, "friction at every level was a concomitant of disintegration in the community." The New England economy was "battered by the impact of radical innovations and disrupted by unforeseen changes in status," and as a result, "social fragmentation snapped communal ties and often cast individuals free but adrift. Attenuation of old responsibilities and weakening of old controls at every level, from state to family, left men to cope alone with increasingly complicated problems arising from industrialization, growth of cities, and integration into broader markets."[158]

Spurred by a new breed of professional politicians, the inarticulate classes, suddenly emancipated, were making themselves heard in councils of state. Imperceptible erosion of regional differences was sweeping aside habits of life and thought rooted in the colonial experience and more than two centuries old. The quiet country village, which had been a fortress in New England for religion, custom, and classes, was disintegrating under the pressure of an impersonal, consolidating urbanization. And a flood of romantic philosophies from abroad, declaring the native virtue of man and the equality of human rights, quickened and exalted such leveling tendencies. Demolished were old-fashioned notions about man's depravity and the natural ordering of classes. Inundated by a wave of skepticism, the Calvinist hell-fires sputtered and went out altogether.

Moreover, these rapid changes taking place throughout the country, in greater or lesser degree, were marked not so much by a sense of loss or confusion, as by a sense of potentiality and expectancy. The Era of Good Feeling following the War of 1812 had blinded men to the risks of the American experiment, revealing only its adventure and romance. A new nation was setting about to build a civilization and culture of its own, with all the self-consciousness and exuberance of youth.

Joseph Story envisioned more than most the individual and cultural problems created for a nation riding the crest of social, political, and economic change, and moderns who share his anxiety over the reckless abandonment of enduring human values would do well to repair to his *Miscellaneous Writings*, a rather profound collection of essays which has scarcely received the recognition it amply deserves. The relevance of Story's animadversions even today is suggested by Robert Nisbet's forthright observation that "The fears of the nineteenth-century conservatives in Western Europe, expressed against a background of increasing individualism, secularism, and social dislocation, have become, to an extraordinary degree, the insights and hypotheses of present-day students of man in society."[159]

[158] Handlin and Handlin, *Commonwealth*, 202.

Unlike many of his contemporaries, Story was painfully aware "that the spirit of the age has broken loose from the strong ties, which have hitherto bound society together by the mutual cohesions and attractions of habits, manners, institutions, morals, and literature."[160] The sudden discovery of romance, of altruism, of optimism, of self-reliance, and individualism—the hallmarks of indigenous Americanism—Judge Story diagnosed as "a general skepticism—a restless spirit of innovation and change—a regretful desire to provoke discussions of all sorts, under the pretext of free inquiry, or of comprehensive liberalism."[161] Like Tocqueville he could put an admonishing finger on the pulse of American character. He deplored the strong disposition in the public mind "to turn everything to a practical account; to deal less with learning and more with experiment; to seek the solid comforts of opulence rather than the indulgence of mere intellectual luxury."[162]

Above all, Story feared the loss of general truths, social and humane, in the flood of speculation and novelty. Sharing with his mentor Burke the same detestation for rationalism, he cautioned against the bold and fearless spirit of speculation, which threatened to destroy reverence for authority and encouraged a cold skepticism regarding established truths of the past. "There is not a remark deducible from the history of mankind more important than that advanced by Mr. Burke," decried Story with a somber alarm in 1826, "that 'to innovate is not to reform.' That is, if I may venture to follow out the sense of this great man, that innovation is not necessarily improvement; that novelty is not necessarily excellence; that what was deemed wisdom in former times, is not necessarily folly in ours; that the course of the human mind has not been to present a multitude of truths in one great step of its glory, but to gather them up insensibly in its progress, and to place them at distances, as guides or warnings to succeeding ages."[163]

With the passing of the years, these democratic trends gained even greater momentum. Story fought them all the way to his grave. "We seem to be borne on the tide of experiment with a rash and impetuous speed," he warned shortly before his death, "confident that there is no risk in our course, and heedless, that it may make a shipwreck of our best hopes, and spread desolation and ruin on every side."[164] How to preserve the continuity of traditional

---

[159] *Community and Power*, 3. See also Russell Kirk, *A Program for Conservatives*, 140–64.

[160] Story, "Literary Tendencies of the Times," A Discourse Pronounced before the Society of the Alumni of Harvard University, at Their First Anniversary, August 23, 1842, *Miscellaneous Writings*, 747.

[161] *Ibid.*

[162] Story, "Characteristics of the Age," *Miscellaneous Writings*, 361.

[163] *Ibid.*, 359.

[164] "Literary Tendencies of the Times," *ibid.*, 747.

values within a context of inevitable change: this, then, was Story's dilemma, the dilemma which has always confronted conservative thinkers.

While the spirit of affluence encouraged criticism and invigorated cultural pursuits, democracy itself, no longer construed as a mere experiment in government, was soon subjected by Story to a more thorough examination of its fundamental moral and metaphysical meanings. The role he was to play in constitutional history as executor of natural law and common law had been cast the moment he took up arms in a general defense of older inherited values. Counteracting *fin de siècle* optimism and the theoretical challenges of Rousseau, Bentham, and their apostles of "progress," Story contributed to America's self-imposed task of creating a new "metaphysic" for democracy by working out of the intellectual materials of the past.

Not all jurists have had a philosophy to guide them in their legal ministerings, but philosophy and religious belief were Story's mace and scepter, the strength of his opinions, and the creative source of his genius. It is clear, from his writings and decisions, that he interpreted democracy and "progress" in the light of natural law, Christianity, and the common law. Rejecting with Marshall the notion that democracy was a safeguard against the danger of arbitrary government, Story's critical test of a healthy society and a sound government was the measure of protection afforded the ancient rights of the common law. At the heart of the political, economic, and social process he perceived the unbidden hand of Providence. "He reverenced all institutions which wore the venerable aspect of time. He knew the 'strength of backward-looking thoughts.' He felt how ephemeral a creature man would be, without the ties which link him to the past and future."[165]

Behind Story's penchant for eighteenth-century ideas and ideals, epitomized by Burke, William Paley, the Augustan poets, Jane Austen, and Scott, all of whom he read and admired, was an insistence upon order and restraint, the essence of the classical spirit.[166] Drawn since school days within the pale of classicism, Story was never without this ultimate criterion of thought and expression. For what he regarded as disorderly aesthetics and the immorality of opportunism, he would substitute classical standards of balance, cultivation, and the ideal of the sympathetic, cosmopolitan gentleman.

But Story's genial temper never permitted him to set his face rigidly against the times, and we often see him partaking of the new as well as the old. Although Blackstone and Coke, who slipped familiarly from his pen, had instilled in him the inherent conservatism of the law, such accouterments never produced a narrow system or slavish submission to precedent. Story's juridical

---

[165] "Biographical Notice of Mr. Justice Story," *American Review, A Whig Journal,* Vol. III (Jan. 1846), 77.

[166] Irving Babbitt, *Rousseau and Romanticism,* 16.

ethic, like the law itself, was flexible and susceptible to modification, as liberty and justice might require. It would be erroneous to think of him solely as an "old fashioned gentleman . . . [who] should have dressed in stockings and knee-breeches and a scarlet coat."[167] He carried with him throughout life an ebullient response to cultural improvements and always had time for every good cause and worthy enterprise. "There was no public meeting for a needed charity, for educational interests, in behalf of art or letters or for the advancement of a conservatively liberal theology, in which his advocacy was not an essential part of the program."[168]

Indeed, the hour of American jubilee was never more eloquently (or reservedly) expressed than in Joseph Story's Phi Beta Kappa address to Harvard in 1826. "Let it not be imagined," he exulted, "that we do not live in an extraordinary age."[169] In evaluating the cultural and intellectual monuments of the day, Story praised the general diffusion of knowledge made possible by freedom of the press. He gloried in many of the new developments in science, philosophy, and literature, and even struck a progressive note in his plea for the intellectual and educational advancement of women.

The shortcomings of the century, however, far outweighed these advantages in Story's mind, and the panegyric soon dropped to a lower register of social criticism. Recognizing that there were obvious advancements in many areas of knowledge, especially in science, Story observed at the same time an increasing ignorance of man's older political and religious institutions. These could only be understood and appreciated through rigorous study, particularly of the great classical thinkers of antiquity. He bemoaned the growing propensity in America to disparage the importance of classical learning. The immense mass of new knowledge had induced only the belief that abstractions and simple generalizations could be applied to complex social problems; that man's institutions could be altered at will. This was a dangerous presumption: nothing should be changed unless one first knows what he is changing. Thus, like Matthew Arnold, who was later engaged in the task of assimilating new knowledge into the intellectual and moral fiber of England, Story advocated a cultural renewal only after criticism had effectively done its work, and believed that perhaps the most worthy ideal for Americans would simply be "to know the best that is known and thought in the world." "Human knowledge," he felt, "whether it be for ornament or use, for pleasure or instruction, is the accumulation of the wisdom and genius of all ages, and is, like the ocean, composed of contributions from infinitely various sources, whose currents

[167] Henry Steele Commager, "Joseph Story," *The Gaspar G. Bacon Lectures on the Constitution of the United States*, 1940–1950 (ed. by A. N. Holcombe), 94.

[168] Peabody, *Harvard Reminiscences*, 58.

[169] "Characteristics of the Age," *Miscellaneous Writings*, 342.

have mingled together from the beginning, and must continue so to do to the end of time."[170]

His heart was clearly not in this present "age of improvement," but in that golden day of the American Revolution, which he fancied most nearly approximated the unapproachable majesty of the Age of Pericles for its balance of precept and performance, its rare combination of acquirements and talents, and its celebrated works and deeds. Although generally pleased with the economic progress of his young republic, he lamented the passing of agrarian beatitude that Jefferson had taught would render life on earth tolerable, perhaps improvable. He was repelled by the political and social consequences of industrialization. To his English friend, Sir William Scott, later Lord Stowell, he wrote in 1820:

We are beginning . . . to become a manufacturing nation; but I am not much pleased (I am free to confess) with the efforts made to give an artificial stimulus to these establishments in our country. The example of your great manufacturing cities, apparently the seats of great vice, and political fermentations, affords no very agreeable contemplation to the statesman or patriot, or the friend of liberty. For myself I would wish my country long to remain devoted to agriculture and commerce, because they nourish a lofty spirit of independence and enterprise, and preserve a sound and healthy population.[171]

Judging from his extreme nationalism, however, Story was apparently oblivious to the pernicious effects of consolidation through economic growth upon the older principles and institutions which he cherished. Despite his reservations, he embraced the idea that in consolidation lay the means of making America the noblest nation in history. At base a firm advocate of growth and expansion, his dream was the creation of a great commonwealth equal in strength and culture to the best of Europe.

Whatever her aspirations for cultural independence, the unweaned colossus of the New World could not escape the fact she was a child of the West. "We are Europe at one remove or two," Howard Mumford Jones rightly insists, "but we are part of Europe still. . . . America is related to Europe by alterations of attraction and repulsion."[172] The links that tie America to Europe, and to England especially, had been substantially weakened in Story's lifetime. "The American Revolution dissolved American ties with the House of Hanover, but its leaders reaffirmed our ties with Brutus and Cato—with thinkers, that is, who really believed in virtue and with patriots who really believed in a republic."[173]

At Waterloo the English had triumphed on the battlefield, only to lose the

170 Story, "Literary Tendencies of the Times," *ibid.*, 745.
171 May 20, 1820, *Life and Letters*, I, 385.
172 *O Strange New World*, 390–91.
173 *Ibid.*, 393.

war for men's minds; the doctrines of Rousseau had reappeared in the respectable dress of traditional English liberalism. America, counseled Judge
Story, must reunite the bonds that join her to England with a discriminating
eye, conserving what is valuable, rejecting what is unworthy, somehow holding fast to the permanent things of her ancestors that are not inconsistent with
the American nature, such as English law, while declaring at the same time
her independence of current English political fermentations. In fine, Story was
the first to admit that many of America's sins—like many of her virtues—
were Europe's doing, and he did not shirk from telling his English friends
so. "I take a lively interest in British Affairs," he wrote Sir Charles Vaughan,
the British ambassador to Washington,

& truly in the present state of the world & especially in America, whatever you do
in England for better or for worse reacts everywhere else; except, that, I fear, we in
America are apt to take pattern from your Radicalism & heed not the many other
excellent lessons, which your example should teach us. I fear the present state of
things, throughout all the civilized world is fraught with imminent hazards to
sound principles & to stable government. There is a restless spirit seized upon the
young, the rash, & the improvident, which makes them uneasy under whatever is
established, however good, & eager for whatever is untried, & experimental. In our
Republic I am sure that we are proceeding in a headlong & a headstrong course of
this sort, which endangers, & I fear, may even subvert our liberties. In short, universal suffrage is here working all the evils, which have led on the people in other
countries under the guidance of false & selfish demagogues, to their own
destruction.[174]

That Story based his cultural nationalism on the "Popian heritage," on the
history of Europe, and on Old World religious and political concepts by no
means made him impervious to America's unique opportunities in the field of
letters. His only criterion, as he stated in his oration on the "Literary Tendencies of the Times," was that "Our just ambition should be to make our literature a component part of the literature of the world, for the use of all nations
and all ages. Let it have the bold impress of American genius, and the masculine vigor, and the brave spirit of inquiry and expression, which fitly belong to
a free government, and an unshackled press."[175] Such was his design in ad-
vising Francis Lieber on the matter of establishing a foreign review in
America, somewhat on the scale of the *British Foreign Quarterly*. "A review of
this sort," wrote Story in 1833, "would, I should imagine, be acceptable in
America & let us into foreign literature through a fairer and better medium
than our present one through England."[176]

[174] Nov. 7, 1837, Charles R. Vaughan Papers, Christ's College, Oxford University
(hereafter cited as Vaughan Papers, Christ's College).

[175] *Miscellaneous Writings*, 770.

[176] To Francis Lieber, July 30, 1833, Story-Lieber Correspondence, Henry E. Huntington Library.

Moving hither and yon in the ebb of classicism, beyond the ever increasing pull of indigenous Americanism, Story could not condone the progressive illuminati, such as Channing, who by this time was urging a complete break with the past;[177] or Emerson, whose famed Phi Beta Kappa address in 1837 proclaimed America's intellectual independence.

Nor could he abide his *avant garde* contemporaries pressing for a transcendental philosophy and a culture more compatible with Jacksonian Democracy. They were not merely "illiterate and vain pretenders," but "minds of the highest order, which are capable of giving fearful impulse to public opinion."[178] Story "sometimes feared that there were not conservative elements among us," his anonymous but intimate biographer noted, "sufficiently strong to counteract the disorganizing influence of the ignorance of the many and the selfishness of the few; and with the whole force of his energetic nature, he denounced the men of talents and education, who lent themselves to destroy what they ought to have upheld."[179] Already, he felt, the new crop of American authors reflected the boundless individualism of the nineteenth century and fell woefully short of traditional standards. Their object was to produce not "what will endure the test of future criticism as what will buoy itself upon the current of a shallow popularity."[180]

Since the early nineteenth century there has been hardly a discourse on the subject of American letters without some confident hymning of glories to come. Walt Whitman sang of himself and of his America, predicting that "Above all previous lands, a great original literature is surely to become the justification and reliance (in some respects the sole reliance) of American democracy."[181] Nor was Whitman the last of the visionaries. In our own day Van Wyck Brooks in his "Letters and Leadership" has practically rewritten Emerson's "American Scholar" in terms of "Democratic Vistas." And yet Ortega y Gasset has asserted, possibly to the credit of literary colonialists like Story, that even now American civilization could not survive if civilization were dead in Europe.

Joseph Story could foresee no future for America that did not operate within the mainstream of Western civilization. American law, as American literature, he realized, grows in native soil bearing the marks of a distinct race of men; but it is also a transplantation of older values as well—an offshoot of the "law of nations" that has descended on Western society through the ages. "In the

---

[177] William Ellery Channing, "On National Literature," *Old South Leaflets*, VI, 341. First printed in the *Christian Examiner*, 1830.

[178] Story, "Literary Tendencies of the Times," *Miscellaneous Writings*, 747.

[179] "Biographical Notice of Mr. Justice Story," *American Review, A Whig Journal*, Vol. III (Jan., 1846), 77.

[180] Story, "Characteristics of the Age," *Miscellaneous Writings*, 360.

[181] *Democratic Vistas*, 5.

next age," he sanguinely wrote Vaughan, "I cannot but believe that the English and American lawyers will be brought into a more friendly communion by labouring earnestly & with a common spirit in the building up & strengthening of the great principles of the common law. It will form a tie between England & America which can never be broken."[182]

Future generations would be indebted to men like Story, Clay, Cooper, Webster, Hawthorne, Calhoun, and others, who tried to maintain a spiritual continuity with the great literary, political, legal, and philosophical traditions of the past. By putting their stock in cultural precedents, these men passed on something more than an inert set of principles. They helped create conditions in which American culture, without ceasing to be national, could flow into the channels of Western culture. Perhaps their efforts explain in part the promptness with which such writers as Emerson and Thoreau were later "discovered" and acclaimed abroad.

Russell Kirk, a critical observer in our own century, sums it up this way: "In the first half of the nineteenth century, when America was rawer, the importance of European ideas was correspondingly greater. They filtered into the United States, often against the protest of an arrogant American public; and the Americans who tempered democratic overconfidence with old-world prudence ought to receive in our generation the thanks denied in their own time."[183]

Story's voice was to the end the voice of an Anglo-American and a cosmopolite. "A thorough New Englander of his time who was yet, also, to his great gain, a man of the world,"[184] was Henry James's opinion. Story once astonished an English visitor at Cambridge by being able to "place" some small street in London, though he had never been there and had never even crossed the sea. "Judge Story," James remarked, "knew his London because, even at that then prodigious distance from it, he had a feeling for it."[185]

It is not in the least peculiar, then, that Story once identified himself more closely with Virginia, whose customs, habits, and traditions were more thoroughly English than any other part of the country. It was the first charter

---

[182] Nov. 7, 1837, Vaughan Papers, Christ's College. "I should rejoice," he wrote Vaughan a decade earlier, upon sending him a copy of Kent's *Commentaries on American Law*, to give to his brother, Justice Vaughan, "in being the instrument of bringing English lawyers acquainted with American Jurisprudence, in which they might perhaps find some things worthy of a note for a Book or a Brief." (Dec. 12, 1828, *ibid*.) "I rejoice that at last a communication is opening between us & the English bar," Story told Richard Peters, "so that we shall not always be total strangers to each other. I cannot but believe, that they, as well as ourselves, would be improved by a frank professional intercourse." (July 27, 1833, Peters Papers, HSP.)

[183] *The Conservative Mind*, 172.

[184] *William Wetmore Story*, I, 22.

[185] *Ibid.*, 13.

of Virginia that had secured to her people "the privileges, franchises, and immunities of native-born Englishmen forever," and the sons of Virginia, like John Marshall, and its adopted sons, like Story, did not easily forget it. Moreover, the American republic, which Story so deeply revered, was in the formative years little more than the state of Virginia writ large, so crucial was the role of Virginia in securing independence and in establishing the union, so dominant were Virginia statesmen in public affairs. Although Story quite properly insisted that his youth had been "little infected with Virginia notions"[186] of the Jeffersonian states' rights variety, he was writing Crowninshield in early 1805 "that Virginia is & always hath been the most patriotic, disinterested and magnanimous state in the Union."[187] And a year later he was still calling himself "really at bottom a Virginian."[188]

THE LAST DAYS OF THE OLD COURT

John Marshall, his Virginia friend, was to him the embodiment of all these values he cherished. Marshall's love of literature and the classics, his "deep-rooted principles," his gentle affections, and, above all, his love of Union and sound constitutional doctrines: these were the attributes of the chief justice which Story admired most. The death of Marshall in 1835 was a blow from which Story never fully recovered. It seemed to symbolize the end of an era, the end of the Constitution.

"I miss the Chief Justice at every turn," Story sadly wrote from the boarding house at which he, Marshall, and the other justices had resided in Washington. "I have been several times into the room which he was accustomed to occupy. It yet remains without an inhabitant, and wears an aspect of desolation, and has a noiseless gloom. The table at which he sat, the chair which he occupied, the bed on which he slept,—they are all there and bring back a train of the most melancholy reflections."[189] "I never hope to look upon his like again."[190]

[186] Story, *Life and Letters*, I, 129.

[187] Jan. 24, 1805, as quoted in Dunne, "Joseph Story: The Germinal Years," *Harvard Law Review*, Vol. LXXV, No. 4 (Feb., 1962), 710.

[188] Story to Crowninshield, Jan. 4, 1806, *ibid*. Crowninshield expressed pro-Virginia sympathies, as did other New England Republicans of the day. "Virginia alone can do nothing to the injury of any part of the Union," he told Story in 1804, "and if she has the power she has not the disposition. I love and respect the members of that State. They are our firmest & best republicans. I never heard them utter a statement hostile to the New England interest." (Nov. 9, 1804, Story Papers, Clements Library.) Weakened by sectional antagonisms, which threatened to dismember the Union, the romance between Story and Virginia gradually faded, as did Virginia leadership over the Republic and the South. On November 24, 1832, South Carolina issued her famous ordinance of nullification, and a few months later Story responded in a moment of forgetfulness that "The Union never has received, & never will receive, a Hearty support South of the Potomac." To Joseph Hopkinson, Feb. 17, 1833, Hopkinson Papers, HSP.

[189] To Harriet Martineau, Feb. 8, 1836, *Life and Letters*, II, 226.

He was devoted to Marshall, whose kindred mind he revered above all others. "I love his laugh," Story had written back in 1808, upon first setting sight of Marshall, "it is too hearty for an intriguer."[191] In his great tribute to Marshall, Story confessed, with characteristic humility, that "While I have followed his footsteps, not as I could have wished, but as I have been able, at humble distances, in his splendid judicial career, I have constantly felt the liveliest gratitude to that beneficent Providence, which created him for the age, that his talents might illustrate the law, his virtues adorn the bench, and his judgments establish the perpetuity of the Constitution of the country."[192]

Thus, in 1835, Story found himself stranded and alone. "The last of an old race of judges," he said he was, the last of a once mighty and dominant class of men who formulated their judicial precepts upon the teachings of the *Federalist*, or so they thought, anyway. There was some speculation that Story would succeed Marshall as chief justice. He was, after all, the most learned and experienced judge on the Court. Indeed, as early as 1823, Charles Jared Ingersoll, Philadelphia lawyer, Democrat, and champion of liberal causes, had confided to Story: "I hope, indeed, to live to see you the Chief Justice of the U.S. The great and just judge who now fills that station may continue there while he will, with all my veneration and heart. But as he is some twenty odd years your senior, it is, I know, the view of many of the bar here abouts that his succession belongs to you."[193]

Andrew Jackson, however, entertained the view that Story's conservative predilections and judicial nationalism disqualified him for the post. "The most dangerous man in America"[194] was the label Jackson pinned on Story, and, indeed, no man was more of a threat to the ideas popularized by Old

---

[190] Story to Martineau, Oct. 8, 1835, *ibid.*, 205.

[191] To Fay, Feb. 28, 1808, *ibid.*, I, 167.

[192] "Life, Character and Services of Chief Justice Marshall," A Discourse Pronounced on the 15th of October, 1835, at the Request of the Suffolk Bar, *Miscellaneous Writings*, 696.

[193] Nov. 6, 1823, Story Papers, Clements Library.

[194] Story to Mrs. Story, Jan. 27, 1833, *Life and Letters*, II, 119. Story actually thought that his title as "the most dangerous man in America" was rather amusing, as did Chief Justice Marshall. "The Court dined on Tuesday last with the President," Story reported on February 2, 1834, "& as only three of the judges were present . . . it was my *official honor* to be placed on the President's right & Judge Baldwin on his left . . . the Chief Justice being placed between the ladies of the Household on the opposite side. I could not but smile that 'the most dangerous man' in the U. States was thus by the President's express direction (for he took [me] under my arm & led me to the table) placed in this post of appointed honour. To do him justice he conducted himself very pleasantly . . . was very affable, & sought to be somewhat marked in his attentions. Of course I met his advances quite at ease. I had a good deal of light conversation with him upon many topics. On the whole my time passed off very agreeably; & the Chief Justice on our return laughed heartily at the success of my courtesy." To Mrs. Story, Feb. 2, 1834, Story Papers, Texas.

Hickory. Jackson's successors were no more inclined to elevate Story to his rightful position. President Polk pledged he would "appoint no man . . . likely to relapse into the . . . doctrines of . . . Judge Story."[195] Story's Whig friends in the legal profession, nevertheless, continued to look upon him as the chief justice, if not in name, then in fact. "There is no place where you are more highly estimated, personally & judicially, than here," wrote Joseph Hopkinson, Philadelphia lawyer, then sitting as a federal district judge. "We look upon you as the successor of Ch. J. Marshall, the heir and defender of his constitutional doctrines & opinions."[196]

Story did not attempt to ingratiate himself with Jackson or conceal his antagonism for Jackson's brand of coonskin democracy. He had seen "the reign of King 'Mob' . . . triumphant"[197] at Jackson's first inaugural celebration, and the reign of the democratic despot in Jackson's presidency. "Though we live under the form of a republic," Story lamented, "we are in fact under the absolute rule of a single man. . . . I seem almost, while I write, to be in a dream, and to be called back to the last days of the Roman republic, when the people shouted for Caesar, and liberty itself expired with the dark but prophetic words of Cicero."[198]

Story also had his reputation of party disloyalty working against his appointment. Upon Marshall's death Josiah Quincy had suggested privately to Harrison Gray Otis that Jackson might say to Story as Pharaoh had said to Joseph, " 'Thou shalt be ruler over my house.' " "Joseph, indeed! Why yes, an excellent comparison," snorted Otis, "Pray, was anything said about his coat of many colors?"[199] The appointment of the Maryland Democrat Roger Taney to the chief justiceship came, then, as no surprise to Story, although he had insisted all along that he was "not conscious of ever having deserted republican principles."[200]

---

[195] As quoted in Carl Swisher, *Roger B. Taney*, 444.

[196] To Story, Mar. 24, 1839, Story Papers, Clements Library.

[197] Story to Mrs. Story, Mar. 7, 1829, *Life and Letters*, I, 563.

[198] To Fay, Feb. 18, 1834, *ibid.*, II, 154. "Andrew Jackson," Arthur M. Schlesinger has written, "convinced Story that the country was 'sinking down into despotism, under the disguise of a democratic government,' and the Whig party supplied the only hope for the future." Story's enmity toward Jackson was in large measure the echo of the American legal profession. "Chief Justice Spencer of New York would speak of 'that barbarian Jackson,' while Chancellor Kent called him 'a detestable, ignorant, reckless, vain & malignant tyrant,' and Chief Justice Daggett of Connecticut confessed in 1832 that he had never felt such forebodings: "The nation is too young, though corrupt enough, for destruction. May Heaven defend us." (Schlesinger, *The Age of Jackson*, 322.) "We are fallen on evil times," Webster wrote Kent, "on times when public men seek low objects, & when the tone of public morals & public feeling is depressed & debased. I hope our children may see a better state of things." Apr. 27, 1832, James Kent Papers, Library of Congress.

[199] Morison, *Harrison Gray Otis*, I, 220–21.

Story continued to serve on the Court, but was soon convinced that resignation rather than defeat and humiliation by Jacksonian appointees was the only honorable choice open to him. He was anxious to devote all his attentions to scholarship and to the Harvard Law School over which he presided. Story reacted violently to the changes in constitutional doctrine under Taney, producing three impassioned dissents in Taney's first term,[201] which signaled the coming of the New Order and the retrogression of conservative judicial nationalism.[202]

Webster, Kent, and other old friends rallied to his cause, but nearly every member of the Court was against him in 1837. Even the Court reporter, Richard Peters, whom he had befriended, apparently sided with the opposition. "I do not undertake to account for the fact, that Mr. Peters should entertain a different opinion from mine, as to the late constitutional decisions," Story wrote Judge Hopkinson. "That he thinks them (as Mr. Biddle suggests) in the highest degree conservative, did greatly surprise me. But I do not know, that I might be surprised at anything. I have long been accustomed to know, that even my best friends some times see with other eyes than mine; & I learn daily more & more to entertain a wide charity for human opinions."[203] Littered with lonely protests, Story's road to retreat ended at a point of despair he had not known since early manhood. The final decade of his life upon the bench, terminated by an intestinal disorder at the age of sixty-six, was not, however, a complete rout, but a strategic withdrawal; for he exerted a powerful influence over the Court and was often able to carry Taney and other Democrats appointed to the Court along with him.[204]

Six months before his death on September 10, 1845, Story despondently wrote to his old friend Bacon that he was prepared to step down from the bench, and would have done so then had Henry Clay been elected president

---

[200] Story to John Brazer Davis, Jan. 3, 1824, Massachusetts Historical Society *Proceedings*, 2nd Series, Vol. XLIX (Oct., 1915–June, 1916), 186.

[201] *New York* v. *Miln*, 11 Peters 102 (1837); *Briscoe* v. *Bank of Kentucky*, 11 Peters 257 (1837); *Charles River Bridge* v. *Warren Bridge Co.*, 11 Peters 420 (1837).

[202] Marshall was the last Federalist left on the Supreme Court, Justice Washington having died in 1829. The death of the chief justice in 1835 marked the beginning of a rapid turnover of personnel that altered the composition of the Court, as well as its doctrines. Gabriel Duval died that same year, which created a second vacancy. Jackson appointed Taney as chief justice, and Duval's position was filled by Philip Barbour, which meant that five of the seven justices were now Jacksonian Democrats, leaving only two Republicans, Story and Smith Thompson. Then in 1837, Congress increased the size of the Court from seven to nine justices, which allowed Van Buren to add two more Democrats, John Catron and John McKinley, to the Court. Between 1835–41, six Democrats were appointed to the Court, all from the South.

[203] Mar. 3, 1837, Hopkinson Papers, HSP.

[204] See Robert J. Harris, "Chief Justice Taney: Prophet of Reform and Reaction," *Vanderbilt Law Review*, Vol. X, No. 2 (Feb., 1957), 227–57.

(in order that Clay could appoint his successor). "Many reasons induced me to this conclusion," he explained. "Although my personal position and intercourse with my brethren has always been pleasant, yet I have been long convinced that the doctrines and opinions of the 'old court' were daily losing ground, and especially those on great constitutional questions. . . . I am the last member now living, of the old Court. . . . I am persuaded that by remaining on the Bench I could accomplish no good, either for myself or for my country."[205]

Believing he had outworn his usefulness, and conscious that other philosophies were gaining wide acceptance which were harmful to the nation, Joseph Story died without ever fully realizing the enduring and often salutary influence of his law upon human events. Even in his eclipse, however, he managed to retain the familiar tone of unflagging confidence, certain to the end that his own purposes and designs, and those of the "old Court," were indisputably correct. At the heart of his disillusionment lay the private acknowledgment that he had failed to convince his countrymen of his own moral and legal constants; that he had been misinterpreted as a man and as a justice; and that he had been relegated prematurely to the annals of history. As he confessed to a visitor from abroad, "I seem a monument of the past age and a mere record of the dead."[206]

A kindly scholar who enjoyed good conversation and books, Joseph Story was probably as famous for his garrulity as for his jurisprudence. He entertained his listeners, recalled one Harvard student, "with an unintermitted flow of wit, humor, anecdote, literary criticism, comments on passing events, talk on the highest themes of thought. . . . He must have read by intuition; for he seemed to have read everything, both old and new. . . . His son is the only other man that I have ever known who could talk almost continuously for several successive hours, and leave his hearers with an appetite for more."[207] "Judge Story was a voluble talker," testified another pupil. He concluded his remarks about William Pinkney by saying, 'As great a man as he was, he had one grievous fault—a fault I advise young men to guard against—he was an interminable talker.' " A smile flitted across the faces of his students. "The Judge broke into a laugh and added, 'It is a great fault no matter who indulges in it!' "[208] Looking back on the days when Story himself was a student of law, his teacher, Samuel Putnam, recalled in 1846 that "While he was in my office, altho' he read much, yet we talked more; and I believe in my heart, that even then he did the greater part of it."[209]

[205] Apr. 12, 1845, *Life and Letters*, II, 527–28.
[206] To Martineau, Feb. 8, 1836, *ibid.*, 226.
[207] Peabody, *Harvard Reminiscences*, 58–59.
[208] Warren, *History of the Harvard Law School*, II, 55.
[209] To William Story, May 28, 1846, Putnam Papers, Essex Institute. Josiah Quincy

Story was sentimental, affectionate, and charitable, by temperament habitually cheerful and sanguine. Benjamin Perley Poore, a Washington journalist and Senate clerk, wrote many years after Story's death that the members of the Marshall Court "were a rather jovial set, especially Judge Story, who used to assert that every man should laugh at least an hour during each day, and who had himself a great fund of humorous anecdotes."[210]

With minor exceptions he remained out of active politics during his career on the high bench.[211] He preferred to attend to his banking interests,[212] promote education,[213] write and lecture to learned societies, and remain near the

---

testified that "As a boy I was fascinated by the brilliancy of his conversation" and recalled that while accompanying Judge Story on one of his many trips from Cambridge to Washington to attend Court, "People who never talked anywhere else were driven to talk in those old coaches; while a ready conversationalist, like Judge Story, was stimulated to incessant cerebral discharges. . . . Judge Story was one of the great talkers at a period when conversation was considered a sort of second profession." (Quincy, *Figures of the Past*, 188, 191, 193.) Another relates that "Judge Story was excessively fond of talking and where counsel were making points which did not command his instant assent, was always ready to anticipate the other side and answer them. There were lawyers who knew how to humor this foible for their own advantage, and, when they saw the threatening avalanche of law learning gathering head and impending from the bench, had the cunning to stand aside and simply help launch it on their helpless adversaries." Thomas Durfee, *Gleanings from the Judicial History of Rhode Island*, 122.

[210] Benjamin Perley Poore, *Reminiscences of Sixty Years in the National Metropolis*, I, 295.

[211] In 1813 he delivered a eulogy in Salem at the burial of Captain James Lawrence, who had been killed in battle between the *Chesapeake* and the *Shannon*. And in December of 1819, he again broke his judicial silence and appeared at a Salem town meeting to deliver an address against slavery and the Missouri Compromise. In 1820 he was elected to represent Salem at the Massachusetts Constitutional Convention, where he delivered speeches on suffrage, on judicial reform, and on the rights of property and of Harvard College. Before his appointment to the Court, Story made frequent appearances at Salem town meetings. "There was one in 1806 where he had written the local remonstrance against European harassment of American shipping. There was one in 1807 when Federalist and Jeffersonian were in rare unanimity to protest a British cannonading of an unsuspecting man-o'-war. There was one a year later when Story helped turn back a censure of Jefferson's embargo, the very law he was soon to undo." (Dunne, "Joseph Story: The Salem Years," *Essex Institute Historical Collections*, Vol. CI, No. 4 [Oct., 1965], 310-11.) Throughout his career on the bench, Story worked quietly behind the scenes with members of the Congress to secure judicial reform and used his influence to obtain federal appointments for his friends. For a discussion, see chapter 7, *infra*.

[212] Story served as the president of the Merchant's Bank of Salem between 1815-35, and from 1818-30 was vice-president of the Salem Savings Bank. In 1820 he drafted a memorial for the merchants of Salem protesting trade restrictions and was also the author of the short-lived Bankruptcy Act of 1841.

[213] Story was elected a member of the Board of Overseers of Harvard College in 1819, and became a Fellow of the Corporation in 1825. "In January, 1825, while yet an overseer, he delivered, and afterwards published, an argument against the memorial of the pro-

law school and at home with his family, believing that "real happiness belongs to private life, and most of all to domestic life."[214] His first wife had died after six months of marriage, and only two of his seven children survived him. These personal misfortunes alone might have embittered the stoutest heart. But his mind, by its native elasticity, soon regained its spring; and though experience had its usual effect in moderating the ardor and extent of his hopes, he was still assuaged by his more temperate aspirations. This feature of his character made him, on the whole, one of the happiest of men.

The moral character of Justice Story may be inferred from the unquestioned fact that everyone with whom he had ever been in the habit of domestic or familiar intercourse, whether friend, clergyman, fellow justice, or student, felt for him the liveliest attachment and the highest confidence and esteem. On the morning of September 12, 1845, the day of Judge Story's funeral, Daniel Webster rose at a meeting of the Massachusetts bar and in a eulogy summed up the private character of his close friend and political compatriot, with these fond remembrances:

We have known of his manner of life, from his youth up. We can bear witness to the strict uprightness and purity of his character; his simplicity, and unostentatious habits; the ease and affability of his intercourse; his remarkable vivacity, amidst severe labors; the cheerful and animating tones of his conversation, and his fast fidelity to friends. Some of us, also, can testify to his large and liberal charities, not ostentatious or casual but systematic and silent,—dispensed almost without showing the hand.[215]

---

fessors and tutors claiming the exclusive right to be elected Fellows of the Corporation, full of curious and recondite learning, upon a subject which, we believe, was never before discussed in America." ("Biographical Notice of Mr. Justice Story," *American Review, A Whig Journal*, Vol. III [Jan., 1846], 76.) In 1829 he became Dane Professor of Law at Harvard. Story held honorary degrees from Harvard, Dartmouth, and Brown, and honorary memberships in quaint-sounding student societies, including the Philomathesian societies of Kenyon College, Pennsylvania College (Gettysburg), and the University of Alabama and the Literary Society of Washington College (Pa.). He was also a co-founder of the Essex Historical Society and a member of the Georgia Historical Society; president of the Unitarian Association; vice-president of the Bunker Hill Monument Association, of the American Antiquarian Society, and of the American Academy of Language and Belles Lettres; Fellow of the American Academy of Arts and Sciences; and a member of the Massachusetts Agricultural Society and of the Board of Trustees of the famous Mt. Auburn Cemetery.

214 Story to Mrs. Story, Feb. 25, 1829, *Life and Letters*, I, 562.
215 As quoted in Story, *Life and Letters*, II, 624.

CHAPTER II

Commentaries on the Natural Law

I once saw a book advertised, entitled "New Views of the Constitution." I was startled! What right has a man to start new views upon it? Speculations upon our Government are dangerous, and should be discountenanced. And, upon this point, Edmund Burke has uttered a brief, but important truth: "Governments are practical things, not toys for speculatists to play with." Nevertheless, governments must often change, in conformity to the demands of the times. I have been in public life forty years, and have seen the union change much. You may think you are at last settled! But no! Our laws are written upon the sands of time, and the winds of popular opinion gradually efface them; new layers are to be made, and your old writing renewed or changed.

JOSEPH STORY, *Life and Letters*

THE paternity of American constitutional limitations and guarantees of individual liberty, as Edward S. Corwin demonstrated in a celebrated essay nearly half a century ago, is shared by a widely divergent group of American and European thinkers.[1] The philosophical, political, and legal traditions from which they spoke embrace a wide range of ideas and institutions, spanning more than two thousand years of historical development in the Western world. It is no exaggeration to say that the task of tracing the pedigree of American constitutional principles is formidable as well as compelling; for there are incalculable dangers to be reckoned with if the derivation, evolution, and content of American constitutional principles are ignored and neglected. If, under the doctrine of the living Constitution, the fundamental law is to suffer frequent and far-reaching judicial reinterpretations, reason and experience would seem to require that a knowledge first be acquired of what has been lost, in order to understand and appreciate what has been gained.[2] It remains, advised one of

---

[1] See Edward S. Corwin, *The Higher Law Background of American Constitutional Law.*

[2] "This fundamental fact of man's unavoidable ignorance of much on which the working of civilization rests," observes Friedrich Hayek, "has received little attention. . . . If we are to understand how society works, we must attempt to define the general nature and range of our ignorance concerning it." Only the foolish and arrogant subscribe to the false and dangerous notion "that man has created his civilization and that he therefore can also change its institutions as he pleases." If man clearly understood how civilization

America's foremost constitutional historians, for us to take advantage of the sources of the Constitution available to us,

and to recall that the words written by old George Mason of Virginia into the first Bill of Rights in this country are still true, that: "No free government or the blessings of liberty can be preserved to any people but by . . . frequent recurrence to fundamental principles." Our political system will break down, only when and where the people, for whom and by whom it is intended to be carried on, shall fail to receive a sound education in its principles and in its historical development illustrating its application to and under changing conditions. "Our country," said Edmund Burke, "is not a thing of mere physical locality. It consists, in great measure, in the ancient order into which we are born."[3]

Of particular significance regarding the origins of Anglo-American law is the reign of Henry III (1216–72). According to Pollock and Maitland, it is probably the most important period in the history of the common law; for "At the end of that period most of the main outlines of our medieval law have been drawn for good and all; the subsequent centuries will be able to do little more than to fill in the details of a scheme which is set before them as unalterable."[4]

The achievement of the thirteenth century, however, involved more than the establishment of a body of rules governing individual relationships in the private sphere of human activity. Thanks to Bracton and those who later followed in his footsteps, the common law from this time forward was also a body of principles and ideas, some of which overlapped the fields of public and private law to form the basis of political and constitutional theory.[5] Principal among these was the natural law, which since the age of Bracton has formed an essential ingredient of the Christian philosophy of law in England.[6]

Drawing frequently from Roman law and such classical thinkers as Cicero and influenced by Christian dogma, the great English commentators and the judges of the King's Courts as late as the nineteenth century openly subscribed to a system of legal ethics and "higher law" based on revelation and reason. Conceived by the Creator and revealed through Scripture, natural law served not only as a standard of justice for the application of common law principles,

---

was maintained, or had deliberately created it in full understanding of what he was doing, then such a notion might have merit; but in truth "we know little of the particular facts to which the whole of social activity continually adjusts itself in order to provide what we have learned to expect." *The Constitution of Liberty,* 22–23, 25. See also Edward M. Sait, *Political Institutions: A Preface,* 10–14.

[3] Charles Warren, *The Making of the Constitution,* 804.

[4] Sir Frederick Pollock and Frederic William Maitland, *The History of English Law before the Time of Edward I,* I, 174.

[5] See, for example, "The Common Law's Contribution to Political Theory," in William Searle Holdsworth, *Some Lessons from Our Legal History,* 57–106; and Roscoe Pound, *The Development of Constitutional Guarantees of Liberty, passim.*

[6] See John C. H. Wu, *Fountain of Justice: A Study in the Natural Law,* 55–131.

but also provided a limitation on political authority. Thus Bracton declared that "The King himself, however, ought not to be under man but under God, and under the Law, because the Law makes the king. Therefore, let the king render back to the Law what the Law gives to him, namely, dominion and power; for there is no king where will, and not Law, wields dominion."[7]

In *Calvin's Case*, decided in 1610, Sir Edward Coke stated that "the law of nature is part of the law of England," and added that "the law of nature is immutable" and "was before any judicial or municipal law."[8] Sir William Blackstone introduced his *Commentaries on the Laws of England* with the confident assertion that "This law of nature ... dictated by God himself, is of course superior in obligation to any other. It is binding over all the globe ... no human laws are of any validity, if contrary to this."[9]

In brief, natural law ideas permeated the whole English legal and constitu-

[7] Henry de Bracton, *De Legibus et Consuetudinibus Angliae* (ed. by George E. Woodbine), III, 0.2 (fol. 5b), quoted by Coke in *Prohibitions Del Roy*, 12 Coke's Reports 63 (King's Bench, 1612). Chancellor Kent agreed with Reeves that Bracton was "the father of the English law." (*Commentaries on American Law* [ed. by Charles M. Barnes], I, 500.) Bracton, "who seems not to have read his contemporary, St. Thomas Aquinas, utilized the Natural Law to achieve the equivalent synthesis in the civil and common law of England. In part he inherited the Natural Law from Canon Law." Peter J. Stanlis, *Edmund Burke and the Natural Law*, 10.

[8] 7 Coke's Reports 1 (King's Bench, 1610); see also Coke's remarks regarding limitations on Parliament in *Dr. Bonham's Case*, 8 Coke's Reports 113 (King's Bench, 1610); and Chief Justice Hobart on the same subject, in *Day* v. *Savadge*, Hobart 85 (King's Bench, 1614); Lord Holt, in *City of London* v. *Wood*, 12 Modern Reports 669 (King's Bench, 1701); *Rex and Regina* v. *Knollys*, 1 Lord Raymond 10 (King's Bench, 1695); *Paty's Case*, 2 Lord Raymond 1105 (King's Bench, 1705); *Ashby* v. *White*, 2 Lord Raymond 938, 3 Lord Raymond 320 (King's Bench, 1703), cited as authority by Justice Holmes in *Nixon* v. *Herndon*, 273 U.S. 536 (1927). In an action of *indebitatus assumpsit* to recover six pounds which the defendant obtained and kept from the plaintiff, Lord Mansfield held in *Moses* v. *Macferlan* that the defendant was "obliged by the ties of natural justice and equity to refund the money." (2 Burrows 1005 [King's Bench, 1760].) In the late nineteenth century, under the influence of positivism and Benthamism, English judges tended increasingly to scoff at natural law and to regard Parliament as the sole source of law. Rejecting Chief Justice Hobart's dictum in *Day* v. *Savadge*, the Court of Common Pleas declared in 1871: "It was once said,—I think in Hobart,—that, if an Act of Parliament were to create a man a judge in his own case, the Court might disregard it. That dictum, however, stands as a warning, rather than an authority to be followed. We sit here as servants of the Queen and the legislature. Are we to act as regents over what is done by parliament with the consent of the Queen, lords, and Commons? I deny that any such authority exists." (*Lee* v. *The Bude & Torrington Junction Ry. Co.* 6 Law Reports 576.) In 1913, Lord Justice Hamilton repudiated Mansfield's holding in *Moses* v. *Macferlan*, and insisted that "whatever may have been the case 146 years ago, we are not free ... to administer that vague jurisprudence which is sometimes attractively styled 'justice as between man and man.'" *Baylis* v. *Bishop of London*, 1 Chancery Division 127 (1913). For a more complete discussion, see Wu, *Fountain of Justice*, 71–101.

[9] (Ed. by William Draper Lewis), I, (cited hereafter as *Commentaries*).

tional system. For more than seven centuries they provided the framework within which the common law was developed. "The validity of a system of natural law," as one student has put it, "was taught, and even taken for granted, by all the great common lawyers from Bracton, Fortescue and Littleton, through Thomas More and Christopher St. Germain, to Coke and on to Holt. . . . [Natural law] was taught at the Inns of Court in the Fifteenth and Sixteenth and Seventeenth centuries when the Inns of Court were a truly legal university. The tradition survived into the eighteenth and nineteenth centuries and is not absent even in the twentieth century."[10]

American legal education carried on the natural law tradition, especially in the early nineteenth century, despite unfavorable odds. Few students received formal instruction in an established school of law, and in most instances their legal training was of the law office variety, which afforded little opportunity for the discussion of theory and principle. Still, they read in the common law, acquainted themselves with Coke and Blackstone, and, consciously or unconsciously, were thus drawn into the mainstream of English legal thought.

Moreover, in the small handful of colleges where law was taught, a lecture course in natural law was invariably a part of the curriculum. In 1789, James Wilson, then an associate justice of the Supreme Court, was appointed to the faculty of the College of Philadelphia, now the University of Pennsylvania, and for a brief period lectured on Blackstone and the natural law, among other subjects, before the course was discontinued.[11] At Harvard College, where Joseph Story reigned over the first truly successful and permanent law school in America, lectures on natural law were regularly delivered by the judge himself as a part of the general course of instruction.[12] James Kent echoed the high ideals of Wilson, Story, George Wythe, and other distinguished teachers of law in early America when he declared in his inaugural address as professor of law at Columbia College that the rising generation of lawyers would have to have their "passions controlled by the discipline of Christian truth" and their minds "initiated in the elementary doctrines of natural and public law," if they were to acquire a profound knowledge of the law "regulated by moral principle."[13] So pronounced was the influence of natural law among prominent

[10] Richard O'Sullivan, *Grotius Society Transactions*, Vol. XXXI (1945), 135, as quoted in Stanlis, *Burke and the Natural Law*, 11.

[11] Chroust, *Rise of the Legal Profession in America*, II, 178–80. As early as 1756, a course in the civil laws was offered at the college, and reading assignments included Grotius' *De jure belli ac pacis* and Pufendorf's *De jure naturae et gentium* (*ibid.*, 176). In 1804, Wilson's lectures were published in Philadelphia. His essay on natural law was the first and one of the few written by an American lawyer. See his "Of the Law of Nature" in *The Works of James Wilson* (ed. by Robert Green McCloskey), I, (hereafter cited as Wilson, *Works*).

[12] For an excellent account of Story's professorship, see Arthur E. Sutherland, *The Law at Harvard*, 92–139.

[13] "A Lecture, Introductory to a Course of Law Lectures in Columbia College, De-

lawyers at this time, in fact, that one member of the profession remarked he took

pride in perceiving that some of our American jurists have been warmly praised by their trans-Atlantic brethren, for their exertions to make jurisprudence in this country a science more equitable and philosophical than it has been regarded in England. This they conceive is to be promoted, as Mr. Du Ponceau has declared, by establishing it as a maxim, "that pure ethics and sound logic are also part of the common law." The parallelism of the Roman code with the natural law has been the boast of its admirers; and it has been the aim of some American jurists, among whom our author is to be numbered, to draw the attention of students to the consideration of that great body of wisdom.[14]

STORY'S NATURAL LAW PHILOSOPHY

Among the American lawyers and judges of this creative and resourceful era in legal development, Judge Story stands out as possibly the most learned and influential defender of the natural law tradition. To Story it was imperative that American lawyers understand natural law in interpreting and applying the principles of the Constitution and the common law. Being "a philosophy of morals,"[15] natural law was to Story the substratum of the legal system, resting "at the foundation of all other laws."[16] He believed with Blackstone that an awareness and appreciation of the natural law was the first step in the science of jurisprudence. The laws of nature stood "supported and illustrated by revelation. Christianity, while with many minds it acquires authority from

livered February 2, 1824," reprinted in part in Perry Miller (ed.), *The Legal Mind in America*, 95–96.

[14] "Review of Professor David Hoffman's Legal Outlines," *North American Review*, Vol. XXX (1830), 139. The book was devoted to a consideration of the elements of natural and political law and was the first of its kind in American law. At the Harvard Law School it was included in the list of recommended readings. See the 1834 curriculum at Harvard, reproduced in Charles M. Haar, *The Golden Age of American Law*, 68–70. David Hoffman, whom Story greatly respected, was professor of law at the University of Maryland from 1816–32. In a published lecture delivered in 1823, Hoffman declared there was a "close connection between Ethicks and Natural Law . . . [and] that ethical and political considerations are nearly akin to the proper studies of the accomplished lawyer." (*A Lecture, Introductory to a Course of Lectures, Now Delivered at the University of Maryland, 1823*, reprinted in part in Miller, *The Legal Mind in America*, 90.) Peter Du Ponceau was a leading lawyer who taught at the Law Academy in Philadelphia, which he founded in 1821. For excellent accounts of early American lawyers, their legal philosophies, and their contributions to American jurisprudence, see Chroust, *Rise of the Legal Profession in America*, II, 173–224, and Miller, *The Legal Mind in America, passim*.

[15] Joseph Story, "The Value and Importance of Legal Studies," A Discourse Pronounced at the Inauguration of the Author as Dane Professor of Law in Harvard University, August 25, 1829, *Miscellaneous Writings*, 534.

[16] *Ibid.*, 533.

its coincidences with the law of nature, as deduced from reason, has added strength and dignity to the latter by its positive declarations."[17]

Nature's rules of human conduct, then, flowed from the same source as God's: revelation and reason. "The law of nature," suggested Story, "is nothing more than those rules which human reason deduces from the various relations of man, to form his character, and regulate his conduct, and thereby insure his permanent happiness."[18] Therefore, he concluded, "Christianity becomes not merely an auxiliary, but a guide, to the law of nature; establishing its conclusions, removing its doubts, and evaluating its precepts."[19]

Thus, Story enunciates with Cicero and the English commentators the doctrine of natural law as the creation of the Divine Mind, the science that teaches men their duties, from whence they derive their rights. This conservative religious orthodoxy, lying at the heart of his natural law philosophy, forms the thesis of his essay "Natural Law," which he wrote for Francis Lieber's *Encyclopedia Americana* in 1832.[20] A genuine exception to the general run of political tracts dealing with natural law in the early nineteenth century, the essay has never been mentioned in any analysis of American political and legal thought or in any discussion of Story's jurisprudence.[21] Yet, this brief exegesis of natural law philosophy, which reached a fairly wide audience,[22] reveals the untapped reservoir of Story's constitutional principles and court decisions, which have become such an integral part of our organic law.

One of the salient features of the first part of the essay is its Thomistic conception of natural law, which is practically inseparable from natural theology, and its equally traditional view of natural law as a body of knowledge "which teaches men their duty and the reasons of it."[23] Natural law "in its largest sense," declared Story, "comprehends natural theology, moral philosophy, and political philosophy; in other words, it comprehends man's duties to God, to himself, to other men, and as a member of political society. The obligatory

---

[17] *Ibid.*, 534.

[18] *Ibid.*, 533.

[19] *Ibid.*, 535.

[20] IX, 150–58. The essay is reprinted in the appendix to this study. Story also wrote many articles on private law for Lieber's *Encyclopedia*. These articles, though written at the behest of Lieber, are unsigned, as Story requested. (See Francis Lieber, *Civil Liberty and Self-Government*, I, 232, n. 14. See also Story to Edward Everett, Nov. 1, 1832, Story Papers, MHS.) The articles are discussed briefly in chapter 7 of this study, note 47.

[21] See, for example, the account of Story's thinking in Morgan D. Dowd, "Justice Joseph Story: A Study of the Legal Philosophy of a Jeffersonian Judge," *Vanderbilt Law Review*, Vol. XVIII, No. 2 (Mar., 1965), 643–62.

[22] "The Encyclopedia 'sold phenomenally.'" (Frank Friedel, *Francis Lieber: Nineteenth Century Liberal*, 79.) "Lieber later estimated that over one hundred thousand sets of the *Encyclopedia* had been sold." John C. Hogan, "Joseph Story's Anonymous Law Articles," *Michigan Law Review*, Vol. LII, No. 6 (Apr., 1954), 883.

[23] "Natural Law," *Encyclopedia Americana*, IX, 150.

force of the law of nature upon man is derived from its presumed coincidence with the will of his Creator."[24] Being, in effect, the law of God, natural law operates as a moral restraint upon human behavior, and "by a right application of his powers and faculties man may always pursue his duty" to obey the will of God and choose good over evil.

"From the moral government of God, and the moral capacity and accountability of man, we deduce his general rights and duties." Using this standard as a guide to explain the true rights and duties of man according to natural law, Story proceeds to enumerate man's "natural duties." All duties, he says, are, like the law of nature from which they emanate, of Divine origin. Man's first duty, which consists of "piety or devotion," is to ascertain and obey the will of God. Hence arises the concomitant duty of society's leaders to encourage public worship and to support religious institutions.[25]

The duties of man toward himself consist of personal holiness, temperance, humility, self-preservation, and personal improvement. Toward other men one has "relative duties," according to Story, which grow out of "the correspondent rights of others." Magistrates, for example, have a duty to exercise power with moderation and mercy as well as justice; whereas citizens have the duty to obey the laws and to support the institutions of society.[26]

Story divides "rights" into those which are "natural" and those which are "adventitious." Natural rights are those resulting from our very condition: the right to life, liberty, and property and the use of air, light, and water. Natural rights, however, are not absolute, for they are subject to qualification when considering man not alone, but as a member of the family and the state. To prevent crime, protect the rights of others, or secure the public safety, life, liberty, and property may justly be taken away by the state. Because these rights are "perfect" or "unalienable," they cannot, however, be rightfully transferred to others. The fruits of one's labor, for instance, should not be given to another individual. "Adventitious" rights are accidental, arise from peculiar situations, and presuppose some act of man. They are "alienable" or "imperfect," and involve the rights of the magistrate, legislator, or elector. Being transferable, they concern primarily political rights rather than civil or natural rights.[27]

In his exposition of the origin of government, Story makes no mention of the social contract and seemingly rejects the distinction between society and government. He traces "The origin of political society ... back to the primitive establishment of families. From the union of a number of related families grew up tribes; and from tribes gradually grew up colonies and nations."[28] Govern-

24 *Ibid.*
25 *Ibid.*, 151.
26 *Ibid.*, 151–52.
27 *Ibid.*
28 *Ibid.*, 153.

ment by consent is but one of three ways by which authority has been legitimized. Established coevally with the civil societies, civil government originally arose "from voluntary consent, or from long acquiescence and prescription, or from superior force."[29]

But whatever the basis of political authority in each particular society, the objects of government are universally the same: to protect life, personal rights, and property, which in a state of nature are wholly insecure. At the same time, "The entering into civil society ... naturally induces the surrender of all those private rights, which are indispensable for the good order, peace and safety of the whole society."[30] It implicitly follows that the majority thus acquires the right to govern, for reasons of justice and expediency. It is proper to inquire, states Judge Story, whether civil government "can ever be justly altered, except by the will of the whole," inasmuch as "civil government is formed by the whole people." His answer is yes, "for by entering into society, men necessarily engage to be governed by the will of the majority, since unanimity in all matters of civil polity is impracticable. The will of the majority or the will of the minority must govern."[31]

This, then, in capsule version, is Story's natural law philosophy. On the surface it would appear that what he has promulgated is only a slight variation of Locke's second treatise. Indeed, the section pertaining to natural rights seems to be a faithful reiteration of Locke. Upon closer inspection, however, we find that the essay, in large measure, is in conflict with Locke's teachings. This becomes clear when the essay is considered within the context of Story's other writings. In addition, there is little in the essay that is either new or original, with the possible exception of a portion devoted to the rights of property, which will be examined later. Story's indebtedness to William Paley, the moral philosopher of the eighteenth century who at this time was quite popular among American lawyers, is freely acknowledged in the opening passage of the essay.[32] Story's speculations on the origin and content of natural law, his emphasis upon duty and restraint, his classification of rights and duties —all this, and more, has been lifted intact from Paley's treatise, *Moral and Political Philosophy*.[33]

[29] *Ibid.*

[30] *Ibid.*, 154.

[31] *Ibid.*

[32] *Ibid.*, 150.

[33] The book was first published in 1785 and went through fifteen editions in England and America in Paley's lifetime. From 1767 to 1775, Paley lectured on ethics, metaphysics, and divinity at Christ's College. His works on theology, which appeared between 1785–1802, were also very widely read in the early nineteenth century. Together with the work on *Moral and Political Philosophy*, they constitute what Paley described as a system, explaining "the evidences of natural religion, the evidences of revealed religion, and an account of the duties that result from both." For a discussion of Paley's theology, see Sir

Like Paley, Story is a product of the Enlightenment, and his view of natural law is a sad commentary on the intellectual confusion of the times. His natural law is two-sided: one half modern in the style of Hobbes, Locke, and even Rousseau; the other half classical and Christian, in the tradition of Cicero, Aquinas, Hooker, and Burke. He seems unaware of the basic conflict between natural law and natural rights. Perhaps, though, it is asking too much that he see this far beyond his age; for this conflict has been persistently misunderstood and misrepresented by many of the natural law thinkers themselves and by many students of political philosophy who, until very recently, were unable to perceive the break in the natural law tradition that occurred in the writings of Hobbes, Locke, and Rousseau. Exhibiting "extensive powers of learned misunderstanding which it possessed to an astonishing degree," John Courtney Murray has noted satirically, "the nineteenth century supposed that the 'law of nature' of the Age of the Enlightenment was the *ius naturale* of an earlier and in many ways more enlightened age."[34]

Properly speaking, of course, there is no single, continuous, and uninterrupted natural law tradition; there are instead various schools of thought on the natural law, the most prominent being classical, Christian, modern, and historical. Not all of these schools can be easily reconciled; indeed recent scholarship demonstrates clearly enough that the doctrines of modern natural rights, though couched in the vocabulary of the natural law, amounted "at bottom to a denial of the natural law."[35] As seen in Locke, for example, the natural law ceases to be the moral basis for positive law, and natural rights are

Leslie Stephen, *History of English Thought in the Eighteenth Century*, I, chapter 7. According to Stephen, Paley's "methods of reasoning lead naturally to the Unitarianism which presents the nearest approach to a systematic evolution of opinion in the latter half of the eighteenth century" (*ibid.*, 420). Paley's *Moral and Political Philosophy* is heavily infused with utilitarianism, which is also reflected in Story's essay. Although Paley relies substantially on the "morality of the Gospel," his system is built on the principle of expediency. "Whatever is expedient," he says, "is right; and the utility of a moral rule constitutes its obligation." Such utility, however, is subordinate to Scriptures. "Paley was as convinced a believer in the utilitarian philosophy as Bentham; but like Burke, he venerated the English Constitution, and he used his philosophy to defend its anomalies." A. V. Dicey, *Lectures on the Relation between Law and Public Opinion in England in the Nineteenth Century*, as quoted in part by Sir William Searle Holdsworth, *A History of English Law*, XIII, 118–19.

[34] *We Hold These Truths*, 299.

[35] Heinrich Rommen, *The Natural Law*, 82. "The modern theory of natural law was not, properly speaking, a theory of law at all. It was a theory of rights." (A. P. D'Entrèves, *Natural Law: An Historical Survey*, 59.) And according to Strauss, "Traditional natural law is primarily and mainly an objective 'rule and measure,' a binding order prior to, and independent of, the human will, while modern natural law is, or tends to be, primarily and mainly a series of 'rights,' of subjective claims, originating in the human will." Leo Strauss, *The Political Philosophy of Hobbes*, xi–xii. See also Strauss, *Natural Right and History*.

substituted, so that the only natural law remaining is the positive law of the state.

At the risk of oversimplification, it may be said that throughout Western history, two hostile traditions of natural law are evident. The older and once dominant traditional natural law, encompassing the classical and Christian schools, subscribed to the view that a Divine Being, ruler of the universe through an eternal and universal law, is the supreme lawgiver, and that natural law is an emanation of God's reason and will. The ancients, the Schoolmen, the English legalists, and Hooker all recognized, as Cicero put it, that "God [is] the framer and proposer of this law."[36] Unlike the modern natural rights concept, which is essentially a secular, individualistic assertion of the claims of man in a world naturalistically conceived—the "state of nature"—traditional natural law was based upon a divinely grounded cosmic order in which man is only a part. It was a natural law grounded in metaphysics, existing not in a mythical state of nature prior to the law, but one which lives, and ought to live, in the law. "Man's nature as well as his ethical goal," argued the traditional thinker, "consists . . . in the subordination or conformity of individual and social life to the general law of the universe."[37]

Often characterized by its rationalism, secularism, and radicalism, the opposing tradition, though observable in the Sophists,[38] did not gain impetus until the seventeenth and eighteenth centuries and is therefore commonly

[36] Cicero, *De Legibus*, II, 10, as cited in Benjamin F. Wright, *American Interpretations of Natural Law*, 5. The Ciceronian doctrine of a universal and immutable natural law, writes D'Entrèves, "passed into the *ius naturale* of the Roman jurists as well as into the teaching of the Christian Church. It is significant that Cicero's definition should have been preserved for us by a Christian writer, Lactantius. It is not surprising that Justinian, the Christian law-giver, should have taken the idea of natural law as the cornerstone of his system." *Natural Law*, 21.

[37] Rommen, *The Natural Law*, 6.

[38] Both traditions, observes Rommen, "are already plainly visible in the first Sophists and in Heraclitus, the great forerunner of Plato" (*ibid.*, 5). Given to reckless criticism of existing society, to demagogy, and paradoxical statements, the Sophists, not unlike their modern intellectual heirs, condemned law as an artificial construct to serve class interests and ridiculed the notion of a higher law. An enemy of the natural law, whose muddled treatment of the tradition is somewhat representative of earlier scholarship, Ritchie nevertheless recognized that "Hobbes, Locke, and Rousseau are modern representatives of the Sophistic stage" and that there is a "similarity in manner of thinking between the Greek Sophists . . . and the advocates of liberal ideas in the seventeenth and eighteenth centuries." (David Ritchie, *Natural Rights*, 25.) "It is sometimes asserted," says John Hallowell, "that if the natural law conviction were true, we should expect all men everywhere to agree upon its content. Since we do not find this universal agreement there is no such thing as natural law or universal justice. Such critics point to the diversity of moral customs throughout the world as though this were a clinching argument. Such criticism is as old as the tradition itself and, though they are rarely identified by the same name, the Sophists are still with us and still repeating the same arguments" (in the Foreword to Yves Simon, *The Tradition of Natural Law: A Philosopher's Reflections* [ed.

referred to as modern natural law—or more correctly, modern natural rights. Modern natural law theories, built around the doctrine of the state of nature, "constituted the first attempt to construct a lay or secularist theory of ethics and politics."[39] In the first place, the state of nature concept used by Hobbes and later modern natural law thinkers was a distortion of Christian theology, which had subdivided nature into pure and fallen, or perfect and imperfect. Hobbes abandoned the subdivisions, denied the importance of the Fall, "and accordingly asserted that what is needed for remedying the State of Nature is not divine grace but the right kind of human government."[40] Moreover, this reconstituted state of nature now became the starting point of natural law speculation. Highly individualistic, the modern school rejected the divine origin of natural law, exalted the autonomy of human reason, and exhorted man to look for a law of nature in a secularized state of nature. Conceived in the mind of man and devoid of theological or historical foundation, the state of nature necessarily varied according to the excogitative genius of each philosopher. He might imagine it "nasty, brutish, and short," or he might imagine it peaceful and pleasant. Thus was the way prepared for a relativistic law of nature, which rested on the shifting sands of a totally subjective "model." Little wonder, then, that the modern concept of natural law, like its intellectual offspring legal positivism, could be manipulated to impugn or to serve any political system, whether it be state absolutism (Hobbes), enlightened despotism (Pufendorf), liberal democracy (Locke), or totalitarian democracy (Rousseau).

Of course, the deadly assault of the state of nature doctrine against the past was not clearly visible until 1789. Hobbes and Locke had at least intimated they were religiously oriented, even though their natural law was essentially a secular, rationalistic doctrine emancipated from the church.[41] "Not until the days of the French Revolution," notes Ernst Troeltsch, "do we find the idea of natural law directed along the line of pure and radical progress, and pressing towards the goal of absolute popular sovereignty within the area of a great modern state; and the French Revolution, for that very reason, marks a break with the Church and the whole of the past."[42]

by Vukan Kuic], viii). "The variety of notions of justice," observes Strauss, "can be understood as the variety of errors." *Natural Right and History*, 98.

[39] Rommen, *The Natural Law*, 79.

[40] Strauss, *Natural Right and History*, 184.

[41] Locke's frequent references to God as the giver of natural law obscured his secularization of it. As Strauss points out, "his natural law teaching concerning the rights and duties of rulers and of subjects was as independent of Scripture as it could possibly be." (*Natural Right and History*, 209.) Furthermore, "Locke's entire political teaching is based on the assumption of a state of nature. This assumption is wholly alien to the Bible." *Ibid.*, 215.

[42] "The Ideas of Natural Law and Humanity in World Politics," Appendix I in Otto Gierke, *Natural Law and the Theory of Society*, 1500–1800 (trans., with an Introduction,

Separating all of the natural law writers into either tradition poses certain difficulties, if only because the governing tradition reaching back to Aristotle and the Stoics, which passed into Roman law and English common law, and attained its most masterly expression in scholasticism, atrophied gradually and almost imperceptibly, leaving major figures such as Hugo Grotius "in the twilight between two great epochs. Still linked by many ties to the preceding age, he yet served to transmit to the natural law theory of the modern period its distinguishing marks: rationalism, sociality, and particular political aims."[43] Two centuries later, the steady erosion of natural law had left Story at the same equinox. "It is not in its content that Grotius' theory of natural law breaks away from Scholasticism," D'Entrèves has observed. "It is in its method . . . . He proved that it was possible to build up a theory of laws independent of theological presuppositions."[44]

To a degree, this is also true of Story, as well as Pufendorf, Burlamaqui, and Vattel,[45] the continental jurists whose systematic works on the law of nations ("the law of nature applied to states") Story has mastered and transmitted to

---

by Sir Ernest Barker), I, 208. "The proclamation of the 'natural, inalienable and sacred rights of man [in 1789] marks the end of an era and the beginning of contemporary Europe." (D'Entrèves, Natural Law, 48.) In a broader sense, writes Eric Voegelin, "The corrosion of Western Civilization through gnosticism is a slow process extending over a thousand years. The several western political societies, now, have a different relation to this slow process according to the time in which their national revolutions occurred. When the revolution occurred early, a less radical wave of gnosticism was its carrier, and the resistance of the forces of tradition was, at the same time, more effective. . . . The English Revolution, in the seventeenth century, occurred at a time when gnosticism had not yet undergone its radical secularization. . . . The American Revolution, though its debate was already strongly affected by the psychology of the enlightenment, also had the good fortune of coming to its close within the institutional and Christian climate of the *ancien regime*. In the French Revolution, then, the radical wave of gnosticism was so strong that it permanently split the nation." *The New Science of Politics*, 188.

[43] Rommen, *The Natural Law*, 74.

[44] D'Entrèves, *Natural Law*, 51–52.

[45] Pufendorf was the first to expound the doctrine of Grotius. "The net result of the age was a disastrous setback, from the opening of the nineteenth century, for the natural-law idea among the modern philosophers and practitioners of law who were unacquainted with the older Christian tradition." (Rommen, *The Natural Law*, 75.) "The doctrine of natural law which is set forth in the great treatises of the seventeenth and eighteenth centuries—from Pufendorf's *De Jure Naturae et Gentium* (1672) to Burlamaqui's *Principes du Droit Naturel* (1747), and Vattel's *Droit des Gens ou Principes de la Loi Naturelle* (1758)—has nothing to do with theology. It is a purely rational construction, though it does not refuse to pay homage to some remote notion of God." (D'Entrèves, *Natural Law*, 52.) Ironically, Pufendorf criticized Hobbes and Grotius for their deviations from the teachings of the church. Burlamaqui's ideas are discussed in Ray Forrest Harvey, *Jean Jacques Burlamaqui: A Liberal Tradition in American Constitutionalism*.

American law through his writings and judicial opinions.[46] Story seems to have absorbed a share of their philosophical methods and rationalistic ideas, despite the stronger influences upon his mind of Christianity, the common law, and such legal and political thinkers as Blackstone and Burke.

It has been observed that Story's rendition of the origin of the natural law appears to be Thomistic. Yet he speaks of a state of nature. He uses the terms "natural law" and "law of nature" interchangeably and is unaware of the fact the latter, which is a semantical innovation of the modern school, is wholly antagonistic toward traditional natural law. He declares that natural law is an emanation of God's will, but, like Grotius and his followers, he slips into the doctrine of nominalism and excludes the possibility that natural law is also an emanation of God's reason.

The Scholastics insisted that natural law was also grounded in essence and reason, not in mere absolute will.[47] And although Story's natural law is not a systematic code of rules and rights, it moves in this direction and is bound up with "particular political aims," which is so typical of the modern school. Throughout his essay, for example, is the underlying assumption that the natural law requires a representative form of democratic government, a vigorous and independent judiciary, separation of church and state, and the enforcement of the obligation of contracts according to the common law principles of interpretation.[48]

[46] References to the writings of the international law philosophers will be found throughout Story's legal treatises, and are too numerous to warrant lengthy citation. But see, for example, Story's *Commentaries on the Constitution of the United States*, I, 136, 138, 192, 292, 293, 384, 412, 434, 437, 438, 439, 441. It is abundantly clear that Pufendorf has influenced both Paley and Story in a number of ways. He commences, for example, by first drawing up a catalog of duties toward God, towards oneself, and towards others that is practically indistinguishable from that offered by Paley and Story. Everyone, he says, must keep his word, must not swear falsely, and must be sincere of speech. His classification of rights is, likewise, the same as that drawn up by Paley and Story.

[47] Rommen, *The Natural Law*, 58–60. If law is will, without any foundation in reality, then it would seem to follow that natural law and positive law have no inner relation to each other. It is thus but a short step to Machiavelli's *The Prince*, Hobbes's *Leviathan*, and the modern doctrines of legal positivism, or the notion that the will of the absolute sovereign is law because no higher norm stands above him. *Ibid.*, 60.

[48] "The decisive differences between this newer natural law and that of the Scholastics," observes Rommen, "are three in number. The first is the individualistic trait manifesting itself in the predominance of the doctrine of the state of nature as the proper place in which to find the natural law. The second is the nominalist attitude which found expression in the separation of eternal law and natural moral law, of God's essence and existence, of morality and law. The third is the resultant doctrine of the autonomy of human reason which, in conjunction with the rationalism of this school, led straight to an extravagance of syllogistic reasoning, of deductively constructed systems that served to regulate all legal institutions down to the minutest detail: the civil law governing debts, property, the family, and inheritances as well as constitutional and international law." *The Natural Law*, 94.

It is not certain to what extent Story accepted the doctrine of natural rights. As noted earlier, his essay on natural law ostensibly supports the Lockean proposition that all men are endowed with the natural rights of life, liberty, and property and that governments are instituted to protect these ends. One gathers the impression, however, that Story has been trapped unwillingly and unwittingly into a philosophical acceptance of the doctrine and has only grudgingly conceded its validity because he does not know how to disprove it. Significantly, he emphasizes duties, in keeping with traditional natural law; and he has not gone so far as Locke, to the extreme position where concern with the "rights of man" and "natural liberties" has effectively eliminated natural law and natural duties.[49]

In his judicial opinions and other writings, "natural rights" are seldom mentioned, and Story much prefers the term "personal rights." In the *Commentaries* he rejects Jefferson's argument that the American Revolution was fought to secure the natural rights of Americans and insists instead that the American patriots were struggling to secure their common law rights.[50] The purpose of government is not to *grant* "natural rights" to each *individual*, said Story on one occasion, it is to *protect* the "personal rights" of the *whole people*: "What are the great objects of all free governments? They are, the protection and preservation of the personal rights, the private property, and the public liberties of the whole people. Without accomplishing these ends, the government may, indeed, be called free, but it is a mere mockery, and a vain, fantastic shadow."[51] In his address as Dane Professor of Law in 1829, Story gives the impression that he actually rejects the doctrine of natural rights, if not philosophically, then on grounds of expediency. "It has been observed by a profound statesman," recalled Story in reference to Burke's *Reflections on the Revolution in France*, "that the abstract perfection of a government, with reference to natural rights, may be its practical defect. . . . Great vigilance and great jealousy are therefore necessary in republics, to guard against the captivations of theory."[52]

There is no doubt, however, that Story stands squarely in the classical and Christian natural law tradition regarding the origin of the state. The Aris-

[49] This is not to say, however, that the notion of natural rights was in principle wholly alien to traditional natural law. What the classical thinkers rejected was an egalitarian natural rights philosophy. "Since the classics viewed moral and political matters in light of man's perfection," Strauss notes, "they were not egalitarians. . . . Since all men are then unequal in regard to human perfection, i.e., in the decisive respect, equal rights for all appeared to the classics as most unjust. They contended that some men are by nature superior to others and therefore, according to natural right, the rulers of others." *Natural Right and History*, 134-35.

[50] I, sec. 157, p. 140. See also ch. 4 of this study, 164.

[51] Story, "The Science of Government," A Lecture Read before the American Institute of Instruction in August, 1834, *Miscellaneous Writings*, 618.

[52] "The Value and Importance of Legal Studies," *Miscellaneous Writings*, 512.

totelian theory of the state, later engrafted on to the Christian interpretation of natural law, was premised on the belief that man is by nature a political and social animal. Except for beasts and gods it was against nature to live outside the community; and only in the community, the highest achievement of man, and the highest expression of natural morality, could man find fulfillment. In traditional natural law the state was thus conceived as the natural expression of man's true self, as the organic development of the polity, originating at the rudimentary stage of family life and progressing to the more complex city-state. The state, in sum, was seen in premodern natural law as an instinctive, unconscious expression of man's conformity to Divine plan, satisfying basic human needs.

Conversely, the modern school depicted the state as an outgrowth of the social contract. Artificial and unnecessary metaphysically, the state according to the moderns was the conscious creation of rational man, who has abandoned a prehistoric, stateless existence by contracting out of a state of nature for the protection of natural rights.

But to conceive of an unhistorical state of nature, as did Locke, where man existed alone in an idyllic state of anarchy, bound to no will but his own, was to Story an illusion. The state did not begin unnaturally, with man contracting himself out of his "natural condition"; and even supposing he did, how could he possibly remove himself from this peculiar situation spontaneously with others? The accomplishment of such a task would require some form of organized activity, an act of government prior to government.

Story thus stood on common ground with Aristotle, Aquinas, Blackstone, and Burke in believing that political society evolved from the early establishment of families and the union of tribes to the higher stage of the nation-state.[53] The doctrine of the social contract, he declared in his *Commentaries on the Constitution*, was unfounded either in reason or history, and its endorsement by some of the first state constitutions in the 1770s served only to obscure the true basis of the citizens' rights: "It would, indeed, be an extraordinary use of language to consider a declaration of rights in a constitution, and especially rights, which it proclaims to be 'unalienable and indefeasible,' to be a matter of contract, and resting on such a basis, rather than a solemn

---

[53] Story, "Natural Law," *Encyclopedia Americana*, IX, 153. "It is no longer possible to think of the State as a conscious invention, suddenly introduced as an antidote to confusion and chaos. The State must have evolved from rudimentary and inchoate beginnings, by a process of growth that was so slow as to have been all but imperceptible." (Edward M. Sait, *Political Institutions*, 104.) Ernest Barker says "*Society* is not constituted, and never was constituted, on any basis of contract." (*Essays on Government*, 92.) Sir Henry Maine's Patriarchal Theory, elaborated in his *Ancient Law* (1861) and *The Early History of Institutions* (1874), also supports the Aristotelian position that the state is an outgrowth of the family, from which the earliest kings derived their authority, as head of a kinship group.

recognition and admission of those rights, arising from the law of nature, and the gift of Providence, and incapable of being transferred or surrendered."[54] In support of his view, Story quoted Burke and Paley at length,[55] repudiated Locke,[56] cited Hume approvingly,[57] and concluded with the observation that "Mr. Justice Blackstone has very justly observed, that the theory of an original contract upon the first formation of society is a visionary notion."[58]

And so it seems in the final analysis there is little in Story's intellectual sympathies that marks him of the modern school. True, a strain of utilitarianism can be found in his thinking; but this is attributable to his profound distrust of the undiluted idealism and "visionary" theories of the natural rights enthusiasts rather than a reformist zeal or empathy with Benthamism. Story, above all, is a practical man whose own brand of idealism is more akin to that of Burke and the defenders of the traditional natural law.

His commitment to the doctrine of natural rights is at best half-hearted; and those rights which he regards as "natural" seem to be essentially the same as the accumulated and prescriptive rights of the common law. On the right of revolution, he is silent. He rejects the social contract. He rejects the ratiocination of the moderns that equality is a natural right. The only real equality among men, he concludes, is moral equality, "the original equality of all mankind in the eyes of the Supreme Being."[59] He apparently accepts the natural right of the majority to govern, but at the same time has little faith in the

---

[54] I, sec. 340, p. 309.

[55] *Ibid.*, sec. 325, pp. 293–94, n. 2. Paley's *Moral and Political Philosophy* clearly "rejects as a fiction or unproved hypothesis the theory of the social contract." (William Edward Hartpole Lecky, *A History of England in the Eighteenth Century*, VI, 22.) Says Paley: Locke's account of a twofold compact, "express, and entered into by the founders of the state ... [and] Tacit, and adopted by all who succeeded the founders ... is false in fact; and, if it were true, it would not be admissible, as it leads to dangerous conclusions. No such compact was ever made; for it could not have been made, without supposing, what is impossible, that savages could deliberate on topics which civil life alone suggested. But though no government began from this origin, some imitation of a social compact might have taken place at a revolution. In these United States, for instance, the people did assemble to elect deputies for the express purpose of forming a constitution; and the deputies so elected did frame a government, and erect a perpetual legislature, invested with the power of making laws, which should be binding on the very people by whom that legislature has been elected. Yet even here much was presumed to be already settled; for even the qualifications of the voters, and the mode of electing the representatives, were modeled after the older forms of government." *Moral and Political Philosophy* (ed. by A. J. Valpy), 190–91.

[56] Story, *Commentaries on the Constitution*, I, sec. 325, p. 293, n. 2.

[57] *Ibid.*, sec. 326, p. 295, n. 1.

[58] *Ibid.*, p. 294. Andrew McLaughlin, in "Social Compact and Constitutional Construction," *American Historical Review*, Vol. V, No. 3 (Apr., 1900), 487, erroneously contends that Story rejected the Aristotelian view of the origin of the state.

[59] Story, "Value and Importance of Legal Studies," *Miscellaneous Writings*, 534.

notion that the majority is always right. He agrees with the framers and Publius that majority rule must be kept under surveillance and carefully restricted. "I know of no despotism so oppressive, or so irresponsible, or so aggravating, as that of the Majority in a Republic," he once remarked. "Numbers give not only a confidence & power, but an indifference to all interests but their own. You have a buoyant spirit, & hope all things & believe all things. So do not I."[60] The clamor for universal suffrage, he once confided to an English friend, was the death rattle in the throat of democracy.

If I were an Englishman I should resist the introduction of both (the Ballot & General suffrage) into the English Constitution. I am sure, that general suffrage would overthrow your government, & soon, in a practical sense, annihilate the monarchy. I believe it would go farther, & greatly endanger, if not overturn all the rights of property. The example in America on this point is not half as strong in their favour, as your Radicals suppose; & if it were, the scheme is ill adapted to any other country than one situated in all respects as America is. Even here, many of our wisest & best men doubt, if it will not ultimately sap all the solid foundations of our liberty & property.[61]

Story apparently also accepts, to a degree, the natural rights of "life, liberty, and property," but like the classical and Christian natural law philosophers, he is no libertarian. It is abundantly clear from his writings and opinions that in Story's view, the primary purpose of government is to establish not only liberty, but also order and justice and to promote among the citizenry public and private virtue, or what Aristotle would describe as the "common good."[62] In

---

[60] Story to Richard Peters, June 14, 1837, Peters Papers, HSP.

[61] Story to Charles R. Vaughan, June 27, 1834, Vaughan Papers, Christ's College. Moreover, Story added, the use of the ballot in America had proved to be of little benefit. "You are aware, that in one half of the States of the Union it has no existence; & to say the least they are quite as democratic in their Elections & Canvasses as any of the rest of the States. I allude to the Southern & Western States. In New England the Ballot generally exists. But there is no pretence, that to any considerable degree it now secures either secrecy or independence of votes. The Voters hinge themselves under their leaders & their party, & most, who are deemed dependent, are kept in constant surveillance from the moment they come to the polls, until their votes are deposited. The colour of the paper, too, is one of many contrivances to defeat all secrecy. And, indeed, I fear, intelligent voters now abstain from the polls from disgust or despair of counteracting the mere partisan movements, which are decisive of the election before a single ballot is cast" (*ibid.*). See also Story's condemnation of tyranny of the majority in his address to the Suffolk bar in 1821, "Progress of Jurisprudence," *Miscellaneous Writings*, 227, quoted on page 272 of this study.

[62] The important fact is often overlooked that Story is one of the authors of the "bad tendency" test of free speech, which the Supreme Court first announced in the landmark decision of *Gitlow* v. *New York*, 268 U.S. 652 (1925). Speaking for the Court, Mr. Justice Sanford upheld the conviction of Benjamin Gitlow under a state criminal anarchy statute for distributing a document similar to the *Communist Manifesto*, and offered as authority Story's interpretation of the First Amendment. Citing Story on the Constitution, Sanford

sharp contrast with Thomas Paine and other libertarians more deeply imbued with the natural rights spirit, who view liberty as the ultimate object of government, Story harbors no intrinsic, doctrinaire aversion to government merely because it restricts liberty; for the best government is not always the least government, Story would agree, when governmental inertia for liberty alone leads to injustices, disorder, or moral impairment. For what purpose does the government act? This, in Story's mind, is the overriding question.[63]

Although framed in the rationalistic mold, Story's natural law ideas more nearly reflect the attitudes and concerns of the traditional natural law writers. His rationalism is undercut by his religiosity and respect for history, precedent, and experience—hallmarks of modern conservatism.[64] Judge Story impugned the idea that a social order, simply because so untrustworthy a faculty as reason finds fault with it, should be rashly amended. He proposed instead a faith in the wisdom of the past and stressed the importance of keeping change within the framework of law and custom. God-fearing, suspicious of drastic innovation, antirevolutionary, critical of egalitarian democracy, he stands with the New England Federalists, with a dying party and a conservative philosophy, in retreat against the radicalism generated by natural rights doctrines. His natural law is in principle allied with the existing political, economic, and social institutions of the young Republic, lending them support and justifying their existence; it is not calculated to tear them down or replace them with new and untried models that would further encourage the leveling tendencies

---

stated: "It is a fundamental principle, long established, that freedom of speech and of the press which is secured by the Constitution does not confer an absolute *right* to speak or publish, without responsibility, whatever one may choose . . . . Reasonably limited, it was said by Story . . . this freedom is an inestimable *privilege* in a free government; without such limitation, it might become the scourge of the republic . . . . Freedom of speech and press, said Story, does not protect disturbances of the public peace or the attempt to subvert the government." (*Ibid.*, 666–67. Emphasis supplied.) Unlike Justice Holmes's "clear and present danger" doctrine, which was more favorable to the libertarian claims of the individual, the bad tendency test, as is evident from the passage quoted above, permitted governmental restriction of *bad* speech, that is, speech "tending to corrupt public morals, incite to crime, or disturb the public peace." Dissenting in the important decision of *Near v. Minnesota*, 283 U.S. 697 (1931), which reversed the conviction of a newspaper publisher, Justice Butler declared: "It is plain that Blackstone taught that under the common law liberty of the press means simply the absence of restraint upon publication in advance as distinguished from liability, civil or criminal, for libelous or improper matter so published. And . . . Story defined freedom of the press guaranteed by the First Amendment to mean that 'every man shall be at liberty to publish what is true, with good motives and for justifiable ends.'" (*Ibid.*, 735.) For a critique of the clear and present danger test, see Walter F. Berns, *Freedom, Virtue, and the First Amendment.*

[63] For an excellent discussion of the functions of authority, see Yves Simon, *Philosophy of Democratic Government*, 1–72.

[64] See Russell Kirk, *The Conservative Mind*, 3–62.

of the times. Notwithstanding the rationalistic bent of his mind, then, Story believed, and rightly so, that he resolutely opposed modern political and legal doctrines originating in natural rights theories. For certain, there is no more worthy a foe of natural rights doctrines in early nineteenth-century America than Mr. Justice Story; for while it is true he did not fully comprehend the natural law tradition, it is also true he understood it better than probably any American of his day.

Perhaps the key to a clear understanding of the man and what he sought to accomplish lies in the fact he identified himself with the natural law tradition and its leading exponents and, in general, was sufficiently well-read in the literature to grasp its essentials and apply them to the legal questions of the day. His mentors were not Hobbes, Locke, Rousseau, Bentham, Austin, or their American pupils, but men of a more conservative caste, men like Coke, Blackstone, John Marshall, and the founding fathers. Among the ancients Cicero was his acknowledged favorite: "He was . . . the most learned and accomplished man of all antiquity, as a statesman, philosopher . . . lawyer & . . . as an orator."[65]

Although the influence of Coke and Blackstone cannot be ignored, surely the individual from whom he drew his greatest inspiration was Edmund Burke. Story's letters, essays, public addresses, and famed *Commentaries on the Constitution* glitter with praises of Burke and frequently refer the reader to many of Burke's works. A perusal of the public addresses, for example, will reveal almost without exception at least one significant reference to the Great Whig. Precisely when Story began reading Burke is uncertain, but by the 1820s he was clearly under Burke's influence. From this time forward and throughout the remainder of his career on the high bench, Story repeatedly invoked Burke's views on the dangers of abstract reason, on the problem of change, on government and politics, on the common law, and on natural law.[66] "Judge Story called on me at my office in New York," Chancellor Kent wrote in 1835 on the flyleaf of his personal copy of Story's *Commentaries on the Constitution.* "His greatest authorities on the Science of Government, as he thinks, are *Aristotle, Cicero,* and *Burke.*"[67]

[65] Story to William Story, Mar. 9, 1835, Story Papers, Texas.
[66] See James McClellan, "Judge Story's Debt to Burke," *The Burke Newsletter,* Vol. VII, No. 3 (Spring, 1966), 583–86.
[67] Note in *American Law Review,* Vol. V (1870), 368–69: "At a recent sale of part of Chancellor Kent's library, in Boston, a copy of *Story on the Constitution* was bought, on the fly leaf of which was discovered this curious note, in the Chancellor's handwriting:—'March 18, 1835. Judge Story called on me at my office in New York. . . . His greatest authorities on the Science of Government, as he thinks, are *Aristotle, Cicero,* and *Burke.* In a French translation of Aristotle on Politics, he found that *Aristotle* treated of representative Government of the People, and said it would not do, and never could do, because the People never could be brought for any length of time to choose the most wise and

By far, Judge Story's most significant debt to Burke was that relating to natural law. "The Natural Law," writes Professor Stanlis, "is fundamental to Burke's conception of man and civil society."[68] And so also was natural law basic to the thought of Joseph Story. Natural law was the nucleus of his legal

---

virtuous men to govern them. Whoever reads Cicero *de Republica* would see the evils of democracy as they are and always will be. He says that Hamilton was the greatest and wisest man of this country. He saw fifty years ahead, and what he saw then, is *fact now*. Next to him in wisdom and sense, intuitive rectitude and truth and judgment is Ch. J. *Marshall*.

" 'He says all sensible men at Washington, in private conversation, admit that the Government is deplorable, weak, factious, and corrupt. That everything is sinking down into despotism, under the disguise of a democratic Government. He says the Sup. Court is sinking, and so is the Judicial in every State. We begin with first rate men for judicial trusts, and we have now got down to third rate. In twenty-five years there will not be a judge in the U.S. who will not be made elective, and for short periods and on slender salaries. Our Constitutions were all framed for man as he *should be*, and not for man *as he is and ever will be*. The Senate of the U. States are discouraged. There are 20 men in that Senate who are as wise and patriotic as any Sages of the Roman Senate, and last year they sustained the Constitution against the President and his collared House of Representatives, and yet *public opinion* remains unmoved, and not shaken and equally devoted to Tyranny and Corruption. . . . He says Ch. J. Marshall has finally come over to the opinion that the *appointing* Power includes the Power of *removal*; and that the President ought not, and has not, according to the Constitution, the Power in himself.' "

[68] *Burke and the Natural Law*, 231. That Burke figures prominently in the natural law controversy of the late eighteenth and early nineteenth centuries has come to be recognized through a better understanding of Burke and of the natural law tradition. For years Burke was identified by utilitarian and positivist scholars, such as John Morley, Leslie Stephen, and Charles E. Vaughan, as an enemy of the natural law, whose political philosophy rested on a sort of mystical "conservative utilitarianism." Recent scholarship, however, has rendered this view of Burke untenable. Burke's concept of natural right, as Russell Kirk has observed, "descended from sources very different from Rousseau's, the great equalitarian's homage to the Divinity notwithstanding . . . Burke's natural right is the Stoic and Ciceronian *jus naturale*, reinforced by Christian dogma and English common law doctrine." (Russell Kirk, "Burke and Natural Rights," *The Review of Politics*, Vol. XIII, No. 4 [Oct., 1951], 442.) Peter J. Stanlis has ably demonstrated in his *Edmund Burke and the Natural Law* Burke's adherence to classical and Christian natural law. See also Strauss, *Natural Right and History*, 294–323; Barker, *Essays on Government*, 219–33. The true state of nature, Burke argued, is civil society; prescription rather than contract is more often the source of legitimacy. "The pretended rights of these theorists are all extremes," he wrote in his *Reflections on the Revolution in France*. "[A]nd in proportion as they are metaphysically true, they are morally and politically false." Writes Professor Strauss, "Burke sided with Cicero and with Suarez against Hobbes and against Rousseau." He "sided with 'the authors of sound antiquity' against 'the Parisian philosophers' and 'the bold experimenters in morality.' " (*Natural Right and History*, 295.) More importantly from the standpoint of his influence on American political and legal development, Burke sided with the natural law jurists, with Coke and Blackstone, the common law and the constitution, against the Benthamite reformers and the natural rights revolutionaries.

philosophy, the creative source of his jurisprudence. Story found Burke to be a powerful antidote to contractual natural rights theories, and in his *Commentaries*, which begin, by the way, with quotations from Cicero and Burke, Story cited Burke extensively in refuting Locke's theory of the social contract. "Mr. Locke is one of the most eminent authors," observed Judge Story, "who have treated on this subject. He founds all civil government on consent. 'When,' says he, 'any number of men have so consented to make a community or government, they are thereby presently incorporated, and make one body politic, wherein the majority have a right to act, and conclude the rest.' " But, retorted Story, "Mr. Burke has, in one of his most splendid performances, made some profound reflections on this subject, the conclusion of which seems to be, that if society is to be deemed a contract, it is one of eternal obligation, and not liable to be dissolved at the will of those who have entered into it."[69]

Story was not, of course, the only or the first American to see through the Lockean illusion. Even before Story made his views known, John Randolph of Roanoke had on repeated occasions attacked the idea of the social contract. Like Story, Randolph looked to the Great English Whig for guidance and through his readings of Burke had reached the conclusion that the majoritarian rule of democracy, built upon a false theory of the origin of government, carried with it the seeds of despotism.[70] Even so, Story was the first to publish his view of the social contract widely in America. As Harold J. Laski perceptively observed while reading Story's *Commentaries*, "It may be said that not until the time of Story did it [the social contract] cease to play an important part in American political theory."[71]

In many of Story's constitutional opinions, to which we shall recur throughout this study in an attempt to uncover the influence of natural law ideas upon his jurisprudence and upon American constitutional development, he frequently prefaced his remarks with the bold assertion that his reasoning was based upon the principles of "natural justice." Significantly, many of these same decisions are not only consistent with Burke's principles but, as will be seen, also play a major role in the evolution of American civil and political liberty, especially in the area of the rights of property and contract, religious liberty, and common law rights in general.

No less important is the fact Story's Burkean natural law influenced him to

[69] *Commentaries on the Constitution*, I, sec. 325, p. 293, n. 2.

[70] Russell Kirk, *John Randolph of Roanoke: A Study in American Politics*, 25. In the interest of accuracy, the first American who actually attacked the foundations of Locke's theory of the social contract was the Tory parson from Maryland, the Reverend Jonathan Boucher. See his *A View of the Causes and Consequences of the American Revolution* (London, 1797), 519. Although not trained in the law, Boucher apparently read Blackstone, as his criticisms are closely analogous to those of the Great Commentator. Compare Blackstone, *Commentaries*, I, 38.

[71] "Social Contract," *Encyclopedia of Social Sciences*, IV, 130.

repudiate not only contractual theories of human rights, but also contractual theories of the American union. It was Story's belief that the Jeffersonian doctrine of states' rights, that is the compact theory of the Union, was an out-growth of the social contract theory. Against the Jeffersonian theory Story placed his own, noncontractual or organic theory of the Union, which he first enunciated in *Martin* v. *Hunter's Lessee*,[72] then later in the *Commentaries*.[73] As one of the prime intellectual leaders of nationalistic thinking, Story pro-vided the Federalist-Whig school with the most acceptable interpretation of the origin and nature of the federal union. It remains to this very day the theoretical basis of nationalist thought.

Regarding himself also as an adept of Hamilton, Madison, and Jay, whose *Federalist* papers formed the backbone of his *Commentaries on the Constitu-tion*, Story labored in the wake of the French Revolution to reinforce the foundations of a disintegrating society and collapsing Constitution under-mined by sectionalism, radicalism, and Jacksonian Democracy. The Glorious Revolution, Burke had asserted, was a revolution prevented. The American Burke, who fully agreed that one revolution was enough, aspired to keep the American experiment within the same evolutionary pattern.

As will later be seen, Story applied his natural law ideas often and en-thusiastically during his judgeship under Marshall and Taney, thereby ac-complishing a twofold purpose. In his opinions and writings he counteracted the American revolutionary practice of hypothesizing civil liberties upon a contractual–natural rights basis and, at the same time, shifted the theoretical basis of positive law from natural rights to natural law and history.[74]

Important as they are, however, these preliminary estimates of Story's con-tributions to American political and legal thought fail to take account of Story's essay on natural law, which is truly the *locus classicus* for his natural law philosophy. Lacking in originality and depth of understanding, peppered

---

[72] 1 Wheaton 304 (1816). See especially 324–25.

[73] I, sec. 352, p. 319. For an analysis of Story's theory of the Union, see chapter 6 of this study.

[74] Although unmindful of the vital distinction between natural law and natural rights, and unaware of the philosophical basis of Story's traditional natural law, Roscoe Pound is partially correct in his contention that during the period of Story and Kent, "Eighteenth-century law and eighteenth-century thinking were passing off the stage in the United States. Kent had given natural law a historical account and was shifting the theoretical basis of positive law from natural law [rights?] to history, from reason to experience [and the natural law philosophy?]. In Story on the Constitution, published in 1833, the transition is complete from an eighteenth-century basis, confirmed by a constitution which declares natural rights [common law liberties?] with a historical [and natural law?] content." (*The Formative Era of American Law*, 144.) Pound's rendition has been widely accepted. See, for example, Elizabeth K. Bauer, *Commentaries on the Constitution, 1790–1860*, 329. For a similar account, see Francis R. Aumann, *The Changing American Legal System: Some Selected Phases*, 129.

with inconsistencies, the essay nevertheless stands out like a ray of light in the midnight hour of American political theory. Without question, it is one of the most complete and knowledgeable statements of the natural law in the early nineteenth century by any American.[75] The Story-Burke contribution to natural law also suggests that the ultimate rejection of contractual natural rights in England and America can be traced to causes other than the destruction of the social contract theory as a logical and acceptable basis for the origin of government—although this surely acted as a catalyst. What seems evident is that Blackstone and earlier English commentators, by implanting deeply and permanently in the minds of English and American lawyers and legislators the traditional natural law, rendered their readers impervious to revolutionary doctrines of natural rights. Both Story and Burke were profound students of Blackstone and the common law. Tenacious of the customary, acutely adept at assimilating the funded wisdom of the past, both plied the natural law concepts inherent in the common law against innovating natural rights ideas, and in so doing brought to light the hidden resources of Anglo-American political and legal thought.

It is not idle to conjecture that the common law, more than any other single factor, ultimately spared the English-speaking peoples of the revolutionary disorders that have plagued continental Europe. The common law, after all, had brought to fruition in England individual liberties only imagined across the channel. The English had little reason to demand through philosophy what they had achieved through practice. Moreover, the frequently noted disregard of political philosophy in America, which at bottom has meant largely a rejection of modern natural rights theories and their ideological offspring, may well be the result of the adoption of the English common law in the colonial era. "Happy is the nation which has no political philosophy," Sir Leslie Stephen once wrote, "for such a philosophy is generally the offspring of a recent or the symptom of an approaching revolution."[76] It is a common rule of civilized man, it would seem, that those who keenly feel the loss of liberty speculate upon it, while peoples harvesting the fruits of freedom seldom pause to chop logic over the value of their institutions.

NATURAL LAW AND COMMON LAW

Throughout its long history, natural law theory has been closely associated with law and morals. Sometimes abruptly and consciously through legislation, at other times silently and piecemeal through the judicial process, the general

---

[75] Story's frequent references to Burke are also instructive; inasmuch as Burke greatly influenced Story, and Story in turn permanently influenced the growth and development of American constitutional law, there is good cause to suspect that Burke's influence on American law has been far more extensive than usually is believed.

[76] *The History of English Thought in the Eighteenth Century*, II, 131.

morality and the higher moral ideals of the natural law philosophy have entered into the law—not simply as abstract theory, but as practical rules of human conduct. This is especially true of English legal history, where natural law and common law have stood in close relation for centuries. "Taken all in all," writes one legal scholar, "the common law has not departed very far from the Christian tradition of the natural law, which does not think of power and rights in isolation from their correlative responsibility and duties."[77] Indeed, the ways in which natural law has influenced common law are myriad. It is no mere coincidence, therefore, that many of the great English jurists and lawyers, especially before the time of Bentham and Austin, were also stalwart champions of natural law. The common law, they knew, had gradually assimilated, to the extent of its capacity, many natural law principles. "To Burke," Professor Stanlis has explained, "the spirit of the natural law was embodied in the rules of equity which governed English common law, and was transmitted through legal precedents and prescription."[78]

Joseph Story's adherence to traditional natural law also influenced his views on common law, and with Burke he looked upon the common law as being in part declaratory of natural law moral precepts.[79] However distinguishable and inseparable in their own right, the Anglo-American systems of public and private law in Story's view should, and to a degree already did, reflect the eternal *jus naturale*. Man-made law is the means by which man essays to conform to natural law. No less Divine, it may be thought of, and interpreted as, the refinement of a grand metaphysical design into a canon of ethics for men of all ages to tender and administer as they see fit. A proper understanding of the law, then, said Story, meant that it should be viewed from two perspectives, the philosophical and the practical:

In its widest extent, it may be said almost to compass every human action; and in its minute details, to measure every human duty. It searches into and expounds the elements of morals and ethics, and the eternal law of nature, illustrated and supported by the eternal law of revelation. . . .

But if we contemplate it in a narrower view, as a mere system of regulation for the safety and harmony of civil society; as the instrument of administering public and private justice; as the code, by which rights are ascertained, and wrongs redressed; by which contracts are interpreted, and property is secured, and the insti-

[77] Wu, *Fountain of Justice*, 59.

[78] *Burke and the Natural Law*, 38.

[79] This view was shared by other American lawyers of the early nineteenth century. The common law, argued one early Connecticut writer, "was derived from the law of nature and of revelation—those rules and maxims of immutable truth and justice, which arise from the eternal fitness of things, which need only to be understood, to be submitted to, as they are themselves the highest authority." Jesse Root, *The Origin of Government and Laws in Connecticut, 1798*, reprinted in Miller, *The Legal Mind in America*, 33.

tutions, which add strength to government, and solid happiness to domestic life, are firmly guarded . . . its dignity may in some measure be lessened, but its design will yet appear sufficiently grand, and its execution sufficiently difficult.[80]

But, cautioned Story, in answer to "those bold projectors," as Kent described them, "who can think of striking off a perfect code of law at a single essay,"[81] philosophical inquiries into the complexities of the common law should be undertaken with modesty and prudence. A striving for total perfection through wholesale reform, querulous and excessive theorizing, constant probing of the common law substructure in search of new ways to install new "rights": these were vain, if not dangerous, practices. Story agreed with Burke that the individual is foolish, although the species is wise; only the reckless and the arrogant pit their minds against the wisdom of the ages. In the words of Sir Matthew Hale, the common law of England was "not the product of the wisdom of some one man, or society of men, in any one age; but of the wisdom, counsel, experience, and observation of many ages of wise and observing men."[82]

Legal philosophers, then, can best serve the cause of good government and rule of law by recognizing their own limitations before assailing those of the common law, which, after all, had withstood the supreme test of time. The common law, Story insisted, evolved as a just and viable system of rights and duties compatible with natural law because practical men, who were "not employed in closet speculations, in the silence of the monastary, or in the seclusion of private life," had nearly always been its administrators. "Common sense has . . . powerfully counteracted the tendency to undue speculation in the common law, and silently brought back its votaries to that, which is the end of all true logic, the just application of principles to the actual concerns of life. . . . Every cause is heard in the presence of men, whom practice and study have made singularly acute and discriminating."[83]

The "acute" and "discriminating" men upon whom Story relies for the proper development of the common law are, of course, the jurists and lawyers privy to its workings—men who, over the centuries, have infused natural law principles into the common law. The enjoyment of liberty and the security of property do not arise from legislative command, as the analytical jurists would contend, but are "traced to the principles of the common law, as it has been moulded and fashioned from age to age, by wise and learned judges."[84] The common law doctrines of precedent and supremacy of law, incorporated in

---

[80] "Value and Importance of Legal Studies," *Miscellaneous Writings*, 534.

[81] Kent, *Commentaries on American Law*, I, 471.

[82] As quoted in Kent, *ibid.*

[83] Story, "Value and Importance of Legal Studies," *Miscellaneous Writings*, 508–10.

[84] Story, "A Course of Legal Study," Addressed to the Students of Law in the United States, by David Hoffman, Professor of Law, in the University of Maryland, *ibid.*, 66.

the general concept of law as a quest for the justice of the Creator, are based on the idea that individual and social conflicts should be resolved by principles reached inductively through judicial experience, and deductively through natural law rather than rules established under the sovereign will of the majority. With Chancellor Kent, J. F. Stephen, and Sir Henry Maine, Story defended judicial empiricism as the method best suited for the growth and protection of individual liberties. Common law rights, he believed, were probably more secure in courts of law than in codes and statutes drawn up by legislative bodies laboring under the pernicious influences of Benthamism and Jeffersonian or Jacksonian Democracy.

The courts themselves, however, offered bleak prospects for the development of an enlightened common law system in America. During the late eighteenth and early nineteenth centuries, according to Roscoe Pound, "Many things had operated to retard a complete and final reception of the English common law."[85] There was, for example, a danger of extreme decentralization through the development of separate local systems. The common law system of central courts, because of geographical conditions and slow, expensive travel, often imposed an intolerable burden upon litigants. One cannot help sympathizing with those who fought the centralizing tendencies of a common law enforced under these primitive conditions. Looking back to the days when he practiced law, Story recalled that "the resources of the country were small, the population was scattered, the business of the courts was limited, the compensation for professional services was moderate, and the judges were not generally selected from those who were learned in the law."[86] Although he seems to have concluded by 1835 that more uniformity in the common law was less urgent than in earlier years,[87] Story continued to fear that sectionalism would destroy what uniformity there was in the young Republic. "American jurisprudence can never acquire a homogeneous character," he admitted, and

[W]e must look to the future rather for increasing discrepancies than coincidence in the law and the administration of the law. This is a consideration of no small moment to us all, lest, by being split up into distinct provincial bars, the profession should become devoted to mere state jurisprudence, and abandon those more enlightened and extensive researches which form the accomplished scholar, and elevate the refined jurist; which ennoble the patriot, and shed a never dying lustre round the statesman. The establishment of the national government, and of courts to exercise its constitutional jurisdiction, will, it is hoped, in this respect operate with a salutary influence.[88]

The debasement of law through a weak, politically controlled judiciary

---

[85] *The Formative Era of American Law*, 145.

[86] *A Discourse on the Past History, Present State, and Future Prospects of the Law*, (cited hereafter as *Past History, Present State and Future Prospects*).

[87] *Ibid.*, 21.   [88] *Ibid.*, 35.

further undermined public confidence in the court system. Adding to this was the problem of the judicial quacks—judges with little or no legal education, or worse yet, with no education at all. To able lawyers like Story and Kent, their presence was a source of no little embarrassment, especially when a defense of the judiciary was needed to check legislative encroachment. "In some parts of the country," Professor Chroust has written in his authoritative study of the American legal profession, "the antagonistic sentiment against the lawyer became one of the chief obstacles to the development of a strong and well-organized judicial system during the early period of American history. In many states the aversion to the lawyer went so far that almost anyone but a trained lawyer was regarded as a fit person to sit on the bench."[89]

Charles Brayton, a judge of the Supreme Court of Rhode Island from 1814 to 1818, was a blacksmith, and the chief justice of that state between 1819 and 1826, Isaac Wilbour, was a farmer. Samuel Randall, an associate justice between 1822 and 1832, was not admitted to the bar until he retired from the bench! The Supreme Court of New Jersey included Isaac Smith, a physician, and Samuel Tucker, another layman. John Louis Taylor, North Carolina's first chief justice, read law "without preceptor or guide, and was admitted to the bar at the age of nineteen."[90] Jeremiah Mason recollected that Lot Hall, a member of the Vermont Supreme Court, was "a man of ordinary talents, little learning, and much industry."[91] John Dudley, a trader and farmer, was an associate justice of the New Hampshire Supreme Court from 1785 to 1797, whose judicial utterances no doubt astonished many a lawyer. "Gentlemen of the jury," he once declared, "you have heard what has been said in this case by the lawyers, the rascals! . . . They would govern us by the common law of England. Common-sense is a much safer guide . . . . There was one good thing said at the bar. It was from Shakspear [sic],—an English player, I believe. . . . It is our duty to do justice between parties, not by any quirks of the law out of Coke or Blackstone,—books that I never read and never will."[92]

---

[89] *Rise of the Legal Profession*, II, 39.

[90] *Ibid.*, 42.   [91] As quoted *ibid.*

[92] As quoted *ibid.*, 42–43. In New Hampshire the need for qualified judges was apparently desperate. Two of the three justices of the superior court after Independence lacked legal training: Mechech Weare, the chief justice, was a theologian, and one of his associates, Mathew Thornton, was a physician who, while hearing a case, displayed "the annoying habit of meditating on some lofty transcendental subject or of perusing a book on philosophy or theology, disdaining to listen to the arguments of counsel." During this same period the duties of attorney general were discharged by Nathaniel Peabody and Jonathan Blanchard, neither of whom had any legal training. In 1782, Samuel Livermore was appointed chief justice, and according to Jeremiah Mason, he had "no law learning . . . and did not like to be pestered with it at his courts." He was succeeded in 1790 as chief justice by Josiah Bartlett, a physician, who remained on the court until 1795. Bartlett's successor was Simeon Olcott, a man "more distinguished for the uprightness of his intentions than for his knowledge of the law." *Ibid.*, 39–41.

To the west, brute strength and a combative skill were apparently the first requisites of judicial craftsmanship. "The judges and juries in buckskin on the whole were shrewd and fearless administrators of justice," writes Chroust.

General Morston Clark, one of the earliest judges in Indiana, was an uneducated backwoodsman, six feet tall, whose judicial costume consisted of a hunting shirt, leather pantaloons, and a fox-skin cap. Although tradition has it that he was completely innocent of all legal knowledge, no lawyer could trifle with him. Another judge, John Lindsay of Versailles, Indiana, is said to have quelled a disturbance in his court by descending from the bench, thrashing the nearest offender into submission, and kicking him out of the door.... Judge Charles Reaume of Wisconsin was a powerfully built man who would openly display his long hunting knife if a litigant so much as showed signs of disputing his authority or of objecting seriously to his rulings.[93]

In courts such as these, the proper administration of the common law was surely a rare occurrence. Fortunately, they were the exception rather than the rule, and with the passage of time, were superseded by more respectable tribunals.

Far more ominous to the friends of ordered liberty were the menacing gestures of radical democrats and pretended patriots, who detested anything English and associated lawyers and the common law with aristocracy, the English monarchy, and tyranny. At the root of the difficulty with the courts, as Story knew from firsthand experience in the Massachusetts legislature, was the widespread aversion to lawyers as a class and the law they upheld—attitudes which kept many an able lawyer from taking the bench. "The popular odium which has been excited against the practitioners in this commonwealth," lamented John Quincy Adams, "prevails to so great a degree that the most innocent and irreproachable life cannot guard a lawyer against the hatred of his fellow citizens.... A thousand lies in addition to those published in the papers have been spread all over the country to prejudice the people against the 'order,' as it has been invidiously called."[94]

During the first one-half century of American independence, it was not unusual to find state legislatures enacting repressive measures against lawyers or to see armed mobs demanding the eradication of the legal profession, setting courthouses afire, and attacking lawyers in the streets.[95]

[93] *Ibid.*, 98.

[94] "Diary of John Quincy Adams," as quoted *ibid.*, 21–22. In 1786, Benjamin Austin, writing under the name Honestus, maintained that all the difficulties of the people in Massachusetts could be traced to lawyers, who should be "annihilated" and "abolished, as being not only USELESS, but a DANGEROUS body to the Republic." Austin's sweeping denunciations were refuted by James Sullivan and Adams. William Duane, a Philadelphia journalist, campaigned against the legal profession and "the inextricable and destructive farrago of the common law" during Jefferson's second administration. *Ibid.*, 19–24.

[95] During Shay's Rebellion the demand was actually made that all lawyers and all

Legislative assaults against the common law itself were the general order of the day; for judicial independence and judge-made law were regarded as anathema to the democratic creed of popular sovereignty. Ironically enough, the common law around which American revolutionaries had rallied in the struggle against England became almost overnight an object of public scorn. Mumblings of discontent in the immediate post-Revolutionary Era, amplified by raucous feuding between Federalists and Jeffersonian Republicans, grew by the turn of the century to vociferous cries for the complete abolition of the common law. Peter Du Ponceau, a leading Philadelphia lawyer, observed as late as 1824 that there was clearly "a spirit of hostility" in America against the common law, which "began in Virginia . . . in consequence of an opposition to the Alien and Sedition Acts," and has since spread to other states, where "attacks upon the Common Law, more or less direct, have appeared from time to time." But in spite of its many faults, its lack of certainty, "and above all the supposed danger to our institutions from its being still the law of a monarchical country," the common law, said Du Ponceau, was preferable to any other. "Were it abolished, a still greater difficulty must arise, to fill up the immense chasm which would be produced in its absence. Not all the codes of all the Benthams would be capable of producing that effect."[96]

Many advocates of code law were, as to be expected, among the fiercest opponents of the common law. To a populace still smarting from the sting of English oppression, caught up in a whirlwind of revolutionary turmoil and general confusion, the wild accusations and visionary schemes of the Benthamites seemed plausible indeed. To members of the bar, nursing along an

inferior courts be eliminated. In New Hampshire and other states, demands were made to suppress the legal profession or to reduce its size and to lower lawyers' fees. In Vermont, courthouses were put to the torch, and the state legislature arrogated to itself the right to modify or set aside all court decisions. The doors of courthouses in New Jersey were nailed shut, and lawyers were publicly assaulted by irate mobs. Rhode Island lawyers were required by the legislature to accept paper money at par value or suffer disbarment, despite the fact a previous act providing for compulsory payment of debts in paper money had been declared unconstitutional in the case of *Trevett* v. *Weeden* (1786). *Ibid.*, 26-27.

[96] Peter Du Ponceau, *A Dissertation on the Nature and Extent of the Jurisdiction of the Courts of the United States, 1824*, reprinted in Miller, *The Legal Mind in America*, 112. The Virginia General Assembly in 1800 instructed its representatives and senators in the federal Congress to oppose all laws founded on the principle that the common law was in force under the United States government. In 1799, New Jersey enacted a law forbidding the bar to cite in court any decision, opinion, or treatise of the common law made or written in England after July 1, 1776. In Pennsylvania a statute passed in 1810, which was not repealed until 1836, forbade the citation of any English decision delivered after July 4, 1776. Similar statutes appeared in Kentucky and Ohio. For a discussion of anti-common law sentiment in early America, see Chroust, *Rise of the Legal Profession*, II, especially 51-72. Jefferson wished to forbid the citation in American courts of any English decisions handed down after Lord Mansfield became chief justice of the King's Bench in 1756. See Jefferson to John B. Cutting, Oct. 2, 1788, *Writings* (Library ed.), XIII, 155.

American common law that was still in its infancy, struggling for recognition and acceptance, the Benthamites were a formidable challenge. More than anyone, American lawyers were acutely aware that in a number of ways, American common law was vulnerable to attack, and that the codifiers stood to profit from long-standing dissatisfaction with the existing legal system.

Perhaps the greatest factor working in favor of the codifiers was simply the intellectual climate of the times—the resentment towards the English, the demand for more democracy, "the example of the French civil code, the enthusiasm for things French following the Revolution and in the era of Jeffersonian democracy, and the [modern] natural law idea that a code could be drafted independent of the historical materials of the law and on a basis of pure reason."[97] In addition, a sense of urgency prevailed throughout the legal profession to enact premature and crude code laws.

American common law, still undeveloped, was inaccessible to many lawyers. Digests, reports, and legal treatises, not to mention the modern tools of the lawyer, were few in number and not always complete or satisfactory. Chancellor Kent remarked that when he went upon the bench, "there were no reports or state precedents. The opinions from the bench were *ore tenus*. We had no law of our own and nobody knew what [the law] was."[98]

Codification of the common law would, it was argued, ameliorate these difficulties by making the law readily available, less uncertain, and more easily understood by lawyers and laymen alike. Above all, codification meant the democratization of the law, and the followers of Bentham were quick to point out the allegedly undemocratic character of the common law both in its content and administration.[99]

Much to their displeasure, the legislative supremacy of the Revolutionary Period, which had effectively bound the courts to the popular will, was gradually receding, owing to the doctrine of separation of powers, the tenacity of an earlier English tradition of judicial independence, and the emergence of a well-organized and increasingly learned profession of lawyers, many of whom were in a position to defend the courts from the bench and the halls of the legislature. (A code drafted by the legislature would strike a blow at judicial discretion and judicial supremacy, restore popular sovereignty to its rightful

[97] Pound, *The Formative Era of American Law*, 145.

[98] As quoted *ibid.*, 128.

[99] "The last argument is," noted one opponent of codification, "that the common or unwritten law 'is inconsistent with the theory of our social compact.' If so, I have only to remark, that it is very strange that the great men of our country, the Washingtons, the Hamiltons, the Madisons, the Marshalls, the Livingstons, the Storys, the Pinckneys and the Taneys, have never discovered, that in carrying out the great principles of the common law, they have been acting in the very face of the Constitutions of our country." Washington Van Hamm, "Codification—Its Practicability and Expediency," *Western Law Journal*, Vol. I (Sept., 1844), 229, reprinted in Haar, *The Golden Age of American Law*, 262.

place in the order of things, and extirpate from the law those English encumbrances carried over from the distant and "unenlightened" past.) Robert Rantoul, a radical Massachusetts Democrat from Salem and fervent supporter of codification, spoke for many of his fellow Benthamites when he bluntly declared in 1836 that

The Common Law sprung from the Dark Ages . . . in the time of ignorance . . . folly, barbarism, and feudality. . . . Judge-made law is *ex post facto* law, and therefore unjust. An act is not forbidden by the statute law, but it becomes void by judicial construction . . . . The judiciary shall not usurp legislative power, says the Bill of Rights; yet it not only usurps, but runs riot beyond the confines of legislative power. . . . No man can tell what the Common Law is; therefore it is not law. . . . The Common Law is the perfection of human reason, just as alcohol is the perfection of sugar . . . . With us, it is subversive of the fundamental principles of a free government. . . . All American law must be statute law.[100]

The ideas of Bentham on code law were first introduced to America by Edward Livingston, a close disciple of Bentham who later became a member of President Jackson's cabinet.[101] Livingston was successful in drafting a code of procedure which the Louisiana legislature adopted in 1805. Then in 1811, the same year Story was appointed to the Supreme Court, Bentham himself wrote to President Madison, offering to codify all the laws of the United States!

[100] Robert Rantoul, Jr., *Oration at Scituate*, reprinted in Miller, *The Legal Mind in America*, 222–27. Rantoul graduated from Harvard in 1826, and was admitted to the Salem bar in 1829 and the Boston bar in 1838. A Jeffersonian and Jacksonian Democrat, he agitated against capital punishment, advocated labor unions, served as legal counsel to the Dorr rebels in Rhode Island, and was an active abolitionist in the anti-slavery movement. Other advocates of codification included Jesse Root, Henry Dwight Sedgwick, Thomas S. Grimké, and David Dudley Field.

[101] Three works by Bentham were devoted wholly to codification: *A General View of a Complete Code of Laws, Pannomial Fragments*, and a short tract on *The Promulgation of Laws and the Reasons thereof with Specimen of a Penal Code*. His attacks on Blackstone appeared in his *Comment on the Commentaries* and *Fragment on Government*. For a discussion of these and other works by Bentham on legal reform, see Holdsworth, *A History of English Law*, XIII, 41–134. Even before the codification "movement" was underway in America, James Wilson and Nathaniel Chipman had broken ranks, calling for emancipation of the American legal mind from the domination of Blackstone. "I cannot," said Wilson, "consider him a zealous friend of republicanism. On the subject of government I think I can plainly discover his jealousies and his attachments. . . . In publick law . . . he should be consulted with cautious prudence." (*Works*, I, 79–80.) In *Chisholm* v. *Georgia*, 2 Dallas 458–59 (1793), Wilson brazenly declared: "A plan of systematic despotism has lately been formed in England. Of this plan, the author of the Commentaries was, if not the introducer, at least the great supporter . . . [H]is doctrines have been, both on the other and this side of the Atlantic, implicitly and generally received by those who neither examined their principles nor their consequences." Blackstone's principles, said Chipman, "are not universal," and "in a democratic republic, they are wholly inadmissible." *Sketches of the Principles of Government, 1793*, reprinted in Miller, *The Legal Mind in America*, 29.

Madison, of course, declined the invitation. Bentham's letter, being quite incoherent, probably persuaded Madison that the existing system made more sense.[102] Undaunted, Bentham's followers and other advocates of legal reform continued their efforts, and in the 1820s interest was again aroused in the possibilities of codification, especially in New York and Massachusetts.

For the first time Judge Story was drawn into the codification controversy. His friend Henry Wheaton, the Supreme Court reporter, was appointed by the New York State assembly in 1825 to assist in revising the state's statutes. No legal dilettante, Wheaton nevertheless deemed it necessary to consult both Story and Bentham on the matter, and to lay before them for critical examination some of the changes proposed by his committee of revisers.[103] With characteristic independence, Story took up a unique position. He openly endorsed codification, but apparently with a view toward conservative ends. Unlike many of his fellow lawyers, who trembled at the bare mention of the word *codify*, Story saw that through codification the common law might actually be strengthened. As long as the legislature limited its task to a rewriting of existing law and did not venture into new areas of law or attempt to devise new rights and duties, the common law principles would remain intact and judicial supremacy would in essence be preserved. Thus understood, codification would amount to little more than legislative ratification of the common law and a continuation of judicial independence. Moreover, codification would reduce the burdens of legal research, which Story had always thought were excessive. The result would allow the lawyer to devote more time to other pursuits, which, it was to be hoped, would expand his mind and his legal practice.

In short, practical and professional considerations rather than a desire to establish natural rights or to democratize the law explain why Story at first favored some codification of the common law, especially in the field of commerce. His stand can be seen from a reading of his letter to Wheaton, written

[102] A portion of the letter is reprinted in John Honnold, ed., *The Life of the Law*, 100–102. "In the light of the style of Bentham's letter," asks Honnold, "should Madison have been concerned about the readability of the codes which Bentham would have produced?" *Ibid.*, 102.

[103] Wheaton had been interested in code law for many years. In 1804 he translated into English the Code Napoléon for publication in the United States, but the manuscript was accidentally lost in a fire. When in England he often visited Bentham, "a charming old man, less dogmatical than expected, who criticized the specimens of the New York *Revised Laws* that had been sent to him in a tone of great politeness, expressing himself satisfied with what the revisers had done, as far as they had attempted to go." (William Beach Lawrence, as quoted in Elizabeth Feaster Baker, *Henry Wheaton, 1785–1848*, 82.) Widely recognized as one of America's foremost authorities on international law, Wheaton wrote two major works on this subject during Story's lifetime. Besides serving as a Supreme Court reporter, Wheaton was also a journalist, historian, diplomat, and biographer of the great Maryland lawyer William Pinkney.

in the fall of 1825, concerning Wheaton's alterations of the committee's draft:

In respect to your proposed revision of the New York Code, from the specimen you sent me I think it will be very valuable. . . . But my opinion does not stop with a mere revision of the Statute Law. I have long been an advocate for a "codification" of the common law, at least of that part which is most reduced to principles & is of daily and extensive application. I do not suppose that such a code would render future legislation unnecessary, or would supersede the necessity of perpetual appeals to courts of justice. So long as human transactions are unlimited & are assuming new courses, & new forms, there must be an infinite diversity in the application of legal principles. Lawyers will always be required for new cases, as they arise. . . . My opinion in favour of a code of the Common Law, therefore, rests on no visionary expectation of a perfect, infallible, or universal system. But I am in favour of a Code, because I think it may reduce to certainty, method, & exactness much of the law, already passed upon by judicial tribunals, & thus give to the public the means, within a reasonable compass, of ascertaining their own rights & duties in many of the most interesting concerns of human life. In the next place I think it would greatly abridge the labours & exhausting researches of the profession. Half our time is now consumed in examining cases . . . . What a great gain it would be for us to have a starting point—something irrevocably fixed as a settled principle. . . . What would be [lost] if our principles of shipping, insurance, & bills of exchange, were reduced to a code, as they are in a most admirable form in the French Code of Commerce?[104]

Two years later, in a letter to Thomas Grimké of South Carolina, Story re-asserted these beliefs, insisting that "A positive code, recognizing in a fixed form & in a lucid method the great principles of commercial law, would of itself be a very great blessing." But again, he stressed the importance of keeping codification within the confines of established law and of giving the judicial branch a free hand in the development of new principles. "In my view," he told Grimké, "the great object of a code, is not & ought not to be, so much the formation of new principles for future cases, as the positive enactment, as fundamental, of those which have been already . . . acted upon, &

[104] Oct. 1, 1825, Henry Wheaton Papers, Pierpont Morgan Library. Story was critical of lawyers who blindly opposed all code law and "incline against all innovations, because they have no confidence in any reforms, & cling with reverence to every thing old. The very clumsiness & awkwardness of the phraseology of the Enactments of the legislature in ancient as well as in modern times has a charm. . . . There is something in the old imputation, that there is no error, which they are not apt to defend, & no improvement, which they do not steadfastly resist." Fearing that he might be misunderstood, Story cautioned Wheaton that he "must not shew this letter at large, for it does not give my views in a manner, which I am satisfied with; but I have no objection, that your colleagues should know my opinions" (*ibid.*). But Perry Miller asserts "Story and his sort endeavored to impose [the burden of scholarship] upon the rising generations in order to stifle any dreams of simplicity." Miller, *The Legal Mind in America*, p. 146, n. 1.

approved." Therefore, he concluded, "A revision of a Code once in fifty years by embodying in a fixed shape the additions of new principles & the limitations & expositions of old ones, made in the intermediate period, by the highest courts of justice, would perpetually bring the law into a state approximating to the exactness of Science."[105]

By the 1830's, however, Story's attitude towards codification had changed considerably. In 1836 he became directly involved in the codification controversy when he was appointed by Governor Edward Everett to head a commission for the purpose of further reducing Massachusetts common law to a systematic code. Instead of welcoming the assignment as a unique opportunity for the advancement of sweeping legal reforms, Story accepted his new task with great reluctance, even questioning the merits of the committee's purpose. His distaste for the whole project he communicated privately to an English friend:

While in England your Courts have by the New Rules given a new organic to special pleading, we in Massachusetts have by a recent statute positively abolished it, & instituted the general issue in all cases. I confess myself opposed to this change. ... I think our recent enactment grows out of a restless love of innovation, combined with a desire in some members of the profession to find an apology for their indolence or want of skill.

A Commission has been appointed by the State of Massachusetts to report to the Legislature on the practicability & expediency of codifying the common law or any part thereof. Much against my will I was placed at the head of the Commission. We shall report favorably to the codification of some branches of the commercial law. But the report will be very qualified & limited in its objects. We have not yet become votaries to the notions of Jeremy Bentham. But the present state of popular opinion here makes it necessary to do something on the subject.[106]

From an analysis of the report,[107] it is clear Judge Story took a moderate

---

[105] Copy of original in Weld-Grimké Papers, William L. Clements Library. Story's letter was a reply to Grimké's *Oration of the Practicability and Expedience of Reducing the Whole Body of the Law to the Simplicity of a Code*, which Grimké delivered before the South Carolina Bar Association on March 17, 1827 (reprinted in Miller, *The Legal Mind in America*, 148–59). Like Story, Grimké was a friend of the common law who favored some codification. Chief Justice Marshall also believed that codification might prove to be beneficial. "I concur entirely in the opinion that the body of the law may be reduced to a code," he wrote to Grimké, "& that great advantages might result from this simplification of those rules which affect every member of Society." Aug. 7, 1827; copy of original in Weld-Grimké Papers, Clements Library.

[106] To James J. Wilkinson, Dec. 26, 1836, Massachusetts Historical Society *Proceedings*, 2nd Series, Vol. XV (1901–1902), 221.

[107] See *Report of the Commissioners*, Appointed to Consider and Report upon the Practicability and Expediency of Reducing to a Written & Systematic Code the Common Law of Massachusetts, signed by Joseph Story (author), Samuel Greenleaf, Theron Metcalf, Charles E. Forbes, and Luther Cushing (Boston: Dutton and Wentworth, 1837),

position. From an earlier belief that "We ought not to permit ourselves to indulge in the theoretical extravagances of some well-meaning philosophical jurists, who believe that all human concerns for the future can be provided for in a code speaking a definite language,"[108] Story concluded that the reduction of all law to a positive form would create an unjust, oppressive, and unwieldy conglomeration of empty mandates. Such a code, he contended, would render provisions for future cases utterly impracticable. It "would be perpetually growing more and more defective, unless resort was had to new legislation."[109] Such legislation, moreover, would, in order to cover all human activity, be so voluminous "that a whole life would be required to master all its provisions, and more than a whole life to accumulate the materials fit for its composition."[110]

Thus, he surmised, it was not possible to reduce the common law of Massachusetts to a written code. It "should be left to its prospective operations in the future (as it has been in the past) to be improved, expanded, and modified to meet the exigencies of society, by the gradual application of its principles in courts of justice to new cases, assisted from time to time, as the occasion may demand, by the enactments of the legislature."[111] Story therefore recommended only the codification of those areas of common law which were "capable of a distinct enunciation," and were already established by judicial decision. Certain areas of law respecting civil liberties, implied contracts, crimes, and rules of evidence were consequently recommended for codification.

Historians reviewing Judge Story's activities in the codification movement have been unable to agree upon his position. According to Perry Miller, "Kent, Story, Hoffman, and their ilk stoutly defended the Common Law as being an accretion of reasonable decisions, and so—once divested of its peculiarly English quirks—already at one with the Law of Nature and therefore not requiring codification."[112] On the other hand, it has been asserted by a number of others that both Story and Kent "believed wholeheartedly in the establishment of codes of law."[113] Somewhere between these two extremes stands Judge Story. While Story may have believed that *some* codification would be bene-

---

reprinted under the title "Codification of the Common Law" in Story, *Miscellaneous Writings*, 698–735.

[108] Story, *Past History, Present State and Future Prospects*, 49–50.

[109] Story, "Codification of the Common Law," *Miscellaneous Writings*, 709.

[110] *Ibid.*, 710.

[111] *Ibid.*, 713.

[112] *The Legal Mind in America*, 93–94.

[113] Elizabeth K. Bauer, *Commentaries on the Constitution, 1790–1860*, 20. Henry S. Commager also gives the impression that Story was at all times a warm supporter of codification. Commager states that "Story early ranged himself on the side of the codifiers" and that Story's report to Governor Everett on the codification of Massachusetts common law is indicative that he favored all such projects, "Joseph Story—A Portrait," *Bacon Lectures*, 79.

ficial, as in the field of commercial law, it is also apparent, especially in the 1830s, that he was highly skeptical of general codification of the common law. No Benthamite, as we have seen, Story favored limited codification for professional more than philosophical or political reasons and regarded most attempts at codification as premature. "In truth," he wrote during these years,

the formation of codes, or systems of general law, for the government of a people, and adapted to their wants, is a business which takes place only in advanced stages of society, when knowledge is considerably diffused, and legislators have the means of ascertaining the best principles of policy and the best rules for justice, not by mere Speculation and theory, but by the results of experience, and the reasoning of the learned and the wise. Those codes with which we are best acquainted, are manifestly of this sort. The Institutes, and pandects, and Code of Justinian were made in the latter ages of Roman Grandeur—nay, when it was far on the decline—not by instituting a new system, but by embodying the maxims, and rules, and principles, which the ablest jurists had collected in different ages.[114]

It seems safe to conclude, therefore, that Story did not regret the failure of the codification movement in nineteenth-century America. He considered all forms of knowledge to be the result of gradual evolution, and law, especially, owed its strength and vigor to past struggle. Theorists and codifiers, in their zeal to revamp the entire legal system for the purpose of establishing new concepts of universal justice, only usher in chaos and greater injustice. The law cannot be built merely on rational principles as Bentham would have it. Sturdy, but delicate, it must be administered by those familiar with its workings, by the lawyers and judges who daily explore its intricate systems. Every good system of laws must be slow in consolidating, said Story.

[T]he rashness of an hour may destroy what ages have scarcely cemented in a solid form. The oak, which requires centuries to rear its trunk, and stretch its branches, and strengthen its fibres, and fix its roots, may yet be leveled in an hour. It may breast the tempest of a hundred years, and survive the scathing of the lightning. It may acquire vigor from its struggles with the elements, and strike its roots deeper and wider as it rises in its majesty; and yet a child, in the very wantonness of folly, may in an instant destroy it by removing a girdle of its bark.[115]

And so, Story would illustrate Jefferson's tree of liberty as the tree of law, the British oak which Burke once described in a famous passage as the shelter

---

[114] "Law, Legislation and Codes," *Encyclopedia Americana*, VII, Appendix, 586. In reviewing Nathan Dane's *General Abridgment and Digest of American Law*, Story quoted with approval Dane's assertion that, before a system of codification could be seriously entertained as desirable, " 'there must be a *national* character . . . . A complete system of law and equity, best calculated to preserve the power of the magistrate and the rights of the people, is the last thing men attain to in society.' " "Digests of the Common Law," *Miscellaneous Writings*, 406–407.

[115] Story, "The Value and Importance of Legal Studies," *Miscellaneous Writings*, 515.

of the British people. Story believed in law as a process of organic growth, as the result of man's endless quest for liberty, justice, and virtue. As Story knew well, codification could be a dangerous short cut to these ends, especially in a country like the United States, where the legal system was undeveloped.

Like the law, governments and constitutions are complex structures, whose many walls, pillars, and hidden underpinnings rest on materials from the distant past. There is no greater fallacy, said Story, than "the common notion that government is a matter of great simplicity. . . . In proportion as a government is free, it must be complicated. Simplicity belongs to those only, where one will governs all."[116]

The assumption that governments and constitutions can be drawn by the guiding hand of the philosopher king, which impelled the Abbé Sieyès to draft constitutions for France and the states of Europe during the French Revolution without deference to prescription, custom, and precedent, Story excoriated as a frightful delusion. Writing to Francis Lieber in 1837 praising his new work, *Political Ethics*, Story expressed these sentiments of Burke, John Adams, and probably Mounier, when he complimented Lieber for producing a book which "puts aside the wild and visionary notion, the parent of so many revolutionary schemes, that the same form of government is equally well suited to all countries and nations."[117] To a large extent, constitutions are indigenous to a particular people, becoming their private, unalienable possession. Their complexity is their guaranty against arbitrary action, as Publius taught, making deliberation not a matter of choice, but of necessity, rendering all change subject to compromise. Like the jurist, therefore, the statesman "must, in some measure, be master of the past, present, and future."[118] We know from history, Story exhorted in his tribute to the Constitution, that

Whatever . . . has been found to work well in experience, should be rarely hazarded upon conjectural improvements. Time, and long and steady operation are indispensable to the perfection of all social institutions. To be of any value they must become cemented with the habits, the feelings, and the pursuits of the people. Every change discomposes for a while the whole arrangements of the system. What is safe is not always expedient; what is new is often pregnant with unforeseen evils, and imaginary good.[119]

Veneration for a system of public and private law that has slowly matured over the years under the supervision of wise and learned men steeped in the natural law tradition: here in essence is the mind and faith of Mr. Justice Story. Rejecting Bentham's allegation that the common law is incompatible

[116] "The Science of Government," *Miscellaneous Writings*, 619.

[117] Aug. 15, 1837, *Life and Letters*, II, 278–79.

[118] Story, "Statesmen—Their Rareness and Importance: Daniel Webster," *New England Magazine*, Vol. VII (Aug., 1834), 93.

[119] Story, *Commentaries on the Constitution*, I, sec. 1904, p. 758.

with democracy, Story sided with Blackstone in arguing "that in every modern government, practically free, the common law rule has prevailed by general consent."[120] He held the view later espoused by Dean Pound that common law, like natural law, "stands beside religion and morality as one of the regulative agencies by which men are restrained and the social interest in general security is protected."[121] And not only does the common law have "the advantage of producing certainty as to rights, privileges, and property," said Story, but it also "controls the arbitrary discretion of judges, and puts the case beyond the reach of temporary feelings and prejudices. . . . [T]he consciousness that the decision will form a permanent precedent, affecting all future cases, introduces necessarily great caution and deliberation in giving it."[122]

In retrospect, however, it would appear that Story's attitudes on codification are not of major significance today; except to show the patterns of his thought, and to illustrate that in spite of his predilection towards judicial supremacy and his general distrust of democratic assemblies, he was nevertheless in support of limited reform of the common law through legislation and did not in doctrinaire fashion oppose (or favor) all attempts at reform. Through his copious and learned decisions, meticulous treatises on the common law, and lectures at the Harvard Law School, Story dispelled much of the confusion and mystery surrounding the "newest" and yet "oldest" common law system in the world and, without realizing it, thereby helped to defeat codification in America.

Let it again be recalled that before the time of Story and Kent, lawyers often possessed only dim knowledge of the American common law. Much of English common law was inapplicable to the American situation, and few had access to the modifications which had been made since the colonial era. Court reports were scarce and digests and treatises were relatively nonexistent. But once these materials became available, the need for code law disappeared, as did the desire for a premature codification of America's unsettled common law. Dean Pound has noted that "more than anything else, the books of our great nineteenth century text-writers saved the common law . . . . If Marshall made our public law, they in almost equal measure made our private law in that they assured it should develop by judicial rather than by legislative empiricism."[123]

NATURAL LAW AND THE CONSTITUTION

"The science of politics . . . like most other sciences has received great im-

---

[120] Story, "Law, Legislation and Codes," *Encyclopedia Americana*, VII, Appendix, 582.
[121] Roscoe Pound, *The Spirit of the Common Law*, 139.
[122] "Law, Legislation and Codes," *Encyclopedia Americana*, VII, Appendix, 582.
[123] "The Place of Judge Story in the Making of American Law," *Massachusetts Law Quarterly*, Vol. I, No. 3 (May, 1916), 135, 140.

provement," Alexander Hamilton assured the people of New York in *The Federalist*, Number 9. The men who drafted the new constitution at Philadelphia, he explained, were well versed in the mechanics of government—in the techniques of separation of powers, checks and balances, judicial independence, and democratic representation:

The efficacy of various principles is now well understood, which were either not known at all, or imperfectly known to the ancients. The regular distribution of power into distinct departments, the introduction of legislative balances and checks, the institution of courts composed of judges, holding their offices during good behavior, the representation of the people in the legislature by deputies of their own election—these are either wholly new discoveries or have made their principal progress towards perfection in modern times. They are *means*, and powerful means, by which the excellencies of republican government may be retained and its imperfections lessened or avoided.[124]

Few would deny the veracity of these remarks today. As political scientists, in the narrow sense of that term, the framers were expert technicians, and a few were even craftsmen; and there is a great deal of truth in Gladstone's statement, uttered in 1878, that the American Constitution "is the most wonderful work ever struck off at a given time by the brain and purpose of man."[125]

As political philosophers, however, the founding fathers were less impressive; for they labored at their magnanimous task of constructing a new government at a time in history of great intellectual confusion, at a time when natural law and natural rights were locked in mortal combat. "It must be pointed out," John Wu has observed, "that although these great men drew their inspiration mainly from the Bible and the common law, they also absorbed to a degree some rationalistic ideas from such authors as John Locke, Grotius, Pufendorf, Rousseau, Montesquieu, and Burlamaqui. With few exceptions, they were not too well acquainted with the scholastic tradition. Because, no doubt, of their historical situation, they were inclined to think more of the natural liberties and rights of man than of the natural law and natural duties."[126]

Sanctioning, as Burke put it, the prescriptive or common law and charter rights of Englishmen, the natural law of the black-letter philosophers ran counter to the newly emerging doctrines of modern natural law declaring the "rights of man," so that, oddly enough, two traditions of natural law had simultaneously found favor among the English intelligentsia in the eighteenth century. Stranger yet, few recognized at the time the inherent incompatibility

---

[124] Modern Library ed., 48–49. Emphasis supplied.

[125] Sir William Gladstone, as quoted in Martin Diamond et al., *The Democratic Republic*, 34.

[126] *Fountain of Justice*, 129.

of the opposing philosophies. Only Blackstone seemed to realize that the common law denied to men the egalitarian rights "inherited" from a pre-existing state of nature. "The principles of Mr. Locke," he observed candidly, "would have reduced society almost to a state of nature; would have levelled all distinctions of honour, rank, offices, and property."[127]

The confusion surrounding the natural law philosophy was no less pervasive in the American colonies, whose leaders were attempting the impossible task of transplanting English common law and the social contract theories of John Locke. Everyone in America was reading Blackstone, as Burke observed, but so also were the pages of Locke's second treatise being scrutinized. The tendency of Americans to misconstrue Locke's ideas, and to twist them to their advantage, added another dimension to the intellectual disorder of the period respecting conflicting natural law doctrines. "American revolutionists, to be sure, hardly qualified as expert contract theorists. Their contribution to any systematic exposition of the social contract was small, indeed almost non-existent. The characteristic American statements were resolutions, instructions to legislators, or newspaper articles, all brief and uninquiring in their references to the contract. The few longer treatments were almost entirely derivative—usually an admitted paraphrase of Locke's second treatise. American spokesmen, moreover, did not always comprehend the contract theory fully. Nearly all of them failed, for example, to distinguish between the separate contracts of society and of government."[128]

[127] *Commentaries*, I, 31. An excellent analysis of Blackstone's political and legal thought is that of Herbert J. Storing in *History of Political Philosophy*, ed. by Leo Strauss and Joseph Cropsey (Chicago, 1963), 536–48. "Blackstone's highest theme," notes Storing, "deals with the relation between natural law and conventional law." In the first chapter of book I, which concerns what he calls the absolute rights of individuals, Blackstone "spends little time . . . with the natural liberty of mankind . . . but moves quickly to the subject of civil rights." He then proceeds "to define the rights of man in terms of the rights of Englishmen" (*ibid.*, 537, 539). See also Daniel J. Boorstin, *The Mysterious Science of the Law*, and Paul Lucas, "Ex Parte Sir William Blackstone, 'Plagiarist': A Note on Blackstone and the Natural Law," *American Journal of Legal History*, Vol. VII (1963), 142–58. Professor Lucas concludes that Bracton and Cicero were Blackstone's two major teachers on the natural law, and "that Blackstone was an adherent of the rational school of the Stoics, of the Germano-English respect for ancient custom, of the medieval civilian and Christian—and Thomistic—traditions of belief in a pre-existent natural law" (*ibid.*, 146). See also Sir Ernest Barker, "Blackstone on the British Constitution," in his *Essays on Government*, 120–53.

[128] Thad W. Tate, "The Social Contract in America, 1774–1787: Revolutionary Theory as a Conservative Instrument," *William and Mary Quarterly*, 3rd Series, Vol. XXII, No. 3 (July, 1965), 376. American Loyalists were equally confused. At least two, Jonathan Boucher and Charles Inglis, rejected Locke and the social contract, only vaguely perceiving, however, the conflict between traditional natural law and modern natural rights. But Peter Van Schaack, the New York Loyalist, revered Locke. William H. Nelson, *The American Tory*, 121, 185–89; see also Leonard Woods Labaree, *Conservatism in Early American History*.

The slogans, the pamphlets, and the public records of the American Revolution reflected the superficiality of political philosophy and left in doubt the whole matter of the exact aims and purposes of the war, and the nature of the liberties Americans were claiming for themselves.

"We assert the rights of Englishmen!" declared the American patriots, at almost the very moment Thomas Jefferson was drafting the Declaration of Independence and committing his countrymen to the rights of man. Evincing little appreciation for the distinction between concrete legal rights of Englishmen, as emphasized by Blackstone, and the more abstract doctrines of natural rights common to all men which Locke stressed, American revolutionaries insisted upon having it both ways.

Future generations could not so easily afford the luxury of theoretical illiteracy, particularly after it was claimed that the Declaration of Independence and the Constitution were in conflict and irreconcilable. The art of muddling: such is one way to describe the talent of American revolutionaries in their confused treatment of the natural law philosophy. Much of their difficulty in understanding natural law and much of their indiscriminate and reckless usage of the word *rights* can be attributed to their inadequacies as philosophers, even though when the time came for calm deliberation and the drafting of a constitution for the new Republic, they exhibited an astonishing degree of knowledge and prudence in pulling together incongruous theories of politics and making them work. As students of government, then, and not as philosophers, they were successful.

Their failure to deal satisfactorily with the overriding issues of natural law and natural rights was destined to haunt America and Europe in succeeding decades. An example may be found in the preambles of the state constitutions of 1776, which became rallying points for the revision of state constitutions some fifty years later.[129] It was especially true on the continent of Europe. No

---

[129] Although differing little in substance from the Constitution and Bill of Rights on the nature and scope of English guarantees of liberty, many state constitutions prior to the War between the States paid lip service to the philosophy of the Declaration of Independence in their preambles. "The constitutions of 1776 [in the southern states] were based upon the theories of natural rights, the doctrine of popular sovereignty, and the social compact. Like the Declaration of Independence, they theoretically recognized the equality of all men, yet their founders did not hesitate to withhold suffrage and other political privileges. . . . Jeffersonian democracy wished to make of the principles of the Declaration of Independence and the Virginia Bill of Rights something more than mere glittering generalities." Thus, after 1800, was begun an attempt to democratize state constitutions, under the claim of natural rights and the contract theory, which ultimately bore fruit in the constitutional conventions after 1830. (Fletcher M. Green, *Constitutional Development in the South Atlantic States, 1776–1860*, 171.) With the rise of abolitionism after 1830, the conflict between the Declaration of Independence and the national Constitution came to the surface, and abolitionists such as William Ellery Channing and William Lloyd Garrison publicly denounced the Constitution, arguing that the "self-evident

doubt many agreed with Friedrich von Gentz that the American revolutionaries made a fatal mistake simply in mentioning natural rights, which, according to Gentz, they neither understood nor actually sought.

Gentz, a close adviser to Metternich and British cabinets and a disciple of
Edmund Burke, published in Germany in 1810 an essay on the "French and
American Revolutions Compared," in which he demonstrated convincingly
that "with regard to the lawfulness of the origin, character of the conduct,
quality of the object, and compass of resistance . . . these two revolutions will
much more to display the contrast, than the resemblance between them."[130]
What disturbed Gentz in particular was the frequent appeal of the French
revolutionaries to the American example, and their misuse of the Declaration
of Independence in support of wild, "revolutionary speculations" and "systematic anarchy." Unfortunately, he wrote,

the Declaration of Independence . . . is proceeded [*sic*] by an introduction, in which
the *natural* and *unalienable* rights of mankind are considered as the foundation of
all government; that after this assertion, so indefinite, and so exposed to the greatest
misconstructions, follow certain principles, no less indefinite, no less liable to be
abused, from which an inference might be drawn of the unlimited right of the
people to change their form of government, and what in the new revolutionary
language, is called *sovereignty*. It is likewise true, that most of the [state] constitutions of the United States, are preceded by those idle *declarations of rights*, so
dangerous in their application, from which so much misery has at a later period
been derived upon France, and the whole civilized world. Much, however, as it
were to be wished, that the legislators of America had disdained this empty pomp
of words, that they had exclusively confined themselves within the clear and lawful
motives of their resistance; a resistance at first constitutional, and afterwards necessary, and within the limits of their uncontrovertible rights, yet it cannot escape the

---

truths" of natural rights in the Declaration were the supreme law of the land. They
would obey and defend, they said, not the legal rights of American citizens, but the
sacred rights of all men. Southerners, led by John C. Calhoun, responded by discrediting
the ideas and ideals of the Declaration of Independence, notwithstanding the fact their
own state constitutions were developing in that direction. See Carl L. Becker, *The Declaration of Independence*, 239-56.

[130] Reprinted from the original translation by John Quincy Adams in Stefan Possony
(ed.), *Three Revolutions*, 95. Gentz, like many intellectuals of the period, was at first
sympathetic towards the French Revolution. Influenced in his younger days by Kant, he
praised the French Revolution as a model for the future, in keeping with Kant's idea that
the state should be reconstructed to conform with reason. But the radicalism of the
Jacobins and Burke's formidable *Reflections on the Revolution in France*, which Gentz
read and later translated into German, turned him against the Revolution. Adams read
Gentz while serving as minister to Prussia, translated the essay into English, and published it anonymously in Philadelphia. Fearing that the false ideas of the French Revolution were taking root in America, Adams hoped the essay would purge from the American mind false notions about the alleged close parentage of the two revolutions.

observation of those, who attentively study the history of their revolution, that they allowed to these speculative ideas, no visible influence upon their practical measures and resolves—they erroneously believed them necessary to justify their first step.[131]

And so it was the French Revolution of 1789, demonstrating clearly enough the perils of natural rights rhetoric, that caused Americans once again to examine the question of "rights" and to ask themselves whether they would settle for the common law rights written into their constitutions[132] or whether they desired to pursue the ideals of the Declaration of Independence, now reaffirmed and revised along more radical lines in the French Declaration of the Rights of Man. Considered from the standpoint of a war of ideas, the American Revolution was refought, though the battle lines were redrawn, and many prominent revolutionaries, such as John Adams and Thomas Jefferson, found themselves in opposing camps.

Independence of the mother country had been secured; the question now presented itself whether a complete break with the past was either necessary or desirable. That American legal institutions, at the level of both public and private law, generally held firm against the radical doctrines of the French revolutionaries and their epigoni is due in no small part to the conservative influence of the Supreme Court in these critical years, and of John Marshall and Joseph Story in particular.

There are certain great principles of government, John Randolph of Roanoke once declared in the Congress, which, if not held inviolate, cease to safeguard individual liberty. And, he added, "if I were Philip, I would employ a man to say it every day."[133] Perhaps also it cannot be too often repeated that there are certain great principles of American government, and of American liberty, that owe their origin and existence to the Constitution rather than to the Declaration of Independence. True, the natural rights theories played a significant part in molding the American revolutionary mind, despite widespread misunderstanding of Locke; and they have continued to exert a powerful influence down to the present, though they are rarely identified as such. But they did not dominate American thinking exclusively, even in 1776; for there was an older, and in many ways more enduring, tradition of English thought in colonial and post-Revolutionary America, which found expression not only in the words of Blackstone and the public records of the Continental Congress,[134] but was permanently infused into the fundamental law more than a decade later.

[131] *Ibid.*, 70–71.
[132] For a discussion of the common law origin of the Bill of Rights, see Pound, *The Development of Constitutional Guarantees of Liberty.*
[133] *Annals*, 12 Congress, 2 sess., 184–85, as quoted in Kirk, *The Conservative Mind*, 134.
[134] See the *Journals of the Continental Congress*, October 14, 1774, in which the Con-

Predominantly legalistic, evolutionary rather than revolutionary, and consistent with traditional natural law principles, this conflicting and more conservative tradition of American political thought tended to rely more heavily on established political institutions and on liberties handed down through the English constitution, the colonial experience, and Anglo-American common law, than on novel theories of government built upon natural rights speculation. There are, then, two opposing "styles of thought" or political traditions emerging from the late eighteenth century, the one deriving from the exponents of natural rights as reflected in the Declaration of Independence, the other from the traditional natural law adherents as reflected in the Constitution. Of course, the true conflict between these two traditions was not realized by American political thinkers until the radicalism of the natural rights doctrines was clearly revealed in the French Revolution, when, for the first time they were implemented in an internal revolt to achieve a reordering of the entire political and social structure. Natural rights, for these purposes, was not attempted in the American states; there the more limited objective of political independence from the mother country was pursued.[135]

But the problem, as one political scientist has put it, is this: "We have all been brought up to believe that the Framers of the Constitution and the Bill of Rights were—though indeed subject to this or that other 'influence'—under the spell of John Locke and of Lockean ideas. . . . We have been brought up to believe further, therefore, that our continuity with the past is somehow through the Framers *and* Locke, who was himself continuous with the past."

However, the logic, and so the conclusion, "involves two whopping big fibs:

---

gress *unanimously* resolved that the colonies were entitled not to the rights of men, but "to the common law of England" and "to all the rights, liberties, and immunities of free and natural born subjects within the realm of England." Declaration and Resolves of the First Continental Congress, reprinted in *Documents of American History* (ed. by Henry Steele Commager), 82–84.

[135] The frequent assertion that the American Revolution, like the French, was a class struggle, remains to this day one of the great folk tales of the American past. The typical Loyalist has been pictured as the Tory gentleman, or as the wealthy Royalist, who lived in a great house, drove about in a fine carriage, and fought the patriots in order to protect special privileges. But, "Of all the approaches that might be used in an attempt to separate intelligibly the Loyalists from their Patriot kinsmen, that of occupation or social class seems the least fruitful. There was indeed a Tory oligarchy, but there was also a Whig oligarchy. . . . Even in New England the Loyalists were hardly the gentry pictured in legend. When an Act of Banishment was passed against some three hundred Loyalists in Massachusetts in 1778, they were listed by trade or profession. About a third were merchants, professional men, and gentlemen; another third were farmers, and the rest were artisans or labourers. . . . Most random lists of Loyalists show even less evidence of gentry than this. Always the gentlemen, esquires, merchants, and the like are far outnumbered by the yeomen, cordwainers, tailors, labourers, masons, blacksmiths, and their fellows." Nelson, *The American Tory*, 85–86.

namely, that the Framers were Lockeans (most of them, for one thing, opposed a bill of rights as part of the Constitution); and that you can establish continuity with the past through Locke."[136] The impress of Locke's doctrines is indeed not readily visible on the face of the Constitution or within any of its principles. One reason is that "In the Federal Convention of 1787 the problem confronting the delegates was strikingly different from that which had faced the members of the Second Continental Congress. . . . [T]he philosophical needs of the occasion were different from those of that period."[137] Independence had already been gained; the convention was not called to protest "acts of tyranny" or violations of "natural rights," but to establish a more stable and effective government, or, as the Preamble stated, "to form a more perfect union, establish justice, insure domestic tranquility, provide for the common defense, promote the general welfare, and secure the blessings of liberty . . . ." It is not unusual, therefore, that the Constitution makes no mention of equal or natural rights, the social contract, or the "right of revolution."

In fact, there is even some disagreement over the nature of the Constitution's commitment to the Lockean principle that the majority has a natural right to rule. Electors, appointed in "Each State . . . in such manner as the legislature thereof may direct," shall vote for president; justices of the Supreme Court shall be appointed by the president, with the advice and consent of the Senate, whose members are to be chosen by the state legislatures. Only in the House of Representatives, "the grand depository of the democratic principle," does the majority have a direct voice; yet section 2 of article 1 gives the several states a free hand in determining the qualifications of those who cast votes for representatives.

All this is not to argue that the Constitution is antidemocratic or undemocratic, but to suggest that, on the whole, there is scant evidence to support the claim that the Constitution fits comfortably within the modern natural rights tradition or that it is the finished product of Locke's teachings. The Constitution, after all, deals mainly with the powers and structure of the national government, not with individual rights.

It is true that Locke favored certain constitutional devices to check power and promote limited government which the framers later adopted—such as separation of powers; but so did a host of other political writers, not all of

[136] Willmoore Kendall, "The Social Contract: The Ultimate Issue between Liberalism and Conservatism," in his *The Conservative Affirmation*, 83–84.

[137] Benjamin F. Wright, *American Interpretations of Natural Law*, 124. "The Virginia Declaration of Rights of 1776 and the state constitutions are, of course, saturated with eighteenth-century ideas and resemble the French Declaration, which was directly influenced by them. But there are few traces of these distinctive traits in our federal Constitution and its amendments, which in contents and theory are nearer to 1689 than to 1776." Herbert W. Schneider, "Philosophical Differences between the Constitution and the Bill of Rights," in Conyers Read (ed.), *The Constitution Reconsidered*, 155.

whom were followers of Locke. In fact, Blackstone appears to have exerted a far greater influence in the young republic of 1787 than Locke with respect to the doctrine of separation of powers. "There were modifications of Montesquieu's thought in the *Commentaries on the Laws of England*, which appeared in 1765–69, and as the *Commentaries* were regarded as authoritative in the American colonies as well as in England, it was often through Blackstone's eyes that the colonists saw the Montesquieu theory."[138] Further, it was Blackstone, not Locke, who expounded "the idea of a partial separation of persons and functions which for him was the basis of a balanced constitution, and a few years later, with some change of emphasis, [was] basically the same doctrine ... used by Madison to explain the nature of the Federal Constitution of the United States."[139]

The Jeffersonian assault against the common law in the early nineteenth century, it should be remembered, was paralleled by an attack on the American doctrine of separation of powers, and those who criticized the adoption and retention of the common law often, in the same breath, and in the name of democracy or natural rights, condemned the Constitution as well. "The Jeffersonians," Professor Vile has noticed, "attacked the Constitution on the grounds that it was the instrument for the reintroduction into America of the ideas of monarchy and aristocracy, and that it was constructed from materials borrowed from the despised English Constitution, instead of being wholly fashioned anew upon American principles."[140]

To associate the Bill of Rights with the natural rights philosophy is equally parlous, in light of the fact that most of the "rights" guaranteed are constitutional and common law rights that evolved independent of Locke's teachings. "The English common law, colonial charters, legislative enactments, and a variety of events in the thirteen colonies were the chief elements contributing to the rationale for a bill of rights."[141] In addition, the Bill of Rights, as will later be shown, was originally intended to be as much a guarantee to the states as it was to the individual that the federal government

---

[138] M. J. C. Vile, *Constitutionalism and the Separation of Powers*, 102.

[139] *Ibid.*, 103.

[140] *Ibid.*, 161. In his later years "Jefferson came to accept that extreme view of a constitutional system of government which Nedham had propounded in 1654, with 'all power flowing in distinct channels' from the people. It was fundamentally the same philosophy as Sieyès had argued before the National Assembly in 1789. It was the complete rejection of checks and balances. . . . The extreme nature of this doctrine was very clear to Jefferson, and he more than once forbad Samuel Kercheval to publish a letter in which it is set out. Although Jefferson was reluctant to acknowledge the doctrine publicly through his letters, the philosophy they contained had been publicly pronounced in America at considerable length by John Taylor, who has been described as 'the philosopher of Jeffersonian Republicanism.'" *Ibid.*, 166.

[141] Robert Allen Rutland, *The Birth of the Bill of Rights, 1776–1791*, v.

would in most instances have no jurisdiction in the general area of civil liberties or personal "rights." Those who maintain that the Bill of Rights is nothing more than a successful attempt to guarantee to each individual his "natural rights" (or common law rights) are thus confronted with the fact that the first eight amendments, although they guarantee each individual that the *federal government* shall not deny the enumerated rights, say nothing about the several *states*—which, by inference, are therefore free to legislate in these areas and to protect or *deny* any one of the personal "rights" listed in the Bill of Rights.

In other words, the Bill of Rights may be construed as a guarantee to the several states that they may define the scope and nature of the civil liberties of their citizens, and that the federal government, by virtue of the Bill of Rights, is denied the power of guaranteeing anyone his civil liberties, except as against federal encroachment. Let it be recalled that in the absence of the Fourteenth Amendment, which restricts the states, uniformity of rights and liberties was largely impossible. Both the Marshall and Taney courts were constitutionally prevented from undertaking a full-scale invasion into the area of civil liberties. Their power to review state practices was limited in large measure to economic and property rights, as the states were generally permitted under the Bill of Rights to deal with civil and political liberties as they saw fit.

If, then, natural rights as proclaimed by Locke are not so obviously inherent in either the Constitution or the Bill of Rights, can it be maintained that the Constitution is a product of the natural law tradition, that it is declaratory of natural law principles? Does the Constitution, being fundamental law, authorize judges as a matter of logical necessity to resort to the natural law in deciding cases?

More than a decade before Joseph Story was appointed to the high bench, debate erupted in the Supreme Court in the famous case of *Calder* v. *Bull* (1798) over the question of the Court's authority to nullify a state law as violative of "the great first principles of the social compact." "I cannot subscribe to the omnipotence of a State legislature, or that it is absolute and without control," argued Justice Samuel Chase. "The people of the United States erected their constitutions or forms of government," he continued, "to establish justice, to promote the general welfare, to secure the blessings of liberty, and to protect their persons and property from violence. The purpose for which men enter into society will determine the nature and terms of the social compact.... There are acts which the federal, or state, legislature cannot do, without exceeding their authority. There are certain vital principles in our free republican governments, which will determine and overrule an apparent and flagrant abuse of legislative power.... An act of the legislature (for I cannot call it a law) contrary to the great first principles of the social compact, cannot be considered a rightful exercise of legislative authority."[142]

Justice James Iredell disagreed. He conceded, "It is true, that some speculative jurists have held, that a legislative act against natural justice must, in itself, be void." But, he insisted, "I cannot think that, under such a government any court of justice would possess a power to declare it so.... The ideals of natural justice are regulated by no fixed standard: the ablest and the purest men have differed upon the subject."[143]

Whatever the merits of Iredell's view, it "was disregarded at one time or another by all of the leading judges and advocates of the initial period of our constitutional history, an era which closes about 1830."[144] In the Marshall and Taney courts the leading advocate of judicial review on natural law principles was Judge Story; but with the arrival of Story on the Court in 1811, the issue assumed broader proportions and shifted unnoticed to different grounds.

Rejecting Chase's Lockean appeal to the "social compact" and Iredell's plea for legislative supremacy, Story turned to traditional natural law and so pursued a different path of reasoning. Locke, who at best only shared the spotlight with Blackstone in the Revolutionary period, and whose influence in 1787 was all the more obscure, faded farther into the background; for Joseph Story openly repudiated Locke's revolutionary doctrines. More than thirty crucial years elapsed in the formative era of American constitutional development while he sat on the high bench wielding as a powerful instrument of jurisprudence the natural law principles of Burke, Blackstone, Coke, and Bracton. Mischievous and defiant state governments, guilty of democratic excesses and violations of liberty and justice, were his usual targets. In this way, the bonds that held the American Constitution to the English constitution from which it sprang, and to the classical and Christian heritage in which it was conceived, were strengthened and reaffirmed.

Although these natural law principles were nowhere stated in the Constitution, Story denied all accusations of judicial usurpation and rejected the charges of his Democratic foes that he distorted the meaning of things. The Constitution, of course, does not specifically authorize the members of the Supreme Court to decide cases upon the principles of natural law or equity; but as one legal scholar has written,

If it is true that precedents are employed only to discover principles, so it is true that principles are employed to discover justice. . . . Nobody claims that the law always achieves ideal moral justice, but whatever the inevitable technicalities of legal science may be, they exist for the prosecution of one aim only, the aim of the judge's office: to do justice between litigants. . . . This dominant purpose all prece-

142 *Calder* v. *Bull*, 3 Dallas 388 (1798).
143 *Ibid.*, 398–99.
144 Edward S. Corwin, *Liberty against Government*, 66.

dents, all arguments, and all principles must subserve. . . . To what, then, do the judges turn? To those principles of reason, morality, and social utility which are the fountainhead of English law and of all law. The judge is not embarrassed by the absence of "authority" in clear cases of this kind, for no authority is needed for the affirmation of the very essence of the law.[145]

This is not to say judges are to disregard the law, scorn all precedent, and in single-minded fashion make justice the sole and deliberate aim in each case, but to emphasize the importance of *justice under law* and the need of keeping law and morality in general harmony and balance; for the intent of the law is not always perfectly clear to the judge, and there will be times when he must rely upon his own intellectual and moral resources in deciding a case. In such instances the principles of natural law, while they may on the one hand serve to expand the power of the judiciary beyond the stated limits of the law, may also operate as a restraining influence by providing, together with as much law and precedent as is available, an objective moral standard by which to weigh the cause of each litigant. Hence obeisance to natural law may actually have the salutary effect of discouraging judicial officers from deciding cases on personal whim or wholly subjective interpretations that fit the needs of the moment.

In any event, the problem of individual interpretation can best be avoided by general adherence to a basic principle deeply rooted in the natural law tradition: to the principle of rule of law which, when properly understood and followed, will in the long run bring about in an indirect way the desired result—justice between men. While there is no denying that a law may be bad and unjust, it is also important to bear in mind that "its general and abstract formulation reduces this danger to a minimum. The protective character of the law, and its very *raison d'être*, are to be found in its generality."[146] In other words, the chances of unjust and oppressive laws are minimized by the passage of laws that are general and equal, so that the real problem of justice is not so much the interpretation of the law as the making of it—at least in a system where the judges do, in fact, feel bound by the intent of the law.

In a profound but much neglected study of this very issue, Friedrich A. Hayek has shown that the principle of rule of law is actually "a doctrine concerning what the law ought to be, concerning the general attributes that particular laws should possess. This is important because today the conception of the rule of law is sometimes confused with the requirement of mere legality in all government action. The rule of law, of course, presupposes complete legality, but this is not enough: if a law gave the government unlimited power to act as it pleased, all its functions would be legal, but it would certainly not be under the rule of law. The rule of law, therefore, is also more than

[145] C. K. Allen, *Law in the Making*, 276–77.
[146] L. Duguit, as quoted in Friedrich A. Hayek, *The Constitution of Liberty*, 210.

constitutionalism: it requires that all laws conform to certain principles"[147]—namely, that they be general and abstract, known and certain, equal, and preferably, that they be interpreted by "independent judges who are not concerned with any temporary ends of government."[148]

Few would deny that the principle of rule of law is inherent in the American Constitution or that members of the Supreme Court would be justified in resting their decisions upon it. The Constitution is a product of the natural law tradition, of the natural law conception that a higher law ought to govern current legislation. "The idea of a constitution, therefore, involves not only the idea of hierarchy of authority or power but also that of a hierarchy of rules of laws, where those possessing a higher degree of generality and proceeding from a superior authority control the contents of the more specific laws that are passed by a delegated authority."[149]

Important as they are in understanding the general theory of the Constitution, the principles themselves do not uniformly explain the *law* of the Constitution. In the formal sense the Constitution is "the nucleus of a set of ideas. Surrounding this and overlapping it to a greater or less extent, is constitutional law, in the formal sense too of a rule of decision. Outside this, finally, but interpreting it and underlying it is constitutional theory, which may be defined as the sum total of ideas of some historical standing as to what the Constitution is or ought to be."[150] In matters of constitutional law, then, as distinguished from constitutional theory, it would seem that a sole reliance upon the general intellectual framework and historical background of the Constitution will not suffice; hence the intent of the framers as regards both the overall objectives of the constitutional framework and the purpose and meaning of each clause, as understood in 1787, must also be determined, in order to comprehend the total design of the fundamental law.

The exigency of the problem is more easily stated than are the means of

---

[147] *Ibid.*, 205.

[148] *Ibid.*, 211. Rule of law and rule of men may thus be distinguished on the basis of the actual content of the law rather than on the method of its enactment. If it is the type of law which, for example, coerces named individuals or discriminates against certain designated segments of society, we may conclude that such a law probably has the effect of being a command by those in a position of power who wish to make others mere tools of their ends. This is the rule of men. If it is the type of law which applies to the general population and merely restrains individual behavior, then it is likely to be rule of law. The fundamental issue is not so much who made the law—though this is important from another standpoint—as what the law is. Hence, democratic assemblies are, conceivably, just as capable as any other type of governing body of violating rule of law. For a closely reasoned analysis of the doctrine of rule of law, see *ibid.*, especially 148–219.

[149] *Ibid.*, 178.

[150] Edward S. Corwin, "Constitution v. Constitutional Theory," *American Political Science Review*, Vol. XIX, No. 2 (May, 1925), reprinted in *American Constitutional History: Essays by Edward S. Corwin* (ed. by Alpheus T. Mason and Gerald Garvey), 101.

solving it; for at each turn and at every level of investigation, beginning with the broader issues of constitutional theory and descending to the narrower questions of constitutional law respecting the proper interpretation of a single phrase, there are almost unsurmountable barriers. Aside from the confusion surrounding the natural law foundations of the Constitution, the complex relationship between democracy and the Constitution has long been a source of confusion and discord in American politics.

Throughout American history the charge has frequently been made, for example, that the Constitution is basically hostile towards democracy and must be evaded or warped in order to permit democracy to function. In the ratification struggle Antifederalists denounced the Constitution as an obnoxious instrument of government calculated to establish rule by aristocracy. Not long ago, Progressives, led by James Allen Smith, were repeating such charges, insisting that the Constitution was a "reactionary" document, wholly unfit for liberal democracy of the twentieth century.[151]

At bottom, the democracy of the Constitution is a question of degree. Inasmuch as the Constitution does tolerate *some* democracy, the real problem, therefore, is whether it tolerates *enough* to justify the assertion of Publius that the framers did in fact establish a "democratic republic." What the framers hoped to achieve was a balance between majority rule and limited government, which would allow for the operation of both under a fundamental law of the land.

This is the problem to which Madison addressed himself in *The Federalist*, Number 51. "In framing a government which is to be administered over men," he observed, "the great difficulty lies in this: you must first enable the government to control the governed; and in the next place oblige it to control itself. A dependence on the people is, no doubt, the primary control of the government; but experience has taught mankind the necessity of auxiliary precautions."[152] Understood, then, as a system of government allowing for limited democracy, wherein the power of the majority would be restricted by "auxiliary" constitutional devices, it would appear that the Constitution, as Martin Diamond has insisted, is now and always has been essentially democratic.[153]

---

[151] More recently, Robert E. Brown, Forrest McDonald, Martin Diamond, and others have challenged this interpretation. See the collection of writings on this subject in Willmoore Kendall and George Carey (eds.), *Liberalism Versus Conservatism: The Continuing Debate in American Government*, 3–58.

[152] (Modern Library ed.), 337.

[153] "Democracy and the Federalist: A Reconsideration of the Framers' Intent," *American Political Science Review*, Vol. LIII, No. 1 (Mar., 1959), 52–68. The latest and most thorough study dealing with this question is that of Paul Eidelberg, who argues that "the Republic established by the Founding Fathers was understood by them to be a *Mixed Regime.*" *The Philosophy of the American Constitution: A Reinterpretation of the Intentions of the Founding Fathers*, 3.

Whether by accident or design, the task of refereeing the game called democracy according to the rules of the Constitution has fallen on the shoulders of the federal judiciary. The task is a difficult one, primarily because the judges often lack clearly stated rules to go by and not infrequently are compelled to rely on their own subjective interpretations, which are often vulnerable to valid criticism. The fundamental principles of the game—separation of powers, checks and balances, federalism—are nowhere spelled out with force and clarity. The wording of the document is frequently vague, and sometimes intentionally so, inviting judicial manipulation. One thinks of the ruling handed down by the framers regarding limitations on Congress' power of taxation, as reported by Madison in his notes on the Federal Convention: "Mr. King asked what was the precise meaning of *direct* taxation? No one answered."[154]

Even when ascertained, the intent of the framers, according to many political scientists and legal scholars, is neither binding nor relevant. Since the turn of the century, powerful influences in American legal circles have been at work—notably legal realism and sociological jurisprudence—which stress the need for constitutional adaptability to current political fermentations, and which denigrate the importance of judicial adherence to long-standing principles of legal justice or the intent of the framers. Constitutional tinkering has become not only a habit, but a standard of judicial excellence. This general trend away from the idea that fixed principles or the original meaning of a clause are binding upon the judges is reflected in the popular slogan, "What's the Constitution among friends?"

Few scholars have exercised a greater influence in the field of constitutional law in recent times than the late Edward S. Corwin. His studies expounding the complexities of constitutional development are legion. But Professor Corwin preached the doctrine of the living Constitution, and he urged students of American government—as well as the judges—to disregard the intent of the framers, particularly when it stood in the way of New Deal reforms.[155] "For many practical purposes," he wrote as early as 1925, "the *Constitution* is the judicial version of it—*constitutional law*. The latter in turn derives in no small part from speculative ideas about what the framers of the constitution or the

---

[154] Session of Tuesday, Aug. 21, 1787, *Debates in the Federal Convention of 1787*, reported by James Madison (ed. by Gaillard Hunt and James Brown Scott), 435. In *Hylton v. United States*, 3 Dallas 171 (1796), it was decided that a tax which could not be conveniently apportioned should not be classified as a direct tax and that direct taxes should include only capitation and land taxes. In *Pollock v: Farmer's Loan and Trust*, 158 U.S. 601 (1895), however, the Court held that a tax on income derived from property was a direct tax and was therefore void because it was not apportioned. See Sixteenth Amendment to the Constitution.

[155] See, for example, Corwin's *The Twilight of the Supreme Court, Commerce Power Versus States Rights, Court over Constitution, and Constitutional Revolution, Ltd.*

generation which adopted it intended it should mean—*constitutional theory*. Such ideas, nevertheless, whatever their historical basis ... have no application to the main business of constitutional interpretation, which is to keep the constitution adjusted to the advancing needs of time."[156] Indeed, he went on to say, deference to the framers' intent frequently contributed "to rendering the written instrument rigid and inflexible far beyond what is the reasonable consequence of its terms." The only proper method of interpreting the Constitution, he concluded, "is that of regarding it as a living statute, palpitating with the purpose of the hour, reenacted with every waking breath of the American people, whose primitive right to determine their institutions is its sole claim to validity as a law and as the matrix of laws under our system. ... If there still must be an appeal to the framers of the constitution, let it be Marshall's appeal: 'The Constitution (was) intended to endure for ages, and consequently to be adapted to the various crises of human affairs.' "[157]

This is legal positivism, pure and simple. In American jurisprudence it may go by another name, "legal realism," or perhaps "sociological jurisprudence," but the results are the same: the separation of law and morality, fact and standard, will and norm, that leads ultimately, as Professor Hallowell observes, to a theory of constitutional interpretation which "is more congenial to despotism than to freedom."[158]

What are "the advancing needs of time"? What transient majorities and public officials declare them to be? Are election issues so clearly defined that judges can accurately follow the will of the majority? And upon what basis can judges claim the authority to define "the advancing needs of time," even supposing they know what they are? To raise such questions is to state the absurdity of Corwin's proposition.

The question unavoidably presents itself: at what point does judicial law-

[156] Corwin, "Constitution v. Constitutional Theory," reprinted in *American Constitutional History*, 108.

[157] *Ibid*. According to Clinton Rossiter, "Most talk about the intentions of the Framers —whether in ... the opinions of judges, or in the monographs of professors—is as irrelavant as it is unpersuasive, as stale as it is strained, as rhetorically absurd as it is historically unsound. No one, surely, can read the records of the Grand Convention ... and not come to this harsh yet honest conclusion." (*1787: The Grand Convention*, 333.) In reply to this astonishing statement, Profesor Eidelberg acutely remarks: "That Rossiter should say *no one* can avoid this 'harsh yet honest conclusion,' when countless judges and professors have done precisely that, is a cause for wonder. And how he would evaluate his own work in view of this 'harsh yet honest conclusion' is another cause for wonder—for he attempts to elucidate the intentions of the Framers for the better part of three hundred pages! Apparently, the only 'clear intent of the Framers,' according to Rossiter, 'was that each generation of Americans should pursue its destiny as a community of free men.' If *this* is their only 'clear' intent, why study their writings? Indeed, if their writings are as obscure as Rossiter here suggests, they are not worthy of being studied at all." *The Philosophy of the American Constitution*, 293–94, n. 3.

[158] John H. Hallowell, *Main Currents in Modern Political Thought*, 358.

making become an intolerable practice in a democratic system of government? Recognizing that they are expected to interpret and apply constitutional rules of varying degrees of obscurity, in deference to an undefined concept of limited democracy, certain members of the Court have from time to time felt obliged to offer principles of constitutional interpretation, if not to relieve their consciences, then their burdens. But even Justice Story, who more than any other member of the Supreme Court succeeded in establishing reasonable and viable principles of construction, was unable to apply them consistently.

A perusal of Story's "Rules of Interpretation" in his *Commentaries on the Constitution*[159] demonstrates clearly enough that strict adherence to a philosophy of narrow or enlarged construction, judicial activism or judicial self-restraint, ultimately fails, if only because there is a time for both, depending upon the constitutional issue, the wording under examination, the context in which it is placed, and the circumstances of the case. The conclusion seems inescapable that there will be moments when the Court is unable to pinpoint the proper constitutional ruling and will of necessity actually make the rule, even to the point of altering the Constitution. Such, it would seem, is a natural and inevitable consequence, given the fact we have a Constitution replete with nebulous phrases, the proper interpretation of which cannot always be determined by going back to contemporary construction or the debates of the federal and state conventions. In this sense the Constitution is, indeed, "what the judges say it is."

Beyond this point, however, judicial constitution-making raises serious problems pertaining to democratic government. We may join the realists in snickering at the judges of the old school like Judge Story, who in their innocence and naïveté sincerely believed that they merely "found" the law when deciding a case and left intact the original understanding of those who framed and ratified the Constitution. But if they did alter the Constitution, it was more likely by accident than design.

The members of the Marshall Court, in fact, did not even have access to the intent of the framers through Madison's notes.[160] They commonly ac-

---

[159] See I, ch. 5, secs. 382–442.

[160] For a number of reasons, Madison refused to publish his notes on the proceedings during his lifetime, and they did not appear before the public eye until 1840—that is, fifty-three years after the Constitution was signed, and all the members of the Convention were no longer living. See the excellent account of all the original sources relating to the Constitution in Charles Warren, *The Making of the Constitution*, 783–804. Interesting it is that Madison (and apparently a few states' rightists of the period) thought that the original intent of the framers should be sought not in the Federal Convention, but in the various state ratifying conventions. "But whatever respect may be thought due to the intention of the Convention which prepared and proposed the Constitution, as presumptive evidence of the general understanding at the time the language was used, it must be kept in mind that the only authoritative intentions were those of the people of the States,

knowledged the binding authority of "original intent" when it could be ascertained and generally followed a philosophy of construction that did not prevent, but at least discouraged and condemned, excessive constitutional tinkering.

Agreed, judges make law, but is this any reason to recommend the practice as a general principle of judicial construction? When the rule *is* clear of doubt, is it not the task of the judge to "find" the law and apply it to the case, as always? Before resorting to an individual interpretation, should not the judge make a sincere and honest attempt to discover the original intent?

A strong nationalist, Joseph Story nevertheless warned against unrestricted interpretation and recognized that there are certain enduring constitutional principles which are valid for all times. His thoughts on this subject are worthy of extended quotation:

The Constitution of the United States is to receive a reasonable interpretation of its language, and its powers, keeping in view the objects and purposes, for which these powers were conferred. By a reasonable interpretation, we mean, that in case the words are susceptible of two different senses, the one strict, the other more enlarged, that should be adopted, which is most consonant with the apparent objects and intent of the Constitution. . . . Of course we do not mean, that the words for this purpose are to be strained beyond their common and natural sense; but keeping within that limit, the exposition is to have a fair and just latitude. . . . On the other hand, a rule of equal importance is, not to enlarge the construction of a given power beyond the fair scope of its terms, merely because the restriction is inconvenient, impolitic, or even mischievous. If it be mischievous, the power of redressing the evil lies with the people by an exercise of the power of amendment. . . . Nor should it ever be lost sight of, that the government of the United States is one of limited and enumerated powers; and that a departure from the true import and sense of its powers is, *pro tanto*, the establishment of a new constitution. It is doing for the people, what they have not chosen to do for themselves.[161]

How far we have departed from these rules of interpretation is suggested by the fact that judges nowadays are openly encouraged to ignore the original intent of the Constitution. But to ignore the original intent of the Constitution is to subvert not only the principle of rule of law, but a principle of democracy. Past misunderstanding has often led to the false assumption that judicial review, considered in the abstract, is essentially undemocratic in that it allows members of the judiciary, who are not elected, to impose their will on the people's representatives. If this were a pure democracy, with one, single

as expressed thro' the Conventions which ratified the Constitution." (Madison to M. L. Hurlbert, May, 1830, as quoted *ibid.*, 800–801, n. 1.) See also Madison to S. H. Smith, Feb. 2, 1827, and to Thomas Ritchie, Sept. 15, 1821, *ibid.* See the criticisms of this position by Story, *Commentaries on the Constitution*, I, sec. 407, pp. 390–92, n. 1.

[161] *Commentaries on the Constitution*, I, secs. 419 and 426, pp. 404, 409–10.

majority governing in the absence of a fundamental law, judicial review would indeed be undemocratic.

But in fact our system of government is run by a coalition of majorities. Different people elect different political officials at different times, and no single official, including the president himself, can in reality speak for "the majority of the American people."

Similarly, members of the Supreme Court are part of the democratic process in that they speak for past majorities. As Justice William Paterson declared many years ago, the Constitution "is the form of government, delineated by the mighty hand of the *people*, in which certain first principles of fundamental laws are established. . . . [I]t contains *the permanent will of the people* and is the Supreme law of the land."[162] It necessarily follows that there is nothing undemocratic about judicial review in principle, in view of the magistrates' obligation "to support and defend" the permanent will of the people in preference to the temporary will of transient majorities.

Similarly, when the Court blindly submits to current policy and *refuses* to exercise judicial review, it may well be committing an undemocratic act by permitting the will of transient or temporary majorities to take precedence over the permanent will of the people, in violation of the supremacy clause.[163] Thus, when the members of the Court openly defy "the permanent will of the people" under the pretext they speak for temporary majorities or the "advancing needs of the time," they violate their oaths of office and subvert a democratic principle of the American political system—a system which, as the Preamble states, was constitutionally ordained by "We the People," meaning the people of each generation, and not merely the people of 1787.[164]

To put it another way: if a coalition of majorities of the moment, speaking through the Congress and the president, cannot override the permanent will of the people (that is, the Constitution) even by accident, there seems to be no justification for arguing that the Supreme Court should be encouraged to achieve the same ends deliberately.

The conclusion is unavoidable: the doctrine of the living Constitution

[162] *Van Horne's Lessee* v. *Dorrance*, 2 Dallas 308 (1795).

[163] For an analysis of the Supreme Court's democratic role in the American political system, see my article on "The Doctrine of Judicial Democracy," *Modern Age*, Vol. XIV, No. 1 (Winter, 1969–70), 19–35.

[164] As Story notes: "The last clause in the preamble is to 'secure the blessings of liberty to ourselves and our posterity.' And surely no object could be more worthy of the wisdom and ambition of the best men in any age. If there be any thing, which may justly challenge the admiration of all mankind, it is that sublime patriotism, which, looking beyond its own times, and its own fleeting purposes, aims to secure the permanent happiness of posterity by laying the broad foundations of government upon immovable principles of justice. Our affections, indeed, may naturally be presumed to outlive the brief limits of our own lives, and to repose with deep sensibility upon our own immediate descendants." *Commentaries on the Constitution*, I, sec. 506, pp. 485–86.

amounts to little more than the willful disregard of the expressed or implied intent of the framers. As a theory of interpretation, it amounts to little more than a general call for unrestricted constitutional change in the name of progress, which flies in the face of fundamental principles upon which the Constitution rests. Supremacy of the Constitution, rule of law, democratic and limited government are not likely to survive in an atmosphere in which a small body of nonelected officials is encouraged to sit as a permanent constituent assembly, rewriting the Constitution "to fit the advancing needs of time."

It is all well and good to keep the Constitution up to date, so to speak, and to recall the advice of Judge Story against excessively narrow construction of the Constitution. "The instrument was not intended to provide merely for the exigencies of a few years, but was to endure through a long lapse of ages, the events of which were locked up in the inscrutable purposes of Providence."[165] But if the Constitution is to bend with the times, so must public officials and the general public bend with the Constitution; for a constitution that is all sail and no anchor will surely be adrift on the open sea, where the currents are strong and the tempests are severe. In the words of Edmund Burke:

One of the first and most leading principles on which the commonwealth and its laws are consecrated, is lest the temporary possessors and life-renters in it, unmindful of what they have received from their ancestors, or of what is due to their posterity, should act as if they were the entire masters; that they should not think it among their rights to cut off the entail, or commit waste on the inheritance, by destroying at their pleasure the whole original fabric of their society; hazarding to leave to those who come after them a ruin instead of a habitation—and teaching these successors as little to respect their contrivances, as they had themselves respected the institutions of their forefathers. By this unprincipled facility of changing the state as often, and as much, and in as many ways, as there are floating fancies or fashions, the whole chain and continuity of the commonwealth would be broken. No one generation could link with another. Men would become little better than the flies of a summer.[166]

[165] *Martin* v. *Hunter's Lessee*, 1 Wheaton 326 (1816).

[166] "Reflections on the Revolution in France," *The Works of Edmund Burke*, II (ed. by Henry Bohn), 366–67.

CHAPTER III

Christianity and the Common Law

> *It should be observed that, if a systematic religion is true at all, intrusion on its part into politics is not only legitimate but is the very work it comes into the world to do. Being, by hypothesis, enlightened supernaturally, it is able to survey the conditions and consequences of any kind of action much better than the wisest legislator. . . . so that the spheres of systematic religion and politics, far from being independent or incommensurable, are in principle identical.*
>
> GEORGE SANTAYANA, *Dominations and Powers*

IN the summer of 1824, Thomas Jefferson wrote a letter to the English radical John Cartwright, in which he impugned the widely held belief of English and American lawyers that Christianity was a part of the common law. Asserting that judges had "stole this law upon us," Jefferson employed his legal skills to trace this "judicial forgery" to Sir Henry Finch's famous work, *The Common Law* (1613), whence it was passed through Hale, Blackstone, and Mansfield to America. In translating an opinion by Prisot[1] in the Yearbook for 1458, which held that the laws of the Holy Church in ancient writing (*en ancien scripture*) were acknowledged by the common law, Finch had erroneously interpreted the phrase "*en ancien scripture*" to mean "in holy scripture," creating the false notion that the common law incorporated the Christian religion.[2]

Thus began a controversy of far-reaching implications respecting church-state relations in America. In the principle that Christianity was a part of the common law, "Jefferson saw the transmitting of the maxim from English to American shores as the transplanting of the seeds of establishment."[3] The

---

[1] Prisot, who had assisted Littleton in the writing of his *Tenures*, was a highly respected lawyer. In 1449 he became chief justice of the common pleas.

[2] Thomas Jefferson to John Cartwright, June 15, 1824, *Writings* (Library ed.), XVI, 42–52. See also Jefferson to John Adams, Jan. 24, 1814, *ibid.*, XIV, 71–79; Jefferson to Thomas Cooper, Feb. 10, 1814, *ibid.*, 85–97. Jefferson's account of "Whether Christianity Is Part of the Common Law" was affixed to his *Reports of Cases Determined in the General Court of Virginia* (1764) and is reprinted in *Writings* (ed. by Ford), I, 360–67.

[3] Mark de Wolfe Howe, *The Garden and the Wilderness: Religion and Government in American Constitutional History*, 28.

unwritten doctrine that an impregnable "wall" was constructed by our constitutional architects, separating religious and governmental affairs, remains to this very day one of the most warmly debated issues in American constitutional law; yet lawyers and judges have almost entirely overlooked the fact that the first great legal debate after the adoption of the Bill of Rights on the question of separation between church and state in America took place between Jefferson and Judge Story.

Not only is Story the only Supreme Court justice who has ever attempted to answer Jefferson, but he is also the first member of the Court to deliver opinions on the subject of religious freedom in America. Foreshadowing the present conflict, Story's opinions and his demurrer to Jefferson are of especial importance today because they are related directly to the proper relationship between the various state governments and religion as understood by the legal profession in the early nineteenth century. They also raise considerable doubts about the constitutional and historical accuracy of the Everson[4] and Mc-Collum[5] decisions, which ushered in the current doctrines, and of the more recent school prayer[6] and Bible-reading cases[7] of 1962 and 1963.

No sooner was Jefferson's letter received by Cartwright than it was published, widely circulated, and brought to the attention of Judge Story by Edward Everett. That Story seized upon this letter as an opportunity to ridicule Jefferson and challenge his invincible influence was probably not surprising even to Jefferson. A long-standing animosity had existed between them since the embargo affair. Like Marshall, Story doubted Jefferson's loyalties to the Union, and he had frequently warned his friends and associates that Jefferson was in all probability the evil-minded genius behind the spreading disintegration of the country.[8] Jefferson's sympathies toward the common law were also suspect, and his unorthodox religious opinions constituted a favorite subject of public gossip. His attack on the principle that Christianity was a part of the common law, then, probably confirmed what Story had suspected all the while.

Story believed Christianity and the common law to be the foundation of the Union, liberty, and social order. So thoroughly convinced was he of the indissoluble bond between Christianity and the common law that his first reaction after hearing of Jefferson's grave accusation was that of sheer incredulity.

[4] *Everson* v. *Board of Education*, 330 U.S. 1 (1947).

[5] *McCollum* v. *Champaign Board of Education*, 333 U.S. 203 (1948).

[6] *Engel* v. *Vitale*, 370 U.S. 421 (1962).

[7] *Abingdon School District* v. *Schempp*, and *Murray* v. *Curlett*, 374 U.S. 203 (1963).

[8] See Marshall to Story, Sept. 18, 1821, Massachusetts Historical Society *Proceedings*, 2nd Series, Vol. XIV, (1900–1901), 330–31; Story to Jeremiah Mason, Jan. 10, 1822, *Life and Letters*, I, 411; Story to Samuel Fay, Feb. 15, 1830, *ibid.*, II, 33; Story to Edward Everett, May 31, 1832, *ibid.*

"It appears to me inconceivable," he wrote in exasperation to Everett, "how any man can doubt, that Christianity is a part of the common law."[9]

Most surely, the Sage of Monticello had worked himself into a difficult position. Even if there had been a mistranslation, the question now seemed moot. His entire argument rested on a selected phrase of a single case decided back in 1458, and the whole weight of authority in the ensuing three and one-half centuries was overwhelmingly on the side of Story. That the members of the judiciary should not permit "offenses which strike at our national religion" to go unpunished was an established principle of English law, Blackstone had explained to English and American lawyers in 1765. The temporal courts, he went on to say, "resent the public affront to religion and morality on which all governments must depend for support." They had in the past, therefore, proscribed "gross impieties and general immoralities" against God and Christianity. One such offense was that of "blasphemy against the Almighty by denying his being or providence; or by contumelious reproaches of our Savior Christ. Whither also may be referred all profane scoffing at the holy scripture, or exposing it to contempt and ridicule. These are offenses punishable at common law by fine and imprisonment . . . for Christianity is part of the laws of England."[10]

Blackstone's remark could not have provoked much comment at the time, for the common law crime of blasphemy was already firmly established when he wrote his *Commentaries*; and there were ample precedents to support him. Although not cited by Blackstone, the first indictment for blasphemy seems to have occurred in 1663, when

the dramatist Sir Charles Sedley and a group of his aristocratic boon-companions exhibited themselves naked on the balcony of a tavern of ill-fame in Covent Garden, before a crowd of several hundred persons. They proceeded to gestures and acts so gross that the crowd stoned them from the balcony and that even the laxest editors of Pepy's *Diary* have not dared to print his description of the scene. Yet the general opinion was, as Pepys regretfully records, that there no longer existed any authority

[9] Sept. 15, 1824, *Life and Letters*, I, 430. "I had not seen Mr. Jefferson's letter, my own newspaper having been mislaid or miscarried, until after you referred me to it. . . . Upon what other foundations [than Christianity] stands her [England's] whole ecclesiastical system? Yet that system is as old as any part of the Common Law which we can clearly trace. Can you believe that when heresy was punishable with death, and Statute Laws were made to enforce Christian rites and doctrines, it was no part of the Law of England, that to revile the established religion was a crime? Prisot did not make, or declare the law, in the case referred to; he spoke to a fact. In his age, England was overrun with all sorts of ecclesiastical establishments, nunneries, and monasteries, and Christianity constituted a great part of the public concern of all men. To suppose it had not the entire sanction of the State, is, with reverence be it spoken, to contradict all history" (*ibid.*). Story frequently stated his Christian beliefs to his friends and associates. See, for example, Story to Chancellor Kent, June 24, 1831, *ibid.*, II, 56.

[10] *Commentaries*, IV, 59.

that could legally repress such outrages on public decency. But under Foster, Lord Chief Justice of the King's Bench, by a bold innovation, promptly created one (17 St. Tr. 155); so Sedley, on being indicted, was fined £500.[11]

Sir Matthew Hale of the King's Bench, however, is generally regarded as having established the common law crime of blasphemy in *Taylor's Case*, and it is this decision, together with the *Woolston* case, which Blackstone cited as precedent. In 1676 a man named Taylor uttered violent and offensive words against religion. He was fined, pilloried three times, and ordered to produce sureties of his good behavior during the rest of his life. Asserting that "contumelious reproaches to God or of the religion established are punishable here," Justice Hale declared that "The Christian religion is a part of the law itself."[12] Thus, through Hale, was created the maxim that Christianity was a part of the common law, and it "acquired a currency which lasted to our own day."[13] Proceeding upon the authority of *Taylor's Case*, the King's Bench upheld the conviction of one Woolston in 1729, who had denounced the biblical narratives in coarse and scurrilous language. The court held that "Christianity in general is parcel of the common law of England; and therefore to be protected by it."[14]

In his brief defending the maxim that Christianity was a part of the common law, Story assailed Jefferson's position on three grounds. Turning to an article he had written in his Common Place Book in 1811,[15] Story, apparently after slight revision, published his reply to Jefferson in the *American Jurist* in 1833.[16]

His first point, sufficient in itself to quash the indictment, was simply that there had been no mistranslation. The case in controversy was a *quare impedit* action against a bishop, recorded in French in 34 Henry VI, 38, 40, which had been brought by one Humphrey Bohun. Claiming to be the patron of a vacant benefice, Bohun had presented a priest to the bishop of Lincoln for institution. But on that very same day another claimant of the same advowson had presented another priest to that bishop. Bohun accordingly sued the rival claimant, the priest, and the bishop. The bishop argued that under ecclesiastical law he was not bound to admit either presentee until the disputed right of patronage had been judicially ascertained, but that the right of presentation lapsed to him in the event the dispute between the two patrons lasted more than six months. In this instance the six-month period had elapsed, and the bishop had exercised his right of presentation.

[11] As related by Courtney Kenny, "The Evolution of the Law of Blasphemy," *Cambridge Law Journal*, Vol. I, No. 2 (1922), 129.

[12] *Taylor's Case*, 1, Ventris 293; 3 Keble 607 (King's Bench, 1676).

[13] Kenny, "Evolution of the Law of Blasphemy," *Cambridge Law Journal*, Vol. I, No. 2 (1922), 130.

[14] *Rex* v. *Woolston*, 2 Strange 832; 1 Barnardiston 162 (King's Bench, 1729).

[15] *Life and Letters*, I, 431, 434.

[16] This article is reprinted in *Life and Letters*, I, 431–33.

Was the secular court of common pleas bound to recognize and enforce this ecclesiastical doctrine, and if so, by what method was it to determine the validity of the bishop's interpretation of it? "The point is," stated Prisot, "whether the law of the Church is as the Bishop says, or not. For if their law is so, we wish to accept it." He then stated the proper method of ascertaining the ecclesiastical law. "As to those laws, which those of holy church have in ancient scripture, it behooves us to give them credence, for this is common law, upon which all manner of laws are founded; and thus, sir, we are obliged to take notice of their law of holy church; and it seems they are obliged to take notice of our law."[17]

To Jefferson's contention that the words *ancien scripture* did not refer to Holy Scriptures or the Bible, but to ancient writings, or the written code of the church, Story replied: "But if this is so, how could Prisot have said they [the words *ancien scripture*] were common law, *upon which all manner of laws are founded*? Do not these words suppose that he was speaking of some superior law, having a foundation in nature or the Divine appointment, and not merely a positive ancient code of the church?"[18] Clearly, then, it was Christian natural law to which the court had referred.

Secondly, continued Story, the legal doctrine that Christianity was a part of the common law did not develop solely from the case in point, but was, in fact, a general principle of English common law. He noted, for example, that in *Taylor's Case* and in *Rex* v. *Woolston*, the court did not cite the disputed case of 34 Henry VI as the basis of the holdings.[19]

Story rested his case finally upon common sense and history:

But independently of any weight in any of these authorities, can any man seriously doubt, that Christianity is recognized as true, as a revelation, by the law of England, that is by the common law? What becomes of her whole ecclesiastical establishment, and the legal rights growing out of it on any other supposition? What of her test acts, and acts perpetually referring to it as a divine system, obligatory upon all? Is not the reviling of any establishment, created and supported by the public law, held a libel by the common law?[20]

In this broader sense of the term *Christianity*, Story was, of course, on solid ground. For centuries ecclesiastics had sat on the English benches fashioning the common law from religious teachings; and even the secular judges dis-

[17] *Ibid.*, 432.

[18] *Ibid.*

[19] *Ibid.*, 433.

[20] *Ibid.* In his inaugural address as Dane Professor of Law at Harvard, Story had earlier taken a similar position as that in his article for the *American Jurist:* "One of the beautiful boasts of our municipal jurisprudence is, that Christianity is a part of the common law, from which it seeks the sanction of its rights, and by which it endeavors to regulate its doctrines. And notwithstanding the specious objection of one of our distinguished statesmen, the boast is as true as it is beautiful. There never has been a period in which the

pensed justice in accordance with the dictates of Christian principles. During the Catholic Middle Ages in particular, the English common law, under the guiding influence of the great lawyers such as Bracton and Fortescue, assimilated Christian ethics and the conceptions of equity and natural law. Their successors carried on the tradition. The debate is thus resolved in part, suggests John Wu, in this manner:

The question has often been asked if Christianity is a part of the common law. It depends on what you mean by Christianity. If you mean a revealed religion, a faith as defined by the Apostles' Creed, it is not a part of the common law in the sense that you are legally bound to believe in it. Christianity as a Faith comes into the courts, not as a law, but as a fact to be taken judicial notice of, on a par with other facts of common knowledge. On the other hand, if you mean by Christianity the fundamental moral precepts embodied in its teachings, it is a part of the common law in the sense that all the universal principles of justice written in the heart of every man are a part thereof.[21]

Although he did not rely on American cases, Judge Story would also have found Chancellor Kent's decision in *People* v. *Ruggles*[22] to be a refutation of Jefferson's theory. In ruling against Ruggles, who had been indicted for profaning Christ and the Virgin Mary, Kent had asserted that even in the absence of a New York statute prohibiting blasphemous language, Ruggles' indictment should stand for the reason that the common law explicitly forbade impious or irreverent references to holy persons. To support this contention, Kent offered a long and impressive roster of distinguished legalists, all of whom seemingly strengthen Story's analysis.

Kent pointed, for example, to *Rex* v. *Williams*, a case involving the publication of Paine's *Age of Reason*, which was tried before Lord Kenyon in 1797 and postulated as an ancient principle that the defaming of Christianity was an offense against the common law, the theory being that whatever strikes at the roots of Christianity tends manifestly to the dissolution of civil government.

Chancellor Kent's biographer, after reading the *Ruggles* decision, concluded that "The tendency of all the authorities, including Blackstone, was to establish beyond all doubt that profane ridicule and contumelious reproaches of Christ

common law did not recognize Christianity as lying at its foundations. For many ages it was almost exclusively administered by those who held its ecclesiastical dignities. It now repudiates every act done in violation of its duties of perfect obligation. It pronounces illegal every contract offensive to its morals. It recognizes with profound humility its holidays and festivals, and obeys them as *dies nonjuridici*. It still attaches to persons believing in its divine authority the highest degree of competency as witnesses; and, until a comparatively recent period, infidels and pagans were banished from the halls of justice, as unworthy of credit." "The Value and Importance of Legal Studies," *Miscellaneous Writings*, 517.

21 John C. H. Wu, *Fountain of Justice*, 215.
22 8 Johnson (N.Y.) 290 (1811).

and of the Holy Scriptures were offenses at common law, whether uttered in words or writings. . . . The Digest of Justinian lent weight to the conclusion that an offense against religion was an offense also against the law."[23]

Even "the polished nations of antiquity," Kent himself noted, discouraged the dangerous practice of permitting "with impunity and under the sanction of their tribunals the general religion of the country to be openly insulted and defamed. The very idea of jurisprudence with the ancient law givers and philosophers embraced the religion of the country;—*Jurisprudentia est divinarum atque humanarum rerum notitia*."[24] To the objection that his opinion might be inconsistent with the American tradition of religious freedom, Kent conceded that "The free, equal and undisturbed enjoyment of religious opinion . . . is granted and secured" but "to revile with malicious and blasphemous contempt the religion professed by almost the whole community is an abuse of that right."[25]

In sum, Kent's decision clearly illustrated that not only was religion a part of the common law, but that it had also been regarded as basic to civil order in Western jurisprudence and political philosophy from the time of ancient civilization, centuries before Sir Henry Finch made his alleged mistranslation. Relying solely on the thesis that Christianity had suddenly been introduced into the English common law by Finch, Jefferson had neglected to consider the all-important fact that much of the common law was actually based on Roman law. Christianity became a part of the common law from the very moment early Roman Catholic churchmen converted the Anglo-Saxons to Christianity and incorporated Roman legal principles into the slowly evolving English system of jurisprudence. Indeed, from the time of the Battle of Hastings, the two coalescing systems of English law "were the Anglo-Saxon, largely formed on the Roman tradition, and the Norman, which was almost wholly the product of the Roman model."[26]

The folly of Jefferson's "discovery," in whatever legal or theoretical sense one wishes to construe it, is suggested not only by Story's devastating critique, but also by the fact it was completely ignored by English and American courts. "With all due respect" to Jefferson, one commentator has written, "it may be said that a more perfect travesty of the doctrine, as held by an intelligent student of law, that religion is a part of the common law, could not be devised."[27] The English reports of the nineteenth century abound in common

[23] John Theodore Horton, *James Kent*, 188.

[24] 8 Johnson (N.Y.) 294.

[25] *Ibid.*   [26] John M. Zane, *The Story of Law*, 230–31.

[27] P. Emory Aldrich, "The Christian Religion and the Common Law," American Antiquarian Society *Proceedings*, New Series, Vol. VI, (Apr., 1889–Apr., 1890), 18. Kenny, however, seems to believe there was a mistranslation; but he does not attempt to answer Story. See Courtney Kenny, "The Evolution of the Law of Blasphemy," *Cambridge Law Journal*, Vol. I, No. 2 (1922), 130.

law prosecutions for blasphemy, and as late as 1917, Prisot's words were quoted in full by Lord Sumner.[28] The only real difficulty experienced in the English courts, it seems, was "whether the common law rendered punishable *all* open expressions of a disbelief in Christianity, or only such as were couched in language so irreverent and scurrilous as to be likely to offend ordinary Christians deeply enough to provoke some of them to a breach of the peace."[29]

Blackstone had indicated that any denial of Christianity was an offense at common law; but in the *Woolston* case, his majesty's judges had clearly stated they did "not meddle with any differences in opinion; we interpose only when the very root of Christianity itself is struck at." The court "desired it might be taken notice of, that they laid their stress upon the word 'general'; and did not intend to include disputes between learned men upon particular controverted points."[30]

With few exceptions, the more restrictive view of Blackstone was rejected in the courts of England and America.[31] In Foote's case, decided in 1882, Lord Chief Justice Coleridge resolved the issue, stating that "If the decencies of controversy are observed, even the fundamentals of religion may be attacked without the attackers being guilty of blasphemous libel."[32] Finally, in 1917, the House of Lords unanimously endorsed Coleridge's judgment in *Bowman* v. *The Secular Society*.[33]

How persuasive was Jefferson's argument among American judges? "On the whole," Mark de Wolfe Howe has written, "Jefferson's effort had little effect on the decision of cases in American courts administering the common law. The judges found it very easy to repeat the old maxim and to find reasons (or other grounds) for discrediting the endeavor of Jefferson. As a consequence, the early State reports are full of cases in which decisions were affected, and sometimes controlled, by the thesis that Christianity is a part of the common law which we have inherited from England."[34]

---

[28] Kenny, "Evolution of Law of Blasphemy," *Cambridge Law Journal*, Vol. I, No. 2 (1922), 131.

[29] *Ibid.*, 128.

[30] *Rex* v. *Woolston*, 2 Strange 832; 1 Barnardiston 162 (King's Bench, 1729).

[31] Neither Story nor Kent followed Blackstone; see, however, the case of *Commonwealth* v. *Kneeland*, 20 Pickering (Mass.) 206 (1838).

[32] See Kenny, "Evolution of Law of Blasphemy" *Cambridge Law Journal*, Vol. I, No. 2 (1922), 138.

[33] Law Reports, Appeals Cases 406 (House of Lords, 1917). This case is remarkably similar to the Girard case, decided by Judge Story in 1844. Here a testator had given his residuary estate upon trust for the Secular Society, one purpose being "to promote the principle that human conduct should be based upon natural knowledge and not upon supernatural belief." The House of Lords ruled that the gift was valid on the ground that the purposes of the society were not unlawful. See Story's opinion, *infra*, pages 131–32.

[34] *The Garden and the Wilderness*, 28. Professor Howe cites Story's article in the *American Jurist*; Chief Justice Clayton's opinion in *State* v. *Chandler*, 2 Harrington (Del.)

SEPARATION OF SECT AND STATE

The Story-Jefferson feud is of no small consequence in assessing Story's position on the separation of church and state. Story's philosophy of law and politics, which ascribed, as did Burke's, a transcendent reality to laws and the state, making them a part of the Divine order, tends to breach the "wall of separation" between church and state. According to Story, we separate political and churchly authority upon considerations of expedience, not for the purpose of achieving a secularized existence. Because the church and state seek the same ends, that is public and private virtue, it is only wise and proper that they assist each other in striving to reach these noble ends. By enforcing the laws, promoting justice, and encouraging the growth of the material and rational conditions for a sound body politic, the state fosters its own general morality, while the church lives not only in partnership, but with it constitutes a spiritual unity. The state is the natural expression of its parts, not an artificial body from which Providence can be excluded. In so far as Christianity represents the indissoluble bond between God, natural law and common law, the state, the guardian of all law, fashions the framework within which our Creator executes his Divine plan. At bottom, church and state are forever united; their total separation impossible. Such would have been Story's reply, one may conjecture, to Jefferson's doctrine that a "wall" must separate church and state.

Now a student of Jefferson, who has reviewed the quarrel between Story and Jefferson, boasts that, whatever the merits of Jefferson's legal argument, he "was ultimately victorious in fact. The religious conditions and convictions of the American people made the orthodox doctrine a practical impossibility, as well as a perversion of the democratic creed. . . . The progress of Jefferson's principle went forward with slight interruptions until, in recent years, the Supreme Court has explicitly recognized his interpretation of the First Amendment—'a wall of separation between church and state'—as the orthodox principle of American institutions."[35]

Professor Peterson's interpretation of the dispute, however, arouses skepti-

---

553 (1837); and Kent's opinion in the *Ruggles* case. But see also *Updegraff* v. *The Commonwealth*, 11 Sergeant & Rawle (Pa.) 394 (1824); *Hale* v. *Everett*, 53 New Hampshire 9 (1868); *Commonwealth* v. *Kneeland*, 20 Pickering (Mass.) 206 (1838). The famous case of blasphemy against Abner Kneeland is discussed at length by Leonard Levy, *The Law of the Commonwealth and Chief Justice Shaw*, 43–58. Blasphemy laws are still found in many states today. The most important decision in recent times involving blasphemy is *State* v. *Mockus*, 120 Maine 84, 113 A. 39 (1921), in which the Supreme Court of Maine upheld the conviction of a man who was accused of ridiculing the Virgin Birth, the death of Christ, the Trinity, and religion in general. It should also be pointed out that in the *Chandler* case, Chief Justice Clayton based much of his opinion on a refutation of Jefferson, whose letter to Cartwright was relied upon by counsel for the defendant.

[35] Merrill D. Peterson, *The Jefferson Image in the American Mind*, 98.

cism. In the first place, Jefferson's principle did not go "forward with slight interruptions," but was in fact abruptly introduced into American law in very recent times. Secondly, as will be shown, Jefferson's interpretation of the First Amendment is not exactly the same as the Supreme Court's. Moreover, Professor Peterson's interpretation casts doubt upon Story's position on the separation of Church and State, and leaves the false impression Story may have championed the doctrines of theocracy. Story's treatises, his speeches, public activities, and judicial decisions, however, clearly indicate that he was firmly attached to the separation of governmental and churchly authority, though not in the absolutist sense.

In a speech before the Essex Historical Society in 1823, Story labelled the theocratic theory of the Puritans a "wretched doctrine,"[36] insisting quite vigorously upon separation of church and state as the best system of free and enlightened government: "The fundamental error of our ancestors, an error which began with the very settlement of the colony, was a doctrine which has since been happily exploded; I mean the necessity of a union between church and state.... The arm of the civil government was constantly employed in the support of the denunciations of the Church; and, without its forms, the Inquisition existed in substance, with a full share of its terrors and violence."[37]

With equal forcefulness Story reiterated the same philosophy in his *Commentaries on the Constitution*: "the history of the world has shown the extreme dangers, as well as difficulties, of connecting the civil power with religious opinions. Half the calamities, with which the human race have been scourged, have arisen from the union of Church and State."[38]

What is important here is that Story did not—and could not, owing to his pietistic views on the natural law—advocate the *absolute* separation of church and state. As a delegate at the Massachusetts constitutional convention in 1820, he voted with his conservative friends to defeat a radical attempt to secure a complete separation of church and state,[39] believing that "the power of the legislature to compel the support of public worship" should be upheld.[40] Significantly, however, Story also wanted to correct the partiality of the old system of assessment of religious dues which had been designed to favor the Congregationalist church.[41]

---

[36] "History and Influence of the Puritans," A Discourse Pronounced at the Request of the Essex Historical Society, September 18, 1828, in Commemoration of the First Settlement of Salem, Massachusetts, *Miscellaneous Writings*, 448.

[37] *Ibid.*

[38] II, sec. 621, p. 97.

[39] *Journal of Debates and Proceedings in the Convention of Delegates Chosen to Revise the Constitution of Massachusetts 1820–1821*, 560 (cited hereafter as *Journal of Debates and Proceedings.*)

[40] *Ibid.*, 562.

[41] *Ibid.*, 567. For a discussion of the arrangement for assessment under the old consti-

On the question of a church-state dichotomy, then, Story took the position that the state ought not to give preference to any specific religious sect, but that it should lend encouragement to the spreading of the Christian religion generally. "It is . . . the especial duty of government," he asserted, "to foster, and to encourage it among all the citizens and subjects. . . . as a matter of sound policy, as well as of revealed truth."[42]

The opinion that the state should be neutral *against* religious belief was unhistorical, according to Story. Christianity should be patronized by the government up to the point where "private rights of conscience" and "freedom of religious worship" are not endangered; but "an attempt to level all religions, and to make it a matter of state policy to hold all in utter indifference, would have created universal disapprobation, if not universal indignation."[43] The only question in Story's mind over the true meaning of the First Amendment to the Constitution was "in ascertaining the limits, to which government may rightfully go in fostering and encouraging religion."[44] He would agree with Jefferson that there must indeed be a "wall of separation" between church and state—but religion cannot be entirely walled out of the life of a nation.

In believing that Christianity ought to be promoted by the state, Story did not advocate that the Christian religion be forced upon an individual against his will, or that persons be punished for refusing to worship God in any particular form or manner. "The duty of supporting religion, and especially the Christian religion, is very different from the right to force the consciences of other men, or to punish them for worshipping God in the manner, which, they believe, their accountability to him requires."[45] This very concept of no preference to any sect, argued Story, was the underlying philosophy of the First Amendment clause of religious freedom: "The real object of the amendment was, not to countenance, much less to advance mohametanism, or Judaism, or infidelity, by prostrating Christianity; but to exclude all rivalry among Christian sects, and to prevent any *national* ecclesiastical establishment, which should give to an hierarchy the exclusive patronage of the national government."[46]

---

tution, see Albert B. Hart (ed.), *Commonwealth History of Massachusetts*, IV, 9–10. "I perceive a proposition in our Legislature to destroy the third article on the public maintenance of religion in our constitution," Story observed in 1832. "It seems to me that there is no end to rash experiments upon all subjects. Who would have thought that so vital an interest to piety, and morals, and independent freedom of opinion, would have been yielded up in the House of Representatives, with so little show of debate?" To Rev. John Brazer, Feb. 16, 1832, *Life and Letters*, II, 82–83.

[42] *Commentaries on the Constitution*, III, sec. 1865, p. 723; sec. 1867, p. 724.

[43] *Ibid*, sec. 1868, p. 726.

[44] *Ibid.*, sec. 1866, p. 723.

[45] *Ibid.*, sec. 1870, p. 727.

[46] *Ibid.*, sec. 1871, p. 728. Emphasis supplied.

THE NO PREFERENCE DOCTRINE
IN THEORY AND PRACTICE

Turning to Story's interpretation of religious liberty as Supreme Court justice, one finds Story consistently adhering to these sympathies expressed in his writings and public utterances. In *Terrett* v. *Taylor*,[47] decided in 1815, a unanimous Court ruled that the legislature of the state of Virginia lacked authority to expropriate land formerly granted to the Church of England. The case, which grew out of Jefferson's war against the Virginia Episcopacy, centered on a statute enacted in 1801 by the Virginia legislature. The legislature, asserting its right to all the property of the Episcopal churches in the various parishes throughout the state, had directed that the church property be sold, the proceeds going for the support of the poor of each parish. Virginia contended that its constitution and bill of rights were inconsistent with its prior act of 1776, which confirmed the rights of the church to its lands and property, and that during the Revolutionary War, all the property cumulatively acquired by the Episcopal churches, under the sanction of the laws, became the property of the state.

Speaking for the Court, Judge Story admitted that the American Revolution might have eradicated the state's patronage of the church—but it did not authorize the confiscation of church property, for this would have been an infraction of the free exercise of religion of the Episcopal church. "It is conceded on all sides that, at the Revolution, the Episcopal Church no longer retained its character as an exclusive religious establishment,"[48] said Story, and the people and their representatives were entirely within their rights "to deprive it of its superiority over other religious sects, and to withhold from it any support by public taxation."[49] On the other hand,

although it may be true that "religion can be directed only by reason and conviction, not by force or violence," and that "all men are equally entitled to the free exercise of religion according to the dictates of conscience," as the bill of rights of Virginia declares, yet it is difficult to perceive how it follows as a consequence that the legislature may not enact laws more effectively to enable all sects to accomplish the great objects of religion by giving them corporate rights for the management of their property, and the regulation of their temporal as well as spiritual concerns.[50]

Thus, Story would conclude that strict obeisance to Jefferson's doctrine of an absolute wall of separation necessitates the annihilation of religion as an institution.

The Episcopal church in Virginia, deriving its rights from the common

[47] 9 Cranch 43 (1815).
[48] *Ibid.*, 48.
[49] *Ibid.*
[50] *Ibid.*, 48–49.

law, depended for its existence upon legislative assistance through the grant of corporate rights, in order that it might adequately preserve its properties. Such cooperation between church and government, rather than hindering the free exercise of religion, aids and ensures it for the benefit of both religion and the state. Nor, Story added, is the free exercise of religion "restrained by aiding with equal attention the votaries of every sect to perform their own religious duties, or by establishing funds for the support of ministers, for public charities, for the endowment of churches, or for the sepulture of the dead."[51]

In *Vidal v. Girard's Executors*,[52] Story, again with the unanimous assent of his fellow justices, established the principle that state assistance to religion must be accomplished in a positive manner. The state of Pennsylvania cannot forbid, he contended, the establishment of a school whose policies toward religion are questionable, perhaps ultimately hostile, so long as Christianity is not openly reviled. The case involved the unusual will of one Stephen Girard of Philadelphia, who, in bequeathing in trust some two million dollars and the residuum of his estate to the public officials of his city, for the establishment of a school for "poor, male, white orphan children," had stipulated that "no ecclesiastic, missionary, or minister of any sect whatsoever, shall hold or exercise any station or duty"[53] in the institution.

Daniel Webster, Story's confidant and colleague, represented the complainants contesting the will, and contended that it was void on various grounds, one being that the flagrant exclusion of members of the clergy from the school was incompatible with the common law and public policy of Pennsylvania. "The idea was drawn from Paine's *Age of Reason*," argued Webster, probably hoping to strike a responsive chord in Judge Story, "where it is said, 'let us propagate morality unfettered by superstition.' Girard had no secrets, and therefore used the words which he considered synonymous with 'superstition,' viz.: 'religious tenets.' "[54] As it stands, said Webster, the clause at issue is as antagonistic toward the Christian religion as though Girard had provided that lectures be delivered against it. The will required that students be permitted at maturity to choose on their own whether to adopt the Christian faith; but, was not a knowledge of man's duty and destiny the earliest principle to be learned by young men, queried counsel? Surely, he concluded, the Court must agree

[51] *Ibid.*, 49.

[52] 2 Howard 127 (1844).

[53] *Ibid.*, 133. Girard's will continues to be a source of controversy and litigation. In *Pennsylvania v. Board of City Trusts of Philadelphia*, 353 U.S. 230 (1957), the Supreme Court ruled that the refusal of the board (a state agency set up to administer the school) to admit two Negro boys constituted a violation of the Fourteenth Amendment. Subsequent efforts by the school to exclude Negroes have also failed to gain the Court's approval.

[54] 2 Howard 174–75.

that Girard's will was a "cruel experiment" calculated to ascertain whether orphans can be brought up without religion.[55]

"The first step of infidelity is to clamor against the multitude of sects," and "if it be said that infidels will not be encouraged, the answer is, that a court can only judge the tendency of measures."[56] The very fact that the will deemed the presence of the clergy as mischievous was tantamount to a sweeping denunciation of the entire clergy, thus rendering the will clearly in opposition to sound public policy. Furthermore, Webster added, Christianity was a part of the public and common law of Pennsylvania: "the charter says that Penn came over to spread the Christian religion; and the Legislatures have often acted upon this principle, as where they punished the violation of the Lords day. That it is a part of the common law, see *Updegraff* v. *The Commonwealth*."[57]

Webster's arguments failed to impress Judge Story. To Chancellor Kent he remarked that "Mr. Webster did his best for the other side, but it seemed to me, altogether, an address to the prejudices of the clergy."[58] Story also wrote to his wife, assuring her he had "ever been a sturdy defender of religious freedom of opinion, and . . . took no small pains to answer Mr. Webster's argument on this point, which went to cut down that freedom to a very narrow range."[59]

Two issues confronted Judge Story: is the Christian religion a part of the common law, and does the common law take cognizance of offenses against the Christian religion? Story accepted Webster's contention that the Christian religion was a part of the common law of Pennsylvania and ought to be a rule of decision in determining the validity of the will, but the proposition had its appropriate qualifications: "we are compelled to admit that although Christianity be a part of the common law of the State, yet it is so in this qualified sense, that its *divine origin* and truth are admitted, therefore it is not to be

[55] Jefferson insisted that where the judgments of young children "are not sufficiently matured for religious inquiries, their memories may here be stored with the most useful facts from Grecian, Roman, European and American history." *Writings*, (Memorial ed.), II, 204.

[56] 2 Howard 174, 176.

[57] *Ibid.*, 177. To his wife, Story wrote: "Mr. Webster began his reply . . . today, and the Court-room was crowded, almost to suffocation, with ladies and gentlemen to hear him. . . . I was not a little amused, with the manner in which on each side, the language of the Scriptures, and the doctrines of Christianity, were brought in to point the argument; and to find the Court engaged in hearing homilies of faith, and expositions of Christianity, with almost the formality of lectures from the pulpit." (Feb. 7, 1844, *Life and Letters*, II, 468.) For a discussion of the political ramifications of the case, see Charles Warren, *The Supreme Court in United States History*, II, 124–33. An excellent analysis of the case is that of Maurice G. Baxter in his *Daniel Webster and the Supreme Court*, 156–68.

[58] Aug. 31, 1844, *Life and Letters*, II, 469.

[59] Mar. 3, 1844, *ibid.*, 473.

maliciously and openly reviled and blasphemed against, to the annoyance of believers or the injury of the public."[60]

Here, however, there was insufficient evidence that Christianity would be openly maligned. The exclusion of the clergy was not necessarily a declamation against religion. "There must be plain, positive, and express provisions, demonstrating not only that Christianity is not to be taught, but that it is to be impugned and repudiated."[61] On its face, said Story, the will does not say there will be no religious instruction, but only that no member of any sect shall retain a position in the school; and a layman might just as well instruct the students in the Christian faith as a minister.

Story upheld Girard's will and refused to explore the issue beyond the confines of Pennsylvania's constitution, its laws and judicial decisions. He denied that the Updegraff ruling cited by Webster was inconsistent with the Court's opinion. In that decision, Story averred, the Supreme Court of Pennsylvania had held that Christianity must be openly inveighed against before one's conduct could be said to transgress sound public policy. "The case of *Vidal* v. *Girard's Executor*," Chancellor Kent assured Story, "is a great case & decided on the clearest and soundest principles."[62]

The *Terrett* and *Girard* cases, together with Story's treatise on the Constitution and public comments, delineate a constitutional theory of religious freedom and establishment. Story's theory discloses a belief in Christianity as the true religion of man and great bulwark of social order. "In a Republic, there would seem to be a peculiar propriety in viewing the Christian religion, as the great basis, on which it must rest for its support and permanence, if it be, what it has ever been deemed by its truest friends to be, the religion of liberty."[63]

Story never uses the phrase "wall of separation," and his ideas sharply clash with the Jeffersonian conception of a total separation between government and religion. He would agree that government and church are separated formally, in order to protect both liberty and Christianity. Nevertheless, civil liberty and religious liberty are mutually dependent, because it is only through the restriction of the state's power and authority that religious liberty can be maintained; and civil liberty is meaningful only where religious liberty is secure.

Religious liberty—the freedom to worship according to the dictates of one's own conscience, to believe or not to believe without threat of punishment or coercion—will be preserved if the authority of the church remains distinct

---

[60] 2 Howard 198. In *Terrett* v. *Taylor*, 9 Cranch 46, Story observed that "At a very early period, the religious establishment of England seems to have been adopted in the colony of Virginia; and, of course, the common law upon that subject, so far as it was applicable to the circumstances of the colony."

[61] 2 Howard 199.

[62] Aug. 8, 1844, Story Papers, Texas.

[63] Story, *Commentaries on the Constitution*, III, sec. 1867, pp. 724–25. Story refers here to Montesquieu's remark "that the Christian religion is a stranger to mere despotic power."

from, and hence limited by, political authority. In carrying out this function, however, the state cannot, while limiting churchly prerogative, encroach upon matters of religion. It cannot expropriate church property, forbid public worship, or seek to destroy the church as an institution. This balance between the two centers of power is upheld by the principle of mutual assistance. The state recognizes, guarantees, and protects the full freedom of the church, ensuring to the church the free exercise of its spiritual mission; the church in turn promotes the general welfare of the community by encouraging a virtuous citizenry, social cooperation, and a respect for authority—a respect more readily attained where the state does not pose itself as a threat to the continued existence of the church. When confronted with moral questions which the church cannot accomplish by itself, the state should not be indifferent or stand aloof, but must in fact actively assist. Such assistance, however, should be given in a general manner to all religions, for the state has no authority to impose or expel a sect. Nor should the state, in aiding religion, attempt to eradicate heresy. As long as dissenters do not openly and viciously attack the Christian religion, Story believed they should be protected by civil authority.

Story's judicial opinions mark the first attempt of a Supreme Court justice to expound the American philosophy of religious liberty and represent the Court's formal baptism of the "no preference" theory in American constitutional history. The origin of the tenet that the encouragement of religion as an institution requires that church property not be expropriated by the government may also be attributed to Story.

While the latter principle is still accepted by the Court,[64] the impact of Judge Story's no preference doctrine upon the present footing of the First Amendment, is less clear. As mentioned earlier, there is on the one hand the innuendo that Story's view of religious establishment is overshadowed by that of Mr. Jefferson.[65] The Supreme Court, on the other, continues to endorse *Terrett* and *Vidal*. In *Everson* v. *Board of Education*,[66] Mr. Justice Black, citing *Terrett* v. *Taylor*, *Watson* v. *Jones*,[67] and *Davis* v. *Beason*,[68] said on behalf of the Court, that

The meaning and scope of the First Amendment preventing establishment of religion or prohibiting the free exercise thereof, in the light of its history and the

---

[64] See, for example, *Ponce* v. *Roman Catholic Church*, 210 U.S. 314 (1907). On the general subject of church property rights, see *Watson* v. *Jones*, 13 Wallace 679 (1872); expanded to include church autonomy over doctrinal disputes in *Presbyterian Church of the United States* v. *Mary Elizabeth Blue Hull Memorial Presbyterian Church*, 393 U.S. 440 (1969); also Paul Kauper, "Church Autonomy and the First Amendment: The Presbyterian Church Case," *The Supreme Court Review* (1969), 347–78.

[65] Peterson, *Jefferson Image in the American Mind*, 92–98.

[66] 330 U.S. 1 (1947).

[67] 13 Wallace 679 (1872).

[68] 133 U.S. 333 (1890).

evils it was designed forever to suppress, have been several times elaborated by the decisions of this Court prior to the application of the First Amendment to the states by the Fourteenth. The broad meaning given the Amendment by these earlier cases has been accepted by this Court in its decisions concerning an individual's religious freedom rendered since the Fourteenth Amendment was interpreted to make the prohibitions of the First Amendment applicable to state action abridging religious freedom. There is every reason to give the same application and broad interpretation to the "establishment of religion" clause.[69]

In *McCollum* v. *Champaign Board of Education*, Mr. Justice Frankfurter cited *Vidal* approvingly in his concurring opinion. He noted that even "before the Fourteenth Amendment subjected the States to new limitations, the prohibition of furtherance by the State of religious instruction became the guiding principle, in law and feeling, of the American people. In sustaining Stephen Girard's will, this Court referred to the inevitable conflicts engendered by matters 'connected with religious polity' and particularly 'in a country composed of such a variety of religious sects as our country.' "[70] In both *Terrett* and *Vidal*, Judge Story argues from the position of the no preference theory; that is, he contends that the prohibition of laws respecting the free exercise of religion simply forbids the extension of preferential aid to a single religious sect. Yet, *Everson* and *McCollum*, aside from the fact they present conflicting interpretations regarding the nature of the wall of separation between church and state,[71] both speak in terms of "no aid of any kind to religion in any form," which flies in the face of Story's opinions in *Terrett* and *Vidal*. The conclusion is unavoidable that the present Court has either misrepresented the position of every justice on the Marshall and Taney courts, and of Story in particular, or has simply given *Terrett* and *Vidal* a superficial reading.

Indeed, the precedents cited by the Court since 1947 in establishment of religion cases are bewildering. *Terrett* and *Vidal* obviously conflict with the absolutist position taken by the Court; and *Engel* v. *Vitale*[72] and *Abington* v. *Schempp*,[73] two more recent opinions, indiscriminately quote *Everson*, *Mc-*

---

[69] 330 U.S. 14–15.

[70] 333 U.S. 215 (1948).

[71] "Taking Everson and McCollum together, it is apparent that the Court had worked itself into an untenable position. The welfare doctrine which was the basis of the ruling in Everson would logically justify almost any legislation and consequently deny any prohibitive effect to the establishment clause. On the other hand, the wall of separation doctrine was so applied in McCollum as to carry the implication that the First Amendment forbids all forms of public aid to religion, however general and nondiscriminatory." George W. Spicer, *The Supreme Court and Fundamental Freedoms*, 137–38.

[72] 370 U.S. 421 (1962).

[73] *Abington School District* v. *Schempp*, and *Murray* v. *Curlett*, 374 U.S. 203 (1963). For an excellent analysis of the Court's decisions regarding religious establishment, and

Collum, and *Zorach* v. *Clauson*[74] with approbation. Jefferson's phrase, "wall of separation," is often repeated by the Court, although it does not appear in the First Amendment and was originally conceived in a private letter.

Few persons other than Jefferson and Madison are ever consulted, although in the *Schempp-Murray* cases Justice Clark quotes an unpublished opinion of Judge Alphonso Taft,[75] who never sat on the Supreme Court, and whose statement neither affirms nor denies Clark's opinion for the Court. And in *McCollum*, Justice Frankfurter refers to President Grant,[76] whose recommendation against the use of federal funds for sectarian education is inapplicable to the issue before the Court involving state assistance to religion. In the two references to Story's decisions, the Court carefully avoided mention of Story's remarks affirming the no preference theory. With one minor exception the Court has made no mention of Story's *Commentaries on the Constitution*.[77]

No less puzzling is the historical evidence offered by the Court in support of the absolutist interpretation of the First Amendment. In every establishment case the Court is at pains to justify its position on historical grounds, and from Justice Black's opinion in *Everson* through Clark's in the *Schempp-Murray* cases, there are lengthy discourses on religious liberty purporting to demonstrate the universal acceptance throughout American history of the Jeffersonian proposition. What strikes the critical student of the Constitution as peculiar is the fact the historical material dredged up by the Court, much of which relates to religious conflict in England in the seventeenth century, is totally irrelevant to the absolutist position the Court is attempting to sub-

---

especially the *Schempp-Murray* cases, see L. Brent Bozell, *The Warren Revolution*, 70–79; see also Charles Rice, *The Supreme Court and Public Prayer*.

[74] 343 U.S. 306 (1952). Justice Brennan cites Vidal in his concurring opinion in *Abington* v. *Schempp* at 243, regarding governmental preference to religious sects. No mention of *Terrett* is made in the Supreme Court's latest decisions dealing with the subject of separation of church and state. For a discussion of the conflicting doctrines formulated in *Everson*, *McCollum*, and *Zorach*, see William Van Alstyne, "Constitutional Separation of Church and State: The Quest for a Coherent Position," *American Political Science Review*, Vol. LVII, No. 4 (Dec., 1963), 865–82, and Spicer, *The Supreme Court and Fundamental Freedoms*, 147–51. In *Abington* v. *Schempp* at 261, Justice Brennan, referring to Spicer's criticisms and to those of Paul G. Kauper ("Church, State and Freedom: A Review," *Michigan Law Review*, Vol. LII, No. 6 [Apr., 1954], 829–48) and George E. Reed ("Church-State and the Zorach Case," 27 *Notre Dame Lawyer*, Vol. XXVII, No. 4 [Summer, 1952], 529–51) says, "I reject the suggestion that Zorach overruled McCollum in silence." Justice Brennan fails to explain why he rejects these criticisms, however.

[75] 374 U.S., 215. Alphonso Taft was the father of William Howard Taft and the grandfather of the late Senator Robert A. Taft.

[76] 333 U.S., 218.

[77] In *McGowan* v. *Maryland*, 366 U.S. 420 (1961) on page 441, Chief Justice Warren quoted Story's remark in the *Commentaries* that the "real object of the [First] Amendment was . . . to prevent any national ecclesiastical establishment, which would give to an hierarchy the exclusive patronage of the national government."

stantiate and invariably refers to the consequences and dangers of political aid to one religious sect rather than religion generally.

Likewise, the absolutist concept embraced by Jefferson was clearly not shared by a large majority of his contemporaries when the Bill of Rights was adopted. Jefferson and Madison were successful in disestablishing the Episcopal church in Virginia in the 1780s, but five states, including Massachusetts, refused to follow suit. This fact has apparently escaped notice in the Court. Pointing to the many state court decisions upholding the thesis that Christianity is a part of the common law, Mark de Wolfe Howe has concluded, "This fact seems to me to constitute persuasive evidence that it was a common assumption in the first decades of the nineteenth century that State governments may properly become the supporters and the friends of religion."[78]

The Court's wall of separation theory is further weakened by an important but almost forgotten document on church-state relations, recently uncovered by this author. It seems that in 1833 a Reverend Jasper Adams delivered a sermon to a convention of the Episcopal church in South Carolina, which was later published under the title "The Relation of Christianity to Civil Government in the United States."[79] The sermon is as perceptive as it is relevant. Reverend Adams was not only an informed critic of the wall of separation theory, but he was apparently also endowed with great powers of foresight. His sermon deals with this very issue of the absolutist versus the no preference theories at both the state and federal levels and, in anticipation of the establishment cases delivered by the Supreme Court since 1947, offers an abundance of evidence to refute the notion that church-state relations in early nineteenth-century America ever followed the absolutist example offered by Jefferson and Madison.

[78] *The Garden and the Wilderness*, 28.

[79] A Sermon Preached in St. Michael's Church, Charleston, February 13, 1833, before the Convention of the Protestant Episcopal Church of the Diocese of South Carolina (Charleston, 1833). Adams' personal copy of the sermon is in the William L. Clements Library, University of Michigan; a copy is also in the College of Charleston Library.

Jasper Adams, a cousin of John Quincy Adams, graduated from Brown University in 1815. After pursuing the study of divinity, he became in 1819 a professor of mathematics and natural philosophy at Brown. For health reasons he went south, where in 1825-26 and 1828-36, he was president of the College of Charleston. He also served as chaplain and professor of moral philosophy at West Point. In 1837 he published his *Elements of Moral Philosophy*, which was well received and contains references to Judge Story's legal treatises on equity and conflict of law. "Though he has written a great deal in the shape of lectures upon morals, history, constitutional and international law," noted a friend of Adams, "he has not published much of his writings, with the exception of the sermons ... [and] his treatise on Moral Philosophy—a work which does him credit in my estimation, for it bases the science of morals more decidedly than Paley has done, upon the only foundation on which it can ever rest—the revelation of God's will by Jesus Christ." Sermon on the Death of the Rev. Jasper Adams, Delivered at Pendleton, by the Rector of Christ Church, Greenville (Charleston, 1842), copy in the College of Charleston Library.

After the American Revolution, Adams observed, "A question of great interest comes up for discussion. In thus discontinuing the connexion between Church and Commonwealth, did these states intend to renounce *all* connexion with the Christian religion? Or did they intend to disclaim all preference of one sect of Christians over another, as far as civil government was concerned; while they still retained the Christian religion as the foundation-stone of all their social, civil and political institutions?"[80] Clearly, said Adams, they adopted the latter position. "In perusing the twenty-four constitutions of the United States . . . we find all of them recognizing Christianity as the well known and well established religion of the communities. . . . The terms of this recognition are more or less distinct in the Constitutions of the different states; but they exist in all of them. The reason why any degree of indistinctness exists in any of them unquestionably is, that at their formation, it never came into the minds of the framers to suppose, that the existence of Christianity as the religion of their communities, could ever admit to a question."[81]

[80] "Relation of Christianity to Civil Government," 6–7. Emphasis supplied. "[B]y the sacrifices of blood and treasure made by our ancestors to establish religious freedom and the free profession of religious faith," said Adams on another occasion, "they never intended to sanction, much less to encourage an utter indifference to all religion. Religious freedom differed, in the view of our fathers, as widely, from indifference to religion, as civil freedom differs from universal license and anarchy." "A Baccalaureate Address," Delivered in St. Paul's Church, November 3, 1835, at the Annual Commencement of the College of Charleston (Charleston, 1835), 12; copy in College of Charleston Library.

[81] "Relation of Christianity to Civil Government," 11. "Nearly all these Constitutions," noted Adams, "enjoin the observance of Sunday, and a suitable observance of this day, includes a performance of all the peculiar duties of the Christian faith. The Constitution of Vermont [art. 3] declares, that every sect or denomination of Christians, ought to observe the Sabbath or Lord's Day, and keep up some sort of religious worship, which to them shall seem most agreeable to the revealed word of God" (*ibid.*, 12). Massachusetts and Maryland do not prescribe the observance of Sunday; but, noted Adams, article 2 of the Massachusetts Constitution declares it to be "the right, as well as the duty of all men in society, publicly and at stated seasons, to worship the Supreme Being," and article 3 states: "As the happiness of a people, and the good order and preservation of civil government, essentially depend upon piety, religion, and morality; and as these cannot be generally diffused through the community, but by the institution of public worship of God, and of public instruction in piety, religion and morality; therefore, to promote their happiness and to secure the good order and preservation of their government, the people of this commonwealth have a right to invest their Legislature with power to authorize and require, and the Legislature shall from time to time authorize and require the several towns, parishes, precincts and other bodies politic, or religious societies, to make suitable provision at their own expense, for the institution of public worship of God, and for the support and maintenance of public Protestant teachers of piety, religion and morality, in all cases, where such provision shall not be made voluntarily. . . . All moneys paid by the subject to the support of public worship, and of the public teachers aforesaid, shall, if he require it, be uniformly applied to the support of the public teacher or teachers of his own religious sect or denomination, provided there be any on whose instructions he attends; otherwise it may be paid towards the support of the teacher or teachers of the parish or

The First Amendment to the federal Constitution, Adams continued, "leaves the entire subject in the same situation in which it found it; and such was precisely the most suitable course. . . . This was too delicate and too important a subject to be entrusted to their guardianship. It is the duty of the Congress, then, to permit the Christian religion to remain in the same state in which it was, at the time when the Constitution was adopted."[82] In conclusion, stated Adams, it should be noted that

From the first settlement of this country up to the present time, particular days have been set apart by public authority, to acknowledge the favour, to implore the blessing, or to deprecate the wrath of Almighty God. In our Conventions and Legislative assemblies, daily Christian worship has been customarily observed. All business proceedings in our Legislative halls and Courts of Justice, have been suspended by the universal consent on Sunday. Christian ministers have customarily been employed to perform stated religious services in the Army and Navy of the United States. In administering oaths, the Bible, the standard of Christian truth is used, to give additional weight and solemnity to the transaction. A respectful observance of Sunday, which is peculiarly a Christian institution, is required by the

---

precinct in which the moneys are raised. And every denomination of Christians, demeaning themselves peaceably and as good subjects of the Commonwealth, shall be equally under the protection of the law; and no subordination of any sect or denomination to another shall be established by law."

Article 55 of the Maryland Constitution requires every person appointed to public office to "subscribe a declaration of his belief in the Christian religion." Both the Massachusetts and Maryland constitutions, moreover, concur in the sentiment of article 6 of the constitution of New Hampshire, that "morality and piety, rightly grounded on Evangelical principles, will be the best and greatest security to government; and that the knowledge of these is most likely to be propagated through a society, by the institution of public worship of the Deity, and of public instruction in morality."

Article 1 of the Connecticut Charter states that it is "the duty of all men to worship the Supreme Being." The constitution of the state of New Jersey declares in article 19 that there shall be no establishment of any one religious sect in preference to another . . . but that all persons professing a belief in the faith of any protestant sect . . . shall be capable of being elected to any office." The constitution of the state of Delaware assumes in article 1 that "it is the duty of all men frequently to assemble together for the public worship of the Author of the Universe; and piety and morality, on which the prosperity of communities depends, are thereby promoted." North Carolina in her constitution, article 32, says "that no person who shall deny the being of a God or the truth of the Protestant religion, or the divine authority of either the Old or New Testament or shall hold religious principles incompatible with the freedom and safety of the State, shall be capable of holding any office or place of trust or profit, in the civil department within this state."

"The principle obtained by the foregoing inductive examination of [some] of our state constitutions," concluded Adams, "is this:—THE PEOPLE OF THE UNITED STATES HAVE RETAINED THEIR CHRISTIAN RELIGION AS THE FOUNDATION OF THEIR CIVIL, LEGAL AND POLITICAL INSTITUTIONS: WHILE THEY HAVE REFUSED TO CONTINUE A LEGAL PREFERENCE TO ANY ONE OF ITS FORMS OVER ANY OTHER." *Ibid.,* 12–13.

[82] *Ibid.,* 13.

laws of all the states. My conclusion, then, is sustained by the documents which gave rise to our colonial settlements, by the records of our colonial history, by our Constitutions of government made during and since the Revolution, by the laws of the respective states, and finally by the uniform practice which has existed under them.[83]

Significant though they are in casting new light upon the original understanding of church-state relations in the formative era, these few remarks excerpted from Adams' sermon are but a sampling of his impressive case against the wall of separation doctrine. Perhaps more revealing and more important, though, are the remarks of those who read the sermon soon after it was published.

Adams, it seems, was anxious to confirm his views and, in pursuance of this end, sent copies of the sermon to leading statesmen and lawyers, requesting that they respond to his arguments and offer their own general observations. Among those who received a copy and commented upon it were Chief Justice Marshall, Judge Story, and James Madison. Both Marshall and Story were in complete agreement with Adams. "The documents annexed to the sermon certainly go far in sustaining the proposition which it is your purpose to establish," wrote Marshall.

No person, I believe, questions the importance of religion to the happiness of man even during his existence in this world. . . . The American population is entirely Christian, & with us Christianity & Religion are identified. It would be strange indeed, if with such a people, our institutions did not presuppose Christianity, & did not often refer to it, & exhibit relations with it. Legislation on the subject is admitted to require great delicacy because freedom of conscience & respect for our religion both claim our most sincere regard. You have allowed their full influence to both.[84]

Judge Story replied more forcefully and directly.

My own private judgment has long been (& every day's experience more & more confirms me in it) that government cannot long exist without an alliance with Religion *to some extent,* & that Christianity is indispensable to the true interests & solid foundation of all governments. I distinguish, as you do, between the establishment of a particular sect, as the religion of this state [Massachusetts], & the establishment of Christianity itself, without any preference of any particular form of it. I know not, indeed, how any deep sense of moral obligation or accountableness can be expected to prevail in the community without a firm foundation of the great Christian truths. . . . Mr. Jefferson has, with his accustomed boldness, denied that Christianity is a part of the Common law, & Dr. [Thomas] Cooper has with even

[83] *Ibid.,* 14–15.

[84] John Marshall to Jasper Adams, May 9, 1833, Clements Library. The letter is a copy of the original and is attached, together with the letters from Story and Madison, to Adams' personal copy of the sermon.

more dogmatism maintained the same opinion. I am persuaded that a more egregious error never was uttered by able men. And I have long desired to find leisure to write a disputation to establish this construction. Both of them rely on authorities & expositions which are wholly inadmissible. And I am surprised that no one has as yet exposed the shallowness of their inquiries. Both of them have probably been easily drawn into . . . such a doctrine by their own scepticism. It is due to truth, & to the purity of the law, to unmask their fallacies.[85]

Then in his eighties, James Madison was the last to reply; but his faculties were unimpaired, and his letter was actually the most extensive and thoughtful of the three. He had not abandoned his original belief that there ought to be a clear separation of church and state; nor had he changed his mind on other matters: at this ripe old age he was still under the influence of Locke and the social contract theory. "Waiving the rights of conscience, not included in the surrender implied by the social state, & more or less invaded by *all* religious establishments, the simple question to be decided," he informed Adams,

is whether a support of this best and purest religion, the Christian religion itself, ought not, *in so far at least as pecuniary means are involved*, to be [promoted] by the government, rather than left to the voluntary provisions of those who profess it. And in this question, experience will be an admitted factor all the more adequate, as the connexion between government & religion, has existed in such various degrees & forms, & now can be compared with examples where the connexion has been entirely dissolved. . . . In the colonial state of this country, there were five examples— Rhode Island, New Jersey, Pennsylvania, & Delaware, & the greater part of New York, where there were no religious establishments, the support of religion being left to the voluntary associations & contributions of individuals; and certainly the religious condition of these colonies, will well be as a comparison, with that where establishments existed.

It is true that the New England states have not discontinued establishments of religion found under very peculiar circumstances; but they have by successive relations advanced towards the prevailing example; & without any evidence of disadvantage, either to Religion or to good government. . . . The apprehension of some seems to be, that Religion left entirely to itself, may run into extravagances, injurious both to religion & social order; but to answer the question whether the interference of government *in any form*, would not more likely to increase than decrease the tendency, it is a safe calculation that in this, as in other cases of excessive excitement, religious sentiment will gradually regain its ascendancy. Great excitements are less apt to be permanent than to vibrate to the opposite extreme . . . . Whilst I thus finally express my view of the subject presented in your Sermon, I must do you the justice to observe that you have very ably maintained yours. I must admit, moreover, that it may not be easy, in every possible case, to trace the line of separation between the rights of Religion & the civil authority, with such distinctions, as to avoid collisions & doubts on ecclesiastical points. The tendency to a usurpation on one side, or the other, or to a conflicting coalition or alliance between them, will be

[85] May 14, 1833, Clements Library.

best guarded against by our entire abstinence of the government, beyond the necessity of preserving public order, & protecting each sect against transgresses on its legal rights by others.[86]

Ostensibly, Madison has insisted upon an absolute separation of church and state. Upon closer examination of his letter, however, it would appear that he has conceded there may be some instances where this is not possible. In the first place, he is concerned primarily with pecuniary aid to religion, and seems to imply that other forms of assistance are not objectionable. What he means exactly by pecuniary aid is not clear, but it seems safe to conclude that he has in mind direct financial grants, such as for the support of salaries or the construction of buildings, and would not extend the meaning of pecuniary aid to include, as does the modern Court, indirect financial assistance that occurs when, for example, public school buildings are used for religious instruction. It should also be noted that Madison is disturbed for the most part over the establishment of specific religious sects by *state* governments and at one point frankly admits that a total separation of church and state is impossible. Why else would he confess that "it is not easy to trace the line of separation in every case"? If there is to be an absolute separation, it would seem to follow that there would scarcely be any difficulty in tracing the line of separation.

But what is perhaps most significant regarding Madison's letter is not what he has said, as what he has neglected to say. The letters of Marshall, Story, *and* Madison all attempt to answer the question of whether there *ought to be* a clear and distinct separation of church and state. No one, including Madison, denies the fact that in many instances such is not the case. Nor does Madison even hint that state aid to one religion or to all religions is unconstitutional; improper, yes, but legal, all the same. And most significantly, Madison does not so much as suggest that aid to religion by the Congress is unconstitutional. Reverend Adams' sermon is packed solid with references to laws passed by the Congress which in varying degrees aid religion. On April 10, 1806, as Adams points out, President Thomas Jefferson signed an act of the Congress providing rules and regulations for officers and enlisted personnel in the army and navy. That act reads:

it is earnestly recommended to all officers and soldiers diligently to attend divine service; and all officers who shall behave indecently or irreverently at any place of divine worship, shall, if commissioned officers, be brought before a general court-martial, *there to be publicly and severely reprimanded by the President*; if non-commissioned officers or soldiers, every person, so offending, shall, for his first offence, forfeit one-sixth of a dollar, to be deducted out of his next pay.[87]

On April 12, 1808, Jefferson signed into law an act providing for the appoint-

---

[86] Sept., 1833, Clements Library. Emphasis supplied.
[87] Adams, "Relation of Christianity to Civil Government," 33. Emphasis supplied.

ment of a chaplain to each brigade of the army. On April 30, 1816, President James Madison signed an act providing chaplains in the two houses of Congress. Now if Jefferson and Madison advocated an absolute separation of church and state, with no aid of any kind to religion generally, why, it may be asked, did they approve such laws? Why does Madison not deny their constitutionality?

These are only a few of the questions that the Reverend Jasper Adams' sermon and the letters of Marshall, Story, and Madison raise. The larger question remains: why has the Supreme Court in effect refused to examine the historical background of the First Amendment?

To comprehend the original understanding of separation of church and state, at least a perusal of the acts of the First Congress, which debated and drafted the First Amendment, would seem in order; but the Vinson and Warren and Burger courts have made no such effort. As a result, state religious practices in the late eighteenth and early nineteenth centuries, as well as the intent of the framers and supporters of the Bill of Rights, have been almost entirely ignored. The Court has, in fact, confined its inquiry into the historical background of the establishment clause to religious persecutions in Europe and the Virginia struggle against the Anglican establishment; and it has interpreted the Virginia experience (through carefully selected statements of Madison and Jeffeerson, against which conflicting statements or practices can be found),[88] to be that of the Congress of 1791, and of the American republic generally.

The likelihood that the Court will in the future reconsider its evidence or examine a document such as the Adams sermon is slim, in light of Justice Clark's statement in the *Schempp-Murray* cases that the Court is weary of historical discussion, and that as far as he and the other members of the Court are concerned, the proper meaning of the establishment clause has forever been settled. Objections by scholars and lawyers to the Court's distortion of history, concluded Clark, "seem entirely untenable and of value only as academic exercises."[89]

FEDERALISM AND THE ESTABLISHMENT CLAUSE

A re-examination of the Story-Jefferson feud about whether Christianity is a part of the common law will, perhaps, throw more light on Story's position then and now, as well as that of Jefferson. What seems clearly evident is that

---

[88] Dissenting in *McCollum*, Justice Reed noted, for example, that "the 'wall of separation between church and state' that Mr. Jefferson built at the University [of Virginia] which he founded did not exclude religious education from that school" (333 U.S. 247). See especially the evidence accµmulated by Rice, *Supreme Court and Public Prayer*, 62–68; see also Francis W. O'Brien, *Justice Reed and the First Amendment*, 131–44.

[89] 374 U.S. 217.

Story and Jefferson were arguing whether there ought to be a separation between the Christian religion and *state* governments. Their argument could not have involved the question of whether religion should be separated from the federal government for two reasons: first, they disagreed over whether Christianity was a part of the *common* law, that is, whether a state court may properly aid religion generally or take cognizance of Christian dogma in rendering decisions. If they had been quarreling over the meaning of the First Amendment, which restricts not the various states, but the federal government, it would seem they would have used the terms *public* law or *constitutional* law, rather than common law.

Secondly, Story and Jefferson were agreed that the federal government had no voice in matters of church-state relations. Jefferson, the states' rightist, firmly agreed with Madison, who wrote in *The Federalist*, Number 45 that "the powers reserved to the several States will extend to all the objects which, in the ordinary course of affairs, concern the lives, *liberties* and properties of the people; and the internal order, improvement and prosperity of the State."[90] Story, the nationalist, embraced the same view: "the whole power over the subject of religion is left exclusively to the State governments, to be acted upon according to their own sense of justice, and the State constitutions."[91] Thus, the question over the extent of interference by the *federal* government in religious matters was not at issue. The real issue was the proper degree of separation between church and state government, since the question concerning separation of church and the national government had already been settled by the First Amendment.

Whether, then, Jefferson's doctrine of an absolute division of church and state has emerged "victorious," as Professor Peterson alleges, is open to debate. To apply Jefferson's wall of separation theory to present cases, as the Supreme

[90] (Modern Library ed.), 303. Emphasis supplied. Professor Corwin, by a different path of reasoning, reaches a similar conclusion. According to Jefferson, says Corwin, "the principal importance of the [First] Amendment lay in the separation which it effected between the respective jurisdictions of state and nation regarding religion, rather than its bearing on the question of the separation of church and state." (Edward S. Corwin, "The Supreme Court as a National School Board," *Law & Contemporary Problems*, Vol. XIV, No. 1 [1949], 14.) "I consider the government of the United States," explained Jefferson, "as interdicted by the Constitution from intermeddling with religious institutions, their doctrines, discipline, or exercises. This results not only from the provision that no law shall be made respecting the establishment or free exercise of religion, but from that also which reserves to the States the powers not delegated to the United States. Certainly, no power to prescribe any religious exercise, or to assume authority in religious discipline, has been delegated to the General Government. It must then rest with the States, as far as it can be in any human authority." To the Reverend Samuel Miller, Jan. 23, 1808, *Writings*, (Memorial ed.), XI, 428.

[91] *Commentaries on the Constitution*, III, sec. 1873, p. 731. Story agreed with Hamilton that the Constitution was in itself a "Bill of Rights," without the first ten amendments. See *Commentaries*, I, sec. 304, p. 277.

Court has done, is to lift it wholly out of context.[92] Jefferson believed that the states were free to prescribe the nature of religious liberty within their respective jurisdictions. Would he also accept the Fourteenth Amendment and the doctrine of incorporation, which introduce the federal judiciary as the final arbiter in religious matters?

The application of the Jeffersonian theory *against* the states, and its utilization by the federal courts in deciding how a state should behave with respect to civil liberties, is wholly contrary to the very basis of the Jeffersonian philosophy of states' rights; and it is incompatible with Jefferson's strong desire to resist the increasing powers of the Supreme Court. To say that the national courts instead of the various state courts should possess final authority in the enforcement of an absolute wall of separation between church and state is similar to arguing that the powers of the states are best preserved by transferring those powers to the federal government. The federalism of the First Amendment is as important as its guarantees of liberty, and the dismissal of this fact has led the judges of the Supreme Court "to disregard—even to distort —the intellectual background of the First Amendment." Unfortunately, the Court has adopted the idea "that the policies of freedom and equality enunciated in 1868 in the Fourteenth Amendment must be read back into the prohibitions of the First Amendment—the familiar process of incorporation carried out, as it were, in reverse. The consequences may be admirable law, but it is . . . distorted history."[93]

At the source of difficulty and widespread misunderstanding concerning the establishment clause, then, is the Fourteenth Amendment. Through the so-called doctrine of incorporation, the Fourteenth Amendment has radically altered the federal structure of the American political system by transferring jurisdiction over civil liberties from the states to the national government— or more specifically, to the federal judiciary. Through an extremely broad interpretation of the word *liberty* in the due process clause of the Fourteenth Amendment, the Supreme Court has gradually "incorporated" the liberties of the First Amendment into the Fourteenth, thereby making them applicable to the states. Hence ultimate authority to determine the nature and extent of civil liberties enjoyed by Americans has been vested in the Supreme Court, whereas before, this awesome power was distributed among the various state judiciaries. The result is that nine individuals possess the enormous power of

---

[92] The phrase is taken from a letter of Jefferson to the Baptist Association of Danbury, Connecticut, 1802, which reads in part: "I contemplate with sovereign reverence that act of the whole American people, which declared that *their legislature* should 'make no law respecting an establishment of religion, or prohibiting the free exercise thereof,' thus building a wall of separation between church and state." (As quoted, with emphasis supplied, in Rice, *Supreme Court and Public Prayer*, 63.) Obviously Jefferson is referring to the Congress, not the state legislatures.

[93] Howe, *The Garden and the Wilderness*, 31.

determining in most cases the range and scope of the civil liberties of every citizen in the United States! That the Fourteenth Amendment and the doctrine of incorporation also nullify the very purpose of the Bill of Rights, which was to guarantee to the individual *and* to the states that the Federal government would have no voice in the general area of civil liberties, except as stipulated in the Constitution itself, is clear enough. The power to expand and contract individual liberties was, in the true sense of that much abused term, the states' right, as determined by the state constitutions and the state bills of rights.[94]

It comes as no surprise, therefore, that there was little debate in the First Congress over the precise meaning of most liberties guaranteed in the Bill of Rights, since the substance of these liberties would be determined at the state level and would, in fact, vary from state to state. Similarly, there was little debate in the ratification struggle over the question of which govenment, state or federal, should possess the power to protect and define civil liberties—simply because most Federalists and Anti-federalists were agreed that this power resided in the states.

It will be recalled that in the Federal Convention, George Mason of Virginia proposed that a declaration of rights be made a part of the Constitution, and that a motion offered by Elbridge Gerry that a committee be appointed to prepare such a statement was voted down *unanimously*. It will also be recalled that the Federalists insisted that there was no need for a bill of rights, that such a declaration would be superfluous or dangerous. Nevertheless, the Federalists bowed to the wishes of the Antifederalists in the ratification fight and, without much of a struggle, agreed to the adoption of a bill of rights. Why were the Federalists so easily won over to a position they had earlier rejected? One reason is that the Bill of Rights changed nothing as far as the constitutional structure was concerned and neither reduced federal power nor increased state power. It simply declared what was already understood, viz., that the national government had no authority in the general area of civil liberties.

What, then, was the real basis of disagreement over the issue of whether or not to adopt a bill of rights? A reading of the documentary material would indicate that the disagreement centered not on the question of political power but on semantics. That is, the Federalists and Antifederalists were in general agreement that the states, not the federal government, would determine under their own bills of rights and state charters the scope and content of civil liberties within their respective jurisdictions. The problem was thus the proper wording of the Constitution regarding the enforcement of civil liberties rather than their actual meaning and content.

[94] See the excellent discussion of the effect of the Fourteenth Amendment upon federalism and the original purpose of the Bill of Rights in Felix Morley, *Freedom and Federalism*, 59–71; see also Edward Dumbauld, *The Bill of Rights and What It Means Today*, 132–39.

If one were to phrase the question as it might have been put in 1787–91: "How can we best guarantee to the people that their civil liberties will be protected, defined, and enforced at the local level? Is a constitution of specific, delegated powers sufficient, or should it be spelled out in print in the form of a bill of rights? In other words, should our bill of rights be implicit or explicit?" This, and little more, is what divided the Federalists and the Antifederalists on the issue of whether or not to adopt a bill of rights.

It is important to emphasize once again that the purpose of the Bill of Rights was twofold: to guarantee to the *individual* that the *federal* government would not encroach upon his civil liberties, and to guarantee to the *states* that the *federal government* would not usurp the states' power over civil liberties. Despite incredible misunderstanding throughout most of American history regarding the basic purposes of the Bill of Rights, the fact remains that the Bill of Rights is essentially a states' rights document. Each amendment was a guarantee to the individual *and* to the states.

Indeed, the federalism of the Bill of Rights was regarded as more important than the protection it afforded to the individual in most of the states at the time of ratification. Six of the states which ratified the Constitution before it went into effect proposed long lists of amendments. "It has frequently been stated that the motive behind these amendments was a desire to secure greater protection for the natural rights of the people. This is true only in part. An examination of the proposals of the first three states to make them, Massachusetts, South Carolina, and New Hampshire, will afford sufficient evidence of the fact that the members of these conventions were much more perturbed about the rights and powers of the states than about the rights of the people."[95] Massachusetts proposed nine amendments, but only the sixth, referring to indictment by grand jury, dealt with individual liberty as such. In one place the short list proposed by South Carolina makes mention of the "freedom of the people," but otherwise it deals with the issue of the "sovereignty of the states." Of the twelve proposed amendments offered by New Hampshire, only the last three have a direct bearing on individual liberty. Only Virginia and North Carolina, it seems, proposed a true bill of rights to the people.[96]

Strange as it may sound today, the First Amendment, although it was a guarantee to the individual that the Congress could not establish a national religion, was at the same time a guarantee to the states that they could, if they desired, establish a state religion.[97] Similarly, the Eighth Amendment, for ex-

[95] Benjamin F. Wright, *American Interpretations of Natural Law*, 146.

[96] *Ibid.*, 147. See *The Debates of the Several State Conventions on the Adoption of the Federal Constitution* (ed. by Jonathan Elliot), I, 319–38.

[97] "The reported debates in the various ratifying conventions . . . reveal that the delegates in the various states generally understood an establishment of religion to mean a sect given preferential legal protection by the government. What these delegates wanted was a guarantee that the new national government would neither set up such a national church

ample, while it protected the individual against cruel and unusual punishments inflicted by the federal government, was also a guarantee to the states that they could mete out punishment as they saw fit. As a matter of law, then, the Bill of Rights could thus be construed as a guarantee to the states that they were free to *deny* civil liberties to their citizens—to deny them the free exercise of religion, to forbid freedom of speech and press, to inflict cruel and unusual punishments, to deprive them of life, liberty, and property without due process of law.

Of course, state constitutions and bills of rights ordinarily prevented in the general course of public affairs any such flagrant denials of individual liberty. But the point is that the Bill of Rights prevented the federal government from interfering with the states in their handling of those liberties enumerated in the Bill of Rights, so that the states could have theoretically, and in accordance with the Constitution, prevented their citizens from enjoying any of the liberties listed in the Bill of Rights had that been their intention.

Extremely significant is the fact the first Congress was presented with a proposal that portions of the Bill of Rights be applied to the states and specifically rejected it. The fifth resolution of James Madison's proposal in the First Congress for a series of amendments which would provide a bill of rights read as follows: "No *State* shall violate the equal rights of conscience, or the freedom of the press, or the trial by jury in criminal cases."[98] The proposal was defeated in the Senate. "This [proposal] is offered," Tucker of South Carolina had wisely observed, "as an amendment to the Constitution of the United States, but it goes only to the alteration of the constitutions of particular States. It will be much better, I apprehend, to leave the State Governments to themselves,

---

nor interfere with the various types of establishments, quasi-establishments, and church-government arrangements existing in the several states. Thus, New Hampshire proposed an amendment which read: 'Congress shall make no laws touching religion . . . .' Since the Constitution of New Hampshire provided special privileges for the Protestant religion, the amendment was very likely aimed at excluding the new government from passing any law that might 'touch' [i.e., alter] their particular type of establishment." (O'Brien, *Justice Reed and the First Amendment*, 134.) The significance of the word *respecting* in the First Amendment may thus be seen: Congress is to make no law respecting (i.e., dealing with the subject of) the establishment of religion, so that existing church-state relations in each state shall remain undisturbed.

[98] From his principal address in the House of Representatives, Apr. 8, 1789, *Annals*, 1 Congress, 1 sess., 435. Note the absence of the establishment clause. One suspects Madison here of clever deceit. The author of the extremely nationalistic Virginia Plan at the Constitutional Convention, he had lost much ground to the states' rightists after the introduction of the New Jersey Plan. Now the moving force behind the adoption of a bill of rights, he had endeared himself to the Antifederalists; yet his proposal, had it been adopted, would have completely undermined the Antifederalist position. Needless to say, his fifth resolution was totally inconsistent with what he had written in the *Federalist* Number 45.

and not to interfere with them more than we already do; and that is thought by many to be rather too much."[99]

The common understanding of the purpose and effect of the adoption of the Bill of Rights was later described by Charles Pinckney in 1800, in these striking words:

When those Amendments became a part of the Constitution, it is astonishing how much it reconciled the States to that measure; they considered themselves as secure in those points on which they were the most jealous; they supposed they had placed the hand of their own authority on the rights of religion and the press, and . . . that they could with safety say to themselves: "On these subjects we are in future secure; we know what they mean and are at present; and such as they now are, such are they to remain, until altered by the authority of the people themselves; no inferior power can touch them."[100]

For nearly a century and a half, the Supreme Court, with only a few scattered dissents, respected these views, thereby securing the object of the Bill of Rights. Speaking for a unanimous Court, Chief Justice Marshall declared in *Barron* v. *The Mayor and City Council of Baltimore* that the first eight amendments "contain no expression indicating an intention to apply them to the state governments."[101] This position was strictly maintained in subsequent decisions involving the First, Fifth, Sixth, Seventh, and Eighth amendments, between 1833 and 1868. In *Permoli* v. *Municipality No. 1 of the City of New Orleans*, for example, Justice Catron upheld for a unanimous Court a city ordinance challenged by the Catholic church, saying, "The Constitution makes no provision for protecting the citizens of the respective States in their religious liberties; this is left to the State constitutions and laws."[102]

But even after the adoption of the Fourteenth Amendment, which forbade any state from denying an individual life, liberty, or property, the Supreme Court continued to follow *Barron* v. *Baltimore*—a fact which strongly indicates that the Fourteenth Amendment was not intended by those who witnessed its creation and sought to interpret its original meaning to defeat the purpose of the Bill of Rights.

[99] In the House of Representatives, Aug. 17, 1789, *Annals*, 1 Congress, 1 sess., 783. Madison unsuccessfully argued that he "conceived this to be the most valuable amendment in the whole list." *Ibid.*

[100] In the Senate, Mar. 28, 1800, *Annals*, 6 Congress, 1 sess., 128. "I appeal to any man," he continued, "who dispassionately peruses the Constitution and its Amendments, and who recollects the mode and reasons of their adoption, to answer if this was not the construction then understood, and which now ought always to be given to them?" (*Ibid.*, 128.) No one answered.

[101] 7 Peters 250 (1833).

[102] 3 Howard 609 (1845). See also *Lessee of Livingston* v. *Moore*, 7 Peters 552 (1833); *Fox* v. *Ohio*, 5 Howard 410 (1847); *Smith* v. *Maryland*, 18 Howard 71 (1855); *Withers* v. *Buckley*, 20 Howard 84 (1857); *Pervear* v. *Massachusetts*, 5 Wallace 475 (1867); *Twitchell* v. *Pennsylvania*, 7 Wallace 321 (1868).

Historical research has since shown, fairly conclusively, that the debates accompanying the proposal and ratification of the Fourteenth Amendment do not justify the doctrine of incorporation.[103] Throughout the late nineteenth and early twentieth centuries, state courts and the Supreme Court adhered to the principle that the Bill of Rights applied only to the federal government. "In at least twenty cases between 1877 and 1907," Charles Warren noted, "the Court was required to rule upon this point and to reaffirm Marshall's decision of 1833."[104] As late as 1922, in *Prudential Insurance Co. v. Cheek*, the Court declared that "neither the Fourteenth Amendment nor any other provision of the Constitution imposes restrictions upon the state about freedom of speech."[105]

Without warning, the Court suddenly reversed more than a century and a half of precedent in 1925 and for the first time announced through dicta that "For present purposes we may and do assume that freedom of speech and of the press—which are protected by the First Amendment from abridgment by Congress—are among the fundamental personal rights and 'liberties' protected by the due process clause of the Fourteenth Amendment from impairment by the states."[106] Probably the most far-reaching and revolutionary decision ever handed down by the Supreme Court in its history, *Gitlow v. New York* attracted little notice at the time. So casual and matter-of-fact was the Court that one suspects the justices themselves did not fully grasp the implications of their own rhetoric. So easily, so fortuitously, was the Bill of Rights thus turned on its head.

How quickly do the aims and accomplishments manifested at a nation's founding soon fade from memory in succeeding generations. Ultimate power to define—and therefore to expand or restrict—civil liberties had silently slipped from the hands of the states to those of the central government, or more precisely, to those of nine individuals sitting on the highest court in the land. A staggering blow had thus been inflicted at the very heart of federalism. Such a drastic and swift rupture with the past could only have succeeded through a profound misunderstanding of the constitutional structure.[107]

Charles Warren, the distinguished historian of the Constitution, was appar-

[103] See, for example, Charles Fairman, "Does the Fourteenth Amendment Incorporate the Bill of Rights? The Original Understanding," *Stanford Law Review*, Vol. II (1949–50), 5–139. The authoritative study, until the publication of Fairman's article, was Horace Edgar Flack's *The Adoption of the Fourteenth Amendment*.

[104] "The New 'Liberty' under the Fourteenth Amendment," *Harvard Law Review*, Vol. XXXIX, No. 4 (Feb., 1926), 436.

[105] 259 U.S. 530 (1922).

[106] 268 U.S. 666 (1925).

[107] The central figure in the creation of section 1 of the Fourteenth Amendment was John Bingham of Ohio, a leader of the Radicals. See Joseph B. James, *The Framing of the Fourteenth Amendment*, 190, regarding "Bingham's confusion on the nature of the Bill of Rights."

ently the only scholar who realized at the time what had happened to the Constitution in the *Gitlow* case. Writing in the *Harvard Law Review* in 1926, Warren observed apprehensively that the Supreme Court had followed *Barron* v. *Baltimore* even after the adoption of the Fourteenth Amendment, "Yet, in this *Gitlow* case, *without even mentioning these previous cases, the Court assumes, without argument,* that this right of free speech is so protected by the Fourteenth Amendment. Thus, by one short sentence, rights, the protection of which have hitherto been supposed to be within the scope of the State courts alone, are now brought within the scope of Federal protection and of the United States Supreme Court."[108] Furthermore, he rightly complained, the Court had distorted the meaning of the word *liberty* by broadening it to include civil liberties. "The phrase, 'life, liberty or property without due process of law,'" Warren pointed out, "came to us from the English common law; and there seems to be little question that, under the common law, the word 'liberty' meant simply 'liberty of the person,' or, in other words, 'the right to have one's person free from physical restraint.' It was not, in any way, the equivalent of 'privileges and immunities.'"[109]

Warren's premonition that the Court had expanded the meaning of the word *liberty* "in a manner which is likely to have important consequences, the extent of which has received little attention as yet,"[110] received little more notice than had the assumptions of the Court in the *Gitlow* decision which had prompted it. In 1931, in *Near* v. *Minnesota*,[111] the Court embarked upon the revolutionary course outlined in *Gitlow* by incorporating freedom of speech and press of the First Amendment into the word *liberty* of the due process clause of the Fourteenth. In subsequent cases the Court added freedom of assembly[112] and freedom of religion.[113] Then, in 1947, the doctrine of incorporation was extended to the establishment clause. Speaking for a divided Court, Justice Black announced in *Everson* v. *Board of Education* that "The First Amendment, as made applicable to the states by the Fourteenth . . . commands that a *state* 'shall make no law respecting an establishment of religion.'"[114]

For the first time the Supreme Court interpreted the establishment clause

[108] "The New 'Liberty' under the Fourteenth Amendment," *Harvard Law Review,* Vol. XXXIX, No. 4 (Feb., 1926), 433. Emphasis supplied.

[109] *Ibid.,* 440. In addition, the due process clause was intended originally to consecrate a mode of procedure rather than a constitutional test of the substantive content of legislation. Edward S. Corwin, *Liberty against Government,* 114.

[110] "The New 'Liberty' under the Fourteenth Amendment," *Harvard Law Review,* Vol. XXXIX, No. 4 (Feb., 1926), 432.

[111] 283 U.S. 697 (1931); see also *Stromberg* v. *California,* 283 U.S. 359 (1931).

[112] *De Jonge* v. *Oregon,* 299 U.S. 353 (1937).

[113] *Cantwell* v. *Connecticut,* 310 U.S. 296 (1940); see also *Hamilton* v. *Regents of the University of California,* 293 U.S. 245 (1934).

[114] 330 U.S. 8 (1947). Emphasis supplied. This assumption was also made in the *Cantwell* case, which, however, involved the free exercise clause.

as a restriction on the *states*. This interpretation in itself was a bold innovation, overturning more than a century of practice which had regularly permitted the states to determine church-state relationships within their jurisdictions. Equally novel was the Court's assertion that the First Amendment "erected a wall between church and state," which prohibited the federal and state governments from giving aid of any kind to religion generally. "Neither a state nor the Federal government," said Justice Black, "can set up a church. Neither can pass laws which aid one religion, *aid all religions*, or prefer one religion over another.... *No* tax in *any* amount, large or small, can be levied to support *any* religious activities or institutions...."[115]

The Court softened the impact of its new view of the establishment clause by upholding the law in question, which had authorized the expenditure of state funds to parents for the cost of transporting their children to parochial schools, as a welfare measure assisting children rather than religion.[116] But the precedent had been established. In the following years the Court successfully implemented its newly articulated doctrines in the *McCollum* case[117] and, more recently, in the school prayer[118] and Bible-reading cases.[119]

Also announced by Justice Black in 1947 was another interpretation of the doctrine of incorporation, which the majority of the Court rejected at this time. Arguing that the entire Bill of Rights rather than the First Amendment alone ought to be incorporated, Black maintained:

My study of the historical events that culminated in the Fourteenth Amendment, and the expressions of those who sponsored and favored, as well as those who opposed its submission and passage, persuades me that one of the chief objects that the provisions of the Amendment's first section, separately and as a whole, were intended to accomplish was to make the Bill of Rights applicable to the states. With full knowledge of the import of the Barron decision, the framers and the backers of the Fourteenth Amendment proclaimed its purpose to be to overturn the constitutional rule that case had announced.[120]

Issued in dissent, Black's sweeping hypothesis, feebly argued, has apparently secured a foothold in the Court. Since 1961 the doctrine of incorporation has been extended beyond the First Amendment to the Fourth,[121] Fifth,[122]

---

[115] *Ibid.*, 15, 16. Emphasis supplied.

[116] Citing Everson, the Court recently sustained a New York law allowing parochial school children to "borrow" without charge secular textbooks approved by local school boards. *Board of Education of Central School District No. 1* v. *Allen*, 392 U.S. 236 (1968).

[117] *McCollum* v. *Champaign Board of Education* (1948).

[118] *Engel* v. *Vitale*, 370 U.S. 421 (1962).

[119] *Abington School District* v. *Schempp* and *Murray* v. *Curlett*, 374 U.S. 203 (1963).

[120] *Adamson* v. *California*, 332 U.S. 71 (1947).

[121] *Mapp* v. *Ohio*, 367 U.S. 643 (1961).

[122] *Malloy* v. *Hogan*, 378 U.S. 1 (1964).

Sixth,[123] Eighth,[124] and Ninth[125] amendments in various other interpretations.

Nonetheless, in Black's contention that section 1 of the Fourteenth Amendment "was intended and understood to impose Amendments I to VIII upon the states, the record of history is overwhelmingly against him."[126] "In the absence of any adequate support for the incorporation theory," concludes Professor Stanley Morrison, "the effort of the dissenting judges in *Adamson* v. *California* to read the Bill of Rights into the Fourteenth amounts simply to an effort to put into the Constitution what the framers failed to put there."[127]

OLD WINE IN NEW BOTTLES

Through an extraordinary accumulation of broad interpretations and historical misrepresentations, the Supreme Court, it would seem, has fabricated a constitutional doctrine nationalizing the Bill of Rights. It is a doctrine which rests upon questionable assumptions. By whatever road one wishes to proceed in order to justify recent decisions involving the establishment clause, he will ultimately be forced to concede that his task is onerous, indeed. Should he begin his quest by turning first to 1789, he is immediately faced with an array of facts that tend to show the very opposite of what he would hope to establish. The common understanding of 1789 and for more than a century thereafter on the

---

[123] *Gideon* v. *Wainwright*, 372 U.S. 335 (1963); *Pointer* v. *Texas*, 380 U.S. 400 (1965); *Parker* v. *Gladden*, 385 U.S. 363 (1966); *Klopfer* v. *North Carolina*, 386 U.S. 213 (1967); *Washington* v. *Texas*, 388 U.S. 14 (1967), *Duncan* v. *Louisiana*, 391 U.S. 145 (1968).

[124] *Robinson* v. *California*, 370 U.S. 660 (1962).

[125] *Griswold* v. *Connecticut*, 381 U.S. 479 (1965).

[126] Fairman, "Does the Fourteenth Amendment Incorporate the Bill of Rights? The Original Understanding," *Stanford Law Review*, Vol. II (1949–50), 139. In matters of constitutional law and history, one must inevitably deal, it seems, with the iconoclasm of Professor Crosskey. In this instance he has urged the rejection of Fairman's findings and has gone so far as to assert that *Barron* v. *Baltimore* was a corruption of the original understanding. In Crosskey's interpretation of Story's position, prior to *Barron*, Story thought the question of whether any provisions in the Bill of Rights applied to the states was "open." Story's analysis of the establishment clause alone indicates otherwise. (See William W. Crosskey, "Charles Fairman, 'Legislative History,' and the Constitutional Limitations on State Authority," *University of Chicago Law Review*, Vol. XXII, No. 1 (Autumn, 1954), 138. See also Charles Fairman, "A Reply to Professor Crosskey," *ibid.*, 144–56. Another scholar has pointed out that "Marshall's serene assertion [in *Barron* v. *Baltimore*] that the Bill of Rights applied only to the general government was but a reiteration of an opinion expressed on circuit during the Burr trial some 26 years earlier. Robertson, *Reports*, I, 99–100. This by itself destroys Crosskey's thesis . . . ." Robert Kenneth Faulkner, *The Jurisprudence of John Marshall*, 61, n. 27.

[127] "Does the Fourteenth Amendment Incorporate the Bill of Rights? The Judicial Interpretation," *Stanford Law Review*, Vol. II (1949–50), 173. According to Alexander M. Bickel (*The Least Dangerous Branch*, 102), Fairman "conclusively disproved Justice Black's contention; at least, such is the weight of opinion among disinterested observers." For an excellent analysis of this issue, see O'Brien, *Justice Reed and the First Amendment*, 112–25.

question of church-state relations seems unmistakably clear: One of the principal underlying purposes of every amendment in the Bill of Rights was to prevent the federal government from usurping the powers of the states over the specifically named guarantees of liberty, and to reaffirm the authority or right of each state to define without federal interference the scope of individual liberty within its own boundaries.

The establishment clause of the First Amendment, applying strictly to the federal government, was designed to prevent the establishment of a national church or religion and to safeguard and leave undisturbed existing relations between church and state at the state and local level. This intent can be shown easily enough not only by the actions and statements of those who framed the Constitution and the Bill of Rights, but by the words in the documents and by the accepted practices of the time, and for a long time thereafter. States were free to aid all religions generally, or if they so chose, as seen in the case of Massachusetts until 1833, to aid one religion in particular; or as seen in the case of Louisiana, to "discriminate" against one religion in particular.[128] In addition, many state courts accepted the doctrine that Christianity was a part of the common law, and punished blasphemy, with and without benefit of statute.

State aid to religion was beyond doubt the rule rather than the exception; but whatever the relation between church and state, as differing from one state to another, the federal government was estopped by the First Amendment from imposing its concept upon the states. Obviously, too, the Bill of Rights was not intended to displace the various state bills of rights, to which the citizens of the various states might turn to ascertain the nature of individual liberty within the state of their residence.

The foregoing would, of course, have less bearing on current decisions involving the establishment clause of the First Amendment if it could be demonstrated satisfactorily that the framers of the Fourteenth Amendment deliberately sought to apply the Bill of Rights to the states and to defeat, therefore, the purpose of the Bill of Rights. But such evidence is scarce, and there is much documentary material, thanks to the efforts of Professor Fairman, which more than suggests that the Fourteenth Amendment was not intended to accomplish the amazing modification of the Bill of Rights it has effected in the last thirty-odd years.[129]

---

[128] See *Permoli* v. *Municipality No. 1 of the City of New Orleans,* 3 Howard 588 (1845). From the standpoint of the Catholic church in New Orleans, in any event, the ordinance was discriminatory, although no specific religious sects were singled out by name.

[129] An excellent, thorough, and richly annotated publication of the congressional debates which led to the proposal and adoption of the Fourteenth Amendment is *The Reconstruction Amendments' Debates* (ed. by Alfred Avins). The general movement away from the idea that fixed principles or the original meaning of a clause is binding on the judges is reflected in the lack of concern over broad judicial interpretations of the

With respect to the establishment clause itself, another constitutional scholar makes the important observation that "a conclusive argument against the incorporation theory, at least as respects the religious provisions of the First Amendment, is the 'Blaine Amendment' proposed in 1875."[130] James Blaine of Maine, we find, introduced a resolution in the Senate that year upon the recommendation of President Grant, which read accordingly, "No *State* shall make any law respecting an establishment of religion or prohibiting the free exercise thereof." Significantly, the Congress which considered the Blaine amendment included twenty-three members of the Thirty-ninth Congress, which passed the Fourteenth Amendment.

Not one of the several Representatives and Senators who spoke on the proposal even suggested that its provisions were implicit in the amendment ratified just seven years earlier. Congressman Banks, a member of the Thirty-Ninth Congress, observed: "If the Constitution is amended so as to secure the object embraced in the principal part of this proposed amendment, it prohibits the States from exercising a power they now exercise." Senator Frelinghuysen of New Jersey urged the passage of the "House article," which "prohibits the States for the first time, from the establishment of religion, from prohibiting its free exercise." Senator Stevenson, in opposing the proposed amendment, referred to *Thomas Jefferson*: "*Friend as he [Jefferson] was of religious freedom, he would never have consented that the States ... should be degraded and that the Government of the United States, a Government of limited authority, a mere agent of the States with prescribed powers, should undertake to take possession of their schools and of their religion.*" Remarks of Randolph, Christiancy, Kernan, Whyte, Bogy, Eaton, and Morton give confirmation to the belief that none of the legislators in 1875 thought the Fourteenth Amendment incorporated the religious provisions of the First.[131]

Fourteenth Amendment, and the concomitant paucity of scholarly works on its legislative history, which would provide the judges with more clearly defined guidelines. A truly comprehensive, authoritative, and satisfactory study of the legislative history of the Fourteenth Amendment has yet to be written.

[130] O'Brien, *Justice Reed and the First Amendment*, 116.

[131] *Ibid.*, 116–17. Emphasis supplied. Two weeks before he introduced his amendment, Blaine sent an "open letter" to the *New York Times*, which clearly reveals that Blaine believed: (1) that the First Amendment was intended to bind Congress only; (2) that by reason of the Tenth Amendment the states were free to establish religions; (3) that the Fourteenth Amendment did not apply to the states so as to forbid either official churches or the public maintenance of sectarian schools. Blaine's letter is reproduced in Francis W. O'Brien, "The States and 'No Establishment': Proposed Amendments to the Constitution since 1798," *Washburn Law Journal*, Vol. IV, No. 2 (Spring, 1965), 188. "A majority of people in any state in this Union can, therefore, if they desire it," said Blaine, "have an established church—under which the minority can be taxed for the erection of church edifices ... this power was actually exercised in many states long after the adoption of the federal constitution, and although there may be no danger of its revival in the future, the possibility of it should not be permitted" (*ibid.*). Between 1876 and 1930, notes O'Brien, nineteen separate amendment proposals were introduced in Congress for the purpose of making the religion provisions of the First Amendment binding upon the states. *Ibid.*, 210.

Nearly every member of the Supreme Court, not to mention those sitting on the state courts, *before* and *after* the adoption of the Fourteenth Amendment, and until 1925, rigorously followed the case of *Barron* v. *Baltimore*. Even more astounding is the fact some twenty years elapsed *after* the doctrine of incorporation came into vogue before it occurred to a member of the Supreme Court that in order to justify the application of any of the first eight amendments to the states, it would first be necessary to establish the fact that the word *liberty* in the due process clause of the Fourteenth Amendment was intended to incorporate a part or all of the Bill of Rights. Instead, the Court assumed that it did, with no mention of previous cases and no supporting arguments. In every case incorporating some provision of the Bill of Rights, from *Gitlow* down through the present, the Court simply declares in its mysterious summary fashion that the liberty in question belongs in the Fourteenth Amendment.[132]

Not until 1947 did any member of the Court attempt to ascertain the proper relationship between the first eight amendments and the Fourteenth as revealed in the utterances and conduct of the framers and backers of the Fourteenth Amendment. In *Adamson* v. *California*, Justice Black endeavored to justify the doctrine of incorporation of the entire Bill of Rights, frankly admitting that the question of whether *Barron* was intended to be overturned "has never received full consideration or exposition in any opinion of this Court interpreting the Fourteenth Amendment."[133] Overruled, in effect, for more than twenty years, the *Barron* decision is at last clearly acknowledged in a *dissenting* opinion; even so, the results of Black's historical investigation have been forcefully challenged, if not refuted, so that a satisfactory defense of the incorporation theory as applied to any portion of the Bill of Rights has yet to be written. It is as though the Court had been handing down decisions for two decades under a certain provision of the Constitution without having bothered to read it and, when finally called upon to do so by one of its own members, simply ignored the problem altogether.

Compounding the phenomena of incorporation, of course, is the overriding question of whether the Fourteenth Amendment was properly ratified in the first place, a question which the Court has, likewise, refused to examine.[134]

[132] There is, of course, the doctrine of "preferred freedoms" enunciated in *Palko* v. *Connecticut*, 302 U.S. 319 (1937). But most of the First Amendment had already been incorporated by this time, and the Palko doctrine was nothing more than an attempt to justify *philosophically* the application of those First Amendment guarantees to the states; it was not an attempt to justify the doctrine of incorporation on legal or historical grounds. Moreover, the *Palko* doctrine is inconsistent with recent cases that have extended the doctrine of incorporation to liberties outside the First Amendment, which the Court indicated in 1937 were not "preferred freedoms."

[133] 332 U.S. 72 (1947).

[134] See, for example, Joseph F. Inghan, "Unconstitutional Amendment," *Dickinson*

Assuming, *arguendo*, the Fourteenth Amendment was deliberately designed to overturn *Barron*, there remains the semantical difficulty of incorporating the establishment clause of the First Amendment into the word *liberty* of the due process clause of the Fourteenth. As Edward S. Corwin and other students of the Constitution have repeatedly demonstrated, the prohibition against the establishment of religion is not an individual liberty like freedom of speech, religion, and press, which an individual may exercise, but a general principle of interpretation which, like the Tenth Amendment, delineates the spheres of power between two levels of authority. Adherence to the principle of separation of church and state is at best a means to individual liberty.[135]

To associate the names of Jefferson or Story with the current decisions respecting an establishment of religion is, then, somewhat presumptuous. It not only assumes their unquestioned deference to the confusion and obliquity which characterize the doctrine of incorporation in all its manifestations, but grossly distorts their constitutional views. It is clear that Judge Story's decisions, which involved state interference in religious affairs, do not properly belong in present majority opinions involving separation of church and state, since they support the no preference theory; and like Jefferson, Story did not believe the national government had direct, plenary authority to enforce a separation between church and state government. In broadening the original sense of Jefferson's phrase, "wall of separation," to encompass an absolute separation between church and all levels of government, the Court has, in effect, made Jefferson a party to the emasculation of his own constitutional doctrines. Thus in the final analysis there is good cause to argue that neither the view of Jefferson nor Story emerged "victorious," and that the present Court has adopted a view of the establishment clause which is wholly anathema to the positions defended by Jefferson and Story.

But this much can be said of Jefferson's alleged triumph over Story: Through *Terrett* v. *Taylor*, Story defeated the Jeffersonian assault against the Virginia Episcopal church, thereby setting a precedent for the governmental protection of church property and assistance to religion. Neither the state nor the federal

---

Law Review, Vol. XXXIII, No. 3 (Mar., 1929), 161–68; James, *The Framing of the Fourteenth Amendment*, 192–93; Flack, *The Adoption of the Fourteenth Amendment*, 161–209.

135 The impossibility of incorporating the establishment clause was pointed out by a law student as early as 1938: "Congress is forbidden to make a law 'respecting an establishment of religion.' But to argue that a state law is void because it is a law 'respecting an establishment of religion' would be pointless: The state law, if bad, must be proved bad not as a law respecting 'an establishment of religion' but because it deprives one of liberty or property without due process. Not every law respecting an establishment of religion would amount to a deprivation of 'liberty' or 'property.'" Vernon L. Wilkinson, "The Federal Bill of Rights and the Fourteenth Amendment," *Georgetown Law Review*, Vol. XXVI, No. 2 (Jan., 1938), 464. See also Bozell, *Warren Revolution*, 79.

courts have ever accepted Jefferson's notion that Christianity is not a part of the common law. The Christian religion was explicitly recognized by English and American jurists as having been incorporated into the common law, and Story affirmed it as a rule of interpretation in the highest tribunal of America, while sustaining Girard's will.

Justice Brewer reiterated Story's doctrine and upheld the Girard will case in *Church of the Holy Trinity* v. *United States*,[136] while holding that Congress could not have intended to make it a misdemeanor for an American church to contract for the services of a Christian minister residing in England, when it passed a statute making it illegal to bring aliens into the country to work. To impute such an intent to Congress would be to ignore the fact that the Americans are a religious people. In presenting evidence of America's religious character, Justice Brewer observed, "Every constitution of every one of the forty-four States contains language which either directly or by clear implication recognizes a profound reverence for religion and an assumption that its influence in all human affairs is essential to the well-being of the community."[137]

Chief Justice Waite and Justice Field applied the principles of Christianity when they struck down the practices of bigamy and polygamy as crimes against "the laws of all civilized and Christian countries. . . . [T]o teach, advise and counsel their practice is to aid in their commission and such teaching and counseling are themselves criminal and proper subjects of punishment. . . . They tend to destroy the purity of the marriage relation, to disturb the peace of families, to degrade woman and to debase man."[138] In speaking out against these practices, the Court was simply echoing Mr. Justice Story. "Marriage is an institution," he had emphatically declared in his essay on natural law, "which may properly be deemed to arise from the law of nature. . . . It secures the peace of society . . . . Polygamy, on the other hand, seems utterly repugnant to the law of nature. . . . If marriage be an institution derived from the law of nature, then whatever has a natural tendency to discourage it, or to destroy its value, is by the same law prohibited."[139]

The dispute between Story and Jefferson narrows down, it would seem, to the question of whether Christianity *ought* to be a part of the common law. Theological considerations aside, one again hesitates to endorse the Jeffersonian view, however, for reasons of public order and political expediency.

In the main, the judicial recognition of Christianity as a part of the common law meant simply that offenses against the fundamental principles of Christianity were punishable at common law. With isolated exceptions the courts

---

[136] 143 U.S. 457 (1891). Citing *Vidal* and the Updegraff ruling, Justice Brewer asserted that "Christianity . . . is, and always has been a part of the common law of Pennsylvania."
[137] *Ibid.*, 470–71.
[138] *Davis* v. *Beason*, 133 U.S. 341.
[139] "Natural Law," *Encyclopedia Americana*, IX, 152–53.

did not seek to use this maxim to infringe upon individual conscience or to eradicate heresy; for that was done through English statute law. The open vilification of the Christian religion was interpreted by the courts in most instances as only that form of speech or action which tended to disturb public morality and order or subvert organized government.[140] Viewed in the light of the First Amendment, therefore, this maxim involved not only the establishment clause, but the free exercise of religion as well.

The free exercise of religion, like speech and press, is not, according to the Supreme Court, an absolute right. "There are certain well-defined and narrowly limited classes of speech, the prevention and punishment of which have never been thought to raise any Constitutional problem. These include the lewd and obscene, the profane, the libelous, and the insulting or 'fighting' words—those which by their very utterance inflict injury or tend to incite an immediate breach of the peace." So stated the Court in *Chaplinsky* v. *New Hampshire*.[141] There appears to be no reason why blasphemous libel should not be considered as a form of speech which, under certain circumstances, would be punishable as tending "to incite an immediate breach of the peace." Conceivably, the Supreme Court in the future could be called upon to uphold a conviction for speech consisting of blasphemous libel in accordance with the principles of the *Chaplinsky* decision.

Blasphemy laws exist at present in many states and forbid the use of profane or obscene language which tends to disparage religion.[142] They are a product of the Christian heritage and of the legal principle that Christianity is a part of the common law. Would the Supreme Court, in sustaining such a law under the *Chaplinsky* doctrine, be supporting order, religion, or both? Although the present Court speaks in terms of an "absolute wall of separation between Church and State," the problems encountered in establishing this doctrine are, it would seem, as many as they are difficult. In more ways than one, the nation at both the federal and state levels refuses to practice what the Supreme Court preaches. Chaplains continue to serve in the armed forces, prayers continue to be read in schools and government buildings, including the houses of Congress and the Supreme Court, and in countless other ways religion is supported by governmental policy.[143]

The Supreme Court has in effect imposed a constitutional theory or standard respecting church-state relations which not only lacks support in American constitutional history, but is in many instances either impossible to follow or

[140] See Aldrich, "The Christian Religion and the Common Law," American Antiquarian Society *Proceedings*, New Series, Vol. VI (Apr., 1889–Apr., 1890), 24–37.

[141] 315 U.S. 571–72 (1942).

[142] See Chester James Antieau, et al., *Religion under the State Constitutions*, 80–83.

[143] Recently the Court ruled that tax exemptions to church property are constitutional. See *Walz* v. *Tax Commission*, 397 U.S. 664 (1970).

openly violated. Despite Supreme Court rulings over the past twenty years, a good case can be made to show that *in practice*, America continues to subscribe to the view of Mr. Justice Story that government should and does aid religion in a variety of ways.

CHAPTER IV

Common Law and Constitution

*Our ancestors were entitled to the common law of England when they emi-
grated, that is, to just so much of it as they pleased to adopt. . . . as to British
liberties, we scarcely know what they are, as the liberties of England and
Scotland are not precisely the same to this day. English liberties are but certain
rights of nature reserved to the citizen by the English constitution, when they
crossed the Atlantic.*

JOHN ADAMS, *Novanglus*, March 13, 1775

Thus, in 1775, John Adams proclaimed the common law of England to be the
law of nature and the birthright of every American. His Tory antagonist
Daniel Leonard (*Massachusettensis*) fully agreed; but it did not necessarily
follow from the premise, argued Leonard, that because Americans were entitled to the rights of Englishmen, they were also exempt from all laws they did
not consent to in person or by representative.[1] As Burke had warned Parliament, however, Americans thought taxation without representation was
slavery; that it was legal slavery was little compensation to their feeling or
understanding.[2] John Adams and those who believed in his cause would not be
argued into slavery.

So the altercation was settled by the Revolution: Americans would adopt
just so much of the common law "as they pleased to adopt." But how much
of English common law would the judges and lawyers who followed in the
footsteps of Adams incorporate into the American legal system? When Judge
Tapping Reeve opened the first American law school in Litchfield, Connecticut, in 1784, could John C. Calhoun, the school's most eminent graduate, return
to South Carolina with the knowledge of how much of the English common
law, in which he was versed, had been transplanted to America? Probably not.

Being geographically isolated in a wilderness quite unlike the bustling streets
of London, or even rural England, the settlers who carved out the roads and
clearings along the eastern seaboard during the seventeenth and eighteenth
centuries were compelled to make the common law applicable to their situation

---

[1] "Massachusettensis," reprinted in *The Political Writings of John Adams* (ed. by
George Peek, Jr.), 35.
[2] Edmund Burke, "Speech on American Taxation," *Works*, I, 383–437.

by modifying it. Knowing no other system, they strove at first to settle their disputes by the hard and fast rules of the common law. But, as time elapsed and English authority became more and more lax, the old rules were changed and new ones adopted, so that, American law on the eve of the Revolution was both an imitation of the common law and a unique legal system—a mosaic of local custom and usage, statute law, and common law.

It was precisely because the common law had changed that Anglo-American understanding steadily deteriorated. Adams was right when he confessed that "as to British liberties, we scarcely know what they are." He could only know what the American liberties were that had evolved out of the common law and the colonial experience. "And indeed," said Blackstone, "it is one of the characteristic marks of English liberty, that our common law depends upon custom; which carries this internal evidence of freedom along with it, that it probably was introduced by the voluntary consent of the people."[3] Common law was an organic system developed over centuries to suit the needs of a particular people under a particular set of circumstances. To suppose it could simply be lifted as a body to an entirely new situation was to misunderstand its very nature and requirement of popular acceptance. American liberties were, in effect, "new" liberties forged out of the common law substance that sailed with the men of the *Mayflower*.

Americans asserted their understanding of common law rights under the paternal vigilance of John Adams and the founding fathers at Bunker Hill and Yorktown. History, however, has shown that revolutions, while they often correct old injustices, also usher in new problems.

In the case of the American Revolution, there was no settlement of the issue over the nature of the common law which Americans had inherited. Few had the leisure, curiosity, or the method to venture a solution; others chose simply to ignore the possibility altogether. Indeed, there were Jeffersonians who opposed the adoption of the common law and aspired to create an entirely new code of rules patterned along the lines of abstract rights, which the common law denied to men. Where the ordinary guides had grown dim or failed, the unprecedented course of the American jurist, who was endowed with the responsibility of providing a legal justification for these newly inspired liberties, was less clear than before. He was a navigator on a strange sea trusting mainly to the instruments and rules of his science for reaching port. Nathan Dane summed up the task of the American lawyer in the introductory essay to his timely *General Abridgment and Digest of American Law*:

At the close of the American revolutionary war, when the United States became an independent nation, it was very material to inquire and to know what was law in them, collectively and individually; also to examine, trace, and ascertain what were the political principles on which their system was founded; and their *moral* char-

[3] Sir William Blackstone, *Commentaries*, I, 63.

acter, so essential to be attended to in the support and administration of this system; especially in selecting from the English laws in force in the monarchy once feudal, those parts of them adopted here, and remaining in force in our republic. . . . No measures had ever been taken to ascertain with any accuracy what part of English law our ancestors adopted in the colonies or provinces.[4]

To men like Story, who wished to build the American constitutional and legal edifice upon common law foundations, the determinations of authority and the lessons of antiquity were here and now, the chart, needle, and plummet. Inspired with the necessary curiosity and leisure, entrusted with the method, Story regarded the extent to which American law was based on English law as a problem demanding immediate attention. An accurate knowledge of the common law origin of American law would ease the herculean task of the inexperienced jurist in determining rules of decision where statutes were wanting. In other words, the substantiation of a theory setting out the general character of the common law which American colonists had brought to their shores could be employed to determine the source from which the "law" is found, and the "rights" to which the litigants were entitled.

STORY'S THEORY OF ADOPTION

From the very outset of his legal studies in 1798, to his final years on the Supreme Court, the problem of adoption stuck like a burr to Joseph Story. Much of his remarkable career centers upon this enigma handed down from the American Revolution. Story was first introduced to the issue, and provided a practical solution, by his Federalist law teacher, Samuel Sewall. "Blackstone shews you what *is* the law of England," Sewall explained,

> whether originating in immemorial usage or in known statutes. There may be some few principles laid down by him which later determinations of the Judicial Courts have disproved, some few provisions which the Parliam't has by Stat[ute] changed or abrogated. But generally speaking you may consider his information as perfectly correct in describing the rules of municipal law as at present understood and practiced in England. Whether it is or is not in every particular is a question of very little use with us: for it is sufficient that the most important & indisputable rules are arranged by him in the order by which they will be most readily conceived, and effectively retained, and that they shew us that system of written & unwritten reason which our fathers brought with them to this Country & very early adopted as the bond of social order & as their noblest inheritance from their native country.

---

[4] As quoted in Joseph Story, "Digest of the Common Law," *Miscellaneous Writings*, 394–95. Dane began the work in the early 1780s. It appeared in eight volumes in 1823–24, with a supplementary volume in 1829, and was the first comprehensive compendium of law produced in America. Dane concerned himself primarily with the American charters, constitutions, statutes, and decisions which had been incorporated along with the common law into American jurisprudence; but he also made occasional references to constitutional law. See also Elizabeth K. Bauer, *Commentaries on the Constitution*, 124–32.

To what extent and in what particulars these rules have been adopted is a question to be fully answered only by experience.

It may be answered generally that all the Rules of the English law, that is of the common or customary as modified by the statute law, in use & force at the departure of our fathers from their native country, & which have been found applicable to the form of society & gov't & the state of property adopted by them in this acquired territory, became the laws of this land & have so continued unless changed by the acts & ordinances which their gov't has had authority to make—to which may be added the changes wrought by the Stat[utes] of the Engl[ish] Parl't in which the colonies were expressly named & which were formerly holden to be binding therein; & some States which on account of their reasonableness and utility were admitted by the Courts of Law here, as modifications of the common law in certain instances, altho[ugh] enacted at much later periods than the emigration of our ancestors. Of the additions to our laws, by the Engl[ish] Parl't subseq't to the emigration, the Act for changing the Style, & Act of Witnesses to Wills and Testaments are as I recollect instances where the colonies were expressly named, & the Statute of Anne for amendments in legal process and the Stat[ute] of Negot'ble Notes are instances where they obtained authority as reasonable & useful by the admission of the Courts of Justice & the acquiescence of the legislative assemblies. Perhaps these two cases are not to be distinguished at this day, because by the maxims maintained at the period of the revolution of the American col[onies] the Parlm't had no authority to bind them in any case whatever; & therefore when such Acts of Parlm't have been conferred here, the admission is less to be ascribed to the naming of the Col[ony] therein, than to the reasonableness and utility of the laws. . . .

[W]hile you shall be acquiring a knowledge of the law of England, you will read in discourse or as occasion may require, the Stat[utes] of the State of Mass[achusetts] & in them you will discover all the local & positive variations of the general system: those variations which are to be argued from neglect or disuse of particular rules will be the subject of some doubt until you shall be more informed by observing the Practice of the Courts & by listening to the conversations or arguments of the professional lawyers.[5]

Sewall's understanding of the problem was in general shared by most members of the bar, at least among Federalists in Massachusetts, and Story made it a permanent part of his legal doctrine. In none of his later treatises did he venture to present a refined theory of the common law origin of American law, but in his *Commentaries on the Constitution* he sketched in an outline, and in his judicial opinions dealt with the question in a variety of circumstances. In his *Commentaries*, Story laid out the general proposition that

In the charters . . . either expressly or by necessary implication it is provided that the laws of England so far as applicable shall be in force there. . . .

And [this] has been the uniform doctrine in America ever since the settlement of the colonies. The universal principle (and the practice has conformed to it) has

---

[5] Sewall to Story, Feb. 12, 1799, Story Papers, Clements Library.

been, that the common law is our birthright and inheritance, and that our ancestors brought hither with them upon their emigration all of it, which was applicable to their situation. The whole structure of our present jurisprudence stands upon the original foundations of the common law. . . . It was not introduced as of original and universal obligation in its utmost latitude; but the limitations contained in the bosom of the common law itself, and indeed constituting a part of the law of nations, were affirmatively settled and recognized in the respective charters of settlement.[6]

A close examination of this statement will show that Story viewed the incorporation of the common law from two perspectives. First, he contended that "the whole structure" of American jurisprudence was based upon the common law, and that certain common law obligations consistent with "a part of the law of nations" were also recognized in the colonial charters. In other words, Story believed that a general body of law, consisting of common law and general legal principles (which would include natural law principles as well as those of the law of nations) constituted the foundation of the American legal system in the several states.

To Jeffersonian Republicans, of course, such an interpretation was wholly unacceptable. Not only did it look favorably upon America's ties with the English and their system of "despotic" laws, but it flatly contradicted a basic premise of the Jeffersonian creed—that the American Revolution was fought to secure the natural rights of men. In a footnote to his general proposition, Story emphasized that the settlers brought with them and struggled to preserve not natural rights but common law rights. Thus, he argued, in spite of "the clearness of this doctrine, both from the language of the charters, and the whole course of judicial decisions, Mr. Jefferson has treated it with an extraordinary degree of . . . contempt."[7]

Quoting at length a letter written by Jefferson to Judge Tyler, Story then proceeded to demonstrate his point. Jefferson's letter read as follows: "I deride with you the ordinary doctrine, that we brought with us from England the common law rights. This narrow notion was a favourite in the first moment of rallying to our rights against Great Britain. But it was that of men, who felt their rights, before they had thought of their explanation. The truth is, that we brought with us the rights of men, of expatriated men."[8] Story rebutted Jefferson's argument by quoting from the *Journal of Congress*, "Declaration of Rights of the Colonies," October 14, 1774. The members of Congress had *unanimously* resolved, Story noted, "That the respective colonies are entitled *to the common law of England*." They did not claim the rights of expatriated men, but the "rights, liberties and immunities of free and natural born subjects within the realm of England."[9]

[6] *Commentaries on the Constitution*, I, sec. 157, p. 140; sec. 158, p. 141.

[7] *Ibid.*, 140.

[8] *Ibid.*

[9] *Ibid.* Story does not discuss the Declaration of Independence.

Secondly, Story deduced that, although the general principles of the common law were established everywhere, the common law, as a body of rules, was not introduced "in its utmost latitude," and only those rules which were "applicable to their situation" were adopted by the colonists. In thus qualifying his general proposition, Story found it necessary to reject a basic rule of the English common law which had long been maintained by English jurists, including Blackstone. Under English common law, he freely admitted, "If an uninhabited country is discovered and planted by British subjects, the English laws are said to be immediately in force there; for the law is the birthright of every subject. So that, wherever they go, they carry their laws with them; and the new-found country is governed by them."[10] This law, however,

requires many limitations, and is to be understood with many restrictions. Such colonists do not carry with them the whole body of the English laws, as they then exist; for many of them must, from the nature of the case, be wholly inapplicable to their situation, and inconsistent with their comfort and prosperity. There is, therefore, this necessary limitation implied, that they carry with them all the laws applicable to their situation, and not repugnant to the local and political circumstances, in which they are placed.[11]

In deference to local and national experience then, Story distinguished between that common law which was *legally* in force and that which was *actually* in operation. From a strictly legal standpoint, all English common law governed the colonies. In reality, however, much of it fell by the wayside or was deliberately rejected. Generally, the principles and rights growing out of the common law were everywhere in force and could not be radically altered by the colonial peoples, as these were immutable. The precise determination of what portions of those less permanent truths had been incorporated, however, did not lend itself to easy analysis.

Story confessed, in fact, there is no answer to the question of how much of the English common law had been adopted during the colonial era. Notwithstanding a general adoption, "it is obvious that the qualifications annexed to it must have given rise to many very perplexing doubts and difficulties."[12] The enactments of colonial, provincial, and state legislatures, together with judicial opinions, had narrowed the areas of disagreement; "yet there still remain some topics of debate upon which it would not be easy to affirm, whether the common law of England had been adopted here or not."[13]

[10] *Ibid.*, sec. 146, p. 132.

[11] *Ibid.*, sec. 148, pp. 132–33.

[12] Story, "Codification of the Common Law," *Miscellaneous Writings*, 700.

[13] *Ibid.* In his *Commentaries*, Story remarks that "it must still remain a question of intrinsic difficulty to say, what laws are, or are not applicable to their situation; and whether they are bound by the present state of things, or are at liberty to apply them in future by adoption, as the growth or interests of the colony may dictate. . . . It is not

In his *Commentaries*, Story made no attempt to discern exactly what portions of the common law were incorporated, but he suggested that "English rules of inheritance and of protection from personal injuries, the rights secured by Magna Charta and the remedial course in the administration of justice"[14] were some examples of those common law rights which were presumptively adopted. In the final analysis, what is to be omitted or retained is a matter of delicate discretion and diversity of judgment.

The distinction which Story makes between this "general foundation of local jurisprudence" common to every colony, and the "actual superstructure" of the laws which differ in "symmetry of design" and "unity of execution"[15] from colony to colony is more fully elaborated in his judicial opinions. Story tackled the problem soon after accepting his judgeship in the case of *Town of Pawlet* v. *Clark*. [16] The case centered upon a charter issued to the town of Pawlet in 1761 by the king of England, through the governor of New Hampshire, in which certain lands were granted as a glebe to the Church of England. The crown, however, made no attempt to erect a church, and no representative of the church was on hand to accept the grant; but in 1802, a society of Episcopalians was organized, which took possession of the property. Meanwhile, Vermont became a state, and Pawlet a town in it. In 1805, Vermont granted

---

perhaps easy to settle, what parts of the English laws are, or are not in force in any such colony, until either by usage, or judicial determination, they have been recognized as of absolute force." (*Commentaries on the Constitution*, I, sec. 149, p. 133.) "Practically speaking it seems to have been left to the judicial tribunals in the colonies to ascertain, what part of the common law was applicable to the situation of the colonies." *Ibid.*, sec. 163, p. 147.

[14] I, sec. 149, p. 133. Story seems to include trial by jury in this classification: "It was under the consciousness of the full possession of the rights, liberties, and immunities of British subjects, that the colonists in almost all the early legislation of their respective assemblies insisted upon a declaratory act, acknowledging and confirming them. And for the most part they thus succeeded in obtaining a real and effective magna charta of their liberties. The trial by jury in all cases, civil and criminal, was as firmly, and as universally established in the colonies, as in the mother country." (*Ibid.*, sec. 165, pp. 148–49.) However, regarding rules of inheritance, the law of descents was not presumed to have been adopted, "and it may now be gathered as the rule of construction, that even in a colony, to which the benefit of the laws of England is expressly extended, the law of descents of England is not to be deemed, as necessarily in force there, if it is inapplicable to their situation; or at least, that a change of it is not beyond the general competency of the colonial legislature." (*Ibid.*, sec. 181, p. 167.) Furthermore, "One of the most remarkable circumstances in our colonial history is the almost total absence of leasehold estates. The erection of manors with all their attendant privileges, was indeed, provided for in several of the charters. But it was so little congenial with the feelings, the wants, or the interests of the people, that after their erection they gradually fell into desuetude." *Ibid.*, sec. 172, pp. 159–60.

[15] *Ibid.*, sec. 163, p. 148.

[16] 9 Cranch 292 (1815).

to the town of Pawlet all lands which the king of England had previously granted to the Episcopalian (Anglican) Church. The recently formed society of Episcopalians refused to surrender the property, and the town of Pawlet thereupon brought an action of ejectment to recover possession of the lot.

The Supreme Court took jurisdiction over the case under the authority of article 3, section 2, which states that the Courts shall have jurisdiction over "controversies between citizens of the same State claiming lands under grants of different States." Story asserted the Court's jurisdiction was applicable where one party claimed land under a grant from the state of New Hampshire, and another claimed it under a grant from the state of Vermont, irrespective of the fact that at the time of the grant Vermont was a part of New Hampshire. According to Judge Story, the question involved grants from two states; for "Although the territory of Vermont was once a part of New Hampshire, yet the State of Vermont, in its sovereign capacity, is not, and never was, the same as the State of New Hampshire."[17]

The second issue of the case concerned the original grant of the king. Was it void for want of a grantee, or, if it could take effect at all, did it not do so as a public reservation, which, upon the American Revolution, devolved upon the state of Vermont? In upholding the claim of the town of Pawlet, Story reasoned that because there was no duly consecrated church established in Pawlet at the time of the charter, the land passed to "pious uses" as a public appropriation. In this respect it would form an exception to the general common law rule which had been incorporated into the state of New Hampshire:

We take it to be a clear principle that the common law in force at the emigration of our ancestors is deemed the birthright of the colonies, unless so far as it is applicable to their situation, or repugnant to their other rights and privileges. *A fortiori* the principle applies to a royal province [New Hampshire] .... The common law, so far as it respected the erection of churches of the Episcopal persuasion of England, the right to present, or collate to such churches, and the corporate capacity of the persons thereof to take in succession, seems to have been fully recognized and adopted. It was applicable to the situation of the province, was avowed in the royal grants and commissions, and explicitly referred to in the appropriation of glebes, in almost all the charters of townships in the province.[18]

Here, however, until a parson should be legally inducted to a new church, the fee of its lands remained in abeyance. A mere voluntary society of Episcopalians, unauthorized by the crown, had no greater claim to the glebe than any other sect in the town.

Thus, concluded Story, whenever an Episcopal (Anglican) church, prior to the Revolution, was erected by the crown in any town, its regularly inducted

---

[17] *Ibid.*, 322–23.

[18] *Ibid.*, 333–34. Justice Johnson concurred. "I see nothing to prevent the legislature itself from making an appropriation of this property." *Ibid.*, 338.

parsons had a right to the glebe in perpetual succession. But where no such church had been established, the state, which succeeded to the rights of the crown, might "alien or encumber" it, if the town assented. However, noted Story in a dictum, a grant of land by a state to a town could not afterwards be repealed so as to divest the town of its rights under the grant.

In *Van Ness* v. *Pacard*,[19] Story found another opportunity to apply his theory of adoption as the basis for decision. Citing this opinion as a classic example of the influence of natural law in judicial decision-making during the early nineteenth century, Roscoe Pound has observed that "the creative spirit of seventeenth century natural law is to be found in the doctrine that the common law was received only so far as applicable to the physical, political, social, and economic conditions of America."[20] In this case, the plaintiff, Van Ness, had leased a certain lot of ground in the city of Washington to the defendant at an annual rental of $112. Pacard took possession of the property and constructed upon the premises a house and stable. These buildings he used to house his family and servants, and in his business of operating a dairy and carrying on a carpentry trade. Thereafter, Pacard removed the buildings to another locale, and the plaintiff brought an action against Pacard for waste committed by him while a tenant. There was no statute authorizing a tenant to remove fixtures which he might erect upon rented property, but Pacard contended that such was the custom, provided it was done before the expiration of the term.

With no statute controlling, Judge Story was compelled to rely upon common law principles in adjusting the claims of the litigants. He admitted that the general rule of the common law is, that whatever is once annexed to the freehold becomes a part of it and cannot afterwards be removed except by him who is entitled to the inheritance. This rule, however, is open to exception:

The Common law of England is not to be taken in all respects to be that of America. Our ancestors brought with them its general principles, and claimed it as their birthright; but they brought with them and adopted only a portion which was applicable to their situation. There could be little or no reason for doubting that the general doctrine as to things annexed to the freehold, so far as it respects heirs and executors, was adopted by them. . . . But between landlord and tenant it is not so clear that the rigid rule of the common law . . . was so applicable to their situation as to give rise to necessary presumption in its favor.[21]

Story then proceeded to point out why the general common law doctrine was not "applicable to our situation." During the colonial period "the country was a wilderness, and the universal policy was to procure its cultivation and

19 2 Peters 137 (1829).
20 *Formative Era of American Law*, 108.
21 *Van Ness* v. *Pacard*, 2 Peters 144–45.

improvement." The object of public policy was the encouragement of agriculture, and Judge Story deemed a law which deterred its development to be unreasonable. "[I]n the comparative poverty of the country, what tenant could afford to erect fixtures of much expense or value, if he was to lose his whole interest therein by the very act of erection? His cabin or log hut, however necessary for any improvement of the soil, would cease to be his the moment it was finished." Story therefore concluded that, unless the common law doctrine has been adopted by a particular statute or judicial decision, it was open to question whether "it ought to be assumed by this Court as a part of the jurisprudence of such state, upon the mere footing of its existence in the common law."[22]

Shortly after the *Pacard* decision, Story once again weighed English common law against the American experience, this time ruling that certain common law rules of evidence had been incorporated into the American law. The issue in *Patterson* v. *Winn*[23] concerned the problem of whether an exemplification (copy) of a grant of land under the seal of the state of Georgia was per se evidence of the original document. Because Georgia had no statutes controlling this question and had never established any rules or customs at variance with the common law, Story therefore assumed that English common law constituted the rule of decision.

We think it clear that by the common law, as held for a long period, an exemplification of a public grant under the seal is admissible in evidence as being record proof of as high a nature as the original. It is a recognition in the most solemn form by the government itself of the validity of its own grant, under its own seal, and imparts absolute verity as a matter of record.

The authorities cited at the bar fully sustain this doctrine . . . . It was to cure this difficulty that the statutes of 3 Edw. VI, Ch. 4, and 13 Eliz., Ch. 61 were passed, by which patentees and all claiming under them were enabled to make title in pleading by showing forth an exemplification of the letters patent, as if the original were pleaded and set forth. These statutes being passed before the emigration of our ancestors, being applicable to our situation, and in amendment of the law, constitute part of our common law.[24]

Justice Johnson, the Marshall Court's most consistent defender of states' rights, dissented on the ground "that were it generally true as laid down, that at common law the copy of the grant was equal in dignity as evidence of the original, still, unless so recognized in Georgia, it is not the law of Georgia."[25] Johnson's point was well taken: In the Pacard case, Judge Story had ostensibly ruled that in the absence of statute, the Court would presume that the common law

[22] *Ibid.*, 145.
[23] 5 Peters 233 (1831).
[24] *Ibid.*, 241.
[25] *Ibid.*, 246.

did not apply;[26] now Mr. Story was holding that in the absence of statute, the Court would presume that the common law rule *did* apply. What was the general principle of judicial construction in federal courts regarding the adoption of the common law in the several states in the absence of statute? Clearly, Judge Story's theory of adoption as applied in these decisions granted wide discretionary authority to the Court in deciding whether a particular state had or had not adopted certain common law rules, or whether such rules were, in the eyes of the Court, "applicable" to the state's situation.

CRIMES AGAINST THE GOVERNMENT: THE *COOLIDGE* CASE

Jefferson's argument that the several states had adopted natural rights rather than common law rights, whatever its philosophical merits, was uniformly rejected in American state tribunals. As a general proposition, and in spite of widespread hostility toward the common law, it was recognized in both state and federal courts, by most Republicans and Federalists, that state jurisprudence rested firmly on a common law basis. Judge Story went farther, we have seen, and argued to the satisfaction of his brethren that members of the Supreme Court might also, as occasion required, have a determining voice in deciding what the common law rule in a state should be.

He was far less persuasive, initially at least, in winning over his fellow justices to the Federalist doctrine that the American Constitution likewise rested on a common law foundation, or that the common law was a source of jurisdiction in cases dealing with common law crimes against the United States. The issue, as Story put it, was simply this: "If then, State Courts may apply the common law to State constitutions, why may not United States Courts apply it to the Constitution of the United States?"[27]

Soon after his appointment, while he was riding circuit in Massachusetts, the case of *United States* v. *Coolidge*[28] came before Judge Story. The question was "whether the Circuit Court of the United States had jurisdiction to punish offenses against the United States, which have not been previously defined, and a specific punishment affixed by some statute of the United States."[29] Although this issue had previously been settled in *United States* v. *Hudson and Goodwin*,[30] Story hoped to reopen it and correct the ruling. He admitted

[26] Technically, the *Pacard* case did not hold that the common law (*qua* common law) was inapplicable. Rather, it held that the common law principle of distinction and differentiation permitted application of a special rule for commercial fixtures. For this point, the author is indebted to Gerald T. Dunne. See also Story's opinion for the Court in *Fairfax's Devisee* v. *Hunter's Lessee*, discussed in chapter 6, *infra*, concerning the applicability of common law rules of inquests of office in Virginia.

[27] Story, *Life and Letters*, I, 299.

[28] 1 Gallison 488; 25 Federal Cases 619, No. 14,857 (1813).

[29] *Ibid.*

[30] 7 Cranch 32 (1812).

that the *Hudson* decision was "entitled to the most respectful consideration; but having been made without argument, and by a majority only of the court, I hope that it is not an improper course to bring the subject again in review for a more solemn decision, as it is not a question of mere ordinary import, but vitally affects the jurisdiction of the courts of the United States; a jurisdiction which they cannot lawfully enlarge or diminish."[31]

Ostensibly, the *Coolidge* case turned on the narrow question of whether the federal courts possessed jurisdiction over common law crimes committed against the United States and in the absence of statute. Story did not urge that the federal courts had a general common law jurisdiction. He only contended they possessed a limited criminal jurisdiction, which was restricted to crimes against the government. "All offenses against the sovereignty, the public rights, the public justice, the public peace, the public trade and the public police of the United States"[32] were, he argued, punishable as public crimes.

Basically, however, the question was not simply whether the courts of the United States had jurisdiction of crimes at common law. As Richard Dana observed many years later while arguing before the Supreme Court in *Swift* v. *Tyson*,[33] the *Coolidge* case "involved the general question [of] whether the common law had been adopted; for if it could be referred to at all, it was equally a source of jurisdiction as it would be the rule of decision."[34] Dana was aware that federal jurisdiction could be extended into civil as well as criminal cases if it was admitted as a general principle that the Constitution was based

[31] 25 Federal Cases 621. The *Hudson and Goodwin* case, notes Professor Crosskey, "arose out of one phase of the extreme inconsistency of Thomas Jefferson and his party, on the subject of freedom of speech and press. For, though the Jeffersonians had protested very loudly that these freedoms were violated when the Sedition Act was passed by Congress, in 1798, their own behavior, after attaining to office, was totally inconsistent with the extreme concern about these freedoms which they had before expressed." (William Crosskey, *Politics and the Constitution*, II, 767.) For a discussion of the cases dealing with the Jeffersonian attack on free speech, see *ibid.*, 754–84. In agreement with Crosskey, Leonard Levy notes that Jefferson approved of Republican prosecutions against Federalist printers, judges, and ministers "until expediency dictated his disapproval some months later." (*Freedom of Speech and Press in Early American History: Legacy of Suppression*, 303.) In 1806, a Federalist newspaper owned by Hudson and Goodwin charged that Jefferson had conspired to grant two million dollars to Napoleon in return for a treaty between France and Spain. The Circuit Court in Connecticut was divided over the question of whether the United States had common law jurisdiction in criminal cases of seditious libel. Both the attorney general and the counsel for the defendants refused to argue the case when it came before the Supreme Court, and Justice Johnson, speaking for an unnamed "majority," ruled that in the absence of statute, federal courts lacked jurisdiction over crimes against the national government. Crosskey is possibly correct in his assertion that the dissenting justices were Marshall, Washington, and Story. Crosskey, *Politics and the Constitution*, II, 782.

[32] 25 Federal Cases 620.

[33] 16 Peters 1 (1842).

[34] *Ibid.*, 12.

upon the common law and permitted the federal judiciary on its own authority and without benefit of statute to punish common law offenses against the United States.

But Story proceeded cautiously in *United States* v. *Coolidge*. He refused to consider the question of "whether the United States, as a sovereign power, have entirely adopted the common law,"[35] or whether an independent body of common law was in force in the federal courts. This exercise in judicial self-restraint regarding jurisdiction did not prevent him, however, from laying down the general rule of constitutional construction that the courts must frequently examine the common law in interpreting the Constitution and the laws enacted under its authority;[36] for "whether the common law of England, in its broadest sense, including equity and admiralty, as well as legal doctrines, be the common law of the United States or not, it can hardly be doubted, that the Constitution and the laws of the United States are predicated upon the existence of the common law."[37]

The inclusion into the Constitution and its amendments of such common law rights as habeas corpus, trial by jury, and other rights (which Story felt were too well known to merit discussion) proved that general common law principles had permeated the thinking of the founding fathers. Common law rights embodying the concept of limited government and rule of law were indisputably the basis of the Constitution in Story's jurisprudence. Surely, it was reasonable to suppose that the judges assigned as guardians of that document were by the nature of their office empowered to punish offenses threatening its continued existence.[38]

Story's circuit court decision came before the Supreme Court for review in 1816, but again no attorneys appeared for the defendant or on behalf of the United States to argue the case, and his holding in *Coolidge* was reversed on the basis of the *Hudson and Goodwin* case.[39] From this decision the Court has never departed. Thus, in the end, the Jeffersonians were victorious in defeating a principle of constitutional law which at an earlier period had not only enjoyed widespread support among Federalists, but had actually been a rule of decision

[35] 25 Federal Cases 619.

[36] Story assured his listeners that the "Courts of the United States are Courts of limited jurisdiction, and cannot exercise any authorities, which are not confided to them by the Constitution and the laws made in pursuance thereof." *Ibid.*

[37] *Ibid.*, 619.

[38] 25 Federal Cases 621. In a charge to the grand jury in 1798, Alexander Addison, president of Pennsylvania's court of common pleas, had stated: "The judicial power of the United States extends to all cases arising under the Constitution, the laws and treaties of the United States. Hence results a jurisdiction to try and punish, as misdemeanors, all acts tending to violate or weaken the authority of the constitution." Judge Addison's Charge to the Grand Jury, September Session, 1798, Addison's *Reports*, Appendix, reprinted in Mark de Wolfe Howe, *Readings in American Legal History*, 349–53.

[39] *United States* v. *Coolidge*, 1 Wheaton 415 (1816).

in the lower federal courts. Looking back on the issue some twenty years later, Story vigorously defended his original position, recalling that

The question, whether the common law is applicable to the United States in their national character, relations, and government, has been much discussed at different periods of the government, principally, however, with reference to the jurisdiction and punishment of common law offenses by the courts of the United States. It would be a most extraordinary state of things, that the common law should be the basis of the jurisprudence of the States originally composing the Union; and yet a government engrafted upon the existing system should have no jurisprudence at all. If such be the result, there is no guide, and no rule for the courts of the United States, or indeed, for any other department of government, in the exercise of any of the powers confided to them except so far as Congress has laid, or shall lay down a rule. In the immense mass of rights and duties, of contracts and claims, growing out of the Constitution and laws of the United States, (upon which positive legislation has hitherto done little or nothing,) what is the rule of decision, and interpretation, and restriction? Suppose the simplest case of contract with the government of the United States, how is it to be construed? How is it to be enforced? What are its obligations? Take an Act of Congress—How is it to be interpreted? Are the rules of the common law to furnish the proper guide, or is every court and department to give it any interpretation it may please, according to its own arbitrary will?[40]

Although following a different and more complex path of reasoning, this was in substance the very same position certain Federalists had maintained when the question was first debated at length in the Congress. Like Story, they based their argument on the doctrine of inherent powers; but some went further by intimating that article 3 of the Constitution specifically conferred common law jurisdiction on the federal courts. One of the great objects of the Constitution, as the Preamble states, declared Harrison Gray Otis in 1798,

is the establishment of justice, and for this purpose a Judicial department is erected, whose powers are declared "to extend to all cases in law and equity, arising under the Constitution, the laws of the United States," &c. Justice, if the common law ideas of it are rejected, is susceptible of various constructions, but agreeably to the principles of that law, it affords redress for every injury, and provides a punishment for every crime that threatens to disturb the lawful operations of government.[41]

[40] Story, *Commentaries on the Constitution*, I, sec. 158, pp. 141–42, n. 2.

[41] *Annals*, House Debates on the Sedition Act, 5 Congress, 2 sess. (July, 1798), 2146–47. The Republican position was presented by Albert Gallatin, *ibid.*, 2156–64. See the analysis of these debates in James Morton Smith, *Freedom's Fetters: The Alien and Sedition Laws and Civil Liberties*, 132–35. Madison vigorously defended the Republican position in his *Report on the Virginia Resolutions of 1798*. (See *Debates in the Several State Conventions*, IV, 561–67.) Earlier discussion on the Constitution and the common law will be found in the letter of James Madison to George Washington, October 18, 1787, in *Documentary History of the Constitution of the United States of America*, IV, 334–36; see also remarks of George Mason and James Iredell in the Ratification debates in *Pamphlets on the Constitution of the United States, Published during Its Discussion by the People, 1787–1788* (ed.

Not all Federalists, however, shared these sentiments, or were as consistent as Story. Certainly Chief Justice Marshall's position on this question of common law jurisdiction constitutes one of the great mysteries of his constitutionalism. His reasons for failing to support his friend Story are by no means clear.

Prior to the enactment of the Sedition Act, federal courts had embraced Judge Story's position in a number of decisions.[42] A chain of precedent was abruptly broken under the pressure of opposition to the Sedition Act, however, when in 1798, Justice Chase ruled in circuit that the United States did not possess criminal jurisdiction based on the common law.[43] Justice Bushrod Washington, the Virginia Federalist, followed suit by ruling in 1804 that federal courts were not authorized to entertain common law indictments for perjury.[44] In *United States* v. *Burr*,[45] a decision, be it noted, which was later cited against Story by counsel in the *Tyson* case,[46] Chief Justice Marshall suggested that common law indictments could not be brought into federal courts; and in *Livingston* v. *Jefferson*,[47] he emphatically stated: "I am decidedly of the opinion that the jurisdiction of the courts of the United States depends, exclusively, on the Constitution and laws of the United States."[48]

---

by Paul Ford), 329–32, 336. The Alien and Sedition Acts expired in 1801. Neither the enactment nor enforcement of these acts, however, settled the question of whether the federal courts had common law jurisdiction. The issue arose again in 1802, when Congress debated repeal of the Adams administration's statute establishing intermediate circuit courts. James Bayard of Delaware presented the Federalist case for common law jurisdiction, and Joseph H. Nicholson of Maryland defended the Jeffersonian position against. See *Annals*, House Debates, 7 Congress, 1 sess. (Feb., 1802), 544, 583, 613–14, 652, 806; reprinted in part, together with the speeches of Otis and Gallatin, in Howe, *Readings in American Legal History*, 337–47. The most complete statement of the Republican position is that of St. George Tucker, in appendix E of his edition of Blackstone's *Commentaries*, V (Philadelphia, 1803), 378–433; reprinted in part with related material in Joseph H. Smith, *Development of Legal Institutions*, 542–44.

[42] See, for example, *United States* v. *Smith*, 27 Federal Cases 1147, No. 16,323 (1793); *Henfield's Case*, 11 Federal Cases 1099, No. 6,360 (1793); *United States* v. *Ravara*, 2 Dallas 297 (1794). In the *Smith* case, it should be noted, the defendant was charged with counterfeiting notes of the Bank of the United States. Representing Smith was the Massachusetts Federalist, Theophilus Parsons, who argued unsuccessfully that federal courts did not have jurisdiction over crimes against the United States. See also *Commonwealth* v. *Schaffer*, 4 Dallas, Appendix XXVI (1797).

[43] *United States* v. *Worrall*, 28 Federal Cases 778, No. 16,766; also reported in 2 Dallas 384. The *Worrall* case, according to Chancellor Kent, "settled nothing, as the Court were divided; but it contained some of the principal arguments on each side of this nice and interesting constitutional question." *Commentaries on American Law*, I, 333.

[44] *Anonymous*, 1 Federal Cases 1036, No. 475.

[45] 25 Federal Cases 55, No. 14,693 (1807).

[46] See the argument of counsel, *Swift* v. *Tyson*, 16 Peters 11.

[47] 15 Federal Cases 660, No. 8,411 (1811).

As conclusive as this may appear on the part of Marshall, it is noteworthy that Marshall had taken an opposite position earlier, which contradicts his judicial opinions. In a letter written in 1800, Marshall stated: "The opinion which has been controverted is, that the common law of England has not been adopted as the common law of America by the Constitution of the United States. I do not believe one man can be found who maintains the affirmative of this proposition." Continuing, Marshall insisted in no uncertain terms that all crimes committed against the United States on the high seas were

clearly punishable in the federal courts . . . . My own opinion is that our ancestors brought with them the laws of England both statute & common law as existing at the settlement of each colony, so far as they were applicable to our situation. That on our revolution the pre-existing law of each state remained so far as it was not changed either expressly or necessarily by the nature of the government which we adopted. That on adopting the existing constitution of the United States the common & statute law of each state remained as before & that the principles of the common law of the state would apply themselves to magistrates of the particular government. I do not recollect ever to have heard the opinions of a leading gentleman of the opposition which conflict with these. M. Gallatin in a very acute speech on the sedition law was understood by me to avow them. On the other side it was contended not that the common law gave the courts jurisdiction in cases of sedition but that the constitution gave it.[49]

What caused Marshall to abandon such a strongly held belief? Whatever the reason, it is curious to note that by 1818, he was clearly sympathetic toward Story's position in the *Coolidge* case, despite his apparent unwillingness to support Story openly or attempt a revision of the *Hudson and Goodwin* decision.[50]

Although Story was unsuccessful in establishing federal jurisdiction over common law crimes through his *Coolidge* opinion,[51] leading lawyers stood

[48] *Ibid.* For additional discussion of the various cases, see Charles Warren, *Supreme Court in United States History*, I, 433–42.

[49] John Marshall to John Jay [?], Nov. 27, 1800, John Marshall Papers, Library of Congress. In the *Hensfield* case, James Wilson, with the concurrence of Justices Iredell and Peters, charged the jury that the law of nature and of nations, plus certain treaties and the president's Proclamation of Neutrality, constituted a "law" within the meaning of the Constitution. But the jury returned a verdict of "not Guilty." Quite clearly, Marshall's sympathies rested with the Court in this case. See his remarks in his *Life of George Washington*, II, 273–74.

[50] See *United States* v. *Bevans*, 3 Wheaton 336 (1818), and *United States* v. *Wiltberger*, 5 Wheaton 76 (1820), in which Chief Justice Marshall expresses discontent over the Court's lack of jurisdiction over common law crimes against the government.

[51] William Alexander Duer clarified the issue and summed it up well in 1843 when he remarked, "The prevailing opinion at present seems to be that, under the Federal Government, the common law, considered as a source of jurisdiction, was never in force, but considered merely as a means or instrument of exercising the jurisdiction conferred by the

faithfully by his side in the ensuing years;[52] and more recently Justice Jackson vindicated Story, in part at least, when he declared in a concurring opinion that "The research of Charles Warren . . . led that scholar to conclude that *United States* v. *Hudson* . . . and *United States* v. *Coolidge* . . . were probably wrongly decided. . . . The error, if it be one, comports, however, with the present tendency to constrict the jurisdiction of federal courts, and I think is likely to survive."[53]

Constitution, it does exist in full validity, and forms a safe and beneficial portion of our national code." (*Course of Lectures on the Constitutional Jurisprudence of the United States*, 54.) Later decisions, however, regard it as well settled by the *Hudson and Goodwin* and *Coolidge* cases that there are no common law offenses against the United States. See, for example, *United States* v. *Britton*, 108 U.S. 199 (1883); *United States* v. *Eaton*, 144 U.S. 677 (1892); *United States* v. *Goodwell*, 243 U.S. 476 (1916); *United States* v. *Flores*, 289 U.S. 137 (1933); *Jerome* v. *United States*, 318 U.S. 101 (1943).

[52] Constitutional commentators were reluctant to accept the *Hudson and Goodwin* and *Coolidge* decisions as definitively settling the question. See William Rawle, *A View of the Constitution of the United States of America*, 258–73; Thomas Sergeant, *Constitutional Law*, 274. In his *Dissertation on the Nature and Extent of the Jurisdiction of the Courts of the United States* (Philadelphia, 1824), 9–10, Peter Du Ponceau made this observation respecting Story's *Coolidge* opinion: "This was an indictment for forcibly rescuing on the high seas, a prize which had been captured and taken possession of by two American vessels, and was on her way, under the direction of a prize master, to the port of Salem for adjudication. Whatever else it might be, it was clearly not a case of common law." Chancellor Kent agreed, citing Du Ponceau approvingly. The *Coolidge* case, he argued, "was clearly a case of admiralty jurisdiction, and the courts of the United States would seem to have had general and exclusive jurisdiction over the case. . . . The courts cannot derive their *right to act* from the common law. They must look for that right to the Constitution and law of the United States. But when the general jurisdiction and authority is given, as in cases of admiralty and maritime jurisdiction, the *rules of action* [i.e., decision] under that jurisdiction, if not prescribed by statute, may and must be taken from the common law, when they are applicable, because they are necessary to give effect to the jurisdiction. . . . Without such a guide, the courts would be left to a dangerous discretion, and to roam at large in the trackless field of their own imaginations." *Commentaries on American Law*, I, 339–41.

[53] *D'Oench, Duhme & Co., Inc.* v. *Federal Deposit Insurance Corp.*, 315 U.S. 469 (1942). Justice Jackson was referring to Charles Warren's landmark essay, "New Light on the History of the Federal Judiciary Act of 1789," *Harvard Law Review*, Vol. XXXVII, No. 1 (Nov., 1923), 49–132. As Warren explained, section 10 of the original draft of this act, which later became section 9, related to the jurisdiction of the district courts. In the draft, district courts were given "cognizance of all crimes and offences that shall be cognizable under the authority of the United States *and defined by the laws of the same*." This would seem to indicate that the framers of the act meant to confine the criminal jurisdiction of the district courts to crimes specifically defined by the Congress. In the Senate, however, an amendment was introduced and passed which struck out the restrictive clause—"*and defined by the laws of the same*"—and left the district courts with jurisdiction over crimes "cognizable under the authority of the United States." A similar restric-

Believing always that he labored in the tradition of John Adams and the founding fathers, Story was content to rest his *Coolidge* case finally on the authority of Adams, whose private secretary had once confided to Story that

While he was Vice President of the United States, and the proceedings were had on *Blount's Conspiracy* before the Senate, this question as to the adoption of the common law was discussed before that body; and his opinion, as that of a great lawyer, (as he certainly was,) and as a great revolutionary patriot, was called for on every side. He rose from his chair, and emphatically declared to the whole Senate, that if he had ever imagined that the common law had not by the Revolution become the law of the United States under its new government, *he never would have drawn his sword in the contest.* So dear to him were the great privileges which that law recognized and enforced.[54]

Story never doubted that Congress had the authority to invest the federal courts with jurisdiction over crimes punishable at common law, and in the end the results sought in the *Coolidge* case were achieved in part through legislative enactment. Once again, it was Judge Story who led the way in finding a solution to the problem which, in the words of one federal judge, was making "a perfect mockery and ridicule" of the national government.[55] In 1825, Congress passed the Crimes Act, drafted by Story and carried through

---

tive clause in the draft was struck out in section 11. "The only meaning that can be given to this action striking out the restrictive words," concludes one legal scholar, "is that Congress did not intend to limit criminal jurisdiction to crimes specifically defined by it. . . . The elision of these words strongly indicates intent to extend jurisdiction to crimes at common law and under the law of nations." Smith, *Development of Legal Institutions*, 551-52.

[54] Story, *Life and Letters*, I, 299-300.

[55] Judge Richard Peters, as quoted in Warren, *Supreme Court in United States History*, I, 441. Because of the Court's ruling in the *Coolidge* case, lamented Peters, "*I cannot carry on the business of my district.* . . . Unless some legislative authority be given to define crimes . . . the whole (or nearly) of our criminal code may be expunged. Treason is defined by the Constitution; but most other crimes are barely named, tho' their punishments are, for the most part, prescribed. We are forbidden to resort to common law for interpretation, and our jurisdiction of crimes punishable at common law is excluded. I live in a district of mixed population; as to seamen particularly, I am subject to constant necessity of taking cognizance of crimes, great and small, without a guide to direct my course. I had little difficulty before the occasion alluded to; but now my hands are tied, and my mind padlocked. . . . Every crime, not defined in our statutes,—murder, rape, all the less offences may be committed with impunity in places under the exclusive jurisdiction of the United States" (*ibid.*). Judge Story complained that the federal courts were crippled by the *Hudson and Goodwin* case: "offenders, conspirators and traitors, are enabled to carry on their purposes almost without check. It is truly melancholy that Congress will exhaust themselves so much in mere political discussions, and remain so unjustifiably negligent of the great concerns of the public." To Nathaniel Williams, May 27, 1813, *Life and Letters*, I, 244.

the Congress by his friend Webster, which gave general jurisdiction to United States courts over certain crimes against the federal government.[56]

There is yet another side to Story's opinion in *United States* v. *Coolidge.* Usually overlooked is the significant precedent Story helped to establish which later played a major role in American constitutional development. This was his premise that the Constitution was "predicated upon the existence of the common law," a premise which counsel strenuously attempted to refute in *Swift* v. *Tyson,*[57] decided in 1842. The *Hudson and Goodwin* and *Coolidge* decisions had merely declared that federal courts lacked common law jurisdiction over crimes against the United States; nothing was said about Story's underlying premise. "These jarring opinions," Kent explained, "have not settled the general question as to the application and influence of the common law, upon clear and definite principles; and it may still be considered *in civil cases*, as open to further consideration."[58] The common law did not provide federal courts with jurisdiction over crimes against the United States; but the question was still open of whether the common law provided federal courts with the rule of decision in a civil case, after jurisdiction had already been obtained under the Constitution.

As the years passed, Story continued to assert this basic premise and, during his last days on the bench, was able to persuade nearly every member of the Court that in certain areas of civil law, it was appropriate for the Court to invoke general principles of law as the rule of decision, the assumption being

[56] Story commented on the bill as follows: "it is still competent for Congress to adopt as to its own powers an exercise of common law principles. . . . [E]xcepting Judge Chase, every Judge that ever sat on the Supreme Court Bench, from the adoption of the Constitution until 1804 . . . held a like opinion [i.e., that the federal courts possessed common law jurisdiction]. Since that time, there has been a difference on the Bench, and it is still a question which we all hold unsettled. I believe, however, that none of us entertain any doubt as to the authority of Congress to invest us with this jurisdiction, so far as it applies to the sovereignty of the United States." (*Life and Letters*, I, 299.) Even before his circuit court ruling in the *Coolidge* case, Story had prepared some "sketches" of a criminal code, which he sent to William Pinkney. (Story to Nathaniel Williams, May 27, 1812, *ibid.*, 244.) Earlier he had implored Williams to "induce Congress to give the Judicial Courts of the United States power to punish all crimes and offenses against the Government, as at common law." (Oct. 8, 1812, *ibid.*, 243.) In 1816, Story forwarded a "manuscript" of a "bill further to extend the judicial system of the United States," the object of which was "to give to the Circuit Court *original* jurisdiction of all cases intended by the Constitution to be confided to the judicial power of the United States, where that jurisdiction has not been already delegated by law." Pinkney was to use this as the basis of a speech to the Congress. (See the remarks of William Story in *Life and Letters*, I, 293–96.) As late as 1842, Story was endeavoring to strengthen the system of laws against common law crimes. See Story to John Macpherson Berrien, Feb. 8, 1842, and July 23, 1842, *Life and Letters*, II, 402–404, 405–406.

[57] 16 Peters 1 (1842).

[58] *Commentaries on American Law*, I, 339. Emphasis supplied.

that common law principles of justice embracing the natural law, the law of nations, and the law of England rested at the foundation of state and federal jurisprudence and were a part of the fundamental law of the land. "It has been repeatedly settled by the Supreme Court of the United States," declared Story in 1838 while riding circuit,

> that if the immediate cause of a loss is a peril insured against, it is no ground of defence, that it was remotely caused by the negligence of the master or crew; the rule being, *Causa proxima, non remota spectatur*. This doctrine being founded, not upon local law, but upon the general principles of commercial law, would be obligatory upon this court, even if the decisions of the state court of Massachusetts were to the contrary; for upon commercial questions of a general nature, the courts of the United States possess the same general authority, which belongs to the state tribunals, and are not bound by the local decisions. They are at liberty to consult their own opinions, guided, indeed, by the greatest deference for the acknowledged learning and ability of the state tribunals, but still exercising their own judgment, as to the reasons, on which these decisions are founded.[59]

Story hoped that the federal courts, like the various state tribunals, could, by such a rule, help to foster the growth of the common law in its new American environment. The overall effect would be uniformity of common law rights, as state and local judges would be encouraged (though not required, of course) to follow the national example and to harmonize their rulings with those of higher federal courts. Hence, instead of dozens of separate common law regulations to clog the wheels of commerce, a single, federal common law would gradually develop, affirming to all the same standard of justice under the Constitution. Such were the aspirations of Judge Story in

[59] *Williams* v. *Suffolk Insurance Co.*, 3 Sumner 270; 29 Federal Cases 1406, No. 17,739 (1838). There were many other precedents for the *Tyson* doctrine established by Story at the lower federal court level before 1842. Story had actually employed the same reasoning as that in *Swift* v. *Tyson* in one of his first decisions. The question before the Court in *Van Reimsdyk* v. *Kane*, 28 Federal Cases 1062, No. 16,871 (1812), was whether a Rhode Island insolvent law could discharge debts contracted by an agent of a Rhode Island firm with a citizen of a foreign country, within the state. Story denied that the Rhode Island law could discharge debts contracted outside the state, but admitted the constitutionality of the statute. In a dictum Story commented upon the effect of such a law in federal courts, where there was a question of diversity of citizenship. He stated that "the laws of the States are to be regarded only as rules of decision, and not as exclusive or peremptory injunctions . . . . Until I should be instructed by the higher court, that I was bound to pronounce in such cases, contrary to the acknowledged principles of national comity, and to acknowledge mere municipal rules as the law of the court, I should have little hesitation in affirming that a discharge under the insolvent law of Rhode Island was not a discharge of the contract in the present suit." See also, for example, Story's opinions in *Donnell* v. *Columbian Insurance Co.*, 2 Sumner 366; 7 Federal Cases 889, No. 3,987 (1836); *Robinson* v. *The Commonwealth Insurance Co.*, 3 Sumner 220; 20 Federal Cases 1002, No. 11,949 (1838). For an analysis of the background of the *Tyson* case, see Crosskey, *Politics and the Constitution*, II, 818–64.

1842, when he handed down the most controversial decision of his career, the famous case of *Swift* v. *Tyson*.

COMMERCE AND THE STATES:
THE *TYSON* DOCTRINE

The case of *Swift* v. *Tyson*[60] involved a bill of exchange, dated 1836 in the state of Maine, which was drawn upon George Tyson,[61] a resident of New York, by Nathaniel Norton and Jarius Keith, as part payment for the purchase of certain lands in Maine. Norton and Keith endorsed the bill to John Swift, in payment of a promissory note due him by Norton and Keith. Tyson, unable to gain title to the lands, subsequently accepted the bill in payment of a protested note drawn earlier by Norton and Keith, which he had paid at the Maine bank. Unknown to Swift when he received the draft, Tyson had already accepted it in payment of the protested note. The draft was dishonored at maturity, and Swift, the holder of the bill of exchange, brought an action against Tyson, the acceptor, to recover the amount of the draft plus interest. Tyson, in turn, pleaded fraud against the drawer of the bill.

The Supreme Court acquired jurisdiction over the case from the litigants' diversity of state citizenship. The issue before the Court, as Judge Story put it, was whether the pre-existing debt, which stood as the basis for payment of Tyson's acceptance of the bill, "constitutes a valuable consideration in the sense of the general rule applicable to negotiable instruments."[62] Under the general rules of commercial law, Story explained, a bona fide holder of a negotiable instrument for a valuable consideration may recover thereon, if he holds title to it without knowledge of any facts which would impeach its validity as between the antecedent parties. He asserted that this doctrine is "so well established, and so essential to the security of negotiable paper, that it is laid up among the fundamentals of the law, and requires no authority or reasoning to be now brought in its support."[63]

Richard Dana, representing Tyson, argued that because the acceptance was made in the state of New York, the contract should be treated as a New York contract. Dana further contended that a pre-existing debt, as expounded by New York courts, did not constitute, in the sense of the general rule, a valuable consideration respecting negotiable instruments. Story side-stepped Dana's argument in what has since been regarded as the only "unconstitutional" decision ever delivered by a Supreme Court justice.[64] Story first examined New York court decisions, concluding the issue unsettled, as "the Court of Errors

[60] 16 Peters 1 (1842).

[61] Appellate case files of the Supreme Court, No. 2125, in the National Archives, show that the spelling is George W. Tysen.

[62] 16 Peters 16.

[63] *Ibid.*, 15.

[64] *Erie Railroad Co.* v. *Tompkins*, 304 U.S. 64 (1938).

have not pronounced any positive opinion upon it."[65] There being no New York statute covering the question before the Court, Story was ostensibly at a loss to render a decision and apply the general commercial rule to the case. If it could be shown, however, that the Constitution was predicated on the common law, Story's problem was solved.

The way had been paved by Judge Story's friend, Richard Dana. Realizing, apparently, that the New York cases were confusing, and that the case would ultimately turn on the question of the common law foundation of the Constitution, Dana invited Story to settle this "whole matter," which "calls for a specific and final decision."[66] He agreed with Story that the states had "inherited" the common law, and that it had been modified in the process "to meet the exigencies of an enterprising people."[67] Dana also agreed with Story's contention in *United States* v. *Coolidge* that clearly defined common law rights, such as trial by jury and habeas corpus, must be interpreted in common law terms. But he disagreed that the Constitution presupposes and is predicated upon the existence of the common law, and cited *United States* v. *Hudson and Goodwin*,[68] *United States* v. *Coolidge*,[69] *United States* v. *Worrall*,[70] and *United States* v. *Burr*.[71] Dana then rested his argument on the following assertion:

If, therefore, in the organization of the federal judiciary, a system of laws is presupposed, it is the American law, which is now as distinct in its character as the English or French; yet, as it is not uniform in the states, the adoption of it in the federal courts could be necessarily subject to some legislative provision, as to the cases and circumstances to which the law should be applicable. . . . Without the aid of a statute the common law cannot be called in aid of the jurisdiction of the courts, or for rules of decision.[72]

Turning to chapter 20, section 34 of the Judiciary Act of 1789, Story proceeded to interpret its provisions broadly. The act provided "that the laws of the several states, except where the Constitution, treaties, or statutes of the United States shall otherwise require or provide, shall be regarded as rules of decision in trials at common law in the Courts of the United States, in cases where they apply." The word *laws* in this section could hardly include within its scope the decisions of local tribunals, because they are not laws "in the

[65] *Swift* v. *Tyson*, 16 Peters 18.
[66] *Ibid.*, 12.
[67] *Ibid.*, 11.
[68] 7 Cranch 32.
[69] 1 Wheaton 415.
[70] 2 Dallas 384.
[71] 25 Federal Cases 55, No. 14,693 (opinion by Chief Justice Marshall). Dana vainly cited Story's remarks in the *Commentaries* and circuit court opinion in the *Coolidge* case with disapproval.
[72] *Swift* v. *Tyson*, 16 Peters 13.

ordinary use of language." On the contrary, "They are often re-examined, reversed, and qualified by the courts themselves. . . . The laws of a State are more usually understood to mean the rules and enactments promulgated by the legislative authority thereof, or long established local customs having the force of laws."[73] Furthermore, added Story, even if the question at bar was settled in New York courts, there was doubt whether the Supreme Court is obliged to follow it, "if it differs from the principles of the general commercial law."[74] Hence, concluded the judge, section 34 applied only to local laws and was not intended to apply to more general matters.

Because the Court could not follow the law of negotiable instruments as laid down by the New York courts, and because there were no controlling statutes, the Court's only alternative was to determine "what is the just rule furnished by the principles of commercial law to govern the case."[75] Assuming, as he had done in *United States* v. *Coolidge*, that the Constitution is predicated upon the existence of the common law, Story based his decision in *Tyson* upon general principles of law. Citing a decision of Lord Mansfield on the law of the sea and quoting an epigram of Cicero on the natural law, he observed that "The law respecting negotiable instruments may be truly declared . . . to be in a great measure, not the law of a single country, but of the commercial world."[76] In deciding for the plaintiff, Story thereby laid down the general rule that in diversity cases at common law, where there was no controlling state statute, federal courts were free to form judgments independent of state court decisions.[77]

At long last Story saw the dream of a lifetime come true: the acceptance of Cicero's magnanimous principle in the highest court in the land. Cicero's doctrine of a law above laws had always been on his lips. It was one of his favorite topics of discussion, and many times he had exhorted members of the legal profession to weigh its merits carefully. It behooved the serious advocate, he once advised an inquiring student of the law, "not to be indifferent to my principle of local law (for law as you remark, is often deemed a 'local view'),

---

[73] *Ibid.*, 18.

[74] *Ibid.*

[75] *Ibid.*, 19. Justice Catron concurred, but was "not prepared to give any opinion, even was it called for by the record."

[76] *Ibid.* "Non erit alia lex Romae, alia Athenis, alia nunc, alia postac, sed et apud omnes gentes, et omni tempore, una eademque lex obtinebit."

[77] During this same term Story reasserted the *Tyson* doctrine and extended it from negotiable paper to all contracts. In interpreting a contract of insurance in *Carpenter* v. *Providence Insurance Co.*, 16 Peters 495 (1842), Story stated that "The questions under our consideration are questions of General Commercial Law, and depend upon the construction of a contract of insurance which is by no means local in character, or regulated by any local policy or customs. Whatever respect, therefore, the decisions of state tribunals may have on such a subject—and they certainly are entitled to great respect—they cannot conclude the judgment of this Court."

[but] you should ever remember that real, solid, permanent fame belongs to higher attainments, to the knowledge of principles, & to that noble jurisprudence, of which Lord Mansfield, quoting Cicero, said that nature was not one law at Rome & another at Athens."[78]

Thus in the *Tyson* case Judge Story linked American capitalism and the American Constitution to an old but timeless principle of the ancient world. The extension of classical concepts into a post-Revolutionary age, wherein a host of authorities had been slowly but surely discarded in the name of progress, was to Story the necessary basis for a sound, ethical, and lasting jurisprudence. Here was a humanistic approach to the law, which could provide man in his new role as popular sovereign with a home in history and a feeling for continuity. Rejected as an antiquated decision of the nineteenth century by modern jurists, the *Tyson* case still stands as a hallmark of enlightened jurisprudence and continues even today to possess a certain enduring quality. Seemingly dead and buried after Justice Brandeis' lethal blow in *Erie Railroad Co.* v. *Tompkins*, the *Tyson* doctrine nevertheless rises from its grave in the form of the Uniform Commercial Code, each new adoption fulfilling Story's ideal of a general and comprehensive body of commercial law throughout the nation.[79]

Although "the chief beneficiaries of the doctrine of *Swift* v. *Tyson* were corporations doing business in a number of states,"[80] Chief Justice Taney and Story's successors subsequently applied the *Tyson* doctrine to matters not wholly of a commercial nature, developing, in effect, a federal common law. The *Tyson* doctrine was applied to wills,[81] torts,[82] real property (titles),[83] mineral conveyances,[84] contracts,[85] and damages,[86] so that by the turn of the century there were twenty-eight various types of cases in which state and fed-

[78] Story to A. D. Alois, Feb. 15, 1832, Story Papers, Yale.

[79] See Gerald T. Dunne, "The American Blackstone," *Washington University Law Quarterly*, Vol. 1962, No. 3 (June, 1963), 329. Federal common law is still applied in several areas, in spite of the *Tompkins* ruling. See Smith, *Development of Legal Institutions*, 574.

[80] Robert H. Jackson, *The Struggle for Judicial Supremacy*, 279. "Such a corporation," Jackson explained, "could claim that it was a citizen only of the state of its incorporation, and so when sued elsewhere, where they did business, they could remove cases freely to the federal courts on the ground of diversity of citizenship. Where the corporation was the plaintiff, it likewise had an advantage. A Delaware corporation suing a New York citizen with respect to a transaction in New York could bring suit there in either the federal or state court; but the defendant could not remove the case from a state to a federal court, being a citizen and resident of the state where suit was brought." *Ibid.*

[81] *Lane* v. *Vick*, 3 Howard 464 (1845).

[82] *Chicago City* v. *Robbins*, 2 Black 418 (1862).

[83] *Yates* v. *Milwaukee*, 10 Wallace 497 (1870).

[84] *Kuhn* v. *Fairmont Coal Co.*, 215 U.S. 349 (1910).

[85] *Rowan* v. *Runnels*, 5 Howard 134 (1847).

[86] *Lake Shore & M.S.R. Co.* v. *Prentice*, 147 U.S. 101 (1893).

eral courts applied different rules of the common law.[87] But almost from its very inception, the *Tyson* decision failed to win the unanimous approval of the Court. Justices Field[88] and Holmes[89] severely criticized Story's doctrine, and in an opinion by Justice Brandeis in *Erie Railroad Co. v. Tompkins*,[90] it was eventually overruled.

There were many who did not mourn its passing. During much of its painful career, the *Tyson* doctrine had suffered from the harsh blows of unfriendly critics. It had been attacked by states' rightists as a usurpation of state power and was said to contravene the Tenth Amendment. Some lawyers complained that it caused confusion. And one member of the Supreme Court raised an interesting objection which would also apply to today's Court because of its active pursuit of uniformity of civil rights under the Fourteenth Amendment and doctrine of incorporation. Suggesting that the *Tyson* doctrine was undemocratic and in conflict with the American system of separation of powers, Justice Jackson questioned "whether the making of uniform rules of law should be entrusted to the Federal judiciary in the fields where the national legislature is powerless to act. . . . [T]he legislature is entitled to share at least equally in the law-making process."[91] Justice Brandeis probably spoke for most members of the legal profession when he declared:

If only a question of statutory construction were involved, we should not be prepared to abandon a doctrine so widely [followed for] nearly a century. But the unconstitutionality of the course pursued has now been made clear. . . . There is no federal common law. Congress has no power to declare substantive rules of common law applicable in a State whether they be local in their nature or "general," be they commercial law or a part of the law of torts. And no clause in the Consti-

---

[87] *The Constitution of the United States of America: Analysis and Interpretation* (ed. by Edward S. Corwin), 604. See also George C. Holt, *The Concurrent Jurisdiction of the Federal and State Courts*, 159–88.

[88] In *Baltimore and Ohio R. Co. v. Baugh*, 149 U.S. 308 (1893), Justice Field dissented from the application of the *Tyson* doctrine in torts, indicating that disregard of state court decisions was unconstitutional.

[89] Justice Holmes suggested in *Black & White Taxicab Co. v. Brown & White Taxicab Co.*, 276 U.S. 518 (1928) in one of his more famous dissents, that the *Tyson* rule was unconstitutional. Holmes deplored the fact that "Books written about any branch of the common law treat it as a unit, cite cases from this Court, from the Circuit Court of Appeals, from the State Courts, from England and the Colonies of England indiscriminately, and criticize them as right or wrong according to the writer's notions of a single theory. It is very hard to resist the impression that there is an august corpus, to understand which clearly is the only task of any court concerned. If there were such a transcendental body of law outside of any particular State but obligatory within it unless and until changed by statute, the Courts of the United States might be right in using their independent judgment as to what it was. But there is no such body of law." See also *Southern Pacific R.R. v. Jensen*, 244 U.S. 205 (1917).

[90] 304 U.S. 64.

[91] *Struggle for Judicial Supremacy*, 280.

tution purports to confer such a power upon the federal courts. . . . [the *Tyson* doctrine] invaded rights which . . . are reserved by the Constitution to the several States.[92]

Both Holmes and Brandeis have contended that Story's decision in *Tyson* was a misinterpretation of the thirty-fourth section of the Judiciary Act of 1789, and refer to Charles Warren's article on the Judiciary Act of 1789 as the basis of their reasoning on this point.[93] As noted earlier, Warren, while searching through the Senate archives, found the original draft of the Judiciary Act of 1789, written in longhand by Oliver Ellsworth, the author of section 34. Ellsworth had struck out the words *statute law* and substituted the word *laws*. According to Warren, this indicated that the originators intended federal courts to follow state court decisions as well as state statutes. Warren's interpretation, according to Charles Haines, is quite "broad," but if accepted, "Justice Story's position was unsound."[94]

Many have also doubted whether the *Tyson* doctrine promoted uniformity, and Edward S. Corwin has even suggested that "In many instances the States followed their own rules of decision even when contrary to the federal rules, so that Justice Story's attempt at uniformity in matters of a commercial nature paradoxically led to a greater diversity and to the mischief in many instances of two conflicting rules of law in the same state."[95]

However, many of the more severe, unmitigated criticisms of the *Tyson* doctrine do not survive the test of analysis and reflect flimsy interpretations of the nature of the Constitution and the Judiciary Act of 1789. There is no question that English common law principles have been incorporated through judicial decisions, statutes, and constitutions into the various states, serving as a basis of interpretation and jurisprudence at the state and local level. But

---

[92] *Ibid.*, 69–70, 77–78.

[93] "New Light on the History of the Federal Judiciary Act of 1789," *Harvard Law Review*, Vol. XXXVII, No. 1 (Nov., 1923), 49.

[94] Charles G. Haines and Foster H. Sherwood, *The Role of the Supreme Court in American Government and Politics, 1835–1864*, 318.

[95] *The Constitution of the United States*, 604. Charles Warren states a similar opinion, "Probably no decision of the Court has ever given rise to more uncertainty as to legal rights; and though doubtless intended to promote uniformity in the operation of business transactions, its chief effect has been to render it difficult for business men to know in advance to what particular topic the Court would apply the doctrine; and the adverse criticisms by Judges and jurists, which have continued to the present day, have had much justification." (*Supreme Court in United States History*, II, 363.) Robert Jackson says there was less uniformity promoted under the *Tyson* doctrine than one might suppose. ("The Rise and Fall of Swift v. Tyson," *American Bar Association Journal*, Vol. XXIV, No. 8 [Aug., 1938], 614.) But according to Harry Schulman ("The Demise of Swift v. Tyson," *Yale Law Journal*, Vol. XLVII, No. 8 [1938], 1348), "To what extent the doctrine of *Swift* v. *Tyson* has promoted uniformity of law is still a mystery." For other representative views, see Smith, *Development of Legal Institutions*, 558, 569.

common law rights also swell the clauses of the American Constitution. The words *common law* even appear in the Seventh Amendment. According to Story, an absolute repudiation of the *Tyson* doctrine is a repudiation of the common law basis of the American Constitution, and such a position Story could not find supported by history.

The assertion that the *Tyson* case was an unconstitutional application of federal rules of decision is irreconcilable with the Supreme Court's own practice. The concept of *stare decisis*, for example, is a general principle of the common law, but is nowhere stated in the Constitution; yet it is a rule of decision which the Court has formally acknowledged since its earliest days. Here are Justice Jackson's views on this point, which correspond closely with those of Judge Story:

I do not understand Justice Brandeis' statement in *Erie R. Co.* v. *Tompkins* . . . that "There is no federal general common law," to deny that the common law may in proper cases be an aid to or the basis of decision of federal questions. . . . The contract clause, article 1, section 10, which prohibits a state from passing any "Law impairing the Obligation of Contracts" is an example of the part the common law must play in our system. This provision is meaningless unless we know what a contract is. The Constitution wisely refrains from saying. . . . [But] This Court has not hesitated to read the common-law doctrine of consideration into the contract clause.[96]

The eminent authority on contract law, Arthur Corbin, who strongly disagrees with the *Tompkins* case, notes that article 3, section 2 of the Constitution, in providing that "The judicial power shall extend . . . to controversies . . . between citizens of different states," does "not prescribe by what law these controversies shall be determined, or to what sources the federal courts may or may not go in determining this law."[97] The *Tyson* doctrine, he asserts, was not an attempt at supervision over state laws and decisions, or an invasion of state authority. "Such a notion vastly overweighs the function of the judges in making law and their power to impose their rationalizations upon other people. The 'judicial power' is the power (and the duty and the necessity) to determine the issues between litigating parties. Upon these, a court does indeed 'impose' its will."[98] Story's doctrine in *Swift* v. *Tyson*, concludes Corbin, simply guarantees that "every litigant's day in court shall be a day in a real court of justice, a court that consults 'all the available data' and reaches its decision as to his rights by that high judicial process that has made constitu-

[96] Justice Jackson, concurring in *D'Oench, Duhme & Co., Inc.* v. *Federal Deposit Insurance Corp.*, 315 U.S. 469–71 (1942).

[97] "The Laws of the Several States," *Yale Law Journal*, Vol. L, No. 5 (1941), 773. Story's doctrine is also defended by Herbert Pope, "The English Common Law in the United States," *Harvard Law Review*, Vol. XXIV, No. 1 (1910), 6–30.

[98] Corbin, "The Laws of the Several States," *Yale Law Journal*, Vol. L, No. 5 (1941), 773.

tions and statutes and the common law render a living service according to the changing needs of men. This is the 'judicial power' that is conferred by our Constitution."[99]

It may well be that, in the long run, individual rights are safest in the local and state courts. But the Supreme Court has acted under the assumption that the states have been the primary offenders against personal liberties. Thus it would appear that the Court's abandonment of common law rights in *Tompkins* to the states, and its elevation of the liberties imbedded in the Bill of Rights to the federal courts, through their incorporation into the due process clause of the Fourteenth Amendment, is somewhat inconsistent. If the states are the transgressors of liberty, why, then, has the Court gone out of its way to abandon common law rights to state tribunals? All this is doubly confusing, of course, because many of the rights which the Court has incorporated are, from an historical standpoint, common law rights. Along this same line of thought, Corbin raises some pertinent questions, which, it might be maintained, not only exculpate Story, but strike at the very heart of the decisions handed down over the past thirty years respecting civil liberties:

The Fourteenth Amendment provides that no state shall deprive a citizen of life, liberty or property without due process of law. "Due process" of what law? Is it not the state law? . . . The Fourteenth Amendment makes the Supreme Court the custodian of "due process," only as against deprivation of life, liberty, and property, not for the purpose of creating a federal general law of "due process." It does not empower the federal court to tell the state court that it must not erroneously *increase* the requirements of due process. Which court was guilty of an "unconstitutional assumption of power"?[100]

The question might also be asked whether Warren's findings in the Senate archives are proof that Judge Story misconstrued the thirty-fourth section of the Judiciary Act of 1789. Warren himself did not contend that the *Tyson* case was unconstitutional. The theory that Ellsworth's elimination of the words *statute law* revealed the true intent of the originators of section 34, prescribing federal courts to follow state decisions as well as state law, is a shimmering exercise in statutory interpretation. Ellsworth may have substituted the word *law* for any number of reasons; perhaps he deleted the words *statute law*

[99] *Ibid.,* 777.

[100] *Ibid.* On page 776, Corbin cites frequent injustices that have occurred under the *Tompkins* ruling. Consider also the fact that the *Tompkins* case "reversed a ninety-six year old precedent which counsel had not questioned . . . for the first and only time in American Constitutional history, it held an action of the Supreme Court itself to have been unconstitutional, to wit, action taken by it in reliance on its interpretation of the 34th Section of the Judiciary Act of 1789, a question which also was not before the Court; and thirdly, it completely ignored the power of Congress under the commerce clause, as well as its power to prescribe rules of decision for the federal courts in the cases enumerated in article III." Corwin, *The Constitution of the United States,* 605–606.

because there were scarcely any current statutes for the Court to follow.[101] Did the members of Congress enacting the Judiciary Act of 1789 command the federal courts to submit to state court decisions, which were generally at that time, and for a long time thereafter, woefully deficient and rudimental? Were court decisions regarded as "laws" in 1789? The principle universally held then by Blackstone and the general legal profession (and later by Story) was that court decisions were not in themselves "laws," but were merely evidence of what the laws are.[102] Unlike such questions as the president's inherent powers, judicial review, and Congress' power to spend for the general welfare, the problem of ambiguity surrounding section 34 has never been fully explored, nor amply debated at the level of "original intention" of the framers. Story's interpretation of its provisions cannot be impugned by the mere stroke of Mr. Ellsworth's pen.

A more powerful defense of Story's position has been made by William Crosskey, who asserts that during the formation of the Union and of the Judiciary Act of 1789, the common law was generally regarded as a single, ascertainable body of customary law and was properly describable as one of "the Laws of the United States." Having fully explored Story's circuit opinions, which seem to indicate to Crosskey that Story almost alone understood the true nature of the Constitution and the intended meaning of section 34 of the first Judiciary Act, Crosskey concludes with dismay that "the Supreme Court, unfortunately, has operated for over a hundred years, upon the utterly false assumption that the Common Law was not, at that time [1789] one of 'the Laws of the United States.' "[103] Crosskey's argument is impressive; and he

[101] It is interesting to note that in his *Coolidge* opinion, Story had argued that some of the provisions of the Constitution can take effect only by recourse to the common law, with respect to the clause in article 3, section 2, which extends the judicial power to all cases in law and equity arising under the Constitution and to admiralty and maritime jurisdiction. The laws and the practices of the various states could not be referred to here, said Story, because in many of them no equity jurisprudence existed, and the maritime law of the states was too unsettled and too imperfect to furnish any basis of interpretation.

[102] In *Swift* v. *Tyson*, 16 Peters 18, Story asserted that court decisions were "at most, only evidence of what the laws are." Sir William Blackstone declared that "the law, and the opinion of the judge are not always convertible terms. . . . we may take it as a general rule, that the decisions of courts of justice are evidence of what is common law." Blackstone, *Commentaries*, I, 61.

[103] *Politics and the Constitution*, II, 902. Crosskey thinks, however, that Story did not base his holding on an interpretation of section 34 of the Judiciary Act, and that Story admitted state court decisions were laws in some cases. While it is agreed that Story decided the case on a broader issue than the Judiciary Act alone, Crosskey's assertion that Story accepted state court decisions as "laws" is a matter of conjecture. Crosskey states that Justice Story did not "deny that the decisions of courts were, *in some sense*, constitutive of 'law'; he seems, instead, to have recognized this rather plainly, declaring only that he did not think the decisions of courts were within the 'more usual,' or 'ordinary,' meaning of the word he was called upon to construe." (*Ibid.*, 858.) Crosskey also seems

has gathered a plethora of evidence to substantiate Story's claim that the Supreme Court had jurisdiction over the common law. From the standpoint of law, Crosskey finds the *Tyson* doctrine consonant with the intentions of the framers and the legal precedents which led to its establishment.

STORY'S THEORY OF ADOPTION RE-EXAMINED

The uncertainty and controversy following in the wake of *Swift* v. *Tyson* is no less extant regarding the theory which Story applied in that case. From the colonial period, through the American Revolution, and up to the present, lawyers, political scientists, and judges have debated the issue over the degree to which American law is founded on the common law of England. According to Zechariah Chafee, Jr., there are three theories of the adoption of English law.[104] One is that of Paul S. Reinsch, who presented the startling conclusion in 1899 that the law adopted by the colonists before Independence was an indigenous, "rude, untechnical, popular kind,"[105] differing markedly from the common law. Julius Goebel, Jr., introduced another theory in 1931, which supported Reinsch's supposition that English common law was abandoned by the colonists. According to Goebel, however, the colonists did not adopt a crude, popular law, but English local law, that is, the law administered in the towns, boroughs, and manor courts.[106] Both Reinsch and Goebel agreed that English common law was ultimately accepted, but they contended it emerged concomitantly with a class of lawyers, trained in its principles and procedures, after the American Revolution.

Chafee credits Judge Story with the third or "orthodox" theory. Although recognizing Story's reluctance to accept inappropriate common law rules, Chafee infers that Story believed the colonists brought the common law with them as a body of case law. At one point he defines Story's theory as "The theory that the common law of England was substantially in force in the

to think that Story outwitted the Jacksonian court and maneuvered it into supporting him by making the inaccurate statement that his opinion was in full accord with *all* the previous opinions decided under section 34 of the Judiciary Act. (See *ibid.*, 860.) Although he quotes Story's remark on natural law, Crosskey takes the position that Story decided the issue strictly on legal grounds, and not on "the nature of law." (*Ibid.*, 858.) What Crosskey apparently means by this is simply that Cicero's general principles were in fact part of the "laws of the United States."

[104] "Colonial Courts and the Common Law," Massachusetts Historical Society *Proceedings*, 2d Series, Vol. LXVIII (Oct., 1944–May, 1947), 132–59.

[105] Paul S. Reinsch, "The English Common Law in the Early American Colonies," *Bulletin* 31 of the University of Wisconsin, Historical Series, Vol. II, No. 4 (Oct., 1899), 8; reprinted in *Select Essays in Anglo-American Legal History*, I, 367–415. Reinsch considers the views of Story and Adams outmoded (*ibid.*, 398).

[106] Julius Goebel, Jr., "King's Law and Local Custom in Seventeenth Century New England," *Columbia Law Review*, Vol. XXXI, No. 3 (Mar., 1931), 417.

colonies from the time of their settlement."[107] He states further that Story's theory "is irreconcilable with the court records, if it means that the common law existed in the colonies in the same way that it did in England."[108] But Chafee holds elsewhere in his essay that "Story's theory has a good deal of truth to it if we define 'the common law of England' more broadly and regard it as a system of principles and rules of action."[109]

Neither of Chafee's conflicting interpretations seems to apply to Story. The Story theory, it will be recalled, was based on two propositions, one theoretical, the other practical. From the doctrine that common law is the birthright of every Englishman and remains in force wherever new lands are inhabited by British subjects, Story acknowledged its assimilation as a matter of legality. Two factors, however, mollified the stringent application of this rule: Circumstances dictated that the whole corpus of English law could not be blended into the rough terrain of the colonial setting; furthermore, the only laws theoretically in force were those which "existed at the time of emigration."[110] At what date the emigration ceased, Story does not say, but it presumably begins in 1607 and extends no farther than the period surrounding the American Revolution of 1776.

As a matter of natural law, English common law was incorporated as a set of principles, usages, and rules of action for the promotion of justice, the governing of the people, and the security of persons and property.[111] Such common law rights as these, including the common law rules for adjudicating these rights—*stare decisis*, rule of reason, and trial by jury[112]—were indisputably adopted in every colony.

The nature of their adoption, and whether the decisions of English courts were incorporated, depended upon their commensurability. As we saw in the last chapter, the Christian religion, being the source of all law in Story's legal philosophy, was surely a part of our common law. Story asserted this doctrine in *Vidal* v. *Girard's Executors*[113] and *Terrett* v. *Taylor*.[114] Its applicability to American jurisprudence, however, was governed by the American experience.

---

[107] "Colonial Courts and the Common Law," Massachusetts Historical Society *Proceedings*, 2d Series, Vol. LXVIII (Oct., 1944–May, 1947), 140.

[108] *Ibid.*, 148.

[109] *Ibid.*, 149.

[110] *Patterson* v. *Winn*, 5 Peters 233.

[111] Charles Haines notes that "The judges in the Colonies frequently indicated their belief in the [classical] natural laws, which were considered true laws, and legislation was thought to be binding only in so far as it was an expression of these laws." *The Revival of Natural Law Concepts*, 53.

[112] In *Parsons* v. *Bedford*, 3 Peters 446 (1830), Story held that the right of trial by jury had been incorporated into the constitutions of every state, and into the Seventh Amendment as a "fundamental guarantee of the rights and liberties of the people."

[113] 2 Howard 127.

[114] 9 Cranch 46.

He believed that, at the state and local level, individuals are forbidden from flagrantly ridiculing the Christian religion; but the American tradition of religious freedom requires a great deal of latitude on the part of the courts in applying this doctrine.

At the constitutional level, Story claimed the First Amendment allows for the promotion of Christianity in general by the national government, but as with the states, forbids the promotion of any one particular sect or the punishment of disbelievers. Regarding the erection of Episcopal churches, the right of the king to present the land for their construction and of the church parsons to take it into possession was a common law principle adopted in the colonies. But if there was no organized church to accept the grant, then the state which succeeded to the rights of the crown might gain control over the land, should the town in which it was located so agree.[115]

According to Story, the common law principle that buildings and other fixtures annexed to leased property cannot later be removed was adopted as a part of our common law; but owing to the widespread poverty during the colonial era, the rule was effective only with respect to laws of inheritance, and not to property law (in relation to landlord and tenant).[116] The states also incorporated the common law principle that an exemplification of a public grant under seal is admissible evidence verifying the original grant. This rule, he contended, constitutes a part of our common law. It was adopted because it became a part of English law before the emigration, and was thereafter suitable to American circumstances.[117]

Being a part of the law of the states, it necessarily follows, in Story's mind, that the common law is also a part of the Constitution, as the latter is an outgrowth of the former, representing the union of the whole. That certain common law principles were incorporated into the federal Constitution, as in state constitutions, is demonstrated, argued Story, by the statements of American revolutionary leaders and such provisions of the Constitution which guarantee federal protection against the violation of habeas corpus and trial by jury. Thus, Story contended that, inasmuch as the common law is a source of judicial interpretation at the state level, then it is also a source of constitutional construction, since both levels of government are predicated upon the general principles of the common law.

Common law, then, is a rule of decision in federal courts and also a basis of federal jurisdiction, where common law questions are involved in absence of controlling statutes. The jurisdiction of federal courts therefore encompasses crimes against the national government that are punishable at common law.[118]

---

[115] *Town of Pawlet* v. *Clark*, 9 Cranch 292.
[116] *Van Ness* v. *Pacard*, 2 Peters 137.
[117] *Patterson* v. *Winn*, 5 Peters 241.
[118] *United States* v. *Coolidge*, 25 Federal Cases 619.

Likewise, said Story, the common law is a rule of decision in diversity cases involving general commercial transactions, where no state laws exist.[119] In accomplishing these ends the Supreme Court fosters uniformity while incorporating the common law into American jurisprudence, thus preserving at the highest level the general principles of the common law.

From this re-examination of Story's judicial opinions and *Commentaries on the Constitution*, it is clear Story believed that those subordinate truths embodied in English statutes and decisions had been adopted with the general principles of the common law. The supposition, however, that Story may have thought "that the common law existed in the colonies in the same way that it did in England,"[120] is at variance with Story's disavowal of outmoded and inapplicable common law rules. Indeed, Story advised the legal profession to ignore such irrelevant and obscure laws and decisions as those respecting tithes, demesne, and English game laws. Toward the conclusion of his review of Nathan Dane's *Abridgment of American Law*, Story lauded the author for omitting those portions of English law not endemic to America. "We can hardly conceive of anything more preposterous," commented Judge Story, "than to engraft on such a work those titles of the English law which have nothing correspondent with them in our country to which they can be applied."[121]

Chafee's further suggestion that Story may simply have regarded the incorporation as an acceptance of the general principles of the common law must also be discarded. Story accepted those English cases that were compatible with the habits and customs of the American people, both before and after the American Revolution.

Zechariah Chafee argues persuasively that Reinsch and Goebel have, in a large measure, overlooked recorded facts, and recommends that more comprehensive examinations of colonial records are needed before any definite conclusions can be drawn respecting the ingredients of colonial American law. Colonial law, deduces Chafee, was apparently a composite of homemade law, Continental law, English common law, and English local law.[122] Yet, as early as 1826, Nathan Dane, with Story's endorsement, had reached an identical conclusion in his *Abridgment of American Law*, after nearly fifty years of research.[123] Chafee may discern an element of truth in Story's "orthodox" theory and in the newer assertions of Reinsch and Goebel,[124] but he avoids the full implication of the Story thesis in arriving at his own synthesis.

[119] *Swift* v. *Tyson*, 16 Peters 1.

[120] Chafee, "Colonial Courts and the Common Law," Massachusetts Historical Society *Proceedings*, 2d Series, Vol. LXVIII (Oct., 1944–May, 1947), 148.

[121] "Digests of the Common Law," *Miscellaneous Writings*, 397.

[122] "Colonial Courts and the Common Law," Massachusetts Historical Society *Proceedings*, 2d Series, Vol. LXVIII (Oct., 1944–May, 1947), 156–59.

[123] Story, "Digests of the Common Law," *Miscellaneous Writings*, 379–407.

What contemporary critics Chafee, Reinch, and Goebel fail to consider in their unsympathetic treatment of the "orthodox" theory is its underlying philosophical assumption. Roscoe Pound has pointed out that Story, Kent, and many other jurists of early nineteenth-century America—and he includes Marshall here as well—frequently identified "the natural rights of man, as declared by the continental jurists, with the immemorial common-law rights of Englishmen, as declared by Coke and Blackstone." When an opportunity was presented "to utilize the peculiar social and political institutions of pioneer America in developing or supplementing the legal materials afforded by the English common law, the continental treatises on commercial law, and comparative law," these jurists often turned to natural law as their theory of judicial decision. Natural law served, in other words, as "a convenient dogmatic justification for the criterion of applicability to American conditions, for the filling up of gaps where English legal precepts were found inapplicable, and for drawing upon the continental commercial law and upon comparative law where English legal materials were not at hand."[125]

Thus it would seem that recent legal scholars have tended to oversimplify the various statements of Adams and Story concerning the origin of American law. According to Adams and Story, the problem of adoption could not be construed in strictly legal terms, and thus the answer did not lie solely in colonial records. When these Massachusetts lawyers proclaimed American inheritance of English common law, they were not referring to the volumes of judicial decisions studiously and silently infused into domestic institutions, but to the aggregate rights emanating from the common law, which, like the natural law, were never abrogated. Case law, digested and compounded into scientific commentaries, was after all, only a microcosm of the macrocosm, reflecting a general "omnipresence" of "natural" rights attained over centuries of history and experience.

[124] "Colonial Courts and the Common Law," Massachusetts Historical Society *Proceedings*, 2d Series, Vol. LXVIII (Oct., 1944–May, 1947), 156.
[125] Pound, *Formative Era of American Law*, 104, 109–10.

CHAPTER V

A Defense of Property

When we call to mind his youth, and remember how earnest and conspicuous he had been on the unpopular side in politics, it will not be a matter of surprise to learn that the news of his appointment fell with something like consternation upon the elder, the more apprehensive, and the more conservative portion of the people of New England.... The public knew him as an enthusiastic partisan; and it is not too much to say that with many there was an apprehension that, in his hands, rights and property would hardly be safe.

GEORGE HILLARD, *Memoirs of Joseph Story*

"I suspect my old political friends thought me somewhat a heretic," wrote Story to Justice Bushrod Washington on January 13, 1821. "But if I may so say in the language of St. Paul, after the way which they call heresy, 'so worship I the God of my fathers,' so do I reexamine the old doctrines of government against the popular speculations & reforms so fashionable in our day."[1] Story was talking about the hostile reaction of his fellow Massachusetts Republicans to the celebrated speech he had recently delivered at the Massachusetts Constitutional Convention in defense of property. Equally surprised by Story's sudden change of heart were his old political foes, who had never imagined Story as a friend of property. "Judge Story has been a most faithful & able champion of every right thing from beginning to end," said Isaac Parker to Harrison Gray Otis after hearing Story's eloquent address, "and really deserves that his former political errors should be entirely forgotten."[2]

More than any other Supreme Court justice of his time, including Marshall, Judge Story stoutly defended the two great principles of Federalist theory: the rights and privileges of private property and the legitimate powers of the national government. Yet Joseph Story was not a man whom the Federalists trusted. He wore the badge of a Jeffersonian Republican and, *ipso facto*, was duly labelled an arch foe of liberty, order, and property. His appointment to the Supreme Court, regarded as little less than a mockery of sound government, deeply shocked the propertied classes of New England society. "I remember my father's graphic account of the rage of the Federalists," recalled Josiah Quincy, "when 'Joe Story, that country pettifogger, aged thirty two,'

[1] Story Papers, NYHS.
[2] Jan. 10, 1821, Otis Papers, MHS.

was made a judge of our highest court."[3] The continued erosion of revolutionary ideals, the steady encroachment of democracy, and the subversion of good Federalist doctrines were the dire consequences of Story's judgeship which the conservative element erroneously anticipated when Story abandoned the Speaker's chair of the Massachusetts legislature to ascend the high bench of the United States Supreme Court in 1811.

New England Republican that he was, and favorite target of Federalist contumely, Story nonetheless pursued the alluring ideals of Washington, Adams, and Hamilton with a dogged consistency throughout his life. Story changed his front but not his ground and outwardly bore a flag of many colors for and against the democratic aspirations of the day. Ultimately, he shifted into the ranks of the old order during the period of adjustment that followed in the wake of the French Revolution. But, as best seen in his admiration and respect for property rights, Story's change of heart was more a matter of degree than principle. His repeated vindications of property, "the theme song of his decisions,"[4] are traceable to the very outset of his political career. As early as 1804, when he delivered his Fourth of July oration, Story had identified himself as a friend of private property, inveighing against old-world monarchy, that vicious system of government under which he feared property rights were in constant jeopardy. "What in truth," he asked the assembled inhabitants of Salem on that celebrated day of Independence, "are the boasted advantages of monarchy? Are civil liberty and personal protection secured? These are the transcendent rights of mankind, without which life itself were a heavy burthen. . . . If the security of property be the object of government, where is the monarch whose rapacity has not trampled on the laws, and wrested from industry its scanty pittance?"[5]

The Fourth of July oration marks the first appearance in his public or private statements of a concern for the protection of property. In the years that separated him from his "radical" youth, he stringently maintained his early attachment to property rights. His pro-Federalist sympathies as Massachusetts legislator eventually attracted the favorable attention of a few prescient Federalists, such as Harrison Gray Otis, who privately admitted that Story possessed "too much sentiment and honor to go *all lengths*."[6] And George Cabot, another leading Federalist, had also perceived an adumbration of conservatism in Story's politics. When Story was retained as counsel in the noted case of *Fletcher* v. *Peck*,[7] along with John Quincy Adams and Robert Goodloe Harper, Cabot recommended to Timothy Pickering that young Story be

[3] *Figures of the Past*, 188.

[4] Henry S. Commager, "Joseph Story," *Bacon Lectures*, 58.

[5] "An Oration," 23–24.

[6] To Robert Goodloe Harper, Apr. 19, 1807, Samuel E. Morison, *The Life and Letters of Harrison Gray Otis*, I, 283.

[7] 6 Cranch 87 (1810).

accepted by the inner circles of the effete Federalist party. "Mr. Joseph Story of Salem goes to Washington as solicitor for the Georgia claimants. Though he is a man whom the Democrats support, I have seldom if ever met with one of sounder mind on the principal points of National policy. He is well worthy the civil attention of the most respectable Federalists; and I wish you to be so good as to say so to our friend Mr. Quincy, and such other gentlemen as you think will be likely to pay him some attention."[8]

Fletcher v. *Peck* was the first case to come before the Supreme Court involving the contract clause, and it is noteworthy that Joseph Story, who would subsequently play a leading role in the constitutional struggle over property rights, appeared in the opening scene of this protracted drama. The source of controversy was an act of the Georgia legislature, passed in 1795, by which extensive tracts of land now comprising Mississippi and Alabama were fraudulently granted to various land speculators. Influenced by bribery, every member of the legislature, save one, participated in the swindle, voting to dispose of some 35,000,000 acres of valuable property at the nominal sum of $500,000. An irate citizenry, aroused against the legislators, endeavored to rectify matters by electing a new legislature, which repealed the grant. In the meantime, however, various agents of the land companies surreptitiously sold much of the land to innocent third parties.[9]

The Salem lawyer rejected states' rights doctrines and pressed for a broad interpretation of the contract clause. Story and Harper contended that the Georgia legislature was forbidden by the Constitution to pass any law impairing the obligation of contracts. A grant was an executed contract, they asserted, "and it creates also an implied executory contract, which is, that the grantee shall continue to enjoy the things granted according to the terms of the grant."[10]

Marshall's indebtedness to counsel was clearly reflected in the unanimous opinion he delivered for the Court.[11] He adopted the doctrine of implied limitations and challenged the validity of the rescinding act on the basis of the inviolable rights of property as well as the constitutional provision for-

[8] Jan. 28, 1808, Henry Cabot Lodge, *Life and Letters of George Cabot*, 377.

[9] For an historical account of the case, see the following: C. Peter Magrath, *Yazoo: Law and Politics in the New Republic. The Case of Fletcher* v. *Peck*; also Charles G. Haines, *The Role of the Supreme Court in American Government and Politics, 1789–1835*, 309–29; Charles Warren, *Supreme Court in United States History*, I, 392–99; Albert J. Beveridge, *The Life of John Marshall*, III, 546–602.

[10] 6 Cranch 123.

[11] According to Charles Haines, Marshall "followed the reasoning of Hamilton that a grant is a contract executed and that the grant involves an implied contract that the grantor will not reassert his right over the thing granted." (*The Role of the Supreme Court*, 325.) Whether Marshall had read Hamilton's remarks on the contract clause is a matter of conjecture, but, certainly, he had listened to the arguments of Story. See also Benjamin F. Wright, *The Contract Clause of the Constitution*, 22.

bidding state impairment of contractual obligations. Following the line of reasoning suggested by Story and Harper, the chief justice defined a contract as "a compact between two or more parties" which may be "either executory or executed."[12] The state grant and the subsequent acceptance by purchase formed in substance an executed contract, the obligation of which continued after the transaction. Marshall also accepted the theory offered in the Story-Harper argument that a legislative grant was not exempt from the obligations of contract, since the constitutional provision made no distinction between public and private contracts, and thus included both, so as to give the widest possible protection to property rights. In voiding the rescinding act, Marshall held for the first time that a legislative grant was a contract, and that a state law conflicting with the Constitution was void.

TERRETT V. TAYLOR:
DARTMOUTH COLLEGE SUB SILENTIO

Untroubled by democratic aspirations or spurious notions about states' rights, Story took his seat on the high bench at the right hand of Marshall and was soon erecting high barriers to state interference with property rights. Two opinions Story delivered in 1815, although they did not directly concern the contract clause, bolstered the precedents he had helped to establish in *Fletcher v. Peck*, and were later relied upon in subsequent decisions upholding the sanctity of contract and rights of property.[13]

The first of these two cases, *Terrett v. Taylor*,[14] involved church property confiscated by the Virginia legislature. Under the terms of an act in 1776, Virginia had confirmed the Episcopal church's rights of property; but this act, together wtih subsequent statutes reaffirming it, was repealed in 1798 as being "inconsistent with the principles of the Constitution and of religious freedom."[15] Three years later the Virginia legislature claimed title to the property

---

[12] 6 Cranch 136.

[13] Story delivered his first opinion upholding the vested rights of property in the First Circuit in *The Society for the Propagation of the Gospel* v. *Wheeler*, 2 Gallison 105, 22 Federal Cases 757, No. 13,156 (1814). Story knocked down a New Hampshire statute allowing land tenants the value of improvements on recovery against them, as a retrospective law violating the New Hampshire Constitution. No contract was involved, and since the *ex post facto* provision of the federal Constitution applied only to criminal cases, Story invalidated the act on the basis of the twenty-third article of the New Hampshire bill of rights, which forbade retrospective laws, civil as well as criminal. "Upon principle," Story added, "every statute, which takes away or impairs vested rights acquired under existing laws, or creates a new obligation, imposes a new duty, or attaches a new disability, in respect to transactions or considerations already past, must be deemed retrospective." *Ibid.*, 767.

[14] 9 Cranch 43 (1815).

[15] *Ibid.*, 48.

and directed the overseers of the poor to sell the lands and use the proceeds of the sale to assist the poor of each parish.

Story struck down the rescinding statute as violating the free exercise of religion and the rights of property guaranteed by the Virginia constitution and bill of rights. Virginia contended that all of the property acquired by the Episcopal church became the property of the state with the advent of the American Revolution. Story admitted that if the church had originally acquired its property through a grant from the king, "there might have been some color (and would have been but a color) for such an extraordinary pretension."[16] The church, however, had acquired the lands over the years through purchase, and such property could not be seized either before, during, or after the Revolution, as "The dissolution of the form of government did not involve in it a dissolution of civil rights, or an abolition of the common law under which the inheritances of every man in the State were held."[17]

Story then focused on the grant of 1776, concluding that the church had been vested with an irrevocable title to its lands. Any legal doctrine sanctioning the capricious repeal of legislative grants, said Story, "would uproot the very foundations of almost all the land titles in Virginia, and is utterly inconsistent with a great and fundamental principle of a republican government, the right of the citizens to the free enjoyment of their property legally acquired."[18] The state's assumption that a legislature was authorized in its sovereign capacity to abrogate statutes creating private corporations, such as the Episcopal church, was an anathema to time-honored standards of civil liberty. "We think ourselves standing upon the principles of natural justice," Story observed, "upon the fundamental laws of every free government, upon the spirit and the letter of the Constitution of the United States, and upon the decisions of most respectable judicial tribunals, in resisting such a doctrine."[19]

A similar issue to that raised in the *Terrett* case confronted Judge Story in *Town of Pawlet* v. *Clark*,[20] in which a town in the state of Vermont attempted to recover under a state grant certain lands originally bestowed upon the Episcopal church by the king of England. Inasmuch as no church was officially consecrated to receive the grant in Pawlet at the time of the royal charter, Story reasoned that the property remained in abeyance. The state, succeeding to the rights of the crown, might "alien" or "encumber" the property with the assent of Pawlet, concluded Story, but the grant to Pawlet could not afterwards be repealed by the state.

The *Terrett* and *Pawlet* decisions not only reaffirmed the doctrines of im-

---

[16] *Ibid.*, 49.
[17] *Ibid.*, 50. Note the use Story makes here of his theory of adoption of the common law.
[18] *Ibid.*, 50–51.
[19] *Ibid.*, 52.
[20] 9 Cranch 292 (1815).

plied limitations and vested rights promulgated by Chief Justice Marshall in *Fletcher* v. *Peck*, but, more significantly, extended the contract clause (by implication) to cover private and public corporation charters. Although framed in general terms, Story's two opinions preempted and anticipated the great *Dartmouth College* case decided four years later.[21] Indeed, Justice Washington, who concurred with the chief justice in *Dartmouth*, thought the doctrines laid down earlier by Story so fully answered the issues raised by the reconstituted trustees of Dartmouth College as to render further discussion almost superfluous.[22] Thus, while Story's first opinion under the contract clause actually appeared in 1819, when he concurred with the chief justice in upholding the charter rights of Dartmouth College against impairment by the state legislature of New Hampshire, Story, in effect, had already brought corporation charters under the protection of the contract clause without so much as a single reference to section 10 of article 1 of the United States Constitution.[23]

MARSHALL AND THE *DARTMOUTH COLLEGE* CASE

That Chief Justice Marshall delivered the majority opinion of the Court in *Trustees of Dartmouth College* v. *Woodward*[24] detracts little, as will be seen,

[21] *The Trustees of Dartmouth College* v. *Woodward*, 4 Wheaton 518 (1819).

[22] *Ibid.*, 663–65. See also Webster's argument as counsel for the defendants. *Ibid.*, 592.

[23] Benjamin F. Wright considers Story's decision in *Terrett* v. *Taylor* as somewhat puzzling, "Puzzling, because here the Court does not apply the contract clause, although in view of the Marshall court's latitudinarian views of that clause it might easily have done so, and the case has, in fact, often been cited by the Court as a contract case." (*The Contract Clause of the Constitution*, 38.) In stating that the Court thought itself "standing . . . upon the spirit and letter of the Constitution," however, Story relied upon the contract clause by implication. Actually, Story's opinion was more latitudinarian than Wright gives credit, as Story also voided the repealing act on grounds of "natural justice," "the decisions of most respectable judicial tribunals," 'upon the fundamental laws of every free government," and upon "the common law of the land." The fact of the matter is that Story had upheld the rights of property upon a broader basis than had Marshall in *Fletcher* v. *Peck* or *New Jersey* v. *Wilson*, 7 Cranch 164 (1812). Furthermore, Story's inclusion of private corporations under the protection of the Constitution can hardly be considered a narrow interpretation. Story's refusal to venture a discussion of the contract clause may be attributed to a variety of causes. First, there is no evidence from the record that counsel on either side raised the issue; secondly, both Justices Johnson and Todd were absent; thirdly, and most important, the principle that property could not be confiscated by the government was a universal concept of free government at the time, a concept so widely accepted that Story felt analysis was unnecessary. Had there been a grant of land, as in *Fletcher* v. *Peck*, Story would surely have based his decision on the contract clause, but here, the Episcopal church had purchased the lands with private funds. The only grant involved was a grant of corporate powers, affirming the church's property rights, that is, affirming a *pre-existing* right. Thus it may be seen that questions involving the obligation of contract were of secondary consideration, and the primary issue was that of vested rights.

[24] 4 Wheaton 518.

from the fact that Judge Story had quietly assumed pre-eminence over the Court in the battle against state interference with the sacred institution of property. The material events precipitating the all-absorbing controversy in the *Dartmouth College* case dated from about the year 1754, when the Reverend Eleazar Wheelock established a school on his estate to train the children of Indians as Christian missionaries.

In order to promote the acquisition of property and financial endowments for the school, Wheelock endeavored to procure private contributions from English citizens, who in turn were to become the trustees of the institution. In return for their contributions, these benefactors were also permitted to choose western New Hampshire as the new site of the school. Wheelock then persuaded the benefactors that the institution should be incorporated to preserve its lands, and in 1769 Wheelock was granted a royal charter incorporating Dartmouth College.

By the terms of the charter, Wheelock was made president with power by his last will to appoint a successor. The college trustees were authorized to select or remove the president and to fill vacancies on the board of trustees. When Wheelock died, his young son, John, succeeded him to the presidency. Soon afterwards, however, the youthful Wheelock found himself pitted against a hostile board of trustees. A fierce pamphlet war ensued of such proportions as to attract the attention of the whole New Hampshire population. Federalists and Republicans, who followed the battle through the political spectrum, identified themselves with the opposing factions and magnified the feud into a campaign issue.

The sequel to the turmoil was a legislative act. A Republican-controlled legislature, following up Wheelock's dismissal in 1815, enacted a law in 1816 which, in effect, not only annulled the royal charter, but also placed the administration of Dartmouth College under legislative control. The name of the school was changed to Dartmouth University. The number of trustees was increased from twelve to twenty-one, and a board of overseers, with a veto power over the acts of the trustees, was created and made responsible for ensuring a presidential report to the governor upon the management of the school. The old trustees, however, refused to acquiesce and remained at their posts, ignoring the ultimatum of the new charter. William Woodward, the college secretary and treasurer, also denied the legality of the new trustees. An action of trover was brought against Woodward, the college secretary and treasurer, for the recovery of the college seal, charter, and record books.

Chief Justice Marshall, speaking for the majority, first answered the question of whether the charter was a contract. Assuming without argument that every necessary ingredient of a contract existed, even though counsel had cogently urged no contract had ever been made, Marshall then inquired whether the royal charter was a contract falling within the purview of the contract clause of the Constitution. He interpreted the clause in the narrowest terms, asserting that the word *contract* should be construed in a "limited sense."[25] The provision of the Constitution prohibiting the legislative impairment of contractual obligations "never has been understood to embrace other contracts than those which respect property,"[26] said Marshall, and such contracts as those comprehending civil institutions and marriages, for example, stood beyond the pale of constitutional protection.

Turning to the charter itself, the chief justice examined its provisions and rejected the contention that Dartmouth College was a public corporation created by a public grant. Because the institution was endowed with private funds, it was a private charter; and it was eleemosynary in nature because it had been founded for the promotion of piety, learning, and the propagation of the Christian religion among the Indians. Nor did the school's acceptance of donations alter the private character of the institution, "for money may be given for education, and the persons receiving it do not, by being employed in the education of youth, become members of the civil government."[27]

Marshall conceded that if there had been no consideration for the agreement, the charter could have been legally repealed, but the incorporation was wholly private; and the incorporating act could not change the charter of the institution, unless gratuitous. The chief justice also conceded that "Had Parliament, immediately after the emanation of this charter, and the execution of those conveyances which followed it, annulled the instrument, so that the living donors would have witnessed the disappointment of their hopes, the perfidy of the transaction would have been universally acknowledged. Yet then, as now, the donors would have had no interest in the property."[28] Nevertheless, asserted Marshall, once a private eleemosynary corporation was established, its creator was without power to subject it to visitation, alteration, or control.

Another concession which Marshall made nearly stripped his entire argument of its rationality. He admitted that probably the preservation of charter rights (exclusive of those regarding property) "was not particularly in the view of the framers of the Constitution, when the clause under consideration was introduced into that instrument";[29] however, he believed every effort should be made to interpret the Constitution in a manner favorable to the rights of property. If the framers had been confronted with the same situation presently before the Court, he felt confident they would have readily acknowledged the correctness of his position.

The chief justice concluded his argument with a discussion of the impairment of the contract. "By the Revolution, the duties, as well as the powers, of

25 *Ibid.*, 628.
26 *Ibid.*, 629.
27 *Ibid.*, 635.
28 *Ibid.*, 643.
29 *Ibid.*, 644.

government devolved on the people of New Hampshire. It is admitted, that among the latter was comprehended the transcendent power of Parliament, as well as that of the executive department."[30] Were it not for the Constitution, forbidding the legislative impairment of contracts, the New Hampshire legislature might have revoked the charter.[31] In substituting the will of the state for the will of the donors, the new charter had altered "every essential operation of the college."[32]

STORY AND THE *DARTMOUTH COLLEGE CASE*

Judging from the events leading up to the arrival of the case on the Supreme Court docket, from certain weaknesses in Marshall's opinion, and from the nature of Story's concurring opinion, it seems clear that both Marshall and Story regarded the former's controlling opinion to be somewhat unsatisfactory, and that Story was, in many respects, the real genius behind the *Dartmouth College* decision. Story was more familiar with the controversy and had previously been appointed by the governor of New Hampshire to the new board of trustees.[33] In fact, Story most likely believed that he would deliver an opinion on the case in the First Circuit.

In agreement with Daniel Webster, who represented the trustees, Story had originally devised a plan by which the rights of all the parties could be tried.

[30] *Ibid.*, 651.

[31] According to Marshall, "The obligations, then, which were created by the charter to Dartmouth College, were the same in the new that they have been in the old government. The power of the government was also the same. A repeal of this charter at any time prior to the adoption of the present constitution of the United States, would have been an extraordinary and unprecedented act of power, but one which could have been contested only by the restrictions upon the legislature, to be found in the constitution of the state. But the constitution of the United States has imposed this additional limitation, that the legislaure of a state shall pass no act 'impairing the obligation of contracts.'" *Ibid.*, 651-52.

[32] *Ibid.*, 652.

[33] Story, however, never accepted the appointment. For a discussion of Story's activities prior to the decision and his collaboration with Webster in planning the legal strategy of the case, see Maurice G. Baxter, *Daniel Webster and the Supreme Court*, 65-109; R. Kent Newmyer, "Daniel Webster as Tocqueville's Lawyer: The Dartmouth College Case Again," *American Journal of Legal History*, Vol. XI, No. 2 (Apr., 1967), 127-47; Haines, *The Role of the Supreme Court*, 391-402; Beveridge, *Life of Marshall*, IV, 223-81. Haines thinks that Story at first sided with the new trustees of Dartmouth College (*The Role of the Supreme Court*, 386, 411), but Beveridge, noting Story's opinion in *Terrett* v. *Taylor*, and the personal correspondence between Webster and Story and Livingston and Story, shows that Story maintained the same position throughout the course of litigation (*Life of Marshall*, IV, 243-44, 257-58, 275). That Story favored the act repealing the old charter was a rumor started by certain New England Federalists, who were unaware of Story's ideas respecting property and judged him solely on the basis of his Republican party affiliations. Beveridge mentions Pickering as one of those who believed the rumors about Story. *Ibid.*, 257-58, n. 4.

Judge Story and the district judge were to disagree *pro forma*, so that the cause could be taken immediately to the United States Supreme Court. With this plan in mind, Webster had instigated three suits in the federal court in New Hampshire, any one of which would have permitted Story to strike down the recently enacted laws upsetting the provisions of the royal charter. But before any of these cases could be brought to trial, the original case presented to the Supreme Court was decided.

Well before the case came before the Supreme Court, Story had privately confided to Webster that he wanted the question placed on the broadest basis possible—encompassing not merely the contract clause, but natural law and the doctrine of implied limitations. On April 28, 1818, Webster wrote to Jeremiah Mason, attorney for the college before the New Hampshire court, the following: "I saw Judge Story as I came along. He is evidently expecting a case which shall present all the questions. . . . The question which we must raise is . . . 'whether by the general principles of our governments, the State legislatures be not restrained from divesting vested rights?' This of course, independent of the constitutional provision respecting contracts. . . . On this question I have great confidence in a decision on the right side."[34]

Marshall hastily wrote his opinion at his home in Virginia, without consulting his brothers on the Court. He was somewhat unsure of himself, it would seem, as evidenced by the fact that upon returning to Washington, he submitted his draft to Story for revision.[35] Story was probably not overly startled by what he read. Abandoning his customary practice of remaining silent when he disagreed with the Chief Justice or the majority opinion, Story had earlier drafted a concurring opinion, which anticipated Marshall's several obvious errors and reinforced Marshall's opinion. So perfectly does Story's

[34] *Private Correspondence of Daniel Webster* (ed. by Fletcher Webster), I, 282–83. "The *Judge* said it was important that a cause should go up, embracing all the questions," Webster wrote to his colleague, Joseph Hopkinson. "I should not have great doubt of *his* opinion, when we get the questions *fairly & broadly up.*" (July 3, 1818, as quoted in Newmyer, "Daniel Webster as Tocqueville's Lawyer," *American Journal of Legal History*, Vol. XI, No. 2 [Apr., 1967], 136.) "Like most of his contemporaries," observes Professor Baxter, Webster "believed there were universal laws of natural justice anterior to positive, man-made law. 'Written constitutions sanctify and confirm great principles,' he said, 'but the latter are prior in existence to the former.' In numerous cases he appealed to natural law as sufficient ground to invalidate legislation. Perhaps the best example is the Dartmouth College Case." *Webster and the Supreme Court*, 37.

[35] "Marshall had prepared his opinion under his trees at Richmond and in the mountains during the vacation of 1818; and he barely had time to read it to his associates before the opening of court at the session when it was delivered. But he afterward submitted the manuscript to Story, who made certain changes." (Beveridge, *Life of Marshall*, IV, 274.) "I am much obliged," wrote Marshall to Story, "by the alterations you have made in the Dartmouth College case & am highly gratified by what you say respecting it." May 27, 1819, Massachusetts Historical Society *Proceedings*, 2nd Series, Vol. XIV (1900–1901), 324–25.

opinion fill in the gaps and correct the mistakes, that it would almost seem he had prior knowledge of Marshall's reasoning and the weaknesses of his opinion.

Erudite and compact, Marshall's reasoning nevertheless carried the seeds of destruction with it, seeds which Mr. Justice Story hastily substituted with carefully assembled common law maxims. Although perhaps the most important decision handed down during his magistracy, Marshall's opinion in the *Dartmouth College* case was open to devastating criticism.[36] It was in many respects as much a handicap as an asset to the protection of property and sanctity of contracts. In addition to being burdened with qualifications and concessions inviting subsequent attack and modification by future courts, the opinion of the chief justice also ignored many of the well-founded arguments of counsel.

The source of weakness in the opinion was Marshall himself, who, in comparison to Story and probably Justice Bushrod Washington, was curiously ill read in the law.[37] The proper disposal of this case, which involved complex questions of contract, required more than a faint acquaintance with the common law, and it is little wonder that Marshall, who, failing to define adequately a contract and its ensuing obligations, was given to incorrect assumptions upon the common law rules governing contracts and was unable to

[36] After poring over the articles criticizing Marshall's opinion in the *Dartmouth College* case, Charles Haines (*The Role of the Supreme Court*, 402–11) assembles more than a dozen complaints against Marshall's reasoning. Haines contends that "Justice Story, however, asserted views which were subject to even stronger condemnation than those of Marshall." (*Ibid.*, 411.) Haines fails to cite a single criticism of Story's opinion.

[37] Beveridge admits that "Indeed, Marshall had no 'learning' at all in the academic sense." (*Life of Marshall*, IV, 60–61.) Beveridge also cites at the same page the opinion of the Boston lawyer George S. Hillard that Marshall "was not, in any sense of the word, a learned man." And Story, though he admired the Chief Justice immeasurably, confessed in his eulogy of Marshall: "That he possessed an uncommon share of juridical learning, would naturally be presumed, from his large experience and inexhaustible diligence. Yet it is due to truth, as well as to his memory to declare, that his juridical learning was not equal to that of many of the great masters in the profession, living or dead, at home or abroad." ("Life, Character and Services of Chief Justice Marshall," *Miscellaneous Writings*, 693.) But Julius Goebel, Jr., has argued that Marshall's learning in the common law was not as inadequate as is generally believed. Goebel notes that Marshall amply cited English precedents in a few of his decisions and often adhered to common law principles. It should be observed, however, that Goebel's evidence is far from conclusive, and that he does not assert Marshall's knowledge of the law was equal to Story's. "But unlike Brother Story, he [Marshall] was incapable of confecting such compendia of learning as *Town of Pawlet* v. *Clark* or the dissent in *Brown* v. *United States* which glitter in the reports like overdecorated Christmas trees." ("The Common Law and the Constitution," *Chief Justice John Marshall: A Reappraisal* (ed. by W. Melville Jones), 120. See, however, Marshall's dissenting opinion in *United States* v. *Dandridge*, 12 Wheaton 64 (1827), which is an impressive display of legal learning and suggests that the chief justice may have been more knowledgeable than is sometimes recognized.

cite a single precedent in support of his decision.[38] True, Marshall could quite successfully deliver opinions on the jurisdictional aspects of the Constitution without regard to the common law, as jurisdiction primarily involves constitutional provisions which generally are unconnected with common law rules. In the *Dartmouth College* case, however, jurisdiction was a secondary consideration; for the basic issues revolved around the contract clause and the common law principles of contract law and corporations.

Solidly reasoned, Story's concurring opinion in *Dartmouth* contained the calm aloofness of the intellectual standing apart to clarify. Keeping an eye on every point, whether obvious or obscure, Story covered the issues ignored or summarily dismissed by the chief justice, with full citation to the English commentators and appropriate Anglo-American decisions. Before examining the issues at bar, Story prefaced his lengthy opinion with "an inquiry into the nature, rights, and duties of aggregate corporations at common law,"[39] to provide a proper background for understanding the royal charter and to clarify the rules governing corporations. Corporations, he explained, were either spiritual or lay. They might again be divided into civil and eleemosynary corporations, the latter consisting of those "constituted for the perpetual distribution of the free alms and bounty of the founder, in such manner as he has directed; and in this class are ranked hospitals for the relief of the poor . . . and colleges for the promotion of learning and piety."[40] Corporations were also classified as public and private. Public corporations generally concerned those founded "for public political purposes only, such as towns, cities, parishes and counties," which had been founded by the state "where the whole interests belong also to the government."[41]

By the common law, observed Story, whenever a private eleemosynary corporation was created by the crown, it was subject to no other control on the part of the crown than what had expressly or implicitly been reserved by the charter itself. This did not mean, however, that such corporations were beyond the reach of the law. "They are subject to the general superintending power of the court of chancery [i.e., the rules of equity], not as itself possessing a visitorial power, or a right to control the charity, but as possessing a general

---

[38] However, Marshall cited two insignificant points of Blackstone universally acknowledged by the legal profession, which he might just as well have omitted.

[39] *Trustees of Dartmouth College* v. *Woodward*, 4 Wheaton 667. Story's interpretation of the common law precedents is supported in R. N. Denham, Jr., "An Historical Development of the Contract Theory in the Dartmouth College Case," *Michigan Law Review*, Vol. VII, No. 3 (1909), 219; see also Warren B. Hunting, *The Obligation of Contracts Clause of the United States Constitution*, Johns Hopkins University *Studies in Historical and Political Science*, Series XXXVII, No. 4. Hunting argues that the extension of the contract clause to public grants had support in contemporary political thought and the common law.

[40] *Trustees of Dartmouth College* v. *Woodward*, 4 Wheaton 668.

[41] *Ibid.*, 669.

jurisdiction in all cases of an abuse of trusts to redress grievances and suppress frauds."[42]

Proceeding to the provisions of the charter, Story noted straightway that no endowment had been given by the crown, and that "no power is reserved to the Crown or government in any manner to alter, amend or control the charter."[43] Marshall's failure to acknowledge the use of reservation clauses was, of course, a serious flaw in his opinion. It would appear the Chief Justice had decided that once the corporation had been created, legislatures were forever denied any power of influencing its *modus operandi*. Confronted with a Hobson's choice, representative bodies might be reluctant to grant certain charters —with the possible consequence of a nationwide retardation of economic development. Story, whose primary concern was the inviolability of contract, demonstrated a willingness to honor "escape" clauses, thereby offering encouragement to the continued enactment of legislative grants, merely stipulating that the legislators adhere to the rules of the common law and the terms of the agreement. Story also succeeded in cushioning the jolt of the chief justice's demands by reminding the states that they were not helpless in the face of prior grants, as certain injustices could be corrected in courts of equity.

With these preliminary observations in view, Story pursued the first question in the case, whether the charter was a contract. Rather than define the term *contract*, Story preferred to quote Marshall's definition in *Fletcher* v. *Peck*, stick to precedent, and attend to the complaint emphasized by counsel, that the contract lacked the necessary element of a valuable consideration. Apparently, his purpose was not so much to clarify Marshall's illustration of the consideration involved in the grant—although he did in fact accomplish this—as to remedy Marshall's dangerous and false presumption, nowhere discernible in the common law, that legislatures were possibly free to revoke gratuitous grants. "In every view of the case," Story surmised, "if a consideration were necessary (which I utterly deny) to make the charter a valid contract, a valuable consideration did exist, as to the founder, the trustees, and the benefactors."[44]

The assumption (made by Marshall) that land voluntarily granted could be resumed at the pleasure of the grantor was "truly alarming," particularly in the United States, "where thousands of land titles had their origin in gratuitous grants of the states."[45] Under long-established rules of the common law, Story demonstrated, once a bona fide contract passed into a grant, the grantor was estopped from recalling the grant of the property, albeit the conveyance may have been purely voluntary. Even a gift, completely executed, was irrevocable.

[42] *Ibid.*, 676.
[43] *Ibid.*, 680.
[44] *Ibid.*, 690.
[45] *Ibid.*, 684.

Engraving of Dr. Elisha Story, by Bousley. (*Courtesy of Peter de Brant*)

Portrait of Sarah Wetmore Story in 1819, by Gilbert Stuart. (*A careful search by the author has failed to disclose the present whereabouts of the original painting. Curators of several well-known museums agree that it is privately owned, but neither the owner's name nor the location of the portrait has come to light.*)

Portrait of Joseph Story in 1819, by Gilbert Stuart. (*Courtesy of Fogg Art Museum, Harvard University*)

Story's home in Salem. (*Courtesy of Essex Institute*)

Portrait of Judge Story by Chester Harding. (*Courtesy of Massachusetts Historical Society*)

Portrait of Judge Story in later life, painted in 1837 by Charles Osgood.
(*Courtesy of the Essex Institute*)

Photograph of William Wetmore Story. (*Courtesy of Peter de Brant*)

Bust of Joseph Story by John Frasee. (*Courtesy of Boston Athenaeum*)

"If, therefore, this charter were a pure donation, when the grant was complete, and accepted by the grantees, it involved a contract . . . and the grantor should not re-assume the grant, as much as if it had been founded on the most valuable consideration."[46]

Having thus extended the contract clause to protect all grants of property, whether founded upon a valuable consideration or gratuity, Story claimed that, nevertheless, there had been a valuable consideration at the conveyance of the charter. Story's reasoning on this point is probably the most ingenious aspect of his opinion, for it allowed him to reassert the doctrine of implied contracts, when actually a discussion of the consideration involved in the contract was unnecessary.

According to Marshall, the consideration consisted of "the objects for which a corporation is created," which "the government wishes to promote. They are deemed beneficial to the country; and this benefit constitutes the consideration."[47] Story, on the other hand, regarded the agreement as a severable contract, with a separate and distinct consideration running between the grantor and President Wheelock, the trustees, and the benefactors. Between the crown and the president the consideration consisted of "the implied stipulations on his part in the charter itself. He relinquished valuable rights, and undertook a laborious office in consideration of the grant of incorporation."[48] In short, the consideration involved more than simply the benefits accruing to the crown; it also concerned the inconveniences incurred by the founder of the institution. With respect to the trustees, the consideration consisted "of services agreed to be rendered by them."[49]

In the offer and acceptance of the charter, then, there were various implied contracts, without which the grant would have been meaningless. Wheelock, for example, impliedly covenanted that if the charter were granted, he would remove the school from his estate to New Hampshire and would relinquish all control over the funds. Most important, however, was the implied contract inherent in the consideration between the various benefactors and the crown.

From the very nature of the case, therefore, there was an implied contract on the part of the Crown with every benefactor, that if he would give his money, it should be deemed a charity protected by the charter, and to be administered according to the general law of the land. As soon, then, as a donation was made to the corporation, there was an implied contract springing up, and founded on a valuable consideration, that the Crown would not revoke or alter the charter, or change its administration, without the consent of the corporation.[50]

46 *Ibid.*
47 *Ibid.*, 637.
48 *Ibid.*, 687.
49 *Ibid.*, 689.
50 *Ibid.*

Story next confronted the issue of whether the contract in this case fell within the prohibitory clause of the Constitution. Repudiating Marshall's vulnerable assumption that the contract clause referred only to private corporations, Story circumscribed the powers of state legislatures regarding both public and private corporations, admitting only, that in a very limited sense, a state legislature might "enlarge, repeal and limit the *authorities* of public officers in their official capacities,"[51] if the state constitution so provided. He denied that such contracts between government and public officers as those involving salaries could be abrogated. "Will it be contended," queried Story, "that the legislature of a state can diminish the salary of a judge holding his office during good behavior?"[52]

Story also pointed out that the Supreme Court had already held in *Terrett* v. *Taylor* and *Town of Pawlet* v. *Clark* that a state legislature could not expropriate the property of a city, town, or other public corporation in revoking a grant. Furthermore, contrary to Marshall's assertion, marriage was also protected by the prohibitory clause. "The truth is," deduced Story,

> that the government has no power to revoke a grant, even of its own funds, when given to a private person, or a corporation for special uses. It cannot recall its own endowments granted to any hospital, or college, or city, or town, for the use of such corporations. The only authority remaining to the government is judicial, to ascertain the validity of the grant, to enforce its proper uses, to suppress frauds, and, if the uses are charitable, to secure their regular administration through the means of equitable tribunals.[53]

When Marshall admitted that Parliament could have perfidiously but legally repealed the grant, he conceded his entire argument to the opponents of the old charter. If the English government was never under any obligation, then it could scarcely be contended that the state of New Hampshire, which succeeded to the rights and *duties* of the crown after the Revolution, had any obligation to maintain the charter. There could be no obligation where there was none before. In refuting Marshall's argument as antagonistic to firmly established principles of the common law, Story surely saved the day for the interests they wished to protect.

Equally important, however, was Story's destruction of Marshall's careless allegation that the prohibitory clause applied only to contracts involving private property rights. Was it true, as Marshall had said, "that no grants are within the constitutional prohibition, except such as respect property in the strict sense of the term; that is to say, beneficial interests in lands, tenements, and hereditaments, which may be sold by the grantees for their own benefit;

[51] *Ibid.*, 694. Emphasis supplied.
[52] *Ibid.*
[53] *Ibid.*, 698.

and that grants of franchises, immunities, and authorities not valuable to the parties as property are excluded from the purview"?[54] Certainly not, argued Story, with ample citation.

Admit that every contract is not sacred, he warned, and serious consequences were sure to follow. Marshall's perfunctory remark was utterly devoid of foundation, either in the common law or the meaning and spirit of the Constitution. "All incorporeal hereditaments," Story insisted, "whether they be immunities, dignities, offices or franchises, or other rights, are deemed valuable in law. . . . Whenever they are the subjects of a contract or grant, they are just as much within the reach of the Constitution as any other grant."[55] And Story might also have added that the entire force of Marshall's argument collapsed under the weight of evidence. Strictly speaking, the new charter did not so much interfere with property—for none was expropriated or changed—as it altered those provisions of the old charter concerning the administration of the college, provisions only remotely concerning the rights of tangible property.

Turning finally to the pertinent contents of the new charter, Story agreed with Marshall they were incompatible with the terms of the old charter and that they modified the obligation of contract, thereby violating the constitution. In parting, Story reassured his audience that he had endeavored throughout the examination of the case to keep his steps *super antiquas vias* of the law, under the guidance of authority and principle. It is not for judges to listen to the voice of persuasive eloquence or popular appeal. We have nothing to do but pronounce the law as we find it; and having done this, our justification must be left to the impartial judgment of our country."[56]

Commenting on Judge Story's opinion, Justice Brockholst Livingston said: "It was exactly what I had expected from you, and hope it will be adopted without alteration. What you say of the contract of marriage, is a complete answer to the difficulty made on that subject."[57] William Prescott remarked that he had read Story's opinion "with care and great pleasure. In my judgment it is supported by the principles of our constitutions, and of all free governments. . . . As one of the public, I thank you for establishing a doctrine affecting so many valuable rights and interests, with such clearness and cogency of argument, and weight of authority. . . . You have placed the subject in some strong, and to me, new lights, although I had settled my opinion on the general question years ago."[58] Story's son thought "it is interesting to compare the two judgments, as evincing the different structure of the two minds. The argument of the Chief Justice is close, logical, and compact, but

---

[54] *Ibid.*
[55] *Ibid.*, 699.
[56] *Ibid.*, 713.
[57] To Story, Jan. 24, 1819, *Life and Letters*, I, 323.
[58] To Story, Jan. 9, 1819, *ibid.*, 324.

somewhat hard and dry. The argument of my father is equally convincing but far more flowing and learned."[59]

And Story himself, hardly oblivious to the significance of the decision, foresaw "the vital importance, to the well-being of society and the security of private rights, of the principles on which that decision rested. Unless I am very much mistaken, these principles will be found to apply with an extensive reach to all the great concerns of the people, and will check any undue encroachments upon civil rights, which the passions or the popular doctrines of the day may stimulate our State Legislatures to adopt."[60] Story's evaluation has stood the test of time. Only recently, it was said by Professor Baxter that

The Dartmouth College case became a landmark in constitutional history, establishing the principle of vested rights of corporations. Not only educational but all types of corporations could now claim the protection of the contract clause against state legislation. In an era of economic expansion such as the early nineteenth century, a legal doctrine of this kind was useful and generally acceptable in spite of criticism then and later. . . . How did the case affect Dartmouth College? Manifestly it saved this institution from being extensively remodeled by the legislature. Instead of becoming a state university, Dartmouth remained a small private New England college with a proud tradition and a distinctive flavor. Indeed later generations of loyal Dartmouth men have felt their alma mater miraculously escaped destruction.[61]

Many lawyers and judges have criticized Marshall's reasoning in *Dartmouth College* v. *Woodward*, and the superiority of Story's opinion, though rarely acknowledged, is nonetheless irrefutable. As Gerald T. Dunne notes, "it has become a virtual convention of economic historiography to begin the American corporate cycle with Marshall's Dartmouth College opinion, and read into it the legal foundations of financial and industrial capitalism. It is true that Marshall implied as much when he made Dartmouth's royal charter a contract between the college and New Hampshire . . . . Nevertheless, he only implied it; his explicit references concern only municipal bodies and private charities. It is in Story's concurring opinion that we find the principle extended to business enterprises."[62] In the words of David Henshaw, a Jacksonian Democrat from Massachusetts, "Judge Story, in the same case, was much more explicit, and develops the doctrine of the Court more boldly than John Marshall."[63]

[59] *Ibid.*, 322.
[60] Story to Chancellor Kent, Aug. 21, 1819, *ibid.*, 331.
[61] *Webster and the Supreme Court*, 106, 108.
[62] "The American Blackstone," *Washington University Law Quarterly*, Vol. 1962, No. 3 (June, 1963), 331.
[63] As quoted, *ibid.* "Thus, beginning in *Terrett* v. *Taylor* and climaxing with his concurring opinion in the Dartmouth College Case, he rejected the ancient communal character of the corporation and substituted a new division of public and private based on the

COROLLARIES TO THE CONTRACT CLAUSE

Whether Marshall himself realized his apparent inadequacies in the field of contract law, it is interesting that Mr. Justice Story was assigned to deliver the next great opinion under the contract clause, in the case of *Green* v. *Biddle*.[64] This case, which broadly extended the protection of the obligation of contracts clause to include valid interstate compacts, originated with the inception of the Union shortly after 1789, when the state of Kentucky separated from Virginia. Under the terms of the separation, they entered into a compact, which was incorporated into the Kentucky Constitution. Article 7 of the compact stated "all private rights and interests of lands . . . derived from the laws of Virginia, shall remain valid and secure under the laws of the proposed state."[65]

But in 1797, Kentucky passed a statute which altered the terms of the compact in a number of ways. Kentucky "squatters" evicted from land owned by any Virginian, for example, were excused from the payment of rents and profits accrued during their occupancy. If they made improvements on the land exceeding its value, the claimant could either reimburse the squatter or convey title to him.

Kentucky passed another statute in 1812, slightly modifying the first, but also intended to encourage the relinquishment of private property to Kentucky citizens. Perhaps the most fundamental change made by the second act was the provision abolishing trial by jury: "The amount of such rents and profits . . .

---

type of property rights involved. Contemporary opinion, friendly and hostile alike, recognized the novel character of his Dartmouth contribution, and this notwithstanding the greater fame of Chief Justice Marshall's opinion." (Dunne, "Joseph Story: The Salem Years," *Essex Institute Historical Collections*, Vol. CI, No. 4 [Oct., 1965], 312.) Oscar and Mary Handlin have stated that "Story's opinion profoundly influenced the American law of corporations. For decades thereafter arguments over what was public and what was private revolved about his definition. In this respect Story was more fortunate in his audience than James Wilson and Thomas Paine who had forty years earlier ineffectually attempted to distinguish between private and public laws." (*Commonwealth*, 168–69.) See also Dunne, "Joseph Story: The Great Term," *Harvard Law Review*, Vol. LXXIX, No. 5 (Mar., 1966), 905–13: David Henshaw, *Remarks upon the Rights and Powers of Corporations* (Boston, 1837), reprinted in part in Joseph Blau, ed., *Social Theories of Jacksonian Democracy*, 163–82.

[64] 8 Wheaton 1 (1823). Benjamin F. Wright considers Story's opinion in *Green* v. *Biddle* "perhaps the most far-fetched, if as it turned out, the least important extension of the contract clause." (*The Contract Clause of the Constitution*, 46–47.) Marshall, it should be noted, delivered another important decision under the contract clause during the same session in which he delivered his controlling opinion in the *Dartmouth College* case. This was the case of *Sturges* v. *Crowninshield*, 4 Wheaton 122 (1819). Speaking for an unanimous Court, Marshall held inoperative a New York insolvency law which allowed a debtor to escape payment.

[65] 8 Wheaton 3.

and also, the value of the improvements, and of the land without the improvements, are to be ascertained by commissioners."[66]

Speaking for a unanimous Court, Story interpreted article 7 of the compact to be a guaranty to all persons deriving titles under the then existing laws of Virginia, to the perpetual enjoyment of their property rights against any future legislative acts of Kentucky. Although the implied base of his opinion was the contract clause, "natural law reasoning still dominated."[67] Every state government, observed the judge, must be regarded as a sovereign entity, endowed with the exclusive right of regulating the descent, distribution, and grants of the domain within its own boundaries. Article 7 did not impinge upon the sovereign powers of Kentucky, but "meant only to provide for the affirmation of that which is the universal rule in the courts of civilized nations professing to be governed by the dictates of law."[68]

The acts of 1797 and 1812, which materially impaired the rights and interests of the rightful owners, were a breach of contract, and consequently void. "They are parts of a system, the object of which is to compel the rightful owner to relinquish his lands, or pay for all lasting improvements . . . without his consent or default."[69] In many cases the improvements would greatly exceed the original cost and value of the lands, and under the laws of Virginia, no such burden was imposed on the owner. He had a right to sue for, recover, and enjoy the property, without any deductions or payments.

The decision was rendered without the occupants being represented by counsel, and Henry Clay, appearing as *amicus curiae*, moved for a rehearing, upon the ground that the cause involved the rights and claims of many Kentucky citizens. The motion was granted, and the case reargued, with Justice Washington delivering the ruling of the Court. Elaborating upon Story's brief opinion, which stuck closely to the actual provisions of the compact, Justice Washington investigated the common law rules of property, ending his analysis with a citation to Pufendorf's concept of natural law, which "lays down in broad and general terms, that fruits of industry as well as those of nature, belong to him who is master of the thing from which they flow."[70]

[66] *Ibid.*, 6.

[67] Gerald T. Dunne, "Joseph Story: The Middle Years," *Harvard Law Review*, Vol. LXXX, No. 8 (June, 1967), 1694.

[68] *Green* v. *Biddle*, 8 Wheaton 12.

[69] *Ibid.*, 15.

[70] *Ibid.*, 80. Story's opinion in the First Circuit, *The Society for the Propagation of the Gospel* v. *Wheeler*, 2 Gallison 139 (1814), may thus be seen as the foundation for *Green* v. *Biddle*. As was true of many of the opinions delivered during the Marshall era, *Green* v. *Biddle* provoked considerable resentment and was regarded by many, especially the inhabitants of Kentucky, as an insult to state sovereignty. One of the factors encouraging this animosity was the erroneous report of many Kentucky newspapers that Justice Johnson dissented, when in fact he concurred. Constitutional historians have repeated the mistake. Charles Warren (*Supreme Court in United States History*, I, 640) says Johnson

For richness of philosophical discourse upon the vested rights of property, *Wilkinson* v. *Leland*, [71] delivered in 1829, stands foremost with *Terrett* v. *Taylor* in the anthology of Story's opinions. Building upon his significant doctrine of implied limitations underscored in the *Dartmouth College* case, Story delivered a vigorous opinion on the rights of property merely through dicta, while holding valid a retrospective law of Rhode Island.

The case sprang from legal complications surrounding the will of one Jonathan Jenckes, a resident of New Hampshire, who died in 1787. By his will he left certain real estate in Rhode Island to his infant daughter and appointed his wife, Cynthia, and one Arthur Fenner, as executrix and executor respectively. Fenner never accepted the appointment, and Mrs. Jenckes alone administered the estate. She proved the will in the proper court of probate in New Hampshire. The estate, however, was insolvent, so she obtained a license in 1790 from the judge of the New Hampshire probate court to sell so much of the real estate of the testator as was sufficient to pay his debts.

Although the property was located in Rhode Island, the will was never proved in that state. In 1791 she sold the property, but the purchasers were not satisfied with her authority to make the sale. To promote the transaction, Mrs. Jenckes entered into a covenant with the purchasers, whereby she promised to procure an act of the Rhode Island legislature, ratifying and confirming the title thus granted. In 1792 the legislature enacted a statute confirming the title, and the descendants of Jonathan Jenckes' daughter brought suit to recover the property.

Judge Story swiftly dismissed the validity of the license obtained in New Hampshire authorizing the sale of property in Rhode Island. "The legislature and judicial authority of New Hampshire," Story said, "were bounded by the territory of that State, and could not rightfully be exercised to pass estates in another State."[72] The questions of the case, therefore, resolved themselves into a consideration of the validity of the Rhode Island act of 1792.

The first objection to the act, that it constituted a retrospective law infringing upon the protected rights of private property, was rejected by Story, though not without ample investigation. He emphatically agreed that retrospective laws were mischievous, and disclosed that he had "felt the full force of the reasoning."[73] Retrospective legislation "is an exercise of power which is of so summary a nature, so fraught with inconvenience, so liable to disturb the security of titles, and to spring by surprise upon the innocent . . . that a legis-

---

dissented. Beveridge (*Life of Marshall*, IV, 381, n. 1) repeats the error, as does Charles Haines (*The Role of the Supreme Court*, 466). Donald G. Morgan (*Justice William Johnson: The First Dissenter*, 185, n. 77) correctly notes that Justice Johnson concurred.

[71] 2 Peters 627 (1829).

[72] *Ibid.*, 655.

[73] *Ibid.*, 656.

lature invested with the power can scarcely be too cautious . . . in the exercise of it."[74]

Shifting to the Rhode Island charter, Story presented through dicta a general theory of legislative powers on the subject of property. His spirited vindication of the sacrosanct nature of property, unrivalled in Supreme Court history, must have touched the heart of every property-minded listener: "In a government [such as Rhode Island] professing to regard the great rights of personal liberty and of property, and which is required to legislate in subordination to the general laws of England, it would not lightly be presumed that the great principles of Magna Charta were to be disregarded, or that the estates of its subjects were liable to be taken away without trial, without notice, and without offense."[75]

Looking upon all democratic aspirations infringing upon the sacred rights of property as calculated to destroy liberty, Story boldly repudiated the notion that economic freedom was inferior to other forms of civil liberty.

That government can scarcely be deemed to be free where the rights of property are left solely dependent upon the will of a legislative body without any restraint. The fundamental maxims of a free government seem to require that the rights of personal liberty and private property should be held sacred. At least no court of justice in this country would be warranted in assuming that the power to violate and disregard them—a power so repugnant to the common principles of justice and civil liberty—lurked under any general grant of legislative authority, or ought to be implied from any general expressions of the will of the people. The people ought not to be presumed to part with rights so vital to their security and well-being, without very strong and direct expressions of such an intention.[76]

Any doctrine differing from that in *Terrett* v. *Taylor*, which held that a grant or title to lands once made to any person or corporation by a legislature was irrevocable, was "utterly inconsistent with the great and fundamental principle of a republican government, and with the right of the citizens to the free enjoyment of their property lawfully acquired."[77]

There was no prior case, said Story, where an act of legislature transferring the property of one person to another without his consent, has ever been sanctioned by a state court. Story and his unanimously agreed brethren "were not prepared, therefore, to admit [as counsel urged] that the people of Rhode Island have ever delegated to the legislature the power to divest the vested rights of property, and transfer them without the assent of the parties."[78]

The second objection to the act of 1792 was rejected by Story. He admitted

[74] *Ibid.*, 657.
[75] *Ibid.*
[76] *Ibid.*
[77] *Ibid.*
[78] *Ibid.*, 658.

"that the title of an heir by descent in the real estate of his ancestor, and of a divisee in an estate unconditionally devised to him is, upon the death of the party . . . immediately involved upon him, and he acquires a vested estate."[79] Such a rule, however, was open to exception where the testator left an encumbered title. At his death Jenckes conferred no title, except what remained after every lien on his estate had been discharged. Retrospective acts, so long as they did not divest the settled rights of property, were constitutional. The sale of the property and ratification by the Rhode Island legislature, rather than destroy the rights of property, merely effectuated them, in a manner beneficial to all parties concerned.

THE *CHARLES RIVER BRIDGE* CASE: STORY IN RETREAT

But the doctrines laboriously built up by Story in *Wilkinson* v. *Leland* and earlier cases plummeted rapidly with the departure of Chief Justice Marshall and the change of Court personnel after 1835—at least in the view of Judge Story.[80] The broad rule of statutory construction guaranteeing the recipient of every legislative grant the protection of his property rights, whether express or implied, against subsequent infringement was promptly repudiated by Chief Justice Taney in *Charles River Bridge* v. *Warren Bridge Co.*[81] In a powerful, exhaustive dissent, Story proudly excoriated the Court in the name of property and the constitutionally protected rights of the common law. This last great undertaking on behalf of property was his best, a *magnum opus* which epitomized years of study spanning more than three decades of dedicated effort.

Believing himself confronted at every turn with obliquity and error, Story

---

[79] *Ibid.*

[80] As early as 1827 serious differences of opinion among the justices began to appear in certain areas of constitutional law, particularly in the area of the contract clause. This was the year in which Marshall and Story, together with Justice Duval, suddenly found themselves dissenting from the majority in the case of *Ogden* v. *Saunders*, 12 Wheaton 213 (1827). Speaking for the three dissenters, Marshall argued that the contract clause protected not only retrospective contracts, but also prospective, so that a New York insolvency law which discharged persons from liability under a contract entered into in that state after the passage of the act, was violative of the Constitution. Story did not become truly alarmed, however, until Chief Justice Taney mounted the high bench following the death of Marshall. Like Story, Marshall became increasingly despondent in the latter years of his judgeship. Beveridge observed that "The last years of Marshall's life were clouded with sadness, almost despair . . . the Supreme Court was successfully defied; his greatest opinion was repudiated and denounced by a strong and popular president; his associates on the Bench were departing from some of his most cherished views." *Life of Marshall*, IV, 518.

[81] *Charles River Bridge* v. *Warren Bridge Co.*, 11 Peters 420 (1837).

annihilated each point Taney advanced by a volley of adverse precedent—to the applause of his friend, Chancellor Kent, who praised the dissent highly. "I have re-perused the Charles River Bridge case," wrote Kent impassionately, "and with increased disgust. It abandons, or overthrows, a great principle of constitutional morality, and I think goes to destroy the security and value of legislative franchises. It injures the moral sense of the community, and destroys the sanctity of contracts. If the legislature can quibble away, or whittle away its contracts with impunity, the people will be sure to follow. . . . But I had the consolation, in reading the case, to know that you have vindicated the principles . . . of the old law, with your accustomed learning, vigor, and warmth, and force."[82] If the needs of a capitalistic society were not on his side—which Story flatly denied—at least the common law fully supported his position.

Story was sure Taney had entrenched himself behind legal fictions; and Taney's economic philosophy was abhorrent to Story beyond measure. To penetrate the heart of the opinion, then, to measure Taney's reasoning with realistic yardsticks, and to remove the outer wrappings and expose the inner fallacies were the tasks which Story set before himself in the *Charles River Bridge* case.

The story of Charles River Bridge goes back to the year 1650, when the Massachusetts legislature granted Harvard College the authority to maintain a ferry between Charlestown and Boston. Then in 1785 the legislature passed an act incorporating the company known as "The Proprietors of the Charles River Bridge," authorizing it to erect a bridge in place of the ferry. Under the charter, which was limited to forty years, the company collected tolls and paid two hundred pounds to Harvard annually. At the expiration of the grant, the bridge was to become the property of the state. In 1792 the legislature extended the charter to seventy years, as compensation for the incorporation of another company, "The Proprietors of West Boston Bridge." But in 1828, before the expiration of the revised charter, the legislature incorporated "The Proprietors of the Warren Bridge," which threatened to destroy the income of the Charles River Bridge.

The proprietors of the Charles River Bridge based their case mainly on two grounds. They first charged that the original grant to Harvard College was irrevocable and exclusive, and that their company, by virtue of the act of 1785, was vested with the same rights. Secondly, they contended that the acts of 1785 and 1792, independent of the ferry right, invested them with the implied guaranty that the legislature would not authorize another bridge, especially a free one, in the same line of travel.

Speaking for the majority, the new chief justice boldly brushed aside established precedents and the doctrine of vested rights. Avoiding throughout his entire opinion *Fletcher* v. *Peck*, the *Dartmouth College* case, and Story's host

[82] To Story, June 23, 1837, *Life and Letters*, II, 270.

of opinions in defense of property, Taney relied on two recent decisions, *Satterlee* v. *Mathewson*[83] and *Watson* v. *Mercer*,[84] in arriving at his first conclusion, that retrospective laws could divest vested rights and not violate the Constitution, unless the obligations of contract had been *explicitly* impaired. To show that they had suffered impairment, Taney demanded that the proprietors of the Charles River Bridge prove by the words of the charter that the legislature covenanted not to establish a free bridge at the place where the new bridge was erected.

The original charter to Harvard College was not at issue, because no rights, by the terms of the second charter, were assigned to the proprietors of the bridge. Once the ferry itself was destroyed, the rights which were incident to it also perished; "and as the franchise of the ferry and that of the bridge are different in their nature, and were each established by separate grants, which have no words to connect the privileges of the one with privileges of the other,"[85] the Court had no reason to associate the two grants. Taney knew of "no rule of legal interpretation which would authorize the Court . . . to infer that any privilege was intended to be given to the bridge company, merely because it had been conferred on the ferry." The charter of Charles River Bridge, he asserted, was an independent grant "which must speak for itself."[86]

Having smoothed the way for a free and unencumbered examination of the act of 1785, Taney now took the risky step of basing his whole argument upon the principles of the common law, thus exposing the body of his opinion to the slashing attack of Judge Story, who, in capacity and training, was unequalled in his knowledge of the common law. Taney cited a recent English case[87] in support of this, his main point in the case: In adopting the English common law, the American system of jurisprudence also incorporated the English rule of statutory construction, which held that legislative acts operate

[83] 2 Peters 380 (1829).

[84] 8 Peters 88 (1834). This case was decided by Judge Story. In 1785, James Mercer and his wife, Margaret, executed a deed of the premises, which belonged to the wife, to one Nathan Thompson in fee. Thompson thereafter reconveyed the property to James Mercer on the same day, the object being to vest the estate in the husband. The certificate of the acknowledgment of the deed of Mercer and his wife to Thompson failed to set forth all the particulars as were required under the laws of Pennsylvania. In 1826, Pennsylvania passed an act designed to cure all defective acknowledgments of this sort. The plaintiffs claimed title to the property under James Mercer, and the defendants as heirs at law of his wife, who died without issue. Story held that the state statute neither divested vested rights nor violated the obligations of contract. The act, said Story, did not violate the contract clause "either in its terms or its principles. It does not even affect to touch any title . . . and only provides that deeds of conveyance . . . shall not be void." *Ibid.*, 111.

[85] 11 Peters 544.

[86] *Ibid.*

[87] *Proprietors of the Stourbridge Canal* v. *Wheely*, 2 Barnewall & Adolphus 793 (King's Bench, 1831).

in favor of the public and against the grantee, if these terms of the contract were ambiguous. This narrow rule of construction, fiercely assailed by Story, had been followed, according to Taney, in *United States* v. *Arredondo*[88] and *Jackson* v. *Lampshire*,[89] and Taney felt it to be an asset to American economic life. "It would present a singular spectacle," he remarked in a dictum,

> if, while the courts of England are restraining, within the strictest limits, the spirit of monopoly, and exclusive privileges in nature of monopolies, and confining corporations to the privileges plainly given to them in their charter; the courts of this country should be found enlarging these privileges by implication; and construing a statute more unfavorably to the public, and to the rights of the community, than would be done in a like case in an English court of justice.[90]

Taney thought the most analogous case to the one then before the Court was *Providence Bank* v. *Billings and Pittman*,[91] which was identical in principle in that it involved an act of incorporation under which the grantees of a bank charter unsuccessfully maintained that the state impliedly agreed not to tax the bank. Again he buttressed his opinion with economic theory, stating that "in a country like ours, free, active and enterprising, continually advancing in numbers and wealth; new channels of communication are daily found necessary, both for travel and trade, and are essential to the comfort, convenience, and prosperity of the people. A State ought never to be presumed to surrender this power."[92]

In a mode of expression which subsequently found reiteration in *Home Building & Loan Association* v. *Blaisdell*,[93] Taney, who only shortly before had rejected the doctrine of implied contract, reintroduced it in a new form, making it favorable to the states rather than the grantee. Conceding almost his entire argument to Story, Taney asserted that the states impliedly withheld certain powers in granting charters, as "The continued existence of a government would be of no great value, if by implications and presumptions, it was disarmed of the powers necessary to accomplish the ends of its creation, and the functions it was designed to perform, transferred to the hands of privileged corporations."[94] Corporations, impliedly limited in the powers which they receive, were, imputed Taney, subject to the changing will of the legislature;

---

[88] 2 Peters 738 (1829).

[89] 3 Peters 280 (1830). Story strongly objected to Taney's citation of the decision in support of his rules of interpretation. "That case does not pretend to inculcate the doctrine that no implications can be made, as to matters of contract, beyond the express terms of a grant." *Charles River Bridge* v. *Warren Bridge Co.*, 11 Peters 640.

[90] *Charles River Bridge* v. *Warren Bridge Co.*, 11 Peters 545–46.

[91] 4 Peters 514 (1830).

[92] *Charles River Bridge* v. *Warren Bridge Co.*, 11 Peters 548.

[93] 290 U.S. 398 (1934).

[94] *Charles River Bridge* v. *Warren Bridge Co.*, 11 Peters 548.

and "while the rights of private property are sacredly guarded, we must not forget that the community also have rights, and that the happiness and well-being of every citizen depends on their faithful preservation."[95]

Armed with these rules of construction, Chief Justice Taney proceeded to apply them to the charter of 1785, effortlessly finding no words in the charter conferring an exclusive privilege on the bridge company. Furthermore, the act of 1792, which authorized the construction of the West Boston Bridge, lessened the profits of Charles River Bridge. This result indicated "that the State did not suppose that, by the terms it had used in the first law, it had deprived itself of the power of making such public improvements as might impair the profits of the Charles River Bridge."[96] Concluding, then, that the incorporation of Warren Bridge was wholly consistent with constitutional stipulations, Taney sealed his case with the stamp of expediency:

And what would be the fruits of this doctrine of implied contracts on the part of the States, and of property in a line of travel by a corporation, if it should now be sanctioned by this Court? . . . Let it once be understood that such charters carry with them these implied contracts, and give this unknown and undefined property in a line of traveling, and you will soon find the old turnpike corporations awakening from their sleep, and calling upon this Court to put down the improvements which have taken their place. . . . We shall be thrown back to the improvements of the last century, and obliged to stand still until the claims of the old turnpike corporations shall be satisfied.[97]

Before entering into a consideration of the primary issue of the case, whether the act of 1828 violated the obligation of contract, Judge Story first scrutinized Taney's rule of interpretation. As proof that the Court must read behind the words of the old charter, infer the true intent of the legislature, "and presume things which the Legislature has not expressly declared,"[98] Story observed that nowhere in the enacting clause of the charter had the legislature even conferred authority upon the corporation to build any such bridge; nor did it state the locale in which the bridge was to be constructed. That such authority was granted, however, was clearly evident by implication and inference.

Asserting, therefore, that the "common rules of interpretation"[99] must be adhered to, Story explained that Taney's rules of interpretation were wholly repugnant to well-established principles of the common law. Certain that "very great errors of opinion have crept into the argument,"[100] he objected to Taney's assumption "that this charter is to be construed as a royal grant, and

[95] Ibid.
[96] Ibid., 550.
[97] Ibid., 552. Justice McLean then delivered a concurring opinion.
[98] Ibid., 587.
[99] Ibid.
[100] Ibid., 588–89.

that such grants are always construed with a stern and parsimonious strictness."[101]

Feeling himself compelled "to go at large into the doctrine of the common law in respect to royal grants,"[102] Story assaulted root and branch the Taney opinion, supporting each devastating blow of logic with an array of common law cases and precedents. He acknowledged the point that royal grants are to be construed most favorably for the king and against the grantee, where there was doubt; but Taney had overlooked the fact that this rule of construction applied only to those cases "where there is a real doubt, where the grant admits of two interpretations, one of which is more extensive, and the other more restricted; so that a choice is fairly open, and either may be adopted without any violation of the apparent objects of the grant."[103] Furthermore, "If the King's grant admits of two interpretations, one of which will make it utterly void and worthless, and the other will give a reasonable effect, then the latter is to prevail."[104] But more important, Taney's rule of construction never applied to royal grants rendered for a valuable consideration; and under such grants as these, "the same rule has always prevailed as in cases between subjects."[105]

Thus, concluded Story, after a prolix analysis of the cases respecting gratuitous royal grants, Taney's doctrine was "exclusively confined to cases of mere donation, flowing from the bounty of the Crown. Whenever the grant is upon a valuable consideration, the rule of construction ceases; and the grant is expounded exactly as it would be in the case of a private grant. Why is this rule adopted? Plainly, because the grant is a contract."[106] This rule was so deeply rooted in the common law, observed Story, that even during the worst ages of arbitrary power, the courts "did not hesitate to declare that contracts founded in a valuable consideration ought to be construed liberally for the subject, for the honor of the Crown."[107]

In all his researches, said the judge, he had not been able to find a single case supporting Taney's doctrine. Cautioning the Court against hasty innovation, Story angrily exclaimed: "I stand upon the old law, upon law established more than three centuries ago, in cases contested with as much ability and learning as any in the annals of our jurisprudence, in resisting any such encroachments upon the rights and liberties of the citizens, secured by public grants. I will not consent to shake their title deeds by any speculative niceties or novelties."[108]

[101] *Ibid.*, 588.
[102] *Ibid.*
[103] *Ibid.*, 589.
[104] *Ibid.*
[105] *Ibid.*
[106] *Ibid.*
[107] *Ibid.*
[108] *Ibid.*, 598.

What was more important, the case did not even involve a royal grant, but a legislative grant, and the rules governing royal grants really had no applicability to the issues before the Court. Legislative grants must receive a reasonable and liberal construction, so that, if either by the express terms of the grant or by inference from the terms, the intent of the contract can be discerned, such intent is to be recognized by the Court. If the terms of the contract were ambiguous and also imposed a burden upon the public, then the contract might be construed in favor of the public; "but at the same time," insisted Story, "there is not the slightest reason for saying, even in such a case, that the grant is not to be construed favorably to the grantee, so as to secure him in the enjoyment of what is actually granted."[109]

Satisfied that Taney's rule of interpretation was now destroyed, Story followed up his attack with a brief sally into the field of politico-economic theory before penetrating the heart of the case. He took issue with each of Taney's assumptions. He denied that the charter restricted legislative power; that it was a derogation of the rights and interests of Massachusetts or the people; that it promoted monopolies; or that it imposed a barrier to the progress of improvement. The grant of a franchise, restricting the legislature only in that the legislature could not again grant what had already been granted, was no different than a grant of land. And the erection of a bridge could scarcely derogate the rights of the people, as it promoted public transportation.

To aid the public, reasoned Story, it was necessary that there be a benefactor, willing to construct the bridge. He would not undertake such a task, however, unless he received in return the exclusive privilege of erecting it and taking toll. Nor was the grant any more a monopoly than a grant of land or patent or copyright, all of which bestowed exclusive rights and privileges. The needs of society demanded that in certain areas of human activity, grantees be given the assurance that the fruits of their industry were guaranteed, as compensation for a task which they would not otherwise undertake. Without this protection enterprisers would turn to other activities, leaving the fate of all public improvements in the hands of government. There was, said Story, "no surer plan to arrest all public improvements, founded on private capital and enterprise, than to make the outlay of that capital uncertain and questionable, both as to security and as to productiveness."[110]

Irrespective of these considerations, upon which, admitted Story, reasonable men might differ, the majority of the Court had lost sight of its judicial responsibilities. The Court had no business considering the political, economic, and social effects of the grant. If the legislature made a grant which involved any or all of the phantom dangers conjured up by the chief justice, "it is not for courts of justice to overturn the plain sense of the grant, because it has been

---

[109] *Ibid.*, 601.
[110] *Ibid.*, 608.

improvidently or injuriously made."[111] The constitutional duty of the Court was to uphold and preserve the obligations of contract, not to usurp the functions of the legislature. "It seems to me to be our duty to interpret laws," chided Story, "and not to wander into speculations upon their policy."[112]

Story now turned to the provisions of the charter. There was no doubt in his mind that it contained the implied obligation on the part of the legislature to abstain from enfranchising another bridge near the Charles River Bridge, the effect of which would be the destruction of the value of the grant. It would be ludicrous to believe the proprietors undertook the task with any other understanding.

Now, I put it to the common sense of every man, whether if at the moment of granting the charter the Legislature had said to the proprietors—you shall build the bridge; you shall bear the burdens; you shall be bound by the charges; and your sole re-imbursement shall be from the tolls of forty years: and yet we will not even guaranty you any certainty of receiving any tolls. On the contrary, we reserve to ourselves the full power and authority to erect other bridges, toll or free bridges, according to our own free will and pleasure, contiguous to yours, and having the same termini with yours; and if you are successful we may thus supplant you, divide, destroy your profits, and annihilate your tolls, without annihilating your burdens: If, I say, such had been the language of the Legislature, is there a man living of ordinary discretion or prudence, who would have accepted such a charter upon such terms?[113]

Story declared that he stood behind *Fletcher* v. *Peck*, which established as a "first principle of justice" that the Court should not "presume that the Legislature reserved a right to destroy its own grant,"[114] and also behind Justice Washington's concurring opinion in the *Dartmouth College* case, in which Washington had remarked that legislative charters amounted "to an extinguishment of the King's prerogative to bestow the same identical franchise on another corporate body, because it would prejudice his former grant. It implied, therefore, a contract not to reassert the right to grant the franchise to another, or to impair it."[115] He moved further into the underlying basis of implied limitations—the common law. It should never be forgotten, he argued, that in construing legislative grants, the common law must be considered; "for the Legislature must be presumed to have in view the general principles of construction which are recognized by the common law."[116]

The common law, fully demonstrated in support of his view, was borne out also in relation to ferries. Applying his theory of the incorporation of the com-

[111] *Ibid.*, 603.
[112] *Ibid.*, 606.
[113] *Ibid.*, 615.
[114] *Ibid.*, 617.
[115] *Ibid.*, 618.
[116] *Ibid.*, 617.

mon law, Story contended that there was an unbroken chain of authorities establishing the doctrine that a franchise granting ferry rights carried with it the implied warranty that a subsequent grant would not be issued so as to impair the profits of the ferry proprietors. This doctrine, he asserted, was "firmly fixed in the common law, and brought to America by our ancestors as part of their inheritance."[117] Refuting counsel's argument at bar that the ancient doctrine of the common law in relation to ferries was not in force, had never been recognized, and that ferries in Massachusetts could be established or removed by the legislature at will, Story showed that in the colonial era, there was no evidence the common law had not been adopted. "For myself, I can only say that I have always understood that the English doctrine on this subject constitutes a part of the common law of Massachusetts."[118]

Story was fully conscious that the crux of Taney's argument was his assertion that an implied limitation existed concerning the extent of power granted by a legislature. "The truth is, that the whole argument of the defendants turns upon an implied reservation of power in the Legislature to defeat and destroy its own grant."[119] This argument, said Story, "seeks to exclude the common law from touching the grant, by implying an exception in favor of the legislative authority to make any new grant. And let us change the position of the question as often as we may, it comes to this, as a necessary result—that the Legislature has reserved the power to destroy its own grant, and annihilate the right of pontage of the Charles River Bridge."[120] If the legislature wished to revoke the charter, the only lawful manner of procedure was to make due compensation to the proprietors; otherwise the new charter amounted to a confiscation of private property. "Are we then to desert the wholesome principles of the common law, the bulwark of our public liberties, and the protecting shield of our private property, and assume a doctrine which substantially annihilates the security of all franchises affected with public easements?"[121]

The argument of the majority assumed that popular assemblies were omnipotent, an assumption refuted by the American experience:

however extensive the prerogatives and attributes of sovereignty may theoretically be, in free governments they are universally held to be restrained within some limits. Although the sovereign power in free governments may appropriate all the property, public as well as private, for public purposes, making compensation therefor, yet it has never been understood, at least never in our republic, that the sovereign power can take the private property of A and give it to B, by the right of "eminent domain"; or that it can take it at all, except for public purposes; or that it can take

[117] *Ibid.*, 620.
[118] *Ibid.*, 634. Note the use Story makes again of his theory of adoption.
[119] *Ibid.*, 637.
[120] *Ibid.*
[121] *Ibid.*, 638.

it for public purposes, without the duty and responsibility of making compensation. ... These limitations have been held to be fundamental axioms in free governments like ours, and have accordingly received the sanction of some of our most eminent jurists.[122]

And, noted Story, these principles had also been incorporated into most of the state constitutions, including that of Massachusetts. Although the Massachusetts legislature possessed unlimited power to grant franchises, it had no legal power to recall them. The Massachusetts bill of rights contained an express prohibition restraining the expropriation of private property, except when taken for public use or with due compensation. Citing *Fletcher* v. *Peck* and the *Dartmouth College* case, Story thus concluded that the statute of 1828 was void under both the constitutions of Massachusetts and of the United States. Any other conclusion, he admonished, would be "utterly repugnant to all the principles of the common law," and might "overturn some of the best securities of the rights of property."[123]

So disheartened was Story by the decision of the Court that he confided to Justice McLean he was seriously contemplating resignation.[124] Not only did the *Charles River Bridge* case represent a new theory of the Constitution, but of the American economic system as well; and Story denied that the general population preferred Taney's novel Jacksonian doctrines to the natural law principle of prescriptive rights. "The opinions have been read by the profession in our neighbourhood," Story informed Peters, the Supreme Court reporter.

I dare say that there is some diversity of opinion among lawyers here, as there has been at Washtn. But I think I may say without hesitation that a very large proportion of all our ablest lawyers think the Court wrong. A number have so said to me; & among them are Mr. J[eremiah] Mason & Mr. Wm. Prescott, whom I think at the head of the profession in America, as men of learning & excellence. But I hear also that those, who deem the court right, are not satisfied with the opinion of the Chief Justice. No one here of any shade or distinction in law thinks the doctrine

---

[122] *Ibid.*, 642.

[123] *Ibid.*, 647. Justice Thompson concurred with Story.

[124] Story to McLean, May 10, 1837, John McLean Papers, Library of Congress. The *Charles River Bridge* case actually confirmed in Story's mind an earlier suspicion "that a spirit of radicalism is not only abroad, adverse to the rights of property, & to the stability of our institutions, but ... is daily gaining ground [in America as well]." (Story to George Ticknor, Dec. 16, 1836, Story Papers, Texas.) No doubt Story read with interest the book of his friend Lieber, *Essays on Property and Labor*, which appeared in 1842. Lieber assured Story that he would profit from a reading of the work, and hoped that it "May ... do some good toward understanding some of the worst theories broached in our period—theories which attack private property, the laws of inheritance, the sacredness of marriage, the stability of society, morality and liberty; which says the very essence of all that is worth living for. Witness the frightful dogmas of the Egalitares." Francis Lieber to Story, Jan. 21, 1842, Story Papers, Clements Library.

"*conservative*"; & it has shaken public confidence in Chartered Rights to the very foundation among all classes.[125]

Daniel Webster conveyed his condolences, assuring the judge that his dissent "is the ablest and best written opinion, I ever heard you deliver. It is close, searching, and scrutinizing; and at the same time full of strong and rather popular illustrations. The intelligent part of the profession will all be with you. There is no doubt of that; but then the decision of the Court will have completely overturned, in my judgment, one great provision of the Constitution."[126]

Charles Sumner, though in sympathy with Jacksonian ideas, confessed to Story that although he had at first favored Taney's opinion, he was "irresistibly carried away by the rushing current of your opinion. . . . The argument from the construction of the King's & also Parliamentary grants, backed by the powerful analogies derived from the franchises of ferries & mills, is loosely & inconclusively met by the Chief Justice." After comparing Story's opinion with Taney's, Sumner "thought of Wilkes' exclamation on hearing the opinions of Ld. Mansfield & his associates in his famous case,—that listening to the latter after the former, was like taking hogwash after champaign."[127] Even those who have violently opposed Story's dissent, such as Louis B. Boudin, confess that it "is probably one of the most learned judicial opinions ever written in this country."[128]

Story's dissent was a brilliant attempt, but unfortunately failed to take account of recent constitutional developments. He surely had the better argument regarding the common law rules of statutory interpretation; but Taney's reliance on a number of cases holding that states withheld certain powers when issuing grants, was not as outlandish as Story supposed. In *Providence Bank*

---

[125] Story to Richard Peters, May 12, 1837, Peters Papers, HSP. Writing to his wife earlier, Story had complained that "A case of grosser injustice, or more oppressive legislation, never existed. I feel humiliated, as I think every one here is, by the Act which has now been confirmed." Feb. 14, 1837, *Life and Letters*, II, 268.

[126] Webster to Story, "Sunday Morning," 1837, *Life and Letters*, II, 268. For an excellent account of Webster's role in the *Charles River Bridge* case, see Baxter, *Webster and the Supreme Court*, 119–35. "[T]he Charles River Bridge stockholders," notes Baxter, "suffered an enormous financial loss. Ironically, the public at Boston in whose interests the Court supposedly delivered a bold stroke, later had to pay tolls to the State to pass over both the Warren and the Charles River Bridges!" *Ibid.*, 135.

[127] Sumner to Story, Mar. 25, 1837, Massachusetts Historical Society *Proceedings*, 2nd Series, Vol. XV, 210-11. "Your opinion is a wonderful monument of juridical learning & science," continued Sumner, "greater by far than Ld Nottingham's in Norfolk's case, or any on the Cholmondelley case. Indeed, I do not know where to turn for its match in all the books." *Ibid.*

[128] *Government by Judiciary*, I, 389.

v. *Billings and Pittman*,[129] decided in 1830 by none other than Chief Justice Marshall, the Court had held that in construing grants, the relinquishment of the power of taxation should never be implied. Marshall's modified rule of statutory construction caught the searching eye of Taney, who quoted Marshall at length in support of his opinion in *Charles River Bridge* v. *Warren Bridge*. Story kept silent about the *Providence Bank* case, concentrating instead on the weaker points of Taney's reasoning.

Thus, in the end, it would seem, Marshall's inadequate preparation in the common law helped to bring about the downfall of vested rights. With Story's acquiescence Marshall unconsciously paved the way for Taney's coup. Steadily, but imperceptibly, the liberal rule of statutory construction favoring the grantee as opposed to the states, had become too liberal, obliging the grantor as well as the grantee. The *Charles River Bridge* case, like earlier decisions on the contract clause, ultimately turned on common law principles of statutory interpretations, and thanks to Marshall, Taney had his choice of the rules to follow.

VIEWS ON PROPERTY AT THE
MASSACHUSETTS CONSTITUTIONAL CONVENTION

A thorough evaluation of Story's philosophy of property would be incomplete without a discussion of his speech on property at the Massachusetts Constitutional Convention in 1820–21, together with some mention of his writings on property during the latter years of his public career. When taken with his opinions, they illustrate his lofty conception of private property as an essential element of a free society. With the possible exception of Webster's speech at the Massachusetts convention and Chancellor Kent's eloquent plea for property at the New York Constitutional Convention of 1821, Story's oft quoted oration touching upon the eternal conflict between the "haves" and "have-nots" is perhaps unparalleled in American history. Venturing to answer arguments that would subsequently be more persuasively leveled by the Marxists and their successors, the Salem philosopher spoke ominously, imploring his fellow citizens to take up their cudgels in defense of property.

Between 1820 and 1830 attempts were made in Virginia, Massachusetts, and New York to remodel state constitutions in the direction of greater popular control.[130] The separation of Maine from Massachusetts in 1820 made further

---

[129] 4 Peters 514. "By and large," argues Professor Baxter, "Story was right about his common law. The more one studies the *Charles River Bridge* case, the plainer it is that the differences between the lawyers and judges on each side came down to the point of economic policy. Story and Webster feared that a decision against the plaintiffs would deter internal improvements. The outlay of new capital would be uncertain, property would be unsafe, stockholders would be alarmed. The old bridge, they thought, was not an odious monopoly (as the Jacksonians labelled it). It was a sign of enterprise and progress, which the state arbitrarily undermined." *Webster and the Supreme Court*, 134.

[130] Debates on these conventions have been reproduced in part in *Democracy, Liberty*

postponement of constitutional reform an impossibility in the Old Bay State,[131] and a convention was reluctantly called to consider a revision of the constitution of 1780.[132] A conservative document written by John Adams, the Massachusetts constitution was a monument to James Harrington's idea that "power follows property." The popular will was sifted through a bicameral legislature, with both houses taking account of the propertied classes. The senate was overrepresented by the eastern seaboard cities, and officeholders were required to meet minimum property qualifications. To discourage further the untrammeled rule of the majority, Adams had designed the constitution with a view toward limited government—through rigorous checks and balances, separation of powers, and rule of law. The constitution provided a strong executive, armed with a liberal veto power, and an independent judiciary appointed for life.

Determined to resist sweeping changes, some of the ablest men in America appeared on behalf of the old constitution, led by the aged Adams himself, who came out of retirement to protect each and every clause of the threatened parchment. Among the younger men laboring at his side were Daniel Webster, Isaac Parker, Josiah Quincy, Leverett Saltonstall, Lemuel Shaw, and the "Republican" delegate from Salem, Judge Joseph Story.

At the outset of the convention, Story was appointed chairman of the committee to consider revision of the judiciary provisions of the old constitution.[133]

---

and Property: The State Constitutional Conventions of the 1820's (ed. by Merrill D. Peterson).

[131] The separation of Maine also gave rise to a controversy analogous to that in the *Dartmouth College* case. In 1833, Story delivered an opinion in the case of *Allen v. McKean*, 1 Sumner 276, 1 Federal Cases 489, No. 229 (1833), in defense of property and contract. Before the separation of Maine, the Massachusetts legislature granted a charter to Bowdoin College, which the Maine legislature altered in 1831, with respect to the election and removal of the college president. Story voided the act on the basis of his concurring opinion in Dartmouth. He reasoned that the Maine act interfered with the vested rights of property, and because it altered the term of the president, it also impaired the obligations of contract. President Allen held office under a valid contract between himself and the governing board of the college, which could not be abrogated except for bad behavior.

[132] For a discussion of the 1780 constitution, see Handlin and Handlin, *Commonwealth*, 1-32.

[133] Story's chief concern was the judiciary, as it had been during his earlier legislative activities in the Massachusetts legislature. He fought for the independence of the judiciary and succeeded in defeating an attempt to limit and control judicial salaries. Standing behind his reasoning in the *Dartmouth College* case, Story asserted that the power of the legislature to limit salaries "was a violation of the contract of every judge now in office with the State; it was a violation of the constitution of the United States, by undertaking to violate one of the most solemn contracts ever entered into." (*Journal of Debates and Proceedings*, 551.) In his report to the convention, Story recommended that the constitutional provision allowing the removal of judges by a bare majority of the legislature be

He was also made a member of the committee concerned with the problem of senate representation. When it was put before the members of the convention in an impassioned speech by the Republican Henry Dearborn that the "aristocratical principle" of property representation in the senate be changed to representation on population by districts, Story rose to a defense of property. Arguments harping on class antagonism had underlined the discussion supporting the change in representation, and Story prefaced his remarks with a denunciation of "this distinction between the rich and poor."[134]

Story then launched into a general defense of the free enterprise system. His audience was reminded that America, unlike the nations of Europe, was a land of opportunity, where each citizen might enjoy the comforts of wealth through personal endeavor. "There is," he boasted, "a gradation of property from the highest to the lowest, and all feel an equal interest in its preservation."[135] Rejecting the notion of class warfare, Story believed that "there is not a conflict, but a harmony of interests between the rich and the poor."[136] It was unrealistic to contend there were great differences in wealth, because in American society, there were no extremes in poverty or wealth.

The beneficiaries of property were the whole population, continued the judge. There were the "opulent and munificent citizens, whose wealth has spread itself into a thousand channels of charity and public benevolence."[137] Those who might otherwise suffer discomfort and neglect benefited from the rich, who gave their fortunes for the construction of churches, hospitals, schools, and asylums. The salutary effects of property were reciprocal; and therefore "Every man, from him who possesses but a single dollar, up to him who possesses the greatest fortune, is equally interested in its security and

---

changed to a two-thirds majority, in order to promote the independence of the judiciary. This proposal was defeated in the convention. Story also urged the convention in his report to abolish the constitutional provision requiring judges to deliver opinions on both public and private matters upon request by the governor or either branch of the legislature, and the convention agreed to submit this proposal to the people in the form of an amendment. A third proposal of Story, to establish courts of equity, was voted down by the delegates. See Story's report as chairman of the committee on the judiciary, *ibid.*, 126–38. Story also supported the amendment recognizing the rights and privileges of Harvard College against legislative meddling. It is interesting to note that Story was silent on the question of suffrage qualifications, but ably defended the representation of property on the question of apportionment. But, according to the Marxist historian, Gustavus Myers, Story's speech, "of an intensely class character," was "an elaborate argument for a continuing property qualification for voters." *History of the Supreme Court of the United States,* 290–91.

134 *Journal of Debates and Proceedings,* 284.

135 *Ibid.,* 285.

136 *Ibid.*

137 *Ibid.*

preservation."[138] Wealth and property, being in a state of flux, could hardly be said to constitute a permanent distinction of families.

Those who are wealthy today pass to the tomb, and their children divide their estates. Property is thus divided quite as fast as it accumulates. . . . Property is continually changing like the waves of the sea. One wave rises and is soon swallowed up in the vast abyss and seen no more. Another rises, and having reached its destined limits, falls gently away, and is succeeded by yet another, which in its turn, breaks & dies away silently on the shore. The richest man among us may be brought down to the humblest level; and the child with scarcely clothes to cover his nakedness, may rise to the highest office in our government. And the poor man, while he rocks his infant on his knees, may justly indulge the consolation, that if he possesses talents and virtue, there is no office beyond the reach of his honorable ambition.[139]

Story did not distinguish between civil rights and property rights. Fused and interdependent, both formed the intricate matrix of personal freedom. "Gentlemen have argued as if personal rights only were the proper objects of government. But what, I would ask, is life worth, if a man cannot eat in security the bread earned by his own industry? If he is not permitted to transmit to his children the little inheritance which his affection has destined for their use?"[140] Determined to "say no more about the rich and the poor," Story concluded with the observation that "The rich help the poor and the poor in turn administer to the rich."[141]

Dearborn's resolution to alter the basis of representation now fell direct prey to Story's umbrage. In the same breath he cheerfully admitted the virtues of popular representation and disparaged Dearborn's proposition that population was in all cases "the safest and best basis of representation."[142] Manchester, England, standing in direct contradiction to such an assertion, was a good example of "Where there are five or ten thousand wealthy persons, and ninety or one hundred thousand of artizans reduced to a state of vice and poverty and wretchedness, which leave them exposed to the most dangerous political excitements. . . . Who would found a representation on such a population, unless he intended all property should be divided among plunderers?"[143]

Such conditions did not exist in Massachusetts, but this did not establish Dearborn's premise as a political axiom. The issue over representation was not "an abstract theoretical question, but depends upon the habits, manners,

[138] *Ibid.*, 286.
[139] *Ibid.*
[140] *Ibid.*
[141] *Ibid.*
[142] *Ibid.*, 288.
[143] *Ibid.*

character and institutions of the people who are to be represented."[144] Story implored his fellow delegates not to throw away their anchor; for there would always be a storm. "The Constitution has gone through a trial of forty years in times of great difficulty and danger."[145] It had survived the odium of party warfare, the War of 1812, emerging "pure and bright and spotless."[146] It was unwise to ignore the benefits of experience "for any theory, however plausible, that stands opposed to that experience, for a theory that possibly may do as well."[147]

He offered his own experience in the Massachusetts legislature as a lesson which all might well reflect upon: "I have always viewed the representation in the House under the present constitution as a most serious evil, and alarming to the future peace and happiness of the State. My dread has never been of the Senate, but of that multitudinous assembly, which has been seen within these walls, and may again be seen if times of political excitement should occur."[148]

Never disturb that which is at rest—such was the advice of Judge Story. Allow Dearborn's resolution to pass, he exhorted, and Massachusetts would suffer the consequence of "new feuds" and "new discontents and struggles for a new convention [which] will agitate the commonwealth."[149] Story regretfully recalled the violence of factional strife which in the past "raged in this State, breaking asunder the ties of friendship and consanguinity."[150] As he had once learned, political fermentation generated animosity and resentment:

I was myself called upon to take an active part in the public scenes of those days. I do not regret the course which my judgment then led me to adopt; but I never can recollect, without the most profound melancholy, how often I have been compelled to meet, I will not say the *evil* but *averted* eyes, and the hostile opposition of men with whom, under other circumstances, I should have rejoiced to have met in the warmth of friendship.[151]

---

[144] *Ibid.* Story added other objections: It has been "asserted that intelligence is the foundation of government. Are not virtue and morality equally so? Intelligence without virtue is the enemy most to be dreaded by every government. . . . While, therefore it may be admitted that intelligence is necessary for a free people, it is not less true that sound morals and religion are also necessary. Where there is not private virtue, there cannot be public security and happiness" (*ibid.*). Story was not opposed to representation on the basis of population in the lower house, but to place the Senate upon the same foundation would destroy "all county lines and distinctions, and break all habits and associations connected with them. They might thus be broken up, but it was by tearing asunder some of the strongest bonds of society." *Ibid.*, 289.

[145] *Ibid.*, 290.

[146] *Ibid.*, 291.

[147] *Ibid.*

[148] *Ibid.*, 293.

[149] *Ibid.*, 294.

[150] *Ibid.*

[151] *Ibid.*

Suggesting that the delegates might better employ their talents in combating poverty rather than uprooting safeguards of property, Story drew his speech to a close with the reminder that as delegates of the Massachusetts citizenry, they legislated not only for past and present, but also for the future generations of the commonwealth:

We have children whom we love—and families, in whose welfare we feel the deepest interest. In the name of heaven, let us not leave to them the bitter inheritance of our contentions. Let us not transmit to them enmities which may sadden the whole of their lives. Let us not . . . in our anger seize upon the pillars of the constitution. . . . I would rather approach the altar of the Constitution and pay my devotions there, and if our liberties must be destroyed, I, for one, would be ready to perish there in defending them.[152]

The Dearborn resolution thereafter came up for a vote and was soundly rejected by a vote of 247 to 164.

Judging from the breadth of Story's judicial opinions upholding the rights of property, there is no question that Story revered the Constitution of the United States with the same intensity as that of Massachusetts: both were designed, with a view toward justice, to protect the institution of property. It will probably seem surprising to present scholars as it undoubtedly was to the Boston lawyers who knew him best, that Joseph Story's contributions to the protection of property as writer, speaker, and judge, transcended those of every other member of the Supreme Court, including John Marshall. And it is plausible to infer that had Story been chief justice and major spokesman for the Court on constitutional issues, the history of vested rights and the contract clause would have followed a slightly different path of development; for while Marshall and Story were closely agreed on the surface, the fact remains that

---

[152] *Ibid.*, 294–95. Story later recalled that his "principal labors were in another body, the great committee on the subject of the representation in the House, whose debates were necessarily private. I there advocated the district system and apportionment of representatives according to population, so as to reduce the representatives to a comparatively moderate manner. . . . I now regret that I did not write out the substance of the speeches which I delivered in the Convention. . . . the best speech which I delivered . . . is scarcely touched in the printed debates. I mean the speech on the question of amending the Constitution so as to allow the Legislature the power to diminish, as well as increase, the salaries of the Judges. . . . [I]ndeed I may say, that not a single speech of mine is given with any thing like fulness or accuracy." ("Autobiography," *Miscellaneous Writings,* 36–37.) Shortly after the termination of the convention, Story wrote: "There was a pretty strong body of radicals, who seemed well disposed to get rid of all the great and fundamental barriers of the Constitution. Another class still more efficient and by no means small in number, was that of the lovers of the people, *alias,* the lovers of popularity." To Jeremiah Mason, Jan. 21, 1821, *Life and Letters,* I, 394–95. See also Story's letter to John Marshall, June 27, 1821, *William and Mary Quarterly,* 2nd Series, Vol. XXI, No. 1 (Jan., 1941), 11–12.

beneath their black-robed unanimity, important differences separated them in no small measure.

There are at least two possible explanations for their differing approaches to the issue of vested rights. As vividly seen in the *Dartmouth College* case, Marshall was no match for Judge Story on the technicalities of the common law. Yet, when we survey the decisions associated with the contract clause, it is Marshall, in a peculiar reversal of roles, who appears the more narrow and legalistic; and as seen in *Terrett* v. *Taylor* and *Wilkinson* v. *Leland*, it is Story, not Marshall, who is most anxious to elevate the doctrine of vested rights to a philosophical plane. Thus it can be seen that Story's penchant for the natural law philosophy, coupled with his broad legal knowledge, led him to view vested rights from a different perspective than Marshall, and to arrive at a somewhat different constitutional position.[153]

It should not be overlooked that Story was eager to establish the rights of property not only on a solid legal foundation, but upon a rational one as well. Nearly half of his essay on natural law is devoted to an analysis of the origins and nature of this sacred institution of liberty. Taking issue with John Locke regarding the origin of property, Story nevertheless agreed with Locke and the whole Anglo-American legal tradition that "One of the great objects of political society is the protection of property."[154] What was truly unique in Story's view of property, however, was his assertion that

Another great object of society is the protection, not only of property in *things*, but of property . . . in *actions*. A great portion of the business of human society is founded upon contracts, express or implied; and these contracts, especially in modern times, constitute the bulk of the fortunes and acquisitions of many persons, from the humblest mechanic up to the most opulent stockholder. The obligation of contracts, or, in other words, the duty in performing them, may indeed, be deduced from the plainest elements of natural law,—that is, if such contracts are just and moral, and founded upon mutuality of consideration . . . [they are] conformable to the will of God, which requires all men to deal with good faith, and truth, and sincerity in their intercourse with others.[155]

The idea that the obligation of contract conformed to the natural law and was a moral duty one covenanted to perform—a moral duty which the Constitution made a legal duty—was also expressed by Story in his *Commentaries*:

The obligation of every contract, then, will consist of that right, or power over my

153 Robert Kenneth Faulkner provides an analysis of the chief justice's philosophy of liberty and property rights in his *Jurisprudence of John Marshall*, 3–44. Faulkner concludes that "Marshall's jurisprudence encourages the 'morals' of the humane, peace-loving, restless and acquisitive modern middle class." *Ibid.*, 34.

154 Story, "Natural Law," *Encyclopedia Americana*, IX, 155.

155 *Ibid.*, 156. However, Story seemed reluctant to accept the legal doctrine that slaves were property, because slavery conflicted with natural law and natural rights. See chapter VII of this study, pp. 297–99.

will or actions, which I, by my contract, confer on another. And that right and power will be founded to be measured, neither by moral law alone, nor by the laws of society alone; but by a combination of the three; an operation, in which the moral law is explained, and applied by the law of nature, and both modified and adapted to the exigencies of society by positive law.[156]

A belief in the sanctity of contract was the fundamental concept introduced by Story in the *Dartmouth College* case which Marshall openly disavowed. Eschewing Marshall's narrow interpretation that the obligation of contract was simply (1) a legal obligation and (2) for the protection of tangible property, Story regarded the obligation as (1) both a legal and moral duty and (2) encompassing the sanctity of contract as well as property. It is Story's philosophy of natural law, then, together with his profound understanding of the common law, which created these differences of opinion with Chief Justice Marshall.

Inherent in Story's decisions, writings, and speeches (and less clearly evident in Marshall's) is Story's predilection to equate property rights with civil rights. In Story's mind all forms of property were sacred, and upon property rested the outer freedoms known together as civil liberties. The validity of this idea, established by ancient philosophers, common law jurists, and statesmen such as Burke and the authors of *The Federalist*,[157] was borne out by experience, reason, and the natural law. The naïve assumption that freedom is possible where property is insecure, was rejected by Story; the power that pulls the purse strings is the power that moves men's minds. Well-acquainted with the economic theories of Adam Smith, Malthus, and Ricardo,[158] Story understood that without an economy upholding property, freedom of any type was nearly impossible. A court failing to defend the inviolability of contract failed to protect property of every sort and ultimately fell down in its duty to protect the personal liberties of man.

Marshall, on the other hand, indicated property to be an end in itself, or at least neglected to establish it as the foundation of all freedom. Story, more

---

[156] Story, *Commentaries on the Constitution*, III, sec. 1272, p. 243.

[157] See James Madison, *The Federalist*, No. 44 (Modern Library ed.), 289-97.

[158] A letter written to his son, William, in 1837, in which Story explains at great length the economic problems accompanying industrialization, particularly with respect to the increasing unemployment of "artizans," shows that Story was familiar with modern economic concepts. To learn more about the subject, Story advised young William to go to the judge's library and examine his collection of works by Malthus, Ricardo, and Adam Smith. (Jan. 28, 1837, Story Papers, MHS.) Story cites Adam Smith prodigiously in his *Commentaries on the Constitution*. But according to Vernon Parrington, Story's "legalism was inveterate; the final, authoritative answer to all questions he discovered in the decision of the courts. Against such a mind, deeply read in the law and with scanty knowledge of economics and political theory, the waves of liberal and romantic thought broke impotently." *Main Currents in American Thought*, 302.

noticeably, acknowledged the suzerainty of higher values, property being only a means to an end. That end was a moral order, a free and just society in which every man was entitled to the rewards of his industry and ability, and to what he had inherited from his ancestors. Marshall's refusal to place the sanctity of contract upon the same moral plane as Story encumbered these exalted goals.

Story, then, defended property on a broader basis, on grounds of freedom, peace, progress, happiness, and as a form of distributive justice, whereby the rich improved not only the character and condition of the poor, but of all humanity. The only form of society he accepted was the free society, which afforded every opportunity to men of ability to rise by their own efforts and assume their natural station in life as leaders of the less fortunate. The only form of government amenable to him was that which honored men's agreements, the fruits of industry, and the accumulations of wealth.

To those who have followed the constitutional development of civil liberties since 1937, the vehemence with which Joseph Story upheld the rights of property and obligations of contract might seem curiously antiquarian. So sweeping, so all-embracing were his opinions protecting the rights and enforcing the duties of property and contract as to appear alien to contemporary concepts of social justice, which place property rights far down the scale of value. Taking his cue from *The Federalist*, which emphasized that under the new compact property would be safe, Story assiduously probed the passages of the Constitution, finding the entire structure honeycombed with safeguards to property. Unlike the modern Court, which has elevated First Amendment freedoms to a higher place of import, Story regarded economic freedom as the desideratum of all liberty. In his inaugural address as Dane Professor of Law, he insisted that

The sacred rights of property are to be guarded at every point. I call them sacred, because, if they were unprotected, all other rights become worthless or visionary. What is liberty, if it does not draw after it the right to enjoy the fruits of our own industry? What is political liberty, if it imparts only perpetual poverty to us and all our prosperity? What is the privilege of a vote, if the majority of the hour may sweep away the earnings of our whole lives, to gratify the rapacity of the indolent, the cunning, or the profligate, who are borne into power upon the tide of a temporary popularity?[159]

Many great fundamental changes in the American Constitution have occurred since 1787, the most important and the most revolutionary being the absorption of First Amendment freedoms into the concept of liberty of the due process clause of the Fourteenth Amendment. The application of the First Amendment to the states ushered in a whole new philosophy of democratic freedom. In 1937, Justice Cardozo enunciated this new philosophy in *Palko* v. *Con-*

---

[159] "Value and Importance of Legal Studies," *Miscellaneous Writings*, 519.

necticut, when he wrote that not all freedoms, including by implication those of property, had been incorporated into the term *liberty* of the Fourteenth Amendment. Only those liberties such as freedom of thought and speech, which formed the "matrix," the indispensable condition of other freedoms, were, he said, essential to "a scheme of ordered liberty."[160]

In effect, Justice Cardozo was following the same perilous course of reasoning laid down by Chief Justice Taney in the *Charles River Bridge* case, that the rights of property, contract, and personal economic freedom rank among the lesser freedoms. In the modern Court this extreme concern over First Amendment freedoms and concomitant indifference toward economic liberties has produced a peculiar double standard of liberty that lacks support either in reason or in the Constitution.

On the one hand, it may be observed that the Supreme Court Reports are bulging with decisions in which the Court has gone out of its way to protect nearly every variety of speech, press, and religious activity against state and federal abridgment. This is not to mention the countless decisions delivered more recently that give broad protection to the accused in a criminal prosecution. Then on the other hand, the Supreme Court Reports reveal not a single case in the last thirty years under the Fifth or Fourteenth amendments in which the Court has struck down economic legislation as violative of substantive due process; and in only one case[161] during this period has the Court invalidated economic legislation under the equal protection clause of the Fourteenth Amendment. "Since about 1937," Professor Robert G. McCloskey has noted with despair, "the Court has been rebuilding its constitutional dwelling place, knocking down a wall here, constructing a new corridor there, in response to a bewildering succession of conflicting impulses. . . . Vast new areas of constitutional supervision have been opened in such decisions as *Palko* v. *Connecticut, Burstyn* v. *Wilson*, and *Brown* v. *Board of Education*, to name only three of many. Other regions, once significant, have been closed off to judicial intervention: the fields of national commerce power and economic due process are the standard examples."[162]

Why should economic liberty be thought of as any less important than other liberties? Citing Holmes and Brandeis, civil libertarians have usually maintained that restrictions on speech and press must be kept to a bare minimum, or prohibited altogether, lest some valuable and important truth be kept from the "market-place of ideas."[163] But as McCloskey observes, "it is not entirely

---

[160] 302 U.S. 325 (1937).

[161] *Morey* v. *Doud*, 354 U.S. 457 (1957).

[162] "Economic Due Process and the Supreme Court: An Exhumation and Reburial," *The Supreme Court Review* (ed. by Philip Kurland) (1962) 34–35.

[163] "[T]he best test of truth," Holmes declared in *Abrams* v. *United States*, 250 U.S. 630 (1919), "is the power of the thought to get itself accepted in the competition of the market." In an age of mass media, propaganda, and news manipulation, Holmes's Wil-

clear why liberty of economic choice is less indispensable to the 'openness' of a society than freedom of expression."[164] Furthermore, Holmes's "market-place" theory of free speech assumes too much: It assumes that every idea is worth a public hearing, that truth will always win out in free and open discussion, and that the ideas expressed in the market place will not otherwise be known unless they are loudly and publicly proclaimed.

On this subject the distinguished British student of politics, Michael Oakeshott, has offered some critical comments which bear repeating: "the current exaggeration over the importance of free speech," he writes, has a tendency to conceal "the loss of other liberties no less important. The major part of mankind have nothing to say; the lives of most men do not revolve around a felt necessity to speak. . . . Nor is it an interest incapable of abuse; when it is extended to the indiscriminate right to take and publish photographs, to picket and enter private houses . . . it begins to reveal itself as a menace to freedom. For most men, to be deprived of the right of voluntary association or of private property would be a far greater and more deeply felt loss of liberty than to be deprived of the right to speak freely."[165]

Nor from a constitutional standpoint does the derogation of property rights seem warranted. The word *property* in the due process clauses of the Fifth and Fourteenth amendments does not rank below liberty. Indeed, the Constitution itself emphasizes property.[166] Article 1, section 10 prohibits the states from impairing the obligation of contracts. The Bill of Rights also protects property; the Fifth Amendment states that no person can be deprived of life, liberty, or property without due process of law and that private property cannot be taken for public use without just compensation; the Seventh Amendment guarantees trial by jury in common law suits involving property. Indeed, property rights were valued by the framers as highly as other rights, and it could be argued that they were considered even more "fundamental" than freedom of speech,

---

sonian idealism appears today as curiously naïve and old fashioned; yet it is an integral part of current constitutional notions respecting First Amendment freedoms. In the *Gitlow* case Holmes went so far as to suggest that freedom of speech was more important than freedom itself. "If in the long run the belief expressed in proletarian dictatorships are destined to be accepted by the dominant forces of the community, the only meaning of free speech is that they should be given their chance and have their way." *Gitlow* v. *New York*, 268 U.S. 673 (1925). That the advocates of proletarian dictatorship might abolish the "market place of ideas" as soon as they achieved victory is a possibility which apparently did not enter into Holmes's charmingly aloof and innocent mind.

[164] McCloskey, "Economic Due Process and the Supreme Court," *Supreme Court Review*, 48.

[165] *Rationalism in Politics*, 43–44. See also Friedrich Hayek, *The Constitution of Liberty*, 11–22; McCloskey, "Economic Due Process and the Supreme Court," *Supreme Court Review*, 46.

[166] See Gottfried Dietze, *In Defense of Property*, 71–92.

religion, press, and assembly, as their protection was already provided for in the original text of the Constitution.[167]

[167] In his study of freedom of speech and press in early America, Leonard Levy demonstrates quite conclusively that these liberties were not intended to "mean advocacy of a freedom broader than that permitted at common law.... [T]he generation which adopted the Constitution and the Bill of Rights did not believe in a broad scope for freedom of expression, particularly in the realm of politics." *Freedom of Speech and Press in Early American History: Legacy of Suppression*, xv, xxi.

CHAPTER VI

The Nature of the Union

We are great ascetics, and even deny ourselves wine except in wet weather. What I say about the wine gives you our rule; but it does sometimes happen that the Chief Justice will say to me, when the cloth is removed, "Brother Story, step to the window and see if it does not look like rain." And if I tell him that the sun is shining brightly, Judge Marshall will sometimes reply, "All the better, for our jurisdiction extends over so large a territory that the doctrine of chances makes it certain that it must be raining somewhere."

JOSEPH STORY, as quoted in Josiah Quincy, *Figures of the Past*

"If we are ever to be a great nation," Judge Story once advised, "it must be by giving vital operation to every power confided to the Government.... I hold it to be a maxim, which should never be lost sight of by a great statesman, that the Government of the United States is intrinsically too weak, and the powers of the State Governments too strong; that the danger always is much greater of anarchy in the parts, than of tyranny in the head."[1] In a firm, indissoluble Union, Judge Joseph Story saw the preservation of civil liberty and the dream of a great American empire. His major concern, during some thirty-four years of vigorous judicial activity, was to strengthen and expand the powers of the federal government; and some would add he did his best to emasculate the powers of the states.

Whether dashing off a letter, pontificating in the classroom, or reading over a lawyer's brief, Story's first thoughts were always of the Union. Few are the opinions of Judge Story in which the powers of the federal government are not affirmed, expanded, or eulogized. Consumed by the dread of secession, again and again he would puncture the inflated doctrines of states' rights, certain that in the end the Union was destined to collapse; but he would not capitulate. His decisions were often greeted by a storm of protests, but rather than turn back, he plunged headlong into the next political crisis.

Instead of discouraging this undaunted New Englander, the powerful arguments emanating from the South merely reaffirmed his undying convictions, urging him to greater exploits. The more he scanned the horizon of federal

[1] *Life and Letters*, I, 296. See also Story to Henry Wheaton, Dec. 13, 1815, *ibid.*, 270–71; *The Federalist*, Nos. 17 and 18 (Modern Library ed.), 101–12.

power, the more channels he discovered in which the states had neglected to defend their interests. Each voyage upon the unknown sea of constitutional power seemed to take him farther from the home port constructed by the founding fathers, until at last he disappeared from sight, taking his beloved Union with him. He has been accused of playing a leading role in bringing about the War between the States;[2] yet his work was not in vain. For every constitutional doctrine he destroyed, he built a hundred in its place, leaving behind a durable, well-constructed wall of precedent under which succeeding generations have since reposed. Indeed, Story's influence on the growth of national supremacy pervades the entire body of American constitutional law.

As in the case of property rights, Story's ideas respecting the nature of the Union can be traced to his Fourth of July oration in 1804. This, his first major public address, was the harbinger of his nationalism, and he never ceased to warn his countrymen in all his political career of the "projects darkly hinted which tend to dissolve the Union, and restore us again to anarchy and confusion."[3]

And countless were the projects that subsequently called Judge Story into action against the states' rightists. He denounced New England secessionists, pilloried the Virginia and Kentucky resolutions, and condemned those who dared question the wisdom of his decisions. To counteract such nefarious schemes, to strengthen the nation, and to preserve the Constitution, Story formulated his own theory of the Union.

At the very start of his judicial career, he laid the groundwork for his nationalism through a natural law and historical interpretation of the Constitution in *United States* v. *Coolidge*[4] and *Martin* v. *Hunter's Lessee*.[5] His circuit opinion in the *Coolidge* case was an early indication not only that he intended to expand the powers of the federal courts by granting them jurisdiction over common law crimes, but also that he was swiftly moving in a direction of judicial nationalism, which, judging from the fact his ruling was

[2] See, for example, Charles Warren, *Supreme Court in United States History*, II, 87; Henry S. Commager, "The Nationalism of Joseph Story," *Bacon Lectures*, 55; William R. Leslie, "The Influence of Joseph Story's Theory of the Conflict of Laws on Constitutional Nationalism," *Mississippi Valley Historical Review*, Vol. XXXV, No. 2 (Sept., 1948), 212–20.

[3] Story, "An Oration," 21–22. States' Rights sympathies were never as strong among New England Republicans as Southern. "I am happy to find your opinions are in accord with mine on the purchase of Louisiana and the Constitutional amendment, and we are not at variance on the repeal of the Bankrupt law," wrote Congressman Crowninshield to Story at this time. "I fully agree with you that we must have a [political] system, it should operate in a uniform and general manner throughout the U. States. . . . The clamour about Louisiana is perfectly ridiculous. The country is of incalculable value." Feb. 13, 1804, Story Papers, Clements Library.

[4] 1 Gallison 488 (1813).

[5] 1 Wheaton 304 (1816).

overruled in the Supreme Court,[6] was unacceptable to his fellow justices. The theory of the Union introduced by Story in the *Coolidge* decision, which finally came to fruition in a different constitutional form in *Swift* v. *Tyson*,[7] was premised on the assumption that the common law was the basis of the American Constitution, both in fact and in theory.

In his first great Supreme Court opinion, *Martin* v. *Hunter's Lessee*,[8] Story announced his second and major theory of the Union. Like that concerning the adoption of the common law, this second theory stemmed from an organic conception of the Union, rejected the Jeffersonian doctrine that American revolutionaries had made a radical break with the past, and upheld the idea that the Constitution was in essence a continuation of pre-Revolutionary principles of law. Story maintained that neither the "rights" embodied in the Constitution nor the *method* by which those "rights" were established was in any way contractual. Precisely how and why Story embraced a noncontractual theory of the Union and how it relates to his ideas concerning natural law and American civil liberties will be more easily seen through an analysis of his opinion in the *Martin* case, and of his rather elaborate exposition of the nature of the Union in his *Commentaries on the Constitution*.

UNDERSTANDING *MARTIN* V. *HUNTER'S LESSEE*

In the beginning the controversy in *Martin* v. *Hunter's Lessee* concerned the common law rights of property and inheritance, and the question of whether those rights had been adopted by the state of Virginia. The case involved substantial tracts of valuable land in the Northern Neck of Virginia, which were originally owned by Lord Fairfax. A Loyalist who fled to England during the American Revolution, Lord Fairfax died in 1781 and devised the property to his nephew, Denny Fairfax, a British subject. In 1782, however, the state of Virginia passed an act voiding the original grant of land to Lord Fairfax. Virginia contended that, under her laws, aliens such as Denny Fairfax could not inherit property, and that various confiscation acts passed during the Revolutionary period (but which were not put into effect) had transferred the property from Lord Fairfax to the state.

David Hunter, who had obtained a grant of 788 acres of the Fairfax lands from Virginia, brought an action of ejectment against Denny Fairfax in the county court at Winchester. The court decided against Hunter, who thereupon appealed to the supreme court of Virginia, which reversed the holding of the lower court. In the meantime the guarantees of the Treaty of Paris affirming titles to land which Virginia had declared forfeited in the confiscatory acts

[6] *United States* v. *Coolidge*, 1 Wheaton 415 (1816).
[7] 16 Peters 1 (1842).
[8] 1 Wheaton 304 (1816).

were reasserted by Jay's Treaty. After years of delay, an appeal was finally taken to the Supreme Court of the United States on a writ of error.[9]

In *Fairfax's Devisee* v. *Hunter's Lessee*,[10] Judge Story reversed the holding of the Virginia Court of Appeals. With Chief Justice Marshall, whose brother was involved in the controversy, and Justice Washington both absent during the argument, the task of writing the Court's opinion devolved upon Judge Story. He briefly examined the original title of Lord Fairfax, concluding that by virtue of the royal charter, Lord Fairfax had been vested with complete possession of the property. Story next examined the title of Denny Fairfax. He based his reasoning in upholding Denny Fairfax's title upon well-documented common law rules. By the common law the general principle was that an alien could purchase, but could not inherit property. However, "in the language of the ancient law, the alien has the capacity to take but not to hold lands."[11] Story admitted that as sovereign, Virginia could legally have seized the lands during the war, "But until the lands are so seized, the alien has complete dominion" over the property and might defend "his title to the lands against all persons but the sovereign."[12] Thus, concluded Story, "Denny Fairfax had a complete though defeasible, title . . . [which] could only be divested by an inquest of office perfected by an entry and seizure."[13] Virginia's failure to confiscate the property during the Revolution therefore left Denny Fairfax in full legal possession of the property.

To the last point, Virginia argued that the common law rules regarding inquests of office had been abolished by statute. Story avoided this contention by invoking his theory of the incorporation of the common law into state jurisprudence. While it was within the power of Virginia to abolish inquests of office, Story claimed that the wording of the statute in question failed to establish clearly that the state legislature had intended to do so. "Upon principles of public policy,"[14] said Story, the Court would not presume that inquests of office had been revoked by the legislature. An inquest of office was "a useful and important restraint upon public proceedings" which prevented "individuals from being harassed by numerous suits," enabled property owners "to contest the question of alienage directly," and discouraged "that corrupt influence which the avarice of speculation might otherwise urge upon the Legislature."[15] Therefore, "The Common law . . . ought not to be deemed to

---

[9] For a more extensive account of the complexities and circumstances surrounding the litigation, see Charles Haines, *The Role of the Supreme Court*, 340–47; Beveridge, *Life of Marshall*, IV, 145–67; Warren, *Supreme Court in United States History*, I, 443–53.

[10] 7 Cranch 603 (1813).

[11] *Ibid.*, 620.

[12] *Ibid.*

[13] *Ibid.*, 622.

[14] *Ibid.*

[15] *Ibid.*, 623.

be repealed, unless the language of a statute be clear and explicit for this purpose."[16]

Thus it may be seen that Story was brazenly imposing the will of the federal judiciary upon the state of Virginia, insisting that Virginia abide by the rules of the common law respecting inquest of office, when actually there was sufficient doubt about whether Virginia desired to maintain such a principle. Confronted, then, with the problem of protecting Denny Fairfax's property as opposed to that of ascertaining the intentions of the state of Virginia, Story chose to utilize federal judicial power and defend property, substituting his own law for that of the Virginia courts.[17] Irrespective of these considerations, Story concluded that it was not necessary to pursue the issues of the case further, as the Court was satisfied that Jay's Treaty "completely protects and confirms the title of Denny Fairfax, even admitting that the treaty of peace left him wholly unprovided for."[18]

Story's ruling ran counter to the decisions of Virginia courts regarding the effect of the confiscation acts and the legal capacity of aliens to inherit property, and the judges of the Virginia Court of Appeals were understandably shaken by Story's haughty disregard for Virginia law. They subsequently agreed to ignore Story's mandate requiring them to enter judgment for the Fairfax devisee, and in seriatim opinions challenged the validity of the Supreme Court's exercise of jurisdiction over state court decisions, thereby raising the question of whether the Judiciary Act of 1789 was constitutional.

Section 25 of the Judiciary Act provided that final judgments in state supreme courts questioning or repudiating the validity of any federal statute, treaty, or clause of the Constitution were subject to re-examination in the Supreme Court of the United States. The Virginia high court, however, claimed that while state judges were obliged to obey the Constitution, laws, and treaties of the United States, they were not bound to obey the Supreme Court's interpretation of them. They argued that state and federal judges were officers of two separate sovereignties, and neither was required to obey the decisions of the other. Congress therefore had no power to enact a law subjecting state court decisions to review by the federal judiciary. In the words of the Virginia Court of Appeals,

---

[16] *Ibid.*

[17] "Story . . . nullified local law and annulled and invalidated Virginia arguments in a sweeping extension of national judicial power. Implicit in the decision was the denial that Virginia was a legal or jurisdictional unit distinguishable from the United States. Implicit also was the scarcely veiled assertion that the Old Dominion was little more than an administrative unit in a constitutionally centralized state." William R. Leslie, "Similarities in Lord Mansfield's and Joseph Story's View of Fundamental Law," *American Journal of Legal History*, Vol. I (1957), 298.

[18] *Ibid.,* 627. Justice Johnson dissented.

the appellate power of the Supreme Court of the United States does not extend to this court, under a sound construction of the Constitution of the United States;—that so much of the 25th section of the act of Congress, to establish the judicial courts of the United States, as extends the appellate jurisdiction of the Supreme Court to this court, is not in pursuance of the Constitution of the United States; that the writ of error in this case was improvidently allowed under the authority of that act; that the proceedings thereon in the Supreme Court were *coram non juridice* in relation to this court; and that obedience to its mandate be declined by this court.[19]

In *Martin* v. *Hunter's Lessee*,[20] Judge Story, again speaking for the Court, upheld the constitutionality of the Judiciary Act and affirmed the Court's power of judicial review over state court decisions. He rejected outright the contention that the states and the national government were equal sovereignties. The Union was not a compact formed by the various states, wherein the contracting parties were free to assert their sovereignty. It was truly a union of individuals in which the Constitution of the American people reigned supreme. The United States Constitution, he postulated, "was ordained and established, not by the States in their sovereign capacities, but emphatically, as the preamble declares, by 'the people of the United States.' "[21]

Here, in distilled version, was Story's theory of the nature of the Union, a theory which he employed throughout his judgeship in defending national power against the powers of the various states. His thesis was that because the Union had been established by the people rather than the states, "it was competent to the people to invest the general government with all the powers which they might deem proper and necessary."[22] By showing that the people intended to empower the Supreme Court with the authority to review state court decisions, Story could thus demonstrate that the Judiciary Act was simply an expression of popular will conforming to the designs of the Constitution. To this task he now turned.

Nowhere in the Constitution was it stated that the Supreme Court should exercise appellate jurisdiction over state courts. Was there any indication from a reading of the Constitution, however, that such a power was legitimate and might be effected by the Congress? Story answered in the affirmative. He admitted that the federal government

can claim no powers which are not granted to it by the Constitution, and the powers actually granted must be such as are expressly given, or given by necessary implication. On the other hand, this instrument, like every other grant, is to have a reasonable construction, according to the import of its terms; and where a power is

---

[19] *Hunter* v. *Martin*, 4 Munford (Va.) 58–59 (1814).
[20] 1 Wheaton 304.
[21] *Ibid.*, 324.
[22] *Ibid.*, 324–25.

expressly given in general terms, it is not to be restrained to particular cases, unless that construction grows out of the context expressly, or by necessary implication.[23]

Taking this rule of construction, Story now turned to the provisions of the Constitution to determine whether "by necessary implication" the Judiciary Act was within the purview of constitutional powers. The powers of the national government, he noted, were "expressed in general terms, leaving to the legislature, from time to time, to adopt its own means to effectuate legitimate objects, and to mold and model the exercise of its powers."[24] With these principles in view, Story proceeded to quote sections 1 and 2 of article 3, which define the judicial power of the Supreme Court. Article 3, he surmised, "is the voice of the whole American people solemnly declared, in establishing one great department of that government which was, in many respects, national, and in all, supreme."[25] This article was a mandate of the people upon the Congress; for "Its obligatory force is so imperative that Congress could not, without a violation of its duty, have refused to carry it into operation."[26]

Thus, Story reasoned that inasmuch as Congress was required to vest the judicial power of the United States, it was therefore the duty of Congress "to vest the whole judicial power. The language, if imperative as to one part, is imperative as to all."[27] Otherwise, he thought, Congress could single out any class of cases, refuse to extend the jurisdiction, and defeat the purposes of the Constitution.[28]

[23] *Ibid.*, 326.

[24] *Ibid.*, 326–27.

[25] *Ibid.*, 328.

[26] *Ibid.*

[27] *Ibid.*, 330.

[28] Addressing himself to this specific point many years later, Story told Judge Joseph Hopkinson that in the case of *Martin* v. *Hunter's Lessee*, the Court held that it was "the *imperative duty* of Congress to vest the appellate jurisdiction in its own courts; & that it would be a violation of their duty to disobey this constitutional requirement. The only point upon which one might pause," he surmised, was that pertaining to the limits of Congress' control over jurisdiction. "If Congress were to make exceptions, co-extensive with the Constitutional provisions, could it be maintained as a constitutional exercise of power? Consider the point. If they may make exceptions short of this, what limit is prescribed as to the nature or extent of those exceptions? The truth is, that the leaving [of] this matter to the discretion of Congress was a great oversight of the framers of the Constitution." (Jan. 22, 1831, Hopkinson Papers, HSP.) Professor Harris correctly observed that "In the whole of his homily on the duty of Congress to create courts and vest in them all of the judicial power they are capable of exercising, Story never went further than to say that such was a moral as distinguished from a legal obligation . . . . Story, therefore, was merely stating with added emphasis the principle first enumerated in the eighteenth number of *The Federalist* and later incorporated in judicial decisions that 'the judicial power of every well-constituted government must be co-extensive with the legislative, and must be capable of deciding every question which grows out of the Constitution and laws.' He was, then, stating a political axiom rather

What, then, was the "nature and extent of the appellate jurisdiction of the United States," which Congress was under an obligation to vest in the federal courts? Generally speaking, it embraced "every case enumerated in the Constitution, which is not exclusively to be decided by way of original jurisdiction."[29] Nothing in the Constitution limited this power or restrained its exercise over state courts. The Constitution stated that the "judicial power shall extend to all cases," and that "in all other cases before mentioned the Supreme Court shall have appellate jurisdiction." It would seem, then, that "It is the case . . . and not the court, that gives the jurisdiction. If the judicial power extends to the case, it will be in vain to search in the letter of the Constitution for any qualification as to the tribunal where it depends."[30] The appellate power of the federal judiciary must extend, then, to such inferior courts as state tribunals, whenever the case involved the Constitution, laws, or treaties of the United States.

The arguments propounded by the Virginia Court of Appeals seemed to Story to violate the unquestioned supremacy of the Constitution in that they rendered impotent the Supreme Court, whose primary duty was the preservation of that supremacy. The underlying fallacy of such reasoning, suggested Story, was the erroneous assumption that state sovereignty equaled national sovereignty: "It has been argued, that such an appellate jurisdiction over State courts is inconsistent with the genius of our governments, and the spirit of the Constitution. That the latter was never designed to act upon State sovereignties, but only upon the people, and that if the power exists, it will materially impair the sovereignty of the States, and the independence of their courts."[31] But Story would not yield to such reasoning. The Constitution, he maintained, was designed to operate on states as well as individuals. "It is crowded with provisions which restrain or annul the sovereignty of the States in some of the highest branches of their prerogatives."[32] Nor did the existence of appellate jurisdiction impair the independence of state judges. Where the powers of the federal government were an issue, state judges were not independent, but, in fact, were bound in obedience to the Constitution, as stipulated by the Constitution itself.

Story believed not only that his constitutional law was sound, but also that it was expedient and practical. Appellate power was necessary to ensure uni-

than enunciating a rule of law. In spite of the fact that Story meant no more than a moral obligation by his references to the duty of Congress to vest all the judicial power in some courts, *Martin* v. *Hunter's Lessee* is the foundation of all arguments against the complete power of Congress to regulate the jurisdiction of the lower federal courts." Robert J. Harris, *The Judicial Power of the United States*, 101–102.

[29] 1 Wheaton 337.
[30] *Ibid.*, 338.
[31] *Ibid.*, 342–43.
[32] *Ibid.*, 343.

formity in decisions respecting federal laws and treaties. Furthermore, "State prejudices, state jealousies and state interests,"[33] constituted a continued threat to the administration of justice. Such controversies as those between states or between individuals and states would, therefore, best be resolved in national tribunals, which were better situated to adjudicate conflicting interests.

Having settled the issues, Story reversed the judgment of the Virginia Court of Appeals and terminated his argument, holding "that the appellate power of the United States does extend to cases pending in the State courts; and that the twenty-fifth section of the Judiciary Act, which authorizes the exercise of this jurisdiction in the specified cases, by a writ of error, is supported by the letter and spirit of the Constitution. We find no clause in that instrument which limits this power; and we dare not interpose a limitation where the people have not been disposed to create one."[34]

That *Martin* v. *Hunter's Lessee* was the most important decision handed down by Story during his entire career is clear enough. "That case decided the very important question of the *right* of Congress to give the Supreme Court *appellate* jurisdiction over the decisions of *State* Courts on constitutional questions," he later explained to Joseph Hopkinson. "The Court of Appeals of Virginia denied the right, & it was very stoutly denied in the argument in the Supreme Court. The opinion, such as it is, goes very elaborately into the doctrine, & I *know*, that, though the Ch[ief] Justice did not sit, he fully concurred in that opinion. On this decision, in effect, rests the whole value & efficacy of our control over the State Courts in their Constitutional decisions. It is *vital* to the government."[35]

Natural law ideas can usually be seen lurking in the background of Story's jurisprudence, and his views on the nature of the Union are no exception to this general tendency. During the first one-half century of the American republic, it should be remembered that it was the Constitution standing alone, not the Constitution pitted against the Declaration of Independence, which provided the first great battleground for the natural rights debates. Until the emergence of the antislavery controversy, following in the wake of the Missouri Compromise of 1820, the whole issue of natural rights and the social contract was tied up with the question of the nature of the Union. As a symbol of egalitarian democracy, the Declaration of Independence was pretty much ignored; even Jefferson himself seemed unaware that the Declaration of Independence, resting on the philosophy of natural rights, was in any way opposed to the principles of the Constitution.[36]

---

[33] *Ibid.*, 347.

[34] *Ibid.*, 351.

[35] Jan. 20, 1830, Hopkinson Papers, HSP.

[36] See Jefferson to James Madison, Aug. 30, 1823, *Writings* (Memorial ed.), XV, 460–64; Jefferson to Henry Lee, May 8, 1825, *ibid.*, XVI, 117–19.

Indeed, before the abolitionists seized upon the Declaration in the antislavery movement, read natural rights into it, and then proclaimed it to be "the supreme law of the land," there had been no noticeable conflict between the Constitution and the Declaration in the American mind; and even when that conflict did arise, the debate was restricted to the question of slavery, and the "natural right" of the Negro to be free. It did not progress to the issue of whether *all* Americans should exercise the same rights everywhere; for in the absence of the Fourteenth Amendment, uniformity of rights and liberties was in most instances constitutionally impossible.

The supervisory control of the Marshall and Taney courts was ordinarily limited to property rights under the contract clause, by virtue of the fact that the Bill of Rights restricted only the federal government and permitted the states to deal with civil and political liberty as they saw fit. In fact, only since the Supreme Court began interpreting the equal protection and due process clauses broadly and applying the Bill of Rights to the states—relatively recent developments—has the federal government, speaking through its judicial branch, been in a position to impose the natural rights philosophy throughout the country or to exercise a dominant voice in the determination of the nature and scope of American civil "rights" and political liberties. Thus it can be seen that the ultimate, face-to-face confrontation between natural rights and the Constitution was postponed throughout most of American history because of Chief Justice Marshall's all-important decision in *Barron* v. *Baltimore*.[37] And when that confrontation did occur, it was the Bill of Rights and the Fourteenth Amendment, serving as the surrogate for the ideas and ideals of the Declaration of Independence, which became, through a liberal interpretation of their provisions, the true vehicles for the implementation of egalitarianism and other natural rights doctrines.[38]

Of course the conflict between the states and the Marshall Court was rarely understood as a conflict over natural law and natural rights; but these ideas were in the political undercurrents all the same, mixed with sectionalism and economic interests, influencing the flow of ideas and events. Many of the very early Jeffersonian states' rightists, quite unlike their more conservative successors such as Randolph and Calhoun, were under the powerful influence of natural rights doctrines—doctrines they were sometimes anxious to apply within their respective states, where they would be beyond the watchful eye of a conservative Court. Likewise, many of these first states' rightists, insisting

[37] 2 Peters 243 (1833).

[38] "A glance at the work of the [Warren] Court," writes Professor Philip B. Kurland, "shows that the Court's most significant innovation has been the emerging primacy of equality as a guide to constitutional decision. . . . [T]he Court, as Mr. Justice Goldberg reported, has chosen to 'recognize the merging of the concepts of liberty and equality.' " "Equal in Origin and Equal in Title to the Legislative and Executive Branches of the Government," *Harvard Law Review*, Vol. LXXVIII, No. 1 (Nov., 1964), 144.

that the Union was a compact of sovereign states, were swayed by contractual theories of government. Such theories they applied to the federal Constitution, in the hope of strengthening the role of the states in the general area of civil and economic liberty, and of weakening the influence of the federal government—the federal judiciary in particular, which stoutly resisted, within the limits of its capacity, egalitarian trends in state after state, even after the Court was packed with Jacksonians.

This is not to say that all early nationalists and states' rightists were natural law and natural rights advocates respectively; indeed, the Republicans on the Court, including Justice Johnson, followed Marshall in nearly all of the major decisions. But there was a pronounced tendency among many of the first nationalists and states' rightists to divide, consciously or unconsciously, over issues that were related in varying degrees to the natural rights controversy. Ironically enough, the first wave of liberalism in American politics after 1787 came under the banner of antifederalism and states' rights. Legislative supremacy and the demand for greater popular control; opposition to much of the common law; political, economic, and social egalitarianism; doctrines of natural rights and states' rights: not infrequently they all went together, hand-in-hand, in the first half of the nineteenth century as part of the intellectual baggage of liberal democracy.

The influence of natural law upon Judge Story's thinking in the case of *Martin* v. *Hunter's Lessee* is not immediately apparent, until one turns to Story's *Commentaries on the Constitution*. Here, at great length, Story repeats his concept of the Union which he enunciated earlier in the *Martin* case. Now according to St. George Tucker, Blackstone's American editor, the American Constitution was an original, federal, and social compact, voluntarily entered into by the states and ratified by the people of the states. The several states and the people thereof thereby bound themselves to each other and to the federal government; and the federal government in turn bound itself to the states and to the people.[39]

This view of the Union, so basic to the states' rights position, was, said Story, neither practical, logical, nor legally justifiable. In the first place it tended to impair and destroy the Constitution's express powers and objects by reducing

[39] It was an *original* compact because the relation between the Colonies and the Mother Country was, according to Tucker, *completely* dissolved by the American Revolution. From that moment, he argued, the original thirteen colonies were sovereign states, possessing all the attributes of sovereignty. It was a *Federal* (i.e., political) compact, formed through an act of the state or body politic; and it was a *social* compact because it was an act of individuals who had joined together to establish a nation, "each individual agreeing with the other to procure the general welfare." Story, *Commentaries on the Constitution*, I, secs. 308-19, pp. 279-87. For an excellent analysis of the various theories of the Union propounded before 1860, including Story's, see Elizabeth K. Bauer, *Commentaries on the Constitution*.

the Constitution to a mere treaty or convention between the states, with no more obligatory force upon each state than suits its pleasure. Such a theory not only allowed each state to judge for itself to what extent it would be bound by the interpretations of the federal government, but it also permitted each state to retain the power to withdraw from the Union and to exercise what amounted to judicial review. Thus Tucker's compact theory of the Union was in essence nothing more than a restatement of the principles of the Articles of Confederation: "For the power to operate on individuals, instead of operating merely on states, is of little consequence . . . if that power is to depend for its exercise upon the continual consent of all the members upon every emergency."[40]

Secondly, continued Story, the compact theory of the Union was not justified by the language of the Constitution.

There is nowhere found upon the face of the Constitution any clause, intimating it to be a compact. . . .On the contrary, the preamble emphatically speaks of it, as a solemn ordinance and establishment of government. The language is, "we the people of the United States, do *ordain* and *establish* this *constitution* for the United States of America." The people do *ordain* and *establish*, not contract and stipulate with each other. The people of the United States, not the distinct people of a *particular state* with the people of other states. The people ordain and establish a "constitution," not a "confederation."[41]

And there were other constitutional provisions that seemed to contradict the compact theory: the Tenth Amendment used the term "delegated" powers. "A contract," said Story, "can in no sense be called a delegation of powers."[42] The compact theory was also inconsistent with the supremacy clause. If the Constitution is the supreme law of the land, queried Story, "how can the people of any state . . . repeal, abrogate, or suspend it?"[43] Moreover, in none of the instruments of ratification by the states was there "the slightest allusion to the instrument, as a confederation or compact of States in their sovereign capacity, and no reservation of any right on the part of any states, to dissolve its connexion or abrogate its assent."[44]

[40] Story, *Commentaries on the Constitution*, I, sec. 322, p. 290.

[41] *Ibid.*, sec. 352, p. 319.

[42] *Ibid.*, sec. 353, p. 321. "The only places, where the terms *confederation* or *compact*, are found in the constitution, apply to subjects of an entirely different nature, and manifestly in contradistinction to *constitution*. Thus, in the tenth section of the first article it is declared, that 'no state shall enter into any treaty, alliance, or *confederation*'; 'no state shall without the consent of Congress, &c., enter into any agreement or *compact* with another state, or with a foreign power.' Again, in the sixth article it is declared, that 'all debts contracted, and engagements entered into, before the adoption of this constitution, shall be valid against the United States under this constitution, as under the confederation.' " *Ibid.*

[43] *Ibid.*, p. 322.

[44] *Ibid.*, sec. 356, p. 324.

The compact theory of the Union was further hindered by the fact that at no time, either before or after the American Revolution, were the states in any way independent or sovereign communities. When colonies, they were subjected to the British crown and limited in their powers by their charters. During the Revolution, they acted in compliance with the recommendations of Congress and proclaimed their independence jointly. The Declaration of Independence, said Story, "was emphatically the act of the *whole* people of the united colonies. . . . It was an act of original inherent sovereignty by the people themselves, resulting from their right to change the form of government."[45] And even during the Articles of Confederation, Story insisted, the states were possessed of a limited sovereignty under a national government.

The idea of a federated compact, then, was based on the assumption that the various states entered into a union with the implied understanding that they reserved to themselves their inherent sovereignty. This Story denied, contending that they could not have entered into a contractual relationship, as their sovereignty was residuary and limited. They were sovereign only to the extent of power given by the federal Constitution and, in fact, had no authority under their separate constitutions to form a contract.[46]

Being rather skeptical of popular sovereignty, Story devoted considerable attention to the point that the sovereignty of the people was latent. The national government was a limited government, and while theoretically the absolute sovereignty of the nation was in the people, the fact remained that the people had elected to impose limitations on themselves through such devices as checks and balances, and the separation of powers. Sovereignty, therefore, was not absolute according to Story, but divisible. The nature of the Union precluded the idea of absolute sovereignty which defenders of states' rights urged through their compact theories. If the states possessed sovereignty, it was a limited sovereignty they shared with the Union. The absolute right to govern remained in the original unity, so that sovereignty in the limited sense was divided, but in the broader sense remained one. Since neither a state nor the inhabitants of a state were wholly sovereign, it was entirely proper to Story that the federal judiciary, representing a higher sovereign, should take jurisdiction over the state courts, when the Constitution, or laws of the national state so authorized.[47]

[45] *Ibid.*, sec. 211, p. 198. Story treats the question of sovereignty under his analysis of the "History of the Revolution and of the Confederation," secs. 198–217, and the question of the "Nature of the Constitution—Whether a Compact," between secs. 306–72.

[46] *Ibid.*, sec. 362, pp. 329–30.

[47] Charles E. Merriam credits Story with predating Calhoun in solving the problem of defining sovereignty in a federal system. "It should not escape notice," he says, "that Joseph Story early distinguished two uses of the term 'sovereignty' in such a way as to obviate the difficulties inherent in the idea of a double supremacy." (*A History of American Political Theories*, 262) Merriam, however, neglects to mention the fact that Story was also the first to destroy the notion that the Constitution was founded upon a "social con-

What, asked Story, was the underlying fallacy of the compact theory of the Union? The answer was clear in Story's mind. These states' rightists were adherents of natural rights doctrines and had mistakenly read the social contract theory into the Constitution. The doctrine of states' rights "seems, indeed, to have its origin in the notion of all governments being founded in compact, and therefore liable to be dissolved by the parties, or either of them."[48] Tucker's assertion that the Union was a social compact, said Story, had no support whatever among reputable students of politics. Unfortunately, "The doctrine maintained by many eminent writers upon public law in modern times, is that civil society has its foundation in a voluntary consent or submission; and, therefore, it is often said to depend upon a social compact of the people composing the nation."[49] John Locke, among others, subscribed to this notion. Nevertheless, replied Judge Story, Burke, Paley, Hume, and Blackstone had successfully refuted it.[50]

Perhaps, then, the American Constitution was, as Tucker also alleged, a *political* compact. Story grudgingly conceded, *arguendo*, that in theory it was possible to found a particular government on the basis of a compact; but, he quickly added, the American Constitution did not easily lend itself to this interpretation. The wording of the document contained no support for such a view. And who were the individuals making this contract? Only a minority of Americans participated in the formation of the Union, or actually consented to live under the new Constitution. Did this mean, then, that all those who did not consent to live under the Constitution, or who were born after the compact was made, were free to disregard the Constitution and to flout its authority? And what about those who did give their consent to obey the new Constitution? "Did the people intend, that it should be thus in the power of any individual to dissolve . . . himself from all obligations and duties thereto, at his choice, or upon his own interpretation of the instrument? If such a power exists, where is the permanence of the government? . . . Where are the duties of allegiance or obedience? May one withdraw his consent today, and reassert it tomorrow?"[51]

Clearly, argued Story, the application of the notion of contract to the Union would lead to chaos. Whatever its merits considered in the abstract—and here Story touched upon the fatal flaw—the compact theory was simply unworkable in practice. If the Union is a compact of the states and the people, then it would follow that dissolution of the Union would result if each *state* was free to

tract." He thus mistakenly believes that Story simply modified the theory, and erroneously concludes that Calhoun went farther than Story by repudiating "altogether the 'natural right' theory of politics." *Ibid.*, 201.

[48] Story, *Commentaries on the Constitution*, I, sec. 359, p. 327.

[49] *Ibid.*, sec. 325, p. 293.

[50] *Ibid.*, pp. 293–94.

[51] *Ibid.*, sec. 332, p. 302.

interpret on its own terms obligations and rights, and that anarchy would result if each *individual* could interpret his own obligations and rights. Both the states and individuals must submit to the Constitution as interpreted by the whole, that is, by the proper tribunals set up by the general government or, failing there, to appeal to the good sense of the majority.[52] Neither a state nor an individual, concluded Story, could secede from the Union. The Union was neither a social compact in which individuals removed themselves from a state of nature nor a political compact between states. If there was any compact at all, said Story, it was, as Nathan Dane declared, "a compact to make a Constitution; and that done, the agreement is at an end."[53]

VARIATIONS ON A THEME OF NATIONALISM

There were, of course, other forces giving impetus to Story's nationalism besides his views on the nature of the Union. Influenced by his environment, Story sprang from an acquisitive class of New Englanders and was keenly desirous of encouraging commerce and trade. He was devoted to "the protection of the great interests of our country—Agriculture, commerce and manufactures,"[54] and frequently advocated exclusive jurisdiction for the federal judiciary in all matters touching upon business transactions. A single example will serve to convey the exuberance of his nationalistic thinking along these lines. In a letter to his friend, Nathaniel Williams, dated February 22, 1815, he wrote:

Let us extend the national authority over the whole extent of power given by the Constitution. Let us have great military and naval schools; an adequate regular army ... [and] a permanent navy; a national bank; a national system of bankruptcy; a great navigation act; a general survey of our ports, and appointments of port wardens and pilots; Judicial courts which shall embrace the whole constitutional powers; national notaries; public and national justices of the peace, for the commercial and national concerns of the United States. By such enlarged and liberal institutions, the Government of the United States will be endeared to the people, and the factions of the Great States will be rendered harmless. Let us prevent the

[52] *Ibid.*, sec. 337, pp. 305–306. Objecting to Rawle's contention that a state was free to secede from the Union, Story countered with the argument that the doctrine of secession was inconsistent with the principle of majority rule, in that it allowed a single individual to subvert the government or a single state to defeat the will of the whole. But, he agreed, "The [whole] people of the United States have a right to abolish or alter the Constitution of the United States." *Ibid.*, sec. 359, p. 327.

[53] *Ibid.*, sec. 337, p. 306, n. 1. Gordon S. Wood contends that the Americans of 1787 rejected the Whig idea of a compact between the rulers and the ruled, and adopted instead the Lockean notion of a contract between individuals. But Wood has apparently not read Story on the Constitution. See *The Creation of the American Republic*, 601.

[54] Story to H. A. S. Dearborn, Sept. 19, 1844, Massachusetts Historical Society *Proceedings*, 2d Series, Vol. LIII (1919–20), 332.

possibility of a division, by creating great national interests which shall bind us in an indissoluble chain.[55]

On the high bench, Story consistently defended the jurisdiction of the federal judiciary over interstate commerce. Chief Justice Marshall is frequently believed to have launched federal supremacy in this area through his opinion in *Gibbons* v. *Ogden*,[56] but, as Charles Warren has noted, "Judge Story is possibly entitled to share in the glory of having aided in writing the opinion in *Gibbons* v. *Ogden*."[57] Warren bases his conclusion on the fact that Marshall, having dislocated a shoulder, was unable to complete the writing of the opinion. The following newspaper account in the *New York Commercial Advertiser*, March 3, 1824, confirms this view: "Inquiries are hourly made respecting the anxiously-looked-for decision of the Supreme Court in this important case. The opinion of the Court has not yet been given, nor do we know when it will be. Judge Marshall, we are informed, had commenced writing the opinion when his labors were interrupted by his unfortunate fall; and it is understood that Mr. Justice Story is now engaged in completing it."[58]

Whatever the nature of Story's contribution in the great steamboat monopoly case, it is clear enough that he supported Marshall's nationalistic interpretation of the commerce clause. In 1837, when *Gibbons* v. *Ogden* was weakened by Justice Barbour's opinion for the Court in *New York* v. *Miln*,[59] Story came

[55] Story, *Life and Letters*, I, 254.

[56] 9 Wheaton 1 (1824).

[57] *Supreme Court in United States History*, I, 608.

[58] As quoted, *ibid*. On February 19, 1824, Judge Story reported to his wife that "On our return home the Chief Justice had the misfortune to stumble over the cellar door of the house from the darkness, by which his shoulder was dislocated, and he received a blow on the head, which occasioned a concussion, that deprived him of his senses for a quarter of an hour. He has been in a good deal of pain all night, but is better this morning & I hope in a day or two will be able to resume his seat." (Story Papers, Texas.) By February 22, however, Marshall's condition had not greatly improved. "The Chief Justice is growing better," wrote Story to his wife, "but still very slowly, & it is somewhat doubtful if he will be able during the residue of the term to engage in active business." (Feb. 22, 1824, *ibid*.) Marshall finally recovered, however, and returned to the Court to deliver the opinion early in March. "The Chief Justice is well enough to health to resume his seat, though he wears his arm in a sling & will be obliged so to do for a long time. The Court is steadily advancing to its business, & we are so steadily engaged in consultations in preparing opinions, that I have no leisure. . . . The great Steam Boat case has been decided & [the] monopoly laws of New York have been declared unconstitutional. This has created a great sensation, though I suppose it hardly attracts much attention in Massachusetts. Mr. Burke very well observed that time and *distance* were very important considerations in all human affairs." (Story to Mrs. Story, Mar. 6, 1824, *ibid*.) The *Minutes of the Supreme Court*, February 1, 1790–August 14, 1828, National Archives, show that between February 19–March 1, the Chief Justice was not present. But he returned on March 2, the same day *Gibbons* v. *Ogden* was delivered.

[59] 11 Peters 102 (1837).

forward in defense of *Gibbons* v. *Ogden*. The problem presented was whether a New York statute requiring the master of a vessel to furnish information about his passengers was a police measure or an unconstitutional regulation of commerce. Building upon the "police power" doctrine introduced by Chief Justice Taney in the *Charles River Bridge* case, Justice Barbour construed the act as a valid exercise of state police power for the protection of the community against paupers and criminals, who were entering New York from foreign lands.

Barbour thought Marshall's opinion in *Gibbons* v. *Ogden* was inapplicable: no federal statute had been enacted conflicting with the New York law. Barbour therefore avoided the issue of whether Congress' power to regulate commerce was exclusive. It seemed reasonable to him that because the states could pass inspection and quarantine laws, that they could also protect themselves against the moral pestilence of vagabonds and "the physical pestilence which may arise from unsound and infectious articles imported, or from a ship, the crew of which may be laboring under an infectious disease."[60] Barbour noted that earlier decisions failed to define the limits of Congress' power to regulate commerce or what was considered as commerce with foreign nations, and thus he felt free to define the subjects of commerce under the control of the states. The states might legislate on any subject concerning "the welfare of the whole people of a state, or any individual within it; whether it respected them as men, or as citizens of the state; whether in their public or private relations; whether it related to the rights of persons, or of property, or the whole people of a state, or of any individual within it; and whose operation was within the territorial limits of the state, and upon the persons and things within its jurisdiction."[61]

Judge Story, dissenting, thought the ruling of the Court conflicted with Marshall's decisions in *Gibbons* v. *Ogden*[62] and *Brown* v. *Maryland*.[63] Whether or not Congress had enacted a statute in opposition to that passed by the New York legislature had little bearing on the case; for "The power given to Congress to regulate commerce with foreign nations, and among the states, has been deemed exclusive."[64] Story, then, deemed Congress' power over interstate commerce as an exclusive power and wished to go beyond the less nationalistic position of the great chief justice. In the *Gibbons* case, it will be recalled, Marshall did not actually hold that Congress possessed exclusive control of interstate commerce. He left the question open of whether, in the absence of federal regulation, the states had any concurrent power in this area.

[60] *Ibid.*, 142–43.
[61] *Ibid.*, 139.
[62] 9 Wheaton 1.
[63] 12 Wheaton 419 (1827). Justice Barbour "distinguished" the *Gibbons* and *Brown* cases from the issues before the Court.
[64] *New York* v. *Miln*, 11 Peters 158.

Proceeding with his dissent, Story advised his brothers to consider the harmful implications of their decision:

Now, if this act be constitutional . . . it will justify the States in regulating, controlling, and, in effect, interdicting the transportation of passengers from one State to another in steamboats and packets. They may levy a tax upon all such passengers; they may require bonds from the master that no such passengers shall become chargeable to the State; they may require such passengers to give bonds . . . they may authorize the immediate removal of such passengers back to the place from which they came. These would be most burdensome and inconvenient regulations respecting passengers.[65]

Although he spoke from a minority position in favoring exclusive federal control over interstate commerce, Story informed the Court that he was not alone in his extreme nationalism: "In this opinion I have the consolation to know that I had the entire concurrence, upon the same grounds, as that of that great constitutional jurist, the late Mr. Chief Justice Marshall."[66]

The Taney Court, however, was unable to resist Story's persistent nationalism, and in 1838, only a year after the *Miln* case, Story again found consolation by expanding federal commerce power in a new direction. The case was *United States* v. *Coombs*,[67] and it involved the Crimes Act of 1825, an act that Story had drafted and his friend Daniel Webster had pushed through the Congress.

The act provided for the punishment of various crimes against the United States and prohibited the theft of goods from wrecked or stranded ships. Coombs was indicted under this act for stealing a quantity of merchandise belonging to the ship *Bristol*, which was stranded on Rockaway Beach, New York. Coombs had taken the goods on the beach, above the high-water mark, and challenged the jurisdiction of the Court on the basis of Story's opinion in the *Thomas Jefferson* case in which Story had ruled that the admiralty jurisdiction of the federal courts was limited to the sea and the tidewaters.[68]

[65] *Ibid.*, 159.

[66] *Ibid.*, 161.

[67] 12 Peters 72 (1838).

[68] *The Thomas Jefferson*, 10 Wheaton 428 (1825). Not surprisingly, Story had followed the English rule then in force. "I am a great friend of the Admiralty jurisdiction," he told Judge Hopkinson, "because it is so full of equity. But I have no inclination to stretch it beyond its legitimate boundaries." (Dec. 22, 1834, Hopkinson Papers, HSP.) "Since receiving your recent letter I have read over the case of the Thomas Jefferson attentively," he wrote Hopkinson a year later. "I know, that it was fully & carefully considered by the whole court, & that it was watched with jealousy by one mind at least, hostile to adm[iralt]y Jurisdiction, Mr. Justice Johnson. There is nothing in that opinion, which I can, or desire to take back, if I could." (Jan. 3, 1835, *ibid.*) Story followed his ruling in the *Thomas Jefferson* case in *Hobart* v. *Drogan*, 10 Peters 108 (1836), and in *Steamboat Orleans* v. *Phoebus*, 11 Peters 175 (1837). All of these cases restricted federal jurisdiction and are generally regarded as an aberration in Story's nationalism. Yet, Story

Story admitted that "the authority of Congress under this clause does not extend to punish offenses committed above and beyond the high-water mark."[69] However, said Story, Congress had full authority to punish the theft of the goods under its commerce powers. "Under the clause of the Constitution giving power to Congress 'to regulate commerce with foreign nations and among the several States,' Congress possessed the power to punish offenses of the sort which are enumerated in the 9th section of the act of 1825."[70] The commerce power, he asserted, did "not stop at the mere boundary line of the State,"[71] and was not confined to acts committed upon the water. "Any offense which thus interferes with, obstructs, or prevents such commerce and navigation, though done on land, may be punished by Congress under its general authority to make all laws necessary and proper to execute their delegated constitutional powers."[72] Justice Story, as one commentator observed, had

---

had a reputation as being a nationalist in the area of admiralty jurisdiction, as witnessed by the following witticism popular in legal circles at the time, which had it that "if a bucket of water were brought into his court with a corn cob in it, he would at once extend the admiralty jurisdiction of the United States over it." (Note in *American Law Review*, Vol. XXXVII, [Nov.–Dec., 1903] 916.) In *Genesee Chief* v. *Fitzhugh*, 12 Howard 443 (1851), Chief Justice Taney abandoned Story's ruling in the *Thomas Jefferson* case and extended the jurisdiction of the federal courts to all the navigable waters of the United States. Justice Daniel dissented and "sharply stressed the novelty of the majority decision: 'I have at least the consolation—no small one it must be admitted—of the support of Marshall, Kent, and Story in any error I may have committed.'" (John P. Frank, *Justice Daniel Dissenting*, 224–25.) Story was generally regarded as the leading American authority in the field of maritime law. See the extensive and detailed correspondence on this subject from Story in the Hopkinson Papers, HSP, especially Story to Hopkinson, December 12, 1831, December 21, 1831, December 12, 1833, December 22, 1834, January 3, 1835, February 9, 1835; see also the letters of Chief Justice Marshall to Story in the Massachusetts Historical Society *Proceedings*, 2d Series, Vol. XIV, 325, 326, 333–34. For a discussion of "Story's aggrandizing efforts on behalf of admiralty" early in his judicial career, see Dunne, "Joseph Story: The Salem Years," *Essex Institute Historical Collections*, Vol. CI, No. 4 (Oct., 1965), 319–22. Story's greatest opinion in admiralty was that in *DeLovio* v. *Boit*, 2 Gallison 398, 7 Federal Cases 418, No. 3,766 (1815). Here, he held that a contract of marine insurance, no matter where executed, was subject to the admiralty jurisdiction. Story spent over a month writing this scholarly and extensive opinion. He amassed all the learning upon the question accessible at the time. In 1870, Justice Bradley, while sustaining the *DeLovio* decision in *Insurance Co.* v. *Dunham*, 11 Wallace 36, remarked: "The learned and exhaustive opinion of Justice Story, in the case of *DeLovio* v. *Boit* . . . has never been answered, and will always stand as a monument of his erudition."

[69] *United States* v. *Coombs*, 12 Peters 78.

[70] *Ibid.*

[71] *Ibid.*

[72] *Ibid.*

"adopted an interpretation of the Commerce Clause which in breadth of congressional power has been rivaled only by decisions in the last two generations."[73]

As the *Tyson* case demonstrates, Story was also desirous of placing banking activities and other related commercial transactions involving the flow and exchange of money under federal supervision. Story was a banker of sorts himself, having served as president of the Merchant's Bank of Salem between 1815 and 1835 and as vice president of the Salem Savings Bank from 1818 until 1830. During his political career in the Massachusetts legislature, he had exerted his influence to obtain acts of incorporation for the State Bank in Boston and the Merchant's Bank of Salem,[74] and thereafter was instrumental in improving the scruples of the Merchant's Bank by eliminating its usurious practices.[75] A supporter of the National Bank, his dissent in *Briscoe* v. *Bank of Kentucky*[76] was to be expected. Here, the Court, speaking through Justice McLean, upheld the right of a state-controlled and state-chartered bank to issue notes of credit.

The case turned on the definition of "bills of credit," which states were forbidden to issue by article 1, section 10 of the Constitution. Justice McLean defined a bill of credit as paper issued by a state, which contained a pledge of its faith and was designed to circulate as money. He conceded that the notes of the Kentucky bank circulated as money and were receivable on public account, but in all other particulars they differed from the bills of credit prohibited by the Constitution. On their face they did not purport to be issued by the state, but by the president and directors of the bank, who, though appointed by the legislature, did not assume to act as agents of the state. Nor did the notes contain a pledge of the faith of the state in any form. Furthermore, the funds of the bank were derived from the state in part only, and the bank could sue and be sued like any private corporation. McLean therefore concluded that the Kentucky act establishing the bank was a constitutional exercise of state power, and that the notes issued by the bank were not bills of credit within the meaning of the prohibition of the Constitution.

Judge Story protested this flagrant evasion of Chief Justice Marshall's hold-

[73] Haines, *The Role of the Supreme Court*, 329.

[74] J. W. Treadwell to William W. Story, Aug. 25, 1847, *Life and Letters*, I, 205. See also Gerald T. Dunne, "Mr. Justice Story and the American Law of Banking," *American Journal of Legal History*, Vol. V (1961), 205–30; and Dunne, "Joseph Story: The Great Term," *Harvard Law Review*, Vol. LXXIX, No. 5 (Mar., 1966), 881.

[75] Treadwell to W. Story, August 25, 1847, *Life and Letters*, I, 205–206. "Judge Story was always an able financier, and from the incorporation of the Merchant's Bank he was a Director, and for many years President; and under his advice, all those illegal and usurious practices then common were discarded and it became a model bank." From the scrapbook of Story eulogies prepared by Simon Greenleaf, as quoted in Bauer, *Commentaries on the Constitution*, 160–61, n. 178.

[76] 11 Peters 257 (1837).

ing in *Craig* v. *Missouri*.[77] As Marshall had explained, bills of credit included any kind of paper intended to circulate as money. Said Story: "The form of the instrument is wholly immaterial. It is the substance we are to look to; the question is, whether it is issued, and is negotiable, and is designed to circulate as currency."[78]

He was willing to accept the issuance of state bank notes by private corporations, private partnerships, or private persons, but here it was abundantly clear that the state of Kentucky was an active participant. "That a State may rightfully evade the prohibition of the Constitution, by acting through the instrumentality of the agents in the evasion, instead of acting in its own direct name, and thus escape from all its constitutional obligations, is a doctrine to which I can never subscribe, and which, for the honor of the country, for the good faith and integrity of the States, for the cause of sound morals and of political and civil liberty, I hope may never be established."[79]

Story reminded his brethren that when this cause was originally argued before the Court a majority of the judges, including Chief Justice Marshall, were decidedly of the opinion that the Kentucky statute was unconstitutional and void. Story pleaded with the Court to join him out of a "profound reverence and affection for the dead"[80] in vindicating the memory of Marshall and to defend the Constitution against state transgression. Had Marshall been living, "he would have spoken in the joint names of both of us. I am sensible that I have not done that justice to his opinion which his own great mind and exalted talents would have. But with all the imperfections of my own efforts, I hope that I have shown that there were solid grounds on which to rest his exposition of the Constitution."[81] But Marshall was gone, and the Taney Court, so it seemed to Story, had turned a deaf ear to the voice of the dead. The doctrines of the Marshall era were to be re-examined in a more favorable light respecting state powers.

Story was the author of the Bankruptcy Act that Congress enacted (despite substantial opposition from the states' rightists) in 1841.[82] Soon called upon to interpret its provisions, Judge Story responded in his usual tropistic manner

---

[77] 4 Peters 410 (1830). The *Craig* case was "distinguished" by Justice McLean. There, Marshall had held that a bill of credit signifies "a paper medium intended to circulate between individuals, and between government and individuals, for the ordinary purposes of society."

[78] *Briscoe* v. *Bank of Kentucky*, 11 Peters 331.

[79] *Ibid.*, 340–41.

[80] *Ibid.*, 350.

[81] *Ibid.*

[82] Story, *Life and Letters*, II, 407. The act was later repealed. Story had been warmly interested in the passage of a bankruptcy bill as early as 1815. (See Story to Henry Wheaton, Dec. 13, 1815, *ibid.*, I, 271. See also Story to Stephen White, Feb. 27, 1820, *ibid.*, 382–83; Story to William Fettyplace, Feb. 28, 1821, *ibid.*, 396–97.) Story's despondency

by vindicating federal primacy. The question raised in *Ex Parte Christy*[83] was whether the Bankruptcy Act authorized district courts to revise state court proceedings in equity relating to the property of bankrupts.

Story, delivering the opinion of the Court, admitted that before the passage of the Bankruptcy Act, the district courts had no equity jurisdiction, since none had been conferred upon them by Congress. But "The obvious design of the Bankruptcy Act," he declared, "was to secure a prompt and effectual administration and settlement of the estate within a limited period. For this purpose it was indispensable that an entire system adequate to that end should be provided by Congress, capable of being worked out through the instrumentality of its own courts."[84] To accomplish this end, Congress had clothed the federal courts with broad powers and jurisdiction. Story therefore concluded that by the terms of the Bankruptcy Act, district courts were permitted to inquire into the validity of liens or mortgages on the property of bankrupts.

Earlier Story had had other opportunities to expound upon the Bankruptcy Act while riding circuit. In *Ex Parte Foster*[85] he upheld the jurisdiction of the

---

at the defeat of an earlier bankruptcy bill, revealed in the last two letters above, was more pronounced in his letter to Rev. John Brazer, February 4, 1827, *ibid.*, 514: "The bankrupt bill has been lost, and under circumstances which will forbid any attempt to revive it for many years. . . . It interferes with State policy, pride, and prejudice; with the interests of some, with the political expectations of others; with the anti-federalism of others; and above all, with that mass of public opinion. . . . I have always had some confidence that a bankrupt law would be passed, but I now begin to believe that the power will, in the National Government, forever remain a dead letter."

[83] 3 Howard 292 (1845).

[84] *Ibid.*, 312. To his son Story wrote: "Yesterday I delivered the opinion of the Court in a great Bankrupt case from New Orleans, embracing the question of the nature and extent of the jurisdiction of the District Court in matters of bankruptcy. It was an elaborate review of the whole statute, and we sustained the jurisdiction of the District Court over all matters whatsoever, and recognized (as indeed was one of the points) the right of the Court to grant an injunction to proceedings and suits in the State courts. The opinion covers the whole ground in Ex Parte Foster, and also in the New Hampshire cases which have been so stoutly contested in the State courts. . . . I took great pains about it, and the Court fully confirmed all my views. Judge Catron alone dissented." To William W. Story, Jan. 1, 1845, *Life and Letters*, II, 509.

[85] 2 Story 121, 9 Federal Cases 508, No. 4,960 (1842). The day before he delivered his opinion in the *Foster* case, Story wrote to Senator John Berrien: "The Bankrupt Act works well. The Courts, at least in my Circuit, are working through all the difficulties incident to the new system. Many interesting questions have arisen in argument, and have been disposed of. I do not hesitate to say that the system is far less defective than the hasty examiner might suppose; and if Congress will let it alone for another year, and leave the Courts to adjust the machinery, probe the defects, and dispel some of the supposed embarrassments which must in all new systems arise in giving them practical operation, I am persuaded that the system will grow popular, and will be one of the most lasting benefits ever conferred upon our country." Apr. 29, 1842, *Life and Letters*, II, 404–405. See also Story to Judge Pitman, Feb. 20, 1842, *ibid.*, 416.

federal courts in determining whether district courts could enjoin state court interpretations on the question of whether creditors were authorized under the Bankruptcy Act to attach mesne profits. Reversing state court decisions, Story held that district courts possessed the full jurisdiction of a court of equity over cases involving bankruptcy. This ruling was unacceptable to Chief Justice Parker of the New Hampshire Supreme Court,[86] and for three years Story and Parker were engaged in a vigorous struggle over this question of jurisdiction, a struggle which the United States Supreme Court finally settled in the case of *Peck* v. *Jenness*.[87]

Certainly Story's training in the English common law provided an additional motivation for resisting the doctrines of states' rights. It is true that by 1835, Story had begun to question the desirability of greater uniformity in the common law, but he never abandoned the idea that the Supreme Court should independently encourage a uniform system of jurisprudence regarding commerce. Seven years prior to the writing of his opinion in the *Tyson* case, Story had wistfully written in a law article:

What a magnificent spectacle will it be to witness the establishment of such a beautiful system of juridical ethics,—to realize, not the oppressive schemes of holy alliances in a general conspiracy against the rights of mankind, but the universal empire of a juridical reason, mingling with the concerns of commerce throughout the world, and imparting its beneficent light to the dark regions of the poles, and the soft and luxurious climates of the tropics. Then, indeed, would be realized the splendid visions of Cicero, dreaming over the majestic fragments of his perfect republic and Hooker's sublime personification of the law would stand forth almost as embodied truth.[88]

He lamented that "American jurisprudence can never acquire a homogeneous character" and that the legal profession might "become devoted to mere State jurisprudence, and abandon those more enlightened and extensive researches which form the accomplished scholar, and elevate the refined jurist." But, he added, "The establishment of the national government, and of courts

---

[86] In *Kittredge* v. *Warren*, 14 New Hampshire 507 (1844), Chief Justice Parker ignored Story's opinion, and held that an attachment of property upon mesne process, made before proceedings under the Bankruptcy Act, was a valid lien under New Hampshire law. In *In re Bellows*, 3 Story 428, 3 Federal Cases 138, No. 1,278 (1844), Story reaffirmed his holding in the *Foster* case. Chief Justice Parker retaliated in *Kittredge* v. *Emerson*, 15 New Hampshire 227 (1844), again repudiating Story's broad view of federal power, which held that federal courts could enjoin the procedure and judgments of state courts. Parker ignored Story's opinion in *Ex Parte Christy*, 3 Howard 292, in *Peck* v. *Jenness*, 16 New Hampshire 516 (1845).

[87] 7 Howard 612 (1849). Justice Grier upheld Story's view that district courts had exclusive jurisdiction over all suits and proceedings in bankruptcy, but deferred to Parker and ruled that the suit pending before the court for common pleas was not a suit in bankruptcy.

[88] *Past History, Present State, and Future Prospects*, 24.

to exercise its constitutional jurisdiction, will, it is hoped, in this respect, operate with a salutary influence."[89]

Toward these goals Story proceeded, and though he failed to achieve them through the *Tyson* case, his cause was a noble cause: to erect an enlightened system of jurisprudence across the North American continent, so that the free-enterprise system might progress in the same spirit of honesty and justice as did his Merchant's Bank in Salem. In their proclivity toward parochialism, poorly trained judges in the state courts, he feared, were too seldom concerned with the universal truths of ancient law and common law and too often inclined to truckle to the will of a people not fully cognizant of their common law rights and duties and their legal heritage.

This same distrust of state courts and desire for uniform rules are discernible in Story's unpopular opinion in *Prigg* v. *Pennsylvania*,[90] which Story delivered along with the *Tyson* case in 1842. The case presented the question of whether a state could enforce the Fugitive Slave Act of 1793 concurrently with the federal government. The constitutional provisions relating to the return of runaway slaves were general, stating simply that slaves escaping from one state to another were to be delivered up to the owner. The Fugitive Slave Act had been enacted to strengthen this provision and to clarify the many difficulties accompanying it, by authorizing the arrest of fugitive slaves and the adjudication of their legal status before federal, state, or municipal courts, whose judges were empowered to issue certificates for the removal of the slave.

In 1826 the state of Pennsylvania enacted a statute to supplement the federal act by providing heavy penalties for persons seizing or removing Negroes who had not been adjudged fugitives from service. Prigg, the agent of a slave owner in Maryland, was indicted under this act for removing a fugitive slave and a child born to her during her absence from Maryland, without obtaining a proper certificate from the Pennsylvania courts.

Should state courts be entrusted with administering the explosive issue of slavery? Absolutely not, argued the spokesman for the Court, Mr. Justice Story. Congress alone was responsible for carrying out the fugitive slave provision of the Constitution, and Congress had covered the whole ground of authority through the Fugitive Slave Act. Not only was Congress' power exclusive, said Story, but it was so exclusive that the states, because they possessed no authority in this area, were under no compulsion to enforce the fugitive slave clause in their courts.

Furthermore, enumerated the Judge, uniformity of legislation and enforcement were requisites which only the national government could provide: "the nature of the provision and the objects to be attained by it require that it should be controlled by one and the same will, and act uniformly by the same system

[89] *Ibid.*, 35.
[90] 16 Peters 539 (1842).

of regulations throughout the Union. If, then, the States have a right, in the absence of legislation by Congress, to act upon the subject, each State is at liberty to prescribe just such regulations as suit its own policy, local convenience, and local feelings."[91] Story emphasized that the Court's invalidation of the Pennsylvania statute should not be interpreted as an abridgment of State police power, as the States "possess full jurisdiction to arrest and restrain runaway slaves, and remove them from their borders."[92] So long as the states did not "interfere with or obstruct the just rights of the owner to reclaim his slave,"[93] they were free to prescribe regulations for the protection of the population against Negro fugitives.[94]

[91] *Ibid.*, 623. William R. Leslie contends that Story's theory of the conflict of laws, which he interprets as meaning that "no person had any rights acquired in another jurisdiction which any court was bound to respect," was the underlying basis of Story's extreme nationalism in the *Prigg* case. This was the English rule, which Story had long admired. Leslie further argues that Story's theory was adopted by Chief Justice Taney in the *Dred Scott* case, and concludes that "It is indeed unjust to belittle Story's stature as a jurist by giving to Taney any of the credit for establishing in this country the principle by which Dred Scott was denied his freedom according to the law of Missouri and of the United States." ("The Influence of Joseph Story's Theory of the Conflict of Laws on Constitutional Nationalism," *Mississippi Valley Historical Review*, Vol. XXXV, No. 2 [Sept., 1948], 212, 220.) Note that as early as 1820, in his dissent in *Houston* v. *Moore*, 5 Wheaton 1, Story had argued that state courts were not obliged to enforce federal laws. In *Testa* v. *Katt*, 220 U.S. 386 (1947), Justice Black, speaking for a unanimous Court, rejected the notion that state courts were not bound to enforce federal criminal law. Such a notion, said Black, ignored the supremacy clause and flew "in the face of the fact that the States of the Union constitute a nation." The *Prigg* case was overruled *sub silentio*.

[92] *Prigg* v. *Pennsylvania*, 16 Peters 625.

[93] *Ibid.*

[94] Not long after he delivered the opinion for the Court in the *Prigg* case, Story wrote to John Berrien of Georgia, who at that time was chairman of the Senate Judiciary Committee. After discussing at some length their collaborative efforts concerning current and prospective legislation dealing with bankruptcy and the criminal jurisdiction of the federal courts, Story turned to the question of fugitive slaves. "In the MSS Bill, which I handed you," he wrote, "the provision was *general*, that *in all cases*, where by the Laws of the U. States, powers were conferred on State Magistrates, the same powers might be exercised by Commissioners appointed by the Circuit Courts. I was induced to make the provision thus general, because State Magistrates now generally refuse to act, & cannot be compelled to act; and the Act of 1793 respecting fugitive slaves confers the power on States Magistrates to act in delivering up Slaves. You saw, in the case of Prigg . . . how the duty was evaded, or declined. In conversing with several of my Brethren on the Supreme Court, we all thought that it would be a great improvement, & would tend much to facilitate the recapture of Slaves, if Commissioners of the Circuit Court were clothed with like powers. This might be done without creating the slightest sensation in Congress, if the provision were made general. . . . It would then pass without observation. The Courts would appoint commissioners in every county, & thus meet the practical difficulty now presented by the refusal of State Magistrates. It might be unwise to provoke debate to insert a Special clause in the first section, referring to the fugitive Slave Act of 1793. Suppose you add at the end of the first section: '& shall & may exercise all the powers, that any State

Story's opinions, particularly in the *Prigg*, *Tyson*, and *Miln* cases, seem to discount the possibility of cooperation between the national and state governments and rigidly divide jurisdictions into compartments, nearly always at the expense of state power. It is no exaggeration to say they do not embody the spirit of federalism and imply a continual aggrandizement of the political state. Extreme though Story's nationalism was, however, it had its limits. Story's main concern was the independence and supremacy of the judiciary. His nationalism was primarily judicial nationalism. His support of presidential and congressional power was strong at times, but lacked consistency. He was quick to assert the judicial prerogative when it was threatened by either of its opposing branches, and, in the latter years of his judgeship, tended increasingly to construe executive and legislative powers more narrowly, half-aware, perhaps, that the formidable powers he had helped to establish might be used against the interests he sought to protect with those powers.

In *Schooner Orono*,[95] decided in 1812, Story, though only recently appointed to the Court, evinced his independence of mind by rebuffing President Madison's bid to reinstate the embargo. The case presented the legal effect of Madison's proclamation for the revival of the embargo system against Great Britain. Such action on the part of the president was not specifically authorized by the act of Congress. Could it be inferred from the enumerated power to suspend the embargo? Story, who had earlier led the fight against the embargo system, did not hesitate. He professed "the most entire respect"[96] for the executive, but with "reluctance"[97] was forced to interpret his powers narrowly.

"I take it to be an incontestable principle," declared the youthful appointee, "that the President has no common law prerogative to interdict commercial intercourse with any nation; or to revive any act, whose operation has expired. His authority for this purpose must be derived from some positive law; and when that is once found to exist, the Court have nothing to do with the manner and circumstances under which it is exercised."[98] The editor of the Federalist newspaper who had predicted in 1808 that Story would "never submit to become a back stairs minion of Executive influence"[99] as a member of Congress

judge, Magistrate, or Justice of the Peace may exercise under any other Law or Laws of the United States.' . . . I hope you will excuse me for the liberty I have taken in making these suggestions. They are dictated solely by the desire to further a true administration of public Justice." (Apr. 29, 1842, John Macpherson Berrien Papers, Southern Historical Collection, University of North Carolina.) William W. Story omitted this portion of the letter in *Life and Letters*, II, 404-405.

[95] 1 Gallison 137, 18 Federal Cases 530, No. 10,585 (1812).

[96] *Ibid.*

[97] *Ibid.*, 531.

[98] *Ibid.*, 530.

[99] As quoted in Warren, *Supreme Court in United States History*, I, 418.

must have been doubly pleased with Story's reassertion of independence on the high court at the expense of Jefferson's successor.

In evaluating Story's nationalism, the rarely discussed case of *Brown* v. *United States*[100] is highly significant in that it dramatically establishes Story as the leading advocate of the school of loose construction very early in the Marshall era. Moreover, it contradicts the frequently asserted, but utterly groundless, assumption that Story was the mere echo of the great chief justice. *Brown* v. *United States*, [101] decided in 1814, came before the Court on an appeal from Story's circuit, where Story had upheld the seizure of British property at the commencement of the War of 1812 by an agent of the executive.

Reversing Story's ruling, Chief Justice Marshall held that the executive's power to confiscate enemy property was an expressed, not an implied power. To be valid, the seizure and condemnation must be authorized by an act of Congress, and no such act had been passed. The declaration of war by Congress could not, said Marshall, "in itself, enact a confiscation of the property of the enemy within the territory of the belligerent,"[102] and the members of the Court were entirely satisfied that the seizure could not be sustained.

Judge Story, however, was not at all satisfied. He offered an extended, scholarly dissent in defense of his circuit decision, insisting that Marshall had misconstrued the common law, the law of nations, and the Constitution. Indeed, said Story, "If the principles of British prize law go further, I am free to say that I consider them as the law of this country."[103] Under the rules of international law, Story argued, the sovereign's subjects "may lawfully seize hostile property in their own defense, and are bound to secure, for the use of the sovereign, all hostile property which falls into their hands."[104] Furthermore, under the war powers of the president, the power of the executive to confiscate enemy property did not depend upon specific legislative authorization, but could be implied from the declaration of war and the duty of the president to enforce the laws of the land. Congress, too, could have authorized the confiscation of property under its power to declare war:

The power to declare war, in my opinion, includes all the powers incident to war, and necessary to carry it into effect. . . . If they [Congress] should authorize the executive "to provide and maintain a navy," it seems to me as clear that he must have the incidental power to make rules for its government. In truth, it is by no means infrequent in the Constitution to add clauses of a special nature to general

100 8 Cranch 110 (1814).

101 *Ibid.*

102 *Ibid.*, 127. It is interesting to note that the attorney general submitted Story's circuit opinion as the government's defense. See *ibid.*, 121.

103 *Ibid.*, 135.

104 *Ibid.*

powers which embrace them, and to provide affirmatively for certain powers, without meaning thereby to negative the existence of powers of a more general nature.[105]

Five years prior to Chief Justice Marshall's decision in *McCulloch* v. *Maryland*,[106] then, Judge Story had already proclaimed the doctrine of implied powers. But more than that, Story went beyond "John Marshall's most comprehensive exposition of the American constitutional system,"[107] by asserting that implied powers did not depend solely upon enumerated powers for their validity, but might be inferred from the "resulting" powers of government.

Four years after his dissent in *Brown* v. *United States*,[108] Story retreated to a more moderate position regarding presidential power in *Gelston* v. *Hoyt*,[109] in which he "strikingly reaffirmed the cardinal principle of the Anglo-Saxon system of the law that no man—not even the President of the United States—is above the law."[110] The problems that Story was asked to resolve concerned the jurisdiction of the Supreme Court and executive power. Revenue officers, who had been sued for damages for seizing a vessel under the neutrality laws, claimed their act was authorized by the express order of the president. Hoyt

---

[105] *Ibid.*, 150. Story also thought "that no subject can commence hostilities or capture property of an enemy, when the sovereign has prohibited it. But suppose he did, I would ask if the sovereign may not ratify his proceedings, and thus by a retrospective operation give validity to them." This statement in Story's dissent was later cited by Justice Grier in *The Prize Cases*, 67 U.S. 635 (1863), as authority for upholding President Lincoln's blockade of southern ports, which Lincoln had undertaken without a formal declaration of war by the Congress.

[106] 4 Wheaton 316 (1819).

[107] Alfred H. Kelly and Winfred A. Harbison, *The American Constitution: Its Origins and Development*, 288. Edward Corwin, who frequently relies upon Story's *Commentaries on the Constitution*, makes this observation: "the latitudinarian conception of 'the judicial power of the United States' was . . . severely restrained by Marshall's conception of some of the [enumerated powers] as set forth in his *McCulloch* v. *Maryland* opinion: This asserts that 'the sword and the purse, all the external relations, and no inconsiderable portion of the industry of the nation, are intrusted to its government'; he characterizes 'the power of making war,' of 'levying taxes,' and of 'regulating commerce' as 'great, substantive and independent powers'; and the power conferred by the 'necessary and proper' clause embraces, he declares, 'all legislative means which are appropriate' to carry out 'the legitimate ends' of the Constitution, unless forbidden by 'the letter and spirit of the Constitution.' Nine years later, Marshall introduced what Story in his *Commentaries* labels the concept of 'resulting powers,' those which 'rather be a result from the whole mass of the powers of the National Government, and from the nature of political society, than a consequence or incident of the powers especially enumerated.' Story's reference is to Marshall's opinion in *American Insurance Company* v. *Canter*, 1 Peters 511 (1828)." Corwin also notes that Story employed the theory of resulting powers in his Prigg decision. (*The Constitution of the United States*, 71–72.)

[108] 8 Cranch 110.

[109] 3 Wheaton 246 (1818).

[110] Warren, *Supreme Court in United States History*, I, 474.

contended that the Supreme Court had no jurisdiction over the case, as the state court had ruled in his favor, the court of errors had affirmed this decision, and the record was no longer in the possession of the court of last resort.

Story, for the Court, held that a writ of error under the Judiciary Act of 1789 could be directed to any court wherein the record could be found, and that if the record had been remitted by the highest court to another court of the state, it could be brought by the writ of error from that court. The writ being properly granted, Story held that United States courts had exclusive jurisdiction over questions of forfeiture under laws of the national government.

Turning to the statute under which the revenue officers justified their act, Story observed that the act merely stipulated that the president was authorized to employ land and naval forces in the seizure and detention of ships. The act did not authorize civil officers to carry out the provisions of this law, concluded Story, and President Madison's order was therefore illegal. "It is certainly against the general theory of our institutions to create great discretionary powers by implication, and in the present instance we see nothing to justify it."[111]

In 1827, however, in *Martin* v. *Mott*,[112] Story returned to his doctrine of implied powers enunciated in the *Brown* case and upheld the right of the president to use his discretion in ascertaining whether the exigencies contemplated in the Constitution justified calling forth the militia. One Jacob Mott, a private in the New York militia, had failed to enter the service of the United States as ordered by the governor of his state, who was acting in pursuance of a requisition by the president. Mott was convicted under court-martial for disobeying the order. He raised some nineteen objections to his conviction, all of which were swept aside by Judge Story, who spoke for a unanimous Court.

Congress, acting under its constitutional powers, had authorized the president in an act of 1795 "to call forth such number of the militia . . . as he may judge necessary to repel such invasion,"[113] and Story interpreted this to mean that "the authority to decide whether the exigency has arisen, belongs exclusively to the President."[114] The exclusiveness of the power, argued Story, "necessarily results from the nature of the power itself,"[115] and it was clearly evident that Congress intended the power to be an emergency power of the executive, to be exercised "under circumstances which may be vital to the existence of the Union."[116]

In the final years of his public career, Story again asserted the superiority of

---

[111] 3 Wheaton, 332–33.
[112] 12 Wheaton 19 (1827).
[113] *Ibid.*, 29.
[114] *Ibid.*, 30.
[115] *Ibid.*
[116] *Ibid.*

the Court over the executive branch in *United States* v. *Dickson.*[117] Here, United States Treasury officers had ruled in an ex parte proceeding against one Dickson that a congressional statute regarding commissions to receivers of public money should be construed in a fashion favorable to the department's accounting procedures. In a suit to recover commission and salary under this statute, Dickson was awarded judgment in a circuit court, which interpreted the act in favor of Dickson, upon a different system of accounting than that employed by the Treasury Department.

Judge Story held for the Court that the Treasury's method of keeping accounts had no effect upon the compensation allowed by law to public officers. "The construction given to the laws by any department of the executive department," observed Story, "is necessarily *ex parte*, without the benefit of an opposing argument . . . and when the construction is once given, there is no opportunity to question or revise it. . . . It is not to be forgotten that ours is a government of laws and not of men; and that the judicial department has imposed upon it, by the constitution, the solemn duty to interpret the laws."[118] Story therefore upheld the circuit court ruling, asserting that that court's interpretation of the statute was more analogous to the intent of Congress than the interpretation offered by the Treasury Department.

There were moments, too, when Story hesitated to interpret broadly the powers of Congress if they encroached upon the ramparts of the judicial stronghold that he stoutly defended. Significantly, Story dissented on this very issue during his last days on the Court. This was the case of *Cary* v. *Curtis,*[119] in which Justice Daniel upheld for the Court an act of Congress requiring customs officials to place all money, which they received for unascertained duties paid under protest, to the credit of the Treasury Department. Justice Daniel held that under this act, an action against the collector of customs duties for the return of such duties would not be entertained, as the act required the collector to turn the money over to the Treasury Department.

From this ruling Story dissented on the ground that the act deprived a citizen of his right to go to court to recover monies illegally collected. The gravamen of the issue, he contended, was "Whether Congress have a right to take from the citizen all right of action in any court to recover back money claimed illegally, and extorted by compulsion, by its officers under color of law, but without any legal authority, and thus to deny them all remedy for an admitted wrong, and to clothe the secretary of the treasury with the sole and exclusive authority to withhold or restore that money according to his own notions of justice or right?"[120]

[117] 15 Peters 141 (1841).
[118] *Ibid.*, 161. See also *Decatur* v. *Paulding*, 14 Peters 497 (1840).
[119] 3 Howard 236 (1844).
[120] *Ibid.*, 252.

Such an act, Story insisted, not only took away from state and national courts their right to interpret the laws by giving executive functionaries final and summary judgment in the collection of all duties, but flagrantly violated the principle of separation of powers. This is "a government where the three great departments, legislative, executive, and judicial, had independent duties to perform"; but, he complained, "the judicial power, designed by the constitution to be the final and appellate jurisdiction to interpret our laws, is superseded in its most vital and important functions."[121]

Only when weighing the legislative powers of the national government against those of the states did Story tend to tip the scales in favor of Congress. Indeed, in vindicating the supremacy of the national government upon questions involving the distribution of powers in the federal system, Story resolutely supported Congress, but again, only with the disapprobation of his less nationalist-minded brethren, who frequently took a dim view of his sweeping constitutional doctrines.

Houston v. *Moore*[122] serves to illustrate once again that in spite of Story's general success in winning a majority of the Court to his view, he often stood alone, stubbornly urging the Court to broaden the base of its jurisdiction. In the *Houston* case, the Court upheld a Pennsylvania statute passed in 1814, which provided that officers and privates of the state militia refusing to serve when called into service upon an order of the president were liable to the penalties defined in the Act of Congress of 1795. Houston, a private in the Pennsylvania militia, was ordered out by the governor in pursuance of a requisition from the president, on July 4, 1814. He neglected to march with his detachment to the appointed place of rendezvous, and was tried and found guilty under the Pennsylvania act. Houston pleaded that the act was unconstitutional.

Justice Washington, on behalf of the Court, admitted that the states had no jurisdiction over members of a nationalized militia and also that Congress had fully exercised its powers over the state militias, by providing through law for the calling forth, organizing, and disciplining of state military personnel in the service of the United States. Washington thought, however, that when called into service, the members of the state militia could not be considered as being in the service until they had mustered at the place of rendezvous. Until that time the states retained concurrent jurisdiction over their militia, and might therefore punish Houston for disobeying the call to action.

In a lengthy, carefully worded dissent, Story rejected the opinion of the Court, asserting the exclusiveness of federal power over state militia who were in the service of the national government. The act of the Pennsylvania legislature, which inflicted the same penalties for the same acts of disobedience as

121 *Ibid.*, 253.
122 5 Wheaton 1 (1820).

Congress' act of 1795, was "an exercise of concurrent authority where the laws of Congress have constitutionally denied it."[123] Federal jurisdiction did not commence at the place of rendezvous, he insisted, but at the call of the president. Although Congress had neglected to provide federal tribunals of court-martial, there was no ground for supposing a resulting trust reposed in the state tribunals to enforce the powers of Congress. "It cannot be pretended," argued Story,

that the states have retained any power to enforce fines and penalties created by the laws of the United States in virtue of their general sovereignty, for that sovereignty did not originally attach on such subjects. They sprung from the Union, and had no previous existence. It would be a strange anomaly in our national jurisprudence to hold the doctrine, that because a new power created by the Constitution of the United States was not exercised to its full extent, therefore the states might exercise it by a sort of process in aid.[124]

The state and federal governments ought to enforce their own penal laws, in their own tribunals. Failure to abide by this principle, Story suspected, would lead to deleterious consequences. How, for example, could the president pardon someone punished by a state? "For if the State legislature can . . . by its own enactment, make it a state offense, the pardoning power of the state can alone purge away such an offense."[125] Or again, "if the state can re-enact the same penalties, it may enact penalties substantially different for the same offense, to be adjudged in its own courts."[126] For these reasons, Story thought the Pennsylvania act should be struck down. From the time Houston was called forth by the president, he was *ab initio* employed in the service of the United States, within the meaning of both the Constitution and the act of 1795.

THE ROAD TO LEVIATHAN

Stripped of their legal covering, Story's opinions on the subject of separation of powers and states' rights reveal the mind of a man with a "mystical sense of nationalism,"[127] who is consumed by the menace of an unrestrained democracy. Like Marshall he considered democracy as something of a euphemism for mob rule and looked upon most elected politicians as unprincipled opportunists, catering to the base emotions of a rowdy populace.[128] He would save

[123] *Ibid.*, 72.
[124] *Ibid.*, 68.
[125] *Ibid.*, 72.
[126] *Ibid.*, 73.
[127] Dunne, "Joseph Story: The Salem Years," *Essex Institute Historical Collections*, Vol. CI, No. 4 (Oct., 1965), 318.
[128] Marshall spoke contemptuously of "the democracy in Virginia" (Marshall to Story, May 27, 1819, Massachusetts Historical Society *Proceedings*, 2d Series, Vol. XIV, 325), and remarked in 1828 that he "had not voted for upwards of twenty years" (Marshall to

men from anarchy and despotism by adherence to the principle of a just order under rule of law. The idea that popular rule was compatible with rule of law seemed unreal to him.

Over and over the state legislatures as well as state courts would verify his solid conviction that the people, their representatives, and their untrained judges were bent upon destroying personal liberty; and with each legislative assault on prescriptive rights and natural law principles of justice, Story hastily erected the judiciary as an unsurmountable barrier of liberty. He fought, for example, against state interference with freedom of religion,[129] the rights and duties of property and contract,[130] the rules and principles of trade and commerce,[131] the regulation and control of the militia,[132] and the rights of inheritance.[133]

He was no less unsympathetic toward Congress and the president if the powers of the judiciary were at stake. Without balance in government, there can be no true law; and without law, no liberty. The judiciary, he believed, was the weakest branch, and Thomas Jefferson its strongest foe. "Mr. Jefferson stands at the head of the enemies of the Judiciary," he once wrote,

and I doubt not will leave behind him a numerous progeny bred in the same school. The truth is and cannot be disguised, even from vulgar observation, that the Judiciary in our country is essentially feeble, and must always be open to attack

---

Story, May 1, 1828, *ibid.*, 336). Marshall strongly favored property qualifications for voters (see Marshall to Story, June 11 and July 13, 1829, *ibid.*, 339–40), and confessed to Story on one occasion that the Constitution "is a subject on which we concur exactly. Our opinions on it are, I believe, identical." (Dec. 25, 1832, *ibid.*, 352). Like Story, Marshall had an early courtship with liberalism, recalling during his youth "the wild and enthusiastic democracy with which my political opinions of the day were tinctured. . . . I sincerely believed human liberty to depend in a great measure on the success of the French Revolution." (John Marshall, *Autobiographical Sketch*, 9, 13.) Arthur N. Holcombe concludes that Marshall was a " 'genuine Conservative' rather than a 'reactionary Rightist.' " ("John Marshall as Politician and Political Theorist," *Chief Justice John Marshall* [ed. by W. Melville Jones], 35.) See also the observations of Beveridge, *Life of Marshall*, IV, 461–518. Robert Kenneth Faulkner offers the unusual thesis that Marshall was a "Lockean Liberal" defending a "Lockean Constitution." *Jurisprudence of John Marshall*, 193–226.

[129] *Terrett* v. *Taylor*, 9 Cranch 43 (1815); *Vidal* v. *Girard's Executors*, 2 Howard 227 (1844).

[130] *Terrett* v. *Taylor*, 9 Cranch 43; *Town of Pawlet* v. *Clark*, 9 Cranch 292 (1815); *Trustees of Dartmouth College* v. *Woodward*, 4 Wheaton 518 (1819); *Green* v. *Biddle*, 8 Wheaton 1 (1823); *Wilkinson* v. *Leland*, 2 Peters 627 (1829); *Charles River Bridge* v. *Warren Bridge Co.*, 11 Peters 420 (1837).

[131] *New York* v. *Miln*, 11 Peters 102 (1837); *Briscoe* v. *Bank of Kentucky*, 11 Peters 257 (1837); *United States* v. *Coombs*, 12 Peters 72 (1838); *Swift* v. *Tyson*, 16 Peters 1 (1842); *Ex Parte Christy*, 3 Howard 292 (1845).

[132] *Houston* v. *Moore*, 5 Wheaton 1 (1820); *Martin* v. *Mott*, 12 Wheaton 19 (1827).

[133] *Fairfax's Devisee* v. *Hunter's Lessee*, 7 Cranch 603 (1813).

from all quarters. It will perpetually thwart the wishes and views of demagogues, and it will have no places to give and no patronage to draw around it close defenders. Its only support is the wise and the good and the elevated in society; and these, as we all know, must ever remain in a discouraging minority in all governments.[134]

On another occasion he remarked: "If the twenty-fifth section is repealed the Constitution is practically gone."[135] In essence, Story meant that the existence of liberty and law depends upon the power of judicial review.

Judicial review was the legal expression of his antipathy toward legislative bodies and executive heads, and it is not difficult to locate the various sources of his unbounded faith in this constitutional doctrine. Blackstone had taught him at an early age of the need for an independent judiciary, free to protect the institution of property, and the rights of the common law. He had learned from experience in the Massachusetts legislature that politicians, driven by the needs of party rather than state, were not inclined to swallow the bitter pill of a nonelective, independent judiciary.

That all men were fit to rule was an idea wholly repugnant to him. Men of humble background, poor education, and narrow outlook were daily increasing in the legislative bodies, men not versed in "the science of government" but in the art of party politics and public opinion. The care and administration of government, he insisted, must be entrusted to men "who have profoundly studied the nature, science, and operations of governments in general; men who intimately understand our relations with foreign states and foreign policy; men who have taken a large survey of all our national interests, agriculture, manufacturing, commercial, political."[136] Men lacking in these attributes were prone to follow the transient wishes of the unthinking majority and were poorly equipped to follow their own sense of what was necessary for society.

Legislators were not meant to be puppets of the people, but, like judges, men of individual conscience, capable of withstanding the odium elicited by unpopular positions on issues affecting the best interests of the country. To Francis Lieber, Story wrote:

As to the right, as it is called, of instruction, we in New England do not admit the doctrine at all; at least, all our sound statesmen reject it as unconstitutional. Mr. Burke, in his address to the electors of Bristol, stated the general principle with great force and correctness. Mr. Giles, of Virginia, in a long address to the Virginia Legislature, in or about 1812, denied it, and reasoned the arguments against it forcibly. I deem the right of instruction, under our constitutions of government, utterly unfounded. It is nowhere given; it is by implication (as I think) denied.[137]

---

[134] To Jeremiah Mason, Jan. 10, 1822, *Life and Letters*, I, 411.

[135] To Professor George Ticknor, Jan. 22, 1831, *ibid.*, II, 49.

[136] "Statesmen—Their Rareness and Importance," *New England Magazine*, Vol. VII (Aug., 1834), 90.

[137] Apr. 10, 1836, *Life and Letters*, II, 230.

But Story knew Burke's doctrine—that the representative of the people was a free agent—had been denied. Burke's concept of disinterested public virtue and nation above party were the distant echoes of another century. The people would control the legislatures and, in their bid for power, would ultimately seize the remaining branches. Already, thought Story, they had captured the presidency. "I fear, as you do," he wrote Hopkinson, "that the theory of the Executive Depart[men]t may be completely broken down by the conduct of a popular, rash, feeble & ambitious President. Nevertheless, the theory is correct; & it is the *People* who are to blame, & will thus become, as they have in all ages been, the diggers of the grave of their own liberties."[138]

The office of the presidency, he warned another colleague, was the "ticklish part of our Constitution. Perhaps it will prove its overthrow."[139] And the judicial branch was no less secure; for "It is . . . a truth, a melancholy & discouraging truth, that the Judiciary of the U.S. has never been a favorite [of the legislature]."[140]

The American party system, then, was to Story a total perversion of the Constitution. By uniting a working majority of the executive and legislative branches, it circumvented the separation of powers and ultimately undermined the independence and integrity of the judiciary. The terrible result: tyranny of majority.

Some visionary statesmen . . . who affect to believe that the legislature can do no wrong, and some zealous leaders, who affect to believe that popular opinion is the voice of unerring wisdom, have, at times, questioned the authority of courts of justice. If they were correct in their doctrine, we might as well be without a written constitution of government, since the minority would always be in complete subjection to the majority; and it is to be feared, that the experience of mankind has never shown that the despotism of numbers has been more mild or equitable than that swayed by a single hand.[141]

Story's opinions surely fulfilled the Federalist plan of an expanding, united commercial nation in which the rights of property would be secure. How far he strayed from the popular consensus is attested by the fact his conservative principles were defeated time and time again at the polls; but at the same time, he took it upon himself to remind the American public, in the teeth of his own sweeping claims for federal judicial power, that the passions of the hour would not be permitted to thwart the principles of limited government.

If Story saved the supremacy of the Constitution and rule of law, he destroyed in part the ideals toward which he aimed. He labored under the false

[138] Nov. 27, 1833, Hopkinson Papers, HSP.

[139] To John Brazer, Feb. 4, 1827, *Life and Letters*, I, 516. See also Story to John Berrien, July 23, 1842, *ibid.*, II, 406.

[140] Story to David Daggett, Nov. 24, 1818, Story Papers, Yale.

[141] Story, "Progress of Jurisprudence," *Miscellaneous Writings*, 227.

assumption that once all state authorities were brought to their knees before a great central power, the democratic principles feared by the founders of the Constitution would be under control. But in this Story's hopes were not fulfilled. He totally misjudged the tendency of his times, which was not toward particularism, but consolidation. He mistook the polarization of power around North and South for a disintegrating process and failed to discern the inroads of unity and consolidation subtly accomplished through the increasing industrialization and democratization of the country which Tocqueville had foreseen.

Democracy acquired a new force while he sat on the Supreme Court, and the federal government became a potential and even real threat to many of the ideas and principles and institutions which he advocated. "The times are so out of joint," he wrote in 1833, "& the spirit of change & restlessness and agitation is so advanced, & the influence of the press is so extensive, I confess myself under no small alarm for the future. . . . I love the law too well not to desire under existing circumstances as few changes on the bench as possible."[142] But the Supreme Court itself became an instrument of, rather than a barrier to, the popular will and proved to be far stronger and hardier than he ever imagined. Why Story did not moderate his intense judicial nationalism in the era of Jacksonian Democracy, when, as he bitterly complained, the federal courts were being overrun by poorly trained Democrats, is a question that must go unanswered.

In attempting to uncover the causes of the War between the States, Lord Acton once wrote that "There was a fundamental error and contradiction in Hamilton's system. The end at which he aimed was best, but he sought it by means radically wrong, and necessarily ruinous to the cause they were meant to serve. . . . For the most conservative and anti-democratic government the most revolutionary basis was sought."[143] To a degree, the same would seem to hold true of Mr. Justice Story.

[142] Story to Charles R. Vaughan, Apr. 25, 1833, Vaughan Papers, Christ's College.

[143] John Emerich Edward Dalberg Acton, "Political Causes of the American Revolution," *The Rambler*, New Series, Vol. V, Part XIII (May, 1861), 17–61. Reprinted in Lord Acton, *Essays on Freedom and Power* (ed. by Gertrude Himmelfarb), 181.

CHAPTER VII

The Story Legacy

Joseph Story was a Salem lawyer whose reputation, considerable as it is, is scarcely commensurate with his influence on our later constitutional development.

VERNON PARRINGTON, *Main Currents In American Thought*

DR. Johnson once observed that Edmund Burke could do everything and anything; that he could have been poet, philosopher, governor, bishop, barrister, or soldier, all with an equally high degree of success. Joseph Story, truly a disciple of Burke, both in his metaphysics and antimetaphysics, nearly accomplished this "whole man" ideal and, in many respects, surpassed his master. Since his death in 1845, however, the reputation of Joseph Story has shrunk with that of Burke and the conservative principles they expounded. Although Story is one of the great jurists of all times, he has been overshadowed by the more spectacular figures of Webster and Marshall and lingers only in the twilight of their glory.

A man who never strutted upon the stage, Story preferred the role of supporting actor and would not protest the fading memory of his stardom. He coveted no foolish civic honors, believing until the end that his fame lay with his students. "If I do not live otherwise to posterity," he once remarked, "I shall at all events live in my children in the law. While that endures I am content to be known through my pupils."[1]

Story pursued quiet scholarship with exemplary diligence. Politics he abhorred. His life was that of a jurist, but that too had its drawbacks, for it kept him in the public eye. He delighted most in trudging across classroom floors, extolling the virtues of the common law and the Constitution.

His intention was to devote the remainder of his active life to the performance of his duties as the head of the law school at Cambridge. He had great confidence in the increasing utility of the law school, not only as a place to acquire knowledge of law, but to instill into the minds of young men, who came from all quarters of the union, correct notions of their political rights and duties, so that when they settled in different parts of this extensive country their influence might be felt in supporting

[1] Story to Charles Sumner, Feb. 10, 1836, as quoted in Elizabeth K. Bauer, *Commentaries on the Constitution*, 337.

our republican institutions and in contributing to the stability and perpetuity of our form of government.[2]

PROFESSOR STORY

"The public seem to suppose that *you* are a worker of miracles," Professor Simon Greenleaf said to his colleague, Judge Story, in 1839. "I rejoice that it is so, & that we have the privilege of imbuing so many minds with sound legal principles & learning. Probably we ourselves do not fully appreciate the influence of this seminary on the institutions of our country."[3] Where Story's influence ends as "founder" of the Harvard Law School, and as the man who revolutionized legal education in America, it is idle to conjecture.

It begins with those who sat at his feet and carried his ideas to the courts, publishing houses, and classrooms of the future. It begins with men such as Rutherford B. Hayes, Benjamin Robbins Curtis, Timothy Walker, Charles Sumner, and Richard Henry Dana, all of whom studied the law under Joseph Story's guidance and direction, and then made their own marks upon the face of America.[4] Story bequeathed to America one of the great law schools of the country. It soon imbibed the nationalist spirit of its founder and became a popular model for legal study throughout the entire country,[5] even forcing

[2] An account of Francis Bassett, for many years clerk of the United States Circuit and District Court of Massachusetts, as quoted in Perley Derby, *Elisha Story of Boston and Some of His Descendants*, 24.

[3] Jan. 29, 1839, Story Papers, Clements Library. Story's activities at the Cambridge Law School, as it was known, are related in Arthur E. Sutherland, *The Law at Harvard*, 92–140; Charles Warren, *History of the Harvard Law School*, I, 417ff.; Anton-Hermann Chroust, *Rise of the Legal Profession*, II, 191–203.

[4] "Walker's most important contribution to the law and his greatest achievement was his *Introduction to American Law*, published in 1837. It was dedicated to Story, the 'Judge, Author, and Teacher . . . by one who has enjoyed the good fortune of being his pupil and friend.'" (Bauer, *Commentaries on the Constitution*, 165.) After leaving Harvard, Walker went to Ohio to teach and practice law. Story tried in vain to coax him back to Harvard. "I rejoice that the West is to gain so worthy a *Son in Law*," he told Walker. "I confess that I have indulged a faint hope, that we might be able to regain you, & that after your wanderings you might be tempted again, 'Here to return & I'm home at last' . . . . The Law School continues to go on well here. We now count 37 students, & most of them are exceedingly industrious & praiseworthy in their studies. We miss you, however . . . . Perhaps by & by the West may repay us for our losses by sending us some of her own children to educate." (Nov. 24, 1830, Timothy Walker Papers, Cincinnati Historical Society.) Dana, who had just returned from two years before the mast when he entered the law school, was overjoyed that he had been "invited to pursue the study of jurisprudence, as a system of philosophy." (Dana, as quoted in Sutherland, *The Law at Harvard*, 127.) But there were others, such as James Russell Lowell, who were not so enthusiastic about the legal study and soon abandoned the law for other pursuits.

[5] "The Board of Trustees of the Indiana University established at this place, have recently connected with that institution, a law school, with a single professorship, to which I have been elected. . . . The Board have left it entirely to me, to fix the course of instruc-

competing law schools in some instances to close their doors forever.[6]

"Truly the stars were in a happy conjunction when the Dane Professorship was founded," Roscoe Pound remarked many years later. "The tradition of the Inns of Court had insured that an Anglo-American academic law school, established and conducted by common-law lawyers, would be a professional school. The philosophical ideas of the time in which Story had been trained had insured that a school under his guidance would be a school of law, not of the rules of law of this or that time or place. The necessities of the time when the school was founded had made it a school of Anglo-American law, in the light of a natural law philosophy and of comparative law, as declaratory of universal principles of natural reason, enabled it to remain a school devoted to a system of the common law that shares with Rome the legal allegiance of the world today."[7]

---

tion, and the rules of discipline. . . . [F]rom your reputation as a judge, a law writer, and professor at Harvard, I have been induced to ask your advice, as to the works which we should adopt as text books, the best modes of instruction, your plan of conducting a moot court, your views of the qualifications necessary to the admission of students, and any suggestion on other subjects, which you may deem useful to me." David McDonald to Story, June 27, 1842, Story Papers, Clements Library.

[6] Chancellor Kent's son complained to Story in 1839 that "Our Newport Law School— of what you once inquired of me—is suspended & virtually extinct, for though my excellent friend B[enjamin] F. Butler dreams of reviving it, I believe it quite past recovery. It failed from the operation of the settled laws of Political economy—the Cambridge Law School sold vastly better law at the same price. How could our competition endure?" (William Kent to Story, Sept. 13, 1839, Story Papers, Clements Library.) Kent came to Harvard after Story's death to assume the Royall Professorship and moved into Story's place of residence on Brattle Street. Even Judge Tapping Reeve's successful law school at Litchfield was no match for the Harvard School, and in 1833 it too closed its doors. The following letter from John Hall, editor of an early law journal, may indicate why. Please be so good, he asked Story, as to send me "some information concerning the law school at Litchfield . . . . As I presume you must have some knowledge of this institution, I take the liberty of asking your opinion on the subject. I have occasionally met with young gentlemen who had attended Judge Reeve's lectures, & who were totally ignorant of the practice, though they seemed to be tolerably well grounded in the theory of law." Nov. 3, 1821, *ibid*.

[7] As quoted in Sutherland, *The Law at Harvard*, 136. In 1781, Isaac Royall left an endowment for a law professorship at Harvard, and in 1815, Isaac Parker, chief justice of the Massachusetts Supreme Judicial Court was appointed Royall Professor, Asahel Stearns becoming his assistant. No more than nineteen students ever enrolled at the law school under Parker and Stearns, and in 1827 Parker resigned. "The first epoch in the history of the Harvard Law School thus ended in complete failure," despite the fact that under Parker and Stearns, Harvard "established the first university school of law in any common law country." (Chroust, *Rise of the Legal Profession*, II, 197.) In 1829, Nathan Dane offered an endowment of $10,000 to establish a professorship, on the condition that Judge Story accept the appointment and lecture on natural law, commercial and maritime law, equity law, and constitutional law. That same year, Story, together with John Hooker Ashmun, the new Royall Professor, started the Harvard Law School toward its

Story's reputation attracted students far and wide, including a substantial number from the South. Charles G. Hooker of Jackson, Mississippi, who was a Harvard law student between 1844 and 1845, recalled that "Judge Story was much beloved by all students, by none more so than the Southern students. I was in the School when he died and no more sincere mourners followed him to the grave than the body of students from the South."[8]

The success of the school under Story's tutelage was remarkable. At the time of his appointment in 1829, only twenty-four students were enrolled, but at his death, enrollment had jumped to 154. He boosted the library of the school, frequently donating his own books to the modest collection.[9] He even offered to sell his library to the corporation at half the replacement cost, in order to provide his students with greater access to the law.[10] And to lessen the expenses of the school, Story, though not a wealthy man, took a low salary for his invaluable services.[11]

The contents of Story's lectures, which he at first "gave twice a week by way of familiar comment on the *text studies*,"[12] are known only to those who attended his classes, as he delivered all but a few extempore. Speaking without notes, he enchanted his students with tales of the "tournament of monarchs and nobles on fields of cloth of gold;—of how Webster spoke in this case, Legaré, or Clay, or Crittenden, General Jones, Choate or Spencer, in that, with anecdotes of the cases and points, and all 'the currents of the heady fight.' "[13] He combined "the two great faculties of creating enthusiasm in study, and establishing relations of confidence and affection with his pupils." Story's

successful ascent to prominence. In 1833, Ashmun died, and was succeeded by Simon Greenleaf, a Maine lawyer. Story was reluctant to leave his home in Salem and to assume this new task; and he confided to friends that he had "been *driven* to accept the Dane Professorship of Law at Harvard University." (Story to Richard Peters, Aug., 1829, Peters Papers, HSP.) "The truth is," he told Joseph Hopkinson, "the founder created it expressly for me, & has confined it to my favorite Law Studies. I have surveyed my task, & though it is formidable, I think that by moderation & patience & diligence I can accomplish it. You need not fear that I shall overwork myself. I shall take counsel of my age & experience. I hope, indeed, that my Labours may not be wholly without some benefit to my profession, as Mr. Dane intimated his wish, that the Lectures shall be ultimately published." Aug. 15, 1829, Hopkinson Papers, HSP.

[8] Warren, *History of the Harvard Law School*, II, 54.

[9] See, for example, the various certificates of appreciation in the Papers of Joseph Story, Library of Congress (cited hereafter as Story Papers, LC).

[10] Story, *Life and Letters*, II, 39–41. The offer was accepted, and Story's extensive collection became the basis of the school's library.

[11] *Ibid.*, 41. "The annual salary received by my father from the College . . . during all his Professorial Life, was one thousand dollars, from which four hundred dollars were deduced for the annual rent of the house, belonging to the University, which he occupied in Cambridge, leaving a net salary of six hundred dollars."

[12] Story to Hopkinson, Nov. 7, 1829, Hopkinson Papers, HSP.

[13] Richard Dana to William W. Story, May 3, 1851, *Life and Letters*, II, 321.

reception at the school upon his return from Washington "was that of a returned father."[14] He was socially communicative with his students and "worshipped by us all." His lectures, in sum, were magnificently taught, interesting, and eloquent, and replete with anecdote and reminiscence, especially when he was expounding the Constitution.[15] His son, the sculptor-writer William Wetmore Story, summarized a lecture he heard as a student at the school:

It was the last lecture of the term, on the Constitution, and it was not probable that the whole class would ever again meet. . . . [H]e slid into a glowing discourse upon the principles and objects of the Constitution; the views of the great men of the Revolution . . . the position of our country; the dangers to which it was exposed; and the duty of every citizen to see that the republic sustained no detriment. He spoke, as he went on, of the hopes for freedom with which America was freighted . . . closing in an exhortation to the students to labor for . . . justice and free principles; to expand, deepen, and liberalize the law; to discard low and ambitious motives in their profession, and to seek in all their public acts to establish the foundations of right and truth.[16]

These were lofty thoughts for the inculcation of young, eager minds; but they reflect more than his affection for the Constitution. One of his most deeply rooted concerns was the rise of an impeccably honest and forthright legal profession, schooled in the philosophy of law and aloof from the sordid realities of party politics. Judge David Cross of Massachusetts, a student of Story's who followed this advice, recalled:

I remember at one time, in talking to us about our future as lawyers, he advised that we eschew all politics and devote our lives entirely to the study and practice of our profession until we had acquired sufficient wealth to live without professional labor, and then at this point I remember very distinctly, with a sort of twinkle in his eye, he said: "Young gentlemen, when you have acquired sufficient competence to live you will not wish to engage in the turmoil, treachery, and disappointments of political life."[17]

Eager that his students should appreciate the social role of law in the maintenance of order and the promotion of justice for the protection of private rights and public liberties, Story believed that with a broad education in legal philosophy, the lawyers and judges would come to grasp his grandiose con-

[14] *Ibid.* "While I know it is the universal voice of all who come under your instruction that they owe this debt of gratitude," wrote one student, "I yet have felt that your very marked kindness & *parental* . . . regard have laid me under a sense of the deepest obligations. . . . The Students one & all feel that you are a father to them & a true estimate of your kindness can be made only by the fact that everyone feels himself the favorite." Allen Ferdinand Owen to Story, Oct. 25, 1839, Story Papers, Clements Library.

[15] Dana to Story, *Life and Letters*, II, 321.

[16] *Ibid.*, 488–89.

[17] As quoted in Warren, *History of the Harvard Law School*, II, 27.

ception of a law above politics, judiciously administered by omnicompetent guardians of the state. "It has been the reproach of our profession in former ages, and is perhaps, true to a great extent in our own times, that lawyers know little or nothing but the law, and *that,* not in its philosophy, but merely and exclusively in its details."[18]

Professor Story feared that few persons, including members of the legal profession, were sufficiently aware of how forcibly, though silently, the law operated upon people's manners, habits, and feelings; of how much one's happiness and virtue depended upon the enlightened administration of justice. Of all the human sciences, none required such multifarious qualifications and extensive attainments as the law. Only half aware of this, too many lawyers, he complained, regarded the law as a means of personal gain and ambition, or political opportunity, and not as a science, requiring a profound understanding of philosophy, history, and human nature. "It is from the want of this enlarged view of *duty,*" Story lamented, "that the profession has sometimes been reproached with a sordid narrowness, with a low chicane, with a cunning avarice, and with a deficiency in liberal and enlightened policy."[19]

Story never stopped believing that party politics was the preoccupation of little minds, the intoxicant of the intellectual amateur, who succumbed to its corruptive influence at the mere whiff of personal gain. Certainly it had no place in the regnant domain of the law. And as "Mr. Burke has somewhat reluctantly admitted, the practice of law is not apt, except in persons very happily born, to open and liberalize the mind exactly in the same proportion as it invigorates the understanding . . . men too much conversant in office are rarely minds of remarkable enlargement."[20]

To a nation whose legislative halls have always been overcrowded with lawyers practicing before the bar of public acclaim, these are truly challenging thoughts. Although annihilated before his very eyes by the forces of Jacksonian Democracy during his later years,[21] Story's ideal of an independent

[18] Story to William W. Story, Jan. 27, 1839, *Life and Letters,* II, 311–12.

[19] "The Value and Importance of Legal Studies," *Miscellaneous Writings,* 527. Emphasis supplied.

[20] *Ibid.*

[21] Unfortunately, anti-common law sentiment was revived during the era of Jacksonian Democracy, and the Harvard Law School, like the legal profession in general, was adversely affected. "If anything can *retard* (stop it you can not) the Jacobinical torrent which is sweeping past and undermining the foundations of . . . our institutions," stated one disturbed lawyer less than a year after Judge Story's death, "the barrier of sound law and conservative influences which the Harvard Law School is building up, will do it." (Handlin and Handlin, *Commonwealth,* 202.) Such influences, however, were neither long lasting nor especially pronounced in the period following Story's departure. The law school fell into a decline from which it did not recover for decades. As late as 1870, the editors of *The American Law Review* (who were Harvard graduates) complained that "For a long time the condition of the Harvard Law School has been almost a dis-

guardian class of virtuous lawyers and judges, endowed with philosophical insight, possesses a certain timelessness and is not far removed from the ideals expressed in Plato's *Republic*. "By his eloquent precepts and his spotless example, he impressed upon his pupils a deep sense of the beauty of a virtuous life; that all professional triumphs were worthless that were not honorably won; and that to be a great lawyer, it was requisite first to be a good man."[22]

THE INVISIBLE HAND

But Story's influence upon the intellectual development of America extends beyond the mere confines of its legal system. Not only his students, but important figures such as Daniel Webster, Francis Lieber, Alexis de Tocqueville, and John Marshall drew their inspiration, and sometimes the bulk of their ideas, from the fertile mind of Judge Story. Story's influence upon Webster and, through Webster, upon the political history of the country, has been frequently noted. In his *Main Currents in American Thought*, Vernon Parrington gave a striking illustration of Story's effect upon Webster, when he noted that Webster's reply to Calhoun's exposition of the concurrent majority was taken from Story's *Commentaries on the Constitution*. Webster delivered his significant speech only a month after the publication of the *Commentaries*, and a comparison of the two documents showed a close similarity between Story's theories of the Union and their presentation by Webster, who "threw Story on the Constitution at Calhoun's theory of compact."[23]

It is nearly impossible to determine with accuracy how much of Webster's constitutionalism was that of Story. Webster never acknowledged his indebtedness to Story and refused to allow the Story letters in his possession to be printed.[24] At the time, only a few were aware of the working relationship be-

---

grace to the Commonwealth of Massachusetts." (As quoted in Sutherland, *The Law at Harvard*, 140.) The damage inflicted on the professional bar associations by Jacksonian Democracy was far more extensive, and in many instances irreparable. "The advent of 'Jacksonian democracy,'" relates Professor Chroust, "probably dealt the death blow to any organization of the legal profession. Statutes throwing the practice of law wide open to all citizens or voters were the common result. . . . Hence it is no mere accident that the New England 'bar organizations' and 'bar meetings' should come to a sudden end during the era of 'Jacksonian democracy.' The Suffolk Bar . . . disbanded in 1836, as did the bar of Cumberland County in Maine. . . . The Bar of Franklin County in Massachusetts disappeared in 1835, and the Bar of Grafton County in New Hampshire ceased to operate in 1838. The Bar of Essex County in Massachusetts miraculously managed to survive until 1856." *Rise of the Legal Profession*, II, 156–57.

[22] "Biographical Notice of Mr. Justice Story, *American Review, A Whig Journal*, Vol. III (Jan., 1846), 77.

[23] Parrington, *Main Currents in American Thought*, II, 312.

[24] Story, *Life and Letters*, II, 408. For an excellent account of the Story-Webster alliance, see R. Kent Newmyer, "A Note on the Whig Politics of Justice Joseph Story," *Mississippi Valley Historical Review*, Vol. XLVIII, No. 3 (Dec., 1961), 480–91.

tween Story and Webster. Secretary of State Louis McLane, however, indicated that he knew of this relationship when he wrote to Martin Van Buren in 1830, "I fear Judge Story is but the wretched tool of Mr. Webster."[25]

A more accurate description of the relationship, however, would seem to be that Webster was the tool of Story. Through Webster, Story was frequently able to influence the Congress to enact legislation favorable to his conservative designs. He drew up an act for the reorganization of the courts, which Webster unsuccessfully attempted to urge upon the Congress in 1825–26.[26] Story drafted the Crimes Act of 1825, which Webster pushed through the Congress as chairman of the House Judiciary Committee. Webster also collaborated with Story at this time in an effort to pass a bankruptcy act: "I should feel greatly obliged to you if in the multitude of your concerns you could find time to make a dft [draft] of a Bankrupt Law. I am pledged to do something on that & I mean to bring it forward early in the session. . . . As far as convenient please place *references* in margin."[27]

Webster was also desirous that Story supply him with ideas respecting the legitimacy and wisdom of internal improvements. "I really wish you could sit down," wrote Webster, and "give me as many *suggestions*, as it wd [would] take you half an hour to write,—either on the power, or the policy—Pray do so if you can."[28] In the Whig campaign against Jackson's bank policy, Webster, as a leading spokesman for his party, delivered a speech in the Congress on the subject of the president's veto. Again, Story was relied upon for Webster's constitutional law. "You may have seen that [veto] message," he wrote Story. "My wish is to give a full answer to its *trash* on the constitutional question. That is Taney's work. The argument, you perceive is, that some powers of the Bank are not necessary, & so not Constitutional. Now, my dear Sir, the object of this is to request you to turn to the message, read this part of it, & give me in a letter of three pages a close & conclusive confutation, and in your way, of all its nonsense in this particular. It will take you less than half an hour."[29]

Story also furnished Webster with arguments relating to international law

---

[25] Charles Warren, *Supreme Court in United States History*, I, 720.

[26] Webster to Story, Dec. 9, 1816, Massachusetts Historical Society *Proceedings*, 2nd Series, Vol. XIV, 399. See also Webster to Story, Dec. 26, 1826, *Private Correspondence of Daniel Webster* (ed. by Fletcher Webster), I, 412–13.

[27] Webster to Story, Nov. 10, 1825, Massachusetts Historical Society *Proceedings*, 2nd Series, Vol. XIV, 405. "Few measures," noted Simon Greenleaf, "affecting either the permanent institutions, or the trade, manufactures, or foreign relations in our country, have been discussed in the halls of Congress during the last thirty years, on which statesmen have not sought the aid of his [Story's] judgment and counsel; and few questions of constitutional law have been there argued upon which the light of his opinion and his suggestions have not been previously sought and most readily imparted." *A Discourse Commemorative of the Life and Character of the Hon. Joseph Story*, 36.

[28] To Story, Apr. 13, 1828, Story Papers, LC.

[29] July 21, 1832, Massachusetts Historical Society *Proceedings*, 2nd Series, Vol. XIV, 408.

and composed drafts of treaties concerning extradition when Webster was involved in negotiations with Lord Ashburton as secretary of state.[30] In fact, even before he became secretary of state and author of the Webster-Ashburton Treaty, Webster had requested information from Story on the subject of boundaries. In 1838 he wrote Story: "Help me to make a speech. I wish to say something on this N.E. Boundary; & I desire to be able to resist, in limine, both on English & American authorities, one of the principal preliminary grounds taken by the English diplomatists. . . . You have the cases . . . . Please refer me to them."[31]

On smaller legal questions, too, Webster frequently sought the advice of his learned friend. "I am puzzled to know how the law stands respecting appeals in equity cases . . . a line this afternoon or tomorrow morning will greatly oblige."[32] Regarding a legal question in the famous Knapp brothers murder trial, Webster wrote: "I pray you collect your thoughts on this point."[33] "Will you have the goodness to give me one hour of your valuable life"[34] on the subject of navigation? Can you furnish me with "a strong case against England on the subject of procuring indemnification for the pirates and murderers"[35] in the Creole mutiny?

A month later Story received a letter from Webster thanking him for his assistance. "I am truly obliged to you for your very satisfactory letter of the 25th of March. The rules of law stated in it are unquestionably stated with great correctness. . . . You can do more for me than all the rest of the world, because you can give me the lights I most want; & if you furnish them I shall be confident they will be true lights. I shall trouble you greatly the next three months. For the present I have to ask that you send me a draft of two articles."[36]

Only a few letters of the Story-Webster correspondence have survived, but what few remain all point to the truth of Rufus Choate's and Theodore Parker's suspicions that Story was the genius behind much of Webster's suc-

---

[30] See Story to Webster, Mar. 26 and Apr. 19, 1842, *The Writings and Speeches of Daniel Webster* (National ed.), Vol. XVI, 364–65, 368–69.

[31] May 12, 1838, Massachusetts Historical Society *Proceedings*, 2nd Series, Vol. XIV, 409.

[32] Webster to Story, Nov. 7, 1821, *Private Correspondence of Daniel Webster*, I, 317.

[33] To Story, Aug. 6, 1830, Massachusetts Historical Society *Proceedings*, 2d Series, Vol. XIV, 408.

[34] Webster to Story, Apr. 16, 1827, *ibid.*, 405. "Let it be devoted to furnishing me with hints & authorities to the following point," continued Webster. "That a right to navigate the upper part of a river (say the St. Lawrence) draws after it a right to go to the ocean. Whatever you *think* or find on this matter let me know by Wednesday or Thursday." Webster signed his letter, "Yr. troublesome friend."

[35] Mar. 17, 1842, *ibid.*, 410.

[36] Apr. 9, 1842, *ibid.*, 410–11.

cess as a lawyer and statesman.[37] In his tribute to Webster as a great American, Story, with characteristic humility, had asserted that Webster, "as a constitutional lawyer and statesman . . . has no compeer in the present day, save only the excellent Chief Justice of the United States."[38] But Theodore Parker knew better: "Mr. Webster was in the habit of drawing from that deep and copious well of legal knowledge, whenever his own bucket was dry. Mr. Justice Story was the Jupiter Pluvius from whom Mr. Webster often sought to elicit peculiar thunder for his speeches, and private rain for his own public tanks of law."[39]

Story's friendship with Francis Lieber, though shorter and less intimate than that with Webster, served as another channel through which the judge spread his doctrines. To what extent Francis Lieber, the editor of *Encyclopedia Americana* who requested the essay on natural law from Story, was under the spell of his contributing author, may be inferred from their extensive correspondence and writings. Shortly after receiving Story's essay, Lieber published his first major work, *A Manual of Political Ethics* (1838). It is evident from a letter written by Story to Lieber on July 30, 1835, that Lieber had informed Story of his plan to produce a work on political philosophy.

Judging from the content of Story's letter, it would appear that Lieber had asked Story to suggest a title for the book. "I think the best, that is, the most attractive title for your work," advised Story, "would be 'Political Ethics, on the Rights & Duties of Citizens in matters of Government'—You see, it is a noble title, but the Explanation seems indispensable, & is short. Nothing better occurs to me at present; but perhaps it may before your work is complete."[40]

Story then proceeds to suggest at great length various subjects which Lieber should consider in the writing of the book. Some mention should be made, urged Story, of "The powers of Government, Separation of Powers, Qualifications for Office, Tenure of Office." Story continued by providing a complete outline for the work: "Universal suffrage. Is it Safe for a Republic"; "Suppose

---

[37] Rufus Choate in his *Discourse Commemorative of Daniel Webster*, delivered at Dartmouth College, July 27, 1853, spoke as follows of the influence of Story on Webster: "I reckon next to his (Jeremiah Mason's) for the earlier time of Webster's life, the influence of the learned and accomplished Jeremiah Smith; and next to these—some may believe greater—is that of Justice Story. . . . he was engaged in many trials in the county of Rockingham, New Hampshire, before Mr. Webster had assumed his established position. Their political opinions differed; but such was his affluence of knowledge already; such his stimulant enthusiasm; and fame, that the influence on the still young Webster was instant; and it was great and permanent." Quoted in Warren, *History of the Harvard Law School*. II, 69.

[38] "Statesmen—Their Rareness and Importance: Daniel Webster," *New England Magazine*, Vol. VII (Aug., 1834), 103.

[39] *Additional Speeches, Addresses, and Occasional Sermons*, I, 170. Parker also observed that Webster "sought to conceal the source of his supplies." *Ibid.*, 171.

[40] Story-Lieber Correspondence, Huntington Library.

voters to be upon different qualifications: as, trade—business—profession—property, &c. Would it serve a better representation of all interests"; "Rights of minority—can the majority justly construe them"; "Distinctions between absolute and limited governments—absolute democracy"; a "chapter on political compromise."[41]

Lieber's work, which incorporated these ideas offered by Story, represents, according to Benjamin F. Wright, "a broader acquaintance with the writings of European political philosophers than did any of the earlier systematic studies published in the country."[42] But, it was Joseph Story, apparently at Lieber's request, who furnished the author with a list of political philosophers to be consulted before undertaking the study; "P.S. The best books which I know of on the subject of Govts are Aristotle on Politics, Cicero; Republic, the Federalist, Delolme on the English Constitution & Paley's Moral Philosophy—Burlamaqui on Natural and Political Law—Vattel—Montesquieu."[43]

Lieber's biographer has recognized that "Story, his colleagues at Harvard Law School, Simon Greenleaf, and his protégé, Charles Sumner, continued to aid Lieber with suggestions and citations," and concludes that "the execution, and, above all, the techniques for preparing the manuscript were Lieber's own."[44] He does not emphasize, however, the extent to which Story's political thought influenced the author and perhaps set the tone of the work itself: "I see you had not only been kind enough to read my very imperfect M.S., but the M.S. had taken hold of your mind, and the very way in which you spoke of the subject on which it treats proves to me both that I had succeeded in representing some points in an original way and that I have been able to carry your mind into my views. . . . I feel ever since that evening a thousand times nearer to you."[45] Lieber dedicated the work to Henry Hallam, an Englishman, and to Joseph Story.

In his second book, *Civil Liberty and Self-Government*, Lieber repudiated the concept of natural rights and advocated instead "Anglican liberties," that is, those liberties secured by common law, statute, and constitution. Lieber's rejection of natural rights has led Benjamin F. Wright to conclude that "Perhaps he had become, sixty years after its publication, a convert to the principles of Burke's *Reflections on the French Revolution*."[46]

---

[41] *Ibid.*

[42] *American Interpretations of Natural Law*, 261.

[43] Story to Lieber, July 30, 1835, Story-Lieber Correspondence, Huntington Library. Frank Freidel, *Francis Lieber: Nineteenth Century Liberal*, 147, notes that "In 1835 Justice Joseph Story encouraged Lieber to undertake the enterprise, helped clarify his ideas, and recommended to him the title, 'Political Ethics.' Indeed, the Justice even prepared an agenda of the principal topics he should cover."

[44] Freidel, *Francis Lieber*, 147.

[45] Lieber to Story, "Monday Morning," 1837, Story Papers, LC.

[46] *American Interpretations of Natural Law*, 266. Lieber frequently asked Story to assist

While the influence of Burke, whom Story recommended to Lieber, is evident in Lieber's works, it would seem more likely that Story, whom Lieber cites constantly in his *Civil Liberty and Self-Government*, is the direct source of "Lieber's concept" of "Anglican liberties."[47] But the influence of Story does not close with natural law. Lieber advocated the independence and supremacy of the judiciary, and a strong national state.

Parrington's conclusion that "Francis Lieber provided a philosophical background that justified [Story's] legal conception of the organic nature of the federal union"[48] fails to account for Story's earlier contributions through his essay on natural law and *Commentaries on the Constitution*. As in the case of Webster, Lieber does not publicly acknowledge any real indebtedness to Story. Again, the precise nature of the latter's influence must in the end rest upon conjecture. Suffice it to say a substantial portion of the ideas offered by Lieber had been enunciated by his friend, Story, years earlier. Building upon Story's precedent, Lieber essentially re-expressed Story's constitutionalism in a new, perhaps more systematic form.

Joseph Story's influence upon the political and legal thinkers of Europe must have been as profound as it was upon Americans. Story maintained an extensive correspondence with many English jurists, with whom he often exchanged views on legal problems. He contributed articles to American, Scottish, German, and French journals,[49] and his contributions as a commentator on the

him in obtaining a professorship at Harvard, but he was unable to secure a post. "Get the means to establish a chair in Pol[itical] Ethics and the Law of Nature," Story told Lieber, "and the next day you shall be appointed professor." Sept. 29, 1842, Story Papers, Clements Library.

[47] In his chapter on the independence of the judiciary and the common law, Lieber relies heavily on Story, citing freely from Story, *Life and Letters*, Story's *Commentaries*, Story's opinions, and Story's essay, "Common Law," in the *Encyclopedia Americana*. (See *Civil Liberty and Self-Government*, I, 220–33.) Lieber, who had a very high opinion of the articles Story wrote for his encyclopedia, uses many of them throughout his work.

[48] *Main Currents in American Thought*, II, 93.

[49] See Story, *Past History, Present State, and Future Prospects*. In a visit to Scotland in 1825, a friend wrote to Story that he had visited privately with two Scottish law lords. "Wheaton's Reports lay on the table and I soon found that the Soliciter General had been looking into cases, and said some civil things of you and Chief Justice Marshall. After dinner the Company retired again to the Library, and I was questioned pretty closely upon the power and Jurisdiction of the United States Court. Luckily for me, having reviewed the Dartmouth College case, I was able to answer their questions. I had remarked, that by the Constitution, the Supreme Court had the power to declare a law of Congress void. Lord Mackenzie stopped me, as though he had misunderstood me, and asked if our Congress were not omnipotent. I replied, that the Court [not on]ly had the power, but had in more than one instance exercized it. And did they submit? was his question. Certainly they did. He paused for a moment, and said there was something sublime in the notion of the Supremacy of the Law. I suppose he had never read the Constitution of the United States; for it seemed to strike him as a new thought." (W. Dutton to Story, July 26, 1825, Story Papers, Clements Library.) Story also wrote in 1836 an article

common law and the American Constitution gave him an international reputation. "Tell Judge Story that I have not seen a Lawyer or a Judge," wrote Webster from London to a friend, "who has not spoken of him & praised his writings. If he were here he would be one of the greatest professional Lions that ever prowled through the metropolis."[50]

Story published his constitutional ideas in four different forms and intended that they reach every level of American society. The three-volume *Commentaries on the Constitution* (1833), designed for the legal profession, was dedicated to Chief Justice Marshall. "It is a question that unavoidably presents itself," exclaimed Edward Everett when he first laid eyes on this monumental work, "now we have the book, How we did without it?"[51] An abridged edition, "for the use of Colleges and High Schools," also appeared in 1833, which was translated into French by Paul Odent in 1843, then into Spanish by Nicholas A. Calvo, an Argentinian, in 1879. Franz Josef von Buss translated the multivolume edition into German in 1838. To promote the teaching of political science, Story expanded his address before the American Institute of Instruction (August, 1834), "The Science of Government As a Branch of Popular Education," and published his *Constitutional Class Book* in 1834.[52]

In 1840, Story published another abridgment of the *Commentaries*, *A Familiar Exposition of the Constitution of the United States: Containing a Brief Commentary on Every Clause, Explaining the True Nature, Reasons, and Objects Thereof: Designed for the Use of School Libraries and General Readers*. The Argentinian José Maria Cantilo translated this work into Spanish in 1863, and it was thereafter distributed throughout the public schools of Argentina. Story's influence in Latin America must have been fairly wide-

---

entitled "The Organization and Jurisdiction of the National Courts of the United States," *Revue Etrangere*, III, 65, and one entitled "American Law," *Kritische Zeitschrift*, IX, I. The original text of the latter (in the hand of Story) was recently discovered in a California library. It is now printed, thanks to the efforts of Professor Kurt Nadelmann, in the *American Journal of Comparative Law*, Vol. III (1954), 9–26.

[50] Copy of letter (in the hand of Story) from Webster to Isaac P. Davis, June 14, 1839, Story Papers, Clements Library.

[51] "Story's Constitutional Law," a review of Story's *Commentaries on the Constitution* in *North American Review*, Vol. XXXVIII (Jan., 1834), 63. (For other early reviews of Story's *Commentaries*, see *American Monthly Review*, Vol. IV [Dec., 1833], 499–513; *American Quarterly Review*, Vol. XIV [Dec., 1833], 327–67; *American Jurist and Law Magazine*, Vols. IX and X [Apr. and July, 1833], 241–88; 119–47.) "Story's *Commentaries on the Constitution* began to appear as authority in arguments of counsel and in opinions from the bench within a year after their publication. . . . [Before 1860] he was cited in four cases in the opinion of the Court, twice in concurring opinions, and eight times in dissents. In all, Story was cited [by bench and bar] in 42 separate cases. . . . The subjects on which Story was used as authority cover almost the entire range of problems of constitutional law." Bauer, *Commentaries on the Constitution*, 352–53.

[52] The address appears in *Miscellaneous Writings*, 614–39.

spread. In Mexico, for example, he was often cited during the constitutional convention which produced the Constitution of 1857.[53]

In fact, it would appear that Story's *Commentaries* were likely to be pressed into service almost anywhere in the world, and for any number of reasons. "I was much amused by what a young friend in the Navy told me," Professor Greenleaf informed Story, "of the use made by a copy of your book on the Constitution, which had found its way to Port Mahon in Minorca. He defended a sailor tried by a naval court martial for manslaughter; & having made known his intention of relying on some want of form in that charge, the Commodore, to prevent any escape *that way*, dissolved the Court, in the midst of the trial, & ordered a new court & new charges! At this new trial he relied on the ground that he had already been in jeopardy, for the same offence; and would have succeeded on this point; when some gentleman from shore sent on board a copy of 'a book they called Story on the Constitution, U.S.,' in which it was read that to entitle to this defence there must have been a previous acquittal or conviction—whereupon he was found guilty—'and I shall charge Judge Story,' he added, 'for those three hundred lashes the poor fellow had to take.' "[54]

Despite unexpected results such as these, Story was surely delighted that his works on the Constitution were offered to foreign readers. On May 9, 1840, he wrote to Lieber: "I do not wonder that you are struck with the barrenness of foreign treatises on Constitutional law; and especially as applied to forms of government like ours. Europeans know little on that subject."[55]

Even Alexis de Tocqueville, who more than any other European succeeded in familiarizing the world with the American Constitution and democractic experiment, seems to have relied upon Story's *Commentaries on the Constitution* for many of his ideas. Tocqueville has frequently been criticized for refusing to acknowledge the sources of his materials. Francis Lippitt claimed that he assisted Tocqueville in preparing materials for the work,[56] and it has been

---

[53] See Kurt H. Nadelmann, "Apropos of Translations (Federalist, Kent, Story)," *American Journal of Comparative Law*, Vol. VIII (Spring, 1959), 204–14, for further discussion of Story's translated works, especially those respecting his treatises on common law; see also Bauer, *Commentaries on the Constitution*, 344–57.

[54] Mar. 2, 1839, Story Papers, Clements Library. [55] *Life and Letters*, II, 330.

[56] George Wilson Pierson, *Tocqueville in America*, 441. Pierson also notes that Tocqueville, "Supposing, apparently, that he was getting an entirely fresh analysis through the uncoloured mind of a college student [Lippitt] . . . actually received instead further translation from Story and Kent and the Federalist. . . . The net result was that either Justice Story or Kent, the old chancellor, might indeed have felt that Tocqueville had borrowed a good deal from them for the pages of his *Democracy*. For what the young Frenchman had actually done was to consult again and again with the Americans who had read their books. . . . In addition to direct and indirect borrowing, therefore, there had been independent judgment. . . . That he agreed with them often, and used them occasionally, was therefore no derogation to his own integrity or intelligence." *Ibid.*, 442.

said that Jared Sparks, and many others also, provided a good part of the matter for *Democracy in America.*[57] Story's son, William Wetmore Story, thought "it is a little singular, that though such extensive use is made of my father's Commentaries on the Constitution . . . no acknowledgment is made, and the Commentaries are scarcely referred to by name."[58]

In a letter to Lieber, Story himself charged that Tocqueville had "borrowed the great part of his reflections from American works, and little from his own observations. The main body of his materials will be found in The Federalist and Story's Commentaries on the Constitution—*sic vos vobis.*"[59] A French journal, *Revue des Deux Mondes*, substantiated Story's claim while reviewing Paul Odent's translation of the *Commentaries*. Story, it was asserted, "has done for the constitutional law of America what William Blackstone did for English law. . . . The author of 'Democracy in America' often relies on Story's authority, particularly in the first part of his book. M. de Tocqueville was fortunate, in finding in the Commentaries of the American Blackstone, a complete view of the legislative powers of the United States."[60] The fact that Tocqueville's analysis of Congress closely resembles Story's is good cause to infer that Tocqueville's work incorporated a substantial amount of Story's *Commentaries*. Indeed, a comparison of the two works fails to produce any discernible differences between them respecting the entire American Constitution. How much of a hand did Story have in the writing of *Democracy In America*?

There is yet another side to Story's wide range of authority. Through personal contact and private correspondence, he exerted a powerful influence over members of the legal profession. From every part of the country they came, to seek his assistance and guidance. Sometimes as strangers, with hat in hand, sometimes as friends or acquaintances, they solicited his opinions on various legal, political, and personal questions of the moment. Enterprising authors, lawyers, state and federal judges, members of the United States Supreme Court: they all came to him with their problems. Each delivery of the mail brought a new bundle of anxious inquiries, and without a word of complaint, Story cheerfully answered them all.

His readiness to offer judgment and advice to members of the legal profession was actually a traditional courtesy Story had extended since 1804. "Be good enough to reply to the following statement," wrote George Prescott. "The wife of A is possessed in fee of a certain farm, and Stock, &c., which A has leased for a yearly consideration for five years. B, a creditor to A, attaches A's rights in the leased premises. What should be the words of the sheriff's return in consequence of the attachment?"[61] On June 14, 1808, Judge Theophilus

[57] *Ibid.*, 440.
[58] Story, *Life and Letters*, II, 329.
[59] May 9, 1840, *ibid.*, 330.
[60] As quoted *ibid.*, 655.
[61] To Story, Mar. 3, 1804, Story Papers, Clements Library.

Parsons requested Story to send him his views on the subject of habeas corpus, in order to obtain bail for one David Rich, who had been charged with assault with intent to commit murder. "I wish you would look into the affairs and direct the enquiry," continued Parsons, "and if it is apparent that no person's life is in hazard from the assault, advise the Justice to bail him."[62] And during the same year, we find the young Salem lawyer and the esteemed Nathan Dane engaged in a most academic discussion of the common law, at a time when the latter was preparing his famed *Digest*.[63]

After Story's appointment to the Court, the variety and number of requests increased steadily. Thomas Green Fessenden wanted to express his "gratitude for your goodness in inspecting my Law of Patents, and for the valuable hints and commendations which you have suggested."[64] Theron Metcalf, who later became a member of the Massachusetts Supreme Judicial Court, would have been very much obliged in 1821 if "you will point out to me the course of reading that will most readily and systematically inform me of the limits of the admiralty jurisdiction, & the admiralty system generally."[65]

[62] Story Papers, LC.

[63] Story to Dane, Nov. 2, 1808, Nathan Dane Papers, Massachusetts Historical Society.

[64] Fessenden to Story, Oct. 1, 1821, Story Papers, Clements Library. See also Fessenden to Story, Oct. 29, 1821, and Jan. 23, 1823, *ibid*. On November 21, 1821, Fessenden told Story that his manuscript was on its way to the publisher, and that he had dedicated the work to Judge Story, adding: "You, sir, have done so much to establish and elucidate correct principles relating to the law of Patents for New Inventions that you are at least entitled to the grateful and public acknowledgment of all, who feel an interest in that branch of jurisprudence" (*ibid*.). See also Benjamin Cozzens to Story, Aug. 8, 1821, *ibid*.; and Frank D. Prager, "Changing Views of Justice Story on the Construction of Patents," *American Journal of Legal History*, Vol. IV (1960), 1–21. Thomas Day wrote to Story in 1823 that he planned to write a supplement to Comyn's *Digest*, and would appreciate any suggestions the judge might have. (Feb. 24, 1823, Story Papers, Clements Library.) See also the letter of C. S. Davis to Story, June 28, 1823, requesting Story to examine a legal manuscript being prepared for publication (*ibid*.). John Bouvier dedicated his famous law dictionary to Story because "I have derived more profit and instruction from your writings than from those of any other American writer." Bouvier to Story, Sept. 19, 1839, *ibid*.

[65] Metcalf to Story, June 2, 1821, Story Papers, Clements Library. See also Metcalf to Story, Aug. 6, 1821, *ibid*., where he seeks assistance on a question of replevin; Jan. 9, 1822, *ibid*., where he again seeks legal advice on a case, having been "encouraged by your suggestions on former occasions." "Can you give me a reference to a case," inquired William Wirt, "said to have been brought against Sir William Scott by some individual whom he had excommunicated . . . ?" (To Story, Jan. 20, 1831, Story Papers, Texas.) See also Story to Leverett Saltonstall, Nov. 4, 1832, Saltonstall Papers, Massachusetts Historical Society, where Story furnishes legal advice on a question of bailments; George W. Christy to Story, Sept. 10, 1842, and Dillon Jordan to Story, Sept. 28, 1842, Story Papers, Clements Library, concerning a point of law dealing with bankruptcy. On April 8, 1843[?], Thomas Johnston, a fledgling lawyer from Kentucky, wrote to Story to tell him that he wished to become a better lawyer, having "come to a determination to

Chief Justice Prentiss Mellen of the Maine Supreme Court had a difficult case involving a will before him. "Permit me to state the case to you and ask you to *un-puzzle me*," he wrote, though realizing "These questions may appear simple to you, versed as you are in all the principles of chancery law."[66] Chief Justice Isaac Parker of the Massachusetts Supreme Court was bogged down in a bewildering property case involving the conveyance of land without title: "We have a case which has puzzled us, & every body concerned in it a great while, and I feel a strong desire to know how it will strike your mind."[67]

The members of the Arkansas Supreme Court were in the midst of a major political crisis in 1842 because of an unpopular opinion they handed down in a case involving a trust estate and needed Story's backing to avoid a purge of the state judiciary by an aroused legislature.[68] The federal district judge in

---

aim at something of a higher grade, of a more aspiring nature, than a mere practicing attorney." Would the learned judge kindly supply him with "a systematick & comprehensive course of legal reading"? *Ibid*.

[66] To Story, Dec. 12, 1825, Story Papers, Clements Library; also Mellen to Story, Oct. 7, 1839, *ibid*. There are many letters from Story to Mellen in the Story Papers, Yale. See especially Story to Mellen, Oct. 7, 1824; July 23, 1830; Aug. 28, 1830; Jan. 29, 1831; and Oct. 9, 1839.

[67] To Story, May 21, 1821, Story Papers, Clements Library; see also Judge Benjamin Franklin of Charleston, S.C., Mar. 12, 1839, requesting legal advice on a property case, *ibid*., and William Gaston, Nov. 16, 1825, *ibid*. In 1833, Gaston was elected chief justice of the Supreme Court of North Carolina. In 1842, Gaston wrote to Story that the state legislature of North Carolina had appointed the governor and judges of the Supreme Court as trustees of the public library, and that $6,000 had been appropriated for the purchase of books, some in the field of law, and that he would like the name of a Boston lawyer who could help him procure the necessary books. (Gaston to Story, Feb. 11, 1842, *ibid*.) In a letter to Senator William Cabell Rives, January 14, 1843, Story offered sound advice which would seem to have no little current significance. "I have read with great satisfaction and pleasure your speech in the Senate on the application of the Smithsonian fund," he wrote. "It seems to me that no distinction can be properly drawn between the diffusion of the physical sciences, and moral and political science, as objects of that bequest. If any is to be drawn, I venture to say that the cultivation of moral and political science with reference to the Institutions and prosperity of our Country is of far greater importance than the physical sciences. If a national library is to be founded, it should embrace all the departments of knowledge—Science, Literature and Art—in all their various forms. . . . [T]he sciences flourish best in the neighborhood of each other . . . [but] Literature and Art are often the Instructors, as well as the hand maids of science. . . . I would lay out as little money as possible in *mere bricks and mortar*. . . . I should deem every dollar expended for show or magnificence a mere waste of that fund. Will you permit me to say that the people want bread and not a stone, knowledge and not colonnades or palaces or halls or vestibules leading to nothing." As quoted in Mortimer D. Schwartz and John C. Hogan, "A National Library: Mr. Justice Story Speaks Out," *Journal of Legal Education*, Vol. VIII, No. 3 (1955), 328–30.

[68] Townsend Dickinson, Thomas J. Lacy to Story, Aug. 23, 1842, Story Papers, Clements Library. "We herewith transmit to you a copy of the opinion of the Supreme Court of this

Providence, Rhode Island, facing an insurrection, had written an anonymous pamphlet dealing with the legal issues of the Dorr's Rebellion, and desperately needed Story's concurrence "upon the constitutional law of the pamphlet."[69] Joseph Hopkinson, the federal district judge in Philadelphia, was in need of legal advice in cases involving admiralty law,[70] criminal law,[71] equity,[72] and probably many other areas of the law.

Members of the Supreme Court, it seems, also habitually relied upon Story for legal assistance. Justice Bushrod Washington, one of the most learned

State," they wrote, "delivered by us a few days since, and respectfully ask you . . . to state in a brief letter . . . your views of its correctness. . . . The opinion has been unacceptable to a portion of the public, and a popular clamor has been raised against it, and in this contest even the purity and uprightness of our own motives have been assailed. Interested men and designing politicians are endeavoring to destroy the independence of the judiciary so that there will be left neither liberty nor law to oppose their unhallowed purposes. . . . The opinion is well received by a large majority of the intelligent and well informed. . . . Our legislature meets in November, and as one of us will again be before that body for re-election, and as the other is anxious for his success, we feel a deep interest in the matter. If we are mistaken, it is because we have been unable to follow the lights of yourself and Chancellor Kent, who have founded and established the principles of chancery jurisprudence for our own country upon an imperishable basis." On December 1, 1842, Dickinson and Lacy wrote to Story thanking him for his "kind favor." *Ibid.*

[69] John Pitman to Story, Jan. 26, 1842, Story Papers, Clements Library. Pitman also wanted to know "whether you think that under all circumstances I have not a right to publish such sentiments without subjecting myself to the charge of having become a 'political judge,' which is the charge now made against me" (*ibid.*). On March 30, 1842, Pitman asked Story to use his influence over Webster to persuade the president of the United States to issue a proclamation to prevent an insurrection (*ibid.*). See *Luther* v. *Borden*, 7 Howard 1 (1849). On October 27, 1825, Pitman wrote to Story for legal advice on an insurance case before him. "You would oblige me by your opinion and a reference to any authorities if there are any." (Story Papers, Clements Library.) "I am much obliged to you for the information you have given me," Pitman wrote on November 8, 1825 (*ibid.*). See also Pitman to Story, Apr. 7, 1842, *ibid.*

[70] Story to Hopkinson, Dec. 16, 1828; Dec. 12, 1831; Dec. 21, 1831; Dec. 12, 1833; Dec. 22, 1834; Jan. 3, 1835, Hopkinson Papers, HSP.

[71] Story to Hopkinson, May 15, 1830, *ibid.*

[72] Story to Hopkinson, June 2, 1832, *ibid.* On March 24, 1839, Hopkinson thanked Story for his assistance, and said, "I shall abide by your opinions." (Story Papers, Clements Library. See also Hopkinson to Story, Mar. 12, 1839 and Aug. 23, 1839, *ibid.*) Story was instrumental in obtaining for Hopkinson his judgeship. In 1826 he had instructed Hopkinson on the procedure to follow to procure an appointment as a United States district attorney. (Story to Hopkinson, Mar. 4, 1826, Hopkinson Papers, HSP.) On March 8, 1826, Story informed Hopkinson that Justices Story, Marshall, and Washington would recommend him to President Adams for appointment to the United States Supreme Court (*ibid.*). In 1827, Story recommended to President Adams that Hopkinson should be appointed to fill the vacancy in the district court (Pennsylvania) caused by the death of Judge Peters. (Story to John Quincy Adams [copy], Jan. 18, 1827, *ibid.*) A year later, Story and Hopkinson celebrated the latter's appointment (which was confirmed by the Senate on February 23, 1829). Story to Hopkinson, Dec. 16, 1828, *ibid.*

members of the Marshall Court, often sent Story exhaustive letters requesting information on complex legal matters.[73] "I have not had time, as yet, to examine the case which you have under advisement," wrote Story to Washington on one occasion, "but I shall come prepared to talk it over with you at our next meeting."[74] Interesting it is that a year before Story handed down his decision in the *Terrett* case, Justice Washington, who strongly supported Story's opinion, first when it was delivered, and again in his own concurring opinion in the *Dartmouth College* case, received an extended analysis from Story on the constitutional question of state impairment of the obligation of contract.[75]

Other members of the Court, namely Justices Barbour,[76] Thompson, and Todd, sought the wisdom of brother Story. "I have a case from the District Court of Connecticut," wrote Justice Thompson, "upon which I find some difficulty. . . . You would oblige me by letting me know your views upon the question."[77] Justice Todd's son wrote to Story that his "father often dwelt with delight upon the intimacy subsisting between you, and his private letters now in my possession establish the same fact."[78]

Even after the appointment of Chief Justice Taney and the rise of the "New Court," Story, although extremely discouraged with the quality and political attitudes of the new appointees,[79] continued to enjoy the admiration and confidence of his brethren. The Jacksonian appointee, John McLean, often disagreed with Story's decisions, but he did not shirk from asking for Story's

[73] See, for example, Washington to Story, Nov. 25, 1824; Nov. 26, 1828, Story Papers, LC.

[74] Dec. 22, 1828, Story Papers, NYHS.

[75] Apr. 21, 1814, *ibid*. Story was replying to Washington's inquiry on the subject of state insolvency laws. "[F]avor me with a copy of the opinion which you shall deliver in the case before you," concluded Story.

[76] Philip Barbour to Story, Feb. 10, 1837, Story Papers, LC.

[77] Smith Thompson to Story, Aug. 7, 1824. Story Papers, Texas. In answer to another request, Story replied: "No case has ever occurred before me, in which a question has been made, whether the Court could order *without* consent any cause to be referred to [a] referee. My opinion is that the Court has no such authority. It is in my judgment at variance with the constitutional provisions respecting a right of trial by jury." (To Thompson, Aug. 17, 1827, Story Papers, Yale.) "I have before me several questions on which I should be much pleased to hear your opinion before deciding them," wrote Thompson on another occasion. Thompson to Story, July 7, 1825, Story Papers, Clements Library; see another inquiry sent by Thompson to Story, Oct. 24, 1825, *ibid*.

[78] C. S. Todd to Story, Feb. 8, 1838, Story Papers, LC.

[79] "I agree with you as to the . . . two new judges," wrote Story to John McLean on May 10, 1837. "An increase of numbers without an increase in strength & ability & learning is a . . . disadvantage. Mr. Smith has declined accepting the office; and I perceive, that Mr. McKinley has been appointed in his stead. I do not know him; but some . . . who do know him, speak of him in *very moderated* terms of praise—so moderated as to leave me to the conclusion that he has not the requisite qualifications for the office." John McLean Papers, Library of Congress.

advice on legal problems beyond his capacity to solve. "I have examined the points suggested by your letter . . . which reached me a few days ago," wrote Story to McLean in 1838, "& I will state to you my *impressions* on them, although I do not pretend to be very confident on the subject."[80] "If your health and engagements shall permit," wrote McLean at a later time, "I should be grateful to know your impressions, as to the points ruled in the bankruptcy case."[81] Justice McLean grew very close to Story and eventually became an admiring disciple. Ultimately, he reached the same conclusion as Story regarding the decline of the Court. "I feel alone without you, and disconsolate," he confided to Story in 1843. "Never have I been so much disgusted as at the present time. I see that the Bench, like the other departments, is to go down."[82]

Just as Story summoned the ghost of John Marshall by expressing the views of the chief justice through post mortem dissents, so, too, did John McLean resurrect Joseph Story, confident that his all-pervading spirit could still influence the members of the Court. Long after Story lay dead and buried, McLean invoked his name in dissenting opinions whenever he sought to venerate a point of law or clarify his own position, thereby demonstrating an abiding belief in the invincibility of his departed friend. "I stand alone," dissented McLean in an 1847 decision, "but I have the satisfaction to know, that the lamented Justice Story, when this case was discussed by the judges of the last term, that . . . one of the last cases which was discussed by him in consultation, coincided with the views . . . [I have] presented."[83]

Chief Justice Taney himself, the Jacksonian Democrat who was supposedly appointed to the Court as an antidote to the Story-Marshall brand of conservative nationalism, soon fell with McLean under the spell of Story and grew increasingly conservative as the years passed. It must have been quite a concession for Story's adversary in *Charles River Bridge* to confess only six years later that he was almost beside himself with anxiety over Story's absence from a session of the Court because of illness.

I need not, I am sure, tell you how much I deplored your absence at the late Term, where questions of great interest from the principles involved as well as the amount of property at stake were almost daily in discussion. And I felt your absence the more sensibly because Brother Thompson was obliged to leave early in the Term. And I have been so accustomed to have you on the one side and him on the other, that with the sincerest respect for my other brethren, I must acknowledge that it was

[80] Apr. 22, 1838, *ibid.*

[81] To Story, Sept. 30, 1843, Story Papers, LC. "I have a question before me involving the rights of securities which gives me some trouble." McLean to Story, Oct. 14, 1839, Story Papers, Clements Library.

[82] Jan. 7, 1843, Story Papers, LC. See also McLean to Story, May 5, 1838, *ibid*. It should be noted that a perusal of the correspondence between Story and his associates fails to produce any evidence that Story relied on his brethren for legal assistance.

[83] *Fox* v. *Ohio*, 5 Howard 440 (1847).

sometimes uncomfortable to feel that you were both absent. . . . You have seen in the newspapers the opinion in the [*Illinois*] case . . . I greatly regretted your absence when that case was under consideration.[84]

Whatever it was that brought about the friendship between Story and Taney— whether it was a growing appreciation for Story's legal knowledge and constitutionalism, his pleasing manner, or simply the temper of the times—it made Taney acutely aware of Story's distinction. When, in the fall of 1845, Taney suddenly realized Story would no longer be with him, he roundly exclaimed: "What a loss the Court has sustained in the death of Judge Story! It is irreparable, utterly irreparable in this generation; for there is nobody equal to him"[85]

STORY AND MARSHALL: THE MYTHS AND THE MEN

But the justice who most frequently relied upon Story was Chief Justice Marshall. As Marshall's biographer has observed, "During the entire twenty-four years that Marshall and Story were together on the Supreme Bench the Chief Justice sought and accepted the younger man's judgment and frankly acknowledged his authority in a variety of legal questions, excepting only those of international law or the interpretation of the Constitution."[86] Again and again Marshall sought the advice of his great friend, Judge Story. "I wish to consult you on a case which to me who am not versed in admiralty proceedings has some difficulty."[87] In another letter Marshall thanked Story for his opinions and asked for Story's views on "another admiralty question of great consequence,"[88] to which Story replied with seven closely written folio pages.[89]

[84] Taney to Story, Mar. 18, 1843, Story Papers, LC. "I was much obliged by your letter containing the references to the late English decisions upon their Pilot laws," wrote Taney to Story in 1842. "I do not mention these difficulties [raised by the case] to give you the trouble of a reply, but in order to call your attention to them while the English cases are fresh in your memory. There is enough of doubt in the case to prevent me from writing out the opinion, until we meet again and have a conference of the Court upon it." June 4, 1842, Story Papers, Clements Library.

[85] To Richard Peters, Nov., 1845, as quoted in Carl Swisher, *Roger B. Taney*, 442. See also Taney to William Story, June 12, 1846, Story Papers, Texas. "Poor Justice Story is no more!" exclaimed Henry Clay. "A great light of law and learning was extinguished by his death." Clay to Richard Peters, Sept. 20, 1845, Peters Papers, HSP.

[86] Albert J. Beveridge, *Life of Marshall*, IV, 120.

[87] May 27, 1819, Massachusetts Historical Society *Proceedings*, 2nd Series, Vol. XIV, 325.

[88] July 12, 1819, *ibid.*, 326.

[89] Story to Marshall, July 26, 1819, *William and Mary Quarterly*, 2nd Series. Vol. XXI (Jan., 1941), 4. "It affords me great satisfaction," said Story, "that the views taken by me of the case formerly stated have in any degree approved themselves to your mind. . . . The maritime law of the continent appears to me better adapted to the general interests of the commercial world, than a narrow adoption of the municipal law of England on this subject. And the authorities are not so stringent that we have no discretion left. Probably your decision will form a leading case for our future government."

In 1821, Marshall requested Story to interpret for him a contract of assignment and discern its effect under a United States statute. Story complied, and Marshall asserted that he would decide the case "in conformity with your opinion."[90] The same year Marshall wrote that he would be most appreciative if Story would assist him with two cases, particularly the second, which "has puzzled me so much that I have taken the case under advisement. . . . You are accustomed to these cases. Will you aid me with your advice?"[91] On December 9, 1823, Marshall again asked for Story's opinion on an admiralty question, frankly admitting that "You are more *au fait* on these questions than I am."[92]

How frequently did Marshall solicit the learning of his esteemed colleague? Let the chief justice himself answer: "I am so accustomed to rely on you for aid when I need it that you must not be surprised at the present application."[93] And on another occasion, Marshall confessed to Story that "Without your vigorous and powerful cooperation I should be in despair, and think the 'ship must be given up.' "[94]

Contrary to Beveridge's assertion, it would seem that in view of the fact Story edited Marshall's opinion in the *Dartmouth College* case, Marshall was also willing to accept Story's authority on questions of constitutional law. In addition, the Story-Marshall correspondence, though most of it has been lost,[95] does not seem to support Beveridge. One might consider this letter from Marshall written in 1831, for example, in which the chief justice informed Story "I have . . . adopted your opinion respecting the admiralty jurisdiction."[96] Similarly, what cases was Marshall referring to in 1829 when he wrote: "I hope your attention has been turned to the two *great* cases *we* have under advisement. I

[90] Marshall to Story, July 13, 1821, Massachusetts Historical Society *Proceedings*, 2nd Series, Vol. XIV, 328.

[91] Sept. 18, 1821, *ibid.*, 331.

[92] *Ibid.*, 334.

[93] Dec. 3, 1834, *ibid.*, 359.

[94] Nov. 10, 1831, *ibid.*, 348.

[95] Ten years after the death of Marshall, his son wrote to Richard Peters, the reporter, and expressed for the Marshalls "our thanks to you for the great interest which you have exhibited in the proposed Biography, and in repeating our earnest wish that it should be undertaken by Judge Story, if he should deem it advisable when he knows that we are almost *entirely* destitute of papers of any interest to the public. . . . While we are very willing to submit for his inspection the few papers which were found loosely scattered in his office, and to make every exertion to procure copies of all addressed by him to others. Great modesty formed a prominent feature of my Father's character which nothing could more clearly indicate than the fact that he never for his own use or that of his friends or children, still less for the eye of the public, preserved any of the numerous letters he received from the warm friends who expressed their admiration & approbation of his character and conduct. The few letters I have were found among old and valueless papers long since thrown aside in old boxes or trunks liable to be used as waste paper." James Keith Marshall to Peters, Apr. 3, 1845, Peters Papers, HSP.

[96] June 26, 1831, Massachusetts Historical Society *Proceedings*, 2d Series, Vol. XIV, 344.

wish you would place your thoughts upon paper."[97] In not a few instances, it would seem, the decisions of Chief Justice Marshall were the result of a collaborative effort.

Many lawyers and constitutional scholars have assumed that Marshall converted Story into a Federalist judge, but there is no question that Story was already a firm advocate of a strong central government and as stalwart a defender of property as any good conservative when he was appointed to the Court.[98] Equally mistaken is the view that Story was dominated by Marshall.[99] While Marshall and Story usually agreed on fundamental issues, nevertheless, there were important differences between them from the very beginning. Story, the extreme nationalist, was frequently impatient with the more cautious, easygoing nationalism of Marshall[100] and, in *Houston* v. *Moore*,[101] dissented from the chief justice and the Court on this very issue. *Brown* v. *United States*[102] serves as still another example of the Marshall-Story breach over the issue of nationalism. Story's concurring opinion in the *Dartmouth College* case, which differs substantially from Marshall's opinion, also demonstrates that on questions of property and contract Story and the chief justice were apparently not in full accord.

On smaller issues, too, the two justices disagreed. Story dissented from Marshall in *The Nereide*,[103] a case of great importance at the time involving prize law, in which he rejected Marshall's holding that a neutral could lawfully place his goods aboard an armed, belligerent ship for conveyance on the ocean. In *United States* v. *Dandridge*,[104] Story reversed Marshall's circuit opinion

[97] July 3, 1829, *ibid.*, 340. Emphasis supplied.

[98] "By 1815 Story had become a confirmed nationalist. The associations with and the well-directed efforts of the leading Federalists, including Marshall and the other members of this party on the Court, as well as the nationalist tendencies which were prevalent following the War of 1812, all combined to carry Story over to the Federalist cause." Charles Haines, *The Role of the Supreme Court*, 336. Beveridge draws the same conclusion: "after Story was made Associate Justice his views became identical with those of Marshall on almost every subject." *Life of Marshall*, IV, 118, n. 1.

[99] Edward Corwin refers to Story as Marshall's "pupil" and asserts that Story, "Still immature, enthusiastically willing to learn, warmly affectionate, and with his views on constitutional issues as yet unformed," fell under Marshall's influence after coming on the Court. *John Marshall and the Constitution*, 116.

[100] "The difference in the positions taken by Marshall and Story on trading with the enemy," notes Professor Newmyer, "was but one of several points of disagreement between the two men which the War of 1812 raised." In *The Bothnea and the Jahnstoff*, 2 Wheaton 169 (1817), for example, Story, the more extreme nationalist, was rebuked by the chief justice. The *Nereide* and *Brown* cases also grew out of that war. R. Kent Newmyer, "Joseph Story and the War of 1812: A Judicial Nationalist," *The Historian*, Vol. XXVI, No. 4 (Aug., 1964), 500.

[101] 5 Wheaton 1 (1820).

[102] 8 Cranch 110 (1814).

[103] 9 Cranch 388 (1815).

[104] 12 Wheaton 64 (1827).

and ruled in a suit brought by the president and directors of the Bank of the United States upon a bond given to the bank to secure the faithful performance of a cashier, that evidence of the execution and its approval by the board of directors did not require a written record. "More than any other judge is Story responsible for abolishing the medieval doctrine which required a corporation to act only by deed under its common seal. . . . and let it be noted, over Marshall's dissent and Blackstone's authority."[105]

On the important question of slavery, Marshall was compelled to restrain his more zealous associate from Salem.[106] Story, well ahead of his time, had demonstrated as early as 1819 that he categorically opposed slavery. In a charge to the federal grand jury at Providence, Rhode Island, in November, 1819, Story declared that the existence of slavery "under any shape is so repugnant to the natural rights of man and the dictates of justice, that it seems difficult to find for it any adequate justification."[107] Condemning both New England and the South as responsible for "this deep pollution" and "loathsome traffic," Judge Story informed his listeners that "the slave trade is . . . repugnant to the dictates of reason and religion, and is an offense equally against the laws of God and man."[108] Story made similar charges at Portland and Boston in 1820, which were given wide publicity throughout New England.[109] Breaking his rule to remain out of politics as a judge, Story stepped down from the bench in 1819 and appeared at an antislavery meeting in Salem to denounce the Missouri Compromise and the extension of slavery into the territories.[110]

Story's antipathy for slavery was reflected throughout his judgeship. In *La Jeune Eugenie* (1822) he invoked natural law, pushed aside established rules of international law, and held that the slave trade violated the "law of nations" and "the great principles of Christian duty, the dictates of natural religion, the obligations of good faith and morality, and the external maxims of social justice."[111] "I read, as you requested, the case of the Brig La Jeune [Eugenie]," wrote Theron Metcalf, "& was exceedingly pleased & instructed. My impressions had been against the doctrine of that case—perhaps relying too much on the dicta of the judges of the King's Bench . . . and upon the long practice of

[105] Gerald T. Dunne, "The American Blackstone," *Washington University Law Quarterly*, Vol. 1962, No. 3 (June, 1963), 332.

[106] Marshall's views on slavery and on the American Indian are discussed in Faulkner, *Jurisprudence of John Marshall*, 49–58.

[107] "Charge to the Grand Jury," quoted in part in *Life and Letters*, I, 336.

[108] *Ibid.*, 340–41.

[109] Story's charge in Portland is printed in full in Story, "Piracy and the Slave Trade," A Charge to the Grand Jury, First Delivered in the Circuit Court of the United States, for the Judicial Circuit of Maine, its First Session in Portland, May 8, 1820, *Miscellaneous Writings*, 122–47.

[110] Story, *Life and Letters*, I, 361.

[111] 2 Mason 409, 26 Federal Cases 832, No. 15,551 (1822).

modern Europe. I do not even now consider myself a competent judge of the question, but all my feelings are with you, & as Mr. Dexter once said, 'if the law is not so, it ought to be.' It certainly is fortunate for yourself as well as for our own country that events have brought you to lead the way in so many important & interesting investigations."[112]

But Chief Justice Marshall refused to accept Story's radical departure from precedent and in *The Antelope*[113] held for the Court that the slave trade was not contrary to international law. In considering the question of slavery, admonished the chief justice, "this court must not yield to feelings which might seduce it from the path of duty, and must obey the mandate of the law."[114]

[112] To Story, May 21, 1822, Story Papers, Clements Library. Before Story handed down his opinion in the *Eugenie* case, William Johnson, the New York reporter, had informed the judge that while in Philadelphia, "and turning over some new Law Books, in the Library of a friend, I met with a case, containing the judgment of Sir William Scott on the very question mentioned in the Newspapers, as having been lately raised before you, in the Circuit Circuit [*sic*] by Mr. Webster. As I had not seen the book anywhere else, I supposed it possible that it had not reached you; & knowing the very high respect which you entertain for the opinions of that great Lawyer, I presumed that you would not be displeased with my introducing this decision to your notice; and that if you had already seen it, you would excuse the freedom I have taken in mentioning the case to you. It was that of a *French* vessel, captured by a British cruiser, for being engaged in the Slave Trade, & condemned in the Vice-Admiralty Court of Sierre Leone. The report is interesting on account of several questions which were discussed; but it is sufficient for my purpose, barely to refer you to the book, 2 Dodson's Adm[iralt]y Rep. 210; The case of the *Louis*, December 1817; & to state that Sir William Scott was of opinion, that being engaged in the Slave Trade was not such a *crime*, as would amount to *piracy*, or to *an offence against the Law of Nations*." (Johnson to Story, Nov. 8, 1821, Story Papers, Clements Library. See the remarks of William W. Story and the letter of Sir William Scott to Judge Story, Jan. 2, 1822, *Life and Letters*, I, 356-57.) "The question would have been simple if the *Eugenie* had been American," notes Professor Maurice Baxter, "for Congress years before had prohibited the slave trade. But two Frenchmen owned the vessel. Did the slave trade violate international law? Could an American prize court invoke such a rule if it existed? Or could a court of this country enforce the laws of France against the trade? Webster's argument was an animated attack on slave traffic, his main purpose to show this trade illicit under international law . . . [and] was contrary to the law of nature, which is part of the law of nations. . . . Justice Story decided the case on much the same grounds urged by Webster." (*Webster and the Supreme Court*, 42.) Story thought "Mr. W[ebster]s argument was truly admirable," and confessed that he "had to decide against Ld. Stowell's *last* judgment, but his former judgment & that of the Court of Appeals delivered by Sir W. Grant are in my favour. I do not affect to be indifferent to the opinion of the public & especially of my friends on the subject. And I should be greatly consoled, if you should agree with me. But if you differ from me, I shall not be surprised, for I am aware that my judgment is often fallible, & I have no right to claim on this subject an unusual accuracy." Story to Jeremiah Mason, Jan. 10, 1822, Jeremiah Mason Papers, New Hampshire Historical Society. Portions of this letter are printed in *Life and Letters*, I, 358, 411.

[113] 10 Wheaton 66 (1825). Story silently acquiesced and did not dissent.

[114] *Ibid.*, 114. Story never conceded that Marshall was correct. See Story to Bacon, Nov.

Although he grew to deplore the violence of the abolitionists and joined with most Whigs in opposing them as a threat to the Union, Story remained a staunch enemy of slavery throughout his life, insisting at the time of his death in 1845 that the annexation of Texas was unconstitutional.[115] In spite of the criticisms that his great opinion in *Prigg* v. *Pennsylvania*[116] was a triumph of slavery, Story was sure that it was a "triumph of freedom."[117]

Thus it may be seen that in many instances Justice Joseph Story, veering sharply from the more moderate chief justice, was actually the leading defender of civil liberties on the Court during the first half of the nineteenth century. He led the fight through his decisions and writings to establish federal protection over the rights of the common law and prevent their debasement at the state level. He defended the academic freedom of Harvard University and

19, 1842, *Life and Letters*, II, 431. Story's opinion in *La Jeune Eugenie* was hailed by the antislavery forces, printed, and offered for sale in the Boston *Daily Advertiser*, January 29 and February 12, 1822. William W. Story relates, however, that many of the newspapers denounced Story for his first charge to the grand jury, "and one among them in Boston, declared, that any Judge who should deliver such a charge, ought to be 'hurled from the Bench.'" On January 23, William P. Mason, the reporter for the circuit court, assured Story that copies of his *Eugenie* opinion would be "sent to the different cities South with the N[orth] A[merican] Review which is just out." (Story Papers, Clements Library.) In *United States* v. *The Amistad*, 15 Peters 518 (1841), Story ordered the release and repatriation of a group of Negro slaves who had taken possession of a vessel in which they were being transported, and had killed the captain and their owners. See also Story's dissent in *Groves* v. *Slaughter*, 15 Peters 449 (1841), in which he asserted that the Mississippi Constitution voided contracts for the purchase of slaves even when brought from a neighboring state, and also Story's controlling opinion in *The Plattsburgh*, 10 Wheaton 133 (1825), in which Story affirmed the condemnation of a slave-trading ship.

[115] See Story to Bacon, Apr. 1, 1844, *Life and Letters*, II, 481; Story to Mrs. Story, *ibid.*, 512; Story to Greenleaf, Feb. 16, 1845, *ibid.*, 514. Story also came to the defense of the oppressed American Indian. See, for example, Story to Richard Peters, June 24, 1831, *ibid.*, 46. "At Philadelphia I was introduced to two of the Chiefs of the Cherokee nation so sadly dealt with by the State of Georgia," Story related to his wife. "I never in my whole life was more affected by the consideration that they and all their race are destined to destruction. And I feel, as an American, disgraced by our gross violation of the public faith towards them. I fear, and greatly fear, that in the course of Providence there will be dealt to us a heavy retributive justice." (Jan. 13, 1832, *ibid.*, 79.) In *Cherokee Nation* v. *Georgia*, 5 Peters 1 (1831), Chief Justice Marshall held that the Court lacked jurisdiction over the case, as the Cherokees were not a foreign nation. Story, joining with Justice Thompson in dissent, was desirous of extending jurisdiction to protect the Indians' rights. See Story to Joseph Hopkinson, Feb. 10, and Feb. 20, 1831, Hopkinson Papers, HSP. Story told Hopkinson that in the *Cherokee* case, the Court "ought not to take jurisdiction in cases of a political & national character, unless that jurisdiction is *clear* & unequivocal" (*ibid.*). Story told Peters that "neither Judge T[hompson] nor myself contemplated delivering a dissenting opinion, until the Ch. Justice suggested to us the propriety of it, & his own desire that we should do it." May 17, 1831, Peters Papers, HSP.

[116] 16 Peters 539 (1842).

[117] Story, *Life and Letters*, II, 392.

Dartmouth and Bowdoin colleges. He delivered the first great opinions on religious freedom. He handed down more and broader defenses of the rights of property and contract than any other member of the Court, and was well ahead of his time as the leading advocate on the Court of freedom for the enslaved peoples of the Negro race. This is truly a remarkable record of accomplishment.

The Marshall Court is best remembered for its contributions to federal supremacy and the sanctity of property; but here, too, Story vigorously challenged the leadership of Chief Justice Marshall. The impress of Story's contributions upon the growth of federal power was surely as permanent and extensive as that of Marshall, covering, it would seem, nearly every expressed and implied power of the American Constitution. His opinion in *Martin* v. *Hunter's Lessee*,[118] as Charles Warren has observed, is "the keystone of the whole arch of Federal judicial power."[119] And Marshall's biographer freely concedes that "Story sped along the path of Nationalism until sometimes he was ahead of the great constructor."[120]

Through his decisions and writings Story established himself as the intellectual leader of the nationalist school. The idea, proposed by Story in the *Martin* decision, of a national union between the people rather than the states became the basis of nationalistic thinking.[121] His *Commentaries on the Constitution*, written for the expressed purpose of destroying the doctrines of nullification and secession, were everywhere regarded as the authoritative statement of the nationalist theory of the Union. "You attach, as I do," he told Judge Hopkinson when the *Commentaries* first appeared, "very little importance[?] to the opinions of Politicians upon the point whether the Constitution is a contract or not. It is a very idle question in itself. But we must not forget, that it has become the leading ground, upon which all the Enemies of the Constitution in the South & West plan the overthrow of the Constitution, & intend to wield up their system of State Rights. Their theory, as theory, is *vox et pretereà nihil*; but it is practically a lever, which is raised to shave down the whole constitution. And so it has hitherto served in the South; for there, *words*

---

[118] 1 Wheaton 304 (1816).

[119] *Supreme Court in United States History*, I, 449.

[120] Beveridge, *Life of John Marshall*, IV, 116.

[121] Citing only Story's *Commentaries* and overlooking the *Martin* decision, Professor J. W. Gough credits Marshall for having first offered the anticontractual view of the Union in 1819 in *McCulloch* v. *Maryland*, 4 Wheaton 316. "It is outside my purpose here to attempt to narrate the history of the state-rights question," says Gough, "but it is worth observing that the position taken up by Story [in the *Commentaries*] was not original, but had been substantially foreshadowed by the judgment of Chief Justice Marshall in *McCulloch* v. *Maryland* in 1819. 'The government of the Union, then,' he declared, 'is emphatically and truly a government of the people.' " *The Social Contract*, 236, n. 2.

[122] Nov. 27, 1833, Hopkinson Papers, HSP.

have, in the soberest sense, become *things*. I felt myself compelled, therefore, once & for all, to endeavor to put the matter right in point of argument."[122]

And that he did. When the southern states embarked upon their disastrous road to secession, they fired their volleys not at Marshall, but in the direction of Judge Story, who was seen as defending every highway of national sovereignty. From every level of the legal profession, Story was regarded in the South as the sinister mind behind the relentless thrust of Yankee oppression. Judge Abel Upshur of the Virginia Court of Appeals, Professor Henry St. George Tucker of the University of Virginia Law School, and the vice president of the southern Confederacy, Alexander H. Stephens:[123] each assailed Story's *Commentaries on the Constitution* and his crucial decision in *Martin v. Hunter's Lessee*.

Story's pre-eminence in the field of vested rights is equally conspicuous. Transcending Marshall's narrower legal approach (excepting, perhaps, *Fletch-*

[123] Among the southern legalists who denounced Story's work as a biased and false interpretation of the nature of the Union were Abel Upshur, *A Brief Enquiry into the True Nature and Character of Our Federal Government: Being a Review of Judge Story's Commentaries* (Richmond, 1840); Alexander H. Stephens, *A Constitutional View of the War Between the States*, 2 vols. (Philadelphia, 1868); Henry St. George Tucker, *Lectures on Constitutional Law* (Richmond, 1843). All three works are devoted primarily to a critical examination of Story's *Commentaries*, and the influence of Tucker over the thinking of southern lawyers is interestingly documented by the 1833 edition of Story's *Commentaries* in the University of Virginia Law School. On the flyleaf of the first volume, a number of unsigned comments on the book are recorded in (fading) ink by students in the following manner: "The Devil himself cd [could] not have written a worse book— 1845." Story's influence seems to have prevailed, however, for below this statement appears the later comment: "I will venture to affirm that the man who wrote the above is a southern fanatic, & a disunionist—1859." Farther down the page, however, is this third comment of a student: "I have had the pleasure of reading the above named book,—& notice with surprise the remarks above—I have only to say that I disagree with both of the gentlemen,—& have but to add that I believe them to be equal—that is their minds tend to the extreme. 1867." The most noteworthy of the criticisms directed against the Story-Marshall decisions, which appeared in the public newspapers, were a series of articles written in 1821 by Judge Spencer Roane of the Virginia Appellate Court, under the pseudonymn of "Algernon Sidney." "I have read the essays in the Richmond Enquirer attacking the Supreme Court," Story wrote Jeremiah Mason. "Those under the signature of Algernon Sidney are as I understand written by Chief Justice Roane. They are exceptionally abusive, & considering he is a Judge, his conduct is most deeply reprehensible. His attack on Judge Johnson is truly in the character of a ruffian." (July 19, 1821, Mason Papers, New Hampshire Historical Society.) For a good general discussion of the southern position, see Walter Hartwell Bennett, *American Theories of Federalism*, 91–161; see also Charles E. Larson, "Nationalism and States' Rights in Commentaries on the Constitution after the Civil War," *American Journal of Legal History*, Vol. III (1959), 360–69. Story's *Commentaries* were still under attack by southern legalists as late as 1899. See John Randolph Tucker, *The Constitution of the United States* (ed. by Henry St. George Tucker), I, 178–324. "At the head of the second [i.e., nationalist] school," said Tucker, "Judge Story is *primus inter pares*." *Ibid.*, 179.

er v. *Peck*), Story combined law and philosophy in vindicating the rights of property, and unlike Marshall, did not restrict himself to cases falling only under the contract clause. It is open to question whether Marshall ever conceived of property rights in the same broad perspective envisaged by Story, and it is doubtful that he was capable of producing a learned, masterful work equal to Story's dissent in the *Charles River Bridge* case. Lacking Story's phenomenal knowledge of the common law, the great chief justice was ultimately forced to seek the assistance of Story to sustain himself in *Dartmouth College* v. *Woodward*.[124]

Still another notable difference between Story and Marshall is the one concerning their opposite approach to that nebulous phrase which can still provoke a heated discussion, the general welfare clause. In few other fields of public law do their nuances assume such significant proportions in our own day and age; for a broad interpretation of the general welfare clause is the desideratum for an important segment of modern social welfare legislation. In the name of Marshall and his doctrine of loose construction, lawyers, jurists, and scholars continually uphold a liberal construction of the Constitution. Also imbued with the spirit of Marshall, so goes it, is a broad interpretation of the general welfare clause.

But there is an abundance of evidence which suggests that Supreme Court decisions in modern times reflect the handiwork of Story more than Marshall. The sweeping and comprehensive decisions handed down nowadays, encompassing the whole moral, economic, and intellectual range of human activity, themselves lack the Marshall touch of moderation and suggest other possibilities. Although here, too, one must venture to generalize with extreme caution, the truth of the matter is that Supreme Court opinions over the past thirty some years have very often been more in keeping with Story's nationalism.

It is not enough, however, simply to say that Marshall broadly construed the Constitution, only with a greater sense of restraint than Story. An exchange of letters between Marshall and Timothy Pickering not only illustrates that the leader of loose construction interpreted one of the most fundamental clauses of the Constitution in its narrowest terms, but also throws light on the general welfare clause itself. For the sake of constitutional history as well as biographical perspective, the correspondence—which took place, incidentally, during the first great debates over nationally sponsored internal improvement programs —is quoted at length below.

SALEM
March 10, 1828

MY DEAR SIR:

Judge Wilson of Pennsylvania, a member of the National Convention, once told me, that after the Constitution had been finally settled, it was committed to him to

[124] 5 Wheaton 518 (1819).

be critically examined respecting its style; in order that the instrument might appear with most perfect precision and accuracy of language. Such is my impression of his meaning. And perhaps no legal composition presents fewer points of disputable construction.

In a copy of the Constitution printed for the use of the Senate, when I was a member, and also in the copy prefixed to the edition of the laws of the United States, in which John B. Colvin was employed, the first clause of the 8th Section, Article I, is thus printed and pointed:

> "Section 8. The Congress shall have power to lay and collect taxes, duties, imposts, and excises; to pay the debts and provide for the common defense and general welfare of the United States; but all duties, imposts, and excises shall be uniform throughout the United States."

It is a year or more since I thought this clause had been misconstrued in consequence of the punctuation; and I made in the margin of my copy, the following footnote: "There should be a comma only after excises: for the meaning intended was evidently this: 'The Congress shall have power to lay and collect taxes, &c. and excises, to pay (i.e. in order to pay) the debts &c.' And the closing passage, 'but all duties' &c confirms this construction: and then the powers necessary 'to provide for the general welfare' are specified."

Today, having occasion to look into the Journals of the Old Congress for 1787, after they had received the Constitution from the Convention, I observed that the clause in question had a comma only after the word excises, in the first line. My edition of the Journals is the first, as printed in 1787, under the eye of the accurate secretary, Charles Thompson. Whether Courts, in construing laws, are ever governed by their punctuation, I do not know: but it would seem that the composition of laws should be clear, independent of the punctuation. I am however inclined to think that the semicolon after excises, has led some persons to view the clause as giving powers almost unlimited; to do any act which had for its object "the general welfare." The very form of the clause favours the construction I put upon it.

The second clause confers the power of borrowing money. And Congress being thus (by these two means of taxing and borrowing) furnished with funds, sixteen additional powers are specifically given, showing how, in the application of those funds, Congress was "to provide for the general welfare" . . . .

TIMOTHY PICKERING[125]

In reply Marshall endorsed the view propounded by Pickering, and sent forth the following:

WASHINGTON
March 18, 1828

My Dear Sir,

I have always supposed that there ought to be a comma instead of a semicolon after the word excises. I have never believed that the words "to pay the debts and provide for the common defense and general welfare of the United States" were to be

[125] Timothy Pickering Papers, Massachusetts Historical Society.

considered as a substantive grant of power, but as a declaration of objects for which taxes &c. might be levied. . . .

I have no doubt of the correctness of your opinion that a general power to make internal improvements would not have been granted by the American people. . . .

JOHN MARSHALL[126]

It is important to note that a host of authorities have supported the orthodox, Pickering-Marshall proposition that the general welfare clause does not constitute a substantive grant of power. In his analysis of the clause, the late Henry St. George Tucker endeavored to prove that Hamilton's plan to draft the clause so as to render it a separate grant of power to the Congress was rejected at the Constitutional Convention six times.[127] Tucker also meticulously searched the records to show that such important figures as James Wilson, Jefferson, Madison, Calhoun, Cleveland, Coolidge, Cooley, Justices Marshall, Taney, Taft, Brewer, Wayne, and Miller all rejected the Hamiltonian thesis.[128]

But Story's position is unique. In his *Commentaries on the Constitution* he denied the soundness of the Hamiltonian argument on the ground that it violated the framers' principle of a government based upon limited powers. At the same time, Story refused to embrace the orthodox interpretation, contending that the words "to provide for the common defense and general welfare" were words of limitation on the taxing power but not on the other seventeen distinct clauses in section 8.[129] According to Tucker's detailed analysis of the problem, Story's construction leads to the same end as Hamilton's, "though by different routes, a government of unlimited powers."[130]

A rather cursory reading of Story's *Commentaries* has placed the Court in a peculiar position. Thus, a century after the *Commentaries* appeared, Story's name was cited in both the majority and dissenting opinions concerning the content of the general welfare clause. In *United States* v. *Butler*,[131] Mr. Justice Roberts adopted the Hamiltonian version (which Story rejected) and stated for the Court: "We shall not review the writings of public men or discuss legislative practice. Study of all these leads us to conclude that the reading advocated by Mr. Justice Story is the correct one." Mr. Justice Stone, speaking for the minority, replied: "That the governmental power of the purse is a great one is not now the first time announced. Every student of government and

[126] *Ibid.*

[127] Henry St. George Tucker, "Judge Story's Position on the So-Called General Welfare Clause," *American Bar Association Journal*, Vol. XIII, No. 8 (Aug., 1927), 468.

[128] *Ibid.*, 468–69. The views of Chief Justices Taney and Taft are cited in the unabridged version of this article. See note 132, *infra.*

[129] See Story, *Commentaries on the Constitution*, I, secs. 906–11.

[130] "Judge Story's Position on the So-Called General Welfare Clause," *American Bar Association Journal*, Vol. XIII, No. 8 (Aug., 1927), 468.

[131] 297 U.S. 66 (1935).

economics is aware of its magnitude and its existence. . . . [B]oth were recognized by Hamilton and Story, whose views of the spending power . . . have hitherto been generally accepted."[132]

And so in seeking justification for a broad rendition of the general welfare clause, the Supreme Court sought the counsel of Judge Story, whose greater nationalism provided the rationale that was demanded and believed necessary. Thus, Story's broad construction of the welfare clause acquired in the twentieth century a significance even greater than it originally possessed in the era of Jackson and the dawn of liberal democracy. Joseph Story, with all his outward vanity and inward humility, would never have suspected that he would be welcomed by the modern Court into its innermost chamber, or that Marshall would be turned out for want of a proper interpretation. It is ironic that a liberal Court, long devoted to sweeping aside obnoxious precedents, should seek support in the works of its most conservative peer.

Comparisons between Story and Marshall could be made interminably, but they all add up to the fact that the greater influence of Chief Justice Marshall and his superiority over Story are too frequently asserted and too seldom proved. It will be recalled that before Story arrived on the high bench, the Marshall Court had not really distinguished itself from earlier courts. The significant nationalist and property opinions came after 1813. The fame of Marshall rests upon his major constitutional decisions, most of which were delivered during this period: *Marbury* v. *Madison*, [133] *Fletcher* v. *Peck*,[134] *Dartmouth College* v. *Woodward*,[135] *McCulloch* v. *Maryland*,[136] *Cohens* v.

---

[132] *Ibid.*, 86–87. The problem of Story on the general welfare clause is further confounded by Tucker's assertion that Story rejected his own theory in a Supreme Court opinion decided subsequent to the publication of the *Commentaries*. In the case of *Dobbins* v. *Commissioners of Erie County*, 16 Peters 448–49 (1842), Justice Wayne said for the Court: "The revenue of the United States is intended by the Constitution to pay the debts and provide for the common defense and general welfare of the United States; to be expended, in particular, in carrying into effect the laws made to execute *all the express powers*, 'and all other powers vested by the Constitution in the Government of the United States.' " One of the judges who concurred in this unanimous opinion was Justice Story. From this, Tucker concludes: "The Madison Papers, the most complete compendium of the formation of the Constitution, were not printed until 1840. They were, therefore, not available to Story, the commentator, in 1833, but were open to Story, the judge, in 1842 . . . and with a judicial instinct worthy of Chief Justice Chase . . . Judge Story, with equal courage, was not afraid or ashamed to renounce his former opinions when he found them based on error." "Judge Story's Position on the So-Called General Welfare Clause," *American Bar Association Journal*, Vol. XIII, Nos. 7–8 (July-Aug., 1927), 363–68; 465–69, reprinted (unabridged) in Document No. 17, United States Senate, 70 Congress, 1 sess., 12.

[133] 1 Cranch 137 (1803).

[134] 6 Cranch 87 (1810).

[135] 5 Wheaton 518 (1819).

[136] 4 Wheaton 316 (1819).

Virginia,[137] and *Gibbons* v. *Ogden*.[138] His opinion in the *Marbury* case, while perhaps his most important, is also one of his most poorly executed, and continues to be severely criticized for its failure to assert that the Court's decision regarding the constitutionality of acts of Congress was binding upon the executive and legislative branches of government.

In fact, Marshall privately admitted later that he did not regard the Court's opinion on constitutional matters to be final with respect to Congress and the president. Nor did Marshall assert that the Court's interpretation was superior to that of Congress or the president. He simply invalidated an act dealing exclusively with the judicial department, claiming only that the judiciary could decide for itself the constitutionality of acts affecting that department.

Furthermore, Marshall's opinion was not particularly novel, in view of the fact that the Court had earlier assumed the right of judicial review in *Hylton* v. *United States*.[139] So weak was the opinion that throughout the nineteenth century Congress and the president continued to regard themselves as equals of, or superior to, the judiciary in determining the constitutionality of legislative statutes. In short, "Marshall's argument in favor of the Court's power to declare an act of Congress void was not of major significance at the time he made it, and the importance of *Marbury* v. *Madison* in the history of judicial review has in fact been somewhat exaggerated."[140]

Marshall's opinion in *Fletcher* v. *Peck*[141] required less originality than is commonly believed, since it is abundantly clear from the record that he followed closely the arguments propounded by Harper and Story as attorneys for the Georgia claimants. The opinion of Marshall in the *Dartmouth College* case was in many respects inferior to Story's concurring one, and Story assisted Marshall in the writing of his controlling opinion.

Furthermore, Story had already covered the ground in *Terrett* v. *Taylor*[142] and *Town of Pawlet* v. *Clark*.[143] Marshall's opinion in *Cohens* v. *Virginia*[144] was significant and probably his best written, but it added little to what Story had established earlier in *Martin* v. *Hunter's Lessee*.[145] The doctrine of implied

137 6 Wheaton 262 (1821).

138 9 Wheaton 1 (1824).

139 3 Dallas 171 (1796). Judicial review had been established in various state tribunals before the *Marbury* case.

140 Alfred H. Kelly and Winfred A. Harbison, *The American Constitution*, 229. See Haines, *The Role of the Supreme Court*, 245–58, for an extended discussion of the criticisms and weaknesses of the *Marbury* case.

141 6 Cranch 87.

142 9 Cranch 43 (1815).

143 9 Cranch 292 (1815).

144 6 Wheaton 264.

145 1 Wheaton 304 (1816). Edward S. Corwin makes this minor distinction: "If Story's argument is defective at any point, it is in its failure to lay down a clear definition of 'cases arising under this Constitution,' and this defect in constitutional interpretation is

powers promulgated by Marshall in *McCulloch* v. *Maryland*[146] was truly important; yet Story enunciated the very same doctrine five years earlier in *Brown* v. *United States*,[147] and without the assent of Marshall. The stature of Marshall cannot rest on *Gibbons* v. *Ogden*,[148] since Story may well have assisted in the writing of the opinion.

An aphorism that has circulated in legal circles for more than a century represents Story as having once said that Marshall was wont to remark, "Now Story, that is the law; you find the precedents for it."[149] Even if Marshall made this statement, perhaps a more accurate one would have it, "Now Marshall, I have established the precedents; you find a case to expound upon them." In a number of cases, Story seems to have anticipated Marshall's every move. Truly the pillar of the Marshall Court, he kept watch over the entire legal system, often pointing the way for Marshall to follow; supplying lawyers, statesmen, philosophers, state and federal jurists as well as his fellow justices with the necessary materials for speeches, books, and court decisions; drafting statutes to be enacted by the Congress; furnishing the legal profession with recondite treatises on nearly every phase of public and private law; and establishing the Harvard Law School as Dane Professor of Law. Yet the great chief justice, so unsure of himself that he must constantly exploit the mind of Mr. Justice Story, is generally believed not only to be the sole founder of American constitutional law, but also to have been Story's master and teacher.

Story's unassuming nature, together with Marshall's self-acclaimed leadership, explain in part the reason for the general obscurity of Story and the

---

supplied five years later in Marshall's opinion in *Cohens* v. *Virginia*." *John Marshall and the Constitution*, 178–79.

[146] 4 Wheaton 316.

[147] 8 Cranch 110 (1814). It has frequently been asserted that Marshall anticipated his decision in the *McCulloch* case fourteen years earlier in the case of *United States* v. *Fisher*, 2 Cranch 358 (1805). True, the chief justice accepted the Hamiltonian theory of loose construction of the necessary and proper clause in this case, but why did he reject it in Story's opinion in the *Brown* decision? The answer seems to be that Marshall was undecided about the proper scope of the elastic clause, or at least had a far narrower view of implied powers than did Story, who advocated that they might be inferred from the "resulting" powers rather than simply those that were enumerated. Clearly, such statements as the following entirely overlook the *Brown* decision: "In fact, nearly fifteen years elapsed [after the *Fisher* case] before Marshall had an opportunity to declare as a principle of constitutional construction the Hamiltonian theory of interpretation of implied powers." Haines, *The Role of the Supreme Court*, 268. For further discussion, see chapter 6 of this study.

[148] 9 Wheaton 1.

[149] As quoted in Corwin, *John Marshall and the Constitution*, 116. Another version describes Marshall as concluding the delivery of his opinions with the remark: "These seem to me to be the conclusions to which we are conducted by the reason and spirit of the law. Brother Story will furnish the authorities." Allan B. Magruder, *John Marshall*, 166. See also John F. Dillon, *John Marshall*, I, 304, 433; II, 116, 477.

greater fame of John Marshall. The record shows that Joseph Story, the unacknowledged legislator of his time, would probably have enjoyed as great a renown as a constitutionalist as the chief justice himself, had the tyranny of title and rank not betrayed him. He accepted a secondary role, never revealed the fact that Marshall and Webster relied heavily upon him for their own constitutionalism and, asking little in return, joined with his countrymen in praise of the Great Constructor.

Perhaps it was fortunate for Marshall's peace of mind that he never fully realized that more than once he was the spokesman for Judge Story. As each important constitutional issue came before the Court, Marshall, being the chief justice, immediately assumed priority and wrote the opinion, without pausing to consider whether Justice Story might not produce a better one. But as Story proved in such cases as *Martin* v. *Hunter's Lessee*,[150] he was fully capable of expounding upon general principles of the Constitution.

It is frequently said that Marshall is to be judged not as a lawyer, but as a judicial statesman. His opinions are regarded as Federalist political opinions. As one observer has noted, however, Story, too, was a statesman. Considering the varied nature of his Whig attachments—as political counselor to state and local interests, as an intermediary of patronage,[151] and as a silent partner of Webster and the Whig leaders—it is clear that Story's quasi-political activities, in tandem with his duties as writer, teacher, and jurist, make him one of the most "pre-eminent of conservative—and Whig—statesmen"[152] of the nineteenth century. Add to this observation the more significant one that Story's opinions embody the quality of statesmanship, perhaps in some instances to a greater extent than those of the chief justice.

In contrast to Marshall, Story spoke as a philosopher. Boldly and skillfully he engrafted natural law upon the fundamental law of the land through his decisions and writings, using the high bench as a platform to expound upon his constitutional and philosophical principles. Like Marshall he frequently employed broad general principles; but unlike Marshall, whose fearless disregard of nonessentials often seems to have been a cover for inadequate learning, Story found the appropriate cases to support those principles. Thus, where Marshall's opinions were baffling, dramatic exercises in logic, Story's were airtight discourses on law and jurisprudence. While it is perhaps a partial observer who makes the following comparison between the opinions of Marshall and Story, this estimate of William Wetmore Story's is nevertheless well taken:

Both are equally logical, clear and conclusive; but there is a warmth and color

---

[150] 1 Wheaton 304.

[151] See the account of R. Kent Newmyer, "A Note on the Whig Politics of Justice Joseph Story," *Mississippi Valley Historical Review*, Vol. XLVIII, No. 3 (Dec., 1961), 485-86.

[152] *Ibid.*, 491.

about my father's judgments which those of Marshall lack. One is a finished drawing in crayon or neutral tint, the other a painting with all the wealth of coloring. . . . Marshall confines his argument to logical statements, stripping it of all that is not strictly necessary, and keeping a narrow course. My father takes a broader sweep, fortifies his reasoning with large learning, and draws contributions from high authorities to strengthen the stream of his argument. . . . Marshall . . . seldom travels beyond the record, and his reasoning is confined to the facts of the case, while my father invariably labors, by bringing together all the learning and power he can command, to establish some principle which shall not only dispose of the particular case, but all others of a similar class. My father's judgments have, therefore, more general value than Marshall's as expositions of the law, at the same time that they are equally conclusive on the special facts of the case.[153]

Story lived somewhat vicariously in the lives of bygone English legalists, sharing their hopes and fears, repeating their doctrines, reproducing their decisions; yet adding individual ideas from his own philosophical convictions and wide experiences under the Constitution. He relied upon his own industry and resources more than Marshall, and realized that the triumph of those "general principles" referred to by Marshall would never survive without the development of an enlightened legal profession and a common law system to support them.

Vernon Parrington proffers the opinion that Story, although a brilliant legalist, was totally devoid of philosophical insight. Inveigled by the severe rationale of the law, overawed by the ermine, the judge, according to Parrington, scrutinized the world as if he were examining a court case. Story had "scanty knowledge of economics and political theory,"[154] concludes Parrington, and fell out of sympathy with his times because he weighed all considerations against outmoded English decisions and the dictates of Tory commentators. Of a similar opinion, Henry S. Commager estimates that Story was singularly inspired by the spirit of the common law. Story rejected liberalism, and it therefore follows in Commager's mind that Story never concerned himself with philosophical problems or the needs of his fellow man. "His reading was confined to law and to belles-lettres; if he had ever heard of Kant or Comte or James Mill he fails to confess it. Even in law his reading, or at least his learning, seemed to lack breadth. He was familiar with Blackstone,

---

[153] *Life and Letters*, II, 579–80. Beveridge gives this perceptive comparison between Story and Marshall: "Where Marshall was leisurely, Story was eager. If the attainments of the Chief Justice were not profuse, those of his young associate were opulent. Marshall detested the labor of investigating legal authorities; Story delighted in it. The intellect of the older man was more massive and sure; but that of the youthful Justice was not far inferior in strength, or much less clear and direct in its operation. Marshall steadied Story, while Story enriched Marshall. Each admired the other, and between them grew an affection like that of father and son." *Life of Marshall*, IV, 96.

[154] *Main Currents in American Thought*, II, 302.

but not, it would seem, with his mighty opponent Bentham. . . . His structure of law was monumental but lacking in any conscious philosophical foundation; it was elaborate but wanting in social orientation."[155]

But if there is one point which this and the preceding chapters have demonstrated, it is that Story cannot be accused of possessing a narrow legalism. As Story evinced in his *Commentaries*, he was well versed in the economic theories of Adam Smith; and he was also familiar with Ricardo and Malthus. From a glance at his judicial opinions, writings, correspondence, and public addresses, there is no doubt that Story possessed, as Francis Lieber realized, a solid foundation in philosophy. Story stated in the preface to the *Commentaries* that the work was based upon *The Federalist* and the decisions of Marshall, but Cicero, Vattel, Hooker, Paley, Montesquieu, Hume, Burke, John Adams, Adam Smith, James Wilson, as well as many of his own opinions, are cited just as frequently. We have seen that the ideas of Plato, Aristotle, Grotius, Burlamaqui, Bacon, Locke, and many others all flow easily from his pen.[156]

Nor was Story unaware of the intellectual movements of his own age. He was an active Unitarian. We recall that he had flirted with Rousseau in his youth, and there is every indication he understood utilitarian doctrines when he was older, especially those of Jeremy Bentham, whom he obviously disliked.[157] And it is plain enough Story was greatly influenced by the modern thinker he admired most, Edmund Burke. Indeed, the mainstay of the *Commentaries* is Burke, whose conservative philosophy Story weaves into the constitutional fabric as though Burke himself had written the document. From the fact Story introduced Burkean natural law into American jurisprudence. one might venture to affirm Story's position of pre-eminence in American political theory. Although he was not an original thinker in philosophy, his essay on natural law alone entitles him to a place of distinction in this area.

Story must be judged, then, not only as a jurist, author, and teacher, but also as a statesman and political and legal theorist. Whereas Marshall and the other members of the Court merely influenced the development of public law from the high bench, Story affected both public and private law in a variety of ways.

[155] "Joseph Story," *Bacon Lectures*, 91.

[156] That Story was familiar with many writings in political philosophy is evidenced by a reading of the "Catalogue of Miscellaneous Books, belonging to the Library of the Late Justice Story" To be Sold at Auction by Phillips & Sampson on Friday and Saturday, April 3 & 4th, 1846 (Boston, 1846). Among the selection offered are works by Burke, Aristotle, Hobbes, Turgot, Calhoun, Cicero, Hume, Thomas Paine, Malthus, John Adams, Sidney, Lord Chesterfield, Godwin, and Fisher Ames. The catalog is in the Story Papers, Essex Institute.

[157] See, for example, Story to James John Wilkinson, Dec. 26, 1836, Massachusetts Historical Society *Proceedings*, 2nd Series Vol. XV, (1901–1902), 221.

"For learning, industry and talent, he is the most extraordinary jurist of the age."[158] So, in 1841, wrote Chancellor Kent, whose estimation has stood the test of time. Lord Campbell of England registered the same opinion in 1842. "I survey with increased astonishment your extensive . . . knowledge of English legal writers in every department of the law," he wrote Story. "A similar testimony to your juridical learning I make no doubt would be offered by the lawyers of France and Germany as well as of America, and we all concur in placing you at the head of the jurists of the present age."[159] Francis Lieber wrote fourteen years later that Story was "perhaps the most enlightened jurist that our land has produced . . . he made a distinct impression on the history of his country, so much so that we know of no foreigner, desirous of becoming thoroughly and comprehensibly acquainted with the United States that leaves his works unstudied. His name will forever grace the list of leading men in a period of our country which we fear was greater than that in which we live."[160] At the turn of the century, another interested observer commented that "Tried by the quantity, quality and variety of his legal work, and by the influence which it has exerted and is still exerting upon the law, he is the foremost jurist America has produced."[161]

[158] Extract from a letter of Chancellor Kent to the editor of the *Louisiana Law Journal*, July 31, 1841, as quoted in Story, *Life and Letters*, II, 648.

[159] Sept. 21, 1842, *ibid.*, 429.

[160] Memorandum, July 30, 1855, Story-Lieber Correspondence, Huntington Library.

[161] Judge William Schofield, "Joseph Story," *Great American Lawyers* (ed. by William Draper Lewis), III, 185. Schofield makes the following refutation of the generally held belief that Story was dominated by Marshall: "During the period covered by his work in the Circuit Court Judge Story wrote opinions in two hundred and eighty-six cases in the Supreme Court. Of these two hundred and sixty-nine are reported as the opinion of the court or of a majority. Three were concurring opinions, and fourteen dissenting opinions. He wrote four [sic] dissenting opinions on questions of constitutional law, one [sic] being in the lifetime of Marshall, in *Houston* v. *Moore*. In *Ogden* v. *Saunders,* the only case in which Chief Justice Marshall was in the minority upon a question of constitutional law, Justices Story and Duvall concurred with him in the question upon which he wrote his dissenting opinion. Judge Story wrote the opinion of the majority of the court in five cases in which Marshall dissented; and in four of the cases in which he dissented during Marshall's life, the Chief Justice wrote the opinion of the majority. This record of his work is a sufficient answer to the assertion sometimes made by lawyers, that Judge Story, after his accession to the bench, was dominated by Chief-Justice Marshall." (*Ibid.*, 150–51. See also the estimate of Story's contributions by Hampton L. Carson, *The History of the Supreme Court of the United States*, I, 234.) "[W]hen some mediocre fluent book has been printed," observed Justice Holmes, "how often have we heard it proclaimed, 'Lo, here is a greater than Story!' But if you consider the state of legal literature when Story began to write, and from what wells of learning the discursive streams of his speech were fed, I think you will be inclined to agree with me that he has done more than any other English speaking man in this century to make the law luminous and easy to understand." Oliver Wendell Holmes, *Collected Legal Papers*, 41.

Story's influence will continue to make itself felt as long as the American republic stands. By his contributions to law, he spread his principles into every niche and corner of American jurisprudence. He combined traditional natural law and the Constitution into a barrier against the rise of tyranny, injustice, and the wholesale alteration of American liberties; but at the same time, he inadvertently prepared the way for the leviathan state through a liberal interpretation of the Constitution. Joseph Story thus bequeathed to America a set of conflicting precedents which are at once friendly and hostile towards limited government.

In promoting public and private virtue and the rights and duties of the common law, he checked state power and scuttled the ambitious schemes of many a Jeffersonian and Jacksonian democrat. In this sense, the Supreme Court under Story and Marshall acted as a conservative force in American politics. Still, it was Story, possibly more than any other judge of his day, who laid the groundwork for the judicial nationalism of the twentieth century which has enabled the Court to act as a liberal, and even radical, force in the American political system.

Being well-read in many areas of knowledge, and equally at home among the sages of antiquity and the black-letter philosophers, Story frequently relied upon the accumulated wisdom of the past as the best material for constructing his ideas. Although he often felt the greatest affinity for the minds of men who had long since passed into the annals of history, he nevertheless had a healthy streak of progressivism in him and hopefully paced at the rear of the march toward democracy, keeping sight of its possibilities as well as its dangers. He walked, then, in the shadow of John Adams, who had taught the value of liberty under practical laws. Law was his religion, and he loved the American Constitution because it was to him a conservative Constitution.

The *Commentaries on the Constitution* was his memorial to that divinely decreed covenant between God and man, and he worshipped at its altar with a religious inspiration. He introduced the American people to that great masterpiece of the founding fathers through the *Commentaries*. With a quotation from Cicero, then Burke, he dedicated his work to the American he admired most, Chief Justice Marshall, built the entire structure on the solid foundation of *The Federalist*, and offered it to his fellow countrymen as the light of their salvation. If asked what he was conserving, he would no doubt have replied simply: the American Constitution, the system most friendly to order and freedom in all the world. If pressed further on the matter, he would probably have dropped his tireless pen, glanced out his study window toward his nearby law school, and reflectively remarked that he stood for the preservation of a still greater constitution, that of civilization.

Appendices
Appendix I: Natural Law

Natural Law, or, as it is commonly called, the law of nature, is that system of principles, which human reason has discovered to regulate the conduct of man in all his various relations. Doctor Paley defines it to be the science, which teaches men their duty and the reasons of it. In its largest sense, it comprehends natural theology, moral philosophy, and political philosophy; in other words, it comprehends man's duties to God, to himself, to other men, and as a member of political society.

The obligatory force of the law of nature upon man is derived from its presumed coincidence with the will of his Creator. God has fashioned man according to his own good pleasure, and has fixed the laws of his being, and determined his powers and faculties. He has the supreme right to prescribe the rules, to which man shall regulate his conduct, and the means, by which he shall obtain happiness and avoid misery. He has given to man the power of discerning between good and evil, and a liberty of choice in the use of those means, which lead to happiness or misery. The whole duty of man therefore consists in two things; first, in making constant efforts to ascertain what is the will of God; and, secondly, in obedience to that will when ascertained.

For the purposes of the present article, we shall assume, without undertaking to prove, that there is a God of infinite power, knowledge, wisdom, benevolence, justice and mercy; that he has created man with suitable powers and faculties to pursue and obtain happiness; that man is a moral, dependent and accountable being; that his soul is immortal; that his ultimate happiness or misery is dependent upon his own conduct; that there is a future state of retribution, in which the inequalities of the present life will be adjusted according to supreme wisdom and goodness; that, by a right application of his powers and faculties, man may always discern and pursue his duty; that virtue, or doing good to mankind in obedience to the will of God, has attached to it the reward of everlasting happiness; and that vice, or doing wrong is disobedience to that will, is, by the very constitution of man's nature, necessarily connected with suffering and misery, directly or ultimately.

AUTHOR's NOTE: The following articles written by Joseph Story have been selected because of their relevance to this book and their general inaccessibility to most readers. All but one are reprinted here for the first time.

"Natural Law," an unsigned article by Joseph Story reprinted from Francis Lieber (ed.), *Encyclopedia Americana. A Popular Dictionary of Arts, Sciences, Literature, History, Politics and Biography, Brought Down to the Present Time: Including a Copious Collection of Original Articles in American Biography* (new ed.; Philadelphia: Desilver, Thomas & Company, 1836), IX, 150–58.

In short, that man cannot be permanently happy by the practice of vice, and must be permanently happy by the practice of virtue. We shall assume these propositions, not because they are not susceptible of complete proof, but because, not being intended to be discussed in this place, they nevertheless form the basis of the subsequent remarks.

From the moral government of God, and the moral capacity and accountability of man, we deduce his general rights and duties.

1. His duties towards God. In the just performance of these duties consists piety or devotion. In a large sense, indeed, every performance of our duty is but a performance of some duty towards God; since it is his will which makes it a duty. But in the restrained sense, in which we are accustomed to use the phrase, we refer it to those duties of which God is peculiarly the object. As he is our Creator, we owe him supreme worship and reverence; as he is our Benefactor, we owe him constant gratitude and thankfulness; as he is our Lawgiver and Judge, we owe an unreserved obedience to his commands. We are frail and dependent beings, and we have constant reason to implore his assistance, his mercy and his forgiveness. Hence arises the duty of prayer, as a solemn recognition of our dependence on God; as a means of religious improvement and of cultivating devout affections; as an effectual instrument of communing with our own hearts; as a source of consolation under the afflictions of life; and as an exercise of piety fitted to give a spiritual elevation to our thoughts, and a livelier and more enduring sense of our duty. From the same causes also flow the duty of public and social worship; of maintaining religious institutions; of aiding in the diffusion of religious knowledge; and of keeping in view, in all our words and actions, an habitual and reverential fear of God.

2. The duties of man towards himself, or those which terminate in himself. Among these we may enumerate the duty of personal holiness; of self-preservation; of temperance; of humility; of personal improvement in knowledge, wisdom and virtue; and of preserving a conscience void of offence towards God and towards man.

3. The duties of man towards other men, or what are called his relative duties, arising from the various relations, which he sustains or may sustain towards others. —Now these duties flow from the correspondent rights of others. And this leads us to the consideration of the different sorts of rights. Rights are usually divided into such as are natural or adventitious, alienable or inalienable, perfect or imperfect. We call those rights natural, which belong to all mankind, and result from our very nature and condition; such are a man's right to his life, limbs and liberty, to the produce of his personal labor, at least to the extent of his present wants, and to the use, in common with the rest of mankind, of air, light, water, and the common means of subsistence. Adventitious rights are those, which are accidental, or arise from peculiar situations and relations, and presuppose some act of man, from which they spring; such as the rights of a magistrate, of a judge, of electors, of representatives, of legislators, etc.

We call those rights alienable, which may be transferred, by law, to others, such as the right to property, to debts, houses, lands and money. We call those rights unalienable, which are incapable by law, of such transfer, such as the right of life, liberty and the enjoyment of happiness.

We call those rights perfect, which are determinate, and which may be asserted by force, or in civil society by the operation of law; and imperfect, those which are indeterminate and vague, and which may not be asserted by force or by law, but are obligatory only upon the consciences of parties. Thus a man has a perfect right to his life, to his personal liberty, and to his property; and he may by force assert and vindicate those rights against every aggressor. But he has but an imperfect right to gratitude for favors bestowed on others, or to charity, if he is in want, or to the affection of others, even if he is truly deserving of it.

It is difficult to make any exact enumeration of what may be deemed the general rights of mankind, which may not admit of some exceptions, or which may not be deemed capable of modification under peculiar circumstances. Thus the most general rights, which belong to all mankind, may be said to be the right to life, to liberty, to property, and to the use of air, light, water, and to the fruits of the earth. And yet, under certain circumstances, life, and liberty, and property, may justly be taken away; as, for instance, in order to prevent crimes, to enforce the rights of other persons, or to secure the safety and happiness of society. And in like manner the free use of air, light and water, may be interdicted.

In regard to imperfect rights, although the sanction is wholly upon the conscience of the party under a sense of religious responsibility, the obligation to perform the duties corresponding to them is, nevertheless, to be deemed as imperative, as if they also possessed the strongest earthly sanctions; since they arise from the commands of God, and are to be done in obedience to his will. Every man is therefore bound to exercise charity in its largest sense; to be just, grateful, kind and benevolent; to promote the general happiness; to speak the truth and to abstain from falsehood; to abstain from oppression, anger, revenge, hatred, malice, slander, uncharitableness, persecution, and every other injurious act or passion. These are duties, which are incumbent on him in respect to all the human race.

There are others, again, which arise from peculiar relations to others; such are those, which belong to him in the character of master or servant, magistrate or subject, parent or child, husband or wife. Among the duties of masters and servants, we may enumerate, on the part of the master, the duty to enjoin on servants no unnecessary labor or confinement, from caprice, or wantonness, or passion; to insult no servants by harsh, opprobrious or scornful language; to refuse them no harmless pleasures; to promote their welfare by all reasonable means. On the part of servants, the duty to be industrious, and punctual in the discharge of their duty, faithful and honest; and to yield a ready obedience to all just commands. On the part of magistrates, the duty of exercising power with moderation and mercy as well as justice. On the part of subjects, the duty of obeying the laws and supporting the institutions of society. On the part of parents, the duty of maintaining, educating, and otherwise providing for the intellectual, moral and physical improvement of their children. On the part of children, the duty to render their parents a just homage, love and reverence, to obey their commands, to lighten their labors, assuage their sorrows, and, as far as may be in their power, to administer to their infirmities, and to sup-

315

port and succor them when in poverty. On the part of husband and wife, the duty to promote domestic peace and harmony; to cultivate mutual love and forbearance; and in prosperity and in adversity, in sickness and in health, in life and in death, to be true, and watchful, and tender, as those whom God has united in bonds of permanent obligation and sanctity.

And this leads us to the consideration of the subject of marriage, and some of the rights and duties flowing from it. Marriage is an institution, which may properly be deemed to arise from the law of nature. It promotes the private comfort of both parties, and especially of the female sex. It tends to the procreation of the greatest number of healthy citizens, and to their proper maintenance and education. It secures the peace of society, by cutting off a great source of contention, by assigning to one man the exclusive right to one woman. It promotes the cause of sound morals, by cultivating domestic affections and virtues. It distributes the whole of society into families, and creates a permanent union of interests, and a mutual guardianship of the same. It binds children together by indissoluble ties, and adds new securities to the good order of society, by connecting the happiness of the whole family with the good behavior of all. It furnishes additional motives for honest industry and economy in private life, and for a deeper love of the country of our birth. It has, in short, a deep foundation in all our best interests, feelings, sentiments, and even sensual propensities; and in whatever country it has been introduced, it has always been adhered to with an unfailing and increasing attachment.

Polygamy, on the other hand, seems utterly repugnant to the law of nature. It necessarily weakens, and, in most cases, destroys the principal benefits and good influences resulting from marriage. It generates contests and jealousies among wives; divides the affections of parents; introduces and perpetuates a voluptuous caprice. It has a tendency to dissolve the vigor of the intellectual faculties, and to produce languor and indolence. It stimulates the sensual appetites to an undue extent, and thus impairs the strength and healthiness of the physical functions. It debases the female sex. It retards, rather than advances, a healthy and numerous population. It weakens the motives to female chastity and to exclusive devotion to one husband. Besides; the very equality in point of numbers of the sexes seems to point out the law of God to be, that one woman shall be assigned to one man. And in point of fact, the countries, where polygamy has been allowed, have been uniformly debased, indolent and enervate, having neither great physical, nor great intellectual ability.

If marriage be an institution derived from the law of nature, then, whatever has a natural tendency to discourage it, or to destroy its value, is by the same law prohibited. Hence we may deduce the criminality of fornication, incest, adultery, seduction, and other lewdness; although there are many independent grounds, on which such criminality may be rested. It follows that the right of divorce must be a very limited right; and that divorces are forbidden by the law of nature except for causes of very extraordinary character. It is manifest, that a power on either side to dissolve the marriage at will, would rob the state of matrimony of many of its principal blessings and advantages. It would deprive one of the parents of the comfort and gratitude of the children of the marriage. It would defeat the main purposes of their union, and weaken all domestic ties between parents and children.

On the other hand, a very restricted allowance of divorces has a natural tendency to preserve peace and concord in families, by perpetuating a common interest, and encouraging mutual forbearance and affection. By denying, except for extraordinary reasons, the right of divorce, we discourage, in a proportionate degree, the desire, as well as the means of accomplishing it. Christianity has confined the right of divorce to the single case of adultery; though the law of nature may perhaps be thought to justify some few other exceptions.

4. We next come to the duties of man as a member of political society. And, here, we shall briefly treat of certain rights and duties, which may arise from the law of nature independent of any organization into political societies, but which more naturally find a place here, because they constitute the principal grounds for such organization. Thus the right of property, the obligation of contracts, the duty of speaking the truth, the sanctity of oaths, with other corresponding duties, strictly speaking, may be perfect in a mere state of nature, without the recognition of any fixed society; for they may exist and have a necessary application independent of such society. But their value and importance are far more felt, and far better provided for, in political society, and, therefore, properly belong to the present head.

1. The origin of political society.—The origin of political society may be traced back to the primitive establishment of families. From the union of a number of related families grew up tribes; and from tribes gradually grew up colonies and nations. Accidental associations for offence or defence may, in some instances, have introduced the first elements of fixed society between strangers; and a sense of mutual interest and mutual dependence may have rendered them permanent. Coeval with the establishment of civil societies was the origin of civil government. Parents, from necessity as well as from prudence, exercised, and were admitted rightfully to exercise, immediate authority and government over their children and families. The patriarch or chief of a tribe, in like manner, exercised authority over those, who were of his blood and lineage. And, silently, the powers of rule or government were either divided as convenience or accident dictated, or were retained by the head, as the common bond of the union of the whole. Sometimes, indeed, government did or might arise from military associations for plunder or protection. And in such cases the strongest, the most intelligent, and the most enterprising and valiant, were the most likely, in the first instance, to be intrusted with the highest powers. The necessity, in all cases, of prompt submission and obedience, in order to accomplish the immediate objects in view, furnished a sufficient excuse, if not just reason, for intrusting the leaders with summary and despotic authority.

2. Governments, then, may be properly deemed to arise from voluntary consent, or from long acquiescence and prescription, or from superior force. The fundamental objects of all civil governments are, or ought to be, to promote the welfare and safety of the whole society. It is obvious, that no single individual can protect himself to the same extent, or by the same means, as an organized society or government can protect him. The latter has the powers, authority, union and resources of numbers. Men enter, then, into civil societies for the protection of their persons, and personal rights and property. In a state of nature, if either be invaded, the only

redress is by the application of positive force by the individual, who is injured. But under the establishment of civil governments, the redress is taken from the individual, and is administered by the government itself through its own functionaries, and according to its regulations, and by the authority and force of numbers. The entering into civil society, therefore, necessarily, or, at least, naturally, induces the surrender of all those private rights, which are indispensable for the good order, peace and safety of the whole society. And, indeed, unless some surrender of powers and rights were made, there could be no such thing as a regular government, since each person would be at liberty to do as he pleased and there would be no such thing as lawful authority on one side to give a rule, or, on the other side, any duty of obedience.

Civil government, then, may be properly said to consist in the exercise of such delegated powers, as are proper or necessary for the safety, protection and happiness of the whole community. And civil liberty may be said to consist in not being restrained by any laws, which are not conducive to the public welfare. We sometimes see governments existing, in which these objects are but imperfectly obtained, and ask ourselves, why they are not changed. There are several reasons, which may help us to a just understanding of the facts, and enable us satisfactorily to solve the inquiry, how it should happen, that governments should fail of attaining the very objects, on which they are founded, and yet be supported by the acquiescence of the people.

In the first place, in every government, there are many persons, who obey from mere prejudice, or the habit of obedience, and from an inherent indisposition to contemplate any thing otherwise than as it at present exists. They do not stop to consider, whether it can be made better or not. They are content, from a *vis inertiae* to let things remain as they are.

In the next place, those whose obedience is governed by reason, are often persuaded to obedience by the consciousness of their own inability to procure suitable changes; by the dread of civil commotions; by doubts as to the method of curing existing evils; and by the persuasion, that in many instances the form of government has become so interwoven with the habits and institutions of the people, that as much mischief as good might be done by a change.

In the next place, in every government, many persons have a direct and positive interest in preserving the government as it is, and even in perpetuating its very corruptions. They may be a favored class, enjoying peculiar privileges, ranks, or patronage; they may have their whole property and importance involved in the existence of the present state of things.

In the next place, the actual moral and intellectual power, and even physical power, of the state in its present organization, may be so combined in the structure of the government, that they may present insuperable barriers to any change. If, for instance, the whole of the privileged classes should happen to be the only educated persons in the nation; if the whole priesthood should depend upon the government for its influence and support, and its exclusive patronage and privileges; if the whole wealth of the community should be lodged in a few hands, and those few should be the very heads of the government; if the military power should be so organized, that it could scarcely find the means, or possess the power, to act except under the existing arrangements;—in any, and in all of these cases, it is easy to perceive, that there would be immense difficulties in introducing any fundamental and salutary change. It could scarcely take place but upon some general convulsion, which could break asunder all the common ties of society.

But it may be asked, as civil government is formed by the whole people, whether it can ever be justly altered, except by the will of the whole. If by the will of the whole be meant the will of each individual singly, it may be answered in the affirmative; for by entering into society, men necessarily engage to be governed by the will of the majority, since unanimity in all matters of civil polity is impracticable. The will of the majority or the will of the minority must govern. If the latter, by a veto, can stop all measures, the majority are governed by them. All reasoning and all principle, therefore, unavoidably lead to the result, that the will of the majority must be deemed the will of the whole for all practical purposes; and as the interests of the whole society require this, it is binding on every part of it.

3. The origin of property. One of the great objects of political society is the protection of property; and many learned discussions have taken place as to the origin and nature of property. Some things are of common and universal use by all mankind, and to such use all mankind have an equal right. Such, generally speaking, are (as we have seen) air, water, and light. Other things belong, exclusively, to one or more persons, and no others have a right to intermeddle with, possess, or enjoy them. Such an exclusive right in things is called *property*.

How did such a right originate? It is plain, that, in a mere state of nature, no man could insist, that he possessed any such exclusive right to things in general; for, if one possessed it, all would equally possess it, which would be the same as to affirm its non-existence. The earth, and its various fruits, herbage and trees; the various inferior animals, such as birds, fishes, and beasts, either for food, or covering, or pleasure, or labor, seem alike to belong to all mankind, and are for the use of all.

To a limited extent, possession and use of a thing must, indeed, confer a temporary or permanent ownership. If, for instance, a man stands or lies on a particular spot of ground, during the time of such occupation, he must have the exclusive right of occupation, for it is indispensable for his immediate use, and no other person can show a better right to it. So if he gathers fruit, for the purpose of eating it, no other person can have a better right to eat it than himself; and he must, therefore, have an exclusive right, because it is necessary to the use. But if he does not hold the fruit to eat it at present, but lays it aside for future consumption, his right to the exclusive use of it is not so clear; it is somewhat more remote; it does not turn upon immediate possession, and immediate use.

It may be said, that he has, by his labor, gathered it, and therefore he has a superior title to it. But, though his labor is his own, it does not follow, that because he bestows it upon another thing, he thereby acquires any exclusive ownership in that thing. It may be extremely inconvenient, and, perhaps, even injurious to the common claims of others, that he should so bestow his labor upon it. They are not, therefore, bound to respect any claim founded upon such labor.

Some persons found the right of property upon a presumed or tacit consent of all mankind, which is a mere theory, and wholly unsupported by any universal facts.

Others found it upon mere occupancy; but that, at most, gives only a present and temporary right, during such occupancy. Others, again, found it upon the very equality of all mankind, and contend that, as God has given all things for the use and necessities of all, each may appropriate to himself whatever is proper to satisfy those necessities. But, even here, he must leave sufficient to satisfy the necessities of others; and they may take, of the stores so appropriated, enough to supply their own necessities. The truth, however, seems to be, that, in a state of nature, each man actually appropriates to himself whatever he desires, and can get; and he then holds it by the title of the strongest; and no other person respects his title any longer than it can be so maintained, though no one can show a better title to it.

As soon as families are formed, the necessity of providing for their own mutual comfort and wants, gradually leads them to hoard up and appropriate food, and other things, for future use. The convenience, and sometimes, the necessity of an interchange of commodities with other families, of which each has a superfluity, leads to an increased accumulation. Possession and power are the guardians of these gathered stores; and a sense of convenience and mutual interest induces every family to regard with respect the commodities in possession of the other.

Thus the first rudiments of exclusive property begin in the fact of actual possession and power, and the title gains strength and permanence from a sense of the beneficial results to the interests of all the neighborhood, and, ultimately, to the whole society, with which each family and tribe are connected. The advantages of the admission of such an exclusive right are soon felt by all reflecting minds, and gradually prepare the way for a more solemn recognition of it. It is perceived, that its tendency is to increase the product of the earth, by creating inducements to plant, when the planter is secured in his exclusive right to the harvest. It also improves the comforts and conveniences of life, and introduces a fit distribution of labor; and it cuts off a great source of perpetual contest and warfare among those, who would, otherwise, be struggling for the common prize. In the ordinary course of things, movables, such as fruits, and flocks, and herds, and fishes, first become property. Land rarely becomes permanent property until a much later period in the history of nations.

4. But, whatever may be the origin of the right to property, it is very certain, that, as it is now recognized and enforced, it is a creature of civil government. Whatever right a man may have to property, it does not follow, that he has a right to transfer that right to another, or to transmit it, at his decease, to his children, or heirs. The nature and extent of his ownership; the modes in which he may dispose of it; the course of descent, and distribution of it upon his death; and the remedies for the redress of any violation of it, are, in a great measure, if not altogether, the result of the positive institutions of society.

Accordingly, we find that, in different nations, all these subjects are regulated in very different manners. In some nations, all the children inherit the property, upon the death of the ancestors; in others, the eldest son only. In some, there is power to dispose of the whole, or of a part only, by will and testament; in others, this power has been denied. In some, the duration of the right of property is perpetual; in others, it is limited. In some, it may be alienated at all times, and in perpetuity; in others, the power of alienation is restrained. In some, long possession confers title; in others, it confers none. Above all, the capacity to dispose of property is variously regulated by civil institutions. It is obvious, that idiots, and madmen, and infants, ought not to be allowed to dispose of property, since they have no rational discretion. But at what period of life shall a man be deemed to possess such discretion? At ten, or twenty, or thirty years of age? Shall it equally apply, at all times, to both sexes, under all changes of condition? In all nations, some peculiar regulations have been adopted to settle these questions, which, by the law of nature, it would not be easy to settle by any uniform and fixed rule. The power of disposing of property is sometimes allowed at eighteen, sometimes at twenty-one, sometimes at twenty-five, and sometimes at thirty years of age. It is sometimes permitted to married women, but it is more commonly denied to them. Who can say, which of these periods is the true one, or which of these privileges is the proper one?

5. Another great object of society is the protection, not only of property in *things*, but of property (if we may so say) in *actions*. A great portion of the business of human society is founded upon contracts, express or implied; and these contracts, especially in modern times constitute the bulk of the fortunes and acquisitions of many persons, from the humblest mechanic up to the most opulent stockholder. The obligation of contracts, or, in other words, the duty of performing them, may indeed, be deduced from the plainest elements of natural law, that is, if such contracts are just and moral, and founded upon mutuality of consideration. It is indispensable to the social intercourse of mankind. It is conformable to the will of God, which requires all men to deal with good faith, and truth, and sincerity in their intercourse with others. It is indispensable in order to prevent injuries to others, whose acts, and interests, and property, may depend upon a strict fulfilment of such contracts.

But, in a state of nature, the obligation of contracts, however perfect in itself, cannot ordinarily be enforced upon the other contracting party to its just extent. The only remedy is positive force; and this, in many cases, is impracticable, and is generally inconvenient. The institution of political society brings the moral, as well as the physical power of the whole in aid of the natural obligation of contracts. The remedy is generally peaceable, perfect and easy.

But it may be naturally asked, what contracts are really obligatory? The true answer, in civil societies, is, all such contracts as the law of the land declares to be obligatory or of which it permits the obligation to be enforced. The true answer, independent of the positive recognitions of civil society, is, all such contracts as are moral, just, practicable, and have been extinguished in any lawful manner. Contracts which are immoral, or which have resulted from fraud or oppression; contracts which require impossible things, or are repugnant to natural justice; or which are founded in essential mistakes, as to persons, characters, or things; or which involve the breach of other paramount obligations, cannot, upon the principles of eternal justice, be obligatory.

6. Without going more at large into the origin and objects of political society, it will be seen, that these objects require the delegation (as has been already intimated)

of certain powers and authorities to those who are to administer the government. The ends required are the preservation of the general rights and the general welfare of the community; and the means to accomplish these ends must be given by the express or implied assent of the governed. The civil powers, which, in every well constituted society, seem indispensable for this purpose, are the legislative, executive and judicial powers.

In order to secure the safety and happiness of the society, it is indispensable, that there should be somewhere lodged a power to make laws for the punishment of wrongs, and for the protection of rights, and for the promotion of the peace, health and good order of the society. And, as there is a perpetual change in human affairs, and laws and institutions which are adapted to one age are partly unfit for another, there must be in the government a power to alter, amend and modify existing laws; —and, as human legislation must necessarily be imperfect, the power to improve it may always be presumed to be useful, since experience often points out mistakes and deficiencies. The power of legislation must, therefore, in its nature, include the power of abolishing, as well as of enacting laws. Again, as the exigencies of the society must require expenses to be incurred, and revenues to be raised to defray those expenses, the power of taxation naturally belongs to the power of legislation, as a means to accomplish the appropriate ends of society.

But, if laws exist, they soon become a dead letter, unless obedience to them can be enforced; for it is found that moral obligation alone is not sufficient to insure a perfect performance of duty. The existence of an executive authority, to which is intrusted the due and vigilant execution of the laws, seems indispensable.

And, as controversies may arise, in a great variety of cases, as to what is the right of one party, and the duty of another; whether property belongs to one party, or to another; whether a contract has or has not been performed; whether a wrong has or has not been done; whether a crime has or has not been committed,—it seems also indispensable, that a power should exist, whose jurisdiction should extend over all controversies of this sort, and should finally decide upon them. This power is the judicial power; and its free, independent and honest exercise is as important to the safety and happiness of society as either of the other two. In short, without a due administration of civil and criminal justice, society is, and can be, of no value. The merit of every government must, therefore, be subjected to this, as the truest test of its real excellence.

7. In what manner these various powers, legislative, executive and judicial, are to be exercised, and to what functionaries they are to be intrusted, depends upon the particular organization of each society or nation, or what is usually called its form or constitution of government. Where the society is small and within a very limited extent of territory, it is possible to have them all exercised in an assembly of the whole people by the whole people. This would be a pure democracy. But it is obvious that though possible, in an exact sense it is scarcely practicable; for all the people of even a small territory can rarely be assembled; some will be absent from accidental circumstances of illness, and age, and more pressing duties. And, probably, in no society whatever were these powers ever, in fact, exercised by the whole people, in

any single assembly; for idiots, madmen, infants, have been universally excluded; and married women, and persons guilty of crimes, have been usually excluded.

The most simple form, in which the powers of government have ever been actually administered, probably is by a majority of that part of the people, which has actually been assembled for such a purpose. And this is, in fact, though in its humblest form, a delegation of the sovereign power of the whole, since it intrusts the authority of the whole to the part, which is assembled. It is also, though in its humblest form, a *representative* government; for the whole are represented by those, who are present. We ordinarily call such a government a *democracy*, or government of the whole people.

But in societies, which are composed of large masses of population, such a form of government is unwieldy, and burthensome, and inefficient. The people are, therefore, driven to a delegation of their authority to a smaller number of persons, who can act as their representatives in the discharge of the legislative, executive and judicial functions.

Sometimes all these powers are concentrated in a single person; and then the government assumes the form of a pure despotism; sometimes they are all exercised by one and the same select body, composed of a few select persons, and then the government is, in form, a pure aristocracy. Sometimes the powers are divided, and distributed among various functionaries, and then the government becomes a mixed form of government.

If the executive power, in such a case, is delegated to a single person, it is then called a *monarchy*, or a *limited monarchy*. If the executive power is exercised by a select body of men, it is called an *aristocracy* or *limited aristocracy*. If the executive power is exercised by a magistrate elected by the people from time to time, and removable by the people, it is sometimes, though not perhaps, with perfect accuracy, called a *republic*, or a *limited republic*. If, in a monarchy, the power of legislation is shared by the representatives of the people, it is called a *mixed monarchy*; if in an aristocracy it is so shared, it is called a *mixed aristocracy*; if in a republic, it is called a *representative republic*.

But it is obvious that all these forms of government may be variously mixed together by delegations and limitations of the executive, legislative and judicial powers, in different proportions; and the actual structure of every government depending upon the choice, or necessities, or prejudices, or accidental combinations, of each society, they do not admit of any determinate classifications. But, whatever be the form of the government, the aggregate exercise of the legislative, executive and judicial powers constitutes what is commonly called the internal sovereignty of a nation.

8. From the nature and objects of civil government, we deduce not only the rights, but the duties of magistracy. These, of course, depend upon the nature of the functions, which belong to the particular department, legislative, executive, or judicial. All magistrates are responsible to God for the due and honest discharge of their duty; and, in republican forms of government, these magistrates are also made, in some shape, directly or indirectly, responsible to the people.

Every civil government is bound to promote the interests of agriculture, commerce and manufactures, as conducive to the strength and happiness of the people. Every government is bound to protect the persons, the personal rights and property of its citizens from violation and injury. Every government is bound to establish courts of justice, to provide for the punishment of crimes, to enforce the obligation of legal contracts, to encourage marriages, to prohibit immorality, to cultivate a sense of religious obligation, to allow a free exercise of religious worship, and a free expression of religious opinion, so far as it is not inconsistent with the public peace and safety. Every government may impose oaths or other solemn affirmations, appealing to the consciences of parties, for the purpose of ascertaining the truth of facts, or to secure the just performance of duties. It may, therefore, reasonably require, that witnesses should be sworn, or otherwise solemnly bound to testify the truth; and it may also reasonably require parties to take promissory oaths and affirmations for the future discharge of official and other duties.

And here ends our imperfect sketch of some of the leading principles of natural law, in their practical application to the relations of man to God, to himself, to other men, and to political society. The consideration of the rights and duties of nations to each other and of their external sovereignty, independence, and equality, belongs to another head, that of law of nations.

Appendix II: A Discourse on the Past History, Present State, and Future Prospects of the Law

In comparing the present state of jurisprudence with that of former times, we have much reason for congratulation. In governments purely despotic the laws rarely undergo any considerable changes through a long series of ages. The fundamental institutions (for such there must be in all civilized societies), whether modelled at first by accident or by design, by caprice or by wisdom, assume a settled course, which is broken in upon only by positive edicts of the sovereign, suited to some temporary exigency. These edicts rarely touch any general regulations of the state, and still more rarely attempt any general melioration of the laws. For the most part they affect only to express the arbitrary will of the monarch, stimulated by some pressing private interest, or gratifying some temporary passion, or some fleeting state policy. There is in such governments what may be called a desolating calm, a universal indisposition to changes and a fearfulness of reform on all sides; on the part of the people, lest it should generate some new oppression, and on the part of the ruler, lest it should introduce some jealousy or check of his arbitrary power.

In such countries the Law can scarcely be said to have existence as a science. It slumbers on in a heavy and drowsy sleep, diseased and palsied. It breathes only at the beck of the sovereign. It assumes no general rules, by which rights or actions are to be governed. Causes are decided summarily and more with reference to the condition and character of the parties, than with reference to principles; and judges are ministers of state to execute the policy of the cabinet, rather than jurists to interpret rational doctrines.

Under such circumstances the lapse of centuries scarcely disturbs the repose of the laws and men find themselves standing in the same crippled posture, which was forced upon their ancestors, long after their sepulchres have mouldered into dust, and the names of the oppressor and the oppressed are sunk into doubtful traditions. The laws of the Medes and Persians were proverbially immutable. The institutions of China have undergone no sensible change since the discovery and doubling of the Cape of Good Hope; and the pyramids of Egypt, lost as their origin is in remote antiquity, are not perhaps of a higher age than some of its customary laws and institutions. And it may be affirmed of some of the eastern nations, that through all the revolutions of their dynasties, it is difficult to point out any fundamental changes in the powers of the government, the rights of the subject, or the laws that regulate the succession to property, since the Christian era.

Reprinted from a pamphlet by Joseph Story (Edinburgh: Thomas Clark, 1835), 61–114.

In free governments, and in those where the popular interests have obtained some representation or power, however limited, the case has been far otherwise. We can here trace a regular progress from age to age in their laws, a gradual adaptation of them to the increasing wants and employments of society, and a substantial improvement corresponding with their advancement in the refinements and elegancies of life. In the heroic and barbarous ages, the laws are few and simple, administered by the prince in person, assisted by his compeers and council. But as civilization advances, the judicial powers are gradually separated from the executive and legislative authorities, and transferred to men, whose sole duty it is to administer justice and correct abuses. The punishment of crimes, at first arbitrary, is gradually moulded in a system, and moderated in its severity; and property, which is at first held at the mere pleasure of the chief, acquires a permanency in its tenure, and soon becomes transmissible to the descendants of those whose enterprise or good fortune has accumulated it.

Whoever examines the history of Grecian, or Roman or Gothic, or Feudal jurisprudence, will perceive in the strong lines, which may every where be traced the truth of these remarks. And it is matter of curious reflection, that while the laws and customs of the East seem in a great measure to have been stationary since the Christian era, those of Europe have undergone the most extraordinary revolutions; attaining at one period great refinement and equity, then sinking from that elevation into deep obscurity and barbarism under the northern invaders, and rising again from the ruins of ancient grandeur to assume a new perfection and beauty, which first softened the features, and then extinguished the spirit of the feudal system.

It is not, however, upon topics of this sort, suggested by a broad and general survey of the past, however interesting to the philosophical inquirer, that I propose to dwell at this time. My purpose rather is, to offer some considerations touching the past and present state of the common law, and to suggest some hints as to its future prospects in our own country, and the sources from which any probable improvements must be derived. In doing this, I shall attempt nothing more than a few plain sketches, contenting myself with the hope of being useful, and leaving to others of higher talents and attainments the more ambitious path of eloquence and learning.

The history of the common law may be divided into three great epochs; the first extending from the reign of William the Conqueror to the Reformation; the second from the reign of Elizabeth to the Revolution, which placed the House of Brunswick on the throne; and the third including the period which has since elapsed, down to our own time.

The first of these epochs embraces the origin and complete establishment of the feudal system, with all its curious burthens and appendages; its primer seizins, its aids, its reliefs, its escheats, its wardships, its fines upon marriages and alienations, and its chivalrous and socage services. Connected with these were the distinct establishment of tribunals of justice, administered first by Judges in Eyre, and afterwards by Courts at Westminster; the introduction of assizes and writs of entry, and the perfecting of all those forms of remedies, by which rights are enforced and wrongs redressed.

Some of the most venerable sages of the law belong to this period; the methodical and almost classical Bracton; the neat and perspicuous Glanville; the exact and unknown author of Fleta; the criminal treatise of Britton; the ponderous collections of Statham, Fitzherbert, and Brooke; and, above all, the venerable Year Books themselves, the grand depositories of the ancient common law, whence the Littletons and the Cokes, the Hobarts and the Hales of later times drew their precious and almost inexhaustible learning. Of these black-lettered volumes few in our days can boast the mastery. Even in England they are suffered to repose on dusty and neglected shelves, rarely disturbed, except when some nice question upon an appeal of death, upon the nature of seizin, or upon proceedings in writs of right calls them up, like the spirits of a departed age, to bear their testimony in the strife.

This, too, was the age of scholastic refinements, and metaphysical subtleties, and potent quibbles, and mysterious conceits, when special pleading pored over its midnight lamp, and conjured up its phantoms to perplex, to bewilder, and sometimes to betray. This, too, was the age of strained and quaint argumentation, when the discussions of the bar were perilously acute and cunning. And yet, though much of the law of these times is grown obsolete, and the task of attempting a general revival is hopeless, it cannot be denied that it abounds with treasures of knowledge. It affords the only sure foundations in many cases on which to build a solid fabric of argument; and no one ever explored its depths, rough and difficult as they are, without bringing back instruction fully proportioned to his labour.

The commencement of the second period is rendered remarkable by the enactment of two statutes, which have probably conduced more than any others to change the condition of real property, and, at the same time that they have facilitated its application to the business and the wants of real life, have in no small degree rendered its titles intricate. I allude to the great statutes of Wills and of Uses in the reign of Henry VIII. The former of them has crowded our books of reports with cases more numerous and more difficult in construction than any other single branch of the law. The latter, followed up by the statute of Elizabeth of Charitable Uses, laid the foundation of that broad and comprehensive judicature, in which equity administers through its searching interrogatories, addressed to the consciences of men the most beneficent and wholesome principles of justice. The whole modern structure of Trusts, infinitely diversified as it is, by marriage settlements, terms to raise portions or to pay debts, contingent and springing appointments, resulting uses and implied trusts,—grew out of this statute, and the constructions put upon it. And it is scarcely figurative language to assert, that the scintilla juris of Chudleigh's case is the spark that kindled that flame, which has burned so brightly and benignantly in the courts of equity in modern times.

Two statutes equally remarkable adorned the close of this second period; the one the statute of Habeas Corpus, the great bulwark of personal liberty, the other the statute abolishing the burthensome tenures of the Feudal Law. These were the triumphs of sound reason and free inquiry over the dictates of oppression and ignorance. They were the harbinger of better days, and gave lustre to an age, which was scarcely redeemed from profligacy by the purity of Lord Hale, and was deeply disgraced by the harsh and vindictive judgments of Lord Jeffries.

Yet, through the whole of this period, we may trace a steady improvement in the great departments of the law. Under the guidance of Lord Bacon the business of Chancery assumed a regular course, and at the distance of two centuries his celebrated Ordinances continue to be the pole-star which directs the practice of that court. A more noble homage to his memory, or a more striking proof of the profoundness of his genius, and of the wisdom and comprehensiveness of his views, can scarcely be imagined. And it may be truly affirmed, that his Novum Organum scarcely introduced a more salutary change in the study of physics and experimental philosophy, than his Ordinances did in the practical administration of equity. The common law, too, partaking of the spirit and enterprise of the times, gradually shifted and widened its channels. Courts of justice were no longer engaged in settling ecclesiastical or feudal rights and services. The intricacies of real actions were laid aside for the more convenient and expeditious trial of titles by ejectment. Assizes and writs of entry fell into neglect, and the subtleties of logic were exchanged for the more useful inductions of common sense. Arguments were no longer buried under a mass of learning; and Reports, instead of overwhelming the profession, as in the pages of the venerable Plowden, with a flood of ancient authorities and curious analogies, began to be directed to the points in controversy with brevity and exactness. Philosophy, too, lent its aid to illustrate the science, and the criminal law, though occasionally disgraced by abuses, was softened by the humanity, illustrated by the genius, and methodised by the labours, of the greatest luminaries of the law.

The third period may not inaptly be termed the Golden Age of the Law; since it embraces the introduction of the principles of commercial law, and the application of them with wonderful success to the exposition of the then comparatively novel contracts, of bills of exchange, promissory-notes, bills of lading, charter-parties, and above all, policies of insurance. Lord Holt, with great sagacity and boldness, led the way to some of the most important improvements by his celebrated judgment in Coggs v. Barnard, in which the law of bailments is expounded with philosophical precision and fulness.

It is true, that the leading maxims are borrowed from the Roman Law; as the beautiful treatise of Sir William Jones sufficiently explains to the humblest student; but the merit of Lord Holt is scarcely lessened by this consideration, since he had the talent to discern their value, and the judgment to transfer them into the English code. The modest close of his opinion in this case shews how little the law on this subject was at that time settled, and how much we owe to the achievements of a single mind. "I have said thus much" (is his language) "on this case, because it is of great consequence that the law should be settled on this point. But I don't know whether I may have settled it, or may not rather have unsettled it. But however that may happen, I have stirred these points, which wiser heads in time may settle." Wiser heads have not settled these points. This branch of the law stands now at the distance of more than a century on the immoveable foundation where this great man placed it, the foundation of reason and justice. And if he had left no other judgment on record, this alone would justify the eulogy of an eminent modern judge, that "he was as great a lawyer as ever sat in Westminster Hall."

The doctrines of the Courts of Equity during this last period have attained a high degree of perfection, though the origin of them must in many cases be admitted to belong to the preceding age. Lord Nottingham brought to the subject a strong and cultivated mind, and pronounced his decrees after the most cautious and painstaking study. Lord Cowper and Lord Talbot pursued the same career with the genuine spirit of jurists. But it was reserved for Lord Hardwicke, by his deep learning, his extensive researches, and his powerful genius, to combine the scattered fragments into a scientific system; to define with a broader line the boundaries between the departments of the common law and chancery; and to give certainty and vigour to the principles as well as the jurisdiction of the latter. Henceforth equity began to acquire the same exactness as the common law; and at this moment there is scarcely a branch of its jurisprudence that is not reduced to method, and does not, in the harmony of its parts, rival the best examples of the common law.

Our own age has witnessed, in the labours of Lord Eldon, through a series of more than twenty-five volumes of reports, a diligence, sagacity, caution, and force of judgment, which have seldom been equalled, and can scarcely be surpassed; which have given dignity, as well as finish, to that curious moral machinery, which dealing in an artificial system, yet contrives to administer the most perfect of human inventions,—the doctrines of conscience ex aequo et bono.

There is another great name, which adorns this period, respecting whom it is difficult to speak in terms of moderated praise, and still more difficult to preserve silence. England and America, and the civilized world, lie under the deepest obligations to him. Wherever commerce shall extend its social influences; wherever justice shall be administered by enlightened and liberal rules; wherever contracts shall be expounded upon the eternal principles of right and wrong; wherever moral delicacy and juridical refinement shall be infused into the municipal code, at once to persuade men to be honest, and to keep them so; wherever the intercourse of mankind shall aim at something more elevated than that grovelling spirit of barter, in which meanness, and avarice, and fraud strive for the mastery over ignorance, credulity, and folly,—the name of Lord Mansfield will be held in reverence by the good and the wise, by the honest merchant, the enlightened lawyer, the just statesman, and the conscientious judge.

The maxims of maritime jurisprudence which he engrafted into the stock of the common law, are not the exclusive property of a single age or nation, but the common property of all times and all countries. They are built upon the most comprehensive principles, and the most enlightened experience of mankind. He designed them to be of universal application, considering, as he himself has declared, the maritime law to be, not the law of a particular country, but the general law of nations. And such under his administration it became, as his prophetic spirit, in citing a passage from the most eloquent and polished orator of antiquity, seems gently to insinuate. *"Non erit alia lex Romae, alia Athenis; alia nunc, alia posthac;*

sed, et apud omnes gentes et omni tempore, una eademque lex obtinebit." He was ambitious of this noble fame, and studied deeply, and diligently, and honestly to acquire it. He surveyed the commercial law of the continent, drawing from thence what was most just, useful, and rational; and left to the world, as the fruit of his researches, a collection of general principles, unexampled in extent, and unequalled in excellence.

The law of Insurance was almost created by him; and it would be difficult to find a single leading principle in the beautiful system that surrounds and protects the commerce of our times, which may not be traced back to the judgements of this surprising man. Of him it cannot be said, *Stat magni nominis umbra.* His character as a statesman and an orator, as the rival and the equal of Chatham and Camden, would immortalize him. But the proudest monument of his fame is in the volumes of Burrow, and Cowper, and Douglas, which we may fondly hope will endure as long as the language in which they are written shall continue to instruct mankind.

I have been drawn into these remarks on the character of Lord Mansfield, beyond the scope of my original intention, by my extreme solicitude to impress the younger members of the profession with a due sense of his learning and his labours. It appears to me, that his judgements should not be merely referred to, and read, on the spur of particular occasions, but should be studied as models of juridical reasoning and eloquence. I know not where a student can learn so much or so well, as in the reports which I have named; and there is scarcely a sentence which dropped from his lips which may not prove of permanent utility to the profession. Our young men of the present day are apt to confine their reading too much to elementary treatises. The utility of these cannot be doubted; but the reports are the true repositories of the law, and of these none are so interesting and so convincing as those which are graced by the persuasive judgements of Lord Mansfield.

The principal improvements in the law during the period which has last past [*sic*] under review, may be summed up under the following heads. 1st, A more enlarged and liberal interpretation of contracts; 2d, The adoption of the great principles of commercial law, borrowed from the usages of merchants, the dissertations and commentaries of foreign jurists, and the inductions of philosophical inquiry; 3d, The enlargement of the remedy by assumpsit, moulding it, as in the action for money had and received, to the most important purposes of a bill in equity; 4th, The reducing of many doctrines of the law to systematical accuracy, by rejecting anomalies, and defining and limiting their application by the test of general reasoning.

Without doubt many of these changes were brought about by the enterprise of commerce, and the philosophizing spirit of the times. The former rendered indispensable the introduction of many general principles to regulate the complicated business of trade, and to protect and encourage navigation. The latter, by accustoming the profession to more comprehensive argumentation, and more perfect generalizations, gradually wore away that exclusive devotion to technical rules and ancient practices, and the narrow policy of the old law, which had been for ages the reproach of the Benchers of Westminster Hall.

The common law had its origin in ignorant and barbarous ages; it abounded with artificial distinctions and crafty subtleties, partly from the scholastic habits of its early clerical professors, and partly from its subserviency to the narrow purposes of feudal polity. When this polity began to decline, the mass of its principles was so interwoven into the texture of the law, and so consecrated by authority, that it became dangerous, if not impracticable, to disentangle it. There was, therefore, a natural jealousy of changes, lest they should work mischiefs in the venerable fabric. It was not until the current of society had taken a new direction, and commerce had worn its channels wide and deep through the whole country, that the necessities of trade compelled the profession to look abroad for doctrines of more general application.

Yet it cannot be denied, that the progress of improvement was slow, and that the genius of Lord Mansfield, by outstripping that of the age at least a half century, accomplished, with brilliant success, what a few may have ventured to hope for, but no one before him was bold enough to execute. The remarks of Mr. Justice Buller, a proud name in the English law, in the case of Lickbarrow v. Mason, fully confirm the views that I have attempted to unfold. "Before that period," says he, "we find that in courts of law all the evidence in mercantile cases was thrown together; they were left generally to the jury, and they produced no established principle. From that time we all know the great study has been to find some certain general principles, which shall be known to all mankind, not only to rule the particular case, but to serve as a guide for the future. Most of us have heard these principles stated, reasoned upon, enlarged, and explained, till we have been lost in admiration of the strength and stretch of the human understanding."

Although the causes to which I have alluded contributed in a high degree to the advancement of the law, yet there is another which, in my judgment, had a decided, though silent, operation in its favor. I refer to the change in the tenure of office, by which the judges, instead of being dependent on the pleasure of the Crown, enjoyed their offices, during good behaviour.

This measure of consummate wisdom forms a part of the solemn act of settlement, which fixed the succession of the throne of England in the house of Hanover, and was adopted not merely to secure the personal independence of the judges, but the purity and independence of the law. The first effect was to check the undue influence of the Crown through its judicial patronage; the next, and not least important, was to restrain the tumultuary excitements of the people. Men, for the most part, are willing to submit to the laws, when faithfully and impartially administered. If they are satisfied that the judges are incorruptible, they acquiesce in their decisions, even when they may suspect them to be erroneous, as the necessary homage by which their own rights and liberties are permanently secured. But if the fountain of justice is impure, and sends forth bitter waters, stained by influences which are not avowed, and yet are scarcely covered; if judges are removed at pleasure, and appointed at pleasure, to gratify a favourite or a faction, an arrogant minister or a violent House of Commons, it is easy to foresee, that jealousy will lead to distrust, and distrust to hatred, and hatred to disobedience, and disobedience to resistance, which, if it stops short of treason, will yet utter itself in deep complaints, until public confidence is universally shaken, and armies become necessary to support the execution of the laws.

Considerations of this sort have always impressed me with the belief, from the first moment that I ventured into the deeper studies of the law, that the independence of the judges is the great bulwark of public liberty, and the great security of property; and that the revolution of 1688 would have been but a vain and passing pageant, a noble but ineffectual struggle against prerogative, if the triumph of its principles had not been secured by this practical means of enforcing them.

Throughout the reigns of both the Charleses and both the Jameses, it is melancholy to remark the perpetual changes on the bench, induced by favouritism, or discontent, or an attempt to overawe the courts. The noble answer of Lord Coke to the inquiry of the kind in the dispute about commendams, what he would do if the Crown, in any case before him, required the judges to stay proceedings, "that he would do that which would befit a judge to do," is worthy of everlasting remembrance. But it was his solitary answer. To the disgrace of the age, all the other judges, intimidated by the king, and his haughty chancellor, "the wisest, greatest, meanest of mankind," promised implicit submission to the commands of the Crown. And even Lord Coke, for his conduct on other occasions, drew from the king the bitter, though perhaps unjust, rebuke, "that he was the fittest instrument for a tyrant that ever was in England."

In the reign of Charles II, the conduct of the Crown was more openly profligate, and its influence exerted to affect the judgments of the courts, even in private suits. It is matter of history, that Sir Edmund Saunders, after having advised the proceedings in the Quo Warranto against the city of London, was promoted to the Chief Justiceship of the King's Bench, not on account of his talents, his learning, or his virtues, but on account of his known devotion to the interests of the Crown. Such are some of the more offensive forms, under which the tenure of offices during pleasure will sometimes exhibit men, from whose elevation of character better things might be expected.

But the more silent and unobtrusive influence of *popular* dependence, though less striking to the vulgar eye, is not less subversive of the great purposes of justice. It is indeed more dangerous to the liberty and property of the people, since it assumes the attractive appearance of obedience to the will of the majority, and thus, without exciting jealousy or alarm, tramples under foot all those who refuse to obey the idol of the day. How can it be reasonably expected, that the law should flourish as a science, when the judges are doomed to resist the humours of the prince, or the clamours of the populace, at the peril of those stations which may constitute their only refuge from pecuniary distress?

If the old tenure of office had remained, we might still have possessed many valuable judgements of the later common law judges. But we should have searched in vain for those bright displays of independence and virtue, for those beautiful arguments in defence of private rights, for those finished illustrations of pure and exalted equity, and for those comprehensive commentaries upon commercial law, which have immortalized their memories. If their places were of any value, they must have resigned them, or remained the timid followers of the old law, without the ambition to improve its doctrines, or the hardihood to encounter the alarm of innovation.

Lord Mansfield would scarcely have sustained himself on the bench, in the midst of so many political and professional foes, to utter the thrilling declaration. "I wish for popularity; but it is that popularity which follows, not that which is run after. It is that popularity which, sooner or later, never fails to do justice to the pursuit of noble ends by noble means. I will not do that which my conscience tells me is wrong upon this occasion, to gain the huzzas of thousands, or the daily praise of all the papers which come from the press. I will not avoid doing that which I think is right, though it should draw on me the whole artillery of libels, all that falsehood and malice can invent, or the credulity of a deluded populace can swallow. I can say with another great magistrate, upon an occasion and under circumstances not un-like, "*Ego hoc animo semper fui, ut invidiam virtute partam, gloriam, non invidiam, putarem.*"

The review, which has been hitherto sketched of the history of the common law, however imperfectly, is confined altogether to British jurisprudence. Before the American Revolution, from a variety of causes which it is not difficult to enumerate, our progress in the law was slow, though not slower perhaps than in the other departments of science. The resources of the country were small, the population was scattered, the business of the courts was limited, the compensation for professional services was moderate, and the judges were not generally selected from those who were learned in the law. The colonial system restrained our foreign commerce, and as the principal trade was to or through the mother country, our most important contracts began or ended there.

That there were learned men in the profession in those times, it is not necessary to deny. But the number was small, and from the nature of the business which occupied the courts, the knowledge required for common use was neither very ample nor very difficult. The very moderate law libraries then to be found in the country would completely establish this fact, if it could be seriously controverted. Our land titles were simple. Our contracts principally sprung up from the ordinary relations of debtor and creditor. Our torts were cast in the common mould of trespasses to lands, or goods, or personal injuries; and the most important discussions grew out of our provincial statutes. Great lawyers do not usually flourish under such auspices, and great judges still more rarely. Why should one accomplish himself in that learning, which is more of curiosity than use? which neither adds to fame nor wealth? which is not publicly sought for or admired? which devotes life to pursuits and refinements not belonging to our own age or country?

The few manuscripts of adjudged cases which now remain, confirm these re-marks. If here and there a learned argument appears, it strikes us with surprise rather from its rarity than its extraordinary authority. In the whole series of our Reports there are very few cases, in which the ante-revolutionary law has either illustrated or settled an adjudication.

The progress of jurisprudence since the termination of the War of Independence, and especially within the last twenty years, has been remarkable throughout all America. More than 150 volumes of reports are already published, containing a mass of decisions which evinces uncommon devotion to the study of the law, and uncommon ambition to acquire the highest professional character. The best of our reports scarcely shrink from a comparison with those of England in the corresponding period; and even those of a more provincial cast exhibit researches of no mean extent, and presage future excellence. The danger, indeed, seems to be not that we shall hereafter want able reports, but that we shall be overwhelmed with their number and variety.

In this respect our country presents a subject of very serious contemplation and interest to the profession. There are now twenty-four States in the Union, in all of which, except Louisiana, the common law is the acknowledged basis of their jurisprudence. Yet this jurisprudence, partly by statute, partly by judicial interpretations, and partly by local usages and peculiarities, is perpetually receding farther and farther from the common standard.

While the States retain their independent sovereignties, as they must continue to do under our federative system, it is hopeless to expect that any greater uniformity will exist in the future than in the past. Nor do I know that, so far as domestic happiness and political convenience are concerned, a greater uniformity would in most respects be desirable. The task, however, of administering justice in the state as well as national courts, from the new and peculiar relations of our system, must be very laborious and perplexing; and the conflict of opinion upon general questions of law in the rival jurisdictions of the different States, will not be less distressing to the philosophical jurist, than to the practical lawyer.

It may not be without utility to glance for a few moments at some of those circumstances, in which the coincidences and differences are most striking and instructive.

1. And first, as to the regulation of the transfers of property. These are either by the descent and distribution of estates, by conveyances inter vivos, or by testamentary dispositions. As to the first, so far as my knowledge extends, the canons of descent in the direct line are the same in all the States. In all the States the children and lineal descendants inherit in coparcency [*sic*], without any distinction as to primogeniture or sex. In descents in the collateral line, there are some peculiar modifications in almost all the States. In some States there is a difference between the half and the whole blood; in others, a difference between inheritances ex parte paterna and ex parte materna; in others, a difference in the order of succession and representation.

From the genius of our political institutions, as well as the habits of the people, there is every probability that inheritances will continue to descend substantially in the same manner, as long as our free governments endure. An attempt to establish the English canons of descent could hardly succeed, but upon the ruins of all those institutions which are considered the best protection of a republican government.

Then, as to conveyances inter vivos. Lands are universally conveyed by a deed, acknowledged by the parties before some competent magistrate, and recorded in some public records kept for the registry of conveyances of this nature. The ceremony of livery of seizin is obsolete, if indeed it have anywhere a legal entity. The common law forms of conveyance are in general use, and the statute of Uses being recognized as a part of the common or statute law of the States, the English doctrines on these subjects are generally adopted.

As to testamentary dispositions. Lands are universally disposable by will. Their ceremonies, by which solemn testaments are evidenced in most of the States, do not materially differ from the English statute on this subject. In Virginia and Kentucky, however, a will wholly written and signed by the testator is good, although there is no subscribing witness. In Louisiana the like provision exists; and it is to be observed, that the preceding remarks are in general inapplicable to this State, whose jurisprudence being founded on the civil law, the forms of conveyances, whether they be donations inter vivos, or donations causa mortis, are regulated in general conformity to the rule of that law.

2. As to commercial law. From mutual comity, from the natural tendency of maritime usages to assimilation, and from mutual convenience, if not necessity, it may reasonably be expected, that the maritime law will gradually approximate to a high degree of uniformity throughout the commercial world. This is indeed in every view exceedingly desirable.

Europe is already, by a silent but steady course, fast approaching to that state, in which the same commercial principles will constitute a part of the public law of all its sovereignties. The unwritten commercial law of England at this moment, differs in no very important particulars from the positive codes of France and Holland. Spain, Portugal, and the Italian States, the Hanseatic Confederacy, and the powers of the North, have adopted a considerable part of the same system; and the general disposition in the Maritime States to acknowledge the superiority of the courts and code of England, leaves little doubt that their own local usages will soon yield to her more enlightened doctrines.

What a magnificent spectacle will it be to witness the establishment of such a beautiful system of juridical ethics,—to realize, not the oppressive schemes of holy alliances in a general conspiracy against the rights of mankind, but the universal empire of juridical reason, mingling with the concerns of commerce throughout the world, and imparting its beneficent light to the dark regions of the poles, and the soft and luxurious climates of the tropics. Then, indeed, would be realized the splendid visions of Cicero, dreaming over the majestic fragments of his perfect republic, and Hooker's sublime personification of the law would stand forth almost as embodied truth, for "all things in heaven and earth would do her homage, the very least as feeling her care, and the greatest as not exempted from her power."

The commercial law of the Atlantic States has indeed already attained to a very striking similarity in its elements. Upon the subject of insurance there is no known difference founded on local usages or statutes. If the law be differently administered, it is not because there is any intention to deviate from the general doctrines of that law, but because the nature and extent of those doctrines have been differently understood. In all the States the same law prevails as to contracts of shipping and affreightment. In most of the States bills of exchange and promissory notes are negotiable, and rest upon the principles which, since the statute of Anne, have won their way into the common law.

Virginia affords the most striking exception to this remark; for there a limited negotiability only is recognized by law, and parties, who are remote indorsers, have no remedy against remote indorsers except by a suit in equity. Massachusetts, as far as I know, stands alone in her local usage of denying days of grace to promissory notes, unless expressed on the face of the contract. And it is seriously wished, that by a legislative act we might fairly get rid of this anomaly, which has not a single ground either of convenience or policy, or antiquity to recommend it.* There are some few other dissonances from the general commercial law, which have existed in some of the States, but it would serve no important purpose to explain them at this time.

3. As to remedies, it would be endless to point out the coincidences and differences between the various States. Remedies are necessarily modified by the wants and manners of the community, and processes, which from habit are thought useful and convenient in one state of society, are rejected as burthensome and injurious in another. In several of the New England States the attachment of real and personal property is allowed upon mesne process, not merely to coerce the appearance of the defendant, but to secure a final satisfaction of the judgement, if the plaintiff recovers in the suit. This process, except so far as it belongs to foreign attachments (analogous to our trustee process) is utterly unknown elsewhere, and the existence of it among ourselves is contemplated with surprise and regret by those who are accustomed to the general processes of the common law. It is thought a hardship, that any person should be liable to be stripped of his property, before it is ascertained judicially that a good cause of action exists against him, and the danger of abuse has been dwelt upon with much emphasis and force.

And yet perhaps the annals of no country present fewer instances of abuse than those of the New England States, which allow this mode of proceeding. Personal arrests are rare here, even when property is not to be found; and it is not perhaps hazarding too much to assert, that the writ of capias has subjected more persons to wrongful imprisonment, than the unjust attachment of property has to serious loss and inconvenience. Yet it cannot be denied, that the latter process is liable to great abuses, and that our exemption from them has resulted principally from the sound discretion and integrity of the Bar. And it is most desirable, that some summary practice, analogous to that of discharging on common bail, should be authorized by the legislature, so that fraud and circumvention and oppression may find it more difficult to obtain undue advantages, and compelled undue compromises under the influence of this dreaded process.

The remedy for trying land titles in all the States in the Union, except Louisiana and some of the New England States, is the English action of ejectment. It is

* Since this address was delivered, a statute has been passed in Massachusetts, providing that grace shall be allowed on all promissory notes, orders, and drafts, payable at a future day certain, in which there is not an express stipulation to tre contrary. St. Mass. 1824, c. 130.

scarcely modified even in its slightest forms, and John Doe and Richard Roe are the familiar guests, *hospites antiqui et constantes,* of the courts on the picturesque banks of the Hudson, the broad expanse of the Delaware and Chesapeake, the sunny regions of the south, and the fertile vales and majestic rivers of the west. In Louisiana, the civil law governs all judicial proceedings, and administers all remedies in personam and in rem. And I cannot help paying my humble homage to the excellence of this code, which, adapting its remedies to the exigency of the case, gives complete relief without trammelling itself with prescribed forms, which often perplex, and sometimes defeat, the ends of justice. In one or two of the adjoining States, the old anomalous proceeding, known as a plea in ejectment, still prevails. The use of writs of entry for the trial of land titles is, I believe, unknown, except in Massachusetts, Maine, and New Hampshire.

Whether we have derived any important benefit from the revival of the old forms of proceeding in real actions, is a question upon which wise men and sound lawyers may probably disagree. If we have disembarrassed them of some troublesome appendages and some artificial niceties, and rendered them more attractive by the simplicity of their structure, still it must be confessed that they are not easily moulded to all the uses which modern conveyances and devises render convenient and necessary. The abandonment of these forms in England, from a general sense of their inadequacy to the purposes of justice, and the adoption there, as well as in most of the American States, of the action of ejectment, which has been ascertained by experience to be a perfect and convenient remedy, do certainly carry a weight of authority against our own practice, which, if it be not difficult to resist, it would at least be safe to follow.

4. As to the structure of land titles, there is a considerable diversity in the States, and in several of them a great departure from the simplicity and certainty of those derived under the common law. I am not aware that in any part of New England any serious difficulties are to be found on this subject, all titles having had their origin in separate grants derived directly from the government or confirmed by it, and having the usual formalities and certainty of grants of the crown at common law, or of grants by private legislative acts. The only questions which have been much litigated are those of boundary, which may and do ordinarily arise under grants between private persons, and of these there have been few of any considerable magnitude.

Far different has been the course of proceeding in some other parts of the Union. Titles there have originated in general laws, under which any person might appropriate the property of the state by following the regulations pointed out by certain statutable provisions. These provisions are very complex, and embrace a variety of stages of title, in each of which the purchaser is obliged to observe great precision, or his rights may be postponed to a puisne holder or claimant. As, therefore, the titles stand upon general laws, and by taking steps to acquire them inchoate rights are obtained, or priorities secured, before the titles are consummated by grants from the government, many very difficult questions have grown up as to the nature, extent, validity, and priority of conflicting titles. A regular grant or patent from the government is no security against other claimants, although it should happen to be prior in point of date to all others. It is liable to be overreached and defeated, sometimes at law and sometimes in equity, according to the local jurisprudence, by prior inchoate rights or equitable claims, whether arising under pre-emptions, or settlements, entries, or other matters, which have been held to confer upon an adverse claimant a legal preference.

These remarks apply with considerable force to the land laws of Pennsylvania, Maryland, North Carolina, and Tennessee. But it is in Virginia, and more especially in Kentucky, which derives its titles under the Virginia land laws, that they are realized in their fullest extent. The system of land titles in Kentucky is indeed one of the most abstruse branches of local jurisprudence, built up on artificial principles, singularly acute and metaphysical, and quite as curious and intricate as some of the higher doctrines of contingent remainders and executory devises. It affords an illustrious example of human infirmity and human ingenuity: of human infirmity in the legislative supposition, that the great statute on which it rests was so certain, as in a great measure to preclude future litigation; of human ingenuity in overcoming obstacles apparently insurmountable, by devising approximations to certainty in descriptions strangely vague and inaccurate, thus preserving the legislative intention, and yet promoting the great purposes of justice.

The vice of the original system consisted in enabling any persons to appropriate the lands of the state by entries and descriptions of their own, without any previous survey under public authority, and without any such boundaries as were precise, permanent, and unquestionable; and the issuing of grants upon such entries without any inquiry as to the true nature, description, and survey of the lands, and without any attempt to prevent duplicate grants of the same property. If we consider, that Kentucky was at this time a wilderness traversed principally by hunters; that many places must have been but very imperfectly known even to them, and must have received different appellations from occasional and disconnected visitants; if we consider, that the lands were rich, and the spirit of speculation was pushed to a most extravagant extent, and that the spirit of fraud, as is but too common, followed close upon the heels of speculation; if we consider the infinite diversity which under such circumstances must unavoidably exist in the descriptions of the appropriated tracts of land, arising from ignorance, or carelessness, or innocent mistake, or fraud, or personal rashness—we ought not to be surprised at the fact, that the best part of Kentucky is oppressed by conflicting titles, and that in many instances there are three layers of them lapping on or covering each other.

The statute to which I have alluded required that the descriptions in the original entry should be so certain, that other purchasers might be able to appropriate the adjacent residuum. The description of the tract might fail in two particulars. *First,* It might be bounded by known objects or boundaries, but yet so general and imperfect, that the description might equally well suit different tracts of land, and thus what has been technically called "identity." *Second,* Or the boundaries might refer to objects so universal as to defy all certainty or to objects not generally known at the time by the particular names given to them, or known generally by another name; and then the description would be fatally defective for want of what is technically called "notoriety!"

Time would fail me to enumerate the doctrines which have started from this origin, or to go over other peculiarities of the system. Perhaps human genius has been rarely more severely tasked or more fairly rewarded, than in its labours on this occasion. The land law of Kentucky, while it stands alone in its subtle and refined distinctions, has obtained a symmetry, which at this moment enables it to be studied almost with scientific precision. But ages will probably elapse before the litigations founded on it will be closed; and so little assistance can be gained from the lights of the common law for its comprehension, that to the lawyers of other states it will forever remain an unknown code with a peculiar dialect, to be explored and studied like the jurisprudence of some foreign nation.

In order to avoid such serious evils, the government of the United States, with a wisdom and foresight which entitles it to the highest praise, has, in the system of land laws which regulate the sales of its own territorial demesnes, given great certainty, simplicity, and uniformity to the titles derived under it. With a few unimportant exceptions, all lands are surveyed before they are offered for sale. They are surveyed in ranges, and are divided into townships, each six miles square, and these are subdivided into thirty-six sections each one mile square, containing six hundred and forty acres. All the dividing lines run to the cardinal points and of course intersect each other at right angles, except where fractional sections are formed by navigable rivers, or by an Indian boundary line. The subdividing lines of quarter sections are not actually surveyed, but the corners, boundaries and contents of these are designated and ascertained by fixed rules prescribed by law; and regular maps of all the surveys are lodged in the proper department of the government.

In this manner, with some few exceptions, the public lands in Alabama, Mississippi, Louisiana, Ohio, Indiana, and Illinois, have been sold; and the system applies universally to all our remaining territorial possessions. The common law doctrines have, in respect to these titles, taken deep root and flourished; and the waters, which divide the states on opposite banks of the Ohio, do not form a more permanent boundary of their respective territorial possessions, than the different origin of their land titles does in the character of their local jurisprudence.

5. Another circumstance, which will probably continue to form a leading diversity in the jurisprudence of the States is the existence of slavery. This condition of society must necessarily involve a great variety of peculiar provisions as to domestic policy and foreign intercourse, as to crimes, rights and duties, to which no parallel can be furnished in States whose constitutions or laws prohibit its introduction and existence. The property in slaves, partaking as it does of the double aspects of real and personal estate, being transmissible by descent, and being sold as personalty; being perpetually in demand and marketable, and of course affording solid revenue and wealth; giving value to lands by increasing the culture of agricultural products; being also of intrinsic value and general necessity in climates, where little or nothing is accomplished by other labour;—it follows, that slavery and its appendages must sink deep into the mass of jurisprudence of the slave-holding states, and furnish much litigation in the shape of contracts, conveyances, torts, or crimes, which other states are happily exempt from, and need not study, either for admonition or instruction.

6. Another diversity, which deserves attention, is the equity jurisdiction, which exists in complete operation in some states, in partial operation in others, and in others again is obsolete, or totally prohibited. In New England no such establishment is known as a separate independent court of equity. In Connecticut and Vermont general equity powers are exercised by the judges of their superior courts; but in all the other New England States equity powers are confined to a few cases which are specified and limited by legislative acts. In Pennsylvania a mixed system exists. No Court of Chancery, or court exercising chancery powers according to the forms and proceedings of that jurisdiction, is known. But in cases where the parties possess rights, which a Court of Equity would recognize and enforce, Courts of Law, following equity in this particular, endeavour to give efficacy to these rights through the instrumentality of remedies at law. Thus, a title to land merely equitable, or resting in a contract, of which a Court of Equity would compel a specific performance, is sufficient to sustain an ejectment at law.

On the other hand, in New York, New Jersey, Maryland, Virginia, and South Carolina, Courts of Equity have a distinct existence and organization, independent of Courts of Common Law; and, as far as I have been enabled to learn, in the remaining States the equity jurisdiction is generally administered by the Courts of Common Law. Wherever the equity jurisdiction is exercised, its admitted basis is the general doctrines of the English Chancery. But it is so modified by local statutes, usages, and decisions, that it would be somewhat hazardous for a lawyer at the chancery bar of Westminster to form an opinion as to the authority to give or to deny relief, however unequivocally those guides might speak, whom he was accustomed to consult.

If I were obliged to speak from my own very imperfect knowledge and experience, I should be compelled to declare, that the deviations in America from the established principles of equity were far more considerable than from those of the common law. A more broad and undefined discretion has been assumed, and a less stringent obedience to the dictates of authority. Much is left to the habits of thinking of the particular judge, and more to that undefined notion of right and wrong, of hardship and inconvenience, which popular opinions alternately create and justify. There are indeed illustrious exceptions to these remarks, which it were invidious to point out, though it be of great importance to follow.

The slight sketches which I have ventured thus to draw of some of the prominent features of state jurisprudence, do, as I think, justify the suggestion already made, that American jurisprudence can never acquire a homogeneous character; and that we must look to the future rather for increasing discrepancies than coincidences in the law and the administration of the law. This is a consideration of no small moment to us all, lest, by being split up into distinct provincial bars, the profession should become devoted to mere state jurisprudence, and abandon those more enlightened and extensive researches which form the accomplished scholar, and elevate the refined jurist; which ennoble the patriot, and shed a never dying lustre round the statesman.

The establishment of the national government, and of courts to exercise its constitutional jurisdiction, will, it is to be hoped, in this respect, operate with a salutary influence. Dealing, as such courts must, in questions of a public nature;

such as concerns the law of nations, and the general rights and duties of foreign nations; such as respect the domestic relations of the states with each other, and with the general government; such as treat of the great doctrines of prize and maritime laws; such as involve the discussion of grave constitutional powers and authorities; —it is natural to expect, that these courts will attract the ambition of some of the ablest lawyers in the different states, with a view both to fame and fortune. And thus, perhaps, if I do not indulge in an idle dream, the foundations may be layed for a character of excellence and professional ability, more various and exalted than has hitherto belonged to any bar under the auspices of the common law; a character in which minute knowledge of local law will be combined with the most profound attainments in general jurisprudence, and with that instructive eloquence, which never soars so high, or touches so potently, as when it grasps principles which fix the destiny of nations, or strike down to the very roots of civil polity.

In comparing the extent of American jurisprudence with that of England, we shall find that if in some respects it is more narrow, in others it is more comprehensive. The whole ecclesiastical law of England, unless so far as it may operate on past cases, is obsolete. The genius of our institutions has universally prohibited any religious establishment, state or national. Nor is there the slightest reason to presume that the imposition of tithes could ever be successfully introduced here, except by the strong arm of martial law, forcing its way by conquest. It was always resisted during our colonial dependency, and would now be thought at war with all that we prize in religion or civil freedom. The numerous questions respecting tithes and moduses, quare impedits, and advowsons and presentations, the fruitful progeny of that establishment, are gone to the same tomb, where the feudal tenures repose in their robes of state in dim and ancient majesty.

In the next place, the right of primogeniture being abolished, and all estates descending in coparceny, and entails being practically changed into fee simple estates, there is no necessity for those intricate conveyances, settlements, and devices, with which the anxiety of parents and friends to provide against the inconveniences of the law have filled all the courts of England. Of this troubled stream of controversy we may indeed say, "it flows, and flows, and flows, and will ever flow on."

In the next place, we are rid not only of the feudal services and tenures, but of all the customary law of our parent country, the ancient demesnes, the copyholds, the manorial customs and rights, and the customs of gavelkind and borough English. The cases in which prerogative or privilege can arise are few, and limited by law. Long terms and leases, and annuities charged on land are rare among us; and the complicated questions of contract and of rent, which fill the books, are of course scarcely heard of in our courts. We have no game laws to harass our peasantry, or to form an odious distinction for our gentlemen; and the melancholy inventions of later times connected with the spring-guns, and the concealed spears, and mantraps, never cross our paths, or disturb our fancies. The penalties of a praemunire cannot be incurred for we neither court nor fear papal bulls or excommunications. Outlawry, as a civil process, if it have a legal entity, is almost unknown in practice. An appeal of death or robbery never drew its breath among us; nor can it now be brought forth to battle in its dark array of armour, to astonish and confuse us, as it recently did all Westminster Hall. These are no small departments of the common law. A few of them, indeed, are almost obsolete in England; but the residue forms a body of principles so artificial and so difficult, that they leave behind them few which can, in these respects, justly claim precedency.

With all these abridgements, however, our law is still sufficiently extensive to occupy all the time, and employ all the talents, and exhaust all the learning, of our ablest lawyers and judges. The studies of twenty years leave much behind that is yet to be grappled with and mastered. And if the law of a single state is enough for a long life of labour and ambition, the task falls still heavier on those who frequent the National Courts, and are obliged to learn other branches of law, which are almost exclusively cognizable there. When it is considered that the equity jurisprudence of the courts of the United States is like that of England, with the occasional adoption of the peculiar equities of local law; and their admiralty jurisdiction takes in its circuit not merely the prize and maritime law, but seizures also for the breach of municipal regulations; when to these are added the interpretation of the treaties and statutes of the United States, and the still more grave discussion of constitutional questions, and the relative rights of states, and their citizens, in respect to other states,—it cannot well be doubted that the administration of justice is there filled with perplexities that strain the human mind to its utmost bearings.

The most delicate, and at the same time the proudest, attribute of American jurisprudence, is the right of its judicial tribunals to decide questions of constitutional law. In other governments, these questions cannot be entertained or decided by courts of justice; and therefore, whatever may be the theory of the constitution, the legislative authority is practically omnipotent, and there is no means of contesting the legality or justice of a law, but by an appeal to arms. This can be done only when oppression weighs heavily and grievously on the whole people, and is then resisted by all, because it is felt by all. But the oppression that strikes at an humble individual, though it rob him of character, or fortune, or life, is remediless; and, if it becomes the subject of judicial inquiry, judges may lament, but cannot resist, the mandates of the legislature.

Far different is the case in our country; and the privilege of bringing every law to the test of the constitution belongs to the humblest citizen, who owes no obedience to any legislative act, which transcends the constitutional limits. Some visionary statesmen, indeed who affect to believe that the legislature can do no wrong, and some zealous leaders, who affect to believe that popular opinion is the voice of unerring wisdom have at times questioned this authority of courts of justice. If they were correct in their doctrine, we might as well be without a written constitution of government, since the minority would always be in complete subjection to the majority; and it is to be feared that the experience of mankind has never shewn that the despotism of numbers has been more mild or equitable than that swayed by a single hand. This heresy, as questionable in point of sound policy, as it is unconstitutional in its language, has hitherto made but little progress among us. The wise, and the learned, and the virtuous, have been nearly unanimous in supporting that doctrine, which courts of justice have uniformly asserted, that the constitution is not the law for the legislature only, but it is the law, and the supreme law, which is to direct and control all judicial proceedings.

The discussion of constitutional questions throws a lustre round the Bar, and gives a dignity to its functions, which can rarely belong to the profession in any other country. Lawyers are here emphatically placed as sentinels upon the outpost of the constitution; and no nobler end can be proposed for their ambition or patriotism, than to stand as faithful guardians of the constitution, ready to defend its legitimate powers, and to stay the arm of legislative, executive, or popular oppression. If their eloquence can charm, when it vindicates the innocent and the suffering under private wrongs; if their learning and genius can, with almost superhuman witchery, unfold the mazes and intricacies by which the minute links of title are chained to the adamantine pillars of the law,—how much more glory belongs to them, when this eloquence, this learning, and this genius, are employed in defense of their country; when they breathe forth the purest spirit of morality and virtue in support of the rights of mankind; when they expound the lofty doctrines which sustain, and connect, and guide the destinies of nations; when they combat popular delusions at the expense of fame, and friendship, and political honors; when they triumph by arresting the progress of error and the march of power, and drive back the torrent that threatens destruction equally to public liberty and to private property, to all that delights us in private life, and all that gives grace and authority in public office.

Something more I would say on this subject, but time fails me, and I feel that I am entering on topics far too grave, and solemn, and delicate, for occasions like the present. May I be permitted, however, to say, that the duty devolved upon the profession in these times is of deep responsibility and interest. It depends upon the present age, whether the national constitution shall descend to our children in its masculine majesty, to protect and unite the country; or whether, shorn of its strength, it shall become an idle mockery, and perish before the grave has closed upon the last of its illustrious founders.

In looking to the future prospects of the jurisprudence of our country, it appears to me that the principle improvements must arise from a more thorough and deep-laid juridical education, a more exact preparatory discipline, and a more methodical and extensive range of studies.

In the first place, it cannot be disguised that we are far behind the English Bar in our knowledge of the practice, and of the elementary forms and doctrines, of special pleading. I do not speak here of the technical refinements of the old law in special pleading, which the good sense of modern time has suppressed; but of those general principles which constitute the foundation of actions, and of those forms by which alone rights and remedies are successfully pursued. There is a looseness and inartificial structure in our declarations, and other pleadings, which betray an imperfect knowledge both of principals and forms; an aberration from settled and technical phraseology, a neglect of appropriate averments, which not only deprive our pleadings of just pretension to elegance and symmetry, but subject them to the coarser imputation of slovenliness. The forms of pleadings are not, as some may rashly suppose, mere trivial forms; they not unfrequently involve the essence of the defense; and the discipline which is acquired by a minute attention to their structure is so far from being lost labour, that it probably, more than all other employments, leads the student to that close and systematical logic, by which success in the profession is almost always secured.

Of the great lawyers and judges of the English Forum, one can scarcely be named who was not distinguished by uncommon depth of learning in this branch of the law, and many have risen to celebrity slowly by their attainments in it. We should blush to be accused of perpetual mistakes in grammatical construction, or of a gross and unclassical style of composition. Yet these are venial errors compared with those with which the law is sometimes reproached. Diffuse and tedious as are the modern English pleadings, it cannot be denied that they exhibit a thorough mastery of the science. We miss, indeed, the close, lucid, and concentrated vigour of the pleadings in the days of Rastall, and Coke, and Plowden, and even of Saunders and Raymond. But our taste is not offended by loose and careless phraseology, or our understanding by omissions, which betray the genuine "crassa negligentia" of the law, or by surplusage so vicious and irrelevant, that one is at a loss to know at what point the pleadings aim, or whether they aim at any.

We ought not to rest satisfied with mediocrity, when excellence is within our reach. The time is arrived when gentlemen should be scrupulously precise in their drafts of pleadings, and when the records of our courts should not be deformed by proceedings which could not stand the most rigorous scrutiny of the common law in form as well as in substance. Exemplifications of our judgements may pass, nay, do already pass, to England, and it ought to be our pride to know that they will not be disgraced under the inspection of the sober benchers of any Inn of Court. We should study ancient forms and cases, as we study the old English writers in general literature; because we may extract from them not only solid sense, but the best examples of pure and undefiled language. There is a better reason still, and that is, that special pleading contains the quintessence of the law, and no man ever mastered it who was not, by that very means, made a profound lawyer.

Another source of improvement is in the more general study of the doctrine of Courts of Equity. I do not here address myself to those who expect to practice in such courts, for to them it is almost unnecessary to say that the study is indispensible. But I address the remark to those who are conversant only with the Courts of Common Law. The principles of equity jurisprudence are of a very enlarged and elevated nature. They are essentially rational, and moulded into a degree of moral perfection, which the law has rarely aspired to. The arguments in courts of this sort abound with new views and elementary discussions. They present strong and brilliant contrasts to some of the perplexed notions of the old common laws; and not unfrequently confirm and illustrate doctrines strictly legal, by unfolding new analogies, and expounding the nature and limits of principles, in a manner full of instructions and interest.

It is a great mistake to confine our juridical researches to the narrow path in which we mean to trade. There is no great mind but that feels itself cramped and fettered by such a course; and no moderate mind but that becomes ground up into the most dusty professional pedantry. The great branches of jurisprudence mutually illustrate and support each other. The principles of one may often be employed with the most captivating felicity in aid of another; and in proportion as the common law becomes familiar with the lights of equity, its own code will become more

344

useful and more enlightened. In our country, the study of equity jurisprudence has not, until within a few years, attracted general attention; and in New England, from causes which have been already alluded to, it has fallen into more neglect than our advances in other branches of the law would justify or excuse.

Connected with this, and as a mine abounding with the most precious materials, to adorn the edifice of our jurisprudence, is the study of the foreign maritime law, and above all of the civil law. Where shall we find more full and masterly discussions of maritime doctrines, coming home to our own bosoms and business, than in the celebrated commentaries of Valin? Where shall we find so complete and practical a treatise on insurance as in the mature labours of Emerigon? Where shall we find the law of contracts so extensively, so philosophically, and so persuasively expounded, as in the pure, moral, and classical treatises of Pothier? Where shall we find the general doctrines of commercial law so briefly, yet beautifully laid down, as in the modern commercial code of France? Where shall we find such ample general principles to guide us in new and difficult cases, as in that venerable deposit of the learning and labours of the jurists of the ancient world, the Institutes and Pandects of Justinian? The whole continental jurisprudence rests upon this broad foundation of Roman wisdom; and the English common law, churlish and harsh as was its feudal education, has condescended silently to borrow many of its best principles from this enlightened code. (See 12 Mod. 482 by Lord Holt) The law of contracts and personalty, of trusts, and legacies, and charities in England, have been formed into life by the soft solicitudes and devotion of her own neglected professors of the civil law.

There is no country on earth which has more to gain than ours by the thorough study of foreign jurisprudence. We can have no difficulty in adopting in new cases, such principles of the maritime and civil laws as are adapted to our wants, and commend themselves by their intrinsic convenience and equity. Let us not vainly imagine, that we have unlocked and exhausted all the stores of juridical wisdom and policy. Our jurisprudence is young and flexible, but it has withal a masculine character, which may be refined and exalted by the study of the best models of antiquity. And the structure of our State and National Governments, while it easily admits of the incorporation of foreign maritime principles, at the same time makes it safe, useful, and commendable.

There is yet another study, which may well engage the attentions of American lawyers, and be, in the language of Lord Coke, both honourable and profitable to them,—I mean the study of the law of nations. This is at all times the duty, and ought to be the pride, of all who aspire to be statesmen; and as many of our lawyers become legislators, it seems to be the study to which, of all others, they should most seriously devote themselves. Independent of these considerations, there is nothing that can give so high a finish, or so brilliant an ornament, or so extensive an instruction, as this pursuit, to a professional education.

What, indeed, can tend more to exalt and purify the mind, than speculations, upon the origin and extent of moral obligations; upon the great truths and dictates of natural law; upon the immutable principles that regulate right and wrong in social and private life, and upon the just applications of these to the intercourse and duties and contentions of independent nations? What can be of more transcendent dignity, or better fitted to employ the highest faculties of genius, than the development of those important truths which teach the duties of magistrates and people, the rights of peace and war, the limits of lawful hostility, the mutual duties of belligerent and neutral powers, and aim at the introduction into national affairs of that benign spirit of Christian virtue, which tempers the exercise even of acknowledged rights with mercy, humanity, delicacy? If the science of jurisprudence be, as it has been eloquently described to be, "the pride of human intellect" and "the collected reason of ages, combining the principles of original justice with the infinite variety of human concerns"; where can we find more striking proofs of its true excellence, than in the study of those maxims which address themselves to the best interests and the most profound reflections of nations, and call upon them, as the instruments of providence, to administer to each other's wants, to check inordinate ambition, to support the weak, and to fence in human infirmity, so that it can scarcely transcend the bounds of established rules, without drawing after it universal indignation and resistance?

Yet how few have mastered the elementary treatises on this subject, the labours of Albericus Gentilis, and Zouch, and Grotius, and Puffendorf, and Bynkershoek, and Wolfius, and Vattel? How few have read with becoming reverence and zeal the decisions of that splendid jurist, the ornament, I will not say of his own age or country, but of all ages and all countries; the intrepid supporter equally of neutral and belligerent rights; the pure and spotless magistrate of nations, who has administered the dictates of universal jurisprudence with so much dignity and discretion in the Prize and Instance Courts of England! Need I pronounce the name of Sir William Scott? How few have aspired, even in vision, after those comprehensive researches into the law of nations, which the introductory discourse of Sir James Mackintosh has opened and explained with such attractive elegance and truth?

Such are some of the studies from which American jurisprudence may, in my humble judgment, derive essential improvements; and I cannot but indulge the belief, that they will be eagerly sought and thoroughly examined by the good and the wise of succeeding ages.

The mass of the law is, to be sure, accumulating with an almost incredible rapidity, and with this accumulation, the labour of students, as well as professors, is seriously augmenting. It is impossible not to look without some discouragement upon the ponderous volumes, which the next half century will add to the groaning shelves of our jurists. The habits of generalization, which will be acquired and perfected by the liberal studies which I have ventured to recommend, will do something to avert the fearful calamity which threatens us of being buried alive, not in the catacombs, but in the labyrinths of the law.

I know, indeed, of but one adequate remedy, and that is, by a gradual digest, under legislative authority, of those portions of our jurisprudence, which under the forming hand of the judiciary, shall from time to time acquire scientific accuracy. By thus reducing to a text the exact principles of the law, we shall, in a great measure, get rid of the necessity of appealing to volumes, which contain jarring and discordant opinions; and thus we may pave the way to a general code, which

346

will present in its positive and authoritative text the most material rules to guide the lawyer, the statesman, and the private citizen. It is obvious that such a digest can apply only to the law, as it has been applied to human concerns in past times; but by revision at distant periods, it may be made to reflect all the light which intermediate decisions may have thrown upon our jurisprudence.

To attempt more than this would be a hopeless labour, if not an absurd project. We ought not to permit ourselves to indulge in the theoretical extravagances of some well-meaning philosophical jurists, who believe that all human concerns for the future can be provided for in a code speaking a definite language. Sufficient for us will be the achievement to reduce the past to order and certainty; and that this is within our reach cannot be matter of doubtful speculation. It has been already accomplished in a manner so triumphant, that no cavil has been able to lessen the fame of the authors.

The Pandects of Justinian, imperfect as they are from the haste in which they were compiled, are a monument of imperishable glory to the wisdom of the age; and they gave to Rome, and to the civilized world, a system of civil maxims which have not been excelled in usefulness and equity. They superseded at once the immense collections of former times, and left them to perish in oblivion, so that, of all ante-Justinianean jurisprudence, little more remains than a few fragments, which are now and then recovered from the dust and rubbish of antiquity, in the codices rescripti of some venerable libraries.

The modern code of France, embracing, as it does, the entire elements of her jurisprudence in the rights, duties, relations, and obligations of civil life; the exposition of the rules of contracts of every sort, including commercial contracts; the descent, distribution, and regulation of property; the definition and punishment of crimes; the ordinary and extraordinary police of the country, and the enumeration of the whole detail of civil and criminal practice and process,—is perhaps the most finished and methodical treatise of law that the world ever saw. This code forms also the law of Holland, and, with comparatively few alterations, has been solemnly adopted as its fundamental law by the State of Louisiana. The materials of it were to be sought for among an almost infinite variety of provincial usages and customary laws, and were far more difficult to reduce into [a] system, than any which belong to the common law.

It is left to the future jurists of our country and England, to accomplish for the common law what has thus been so successfully demonstrated to be a practical problem in the jurisprudence of other nations,—a task which the modest but wonderful genius of Sir William Jones did not scruple to believe to be within the reach of a single mind successfully to accomplish.

I have thus endeavoured, not as I could wish, but as I have been able, amidst the cares of Private life, and the distractions of official business, to give some imperfect sketches of the past history of the law, of its future prospects, and of the sources whence we may derive improvement. May I add, in the language of the eminent living jurist (Sir James Mackintosh, Introd. Disc. 51) whom I have already cited, that "there is not, in my opinion, in the whole compass of human affairs, so noble a spectacle as that which is displayed in the progress of jurisprudence, where we may contemplate the cautious and unwearied exertions of a succession of wise men through a long course of ages, withdrawing every case, as it arises, from the dangerous power of discretion, and subjecting it to inflexible rules, extending the dominion of justice and reason, and gradually contracting within the narrowest possible limits the domain of brutal force and of arbitrary will."

If, in the discussion of these topics, I have suggested a single hint that may cheer the student in his laborious devotion to the elements of the law, or have awakened in the mind of a single advocate another motive to quicken his eloquence or zeal, my humble labour will not be without its consolations. We are all bound by the strong ties of civil obligation, by professional character, by patriotic pride, and by moral feelings to cultivate and extend this interesting science.

No Bar in America is more justly entitled to public confidence, than that of my native State; and none may more justly claim respect for its moral, literary, and juridical elevation, than that which I have now the honour to address. Much, however, remains to be done to satisfy a just ambition for excellence; and every day's experience admonishes us that life is short and art is long, furnishing motives at once to excite our diligence, and to restrain an undue ardour in any human pursuit.

When, indeed, I look round and contemplate the ravages which death has made during my own brief career, not only among the sages of the law, but among those in the fresh bloom of youth, just struggling for distinction, the consideration fills me with the most profound melancholy. Since we were convened here on the last anniversary, the modest and accomplished Gallison has closed his useful life, and buried with him many a brilliant hope of his parents, friends, and country. I will not dwell upon his distinguished talents and virtue, his blameless innocence of life, his elevated piety, his unwearied diligence, his extensive learning, his ardent devotion to literature, his active benevolence, exhausting itself in good deeds, and "blushing to find it fame." You knew him well, and your sympathies have mingled with the tears and sorrows that embalm his memory.

But I may propose him as an example polished, if not perfect, of that excellence which the studies I have this day ventured to recommend are calculated to produce. Tacitus has recorded with affectionate solicitude the life and character of Agricola. May I be permitted to borrow from his admirable page a single passage, to grace the memory of my lamented friend and pupil. "*Placide quiescas, nosque, domum tuam, ab infirmo desiderio et muliebribus lamentis ad contemplationem virtutum tuârum voces, quas, neque lugeri, neque plagi, fas est; admiratione, te potius quam temporalibus laudibus, et, si natura suppeditet, aemulatione, decoremus. Is verus honos, ea conjunctissimi cujusque pietas.*"

We, too, must soon pass away to the tomb, where our friends and instructors, the Ameses, the Sullivans, and the Dexters, the Lowells, the Danas, the Parsonses, and the Sewalls, are gone before us. We cannot be indifferent to the fate of our children or our country, and the happiness, as well as the honour of both, is indissolubly connected with the faithful administration of justice. Nor ought we to disguise that that science, which has been the choice of our youth and the ambition of our manhood, has much in its milder studies to soothe and cheer us in the infirmities of old age. Nor can it be deemed a human frailty, if, when we take our last farewell of the law, we "cast one longing, lingering look behind," and bless those rising lights which are destined to adorn our judicial tribunals, however dimly they may be described by our fading vision.

May our successors in the profession look back upon our times, not without some kind regrets, and some tender recollections. May they cherish our memories with that gentle reverence which belongs to those who have laboured earnestly, though it may be humbly, for the advancement of the law. May they catch a holy enthusiasm from the review of our attainments, however limited they may be, which shall make them aspire after the loftiest possessions of human learning. And thus may they be enabled to advance our jurisprudence to that degree of perfection which shall make it a blessing and protection to our own country, and excite the just admiration of mankind.

Appendix III: Law, Legislation, and Codes

(The interest now felt in law and legal reforms must be our apology for the length of the present article. As we have thought that the views entertained respecting legislation and jurisprudence by the civilians on the continent of Europe might be not uninteresting to our readers, the article which treats of them in the *Conversations-Lexikon* has been translated and forms the first part of the present article, extending as far as the break on page 581 [page 357]. The remainder, giving the common law view of the subject, and treating particularly of codification, is by an eminent American jurist.)

1. Laws are the very soul of a people; not merely those which are contained in the letter of their ordinances and statute books, but still more those which have grown up of themselves from their manners, and religion, and history. Several modern jurists, as John G. Schlosser and Hugo, have shown how little, in legislation, caprice can prevail over the silent but irresistible influence of public opinion. And even the authors of the Code Napoleon have said, with no less elegance than truth, that no legislator can escape that invisible power, that silent judgment of the people, which tends to correct the mistakes of arbitrary legislation, and to defend the people from the law, and the lawgiver from himself.

Frequent experiments have shown that laws, at variance with the manners and religious views of a people, cannot be forced upon them, however well meant, and however beneficial may have been their influence upon other nations; and that, by means of laws, a legislator can no more elevate his countrymen to a higher degree of refinement, without passing through the intervening steps, than he can reduce them again to a condition above which they have risen in the natural course of events.

Hence Frederic II of Prussia was more happy in his reforms than Joseph II. For it was by no means the intention of the Prussian legislator to give his subjects a new system of law, but rather to sanction that which they already possessed; to adapt the letter of the ancient laws to the notions of right which had gained a footing in the spirit of the nation, and, above all, to remove those uncertainties which had necessarily sprung from the use of a foreign code, which had checked improvement in practice.

Unsigned article by Joseph Story, reprinted from Francis Lieber (ed.), *Encyclopedia Americana*. A Popular Dictionary of Arts, Sciences, Literature, History, Politics and Biography, Brought Down to the Present Time: Including a Copious Collection of Original Articles in American Biography (Philadelphia: Desilver, Thomas & Company, 1831), VII (appendix), 576–92. [The portion written by Story begins on p. 357.]

Indeed, it is not the duty of a skilful legislator to create new laws; but only to develop those which existed prior to any express recognition, and to introduce, with prudence, those positive rules which cannot be deduced from general principles; as the determination of the length of minority, the period of superannuation, the amount of punishments, etc.; in which the principles of natural right are reduced to a practical application. To the province of the practical legislator belong also those forms which are required in the application of legal principles; as the formalities of contracts and of judicial processes, and the rules of evidence, in all which it should be kept in mind that these positive institutions do not, of themselves, constitute law, but are the mere mechanism to facilitate the use of it. They should be viewed only as the means of promoting a higher end. The view of the original ground of laws is a point on which not only the schools of European jurists differ, but on which the most important principles of public law come into collision.

2. The schools of modern jurisconsults may be reduced, in reference to their principal characteristics, to four, although these are variously modified, and, in many respects, run into one another. In the last century, with few exceptions, the *practical* school predominated, which, on the one hand, esteemed the authority of courts and individual jurists higher than the law, and, on the other, was influenced, in an important degree, by philosophy, particularly that of Leibnitz and Wolf. Arguments were, for the most part, drawn with great logical precision, from the nature of the case.

The members of this school felt themselves justified in departing from the letter of the written law, either whenever it seemed not adapted to the existing case, or reference could be made to the decisions of courts on the same point. By this school were introduced a multitude of new opinions, supposed equities, and milder punishments; and their fundamental views were not altogether erroneous. They proceeded on the true notion, that the laws of a people are the result of its own peculiar character, and must take their hue from this. They tried to help the letter of the old laws by deductions from the nature of things, and, by adhering to precedents, to attain to that harmony in the administration of justice, which alone can secure the public confidence.

The influence exerted by this school on the legislation of the eighteenth century was very great, particularly through Nettelbladt and Daries; and the code of Prussia, in particular, may be considered as its work. But it wanted a proper system of judicial tribunals, to prevent that fluctuation in practice, in consequence of which all certainty, in regard to law, was lost, so that the result of the decision of the simplest cause could hardly be conjectured beforehand.

The practical school was divided again into two parties, which agreed only in this, that the jurisconsults, or the judges, might look beyond positive law; but were opposed to each other in so far that one party recognised nothing but the authority of some favorite casuist, and the usage of courts; the other regarded natural right, and what they called *reasonableness*, as the basis of all their decisions. The former almost always carried the day; for it often happened that the latter opposed them only till they had become familiar with the routine of practice, and felt themselves at home in it.

351

In the last 10 years of the eighteenth century, new views suggested themselves to the *philosophical* jurists. A more perfect and living philosophy had examined afresh the foundations of science. Many a fabric was shattered, which had preserved the appearance of soundness only in consequence of negligence. At the same time, society took a new turn, and every thing seemed aiming at an ideal perfection. All former obstructions in the way of legal reform appeared to be set aside. France became a republican state, and the doctrines of natural right were introduced into practice. But things have changed again, so that philosophical law has made but little advance, and has gained but little influence in courts of justice. Philosophical treatises, however, have appeared on some departments; as on criminal law, on civil process, and particularly on public and ecclesiastical law. But such works can have no real value without a profound and accurate treatment of positive law, and have, therefore, produced but little effect.

The difference of opinion, in the two parties above-mentioned, has been of practical importance only on one occasion, viz. when it was proposed to prepare new bodies of law for Germany, or to take from the French legislation (which deserves so much respect in regard to public law), the rules of civil and penal law, and the forms of procedure. This plan presupposed that a code might be formed on purely philosophical principles, which, being adapted to mankind in general, would suit all nations and all times, and become the basis and essence of every other. Corrections might be made in this ground-work by degrees, as the development of the science of law pointed out deviations from the requisitions of natural justice; and the peculiarities of the legislation of each people might be added. For even those who believed that all positive legislation was based on a foundation so unalterable and eternal, could not help seeing that the additions to be made, for the purposes of practical application, must be drawn from empirical premises, which were neither suited to all people, nor constant to any given people; so that such a code, drawn from natural law, must still leave a wide field for positive legislation. This view was taken, particularly in considering the value of the French codes, the adoption of which, in Germany, had been recommended. It was inquired whether the civil code of Napoleon had solved the great problem how to establish a code based on natural justice, and capable of so universal application as to be equally adapted to people living on the Vistula and the Seine, on the Elbe, and Po, and Tiber. It was soon perceived that the Code Napoleon did not reach this ideal.

On this occasion, the contest between the philosophical and historical jurisprudence came up, which was afterwards particularly revived by Savigny's *Vom Beruf unserer Zeit zur Gesetzgebung*, 1815 (the Call for Codification in our Times). The peculiar characteristic of this third school of modern jurists—the *historical*—is, that they regard no legal principles as capable of universal and unconditional application. They view law as a mere result of the accidental relations of a people, and as changing with them. According to the principles of this school, every thing may be right, even slavery and many other things, which the philosophical school declares to be a violation of the universal rights of man, and absolutely wrong. The historical school allows a very narrow sphere to that legislation in which law is based on the will of the lawgiver, and a very large one, on the contrary, to the customary law, which commences and perpetuates itself by popular usage, and the decisions of courts. Its ideal is the Roman law, as it is presented in the writings of jurists before Justinian. Every innovation in the law on the part of government, it regards as dangerous; and especially new codes, which interrupt the silent growth of legal rules in a country.

So far, this school agrees with the views of the practical school above-mentioned, from which, in fact, it originated. But it rejects all reasons deduced from a supposed nature of things (or, indeed, from philosophical opinions of right), and derives existing law, not from the decisions of courts and colleges, in which it perceives many glaring errors, but from ancient laws and law-books. It regards as truly right, not what modern times have recognised and followed as right, but what they would have esteemed right, if they had properly understood the ancient sources; and therefore considers that all improvement must be the result of a thorough examination of history. Notwithstanding the manifest inconsistency of this reasoning,—since, if the system of law, in any country, is formed by self-development, the newest shape is always the only one that ought to be recognised, and the present cannot be explained from the past,—this view has met with much acceptance, since it avers that whatever is, is right, from the very fact that it is; and in history, by which almost any principle may be proved or refuted at pleasure, it finds a means of crushing every desire of reform; but it is most favored because it declares all efforts for something higher to be both foolish and wrong.

This view, however, has, doubtless, already reached its acme. It has the merit of having directed to the only successful way of understanding laws by the aid of history; but the erroneous expectation cannot long be maintained, of discovering what should be, from knowing what is, and how that which is, grew up. For, although we may be set in the right way by history, yet nothing but philosophy can direct us to the proper end. History and philosophy supply each other's defects, and either of them, by itself, leads to partial views. It is only together that they can teach us the true science of law, and impart the wisdom requisite for legislation.

A fourth view has been advanced, in modern times, which may be termed the *strict judicial (legistic)*. Justly offended at the authority over the laws assumed by the practical school, and the uncertainty which had resulted from the fluctuations of their practice, impatient of the toilsome researches of a historical jurisprudence, and convinced that the philosophical school could afford materials to the legislator only, and not to the judge, a respectable number of jurists abandoned the authority of existing practice, and returned to the positive laws, though less to the spirit of them than the letter, and frequently to the letter of those laws of which the existence was scarcely known among the people.

Much has been said of the injury which attends a sudden change of the laws, by introducing a new code. But, if the object of such a code is to confirm and sanction the ideas of right already prevalent among a people, it can never bring with it consequences so pernicious as followed the calling up from oblivion, the adopting into use, of antiquated laws, Roman forms and subtleties, and the cruel penal laws of the sixteenth century. In case of the literal application of these old laws, no regard can be paid to the circumstances of the age or to the peculiar character of the particular ordinances; and, in consequence of the incompleteness and want of technical accuracy in the ancient legislation, the laws of the empire, the old and new ordinances of particular countries, papal ordinances, Roman constitutions, and fragments of legal writers, are unavoidably mixed up in the most embarrassing confusion, to form a mosaic, which has the outward appearance of an organized whole, but is wholly destitute of inward, living energy.

The historical school is right in maintaining that laws can be properly comprehended only by an historical examination of their development; but it has fallen into the error of the *legistic* school, in asserting that the deficiencies which are found in every positive institution should be supplied, not from the fountain of all right, but either by the aid of historical hypotheses, which attribute the most artificial systems to nations in the early periods of civilization, or by heterogeneous additions from wholly different systems of legislation. In so doing, the historical school have particularly forgotten that the objects of their veneration, the juridical classics of Rome, owed their greatness to a perpetual habit of reverting to the maxims of natural law (their *aequitas*).

Even the Roman lawyers recognised a universal right, which exists prior to all positive legislation, and without it, and, at the same time, in and with it—the rule of conduct wherever the precepts of positive law have not yet reached. There is an important difference between a maxim of law created by a positive ordinance, and one only acknowledged by it as already existing in natural equity. In the first case, the law cannot extend beyond the immediate object of its creation: in the second, it is of universal application. Of special importance is this distinction in deciding concerning relations and acts without the bounds of a state,—for example, a crime committed abroad,—cases in which positive law has a very limited application. But, however narrow the last-mentioned *legistic* view may be, it has effected much good, by bringing to light the imperfection, and, in some senses, the utter worthlessness, of the existing positive law, and thus aided to promote the reform, which, in several German states, is so necessary.

3. If the question should arise, From what public organ the improvement of laws should proceed, it may be answered, The various juridical theories exhibit a great practical difference. But, at least, the two principal parties—the historical and philosophical—are perfectly agreed in the opinion, that mere caprice, which sees in laws only a means of promoting its own favorite ends, should be, as far as possible, excluded: and it is also agreed, that legislation is an office with which neither the judiciary nor the executive departments can be concerned, without injury to each of them. Nothing can defend men from the arbitrary exercise of power but a separation of the executive, legislative and judicial authorities; for in no other way can each of these three powers be kept within its natural limits.

The great discrepancy, both in the intrinsic nature of these powers, and in the character of their results, makes it important that each of them should be administered by a separate organ. To govern is the business of the state. The executive government is the organ of the people's will. The characteristic of its acts is command. Such commands, however, are not irrevocable, for, at any movement, they may be repealed. Opinions contrary to them may be advanced; and, if they encroach on previous rights, the aid of courts may be enlisted in opposition to them. Law, on the contrary,—and, on this point, the philosophical and historical jurisprudence agree,—is founded, not upon any will, but on the discovery of a right already exist-

354

ing, which is to be drawn either from the internal legislation of human reason, or the historical development of the nation. The law, too, is not irrevocable, nor can any sanction make it so; but, as long as it exists, it is of irresistible and universal force. Finally, the judicial decision is binding only on those who have occasioned its application by resorting to judicial proceedings; but, for such, it is an unchangeable rule, and no power whatever can subvert it.

The different character of these public functions must not only be obvious in their external forms, so as to be understood by every one who would know his duty, but the very nature of the provisions which they require for their operation is so different as to furnish sufficient ground for making the executive, legislative and judicial departments distinct in their organization. But it is a great error of modern (constitutional) politics, that they have conceived of this division of duties, as if all connexion and mutual influence of the three powers must be done away; hence the election of judges by the people, and a legislation which could be neither urged nor restrained by the executive (no veto, or only a limited one). This very naturally produced political dissensions, which could only end in the ruin of the state. But, if the executive power is what it ought to be, nothing can be done in the commonwealth without its orders; and both the legislative and judiciary departments must receive from it the impulse of their activity. The convocation of the legislative body, and the proposal of laws, belong to it; and without its consent, no law can become obligatory upon the people. The execution and promulgation of the laws necessarily rest with the executive, and are necessarily joined with an unlimited veto. On the other hand, the influence of the executive government on the legislative should be merely a negative influence, and on the administration of justice, a formal one; i.e. no law should be passed without its consent, and the judges should receive their offices from the executive, while the executive is to see that they do their duty; but how they shall speak cannot be prescribed to them.

This is the only means by which unity and harmony, in the action of the public authorities, can be maintained, while every branch of power is supported by the other, and kept in the right path. The entire separation of these three powers is an error which, wherever it has existed, in ancient or modern times, has brought upon the people as great sufferings as if they had been subject to an arbitrary and unlimited dominion.

4. The historico-philosophical view of the sources of laws leads us to results concerning the organization of the legislative authorities, which, it is to be regretted, have been often too much overlooked. The consequence of the unreasonable notion, that legislation is an act of the will, was an idea that the general will of the people might be ascertained, if all the different interests to be found in the people could be brought together; or, as this is, in fact, impossible, it was considered sufficient to unite, in representative assemblies, the most important interests—those of agriculture, commerce and manufactures. In respect to the administration of government, and the judicious choice of means to promote the high ends of the state, this sort of representation may be found sufficient. But, when the question is respecting the establishment of laws, in the highest sense of the word, the most comprehensive intelligence is required. A popular representation, for this purpose, should not represent the fluctuating, capricious will of the people, influenced, as it is, by interest,

prejudice and passion. On the contrary, it should be a mirror to reflect all the intellectual power of the nation. Consequently the representatives should be chosen from the most learned, and enlightened, and experienced men, who have the best opportunity to become acquainted with the wants of the people and the defects of the existing laws.

That it cannot be concluded that a man possesses these qualifications, because he owns a piece of ground, is very clear. And it is equally manifest, that it is a great mistake to esteem such a possession a security for good intentions. Disinterestedness is no consequence of wealth, but of the habit of self-denial; and he learns it much more perfectly who has been inured to it from his youth, than one who has, perhaps, never known a want. To regard landed proprietors as the proper citizens, and others as mere tolerated tenants of the state, is an absurdity. Landed property is the offspring of the state, and not *vice versa*; and the state cannot so distribute the soil, that it may depend on the will of the owner to deprive others of the means of subsistence. The more a natural, distinct interest separates landed proprietors, and, indeed, in some sense, the cultivators of the soil also, from the rest of the community, the more should it be made a main object of public institutions to prevent one party from gaining a decided and permanent superiority. But political institutions now have frequently the opposite tendency—a circumstance which, in some places, has had a remarkable influence on taxation.

The second consequence, resulting from the view of legislation here proposed, is, that the number of representatives needs not be proportionate to the number of the people. In a large state, a larger number of deputies is not needed to represent the intellectual capacity of the people; and a small state, if it regards the ends of legislation, properly needs as many persons in its representative assembly as the larger. For it should comprehend so many different kinds of knowledge and talent, that no subject may arise on which a judicious decision cannot be made by the body, by the aid of persons within itself; and that the laws may all have the stamp of moderation, arising from due attention to all interests, which often leads, though by no means necessarily, to half measures. This is the greatest difficulty for smaller states, and they can only prevent it by accommodating their legislation to that of their neighbors.

The management of the public affairs of communities, from the village up to the state, cannot be called legislation, in the sense in which we are now considering the subject: these may be suitably administered by even the smallest state. But if a small state undertakes to establish a peculiar system of civil rights, of legal procedure, of penal laws, etc., it will receive less advantage from such an insulated system than of injury, from the bars to intercourse with its neighbors, which must result from such institutions. Hence it is altogether desirable that, in states which are only minor divisions of one nation, having the same religion, manners and cultivation, the municipal laws, and the institutions for their administration, should, as far as possible, be made common to the whole, although matters of political administration might be kept distinct. Thus they might secure to themselves the advantages enjoyed by larger states, in the preparation of like laws by experienced colleges (as the French council), or by juridical commissions, so as to be accommodated to all the existing institutions. Representative assemblies would be freed from the embarrassment of deliberating and deciding upon topics, of which perhaps few, perhaps not a man among them, has any knowledge.

But this is not to be observed in small states only: very large ones sometimes suffer still more from this evil; for though, on one side, the mass of knowledge united in the body is greater, on the other, a greater number of ignorant men embarrass and confuse: and while too many take part in making laws, but few take an interest in the subject. The thoughtlessness with which this important duty has been performed in England till the present time, is shown by Miller, in an Inquiry into the present State of the Statute and Criminal Law of England (London, 1822). The people of England, therefore (the paradise of the customary law), are at length beginning to feel the urgent need there is of reducing the chaos of single enactments into general codes. This is called the *consolidation of laws*. Several learned individuals have undertaken to make such compends. (So far the German article.)

We now propose to offer some observations, explanatory of the views of lawyers accustomed to the jurisprudence of the common law, on this interesting subject. Civilians are (it seems from the preceding part of this article) divided into several schools, professing different opinions, and actuated by different principles. The course of the common law naturally leads those who are engaged in its studies to take practical rather than theoretical views of almost every department of it. Hence they can hardly be said to be divided into different schools, or to indulge much in what may be called *philosophical, historical* or *antiquarian* inquiries. The actual system, as it exists, is that which they principally seek to administer; and it is only occasionally that very gifted or bold minds strike out into new paths, or propose fundamental reforms. In the present age, however, a spirit of inquiry is abroad, and the value and extent of codification have, among other topics, been matter of warm controversy among practical lawyers, as well as practical statesmen. We shall speak of this subject in the sequel.

Legislation, in its broadest sense, includes those exercises of sovereign power, which permanently regulate the general concerns of society. Its chief object is to establish laws. And by a *law*, we understand a rule, prescribed by the sovereign power of a state to its citizens or subjects, declaring some right, enforcing some duty, or prohibiting some act. It is its general applicability, which distinguishes it from a single edict, or temporary and fugitive order of the sovereign will. It is supposed to furnish a permanent and settled direction to all who are embraced within its scope. It is not a sudden executive direction, but an annunciation of what is to govern and direct the rights and duties of the persons to whom it applies, in future. The rule being prescribed, it becomes the guide of all those functionaries who are called to administer it, and of all those citizens and subjects upon whom it is to operate. Neither is supposed to be at liberty to vary its obligations, or evade its provisions.

But as, in the ordinary course of affairs in free governments, every person has a right, where the matter admits of judicial discussion, to litigate the question, what are the true object and meaning of a law, and how far it bears upon his rights, privileges, or duties,—it is understood that in free governments, and especially in republics, the ultimate adjudication of what the law is, and how far it applies to a given case, is to be definitively settled by the judicial department of the government. It would be obviously unfit for the legislative department to settle retrospectively, as to past cases, what was its own meaning, its true office being to prescribe rules for the future. And though the executive department may, in the first instance, settle for itself what the law requires, its decisions cannot, and ought not to be final; for it has no means to call the proper parties before it to litigate the question, and no power to decree any judgment. Its proper function is to administer the law, and not to make it; to act upon its true construction, and not to fix it. Otherwise, the fundamental principle of a republican government would be overturned; and laws would be, not settled rules of action to be judged of by courts upon the litigation of parties, deriving their rights from, or in opposition to them; but would be arbitrary decisions of the sovereign power, without appeal and without inquiry.

In the American states, this principle is thought so fundamental, that our constitutions of government expressly separate the legislative, executive and judicial departments from each other, and assign to each appropriate duties. It is thought that in no other way can the private rights and the public liberties of the people be secure. A departure from this doctrine would be deemed a direct advancement towards despotism.

When, then, in America and England, it is asked what the law is, we are accustomed to consider what it has been declared to be by the judicial department, as the true and final expositor. No one is at liberty to disregard its exposition. No one is deemed above or beyond its reach, as thus declared. If it is supposed to be misconstrued, or rather, not to carry into full effect the legislative will, a new or declaratory law is passed, and furnishes the appropriate remedy. And this leads us to remark, that the difference between civilians and common lawyers, in respect to the value and obligatory force of former decisions (which we call *precedents*), is most important. The opinion of no jurist, however high or distinguished is his reputation or ability, is of the least importance in settling the law, or ascertaining its construction, in England or the United States. So far as he may, by his arguments, or counsels, or learning, instruct the court, or enlighten its judgments, they have their proper weight. But if the court decide against his opinion, it falls to the ground. It has no farther effect. The decision becomes conclusive and binding, and other courts are governed by it, as furnishing for them the just rule of decision. No court would feel itself at liberty to disregard it, unless upon the most urgent occasion, and when it interfered with some other known rule or principle; and even then, with the greatest caution and deference.

In countries where the common law prevails, it is deemed of infinite importance, that there should be a fixed and certain rule of decision, and that the rights and property of the whole community should not be delivered over to endless doubts and controversies. Our maxim, in truth, and not in form merely, is, *Misera est servitus, ubi jus est vagum aut incertum.* All this (it seems) is different in the civil law countries. There, the celebrity of a particular jurist may introduce a decisive change in the rule, or at least in the administration, of the law; and even different schools of opinion may prevail in different ages. Precedents have not, as with us, a fixed operation and value; and judicial tribunals consider, that a prior decision governs only the particular case, without absolutely fixing the principles involved in it. The practice under the common law has been found to be very beneficial; and, experience having given it a sanction and value which supersede all theory and reasoning about it, it is not often that the matter is discussed upon abstract or philosophical views. But there are many grounds, which might be urged in support of this practice, which are capable of vindicating it in the most philosophical discussions.

The question, in its most general form, must involve this inquiry, What is best for society, with a view to its interests, its security, its permanency? Now, it may not be irrelevant to remark, that in every modern government, practically free, the common law rule has prevailed by general consent; and in those of the American states which were formerly under the civil law jurisdiction, there has been no desire ever expressed to retain their own rule. On the contrary, the common law rule has been eagerly adopted. It is not our purpose to enter into a review of all the grounds on which the common law rule might be vindicated; but there are one or two which deserve attention.

In the first place, the rule has the advantage of producing certainty as to rights, privileges and property. In the next place, it controls the arbitrary discretion of judges, and puts the case beyond the reach of temporary feelings and prejudices, as well as beyond the peculiar opinions and complexional reasoning of a particular judge; for he is hemmed round by authority on every side. In the next place, the consciousness, that the decision will form a permanent precedent, affecting all future cases, introduces necessarily great caution and deliberation in giving it. If the case only were to be decided, it might be disposed of upon sudden impressions, and upon circumstances of hardship or compassion, or kindness, or special equity. But as the principles involved in it are to govern all future cases, and those principles must be derived from other analogies of the law, and be consistent with them, there are very strong restraints upon the judgment of any single judge. And there can be no permanent evil attendant upon any adjudications of this sort; for the legislative power may always apply the proper amendatory corrective at its will. And if the judges are actuated by corrupt motives, they may be removed by impeachment.

It is no small proof that the system works well, that, in the course of many ages, very few decisions (comparatively speaking) have been overturned by the courts themselves, and that the legislature has not often found it necessary to change the rule prescribed by the courts. In fact, positive laws have been amended a hundred times, by the legislature, where one judicial rule has been interfered with. The changes which have been wrought in the fabric of the laws, have not so much arisen from misapplication of principles by the courts, as from the new state of society having rendered the old institutions and laws inexpedient or inconvenient.

The circumstances which have been thus alluded to, have introduced a general and settled course of interpreting the laws, in countries governed by the common law. No such thing is known, in our jurisprudence, as a philosophical, or historical, or practical school of interpretation. And our laws are not subject to any varieties of interpretation grounded upon the present predominance of either of them. Certain maxims were early adopted, and they have never been departed from. Supplementary and auxiliary maxims of interpretation have necessarily been introduced. But, when once incorporated into the system, they have been deemed conclusive and obligatory. The sense of a law once fixed by judicial interpretation, is for ever deemed its true and only sense.

Among the rules of interpretation belonging to and fixed in the common law, we shall enumerate a few, some of which, indeed, may be truly said to belong to the universal elements of rational jurisprudence. It is, perhaps, the exactness and uniformity with which they are applied, by our judicial tribunals, which gives them their principal value.—Laws may be divided into the following classes: declaratory laws; directory laws; remedial laws; and prohibitory and penal laws. Declaratory laws, except so far as they operate upon future rights, are not within the scope of the legislative power in the United States. Our legislatures can only declare what the law shall be, not what it has been, or is; how it shall govern rights in future, not how it shall act upon the past. Directory laws are those which prescribe rules of conduct, or limit or enlarge rights, or point out modes of remedy. Remedial laws are those whose object it is to redress some private injury, or some public inconvenience. Prohibitory and penal laws are those which forbid certain things to be done or omitted, under a penalty, or vindicatory sanction.

In the nature of things, there is not any indispensable reason why the same rule should be uniformly applied in the interpretation of all of these different sorts of laws. We shall see that the common law allows some distinction in this respect. The fundamental maxim of the common law, in the interpretation of statutes, or positive laws, is, that the intention of the legislature is to be followed. This intention is to be gathered from the words, the context, the subject matter, the effects and consequences, and the spirit or reason of the laws. But the spirit and reason are to be ascertained, not from vague conjecture, but from the motives and language apparent on the face of the law.

1. In respect to words, they are to be understood in their ordinary and natural sense, in their popular meaning and common use, without a strict regard to grammatical propriety or nice criticism. But the ordinary sense may be departed from, if the context or connexion clearly requires it; and then such a sense belonging to the words is to be adopted as best suits the context.

2. Again: terms of art and technical words are to be understood in the sense which they have received in the art or science to which they belong.

3. If words have different meanings, and are capable of a wider or narrower sense, in the given connexion, that is to be adopted which best suits the apparent intention of the legislature, from the scope or the provisions of the law.

4. And this leads us to remark, that the context must often be consulted, in order to arrive at a just conclusion, as to the intent of the legislature. The true sense in which particular words are used in a particular passage, may be often determined by comparing it with other passages and sentences, when there is any ambiguity, or intricacy, or doubt, as to its meaning.

5. And the professed objects of the legislature in making the law often afford an excellent key to unlock its meaning. Hence resort is often had to the preamble of a statute, which usually contains the motives of passing it, in order to explain the meaning, especially where ambiguous phrases are used.

6. For the same purpose, the subject matter of the law is taken into consideration; for the words must necessarily be understood to have regard thereto, and to have a

larger or narrower meaning, according as the subject matter requires. It cannot be presumed, that the words of the legislature were designedly used in a manner repugnant to the subject matter.

7. The effects and consequences must also be taken into consideration. If the effects and consequences of a particular construction would be absurd, and apparently repugnant to any legislative intention deducible from the objects or context of the statute, and another construction can be adopted, which harmonizes with the general design, the latter is to be followed. But in all such cases, where the effects and consequences are regarded, they are not permitted to destroy the legislative enactment, or to repeal it, but simply to expound it. If, therefore, the legislature has clearly expressed its will, that is to be followed, let the effects and consequences be what they may. But general expressions, and loose language, are never interpreted so as to include cases which manifestly could not have been in the contemplation of the legislature.

8. The reason and spirit of the law are also regarded; but this is always in subordination to the words, and not to control the natural and fair interpretation of them. In short, the spirit and the reason are derived principally from examining the whole text, and not a single passage; from a close survey of all the other means of interpretation, and not from mere private reasoning as to what a wise or beneficent legislature might or might not intend. Cases, indeed, may readily be put, which are so extreme, that it would be difficult to believe that any rational legislature could intend what their words are capable of including. But these cases furnish little ground for practical reasoning, and are exactly of that class, where, from the generality of the words, they are capable of contraction or extension, according to the real objects of the legislature. These objects once ascertained, the difficulty vanishes. This natural, and sometimes necessary limitation upon the use of words in a law, we often call construing them by their *equity*. In reality, nothing more is meant, than that they are construed in their mildest, and not in their harshest sense, it being open to adopt either.

9. For the same purpose, in the common law, regard is often had to antecedent and subsequent statutes upon the same subject; for, being *in pari materia*, it is natural to suppose, that the legislature had them all in their view in the last enactment, and that the sense which best harmonizes with the whole, is the true sense.

10. For the like reason, words and phrases in a statute, the meaning of which has been ascertained (especially in a statute on the same subject), are, when used in a subsequent statute, presumed to be used in the same sense, unless something occurs in it to repel the presumption.

11. As a corollary from the two last rules, it is a maxim of the common law, that all the statutes upon the same subject, or having the same object, are to be construed together as one statute; and then every part is to be taken into consideration.

12. Another rule is, to construe a statute as a whole, so as, if possible, or as nearly as possible, to give effect, and reasonable effect to every clause, sentence, provision, and even word. Nothing is to be rejected, as void, superfluous or insignificant, if a proper place and use can be assigned to it.

13. If a reservation in a statute be utterly repugnant to the purview of it, the reservation is to be rejected; if the preamble and the enacting clauses are different,

361

the latter are to be followed. But the reservation may qualify the purview, if consistent with it, and the preamble control the generality of expression of the enacting clauses, if it gives a complete and satisfactory exposition of the apparent legislative intention.

14. The common law is also regarded, as it stood antecedently to the statute, not only to explain terms, but to point out the nature of the mischief, and the nature of the remedy, and thus to furnish a guide to assist in the interpretation. In all cases of a doubtful nature, the common law will prevail, and the statute not be construed to repeal it.

15. Hence, where a remedy is given by statute for a particular case, it is not construed to extend so as to alter the common law in other cases.

16. Remedial statutes are construed liberally; that is, the words are construed in their largest sense, so far as the context permits, and the mischief to be provided against justifies. By remedial statutes, we understand those whose object is to redress grievances, and injuries to persons, or personal rights and property, in civil cases. Thus, statutes made to suppress frauds, to prevent nuisances, to secure the enjoyment of private rights, are deemed remedial.

17. So statutes are to be construed liberally which concern the public good; such as statutes for the advancement of learning, for the maintenance of religion, for the support of the poor, for the institution of charities.

18. The general rule is, that the sovereign or government is not included within the purview of the general words of a statute, unless named. Thus, a statute respecting all persons generally, is understood not to include the king. He must be specially named. But, nevertheless, in statutes made for the public good, which are construed liberally, the king, although not named, is often included by implication.

19. On the other hand, penal statutes, and statutes for the punishment of crimes, are always construed strictly.—The words are construed most favorably for the citizens and subjects. If they admit of two senses, each of which may well satisfy the intention of the legislature, that construction is always adopted which is most lenient. No case is ever punishable, which is not completely within the words of the statute, whatever may be its enormity. No language is ever strained to impute guilt. If the words are doubtful, that is a defence to the accused; and he is entitled, in such a case, to the most narrow exposition of the terms. This rule pervades the whole criminal jurisprudence of the common law, and is never departed from under any circumstances. It is the great leading principle of that jurisprudence, that men are not to be entangled in the guilt of crimes upon ambiguous expressions. But it is not to be understood, that the statute is to be construed so as to evade its fair operation. It is to have a reasonable exposition, according to its terms; and, though penal, it is not to be deemed odious.

20. Private statutes, also, generally receive a strict construction; for they are passed at the suggestion of the party interested, and are supposed to use his language.

21. Statutes conferring a new jurisdiction, and, especially, a summary jurisdiction contrary to the general course of the common law, are construed strictly. They are deemed to be in derogation of the common rights and liberties of the people under the common law, and are on that account jealously expounded.

There are many other rules, of a more special character, for the construction of statutes, which the extreme solicitude of the common law to introduce certainty, and to limit the discretion of judges, has incorporated into its maxims. But they are too numerous to be dwelt upon in this place. They all, however, point to one great object—certainty and uniformity of interpretation; and no court would now be bold enough, or rash enough, to gainsay or discredit them. On the contrary, it is the pride of our judicial tribunals constantly to resort to them for the purpose of regulating the necessary exercise of discretion in construing new enactments.

The legislative power of a government is generally coextensive with its sovereignty; and therefore embraces every thing which respects the concerns of the society. But it is in fact employed, if not universally, at least generally, in mere acts of amendment and supplement to the existing laws and institutions. Its office is ordinarily not so much to create systems of laws, as to supply defects, and cure mischiefs in the systems already existing. The question is often discussed in our day, how far it is practicable to give a complete system of positive law, or a complete code of direct legislation. And, if practicable, the farther question arises, how far it is desirable, or founded in sound policy. These questions have been the subject of ardent controversy among the civilians and jurists of the continent of Europe, living under the civil law; and, as may well be supposed, different sides have been taken by men of distinguished ability and learning; and the controversy is, and probably for a long period will be pursued with great animation and powers of reasoning.

In the countries governed by the common law, and especially in England and the United States, the same questions have of late been matter of wide discussion among the legal profession, as well as among statesmen, and a great diversity of opinion has been exhibited on the subject. It will be our object, in the sequel of these remarks, to put the reader in possession of some of the main grounds of the controversy.

The legislation of no country, probably, ever gave origin to its whole body of laws. In the very formation of society, the principles of natural justice, and the obligations of good faith, must have been recognised before any common legislature was acknowledged. Debts were contracted, obligations created, property, especially personal property, acquired, and lands cultivated, before any positive rules were fixed, as to the rights of possession and enjoyment growing out of them. The first rudiments of jurisprudence resulted from general consent or acquiescence; and when legislation began to act upon it, it was rather to confirm, alter, or add to, than to supersede, the primitive principles adopted into it.

We, in fact, know of no nation, or, at least, of no civilized nation, whose history has reached us, in which a positive system of laws for the exigencies of the whole society was coëval with its origin; and it would be astonishing if such a nation could be found. Nations, in their origin, are usually barbarous or rude in their habits, customs and occupations. They are scanty in population and resources, and have neither the leisure, nor the inclination, nor the knowledge, to provide systems for future use, suited to the growing wants of society, or to their own future advancement in the arts. A few positive rules suffice, for the present, to govern them in their most pressing concerns; and the rest are left to be disposed of according to the habits and manners of the people. Habits soon become customs; customs soon becomes rules; and rules soon fasten themselves as firmly upon the existing institutions, as if they were positive ordinances. Whenever we trace positive laws, in the early stages of society, they are few, and not of any wide extent; directions for special concerns, rather than comprehensive regulations for the universal adjustment of rights.

No man can pretend that, in Asia, any such universal rules were established by positive legislation, at the origin of the great nations by which it is peopled. The instructions of Moses, as promulgated by divine authority, for the government of the Jews, are not (as every one perceives) designed for every possible exigency of contract, or right, or injury, or duty, arising in the course of the business and history of that wonderful people. They are rather positive precepts, adapted to great occasions, and to govern those concerns which respected their wants, their spiritual advancement, and their duties as the chosen people of God.

The Greeks are not known to us, in their early or later history, as having had a code of universal extent. The Romans, in their early history, had few positive laws; and those seem to have been borrowed from other sources.

We often, indeed, see it stated, that the common law of England was originally formed from statutes now obsolete and unknown. But this assertion is wholly gratuitous. There is no reason to suppose that, in the early history of its jurisprudence, more was done than is usual in other nations, at the same period of their progress, such as the promulgating of some leading regulations, or the forming of some great institutions for the security of the public. In fact, a great portion of the English common law is of modern growth, and can be traced distinctly to sources independent of legislation. The commercial law of England is not two centuries old, and scarcely owes any thing important to positive legislation.

In truth, the formation of codes, or systems of general law, for the government of a people, and adapted to their wants, is a business which takes place only in advanced stages of society, when knowledge is considerably diffused, and legislators have the means of ascertaining the best principles of policy and the best rules for justice, not by mere speculation and theory, but by the results of experience, and the reasoning of the learned and the wise. Those codes with which we are best acquainted, are manifestly of this sort.

The institutes, and pandects, and code of Justinian, were made in the latter ages of Roman grandeur—nay, when it was far on the decline—not by instituting a new system, but by embodying the maxims, and rules, and principles, which the ablest jurists had collected in different ages, and from all the various lights of reason, and juridical decision, and general experience. No man imagines that Rome, in her early history, was capable of promulgating, or of acting upon, such a system. And this system, large as it was, has no pretension to be deemed complete, even for Rome itself. It left an infinite number of human concerns undecided by its text, which were, of course, to be submitted to judicial decision, and to receive the judgment of the wise men, who should be called, from time to time, to declare the law *ex aequo et bono*.

It may indeed be assumed, as a general truth, that the body of every system of law which has hitherto governed human society, had its origin as customary law; and if it has ever assumed the form of positive legislation, it has been to give it greater sanctity and extent, as well as greater uniformity of operation. This is certainly true in respect to the common law. That system, as administered in England and the U. States, is, as compared with the positive code, or statutes, of an immeasurably wider extent, both in its principles and its practical operation. A man may live a century, and feel (comparatively speaking) but in few instances the operation of statutes, either as to his rights or duties; but the common law surrounds him, on every side, like the atmosphere which he breathes.

Returning, then, to the question before stated, it may be inquired, whether it be practicable, in a refined and civilized state of society, to introduce a positive code, which shall regulate all its concerns. That such a code could be formed in a rude or barbarous age, so as to be adapted to all their future wants and growth, in passing from barbarism to refinement, seems absolutely incredible. That it could be formed in a refined age, when learning, and large experience, and enlightened views, and a sagacious forecast, might guide the judgments of the legislature, is the point before us.

In the first place, it has never yet been done by any people, in any age. The two most illustrious instances of codification are that of Justinian and that of Napoleon. Neither of these purports to be a complete system of laws and principles, superseding all others, and abolishing all others. As far as they go, they purport to lay down positive rules to guide the judgment of all tribunals, in cases within them. But other cases are left to be decided as they may arise, upon such principles as are applicable from analogy, from reasoning, from justice, from the customary law, or from judicial discretion. A positive prohibition to decide in cases not provided for by these codes, is not contained in either.

But is it possible to foresee, or to provide beforehand, for all such cases? Society is ever varying in its occupations and concerns, in its objects and its pursuits, in its institutions, its pleasures, its inventions, its intelligence, and, in short, in innumerable relations and diversities of measures and means. How is it possible to foresee, or to limit, these relations or diversities? How is it possible, especially in free governments, to reduce all human acts to the same positive elements? to prevent contracts, and obligations, and rights, and equities, and injuries, and duties, from becoming mixed up in an infinite series of permutations and combinations? Until it has been ascertained what are the utmost limits of human relations, and those limits, with all their intermediate details, can be clearly defined, in every shade of difference, how can any system of laws be adequate to provide for, or to guard them, or to fix the rights growing out of them?

To suppose that man is capable of all this, is to suppose that he is omniscient, all-wise, and all-powerful; that he is perfect, or that he can attain perfection; that he can see all the future in the past; and that the past is present to him in all its relations. The statement of such a proposition carries with it its own refutation. While man remains as he is, his powers, and capacities, and acts, must forever be imperfect.

But it may be said, that a positive code may be framed, and a declaration made that it shall be deemed the sole guide and rule, and that all other rules shall be prohibited. Certainly this may be done. But the effect of this would be, not to form a perfect code for all the future exigencies of society; but to declare that whatever was left unprovided for in the code, should be neither matter of right nor wrong. It would be to declare, that, as to all other transactions, now and hereafter, society should be utterly lawless; and, of course, it would be to declare, that a system confessedly imperfect, and not meeting the wants or exigencies, the rights or the wishes of society, should still govern it. What would this be, but to provide a bad code for human concerns, which it could not measure or manage?

From these considerations, we may assume it as a concession granted on all sides, that a perfect code, to regulate all present, and, a *fortiori*, all future concerns of any civilized society, by positive rules, applicable to them, is morally impossible. The only real question is, whether a positive code can be provided, adequate, in a general sense, to the present known wants of society. That codes may be formed, more or less comprehensive, to regulate many or few concerns, to supply defects, or to give symmetry and order to the law on particular subjects, cannot be doubted. It has been often done. Perhaps no civilized nation has ever existed, in which there was not, at the same time, a written and an unwritten law, or, in other words, a rule of positive institution and a rule of customary law.

All special decrees and ordinances of the sovereign power are of the former kind. Many subjects are of such a nature as to require some positive rule, seeing that natural law cannot fix them upon any invariable basis. For example, there is nothing in the nature of things by which we can say, that land shall, in all possible states of society, descend to the possessor's heirs, or who those heirs shall be; that he shall have a right to dispose of them by testament or deed, and how that testament or deed shall be evidenced; whether bills of exchange and promissory notes shall be negotiable or not, and to what extent binding upon the parties. These subjects, in the origin of a society, must either be positively provided for, or no rights can exist (strictly speaking) until they have become, by usage, fixed in a particular form. But most nations, with whose history we are acquainted, have had many positive laws. And to suit their institutions to the exigencies of society, in all its changes, there must be ordinances to change the old and to frame new rules.

In ancient Rome, in the modern governments of continental Europe, and especially in France and in England, great alterations have, from time to time, been made in the existing system of laws. Fundamental laws have been abrogated; amendatory provisions have been established; existing rules have been methodized, confirmed, explained, and limited; and new rules prescribed for new cases. The ordinances of Louis XIV, of 1673 and 1681, on the subject of maritime and commercial affairs, are striking instances of this sort. The abolition of feudal tenures; the regulation of uses and charities; the alliance of last wills and testaments, made in a prescribed mode; the provisions to suppress frauds, in the statute of frauds; the registration of conveyances of lands; the negotiability of promissory notes; and, above all, the positive enactments, various and almost innumerable, in the criminal code, are illustrations of the same fact, in the history of English legislation. All these statutes furnished, to a limited extent, a code on the particular subject. And we have recently seen, in the consolidation of the criminal laws of England into a few statutes, under the auspices of Sir Robert Peel, a striking instance of substantive codification of the criminal law of England, in many of its most important provisions.

But the objections often urged against codes, are not meant to be applied to legislation of this sort, but to systems, which are promulgated for the government of the great concerns of nations, in all their various departments and interests. How far this can be done, has been a matter of considerable theoretical discussion. But the question has been practically answered by the celebrity of several positive codes. And among those whose success and wisdom have been most generally acknowledged, are the code of Justinian and the code of Napoleon. That either of them furnishes complete rules for all the concerns of society, or excludes the necessity of judicial interpretations, or positive legislation, cannot be affirmed. That each of them covers a vast mass of the ordinary concerns of society, and fixes, positively and clearly, a great many wrongs and rights, and points out the proper redress, in cases where rights are to be vindicated and wrongs repressed, cannot well be denied. The question, then, is fairly presented, how far codes of this sort (the only ones which, in the actual state of society, are morally possible) are desirable, and founded in sound policy. It is here, that the advocates and the opponents of codes, under the jurisprudence of the common law, meet on debatable ground.

The lovers of ancient institutions, of existing laws, of customary principles, oppose codes as inconvenient and unnecessary. They hold them to be inconvenient, because they fix a stubborn rule, which shall govern future cases, instead of leaving them open to the free operations of the common law, which adapts itself to all the circumstances of the age. They maintain, also, that codes are unnecessary; for, so far as there is any rule, it is already known in the common law; and positive legislation cannot make it more so. It is added (and it is true), that law is gradually formed, and must differ in different ages, according to the different circumstances of society; that it must be varied according to the progress or regress of a nation; that it can rarely settle comprehensive principles; and must, by degrees, thread its way through the intricacies of human actions; and that an inflexible rule might work quite as much mischief as none at all; that no legislature can make a system half so just, or perfect, or harmonious, both from want of time, and experience, and opportunity of knowledge, as judges, who are successively called to administer justice, and gather light from the wisdom of their predecessors.

Most, if not all, of these suggestions, may be admitted to be correct, and yet they do not settle the controversy. In the first place, the objectors must admit, that, under the common law, there are positive statutes, which regulate many great concerns and rights of the countries governed by it. The descent and distribution of real estates, the making of last wills and testaments, the forms and ceremonies attendant upon conveyances of real estate, to say nothing of other important subjects, are, in every one of the U. States, provided for by positive statutes. Here we have a rule, which is absolute and inflexible. To say that, if found inconvenient, it may be altered, so as to suit the future interests of the particular state, is, in effect, no argument at all; for the same may be said as to any provision of a systematic code. No code is supposed to be unalterable.

Again, if it be said, that the legislature may, and often does, in an early stage of society, fix great principles and institutions, and then leaves the rest to judicial decisions, and thereby shows its wisdom, the true answer is, that the same reasoning applies to all codes, however extensive, if they leave the judicial tribunals at liberty to decide upon new cases, not governed by, or necessarily included in, the terms of the code. So far as the legislature has laid down principles (whether more or less extensive is of no consequence), these govern; beyond them, all is left as before.

Again, the common law is itself, as far as it goes, a system of rules. These rules are fixed, certain, and invariable, as to all cases falling within them. They are quite as unyielding as any code can be. When the common law has declared that the eldest son shall be the sole heir, and that the half-blood shall not inherit, a court has no more liberty to depart from these rules, or to refuse to apply them to any case falling within them, upon any notion of hardship, or inconvenience, or ill adaptation to the exigencies of society, than it has a right to say, that a last will and testament shall be good, though not executed according to the requirements of a statute. In each case, it is bound, and bound to the same extent.

If the question were, whether a positive code should contain a clause prohibiting courts of justice from deciding upon cases not within the purview of the code, there might be much to urge against the policy and reasonableness of such a clause; but it would furnish no objection to other parts of the code. The only point, with reference to a code, which, under this aspect, would deserve consideration, is, how far it would be desirable to provide for cases which may be foreseen, but have not, as yet, actually been subjected to legislative decision. On one side, it may be said, that it would be best to leave all such cases to be decided, as they arise, upon the result of human experience and human judgment, then acting upon all the circumstances. On the other hand, it may be said, that it is better to have a fixed, present rule, to avoid litigation, and to alter it in future, if unexpected inconveniences should arise. The reasoning on each side is sound, when applied to particular cases. On each side, it admits of question, when applied to all cases. It may be best, in many cases, to leave the rule to be made, when the case arises in judicial controversy. In others, it may be far better to establish a present rule, to clear a present doubt, or fix a limit to what is now uncertain.

Take the case of a bill of exchange, or promissory note; and suppose the question were, at what time demand of payment should be made, when it was payable on time, and no rule existed, and yet there was an immense amount of property dependent upon having a fixed, uniform rule; and, until so fixed, there must be endless litigation. Can any one doubt of the benefit of a rule, such as is now fixed in the commercial law of our country, for the purpose of securing certainty, viz. that payment must be demanded on the day on which it becomes due. On the other hand, suppose it were now proposed to make a law, fixing what should be the rate of wages in all future times, in all private employments; would it not, at once, occur to be impolitic to act upon a rule, the effects of which might immediately, or in future, press unequally and injuriously upon different interests in society? Again, it is said to be unnecessary to reduce the rules of the common law to a code, for they are as certain now as they would be in a positive code. They are even more so, because the legislature cannot be presumed able to lay down a positive rule, with all the limitations and qualifications of the common law.

Now, both of these suggestions admit of a satisfactory answer. If the rule exists, and has certainty in the common law, it can be stated. If there are any known exceptions, limitations and qualifications, upon a rule, those also can be stated. If nothing beyond a particular limit is known, then legislation can, at least, go to that limit. And as to all other cases, the same uncertainty exists, both at common law and in legislation. The difficulty of the argument consists in assuming, that, because the legislature has prescribed the same rule as the common law, the courts are thereby prohibited from doing what they possessed the power to do before, in the absence of any rule, viz. to find out what is the rule that ought to govern. Now, the legislature may as well leave this power in the courts, after a code, as the common law; and it will be best, unless there is a positive prohibition to the contrary.

The other part of the suggestion applies only to the point, whether the code is well or ill formed by the legislature. If badly formed, it will, of course, be proportionally bad; but that furnishes no objection to a code, but to the mode in which it is executed.

Then, again, as to the suggestion that it is unnecessary, because the rule already exists in the common law, and has certainty: to this several answers may be given. In the first place, if it be conceded, that there is entire certainty in the rule, at common law, there can be no harm in making the rule positive. It may do good; for it will instruct many, in and out of the profession, in respect to their rights and duty, who are now sadly ignorant of both, or are liable to be misled by their imperfect inquiries, or their limited sources of information.

Every man may be able to peruse a concise text; but every man may not have leisure or ability to study a voluminous commentary. Besides, even in relation to the doctrines of the common law, many of them lie scattered in different cases, and many of them are not so clear as not to admit of different interpretations, by minds of different learning and ability. Even lawyers of great research and accuracy, especially where the doctrine, though on the whole clear, is matter of deduction and inference, may not, at once, come to the correct conclusion; and others of less learning and ability may plunge into serious errors. Now, it would be no small gain to have a positive text, which should give, in such cases, the true rule, instead of leaving it open to conjecture and inference by feeble minds.

Again, there are many subjects of great intricacy and complexity, which can be fully mastered only by very able minds, resting, as they do, upon nice, and, sometimes, upon technical reasonings, not seen by the common reader. In such cases, the text may admit of very exact statement, but the commentaries necessary to deduce it, may be exceedingly elaborate. The demonstration, or last result, may be clear, but the steps in arriving at it, exceedingly perplexed and embarrassing. It may require an analysis by the greatest minds to demonstrate; but, when once announced, it may be understood by the most common minds. For instance, the subject of contingent remainders and executory devises is of uncommon complexity in the common law, and many a lawyer may read Mr. Fearne's admirable treatise on the subject, without feeling competent to expound all its doctrines. And yet, put every principle into a positive text, with all its limitations and restrictions (not to be made out by argument and inference, but given in a direct form), and his labors and his reasoning would be materially abridged, and certainty exist where darkness before overshadowed his mind.

Again, the common law has now become an exceedingly voluminous system; and as its expositions rest, not on a positive text, but upon arguments, analogies and commentaries, every person, who desires to know much, must engage in a very extensive system of reading. He may employ half his life in mastering treatises the substance of which, in a positive code, might occupy but a few hundred pages. The codes of Justinian, for instance, superseded the camel-loads of commentaries, which were antecedently in use, and are all now buried in oblivion. The Napoleon codes have rendered thousands of volumes only works of occasional consultation, which were before required to be studied very diligently, and sometimes in repeated perusals.

Again, what is to be done in the common law, where there are conflicting decisions on the same point, or converging series of opposite doctrines, approaching towards a conflict? The rule is here confessedly uncertain. Why should not the legislature interfere, in such a case, and fix a rule, such as, on the whole, stands upon the better reasoning, and the general analogies of the law? In point of fact, this is often done. Declaratory laws, in form, are unusual among us; but laws to clear doubts and difficulties are very common. Such interferences ought, doubtless, to be made with caution and prudence, and great deliberation. But this furnishes no just objection to a reasonable exercise of the power.

But in the practice under the common law, there is a still stronger ground for interference. In the first place, what the common law is, is always open to question; and if authorities are suggested on either side, it is common enough to find the rule deduced from them, doubted, denied, or explained away, by parties in an opposite interest. Courts are bound to hear as well as to decide; and although a court may think the rule of the common law clear, from their own prior researches and reasoning, it will rarely feel at liberty to stop eminent counsel, when they deny the rule, or seek to overthrow the authorities and reasonings by which it is supported. The spirit of our tribunals and the anxious desire, not only to do, but to appear to do justice, lead to a vast consumption of time in these discussions. If the legislature had once recognised the rule in a positive code, there would be an end of all such reasoning. The only question which could remain, would be, whether the rule were applicable to the case.

In the next place, there are, upon some doctrines of the common law, a vast multitude of authorities to examine, compare and understand, which requires not only great diligence, but great skill. In some cases, there are shades of difference fit for comment; in others, *obiter dicta*, which are to be qualified; in others, doubts thrown out upon collateral heads; in others, reasoning not altogether satisfactory. Under such circumstances, what is to be done? The advocate on the one side comments on every case, and the language of every judge, which furnishes any color of support for his client. His arguments must be met and answered on the other side, not only because no advocate can know what the judges will decide, but what will be the influence upon their minds of a *dictum*, or doubt, or incidental remark or reason. It is indispensable, therefore, to examine the whole, although, perhaps, neither party doubts what the amount of authority, on the whole, supports. On one point (we believe) a learned English judge said, many years ago, that there were then more than 170 authorities. It is most probable that the number is now doubled; and yet, upon this very point, a legislative enactment of three lines might put controversy at rest for ever.

Perhaps no man in or out of the legal profession would now doubt what the rule ought to be. The difficulty is, that a rule has either been adopted which works inconveniently in particular cases, or a rule has grown out of a hasty adjudication, which subsequent judicial subtility has been desirous of escaping from; but it is not easy to do so, without breaking in upon the acknowledged force of the rule. Hence distinctions, nice, and perhaps, not very satisfactory, are found, as blemishes in some parts of the law, which need the legislative hand to extirpate or correct them.

But it has been urged, as has been already incidentally noticed, that it is a great advantage to have law a flexible system, which will yield to the changing circumstances of society; and that a written code gives a permanence to doctrines, which would otherwise be subject to modification, so as to adapt them to the particular character of the times. This objection has been already in part answered. In respect to the common law doctrines, they cannot now be changed, whatever may be the changes of society, without some legislative enactment. They furnish a guide to all cases governed by them, until the legislature shall promulgate a new rule. Courts cannot disturb or vary them; and the question of their application to new cases is equally open, whether there be, or be not a code. The legislature can, with the same ease, vary its code as its common law. It can repeal, amend, or modify either.

But another principal objection is often suggested, and that is, that all parts of the common law are not in a state susceptible of codification; and that, as we cannot form a complete system of it, one great object of a code must fail. It may be admitted, that some parts of the common law are too imperfectly settled in principles, and too little understood in practice, to allow of any exact codification. But these parts are principally obsolete, or of rare occurrence and application in the common business of life; so that, if they admitted of being reduced to a text, it may be well doubted if they were important enough to deserve it. There are other parts, again, which have grown up in modern times, which may be admitted to be yet in an immature and forming state, in respect to which, perhaps, it were better to wait the results of experience, than to anticipate them by positive law.

Conceding all this, it falls far short of establishing the inutility of a code in other departments of the common law, not open to the like objections. Because we cannot form a perfect system, does it follow that we are to do nothing? Because we cannot, without rashness, give certainty to all possible or probable details of jurisprudence, shall we leave every thing uncertain and open to controversy?

There is not a single state of the Union that has not repeatedly revised, changed, and fixed, in a positive code, many of its laws. The criminal code has almost every where received, in some of its principal branches, a methodical form. Virginia, long ago, reduced some important portions of her law to a positive text. New York has recently gone much farther, and, in the form of a revised code, made very extensive alterations in her common law, as well as in her statuable law.

England, in our own time, has consolidated the most important heads of her criminal jurisprudence, in a new and methodized text. No man can doubt, that revisions of this sort may be useful, and, indeed, indispensable for the wants and improvements of society, in its progress from one stage to another. The question of more or less is a mere matter of expediency and policy. It is not a little remarkable, that, in England, almost every change in the general structure of her laws, by positive legislation, has, in all ages, met with a similar objection and resistance, and, when once adopted, has been generally, if not universally satisfactory.

But there are many branches of the common law which can, without difficulty, be reduced to a positive text. Their main principles are embodied in treatises, accurate and full, and there can be no want of learned men ready to form an outline of them for the consideration of the legislature. Our commercial law is generally in this state. The law of bills of exchange and promissory notes, of insurance, of shipping and navigation, of partnership, of agency and factorage, of sales, of bailments, and many kindred titles, admits of codification to a very high degree of certainty; and yet, in these branches, there is still room enough to controvert particular decisions and authorities, to make it desirable to give a positive sanction to the better doctrine, and thus to save the profession from laborious researches, and the public from expensive litigation.

The ordinance of Louis XIV, on commercial law, dried up a thousand sources of disputation; and the present code of commerce of France has settled, in a positive manner, most of the questionable points, which had been found unprovided for by that ordinance, and were resigned to judicial decision in the intermediate period. Besides, a code furnishes the only safe means of incorporating qualifications upon a general principle, which experience has demonstrated to be proper and politic. Courts often lament that a principle is established in too broad terms for the public good, and yet do not feel themselves at liberty to interpose exceptions which the principle does not sanction.

This article has already spread out into a great length, and must now be closed. The result of the whole view, as to codes, is, that neither the friends nor the opponents of them are wholly right in their doctrines or their projects; that, in every civilized country, much may be done to simplify the principles and practice of the law by judicious codification, and to give it uniformity and certainty; that How much ought to be done? is a question not admitting of any universal response, but is, or may be, different as to different countries, or, in different ages, as to the same country; that every code, to be useful, must act upon the existing institutions and jurisprudence, and not, generally, supersede them; that what, with reference to the customs, habits, manners, pursuits, interests, and institutions of one country, may be fit and expedient, may be wholly unfit and inexpedient for another; and that the part of true wisdom is, not so much to search out any abstract theory of universal jurisprudence, as to examine what, for each country in particular, may best promote its substantial interests, preserve its rights, protect its morals, and give permanence to its liberties.

Appendix IV: Statesmen—Their Rareness and Importance:
Daniel Webster

One of the first reflections, which occurs to an intelligent observer of the actual political condition of the United States, is, that we have few, very few statesmen. We have party men and party leaders in abundance; we have politicians of all sorts and kinds, who make a trade or a pleasure of the vocation; and we have demagogues of every rank and degree, from those who guide, direct, and control the political arrangements of a city, down to those, who become the humble echoes of their masters at the village inn, or the village post-office, near the cross-roads.

We are a most busy, inquisitive, and, one might almost say, meddlesome people in all public affairs, state and national, public and municipal. We discuss them; we form opinions; we vote in masses at the polls; we insist upon a voice in all matters; and we are quick to act, and slow to doubt upon any measure, which concerns the Republic. Many are eager for office; few, comparatively speaking, decline it; and, in the course of a moderately long life, multitudes are called to political offices and duties.

This is all very natural, nay, almost unavoidable, considering the popular character of all our institutions. The people are entrusted with all the leading powers of legislation and government. They frame their constitutions; appoint their rulers; select their representatives, and through them carry on the whole business of government, from that of the smallest municipality to that of the whole nation. It is, therefore, not only wise, but it is necessary, that they should bestow much time upon public men and public measures, and inquire into, and sift the tendency of all, that is done, and all that is said.

Under such circumstances it might well be supposed, that we should have, in every part of the land, crowds of men deeply versed in public affairs. And yet one of the most lamentable truths, which meets us on every side, as we turn, is, that we have had, for many years past, but few statesmen.

By statesmen, I do not, of course, mean men, who can speak fluently, or even eloquently, in the occasional debates in Congress, and in the state legislatures. There is certainly no lack of these, as our long debates and over-loaded presses abundantly establish. Indeed, it is probably true, (as has been often asserted) that no people exceed the Americans in facility and exuberance of speech; and no people use this facility and exuberance upon more public occasions, from the stump orator, at home, to the representative in the national legislature. But by statesmen I mean men, who

Unsigned article by Joseph Story reprinted from *The New England Magazine*, Vol. VII (Aug., 1834), 89–104.

have profoundly studied the nature, science, and operations of governments in general; men, who intimately understand our relations with foreign states and foreign policy; men, who have taken a large survey of all our national interests, agricultural, manufacturing, commercial, political; men, who have not only acquired some knowledge of the theory of statistics and political economy, but who have had a thorough experience in public business and public measures; men, in short, who may safely be entrusted with public affairs, because they have high talents and solid acquirements, and unite with these a liberal spirit, a thorough acquaintance with the details, as well as with the principles of government, and a lofty ambition, as well as an honest purpose, to serve their country, and to give permanence to its institutions and interests. Such men, and no other men, are entitled to the character of statesmen.

Of such men no country on earth has so much need as our own. In despotic governments, where all power is concentrated in a single sovereign, such men are of occasional use, when important changes in policy are contemplated, or great emergencies call for extraordinary resources and arrangements. But, in the common course of things, in such governments, few innovations are proposed or sanctioned. The stream of public policy moves on within its old and accustomed banks, sluggishly or rapidly, according to the times and the seasons. But the embankments are sufficient for either; or if there be an occasional inundation, it does little more than create a temporary and silent sympathy for the sufferers; and then all moves on again as before.

In a limited monarchy, such, for instance, as the government of Great Britain, there is great use for statesmen; and, it may be added, that great use is made of them. In former times, indeed, court favorites and court cabinets, "the power, behind the throne, greater than the throne itself," could do much. But, even then, in perilous times, there was always need of pilots, who could weather the storm; and, if they could not be purchased upon the ordinary terms of court favor and patronage, the crown was compelled to take them upon their own terms.

And, in our day, they have become indispensable parts of the public machinery. If war is to be declared, or peace is to be concluded; if there is to be a reform in Parliament, or in the law, or in the revenue, or in foreign policy; statesmen must lead the crown, and not the crown lead statesmen. The rights of the people must be guarded and maintained; and they must feel themselves to be fully represented in the House of Commons. The members of the latter will not now suffer themselves to be dragooned into measures at the mere beck of the crown. They require reasons, and satisfactory reasons, from ministers, who are statesmen; and they scruple not to advise the crown to dismiss ministers, when they are incompetent, or they do not possess the confidence of the nation. And, what to Americans may sound strange, the crown listens to the advice. The interests of the whole nation are not to be sacrificed to the wishes or passions of the king and his courtiers. They, who hold the purse, will regulate the sword, and the patronage, and the measures of the government. Earl Grey and Lord Brougham (who are now veterans in the public service) are as necessary to William IV as Mr. Canning, and Lord Castlereagh, and the Duke of Wellington were to George IV in the main purposes of carrying on the government of the empire.

What is true in the limited monarchy of England, as to the necessity of statesmen, is far more true of a republic. There, they are indispensable to carry on only a portion of the machinery. Here, they must guide and manage the whole. There, the people are a part only of the government. Here, the people are the whole, or rather control the whole. There, with some impulses from the people, through the House of Commons, the king can keep every thing in its own place. Here, every thing that is done, daily, nay, hourly, for better or for worse, must be done by the people through their chosen agents. There is, therefore, a perpetual necessity for watchfulness, intelligence, activity, public spirit, and, though last, not least, of integrity and virtue to keep the country in the track of its true interests. Folly or ignorance, rashness or recklessness, the pride of power or the corruptions of office, may endanger our rights and liberties, and cut us adrift from all that is safe and suitable to our condition.

Besides these general considerations, there are others peculiar to us, calling for various and extraordinary abilities in our statesmen. Our form of government, however excellent and admirable in its structure, is confessedly new. It is a great experiment in the history of nations. Its success will cover us with glory, as well as secure us in happiness; its failure will spread a gloom over the human race, as well as involve our own ruin. In such a state of things, all the sagacity, experience, coolness, and prudence, belonging to the wisest and best heads, are indispensable to us. We have our all at risk in the voyage without insurance; and we must always keep on board the ship of state, not only a competent crew to work the ship, but the most cautious of the skillful, as well as the truest of the best, to keep her in good trim, and secure her from shipwreck on the new coasts of the ocean, which we traverse without experienced pilots, upon a voyage partly of discovery, and partly of profit.

We have a most complicated government, composed of different sovereignties, in many respects independent; connected with, and to a limited extent controled by, a national sovereignty. The boundaries between the powers of the states and those of the nation are undefined; and, perhaps, in some degree, must forever remain undefinable; for they almost necessarily run into each other. The lights and the shades are infinitely blended, and the dividing points between them are evanescent. No administration on earth is called to the performance of so many delicate duties, where there are so many diversities of interests, of institutions, of employments, of feelings, of local jealousies and attachments, and of sincere and irrepressible differences of opinion. No where are there so many occasions for mutual sacrifices of opinion, for enlarged notions of public policy, and for a wise and moderate course of general legislation.

That, under such circumstances, we should have comparatively few statesmen, is a seeming paradox, since occasions so constantly arise, in which their importance and usefulness must be severely felt. It seems a contradiction of the well-known doctrine in political economy, that the supply should not always be proportional to the demand, or rather that they should not reciprocally produce each other. But the truth is, that it is, when thoroughly examined, rather an illustration of, than an exception to, the doctrine. The demand, in order to create the supply, must be general, not local; it must be uniform, not casual; it must be permanent, and not merely temporary and capricious. It must justify, if one may so say, the outlay of time and capital, and bring sure returns, if they are distant, and the growth is slow, and the arrangements previously required are extensive.

Now, in the first place, it needs scarcely be said, that statesmen are not the growth of a day, or of a year, or even of several years. There must be a rare combination of eminent qualifications, genius, judgement, extensive knowledge, various experience, a devoted industry, and even an enthusiasm for public affairs. There must be honesty and disinterestedness of purpose, a purified ambition, great firmness, and, at the same time, great flexibility of mind. And, above all, there must be a long and severe training in public life, an intimate familiarity with its various duties, and a ready tact in seizing upon all the proprieties of the occasion to get rid of dangerous and critical excitements, and to forward wise measures, without shocking popular prejudices.

A statesman must, in some measure, be master of the past, present, and future. He must see what is behind, as well as before. He must learn to separate the accidental in human experience, from that which constitutes the cause or the effect of measures. He must legislate for the future, when it is, as yet, but dimly seen; and he must put aside much, which might now win popular favor, in order to found systems of solid utility, whose results will require ages clearly to develop; but still, whose results are indispensable for the safety, the glory, and the happiness of the country.

It has been said, that confidence is a plant of a slow growth; but it may be said, with still more truth, that statesmanship is a plant of the slowest growth. It requires a hardy and vigorous soil, and it must stand many a tempest of icy coldness, and of blasting heat. How few, then, can afford to take such risks, to encounter such chances, to submit to such discipline, and to expend life in pursuits, which, after all, may yield nothing but disappointment? Have republics, in ancient or modern times, been renowned for their constancy and affection towards patriots? Has Athens been alone tired of hearing Aristides called the just, or Demosthenes the eloquent, or Socrates the wise, or Aristotle the great?

In the next place, it is a common, though most mischievous error, that a popular government does not require even high, much less the highest talents to administer it. And in no country has this notion been more extensively believed and acted upon than in America. The people here have been so long and so often told, that they could never mean wrong, and, therefore, could never act wrong, that they were too wise not to choose competent rulers, and too watchful ever to be betrayed or injured by them, that to doubt their infallibility in choice or in judgement is, in the present times, no ready passport to popular favor.

Nothing is more familiar now, than the remark, that there is no mystery in our government. That all lies clear and on the surface. That honesty of purpose, and reasonable intelligence, will secure the just operations of all our public institutions. That the machinery of our constitution has been so well constructed and so skillfully arranged, that it will go on steadily with very little help; and that the most we want is the attention of industrious minds to repair small breaches, and put oil on the friction wheels. Nay, this is turned into a matter of public boast; and it is boldly asserted, that it is a proof of the weakness and mal-adaptation of any government, that high talents and long experience are required to administer it. Few persons have visited Washington, of late years, who have not heard very audible declarations of this sort in the rank and file of parties; and, even near home, it is no bad topic for a college declamation, or a speech at the hustings.

In the next place, in all popular governments, and especially in one like our own, a confederated republic, there is always a very numerous body of men, who, from various causes, are ever on the alert for office, or for popular favor. Some desire it from super-abundance of leisure; some from the desire of profit, and a distressing poverty of means; some from a stirring and ill-directed ambition; some from the pride of consequence; and not, to enumerate more, some from the solid power of patronage, which it confers or exhausts.

Now, it cannot be disguised, that with such hosts in the field, the highest candidates in the race have little chance of success, and find obstructions on every side, from rivals or enemies, from the arts they disdain to practise, or the pretensions they decline to put forth. The real statesman is willing to win public favor only by fair means; by high character, inflexible virtue, fixed principles, and a liberal and enlightened policy. He is conscious of his own humiliation and dishonor, when he rises by subterfuges and intrigues. But the demagogue, like the courtier, can unscrupulously employ all means, which subserve his main purpose. He looks steadily to the'end. The triumph is to be secured; fairly, if it may, but at all events it must be secured. In such a contest, with such unequal means of influence, what chance is there of success for those, who are best qualified for public honors? They know their fate, and they often withdraw from the canvass.

And, not to dwell upon many other grounds, in the rear of these causes comes the overwhelming spirit of party, which substitutes devotion to the party for the good of the country; and which neither acknowledges, nor respects any candidates but those, who are found close wedged in its own ranks. Such combinations are the natural growth of all free governments. They are founded in the very nature of man. They are the most facile means to gain and to perpetuate power without merit, in the same hands. They rally under their standard, all the ambitious, and restless, and disaffected, who have encountered disappointment, or insist on public office, as well as ready materials of many other sorts.

The few are thus enabled, gradually, but irresistibly, to secure to themselves the monopoly of public office and patronage; and the many are drilled in the ranks with the privilege to vote for those, who have already been selected for them, and with a certainty of political denouncement, if they dare to doubt, much less to act, in opposition to the voice of the party. If the party constitutes, at the moment, the majority of the state or nation, it assumes the imposing name of "the People," and all its acts are the acts of the people. If, unluckily, it should sink into a minority, it is compelled to submit to the less grateful appellation of being "a faction."

How far this has been, or is likely, hereafter, to be true, in our country, it is unnecessary to say. It is a dangerous topic for comment or examination. *Incedimus per ignes suppositos cineri doloso*. But it will be easy to see, that in the same proportion, that party spirit obtains a predominance in any free government, and secures its own steady triumph, just in the same proportion it will suppress or dispense with the services of statesmen. If it needs them, it will unwillingly grudge the proper reward; and it can scarcely secure them long without bringing the favored man down to its own level, or surrendering its own sovereignty. The latter must be a moral miracle. The former has but too often proved a melancholy truth, "to point a moral, or adorn a tale."

But it may be asked, for what purpose are these reflections made, and to what object do they tend? They are made to excite my countrymen to the importance and value of rearing and perpetuating a large class of statesmen,—real, pure, effective statesmen. If our republic falls, it will, probably, fall from a general imbecility, brought on by its powers being entrusted to incompetent rulers, or being wielded by corrupt ones. We have no permanent rewards to bestow upon statesmen for their services. They cannot become the founders of great families, or the possessors of hereditary rank. It is wise, that it should be so. But we can promote them to public honors, when they deserve them; we can cheer them for their labors and their sacrifices; we can protect their reputations from unjust censure; we can exercise a generous candor in scanning their actions; we can evince towards them a lively gratitude; we can bear them on our lips while living; we can embalm their memories when dead, if not in costly monuments, at least in our affections and our public records. These are rewards best suited to elevated minds; and they have been those, which patriots in all ages have been most solicitious to acquire and to hold.

I have been led to these remarks, however, not so much by any general views of the subject, as by the immediate contemplation of the character and services of a great statesman now living. I mean DANIEL WEBSTER. I do not propose to write his life, or his eulogy; that duty will belong to abler hands, at some future day, after he shall have passed from the present scenes of action, and shall have become the appropriate theme of the historians of his country. Nor do I propose to sketch his biography, or his rise and progress from the comparative obscurity of private life, to the wide circle of his present fame. This has been already done, so far as it may now be fitly done, by one of the ripest scholars of the age, and in a manner which cannot be surpassed. What I propose is, rather to bring before my countrymen a slight sketch of some of the prominent features of his political life, as an incitement and admonition to the young and ambitious, and a consolation and hope to the old and the contemplative.

Mr. Webster is now about fifty-two years of age; and his first entrance into public life was about twenty-two years ago, as a Representative in Congress from New-Hampshire, the state in which he was born, and received his education, and of which he is, and has long been, one of the proudest ornaments. Whether the state has duly appreciated or thoroughly felt the full value of such a distinction, is a matter, which her own citizens must decide for themselves, and constitutes no point for examination in the present remarks.

At the age of thirty, in a most trying and critical period, just after the commencement of the late war with Great-Britain, Mr. Webster came into the public councils. With the exception of a few intervals, he has ever since been engaged in public affairs. His reputation, therefore, such as it is, is not of a mushroom growth, the sudden production of the hot-bed heats of popular favor, or the stinted and unhealthy upstart of the way-side. He has had a large survey of public cares and public duties, in times of war and of peace, in minorities and majorities, as a leader with, and as a leader against, administrations. His political studies have been nourished and matured by the lucubrations and practice of more than twenty years, a period assigned by the great masters in his own profession, as that fit for a lawyer, who seeks and would secure eminence.

How he has borne himself through all these various scenes, is matter, not merely of curiosity, but of intense interest. Has he been consistent? Has he been firm and frank? Has he been true to his friends and his principles? Has he been true to his country and its institutions? Has he been devoted to the mere objects of party, or to sectional and local interests? Or has he,—as public duty required,—represented the nation, and maintained the integrity of its interests at home and abroad? Has he been the advocate of a broad and comprehensive policy, fit for the North and the South, the East and the West? Or has he contented himself with patronizing and enforcing the exclusive claims of his own state, or district; or narrowed himself down to the more facile and familiar ambition of less gifted minds,—the support of mere private claims and private projects,—as if he were the retained counsel of his constitutents?

In short, has he been the ready and staunch advocate of national measures, national rights, constitutional principles, and liberal systems? Or the flexible supporter of every project, enjoying a temporary popularity, and fluttering for its hour in the sunshine of executive patronage? These are questions, which naturally occur with reference to the characters of all public men; and they acquire extraordinary importance in estimating the merits of statesmen.

Consistency is, doubtless, a quality of no inconsiderable value, as a test of character, and often rises into a high virtue. He, who is ever veering about with every wind of doctrine and opinion, is possessed of feeble judgement, or feeble principles, or both. He wants constancy or clearness of mind, and may often be open to the stronger reproach of a deficiency of morals. As a guide or an example, he is equally unsafe; and it is difficult to say, whether he does most injury as a friend or a foe, as a supporter or as an opponent of government.

But consistency of character and consistency of opinion are not necessarily identical. Never to change an opinion, would be as remarkable, nay, as unworthy, in a wise man, as never to be stable in any opinion. Inflexibility in maintaining opinions once taken up, whatever may be the change of circumstances, and without regard to them, degenerates into mischievous obstinacy and wrong-headed perseverance. It would be strange, if a man should never profit by his own experience, or by that of others; that he should learn nothing, and forget nothing; that, at twenty, he should be as ripe and correct as at forty.

And, to bring the case home, that when he begins political life, he should be so wise, that there should be nothing to learn, and that, in the most complex and difficult of all human transactions, the constant permutations and new combinations of society should introduce no new elements of opinion or action. The statement of such a case carries its own refutation along with it. Human wisdom is the aggregate of all human experience, constantly accumulating, and selecting, and re-organizing its own materials.

It would be little praise to Mr. Webster to say, that he has always entertained the same opinions upon all political subjects. Like other great minds of his own and former times, like Burke, and Pitt, and Fox, and Wellington, and Canning, he has, doubtless, modified some, and changed other opinions. But this change has been the result, not of accident, or interest, but of enlarged knowledge and comprehensive genius acting upon ample means of study and practice. It has been a slow and silent growth, and, therefore, vigorous and solid. It has gradually mixed in with the great principles upon which he began life, and has not superseded them.

The friends to whom he was attached in his youth have never deserted him, nor he them. He may have differed from them on many occasions; but it has been a difference, which created no hostility and lost no confidence. It was merely the exercise of that candid judgement, which claims the right to decide for itself, and freely concedes the same right to others.

Perhaps few men, in so long a career, in so critical a period, have ever maintained so general a consistency of opinion. None, certainly, have maintained more consistency of character. If the cause of all this be sought, it will be found in the peculiar characteristics of Mr. Webster's mind. It is marked by sagacity, caution, accuracy, foresight, comprehensiveness, laborious research, and untiring meditation, as well as by various genius. In short, he possesses that undefinable quality, called WISDOM, in an eminent degree, the joint result of the original texture of his mind, and its severe use and discipline in accurate observations of public affairs.

Let us look a little more closely into his political life, and see if it does not justify these remarks. He came into public life during a period, when his country was at war; and he was chosen as an opponent of the then administration, and as an advocate for peace with Great-Britain. Did he launch into an indiscriminate hostility to the government? Did he support the claims of Great-Britain and repudiate our own? No. He was ready to give his aid for all public measures, useful, and, in his judgement, effective, to carry on the war and to secure peace.

He was against land hostilities, upon the Canadian frontiers, as at once perilous and exhausting. But he was for some defence throughout the land, and for active warfare, where it might be formidable, upon the ocean. He was for a navy to protect us at home, and to carry on retaliatory operations upon the most vulnerable points of our enemy, her commerce and shipping. The main object of the administration seemed to be to maintain the warfare on land. He held it the truest policy to wage it at sea. Was he wrong? Will any man now coolly say, that this was not the best and the safest course? Is it not now a fact in history, which could then only be conjectured, that Great-Britain was mainly pressed to peace by our successful depredations upon her commerce in every sea? Premiums rose, at Lloyd's Coffee-House, from five per cent to thirty-three per cent on maritime risks; and the merchants and ship-owners, who were most clamorous for war in England, became anxious for peace.

The American administration were exceedingly distressed for revenue, the very sinews of war. The credit of the government was sunk to the lowest ebb; its own paper currency and treasury notes, payable in one year, with a fair interest, encountered the enormous depreciation of *fifty* per cent. Under such circumstances, a resort to a national bank seemed indispensable to save the government from bankruptcy. It was, accordingly, proposed by the friends of the administration.

Mr. Webster, on that occasion, acted with the patriotic spirit, which a regard to the public welfare demanded, and without reference to party. The bank, proposed by the government, was with a capital of fifty millions, nine-tenths of which was to be depreciated paper of the government itself. To such a moneyed institution, on such a basis, Mr. Webster was opposed, because it would essentially aggravate all the evils of a *paper* currency, and would render a return to specie payments, then suspended by many of the state banks, absolutely impracticable. But he avowed himself the firm friend of a national bank, both as constitutional and expedient, nay, as indispensable to the operations of the government. And he pledged himself to support a proper national bank, which should be brought forward upon a money basis, and gave the outline of a plan in proof of his sincerity.

That plan, upon the defeat of the paper bank scheme, was brought forward by the friends of the administration, and was steadily and successfully supported by Mr. Webster. It passed both Houses of Congress, and failed afterwards solely by the negative of the then President. In this respect, he followed out the doctrine, which, in a speech made but a short time before, he avowed as his leading principle of action. "The humble aid (said he) which it would be in my power to render to measures of government, shall be given cheerfully, if government will pursue measures, which I can conscientiously support."

Peace soon followed, and with it the project of a national bank was for a time laid aside. When, however, it was again revived in 1816, Mr. Webster adhered to his former doctrines; but the plan, containing some features, especially as to the appointment of government directors,—a measure most questionable in its use, as well as in its abuse,—which he disapproved, he refused to give it his support.

But as soon as it became a law, he took every measure to give it efficiency and strength, so that it might afford a solid and secure currency to the whole country. He, therefore, brought forward a resolution requiring all duties and revenues, payable to the government, to be paid in specie, or in the notes of banks, whose paper was equal to and convertible into specie.

At this time the depreciation of the bank paper of the state banks, which had suspended specie payments, was enormous. The paper of the banks in New-York was about eighteen per cent below par; that of the banks of Philadelphia about twenty per cent; that of the banks of Baltimore about twenty-five per cent. In New-England, there had been no suspension of specie payments; and the consequence was, that duties and revenues, collected in Massachusetts, were twenty-five per cent higher than in Baltimore, where the local depreciated currency was received at par. This was a flagrant breach of the constitution, in its just spirit; for that required all duties to be uniform, and without preference of states. But in this manner the most important advantages were given to the ports of those states, where the depreciation was greatest.

The resolution of Mr. Webster passed; and to that resolution, and the existence of a national bank, we are indebted for the sound, uniform, and excellent currency, which has ever since pervaded the whole country.

Soon after this period Mr. Webster removed to Boston, and for a time retired from the public councils, devoting himself to the arduous duties of his profession. It is not my design to enter upon this subject, or to speak of his distinguished services at the bar, various and interesting as they have been, which have long since placed him among the first, if not the very first in the country. If he is not before all others, it may truly be said, that he is not behind any one in forensic powers and fame, in the general estimation of the profession.

When Mr. Webster again resumed public life, about the year 1823, other duties and other measures of great magnitude agitated the public councils. Among other topics of great interest was that of the arrangements of the Tariff, a subject, which has since become the foundation of some of the most heated controversies in Congress, known to our public annals. Upon this subject, it has often been suggested, that the opinions of Mr. Webster have undergone some modifications. It is, probably, true, that they have so. But these modifications are far less extensive, than is commonly, though erroneously supposed. They are modifications of opinion, connected with and derived from essential changes, not only in our foreign and domestic policy, but in the commercial and political policy and intercourse of the whole world.

A statesman, who should disregard such changes, and omit to provide for them, who should refuse to adopt measures to prevent foreign inequalities, or the sacrifices of domestic interests, from an obstinate adherence to theory, or to measures, which had ceased to be practicable, or if practicable, were constantly working mischievous results, would be unworthy of the name. He would be a bigot, and not a patriot; not "too fond of the right, to pursue the expedient;" but too indifferent to human sufferings to make any effort to redress them, or too wise in his own conceit to gather wisdom from general experience. Such a man would suffer a city to be inundated by a ruinous flood, rather than have an embankment of his own construction doubted in its sufficiency.

When, at an earlier period, Congress were pressed to give a preternatural energy and encouragement to domestic manufactures, to the apparent injury of our commerce, then just recovering from the heavy blows inflicted on it by the war with Great-Britain, Mr. Webster, though a decided friend to manufactures and agriculture, as well as to commerce, was unwilling to try the experiment at such a time, and under such circumstances. All Europe had then ceased to be belligerent, and was struggling in an uncompromising rivalry with our crippled commerce. He thought that manufactures, under the existing state of things, would rise as fast as they could be permanently sustained; that a quick growth might be mischievous to their ultimate prosperity; and at all events, that any sudden change of policy afterwards might involve them in sudden ruin; a change, in a government like ours, always to be feared, and always to be provided against.

Who, looking to all the intervening difficulties, which have since arisen, can say, that there was not much of political foresight and sagacity in all this? At that time, Mr. Webster shared the opinion in common with many of the ablest and best statesmen in the country.

But the system was adopted. Immense capital was embarked in manufactures; and new embarrassments arose from foreign competition, to an extent which no one had previously imagined could possibly exist. Mr. Webster then acted as a statesman should act. He determined to sustain the interests, which had been thus created by the public patronage. He would not consent to destroy, what Congress had pledged itself to support. His object was to give relief where it was needed, and to frame a tariff upon principles adapted to our necessities, our interests, and our permanent pursuits. That he did not accomplish all that he desired, is true. But whoever reads his printed speeches upon this subject, will find them full of profound reasoning, and accurate knowledge of political economy.

Indeed, one of the peculiarities of Mr. Webster's character is, that he draws practical materials freely from all other minds and sources, to give more clearness and certainty to the operations of his own thoughts. Guided by the results of the same enlightened experience, he is now known as one of the firmest and most active friends of the domestic system, as one embedded in the vital interests of the country.

It was about this period, while in the House of Representatives, that Mr. Webster performed one of the most meritorious and valuable labors of his life, a labor, which few can duly appreciate, because it carries with it no general applause; but it, at the same time, deserves the highest praise, from the unostentatious and silent good, which it confers upon the whole community.

I speak of his revision of the criminal code of the United States, which makes provision for the numerous defects and omissions, which must be found in a code made in the year 1790, in the infancy of the national government, and left, without any substantial amendments, until the year 1825. The amendatory act of 1825, which was carried through Congress by his steady and manly devotion to it, though it consists of twenty-six sections, is but a part of the plan which he had sketched of a criminal code. But it contains all, which he then thought could be obtained, without putting at risk the success of the whole revision.

In truth, so little interest do the members of Congress feel in mere civil or criminal legislation, applicable to judicial tribunals, that the very circumstance, that any proposed system is comprehensive and full, ordinarily furnishes a fatal obstacle to its passage. It requires too much time to examine; it catches no popular feelings; it engages no ardent supporters. It is a matter of dry duty, to be postponed to some more convenient season, which never does and never can arrive. To many persons, who may read these pages, it will, probably, be new, that the thing has been done at all, much more, that it has been done by Mr. Webster. Yet it may be told them truly, that their persons, and property, and rights on the broad ocean, as well as on land, are rendered far more secure than they were before, by his untiring industry.

He, who has so often and so eloquently defended the rights of the government and the people, in the halls of legislation, has performed not less important duties in the committee room, in maturing measures, and collecting facts, and suggesting inquiries.

But the field of Mr. Webster's labors, in which his great talents are best known, and have been most successful, are, beyond all question, the struggles he has maintained, at all times, for the constitution in its true, broad, and genuine spirit. On all occasions, he has stood forth, through evil report and good report, its champion and its friend. He has never approved any other exposition than its own text, read by the lights of common sense and historical illustrations. He has had no ingenious theories to support, no paradoxes to display, no local glosses to interpret, and no little expedients to expand or contract it according to the interests of party. As he read it, when he first came into public life, so he reads it now, with those more comprehensive means of exposition only, which a more intense study and a profound reverence for it naturally produce in great minds.

He is not among those, who seek to enlarge its text beyond its fair import. Neither will he consent to cripple it, by stripping it of powers clearly defined, or necessarily implied. In these doctrines, Mr. Webster has been uniform and inflexible, at all times and in all places.

Take him, for instance, in the forum, in one of his earliest and proudest efforts, the Dartmouth College case, or in the National Bank case, or in the Steam-boat Monopoly case; or take him in the Senate, in his magnificent speeches in answer to Col. Hayne, or in support of the Force Bill,—as it is called; or in any of his later struggles, still fresh in our memories, upon great constitutional controversies. Every where, you will find the same principles of exposition, the same luminous course of reasoning, the same compact and irresistible logic, the same commanding eloquence and energy of expression.

His thoughts and opinions upon the constitution run in the same channel with those of its great authors and earliest interpreters. He belongs to the school of Washington, and Jay, and Hamilton, and Madison, and Marshall. He argues, like one in earnest, and determined to maintain constitutional powers and duties; he defends, like one, who believes the constitution to be the last refuge and hope of our political liberty; and he places himself in the breach, to meet every attack, and to surrender nothing to party assaults from without, or to discontented murmurs from within.

It may be affirmed, without fear of contradiction, that in the general estimate of his countrymen, as a constitutional lawyer and statesman, he has no compeer in the present day, save only the excellent Chief Justice of the United States,—*clarum et venerabile nomen*. To him, if one may so say, Mr. Webster seems silently to appeal in all his constitutional arguments, as one able to comprehend and analyze them, and with a consciousness, that what he asserts, can scarcely fail to receive his decisive approbation.

But it is time to conclude these hasty and imperfect sketches. To Mr. Webster, for his public services, his country owes a debt of gratitude, which it cannot easily repay,—a debt of gratitude, not merely for what he has done; but (what is little understood by the people at large,) for what he has silently or openly prevented from being done. Half the labors of a great statesman consist in silently averting public calamities, intentional or accidental; the other half, though more attractive, as positive and active good, is scarcely more important or more permanently useful.

To such a man, a public station is not only a post of observation and responsibility, but also of enormous sacrifices of private ease and private interest. Who can estimate the loss of professional practice and emolument of Mr. Webster, acknowledgedly at the head of his profession, during his long attendance at Washington? If he should now retire, how could his place be adequately supplied? I hope, earnestly hope, for the honor of my country, nay, for its honest interests and permanent prosperity, that he may long remain in the public councils. But I will not disguise my conscientious opinion, that, in so doing, he puts at hazard some of the pecuniary inheritance due to his talents, and those solid consolations of property, which add to the dignity of old age a sense of personal independence, and a sweet and tranquilizing freedom from anxiety, which all men covet and few obtain.

What motive can such a man have, with his hard-earned honors, now thick about him, to remain in Congress, but a strong sense of public duty, and a pure and exalted patriotism? No station can add substantially to his fame, though there is no station which would not be illustrated and sustained by his talents.

Bibliography
I. Manuscript Sources

A. *Government Records and Documents, National Archives*

Acceptances and Orders for Commissions, Department of State, 1789–1829.

Appellate Case Files, United States Supreme Court, 1792–1831.

Letters of Application and Recommendation during the Administration of Thomas Jefferson, 1801–1809 (Appointment Papers).

Minutes of the United States Supreme Court, February 1, 1790–August 4, 1828.

Miscellaneous Letters, Record Group 59, General Records, Department of State.

Miscellaneous Permanent Commissions, Vol. C (March 26, 1801–November 17, 1812), Department of State.

B. *Story Correspondence*

Papers of Joseph Story, William L. Clements Library, University of Michigan.

Papers of Joseph Story, Essex Institute.

Papers of Joseph Story, Harvard College Library.

Papers of Joseph Story, Library of Congress.

Papers of Joseph Story, Massachusetts Historical Society.

Papers of Joseph Story, New-York Historical Society.

Papers of Joseph Story, University of Texas Library.

Papers of Joseph Story, Yale University Library.

Story-Lieber Correspondence, Henry E. Huntington Library.

C. *Correspondence of Contemporaries*

Papers of John Macpherson Berrien, Southern Historical Collection, University of North Carolina.

Papers of Nathan Dane, Massachusetts Historical Society.

Fogg Papers, Maine Historical Society.

Papers of Joseph Hopkinson, Historical Society of Pennsylvania.

Papers of James Kent, Library of Congress.

Papers of John Marshall, Library of Congress.

Papers of Jeremiah Mason, New Hampshire Historical Society.

Papers of John McLean, Library of Congress.

Papers of Harrison Gray Otis, Massachusetts Historical Society.

Papers of Richard Peters, Historical Society of Pennsylvania.

Papers of Timothy Pickering, Massachusetts Historical Society.

Papers of Samuel Putnam, Essex Institute.

Papers of Leverett Saltonstall, Massachusetts Historical Society.

Papers of Charles R. Vaughan, Christ's College, Oxford University.

Papers of Timothy Walker, Cincinnati Historical Society.

Papers of Alexander C. Washburn, Massachusetts Historical Society.

Weld-Grimké Papers, William L. Clements Library, University of Michigan.

Papers of Henry Wheaton, Pierpont Morgan Library.

D. *Unpublished Dissertation*

Newmyer, R. Kent. "Joseph Story: A Political and Constitutional Study." Unpublished Doctoral Dissertation, University of Nebraska, 1959.

II. PRIMARY PRINTED SOURCES

A. *Story Correspondence*

Life and Letters of Joseph Story. Ed. by William W. Story. 2 vols. Boston, 1851.

Letters to and from Story in Massachusetts Historical Society *Proceedings,*
Second Series. Vols. XIV (1900–1901); XV (1901–1902); XLIX (1915–16);
LII (1918–19); LIII (1919–20); LXVII (October, 1941–May, 1944).

Letters from Story to John Marshall. *William and Mary Quarterly,* Vol. XXI,
2nd Series, No. 1 (January, 1941), 1–26. Reprinted in Charles Warren, "The
Story-Marshall Correspondence, 1819–1831," *Anglo-American Legal History
Series.* Series No. 1, No. 7. New York, 1942.

B. *Selected Writings of Story*

"American Law." Reprinted in *American Journal of Comparative Law,* Vol. III
(1954), 9–26.

Commentaries on the Constitution of the United States. 3 vols. Boston, 1833.

*A Discourse on the Past History, Present State, and Future Prospects of the
Law.* Edinburgh, 1835.

"An Eulogy on General George Washington," Written at the Request of the
Inhabitants of Marblehead and Delivered before Them on the Second Day of
January, 1800. Salem, 1800.

"Law, Legislation and Codes," *Encyclopedia Americana* (1st ed.; Philadelphia,
1829–33), VII, Appendix, 576–92.

The Miscellaneous Writings of Joseph Story. Ed. by William W. Story. Boston,
1852.

"Natural Law," *Encyclopedia Americana* (1st ed.; Philadelphia, 1829–33), IX,
150–58.

"An Oration," Pronounced at Salem, on the Fourth Day of July, 1804, in
Commemoration of Our National Independence. Salem, 1804.

The Power of Solitude. Salem, 1804.

"Statesmen—Their Rareness and Importance: Daniel Webster," *New England
Magazine,* Vol. VII (August, 1834), 89–104.

C. *Collected Works and Correspondence of Contemporaries*

The Writings of John Quincy Adams. Ed. by Paul L. Ford. 7 vols. New York,
1913–1917.

The Works of Edmund Burke. Ed. by Henry Bohn. 6 vols. London, 1854.

The Writings of Thomas Jefferson. Ed. by Paul L. Ford. 10 vols. New York,
1892–1899.

The Writings of Thomas Jefferson. Library Edition. 20 vols. Washington, 1903.

The Writings of Thomas Jefferson. Memorial Edition. 20 vols. Washington,
1903.

Private Correspondence of Daniel Webster. Ed. by Fletcher Webster. 2 vols. Boston, 1857.

Writings and Speeches of Daniel Webster. National Edition. 18 vols. Boston, 1903.

The Works of James Wilson. Ed. by Robert Green McCloskey. 2 vols. Cambridge, 1967.

D. *Memoirs, Diaries, Sermons, and Speeches*

Adams, Jasper. "A Baccalaureate Address," Delivered in St. Paul's Church, at the Annual Commencement of the College of Charleston. Charleston, 1835.

————. "The Relation of Christianity to Civil Government in the United States," A Sermon Preached in St. Michael's Church, before the Convention of the Protestant Episcopal Church of the Diocese of South Carolina. Charleston, 1833.

Derby, Perley. *Elisha Story of Boston and Some of His Descendants*. Salem, 1915.

The Diary of William Bentley, D.D. 4 vols. Salem, 1905–1914.

Greenleaf, Simon. *A Discourse Commemorative of the Life and Character of the Hon. Joseph Story*. Boston, 1845.

Marshall, John. *Autobiographical Sketch*. Ann Arbor, 1937.

Parker, Theodore. *Additional Speeches, Addresses, and Occasional Sermons*. 2 vols. Boston, 1855.

Peabody, Andrew. *Harvard Reminiscences*. Boston, 1888.

Poore, Benjamin Perley. *Reminiscences of Sixty Years in the National Metropolis*. 2 vols. Philadelphia, 1886.

Quincy, Josiah, Jr. *Figures of the Past*. Boston, 1883.

"Sermon on the Death of Rev. Jasper Adams," Delivered at Pendleton by the Rector of Christ Church, Greenville. Charleston, 1842.

Story, William Wetmore. *Conversations in a Studio*. 2 vols. Boston, 1890.

III. Newspapers

Boston *Daily Advertiser*, 1813–1929.

Columbian Centinel (Boston), 1784–1840.

Independent Chronicle (Boston), 1776–1840.

Pittsfield *Sun*, 1800–1906.

Salem *Gazette*, 1790–1908.

Salem *Register*, 1802–1807.

IV. State and Federal Documents

Annals of the Congress of the United States, 1789–1825. 10 vols. Washington, 1834–1856.

The Constitution of the United States of America: Analysis and Interpretation. Ed. by Edward S. Corwin. Washington, 1953.

Debates in the Federal Convention of 1787, Reported by James Madison. Ed. by Gaillard Hunt and James Brown Scott. New York, 1920.

The Debates of the Several State Conventions on the Adoption of the Federal Constitution. Ed. by Jonathan Elliot. 5 vols. Philadelphia, 1836.

Democracy, Liberty, and Property: The State Constitutional Conventions of the 1820's. Ed. by Merrill D. Peterson. Indianapolis, 1966.

Documentary History of the Constitution of the United States of America. 5 vols. Washington, 1894–1905.

Documents of American History. Ed. by Henry Steele Commager. New York, 1968.

Journal of Debates and Proceedings in the Convention of Delegates, Chosen to Revise the Constitution of Massachusetts, 1820–1821. Boston, 1853.

Pamphlets on the Constitution of the United States, Published during Its Discussion by the People, 1787–1788. Ed. by Paul L. Ford. Brooklyn, 1888.

The Reconstruction Amendments' Debates. Ed. by Alfred Avins. Richmond, 1967.

V. Articles

Acton, John Emerich Edward Dalberg. "Political Causes of the American Revolution," *The Rambler*, New Series, Vol. V, Part XIII (May, 1861), 17–61. Reprinted in Lord Acton, *Essays on Freedom and Power.* Ed. by Gertrude Himmelfarb. New York, 1960.

Aldrich, P. Emory. "The Christian Religion and the Common Law," American Antiquarian Society *Proceedings*, Vol. VI, New Series (April, 1889–April, 1890), 18–37.

"Biographical Notice of Mr. Justice Story," *American Review, A Whig Journal*, Vol. III (January, 1846), 68–82.

Chafee, Zechariah, Jr. "Colonial Courts and the Common Law," Massachusetts Historical Society *Proceedings*, Vol. LXVIII (October, 1944–May, 1947), 132–59.

Channing, William Ellery. "On National Literature," *Old South Leaflets*, Vol. VI (Boston, 1903), 333–60.

Commager, Henry Steele. "Joseph Story," *The Gaspar G. Bacon Lectures on the Constitution of the United States, 1940–1950.* Ed. by Arthur N. Holcombe. Boston, 1953.

Corbin, Arthur. "The Laws of the Several States," *Yale Law Journal*, Vol. L, No. 5 (1941), 762–77.

Corwin, Edward S. "Constitution v. Constitutional Theory," *American Political Science Review*, Vol. XIX, No. 2 (May, 1925), 290–304. Reprinted in *American Constitutional History: Essays by Edward S. Corwin.* Ed. by Alpheus T. Mason and Gerald Garvey. New York, 1964.

———. "The Supreme Court as National School Board," *Law & Contemporary Problems*, Vol. XIV, No. 1 (1949), 3–22.

Crosskey, William W. "Charles Fairman, 'Legislative History,' and the Constitutional Limitations on State Authority," *University of Chicago Law Review*, Vol. XXII, No. 1 (Autumn, 1954), 1–143.

Denham, R. N., Jr. "An Historical Development of the Contract Theory in the Dartmouth College Case," *Michigan Law Review*, Vol. VII, No. 3 (1909), 201–25.

Diamond, Martin. "Democracy and the Federalist: A Reconsideration of the Framers' Intent," *American Political Science Review*, Vol. LIII, No. 1 (March, 1959), 52–68.

Dowd, Morgan D. "Justice Joseph Story: A Study of the Legal Philosophy of a Jeffersonian Judge," *Vanderbilt Law Review*, Vol. XVIII, No. 2 (March, 1965), 643–62.

———. "Justice Joseph Story and the Politics of Appointment," *The American Journal of Legal History*, Vol. IX (1965), 265–85.

Dunne, Gerald T. "The American Blackstone," *Washington University Law Quarterly*, Vol. 1962, No. 3 (June, 1963), 321–37.

———. "Joseph Story: 1812 Overture," *Harvard Law Review*, Vol. LXXVII, No. 2 (December, 1963), 240–78.

———. "Joseph Story: The Germinal Years," *Harvard Law Review*, Vol. LXXV, No. 4 (February, 1962), 707–54.

———. "Joseph Story: The Great Term," *Harvard Law Review*, Vol. LXXIX, No. 5 (March, 1966), 877–913.

———. "Joseph Story: The Middle Years," *Harvard Law Review*, Vol. LXXX, No. 8 (June, 1967), 1679–1709.

———. "Joseph Story: The Salem Years," *Essex Institute Historical Collections*, Vol. CI, No. 4 (October, 1965), 307–32.

———. "Joseph Story's First Writing on Equity," *American Journal of Legal History*, Vol. XIV, No. 1 (January, 1970), 76–81.

———. "Mr. Justice Story and the American Law of Banking," *American Journal of Legal History*, Vol. V (1961), 205–30.

Everett, Edward. "Story's Constitutional Law," *North American Review*, Vol. XXXVIII (January, 1834), 63–84.

Fairman, Charles. "Does the Fourteenth Amendment Incorporate the Bill of Rights? The Original Understanding," *Stanford Law Review*, Vol. II (1949–50), 5–139.

———. "A Reply to Professor Crosskey," *University of Chicago Law Review*, Vol. XXII, No. 1 (Autumn, 1954), 144–56.

Gentz, Friedrich von. "French and American Revolutions Compared," *Three Revolutions*. Ed. by Stefan Possony. Chicago, 1959.

Goebel, Julius, Jr. "The Common Law and the Constitution," *Chief Justice John Marshall: A Reappraisal*. Ed. by W. Melville Jones. Ithaca, 1956.

———. "King's Law and Local Custom in Seventeenth Century New England," *Columbia Law Review*, Vol. XXXI, No. 3 (March, 1931), 416–48.

Harris, Robert J. "Chief Justice Taney: Prophet of Reform and Reaction," *Vanderbilt Law Review*, Vol. X, No. 2 (February, 1957), 227–57.

Hogan, John C. "Joseph Story's Anonymous Law Articles," *Michigan Law Review*, Vol. LII, No. 6 (April, 1954), 869–84.

Holcombe, Arthur N. "John Marshall as Politician and Political Theorist," *Chief Justice John Marshall: A Reappraisal*. Ed. by W. Melville Jones. Ithaca, 1956.

Hunting, Warren B. *The Obligation of Contracts Clause of the United States Constitution*. Johns Hopkins University *Studies in Historical and Political Science*, Series XXXVII, No. 4. Baltimore, 1919.

Inghan, Joseph F. "Unconstitutional Amendment," *Dickinson Law Review*, Vol. XXXIII, No. 3 (March, 1929), 161–68.

Jackson, Robert H. "The Rise and Fall of Swift v. Tyson," *American Bar Association Journal*, Vol. XXIV, No. 8 (August, 1938), 609–14, 644.

Kauper, Paul G. "Church Autonomy and the First Amendment: The Presbyterian Church Case," *The Supreme Court Review* (1969), 347–78.

———. "Church, State and Freedom: A Review," *Michigan Law Review*, Vol. LII, No. 6 (April, 1954), 829–48.

Kelsen, Hans. "The Pure Theory of Law." Trans. by C. H. Wilson. *Law Quarterly Review*, Vol. L (1934), 474–98; Vol. LI (1935), 517–35.

Kenny, Courtney. "The Evolution of the Law of Blasphemy," *Cambridge Law Journal*, Vol. I, No. 2 (1922), 127–42.

Kirk, Russell. "Burke and Natural Rights," *The Review of Politics*, Vol. XIII, No. 4 (October, 1951), 441–56.

———. "Segments of Political Science Not Amenable to Behavioristic Treatment," *The Limits of Behavioralism in Political Science*. Ed. by James C. Charlesworth. Philadelphia, 1962.

Kurland, Philip B. "Equal in Origin and Equal in Title to the Legislative and Executive Branches of the Government," *Harvard Law Review*, Vol. LXXVIII, No. 1 (November, 1964), 143–76.

Larson, Charles E. "Nationalism and States' Rights in Commentaries on the Constitution after the Civil War," *American Journal of Legal History*, Vol. III (1959), 360–69.

Laski, Harold J. "Social Contract," *Encyclopedia of Social Sciences*, Vol. IV (New York, 1937), 127–31.

Leonard, Daniel. "Massachusettensis." Reprinted in *The Political Writings of John Adams*. Ed. by George Peek, Jr. New York, 1954.

Leslie, William R. "The Influence of Joseph Story's Theory of the Conflict of Laws on Constitutional Nationalism," *Mississippi Valley Historical Review*, Vol. XXXV, No. 2 (September, 1948), 203–20.

———. "Similarities in Lord Mansfield's and Joseph Story's View of Fundamental Law," *American Journal of Legal History*, Vol. I (1957), 278–300.

Lorenzen, Ernest G. "Story's Commentaries on the Conflict of Laws—One Hundred Years After," *Harvard Law Review*, Vol. XLVIII, No. 1 (November, 1934), 15–38.

Lucas, Paul. "Ex Parte Sir William Blackstone, 'Plagiarist': A Note on Blackstone and the Natural Law," *American Journal of Legal History*, Vol. VII (1963), 142–58.

McClellan, James. "The Doctrine of Judicial Democracy," *Modern Age*, Vol. XIV, No. 1 (Winter, 1969–70), 19–35.

———. "Judge Story's Debt to Burke," *The Burke Newsletter*, Vol. VII, No. 3 (Spring, 1966), 583–86.

McCloskey, Robert G. "Economic Due Process and the Supreme Court: An Exhumation and Reburial," *The Supreme Court Review* (Chicago, 1962), 34–62.

McLaughlin, Andrew. "Social Compact and Constitutional Construction," *American Historical Review*, Vol. V, No. 3 (April, 1900), 467–91.

Miller, Arthur S., and Ronald F. Howell. "The Myth of Neutrality in Constitutional Adjudication," *University of Chicago Law Review*, Vol. XXVII, No. 4 (Summer, 1960), 661–95.

Morrison, Stanley. "Does the Fourteenth Amendment Incorporate the Bill of Rights? The Judicial Interpretation," *Stanford Law Review*, Vol. II (1949–1950), 140–73.

Murray, John Courtney. "Law or Prepossessions?" *Law & Contemporary Problems*, Vol. XIV, No. 1 (1949), 23–43.

Nadelmann, Kurt H. "Apropos of Translations (Federalist, Kent, Story)," *American Journal of Comparative Law*, Vol. VIII (Spring, 1959), 201–14.

———. "Joseph Story's Contributions to American Conflict Law: A Comment," *American Journal of Legal History*, Vol. IV (1961), 230–53.

———. "Marginal Remarks on the New Trends in American Conflicts Law," *Law & Contemporary Problems*, Vol. XXVIII, No. 4 (Autumn, 1963), 860–69.

Newmyer, R. Kent. "Daniel Webster as Tocqueville's Lawyer: The Dartmouth College Case Again," *American Journal of Legal History*, Vol. XI, No. 2 (April, 1967), 127–47.

———. "Joseph Story and the War of 1812: A Judicial Nationalist," *The Historian*, Vol. XXVI, No. 4 (August, 1964), 486–501.

———. "Joseph Story on Circuit and a Neglected Phase of American Legal History," *American Journal of Legal History*, Vol. XIV, No. 2 (April, 1970), 112–35.

———. "A Note on the Whig Politics of Justice Joseph Story," *The Mississippi Valley Historical Review*, Vol. XLVIII, No. 3 (December, 1961), 480–91.

"Note," *The American Law Review*, Vol. V (1870), 368–69.

O'Brien, Francis W. "The States and 'No Establishment': Proposed Amendments to the Constitution since 1798," *Washburn Law Journal*, Vol. IV, No. 2 (Spring, 1965), 183–210.

Pope, Herbert. "The English Common Law in the United States," *Harvard Law Review*, Vol. XXIV, No. 1 (1910), 6–30.

Pound, Roscoe. "The Place of Judge Story in the Making of American Law," *Massachusetts Law Quarterly*, Vol. I, No. 3 (May, 1916), 121–140.

Prager, Frank D. "Changing Views of Justice Story on the Construction of Patents," *American Journal of Legal History*, Vol. IV (1960), 1–21.

Reed, George E. "Church-State and the Zorach Case," *Notre Dame Lawyer*, Vol. XXVII, No. 4 (Summer, 1952), 529–51.

Reinsch, Paul S. "The English Common Law in the Early American Colonies." *Bulletin* 31 of the University of Wisconsin Historical Series, Vol. II, No. 4. Reprinted in *Select Essays in Anglo-American Legal History*, Vol. I. Boston, 1908.

"Review of Professor David Hoffman's Legal Outlines," *North American Review*, Vol. XXX (1830), 135–60.

"Review of Story's Commentaries on the Constitution," *American Monthly Review*, Vol. IV (December, 1833), 499–513.

"Review of Story's Commentaries on the Constitution," *American Quarterly Review*, Vol. XIV (December, 1833), 327–67.

"Review of Story's Pleadings," *The Monthly Anthology and Boston Review*, Vol. II (1805), 482–88.

Schneider, Herbert W. "Philosophical Differences between the Constitution and the Bill of Rights," *The Constitution Reconsidered*. Ed. by Conyers Read. New York, 1938.

Schofield, William. "Joseph Story," *Great American Lawyers*. Ed. by William Draper Lewis. 3 vols. Philadelphia, 1908.

Schulman, Harry. "The Demise of Swift v. Tyson," *Yale Law Journal*, Vol. XLVII, No. 8 (1938), 1336–53.

Schwartz, Mortimer D., and John C. Hogan. "A National Library: Mr. Justice Story Speaks Out," *Journal of Legal Education*, Vol. VIII, No. 3 (1955), 328–30.

Storing, Herbert. "William Blackstone." *History of Political Philosophy*. Ed. by Leo Strauss and Joseph Cropsey. Chicago, 1963.

"Story's Commentaries—Vol. I," *American Jurist and Law Magazine*, Vol. IX (April, 1833), 241–88.

"Story's Commentaries—Vols. II and III," *American Jurist and Law Magazine*, Vol. X (July, 1833), 119–47.

Tate, Thad W. "The Social Contract in America, 1774–1787: Revolutionary Theory as a Conservative Instrument," *William and Mary Quarterly*, 3rd Series, Vol. XXII, No. 3 (July, 1965), 375–91.

Troeltsch, Ernst. "The Ideas of Natural Law and Humanity in World Politics," Appendix I in Otto Gierke, *Natural Law and the Theory of Society, 1500–1800*. Translated with an Introduction by Ernest Barker. 2 vols. Boston, 1934.

Tucker, Henry St. George. "Judge Story's Position on the So-Called General Welfare Clause," *American Bar Association Journal*, Vol. XIII, Nos. 7–8 (July–August, 1927), 363–68, 465–69.

Van Alstyne, William. "Constitutional Separation of Church and State: The Quest for a Coherent Position," *American Political Science Review*, Vol. LVII, No. 4 (December, 1963), 865–82.

Warren, Charles. "The New 'Liberty' under the Fourteenth Amendment," *Harvard Law Review*, Vol. XXXIX, No. 4 (February, 1926), 431–65.

———. "New Light on the History of the Federal Judiciary Act of 1789," *Harvard Law Review*, Vol. XXXVII, No. 1 (November, 1923), 49–132.

Wilkinson, Vernon L. "The Federal Bill of Rights and the Fourteenth Amendment," *Georgetown Law Review*, Vol. XXVI, No. 2 (January, 1938), 439–67.

VI. BOOKS

Adams, Henry. *History of the United States of America*. 9 vols. New York, 1890.

Allen, C. K. *Law in the Making*. Oxford, 1951.

Antieau, Chester James, et al. *Religion under the State Constitutions*. Brooklyn, 1965.

Aumann, Francis R. *The Changing American Legal System: Some Selected Phases*. Columbus, 1940.

Babbitt, Irving. *Rousseau and Romanticism*. New York, 1919.

Baker, Elizabeth Feaster. *Henry Wheaton, 1785–1848*. Philadelphia, 1937.

Barker, Ernest. *Essays on Government*. London, 1960.

Bauer, Elizabeth K. *Commentaries on the Constitution, 1790–1860*. New York, 1952.

Baxter, Maurice G. *Daniel Webster and the Supreme Court*. Amherst, 1966.

Becker, Carl L. *The Declaration of Independence*. New York, 1948.

Bennett, Walter Hartwell. *American Theories of Federalism*. Tuscaloosa, 1964.

Berns, Walter F. *Freedom, Virtue, and the First Amendment*. Baton Rouge, 1957.

Beveridge, Albert J. *The Life of John Marshall*. 4 vols. Boston, 1916.

Bickel, Alexander M. *The Least Dangerous Branch*. Indianapolis, 1962.

Blackstone, Sir William. *Commentaries on the Laws of England*. Ed. by William Draper Lewis. 4 vols. Philadelphia, 1902.

Blau, Joseph L., ed. *Social Theories of Jacksonian Democracy*. New York, 1947.

Boorstin, Daniel. *The Mysterious Science of the Law*. Cambridge, 1941.

Boucher, Jonathan. *A View of the Causes and Consequences of the American Revolution*. London, 1797.

Boudin, Louis. *Government by Judiciary*. 2 vols. New York, 1932.

Bozell, L. Brent. *The Warren Revolution*. New Rochelle, 1966.

Bracton, Henry de. *De Legibus et Consuetudinibus Angliae*. Ed. by George Woodbine. New Haven, 1932.

Bryce, James. *The American Commonwealth*. 2 vols. New York, 1911.

Carson, Hampton L. *The History of the Supreme Court of the United States*. 2 vols. Philadelphia, 1902.

Chroust, Anton-Hermann. *The Rise of the Legal Profession in America*. 2 vols. Norman, 1965.

Corwin, Edward S. *Commerce Power Versus States Rights*. Princeton, 1936.

———. *Constitutional Revolution, Ltd.* Claremont, 1941.

———. *Court over Constitution*. Princeton, 1938.

———. *The Higher Law Background of American Constitutional Law*. Ithaca, 1955.

———. *John Marshall and the Constitution*. New Haven, 1919.

———. *Liberty against Government*. Baton Rouge, 1948.

———. *The Twilight of the Supreme Court*. New Haven, 1934.

Crosskey, William. *Politics and the Constitution*. 2 vols. Chicago, 1953.

D'Entrèves, A. P. *Natural Law: An Historical Survey*. New York, 1965.

Diamond, Martin, et al. *The Democratic Republic*. Chicago, 1966.

Dietze, Gottfried. *In Defense of Property*. Chicago, 1963.

Dillon, John F. *John Marshall*. 2 vols. Chicago, 1903.

Duer, William Alexander. *Course of Lectures on the Constitutional Jurisprudence of the United States*. New York, 1843.

Dumbauld, Edward. *The Bill of Rights and What It Means Today*. Norman, 1957.

Durfee, Thomas. *Gleanings from the Judicial History of Rhode Island*. Providence, 1883.

Eidelberg, Paul. *The Philosophy of the American Constitution: A Reinterpretation of the Intentions of the Founding Fathers*. New York, 1968.

Faulkner, Robert Kenneth. *The Jurisprudence of John Marshall*. Princeton, 1968.

The Federalist. Modern Library Edition.

Flack, Horace Edgar. *The Adoption of the Fourteenth Amendment*. Baltimore, 1908.

Frank, John P. *Justice Daniel Dissenting*. Cambridge, 1964.

Friedel, Frank. *Francis Lieber: Nineteenth Century Liberal*. Baton Rouge, 1947.

Gough, J. W. *The Social Contract*. London, 1957.

Green, Fletcher M. *Constitutional Development in the South Atlantic States, 1776–1860*. Chapel Hill, 1930.

Haar, Charles M. *The Golden Age of American Law*. New York, 1965.

Haines, Charles G. *The Revival of Natural Law Concepts*. Cambridge, 1930.

———. *The Role of the Supreme Court in American Government and Politics, 1789–1835*. Berkeley, 1944.

———, and Foster H. Sherwood. *The Role of the Supreme Court in American Government and Politics, 1835–1864*. Berkeley, 1957.

Hall, Edward Hagaman. *A Guide to the Cathedral Church of Saint John the Divine in the City of New York*. New York, 1942.

Hallowell, John H. *Main Currents in Modern Political Thought*. New York, 1950.

———. *Moral Foundation of Democracy*. Chicago, 1954.

Handlin, Oscar, and Mary Handlin. *Commonwealth: A Study of the Role of Government in the American Economy: Massachusetts, 1774–1861*. New York, 1947.

Harris, Robert J. *The Judicial Power of the United States*. Baton Rouge, 1940.

Hart, Albert B. *Commonwealth History of Massachusetts*. 5 vols. New York, 1930.

Harvey, Ray Forrest. *Jean Jacques Burlamaqui: A Liberal Tradition in American Constitutionalism*. Chapel Hill, 1937.

Hayek, Friedrich A. *The Constitution of Liberty*. Chicago, 1960.

Holdsworth, William Searle. *A History of English Law*. 14 vols. London, 1903–1952.

———. *Some Lessons from Our Legal History*. New York, 1928.

Holmes, Oliver Wendell. *Collected Legal Papers*. New York, 1952.

———. *The Mind and Faith of Justice Holmes*. Ed. by Max Lerner. Boston, 1943.

Holt, George C. *The Concurrent Jurisdiction of the Federal and State Courts*. New York, 1888.

Honnold, John, ed. *The Life of the Law*. New York, 1964.

Horton, John Theodore. *James Kent: A Study in Conservatism*. New York, 1939.

Howe, Mark de Wolfe. *The Garden and the Wilderness: Religion and Government in American Constitutional History*. Chicago, 1965.

———. *Readings in American Legal History*. Cambridge, 1949.

Jackson, Robert H. *The Struggle for Judicial Supremacy*. New York, 1941.

James, Henry. *William Wetmore Story and His Friends*. 2 vols. New York, 1903.

James, Joseph B. *The Framing of the Fourteenth Amendment*. Urbana, 1956.

Jones, Howard Mumford. *O Strange New World. American Culture: The Formative Years*. New York, 1964.

Kelly, Alfred H., and Winfred A. Harbison. *The American Constitution: Its Origins and Development*. New York, 1955.

Kendall, Willmoore. *The Conservative Affirmation*. Chicago, 1963.

————, and George Carey, eds. *Liberalism Versus Conservatism: The Continuing Debate in American Government.* Princeton, 1966.

Kent, James. *Commentaries on American Law.* Ed. by Charles M. Barnes. 4 vols. Boston, 1884.

Kirk, Russell. *The Conservative Mind.* Chicago, 1953.

————. *John Randolph of Roanoke: A Study in American Politics.* Chicago, 1964.

————. *A Program for Conservatives.* Chicago, 1954.

Labaree, Leonard Woods. *Conservatism in Early American History.* New York, 1948.

Lecky, William Edward Hartpole. *A History of England in the Eighteenth Century.* 7 vols. London, 1911.

Levy, Leonard W. *Freedom of Speech and Press in Early American History: Legacy of Suppression.* New York, 1963.

————. *The Law of the Commonwealth and Chief Justice Shaw.* Cambridge, 1957.

Lieber, Francis. *Civil Liberty and Self-Government.* 2 vols. Philadelphia, 1853.

————. *A Manual of Political Ethics.* 2 vols. Philadelphia, 1890.

Livermore, Shaw. *Twilight of Federalism.* Princeton, 1962.

Lockmiller, David A. *Sir William Blackstone.* Chapel Hill, 1938.

Lodge, Henry Cabot. *Life and Letters of George Cabot.* Boston, 1877.

Magrath, C. Peter. *Yazoo: Law and Politics in the New Republic. The Case of Fletcher v. Peck.* Providence, 1966.

Magruder, Allan B. *John Marshall.* Boston, 1885.

Marshall, John. *Life of George Washington.* 2 vols. Philadelphia, 1832.

Merriam, Charles E. *A History of American Political Theories.* New York, 1903.

Miller, Perry, ed. *The Legal Mind in America.* Garden City, 1962.

Morgan, Donald G. *Justice William Johnson: The First Dissenter.* Columbia, 1954.

Morison, Samuel Eliot. *The Life and Letters of Harrison Gray Otis, Federalist, 1765–1848.* 2 vols. Boston, 1913.

Morley, Felix. *Freedom and Federalism.* Chicago, 1959.

Murray, John Courtney. *We Hold These Truths.* New York, 1960.

Myers, Gustavus. *History of the Supreme Court of the United States.* Chicago, 1918.

Nelson, William H. *The American Tory.* Oxford, 1961.

Nisbet, Robert A. *Community and Power.* New York, 1962.

Oakeshott, Michael. *Rationalism in Politics.* New York, 1962.

O'Brien, Francis William. *Justice Reed and the First Amendment.* Washington, 1958.

Page, Thomas Nelson. *The Old South: Essays Social and Political.* New York, 1892.

Paley, William. *Moral and Political Philosophy.* Ed. by A. J. Valpy. Philadelphia, 1845.

Parrington, Vernon. *Main Currents in American Thought, 1800–1860: The Romantic Revolution in America.* New York, 1927.

Patterson, Edwin W. *Jurisprudence: Men and Ideas of the Law.* Brooklyn, 1953.

Peterson, Merrill D. *The Jefferson Image in the American Mind.* New York, 1960.

Pierson, George Wilson. *Tocqueville in America.* New York, 1959.

Plumer, William, Jr. *Life of William Plumer.* Boston, 1847.

Pollock, Frederick, and Frederic William Maitland. *The History of English Law before the Time of Edward I.* 2 vols. Cambridge, 1905.

Pound, Roscoe. *The Development of Constitutional Guarantees of Liberty.* New Haven, 1957.

——. *The Formative Era of American Law.* New York, 1950.

——. *The Spirit of the Common Law.* Boston, 1921.

Rawle, William. *A View of the Constitution of the United States of America.* Philadelphia, 1829.

Rice, Charles. *The Supreme Court and Public Prayer.* New York, 1964.

Ritchie, David. *Natural Rights.* New York, 1924.

Robinson, William A. *Jeffersonian Democracy in New England.* New Haven, 1916.

Rommen, Heinrich. *The Natural Law.* St. Louis, 1947.

Rossiter, Clinton. *1787: The Grand Convention.* New York, 1965.

Rutland, Robert Allen. *The Birth of the Bill of Rights, 1776–1791.* Chapel Hill, 1955.

Sait, Edward M. *Political Institutions: A Preface.* New York, 1938.

Schlesinger, Arthur M., Jr. *The Age of Jackson.* Boston, 1945.

Sergeant, Thomas. *Constitutional Law.* Philadelphia, 1830.

——. *Dissertation on the Nature and Extent of the Jurisdiction of the Courts of the United States.* Philadelphia, 1824.

Simon, Yves. *Philosophy of Democratic Government.* Chicago, 1951.

——. *The Tradition of Natural Law: A Philosopher's Reflections.* Ed. by Vukan Kuic. New York, 1965.

Smith, James Morton. *Freedom's Fetters: The Alien and Sedition Laws and Civil Liberties.* Ithaca, 1956.

Smith, Joseph H. *Development of Legal Institutions.* St. Paul, 1965.

Spicer, George W. *The Supreme Court and Fundamental Freedoms.* New York, 1967.

Stanlis, Peter J. *Edmund Burke and the Natural Law.* Ann Arbor, 1958.

Stedman, Edmund Clarence, and Ellen Mackay Hutchinson, eds. *A Library of American Literature.* 11 vols. New York, 1891.

Stephen, Leslie. *The History of English Thought in the Eighteenth Century.* 2 vols. New York, 1902.

Stephens, Alexander H. *A Constitutional View of the War between the States.* 2 vols. Philadelphia, 1868.

Storing, Herbert, ed. *Essays on the Scientific Study of Politics.* New York, 1962.

Strauss, Leo. *Natural Right and History.* Chicago, 1953.

——. *The Political Philosophy of Hobbes.* Chicago, 1952.

Sutherland, Arthur K. *The Law at Harvard.* Cambridge, 1967.

Swisher, Carl. *Roger B. Taney.* New York, 1935.

Tocqueville, Alexis de. *Democracy in America.* Ed. by Phillips Bradley. 2 vols. New York, 1948.

Tucker, Henry St. George. *Lectures on Constitutional Law.* Richmond, 1843.

Tucker, John Randolph. *The Constitution of the United States.* 2 vols. Ed. by Henry St. George Tucker. Chicago, 1899.

Upshur, Abel. *A Brief Enquiry into the True Nature and Character of Our Federal*

Government: Being a Review of Judge Story's Commentaries. Richmond, 1840.
Vile, M. J. C. *Constitutionalism and the Separation of Powers.* Oxford, 1967.
Voegelin, Eric. *The New Science of Politics.* Chicago, 1952.
Warren, Charles. *History of the Harvard Law School and Early Legal Conditions in America.* 3 vols. New York, 1908.
————. *The Making of the Constitution.* Cambridge, 1937.
————. *The Supreme Court in United States History.* 2 vols. Boston, 1922.
Whitman, Walt. *Democratic Vistas.* New York, 1949.
Wright, Benjamin F. *American Interpretations of Natural Law.* Cambridge, 1931.
————. *The Contract Clause of the Constitution.* Cambridge, 1938.
Wu, John C. H. *Fountain of Justice: A Study in the Natural Law.* New York, 1955.
Zane, John M. *The Story of Law.* New York, 1927.

VII. Cases Cited

A. *American*

Abington School District v. *Schempp,* and *Murray* v. *Curlett,* 374 U.S. 203 (1963).
Abrams v. *United States,* 250 U.S. 616 (1919).
Adamson v. *California,* 332 U.S. 46 (1947).
Allen v. *McKean,* 1 Federal Cases 489, No. 229 (1833).
American Insurance Co. v. *Canter,* 1 Peters 511 (1828).
Anonymous, 1 Federal Cases 1032, No. 475 (1804).
The Antelope, 10 Wheaton 66 (1825).
Baltimore and Ohio R.R. Co. v. *Baugh,* 149 U.S. 308 (1893).
Barron v. *The Mayor and City Council of Baltimore,* 7 Peters 243 (1833).
In re Bellows, 3 Federal Cases 138, No. 1,278 (1844).
Black & White Taxicab Co. v. *Brown & Yellow Taxicab Co.,* 276 U.S. 518 (1928).
Board of Education of Central School District No. 1 v. *Allen,* 392 U.S. 236 (1968).
The Bothnea and the Jahnstoff, 2 Wheaton 169 (1817).
Briscoe v. *Bank of Kentucky,* 11 Peters 257 (1837).
Brown v. *Maryland,* 12 Wheaton 419 (1827).
Brown v. *United States,* 8 Cranch 110 (1814).
Calder v. *Bull,* 3 Dallas 388 (1798).
Cantwell v. *Connecticut,* 310 U.S. 296 (1940).
Carpenter v. *Providence Insurance Co.,* 16 Peters 495 (1842).
Cary v. *Curtis,* 3 Howard 236 (1844).
Chaplinsky v. *New Hampshire,* 315 U.S. 568 (1942).
Charles River Bridge v. *Warren Bridge Co.,* 11 Peters 420 (1837).
Cherokee Nation v. *Georgia,* 5 Peters 1(1831).
Chicago City v. *Robbins,* 2 Black 418 (1862).
Chisholm v. *Georgia,* 2 Dallas 419 (1793).
Ex Parte Christy, 3 Howard 292 (1845).
Church of the Holy Trinity v. *United States,* 143 U.S. 437 (1891).
Cohens v. *Virginia,* 6 Wheaton 262 (1821).
Commonwealth v. *Kneeland,* 20 Pickering (Mass.) 206 (1838).
Commonwealth v. *Schaffer,* 4 Dallas, Appendix XXVI (1797).
Craig v. *Missouri,* 4 Peters 410 (1830).

Davis v. *Beason,* 133 U.S. 333 (1890).

Decatur v. *Paulding,* 14 Peters 497 (1840).

De Jonge v. *Oregon,* 299 U.S. 353 (1937).

DeLovio v. *Boit,* 7 Federal Cases 418, No. 3,766 (1815).

Dobbins v. *Commissioners of Erie County,* 16 Peters 448 (1842).

D'Oench, Duhme & Co., Inc. v. *Federal Deposit Insurance Corp.,* 315 U.S. 469 (1942).

Donnell v. *Columbian Insurance Co.,* 7 Federal Cases 889, No. 3,987 (1836).

Engel v. *Vitale,* 370 U.S. 421 (1962).

Erie R.R. Co. v. *Tompkins,* 304 U.S. 64 (1938).

Everson v. *Board of Education,* 330 U.S. 1 (1947).

Fairfax's Devisee v. *Hunter's Lessee,* 7 Cranch 603 (1813).

Fletcher v. *Peck,* 6 Cranch 87 (1810).

Ex Parte Foster, 9 Federal Cases 508, No. 4,960 (1842).

Fox v. *Ohio,* 5 Howard 440 (1847).

Gelston v. *Hoyt,* 3 Wheaton 246 (1818).

Genesee Chief v. *Fitzhugh,* 12 Howard 443 (1851).

Gibbons v. *Ogden,* 9 Wheaton 1 (1824).

Gideon v. *Wainwright,* 372 U.S. 335 (1963).

Gitlow v. *New York,* 268 U.S. 652 (1925).

Green v. *Biddle,* 8 Wheaton 1 (1823).

Griswold v. *Connecticut,* 381 U.S. 479 (1965).

Groves v. *Slaughter,* 15 Peters 449 (1841).

Hale v. *Everett,* 53 New Hampshire 9 (1868).

Hamilton v. *Regents of the University of California,* 293 U.S. 245 (1934).

Henfield's Case, 11 Federal Cases 1099, No. 6,360 (1793).

Hobart v. *Drogan,* 10 Peters 108 (1836).

Home Building & Loan Assn. v. *Blaisdell,* 290 U.S. 398 (1934).

Houston v. *Moore,* 5 Wheaton 1 (1820).

Hunter v. *Martin,* 4 Munford (Va.) 1 (1814).

Hylton v. *United States,* 3 Dallas 171 (1796).

Insurance Co. v. *Dunham,* 11 Wallace 36 (1870).

Jackson v. *Lampshire,* 3 Peters 280 (1830).

Jenness v. *Peck,* 7 Howard 619 (1849).

Jerome v. *United States,* 318 U.S. 101 (1943).

La Jeune Eugenie, 26 Federal Cases 832, No. 15,551 (1822).

Kilham v. *Ward,* 2 Tyng (Mass.) 236 (1806).

Kittredge v. *Emerson,* 15 New Hampshire 227 (1844).

Kittredge v. *Warren,* 14 New Hampshire 507 (1844).

Klopfer v. *North Carolina,* 386 U.S. 213 (1967).

Kuhn v. *Fairmont Coal Co.,* 215 U.S. 349 (1910).

Lake Shore & M.S.R. Co. v. *Prentice,* 147 U.S. 101 (1893).

Lane v. *Vick,* 3 Howard 464 (1845).

Lessee of Livingston v. *Moore,* 7 Peters 552 (1833).

Livingston v. *Jefferson,* 15 Federal Cases 660, No. 8,411 (1811).

Luther v. *Borden,* 7 Howard 1 (1849).

Malloy v. *Hogan*, 378 U.S. 1 (1964).

Mapp v. *Ohio*, 367 U.S. 643 (1961).

Marbury v. *Madison*, 1 Cranch 137 (1803).

Martin v. *Hunter's Lessee*, 1 Wheaton 304 (1816).

Martin v. *Mott*, 12 Wheaton 19 (1827).

McCollum v. *Champaign Board of Education*, 333 U.S. 203 (1948).

McCulloch v. *Maryland*, 4 Wheaton 316 (1819).

McGowan v. *Maryland*, 366 U.S. 420 (1961).

Morey v. *Doud*, 354 U.S. 457 (1957).

Near v. *Minnesota*, 283 U.S. 697 (1931).

The Nereide, 9 Cranch 388 (1815).

New Jersey v. *Wilson*, 7 Cranch 164 (1812).

New York v. *Miln*, 11 Peters 102 (1837).

Nixon v. *Herndon*, 273 U.S. 536 (1927).

Ogden v. *Saunders*, 12 Wheaton 213 (1827).

Steamboat Orleans v. *Phoebus*, 11 Peters 175 (1837).

Schooner Orono, 18 Federal Cases 530, No. 10,585 (1812).

Palko v. *Connecticut*, 302 U.S. 319 (1937).

Parker v. *Gladden*, 385 U.S. 363 (1966).

Parsons v. *Bedford*, 3 Peters 446 (1830).

Patterson v. *Winn*, 5 Peters 233 (1831).

Pennsylvania v. *Board of City Trusts of Philadelphia*, 353 U.S. 230 (1957).

People v. *Ruggles*, 8 Johnson (N.Y.) 290 (1811).

Permoli v. *Municipality No. 1 of the City of New Orleans*, 3 Howard 588 (1845).

Pervear v. *Massachusetts*, 5 Wallace 475 (1867).

The Plattsburgh, 10 Wheaton 133 (1825).

Pointer v. *Texas*, 380 U.S. 400 (1965).

Pollock v. *Farmer's Loan and Trust*, 158 U.S. 601 (1895).

Ponce v. *Roman Catholic Church*, 210 U.S. 314 (1907).

Presbyterian Church of the United States v. *Mary Elizabeth Blue Hull Memorial Presbyterian Church*, 393 U.S. 440 (1969).

Prigg v. *Pennsylvania*, 16 Peters 539 (1842).

The Prize Cases, 67 U.S. 635 (1863).

Providence Bank v. *Billings and Pittman*, 4 Peters 514 (1830).

Prudential Insurance Co. v. *Cheek*, 259 U.S. 530 (1922).

Reynolds v. *United States*, 98 U.S. 145 (1879).

Robinson v. *California*, 370 U.S. 660 (1962).

Robinson v. *The Commonwealth Insurance Co.*, 20 Federal Cases 1002, No. 11,949 (1838).

Rowan v. *Runnels*, 5 Howard 134 (1847).

Rust v. *Low*, 6 Tyng (Mass.) 90 (1809).

Satterlee v. *Mathewson*, 2 Peters 380 (1829).

Smith v. *Maryland*, 18 Howard 71 (1855).

The Society for the Propagation of the Gospel v. *Wheeler*, 22 Federal Cases 747, No. 13,156 (1814).

Southern Pacific R.R. Co. v. *Jensen*, 244 U.S. 205 (1917).

State v. *Chandler*, 2 Harrington (Del.) 553 (1837).

State v. *Mockus*, 120 Maine 84, 113 A. 39 (1921).

Stromberg v. *California*, 283 U.S. 359 (1931).

Sturges v. *Crowninshield*, 4 Wheaton 122 (1819).

Swift v. *Tyson*, 16 Peters 1 (1842).

Terrett v. *Taylor*, 9 Cranch 43 (1815).

Testa v. *Katt*, 220 U.S. 386 (1947).

The Thomas Jefferson, 10 Wheaton 428 (1825).

Town of Pawlet v. *Clark*, 9 Cranch 292 (1815).

Trustees of Dartmouth College v. *Woodward*, 4 Wheaton 518 (1819).

Twitchell v. *Pennsylvania*, 7 Wallace 321 (1868).

United States v. *The Amistad*, 15 Peters 518 (1841).

United States v. *Arredondo*, 2 Peters 738 (1829).

United States v. *Bevans*, 3 Wheaton 336 (1818).

United States v. *Britton*, 108 U.S. 199 (1883).

United States v. *Burr*, 25 Federal Cases 55, No. 14,693 (1807).

United States v. *Butler*, 297 U.S. 66 (1935).

United States v. *Coolidge*, 25 Federal Cases 619, No. 14,857 (1813).

United States v. *Coolidge*, 1 Wheaton 415 (1816).

United States v. *Coombs*, 12 Peters 72 (1838).

United States v. *Dandridge*, 12 Wheaton 64 (1827).

United States v. *Dickson*, 15 Peters 141 (1841).

United States v. *Eaton*, 144 U.S. 677 (1892).

United States v. *Fisher*, 2 Cranch 358 (1805).

United States v. *Flores*, 289 U.S. 137 (1933).

United States v. *Goodwell*, 243 U.S. 476 (1916).

United States v. *Hudson and Goodwin*, 7 Cranch 32 (1812).

United States v. *Ravara*, 2 Dallas 297 (1794).

United States v. *Smith*, 27 Federal Cases 1147, No. 16,323 (1793).

United States v. *William*, 28 Federal Cases 614, No. 16,700 (1808).

United States v. *Wiltberger*, 5 Wheaton 75 (1820).

United States v. *Wonson*, 28 Federal Cases 745, No. 16,750 (1812).

United States v. *Worrall*, 28 Federal Cases 774, No. 16,766 (1798).

Updegraff v. *The Commonwealth*, 11 Sergeant & Rawle (Pa.) 394 (1824).

Van Horne's Lessee v. *Dorrance*, 2 Dallas 308 (1795).

Van Ness v. *Pacard*, 2 Peters 137 (1829).

Van Reimsdyk v. *Kane*, 28 Federal Cases 1062, No. 16,871 (1812).

Vidal v. *Girard's Executors*, 2 Howard 127 (1844).

Walz v. *Tax Commission*, 397 U.S. 664 (1970).

Washington v. *Texas*, 388 U.S. 14 (1967).

Watson v. *Jones*, 13 Wallace 679 (1872).

Watson v. *Mercer*, 8 Peters 88 (1834).

Wilkinson v. *Leland*, 2 Peters 627 (1829).

Williams v. *Suffolk Insurance Co.*, 29 Federal Cases 1406, No. 17,739 (1838).

Withers v. *Buckley*, 20 Howard 84 (1857).

Yates v. *Milwaukee*, 10 Wallace 497 (1870).

Zorach v. *Clauson*, 343 U.S. 306 (1952).

B. *English*

Ashby v. *White*, 2 Lord Raymond 938, 3 Lord Raymond 320 (King's Bench, 1703).

Baylis v. *Bishop of London*, 1 Chancery Division 127 (1913).

Bowman v. *The Secular Society*, Law Reports, Appeals Cases 406 (House of Lords, 1917).

Calvin's Case, 7 Coke's Reports 1 (King's Bench, 1610).

City of London v. *Wood*, 12 Modern Reports 669 (King's Bench, 1701).

Day v. *Savadge*, Hobart 85 (King's Bench, 1614).

Dr. Bonham's Case, 8 Coke's Reports 113 (King's Bench, 1610).

Lee v. *The Bude & Torrington Junction Ry. Co.*, 6 Law Reports 576 (Common Pleas, 1871).

Moses v. *Macferlan*, 2 Burrows 1005 (King's Bench, 1760).

Paty's Case, 2 Lord Raymond 1105 (King's Bench, 1705).

Prohibitions Del Roy, 12 Coke's Reports 63 (King's Bench, 1612).

Proprietors of the Stourbridge Canal v. *Wheely*, 2 Barnewall & Adolphus 793 (King's Bench, 1831).

Rex and Regina v. *Knollys*, 1 Lord Raymond 10 (King's Bench, 1695).

Rex v. *Williams*, 26 State Trials 653 (King's Bench, 1797).

Rex v. *Woolston*, 2 Strange 832; 1 Barnardiston 162 (King's Bench, 1729).

Taylor's Case, 1 Ventris 293; 3 Keble 607 (King's Bench, 1676).

Index

Hobart, Chief Justice: 63n.
Hobart v. *Drogan*: 255n.
Hobbes, Thomas: 69ff., 310n.
Hoffman, David: 65n., 95
Holcombe, Arthur: 270n.
Holmes, Oliver W.: 63n., 78n., 184–85, 235–36, 311n.
Holt, John: 63n., 64
Home Building & Loan Assn. v. *Blaisdell*: 218
Homer: 8
Hooker, Charles G.: 277
Hooker, Richard: 69–70, 260, 310
Hopkinson, Joseph: 56–57, 203n., 244n., 246, 255n., 256n., 272, 277n., 291, 300
Horace: 6, 8
Houston v. *Moore*: 262n., 268–69, 270n., 296, 311n.
Howe, Mark de Wolfe: 125, 136
Hume, David: 76, 251, 310
Hunter, David: 240
Hunter v. *Martin*: 243n.
Hunting, Warren: 205n.
Hylton v. *U.S.*: 112n., 306

Indiana University: 275n.
Ingersoll, Charles Jared: 55
Inglis, Charles: 100n.
Insurance Co. v. *Dunham*: 256n.
Iredell, James: 108, 173n., 175n.

Jackson, Andrew: 45n., 55–56, 281; *see also* Jacksonian Democracy
Jackson v. *Lampshire*: 218
Jackson, Robert: 183ff.
Jacksonian Democracy: 44, 82, 86, 224, 273, 280n.
James, Henry: 5, 53
Jay Treaty: 241–42
Jay, John: 82
Jefferson, Thomas: 5, 59n., 96, 246, 304; appoints Joseph Story commissioner in bankruptcy, 26–27; criticizes Story for opposing embargo, 36–37; opposes Story's appointment to Supreme Court, 39–40; opposes lawyers and national judiciary, 39, 89n., 270; natural rights ideas of, 74, 164; views on separation of powers, 106n.; rejects doctrine that Christianity is part of common law, 118ff.; criticized by

Story, 119, 164; views on religious establishment, 129, 141–42; distortion of his constitutional theories, 156; views on free speech, 171n.; *see also* natural law, Joseph Story, Jeffersonian Democracy
The Thomas Jefferson: 255
Jeffersonian Democracy: 86; *see also* Republican party
Jerome v. *U.S.*: 176n.
Johnson, Samuel: 274
Johnson, William: 167n., 169, 171n., 199n., 212n., 248, 255n., 289n., 298n.
Jones, Howard Mumford: 50
Jones, Walter: 277
Jordan, Dillon: 289n.
Judges: *see* Courts
Judicial Review: 116, 244–45, 271–72, 285n.
Judiciary: *see* Courts
Judiciary Act of 1789: 181, 185, 187–88, 242, 266, 271
Judiciary Act of 1802: 33
Junius: 10
Justinian, Digest of: 70n., 124

Kant, Immanuel: 102n., 309
Kauper, Paul: 135n.
Kennedy, John Pendleton: 16
Kent, James: 53n., 63n., 64, 79, 82n., 86, 87, 98, 193, 226, 287n., 291n., 311; difficulties with legal study, 13; opposes Andrew Jackson, 56n.; views on codification of common law of, 85, 95; opinion in *People* v. *Ruggles* of, 123–24, 126n.; comment on *Vidal* v. *Girard's Executors* of, 132; comment on common law jurisdiction of federal courts of, 174n., 178; comment on Charles River Bridge case of, 216; *see also* Joseph Story
Kent, William: 276n.
Kenyon, Lord: 123
Kercheval, Samuel: 106n.
Kilham v. *Ward*: 25n.
King, Rufus: 112
Kirk, Russell: 50, 80n.
Kittredge v. *Emerson*: 260n.
Kittredge v. *Warren*: 260n.
Klopfer v. *North Carolina*: 152n.
Knapp Brothers Trial: 282
Kneeland, Abner: 126n.
Kuhn v. *Fairmont Coal Co.*: 183n.
Kurland, Philip B.: 247n.